HIDDEN®
Florida

"One of the rare guides that actually lives up to its billing."
—*New York Daily News*

"It's a guide to the Florida beyond the billboards, mega-attractions and traffic-snarled cities."
—*Atlanta Journal and Constitution*

"This book goes into considerable detail on the state's history and geology and details sights, accommodations, dining spots, nightlife, trails, camping and motoring."
—*Toronto Star*

"Where else could you find out about Grandma Newton's Bed and Breakfast in the Everglades or Lone Cabbage Fish Camp near Cocoa?"
—*New Orleans Times Picayune*

"In addition to major attractions, it leads readers to little-known towns, secluded beaches and remote wilderness areas."
—*Washington Times*

"There are numerous consumer travel guides to Florida; *Hidden Florida* is one of the best."
—*Jewish Weekly News*

HIDDEN®
Florida

FIFTH EDITION

Ulysses Press®
BERKELEY, CALIFORNIA

Published by:
ULYSSES PRESS
P.O. Box 3440
Berkeley, CA 94703-3440

Library of Congress Catalog Card Number 96-60706

ISBN 1-56975-073-4

Printed in Canada by Best Book Manufacturers

10 9 8 7

EDITORIAL DIRECTOR: Leslie Henriques
MANAGING EDITOR: Claire Chun
PROJECT DIRECTOR: Lily Chou
COPY EDITOR: David Sweet
EDITORIAL ASSOCIATES: Toby Bielawski,
    Deema Khorsheed, Natasha Lay,
    Naomi Canchela, Phoebe McClure,
    Nicole O'Hay
TYPESETTER: Kenya Ratcliff
CARTOGRAPHER: Robert Lettieri
COVER DESIGN: Sarah Levin
INDEXER: Sayre Van Young
COVER PHOTOGRAPHY: Front: Doug Perrine
    Circle and back: Doug Perrine
    Back: Robert Holmes
ILLUSTRATOR: Timothy Carroll

Distributed in the United States by Publishers
Group West, in Canada by Raincoast Books,
and in Great Britain and Europe by World
Leisure Marketing

To Judith Kahn,
for your dedication, wisdom and wit.

What's Hidden?

At different points throughout this book, you'll find special listings marked with a hidden symbol:

◄ HIDDEN

This means that you have come upon a place off the beaten tourist track, a spot that will carry you a step closer to the local people and natural environment of Florida.

The goal of this guide is to lead you beyond the realm of everyday tourist facilities. While we include traditional sightseeing listings and popular attractions, we also offer alternative sights and adventure activities. Instead of filling this guide with reviews of standard hotels and chain restaurants, we concentrate on one-of-a-kind places and locally owned establishments.

Our authors seek out locales that are popular with residents but usually overlooked by visitors. Some are more hidden than others (and are marked accordingly), but all the listings in this book are intended to help you discover the true nature of Florida and put you on the path of adventure.

Write to us!

If in your travels you discover a spot that captures the spirit of Florida, or if you live in the region and have a favorite place to share, or if you just feel like expressing your views, write to us and we'll pass your note along to the author.

We can't guarantee that the author will add your personal find to the next edition, but if the writer does use the suggestion, we'll acknowledge you in the credits and send you a free autographed copy of the new edition.

ULYSSES PRESS
3286 Adeline Street, Suite 1
Berkeley, CA 94703
E-mail: ulypress@aol.com

Contents

Maps

Special Features

OUTDOOR ADVENTURE SYMBOLS

The following symbols accompany national, state and regional park listings, as well as beach descriptions throughout the text.

🏕	Camping		Waterskiing
	Hiking		Windsurfing
🚲	Biking		Canoeing or Kayaking
	Horseback Riding		Boating
	Swimming		Boat Ramps
	Snorkeling or Scuba Diving		Fishing
	Surfing		

ONE

Florida Dreaming

Florida. Even its colorful name conjures up a variety of visions—delicate orchids, waving palms, tropical waters, white sands, fresh orange juice and, especially for winter-dodgers, welcome and dependable warmth. Shaped like a green thumb pointing into the sea, Florida is probably the United States' most recognizable piece of land. A century of dynamic public relations has also kept Florida in the public eye, from the heralding of the first railroads that carried vacationers deep into tropical paradises to the newest Disney ventures that now reportedly attract more visitors than any other spot in the world.

To squeeze a place like Florida into one book is like trying to compress a bushel of oranges into a can of concentrate. From the Georgia line to the outermost of the Dry Tortugas, from historic Pensacola to bustling, rhythmic Miami, Florida has so many dimensions that to discover them all would require return visits—many, many of them. Though no spot in the state is more than 60 miles from salt water, the beaches differ greatly from coast to coast. Of the many freshwater lakes, springs, streams and rivers, each has its own unique character, inhabitants and delights. Even the cities are all different, from gracious Old South Tallahassee to booming Fort Lauderdale to historic Key West.

Old and new are celebrated fervently in Florida. Exhibits of Spanish treasures, re-enactments of pirate invasions and hikes along trails once trekked by early explorers carry you back into the state's colorful and fascinating past, while cutting-edge tours of the Kennedy Space Center and mind-boggling EPCOT experiences thrust you into the anything-is-possible future. Getting in, out and around Florida is easy, too. Modern highways zip up and down and across the entire state; major airlines and trains keep the runways and tracks humming.

Yet, despite its rapid development, its remarkable tourism and its "upfrontness," Florida still possesses many hidden treasures. If you leave the massive freeways and look beyond the billboards, meander down the city side streets, walk the wilderness trails and visit the small towns, you will find them.

This book is designed to help you explore this great state. It will take you to countless popular spots and offer advice on how best to enjoy them. It will also lead you into many off-the-beaten-path locales, the places one learns about by talking with folks at the local café or with someone who has lived in the area all his life. It will acquaint you with the state's history, its natural habitats and its residents—both human and animal. It will recommend sights that should not be missed. It will suggest places to eat, to lodge, to play, to camp, with consideration for varying interests, budgets and tastes.

The traveling part of the book begins in Miami, presenting in Chapter Two the delights of this ever-popular, multifaceted city with its glittering beaches and Latin beat. Chapter Three heads up the Atlantic Gold Coast, through Palm Beach and Fort Lauderdale, along the pièce de résistance beaches that have attracted some of Florida's wealthiest visitors and residents. The future and the past are presented in Chapter Four, which explores space technology and fishing villages as it travels the East Coast for 300 miles through Daytona, Jacksonville and historic St. Augustine. Central Florida's horse farms and cattle ranches, Lake Okeechobee, the beautiful Ocala National Forest and, of course, Walt Disney World are only a sampling of the startling contrasts you will discover in Chapter Five.

Chapter Six heads south into the Everglades region and then down through the jewel-like Florida Keys. Artful Sarasota, urban St. Petersburg and Tampa, and isolated Cedar Key are some of the places Chapter Seven explores as it travels along the popular gulf beaches and into the rural inland areas of the West Coast. Chapter Eight traverses the Panhandle from the Suwannee River to the Alabama line, visiting Tallahassee and Pensacola, white quartz-sand beaches and inland parks, forests, springs and rivers.

What you choose to see and do is up to you. The old cliché that "there is something for everyone" pretty well rings true in Florida. It is proven by the numbers of retired people who return annually or settle down here, by the families who pour in each summer as soon as school is out, by the sportsfolk and sports fans, by the lovers of the out-of-doors as well as the fanciers of the fast lane. For sun-worshippers, there are few places more satisfying than the Sunshine State.

There is a saying that promises, "Once you get Florida sand in your shoes, you will always return." Many visitors will swear it's true, and so will thousands of permanent residents who have wended their ways here from all over the country and the world and hope to stay forever. May it prove true for you, too.

▼▼▼▼▼▼▼▼▼▼▼▼▼▼▼
The Story of Florida

GEOLOGY

Compared to most land masses, Florida is a mere child, having emerged from the sea as recently as 20 to 30 million years ago. For eons its bedrock lay beneath the warm ocean waters, slowly collecting sediment and forming limestone deposits that would one day break the surface and become a new land. Washed by waves, worn by wind and rain, the mass alternately enlarged and shrank as Ice Age glaciers formed and reformed, intermittently raising and lowering the level of the sea. Following the Ice Age, centuries of heavy rain filled limestone scars and caves created by the changing seas. Springs appeared—hints of the giant aquifers that were aborning underground.

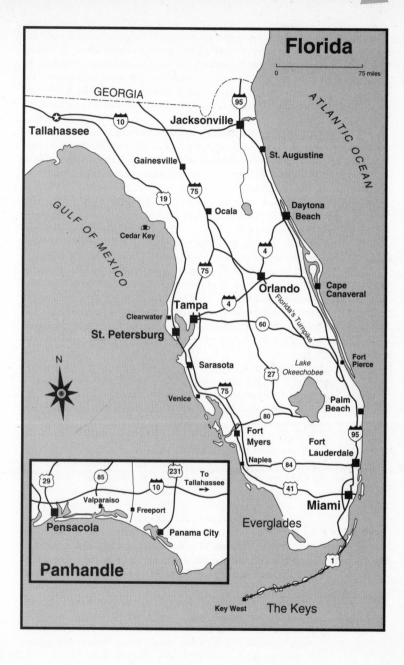

Florida

0 _____ 75 miles

GEORGIA

Tallahassee

Jacksonville

St. Augustine

Gainesville

Ocala

Daytona Beach

GULF OF MEXICO

Cedar Key

ATLANTIC OCEAN

Orlando

Cape Canaveral

Tampa

Clearwater

St. Petersburg

N

Sarasota

Lake Okeechobee

Fort Pierce

Florida's Turnpike

Venice

Palm Beach

Fort Myers

Naples

Fort Lauderdale

Pensacola

Valparaiso

Freeport

Panama City

To Tallahassee

Panhandle

Everglades

Miami

Key West

The Keys

The constant wearing by warm sea waves, wind and rain has resulted in a land that often seems as level as a banquet table. The state's highest point, an unspectacular 345 feet, is found near its far northern border, where rolling hills provide relief from the monotonous flatness.

East of the Keys lies the only living coral reef in the continental United States.

But the limestone that serves as anchor—much of it covered with sand, some with red clay or soils rich enough to nourish superb vegetables and fruits—offers up a variety of treasures beneath its ever-eroding, brittle crust. In some places fresh water bubbles up in tiny sinkholes and sensational springs; in others, bones of mammoths attest to a busy Pleistocene period; elsewhere, rich phosphate rock summons new mining enterprises.

While not readily apparent to the casual traveler, the state is usually divided into several basic land regions that can be identified with closer examination. Like a watery fringe, the Atlantic and Gulf coastal plains surround the state, extending inland as far as 60 miles in some places. Mostly level and low, they are often wooded and dense; offshore they take the form of sand bars, coral reefs, lagoons and islands. The farthest bit of fringe, the Florida Keys, consist of oolitic limestone and coral rock.

The southernmost mainland region, the Lake Okeechobee–Everglades Basin, contains the state's major swamp area, though great portions have been drained and converted to agricultural land. This area is dominated by the Everglades, a giant "river of grass" flowing from Lake Okeechobee, and its neighboring Big Cypress Swamp.

The central ridge and lakes region extends through the middle of the state from the Okefenokee Swamp southward to Lake Okeechobee. Dotted with numerous lakes, this gently rolling area also offers up clear, cold springs.

In the north, the Tallahassee Hills region is a narrow, eroded plateau running about 100 miles from east to west. Next to it lie the Marianna lowlands, filled with sinkholes caused by the dissolution of the limestone strata. Between the Perdido and Apalachicola rivers in the Panhandle, the western highlands rise to the state's highest elevations. Streams and clear rivers meander here between broadly rolling hills and empty into the ever-present sea.

HISTORY

EARLY EXPLORATION   Modern archaeologists tell us that human beings have been harvesting the waters, roaming the hills and wading the swamps of Florida for at least 12 centuries. Little remains of the early wanderers but bits and pieces of tools and artifacts, mystifying mounds and occasional piles of refuse deposited by generations of these early partakers of oyster-on-the-half-shell. When Europeans arrived in Florida, they encountered a number of resident American Indian tribes. Apalachees roamed western regions;

Timucuans spread from east of the Aucilla River down to Tampa Bay; warlike Calusas resided in the Everglades. Smaller tribes such as the Tequestas and Ais struggled among the larger groups.

Written Florida history begins in 1513 when Juan Ponce de León arrived on the northeastern coast, probably near present-day St. Augustine, and claimed the land for Spain. Lovely legend tells us he was searching for a bubbling magical "fountain of youth," although one suspects he might have been equally contented with a great cache of gold, also purported to be lying in wait for ambitious treasure-seekers. Though Ponce de León was to fulfill none of his dreams, he did grace the territory with its romantic name, "Florida," in honor of Spain's Easter holiday, *Pascua Florida*, or "feast of flowers."

Ponce de León left, after exploring the eastern coast, to return again in 1521, this time with the hopes of setting up a little colony on the southwestern side of the peninsula. Unfriendly American Indians soon squelched this plan, but by then Florida's reputation as a place worth struggling to gain had begun to take hold. Cabeza de Vaca came and took back tales of his wanderings among the Indians; Hernando de Soto explored from present day Tampa Bay to Tallahassee before dying of fever. In 1559, Tristan de Luna tried to set up a colony on Pensacola Bay, but hardships and hurricanes put an end to the struggles after only two years.

Within a few years of de Luna's efforts, the French began exploring Florida. René Goulaine de Laudonnière established a little bastion, Fort Caroline, at the mouth of the great northward-flowing St. Johns River. These French inroads challenged the Spanish to work even faster and harder. In 1565, Pedro Menéndez de Aviles arrived on the northeast coast and established what would become the first permanent settlement in the present-day United States—St. Augustine.

Menéndez promptly set about removing the French, converting Fort Caroline into San Mateo, only to see it recaptured with much loss of life two years later. But Spanish progress continued across northern Florida in the form of a chain of forts and missions established to convert the American Indians to Christianity. With the Spanish grip seemingly secure, the English steered clear of Florida. They established their first colonies far to the north, away from the threat of Spanish power, although Sir Francis Drake did manage to raid struggling St. Augustine in 1586.

By the early 1700s, English colonists began causing trouble for the Spanish, particularly in present-day South Carolina and Georgia. Little by little, they trickled south, laid waste the missions between St. Augustine and Pensacola, destroyed the little "first colony" and killed many of the American Indians. Meanwhile, the French had their eyes on Florida's far western coast; they captured Pensacola in 1719. As Spain's hold grew weaker, England's desire for the territory strengthened. Finally, in 1763, following the devastating Seven Years' War, Spain traded Florida for Cuba, abandoning the glorious dreams of eternal youth, gleaming treasure and religious conversion for which her explorers, settlers and missionaries had struggled.

WAR AND CONFLICTS WITH THE AMERICAN INDIANS   England had great plans for Florida. The territory was divided into two sections—East and West Florida—with capitals at St. Augustine and Pensacola. Settlers were promised land grants and other benefits; areas were mapped in detail; tentative peace was made with some of the Creek Indians, who had been gradually moving into the territory and down the peninsula. But the English were able to fulfill few of their hopes in Florida, since they had to turn their attention to the American Revolutionary War.

Today, American Indians number about 2900, living in two separate groups: 2500 Seminoles and 400 Miccosukees. Many still follow the traditional Everglades lifestyle.

Though both East and West Florida remained loyal to the British, when the dust had cleared following the American Revolution, Spain had regained the two territories and their capitals. Colonizing began in earnest. Spain offered generous land grants both to its own people and to the new Americans. Florida also became an accessible and safe haven for escaping slaves from the new states.

Conflict between American Indians and settlers, which had raged through much of Florida's brief history, became more and more serious. By this time, most of the original tribes had been killed or scattered, victims of European exploration, raids and wars, but as the 18th century progressed, more Creek and other southeastern Indians had been filling the void. They became known as "Seminoles," a name derived, most likely, from "siminoli," meaning exiles or wanderers. On a pretext of hunting down runaway slaves, Andrew Jackson led troops into northern Florida in 1817 and attacked American Indian settlements, precipitating the First Seminole War.

Wars with the American Indians and other assorted skirmishes and problems finally encouraged Spain to sell the territory to the United States in 1821. Andrew Jackson became the first territorial governor. The two "Floridas" were united for good. Two men were assigned the task of locating a new capital. Setting out in opposite directions, one from St. Augustine and one from Pensacola, they rendezvoused among the rolling hills of the central Panhandle, where Tallahassee became the seat of government.

As in many other parts of the country, the American Indians struggled to hold onto their homeland. But the settlers found them an "annoyance" and the government decided to have them removed to Indian Territory west of the Mississippi. As president in 1835, Andrew Jackson declared the Second Seminole War, hoping to get rid of the American Indians in short order. But he had not reckoned with the Seminoles' commitment to fight for what was theirs. From their midst rose a powerful leader, Osceola, whose skill and dedication gained respect even from those who fought against him. Only after investing seven years, 1500 lives and $20 million was the government able to declare a victory. At last, under dreadful conditions, most of the surviving Seminoles were removed to Indian Territory.

Several hundred American Indians, however, escaped into the Everglades to spend the rest of the century living a nomadic life in the swamp. They finally resumed official relations with the United States in 1962, 125 years after their self-imposed independence.

In 1845, Florida became a state with a plantation-type economy and a population centered mostly in its northern regions. Though it seceded from the Union during the Civil War, no major battles were fought within its borders and Reconstruction was somewhat less painful than in many other southern states. Even after the war, northern Florida remained an agricultural belt. Its hardworking farmers and later rural settlers became known as "crackers," a nickname of debated origin but one that has come to be associated with folks whose roots lie deep in Florida soil.

TREASURE ALONG THE COASTS   Not until the 1880s would the peninsula to the south begin to reveal its tremendous treasures. At this time, two millionaires with dreams as grand as Ponce de León's made accessible the sea-surrounded paradise and set in motion a land development that, though it has had some tough moments of hesitation, has steamrolled through the 20th century.

It all began when Henry B. Plant and Henry Flagler built railroads down each coast, establishing lavish resorts in tropical settings that attracted visitors, speculators—and the thousands of workers that such projects require. This increasing accessibility also opened up new industries such as phosphate mining, sponge fishing, cigar making and citrus growing. Immigrants, attracted by the new industries, settled in various regions where some of their descendants still reside today. Greek sponge fishers established a major industry at Tarpon Springs. Cubans and Spaniards came to work at the cigar factories at Ybor City in Tampa. Other communities were established by Scots, Jews and Slovaks.

Swamps were drained and more rich farmland became accessible. Real estate boomed until 1926, when, with the rest of the country, it busted. Depression, hurricanes and the Mediterranean fruit fly all took their toll until World War II. Then the all-weather state became a major military training ground and the economy began climbing once again.

MODERN TIMES   The years since the war have been one continuous boom, filled with promise and prosperity. As some of the old industries continue to thrive, new ones—from international banking to electronics and plastics—move in with a steady flow. Most spectacular of these is space exploration, headquartered at Cape Canaveral.

Over 40 million tourists come to Florida each year, attracted as always by the warm winter climate and the beaches. But new dimensions have been added even to tourism with the coming of professional sports, renewed emphasis on the state's colorful history and, above all, sophisticated theme parks such as Walt Disney World and EPCOT Center.

The permanent population is also swelling as dramatically as waves in a hurricane. Large influxes of Cuban refugees in the early 1960s and in 1980 have changed the face of Miami. Central Americans are also arriving in search of new lives. Retirees contribute to Florida's senior population—larger than that of any other state—which brings with it increased leisure time, volunteer manpower and a growing need for health care. By the year 2000, it is expected that more new people will be moving into Florida than to any other state in the nation, making it not only one of the most populous states, but also one of the most diverse.

Dreams of gold and eternal youth have been replaced by promises of dollars, pleasant retirements and the good life in a land where the sun almost always shines and snow almost never falls. But there is a nagging cloud on the horizon that may affect Florida's future as forcefully as the explorers and the railroads impacted her past. It is a cloud observed by many who feel Florida has grown much too fast, that care and caution have been thrown to the winds of profit and growth. In its shadow are predictions of what could happen one day to a land that has developed too quickly, whose supply of crystal water has gone unchecked, whose pollution may kill the hand that feeds.

But there are encouraging signs. In 1968, Florida wrote a new constitution with the coming century in mind. Recent actions at the capital have resulted in the state's acquiring more wild areas and preserves. Archaeological exploration of Spanish missions, American Indian sites and shipwrecks has kindled interest in forgotten history. Florida heritage is rich. It may well have much to teach about where the real treasures lie.

Flora and Fauna

▼▼▼▼▼▼▼▼▼▼▼

Lying on the edge of the tropic latitudes, Florida boasts a "best of both worlds" plant life. Pines are the most prolific; pine forests cover most of north and northwest

FLORA   Florida, where sweet gum, red maple and tulip trees also abound. The majestic sabal palm, Florida's state tree, is widely distributed in the state, flourishing in many types of soil.

Other dominant trees include magnolia and cypress, Florida hickory and numerous varieties of oak. Caribbean representatives, abundant in the subtropical regions to the south, include mahogany, gumbo-limbo and many other species of palm, including the handsome royal palm. Cabbage palmetto can be found in coastal regions throughout the state. Because lumbering was one of the state's earliest industries, few virgin stands remain.

> At least 344 species of trees, about 80 percent of those native to the United States, grow here.

Many Florida plants are sensitive to subtle changes in moisture, resulting in river bottoms and low hammocks full of water oaks and varieties of gum, river banks and lake shores abundant in cypress, and high, dry regions supporting pines, post oak and turkey oak. Wildflowers, many of them natives, may be found in any season. Bladderwort, duckweed and wild iris thrive in marshes and shallow water. Beautiful but not beloved, the fast-growing flowering water hyacinth can choke whole rivers and streams in a short time.

To the south, especially in the Everglades, native orchids and air plants provide an exotic beauty. The rolling northern regions are noted for abundant displays of azaleas and camellias. Oleanders, hibiscus, poinsettias, gardenias, jasmine, trumpet vine and morning-glory thrive almost everywhere. For brilliant floral displays, nothing can match a blooming royal poinciana or a colorful shower of bougainvillea, common where temperatures do not dip too low.

Hurricane Andrew in 1992 changed the habitat in much of the Everglades. The hurricane's high winds sheared off the leafy treetops, exposing the forest floor, which had been shaded from the blazing Florida sun. Low-lying plants such as orchids and ferns are slowly adapting to the sun, while fallen trees are regenerating from their remaining planted roots. This is an interesting time in the Everglades, a time of transition for much of its tropical life.

Early Florida explorers reported amazing numbers of animals everywhere they went. Even veteran travelers living today can recall the abundance of birds soaring above the Tamiami Trail when it was still a new roadway. Today, 90 percent of Everglades birds are gone, and ever-increasing civilization has reduced the mammal and reptile population considerably. However, in the protected areas where natural habitats remain, native wildlife still thrives and Florida continues to be a zoological wonderland.

FAUNA

There are numerous land mammals still found in the state, including the black bear, gray fox, puma and wild cat. The Florida panther is among the rarest. Deer are common in many regions, except for the tiny Key deer, whose dwindling population is now limited to one spot in the Florida Keys. Abundant are squirrels, rabbits, raccoons and opossums; less prolific are otters and minks, long trapped for their pelts. Armadillos poke around noisily for insects; feral hogs can be encountered in many wooded areas.

Once common in Florida but long a victim of civilization, the gentle manatee, or sea cow, is dwindling in numbers despite efforts to save it. These bulky, homely animals may be observed in several protected areas. They often feed trustingly at the water's surface close to boaters and fishermen, where they can become victims of motor blades and abandoned tackle.

Alligators live in lakes, rivers and marshy areas throughout the state. Long protected by law, they can be seen in various parks as well as in the wild and, for safety, should be respected. Their cousin, the American crocodile, is endangered and rare.

A variety of snakes thrive in Florida; the venomous ones include rattlesnake, coral snake, cottonmouth moccasin and copperhead. Frogs, lizards and turtles, including loggerhead sea turtles, can often be seen.

Birdwatchers have listed over 400 species and subspecies of birds throughout the state. In marshes and swamps one can often spot ibis, herons and egrets. Ospreys nest on telephone poles in the Keys. Endangered species such as woodstorks are drastically reduced in number, but are still present in the Everglades. Florida also boasts 800 mated pairs of bald eagles—second only to Alaska.

Coastal regions abound in shore birds such as the brown pelican, varieties of gull, sandpipers and terns. Ducks, geese and many other migratory birds make their winter homes in Florida. Natural rookeries, protected sanctuaries and a thriving Audubon Society contribute to the maintenance of the rich bird life in the state.

One of Florida's most popular mammals resides in the sea. The sleek bottle-nosed dolphin, popular with humans because of its high intelligence and playfulness displayed in captivity, can also present an enchanting spectacle as it sports alongside a beach or among boaters in a bay.

NATURAL HABITATS

Human beings have altered so much of Florida that it's almost possible to believe condominiums and sprawling resort complexes have replaced whatever natural environs once existed. Fortunately, this is not entirely so. A broad variety of habitats still exists, many

FLORIDA'S FRAGILE NURSERIES

Many Florida habitats are watery affairs. The coastal zones along the Gulf of Mexico and the Atlantic Ocean include mangrove swamps, salt marshes and the barrier islands. Here, estuaries—complex and delicately balanced ecosystems formed where fresh and salt water mix—are born. They are crucial and fragile nurseries for many important species.

of them protected in the state's numerous parks and preserves. The Sunshine State boasts more than 8000 miles of tidal coastline and hundreds of freshwater lakes, ponds and springs.

Throughout the state lie swamps of many varieties, each distinctive and curiously mysterious. For example, on the Georgia line lies the Okefenokee Swamp, a cypress bog with towering trees. Dwarf cypress, on the other hand, distinguishes swamps of the Everglades. Flood plain swamps along river banks often lie underwater for several months. Shrub bogs are often found in pine forests.

Pinelands make up Florida's most extensive habitats. Slash pine flatwoods abound in the state's national forests, where trees are tall and close above low, dry ground or dense, swampy areas. Longleaf pines dominate sandhill communities, creating parklike forests on rolling sandy hills. Sand pine scrub, unique to Florida, is probably a remnant of an ancient desert scrub that once covered portions of California, Mexico and dry areas of the Gulf. Today it can be found along the coast and on ancient central Florida dunes.

Hardwood hammocks, or forests, are where the big trees reside. They are quite varied and may be found in many differing forms throughout the state. The hammocks are home to much of Florida's great array of wildlife. Near the shore lie coastal and lowland hammocks, abundant in cabbage palms, oaks and red cedars. From the red clay soil in the central Panhandle grow the southern mixed hardwoods, the tag-end of the forests of the Appalachian range. Massive spreading live oaks, draped with hoary Spanish moss, are found in live oak hammocks throughout the state. Tropical hammocks of southern Florida are perhaps the most intriguing, for here northern and Caribbean trees grow together—live oaks side-by-side with gumbo-limbo, mahogany and poisonwood.

Other habitats, each with their own character, include savannahs, coral reefs beneath the surface of the Atlantic Ocean, native prairies, freshwater marshes and the unique Everglades.

Where to Go

Selecting Florida as a vacation destination is easy; deciding where to go is another matter. The state is so vast and varied that it would take many visits to experience all it has to offer. To help you decide, here are brief descriptions of the regions presented in this book, but they are only teasers. To get the whole scoop, read the more detailed introductions to each chapter, then delve into the material on the regions that appeal to you most.

This book begins in Miami, heads northward up the East Coast, then explores Central Florida. Next it heads south and west to the Everglades and Keys, then travels up the West Coast and finally makes a zigzag journey across the Panhandle. Each area is distinctive; put together they create a rich tapestry of the urban, the wild and the historical.

Miami is the stuff that brochures and television shows are made of. If you fly in, you will likely get a good view of glittering Miami Beach and the glorious Atlantic that attracts millions of visitors each year. You will also see the massive hotels and condominiums that hide the coastal expanse from all but the guests. The area is most definitely urban. Spanish is spoken as freely as English, a sign of the growing Latin American population. Latino entertainment and businesses, Cuban-style food, and ethnic music and language give sections of Miami the feel of a cosmopolitan Latin city.

Along the Atlantic, the **Gold Coast** stretches northward from the outskirts of Miami to Jupiter Inlet. Beautiful beaches and constant development mark much of this region, whose two major cities are booming Fort Lauderdale, with its miles of navigable canals, and wealthy, exclusive Palm Beach. Communities surrounding these two anchors reflect varying personalities, but just about everywhere tourists descend in winter to bask on the beaches.

The **East Coast**, stretching about 300 miles, has areas that are developing with a vengeance. But it also includes regions of near repose, especially in the area up toward the Georgia line. Ocean beaches are accessible along nearly the entire route, from auto-crazy Daytona Beach through old-fashioned fishing villages to almost-hidden Amelia Island. History is celebrated in St. Augustine and is being made at the Kennedy Space Center at Cape Canaveral. The busy seaport of Jacksonville is the major city along this coast.

Even though it boasts no beaches, perhaps the greatest variety of all can be found in **Central Florida**. Here cattle and horses graze on rolling hills, and the beautiful St. Johns River winds northward through the Ocala National Forest, where springs bubble like crystal. Citrus reigns in many areas. Lake Okeechobee struggles for survival as it nourishes fabulous farms. But the single resident of Central Florida that put the place securely on the globe's tourist map is Walt Disney World, near Orlando and Kissimmee. Sleepy towns have become cosmopolitan centers as visitors flock from across the world to this irresistible attraction.

Just beyond Miami's city lights, to the west and south lie the **Everglades and Keys,** two distinctive gifts of nature. Despite its swampy environment, the Everglades is a paradise for nature lovers and birdwatchers, offering up secrets found nowhere else on earth. To the south, the Florida Keys lie like a chain of island beads dividing the Gulf of Mexico from the Atlantic Ocean. Paralleling their eastern shoreline, the only living coral reef off the mainland United States attracts divers and explorers of every level of expertise.

The **West Coast**, from Marco Island to Cedar Key, varies greatly in pace and environment. From Fort Myers up through the Tampa/St. Petersburg area, growth abounds and travelers flood the region in the high season. But many of the communities, such as Sarasota, Tarpon Springs and isolated Cedar Key, have managed to keep their charm. Gulf beaches are fine along most of this coastline, until you reach the marshy spot where the highway veers inland. Here the pace slows down a bit, and wilderness areas offer experiences with an earlier, more natural Florida.

The **Panhandle** area includes everything north and west of the Suwannee River all the way to the Perdido River near historic Pensacola. Except for a few glitzy stretches of developed Gulf shore west of Panama City, the Panhandle reflects much of Old Florida. There are deep forests, clear springs, incredibly beautiful white sand beaches, freshwater lakes and rivers and historic sites. Tallahassee, the state capital, is a mixture of new cosmopolitan and Old South. An author once dubbed this region "the other Florida," and so it remains today.

It's said that a daily newspaper, vowing to give away free editions on days when the sun refused to shine, had to keep its promise no more than four times in any one year. No wonder Florida is called the Sunshine State. The weather stays balmy nearly all year in most regions, boasting a pleasant semitropical atmosphere. While Florida can also get both colder and hotter from time to time than one might expect, the state justifiably claims year-round weather nearly as perfect as can be found in the continental United States, especially for lovers of warmth and sun.

▼▼▼▼▼▼▼▼▼
When to Go

SEASONS

Generally the "shoulder seasons," spring and fall, bring the most pleasant days and nights in all but the southernmost regions of Florida, where winter is the favored time. Throughout the state, summers tend to be wet, hot and humid. Winters are drier, mild and sunny with moderate readings, though in the northern regions there can be periods when temperatures drop into the 20s and even occasional snow. From Central Florida southward, freezing can occur occasionally in all but the most southerly regions.

Curiously, with an average rainfall of 53 inches, the "Sunshine State" is also one of the nation's wettest. But rainfall is uneven: an area may be suffering drought conditions, only to have many inches of precipitation dumped on it from an offshore hurricane.

In general, southern Florida's winter high temperatures average in the upper 70s, with lows dropping only into the 50s. Northwest Florida has winter highs averaging around 67° and lows averaging 44°. Central Florida's temperatures range appropriately between those of its northern and southern neighbors. Summer temperatures are far more uniform throughout the state; average highs hover around 90° with lows seldom falling below 70°. While summer can bring hot afternoons, offshore breezes keep life comfortable in most regions near the coast.

Hurricanes, though they can be devastating, need not keep one away during the fall. Usually developing in September, hurricanes have also been known to occur much later. (Ironically, the worst storm in decades, Hurricane Andrew, which struck here in 1992, occurred in August.) Unlike many other weather phenomena, they come with plenty of warning, allowing visitors either to batten down or depart for inland locations.

Generally temperate seasons, refreshing cold springs, breezy beaches and an abundance of air-conditioning all contribute to making Florida a good year-round destination.

CALENDAR OF EVENTS

If life is a cabaret, then Florida is a fiesta. There are annual celebrations of just about everything from pirates to possum. Check with local chambers of commerce (listed in regional chapters of this book) to see what will be going on when you are in the area. Below is a sampling of some of the biggest events.

JANUARY   **Miami**   One of the largest post-season football games, the **Orange Bowl Classic**, kicks off the New Year. The **Art Deco Weekend Festival**, with the "Moon Over Miami Ball," takes place in South Miami Beach.

East Coast   Jacksonville's **Gator Bowl Classic** kicks off the New Year at the Jacksonville Municipal Stadium, a.k.a. Gator Bowl Stadium.

West Coast   The blessing of the sponge fleet, diving for the cross, a parade, Greek foods and festivities mark **Epiphany Day** in Tarpon Springs.

FEBRUARY   **Miami**   Over 300 artists and more than a million visitors celebrate the annual **Coconut Grove Arts Festival**. The **Miami International Boat Show** at Miami Beach displays craft from just about every major manufacturer and offers free sailing clinics.

East Coast   The **Daytona 500** marks the culmination of **Speed Weeks** with a 200-lap stock car race at the Daytona International Speedway. Motorcyclists from across the country also descend on Daytona for the races and festivities of **Bike Week**.

West Coast   The **Edison Pageant of Lights** commemorates Fort Myers' most famous resident. A pirate ship and accompanying flotilla invade Tampa to kick off the **Gasparilla Invasion and Parade**, as business folk turn pirate for a day.

MARCH   **Miami**   A nine-day Latino celebration, **Carnival Miami**, culminates with a dynamic block party known as **Calle Ocho**. Key Biscayne's **Lipton International Players Championship** features top international tennis players. Race cars whiz through the Homestead Motor Sports Complex during the first weekend in March at the **Miami Grand Prix**.

Central Florida   Top performers play at the **Kissimmee Bluegrass Festival**.

Everglades and Keys   Shell blowers participate in Key West's **Conch Shell Blowing Contest**.

West Coast   A **Medieval Fair** brings jousters, minstrels and fair damsels to the grounds of the Ringling Museum in Sarasota.

Gold Coast   The **United States/National Club Team Championship** is a world-class croquet event held in Palm Beach Gardens.

APRIL

East Coast   The **Bausch & Lomb WITA Tennis Championship** on Amelia Island draws top national and international talent.

Central Florida   At Lake Wales, the **Bok Tower Easter Sunrise Service** followed by carillon music has been celebrated since the 1940s.

Everglades and Keys   Runners set out from Marathon for a dash over the sea in the annual **Seven Mile Bridge Run**.

Panhandle   **Chautauqua** lives again at DeFuniak Springs, once winter home of the great American cultural movement. Festivities include canoe races, live music and fireworks. You can see daring feats at the "greatest collegiate show on earth," **Florida State University's "Flying High" Circus Homeshow** in Tallahassee.

Gold Coast   Florida's largest outdoor jazz festival, **Sunfest** at West Palm Beach, features top names and offers plenty of side events.

MAY

East Coast   St. Augustine puts on the **Seafood Festival** featuring seafood, sailboat races and rubber alligator races.

Everglades and Keys   The annual **Key West Fishing Tournament** has nine divisions and is held throughout the Lower Keys from May to November.

Miami   **Gay Pride Week** features live entertainment, dancing, booths and a Sunday parade. On alternating years the event takes place in Fort Lauderdale.

JUNE

Panhandle   **The Fiesta of Five Flags** in Pensacola is a week-long celebration with historic re-enactments, sporting events, art shows and more.

Many communities celebrate the **Fourth of July** with parades, fireworks and other festivities.

JULY

East Coast   For fast cars and lots of action, be at the **Pepsi 400 Nascar Winston Cup Series** in Daytona Beach. **Jazz Matazz**, a two-day jazz festival, takes place in Ormond Beach.

Central Florida   The **Silver Spurs Rodeo** in Kissimmee has ropin', ridin' and square dancin'.

Everglades and Keys   South Florida ethnic groups join together at the Miccosukee Indian Village for the **Miccosukee Annual Inter-**

national Crafts and Music Festival. Storytelling, arm-wrestling, fishing tournaments and look-alike contests highlight Key West's week-long **Hemingway Days**, honoring the man and his works.

Panhandle Pensacola's **International Billfish Tournament** is one of the largest on the Gulf, with awards exceeding $150,000.

AUGUST

Miami Jamaican foods, arts and live music by internationally acclaimed artists and local bands make up the **Miami Reggae Festival**.

Gold Coast A sandcastle contest, winetasting and a crafts fair are a few of the festivities during the month-long **Boca Festival Days** in Boca Raton.

SEPTEMBER

Central Florida In Bartow, the **Annual Bartow Youth Villa Golf Classic** benefits youth projects with a golf tournament, dance, fashion show and more.

Panhandle For two weekends, the **Pensacola Seafood Festival** celebrates one of the state's oldest industries.

OCTOBER

Miami Latin residents celebrate during Miami's **Latino Heritage Festival**, and music such as calypso, soca and reggae highlight the **West Indian American Miami Carnaval Extravaganza**.

East Coast From the end of October to the beginning of November, the **Jacksonville Jazz Festival** is a free outdoor event in Jacksonville's Metropolitan Park with top-name performers.

Everglades and Keys During **Fantasy Fest**, a ten-day Mardi Gras in Key West, revelers dress up according to the year's theme. The highlight of the week is the Twilight Fantasy Parade.

West Coast Tampa, nicknamed "The Big Guava" by locals, is overrun with costumed citizens during the **Guavaween** carnival and parade.

Panhandle The banks of the Suwannee River are a perfect setting for the **Bluegrass Festival** at Spirit of the Suwannee Campground in Live Oak.

NOVEMBER

Miami Adult and children's choirs, jazz trios, the Greater Miami Symphonic Band and over 30,000 Christmas-colored bulbs combine to create the **Miami Lakes Festival of Lights**.

Gold Coast Fort Lauderdale's Bubier Park hosts the **Riverwalk Blues Festival**, featuring both national and local blues bands.

Panhandle The **Annual Florida Seafood Festival** at Battery Park in Apalachicola is the oldest maritime celebration in the state of Florida and honors one of the area's most thriving industries. Watch the crowning of King Retsyo (that's "oyster" spelled backward) and Miss Florida Seafood. Artists from all across the country congregate in Pensacola's Seville Square for the **Great Gulf Coast Arts Festival**.

Candlelight tours, parades and Santa festivals highlight many communities throughout December. **DECEMBER**

Miami   **Art in the Heart of Miami Beach** has an art and entertainment lineup. In Coral Gables, the **Junior Orange Bowl International Championships** draws hundreds of under-18 players from around the world including the United Kingdom, Taiwan, Sweden and Africa.

Panhandle   Sparkling sea craft parade on the Intracoastal Waterway for the **Pensacola Beach Christmas Parade and Decorated Boat Procession**.

For a free copy of the *Florida Vacation Guide*, contact the **Florida Tourism Industry Marketing Corporation**. Most small towns have chambers of commerce or visitor information centers; many of them are listed in *Hidden Florida* under the appropriate regions. ~ P.O. Box 1100, Tallahassee, FL 32302; 904-488-5607.

Before You Go

VISITORS CENTERS

For visitors arriving by automobile, Florida hosts five **Welcome Centers** that provide fresh orange juice, maps and lots of guidance from 8 a.m. to 5 p.m. daily. These are located near the border on Route 10, west of Pensacola; in the new Capitol Building, Tallahassee; on Route 75, north of Jennings; on Route 95, near Yulee; and three miles north of Campbellton on Route 231.

Unless you plan to spend your Florida trip dining in ultra-deluxe restaurants, you'll need much less in your suitcase than you might think. For most trips, all you'll have to pack are some shorts, lightweight shirts or tops, cool slacks, a couple of bathing suits and cover-ups, and something *very casual* for any special event that might call for dressing up. **PACKING**

The rest of your luggage space can be devoted to light "beach reading" and a few essentials that should not be forgotten (unless you prefer to shop on arrival). These include good sunscreens (preferably not oils), high-quality sunglasses and some insect repellent, especially if you are traveling in the summer or heading to the far south even in winter. If you're planning to spend a lot of time outdoors—where fire ants or stinging jellyfish might be a concern—take along a small container of a papain-type meat tenderizer. It won't keep the varmints away, but it will ease the pain should you fall victim.

Take along an umbrella or light raincoat for the sudden showers that can pop out of nowhere. If you visit North or Central Florida in the winter, you would be wise to take a warm jacket or coat. Even in the far south, a sweater can be welcome on occasional winter days.

Good soft, comfortable, lightweight shoes for sightseeing are a must. Despite its tropical gentleness, Florida terrain doesn't treat bare feet well except along the shore or beside a pool. Sturdy sandals will do well. If you plan to do any hiking in the wetlands (and wetlands can show up where you least expect them), wear canvas shoes that you don't mind wading in.

Serious scuba divers will probably want to bring their own gear, but it's certainly not essential. Underwater equipment of all sorts is available for rent wherever diving is popular. Many places also rent beach toys and tubes for floating down rivers. Fishing gear is also often available for rent.

Campers will need basic cooking equipment and, except in winter, can make out fine with only a lightweight sleeping bag or cot and a tent with good screens and a ground cloth. A canteen, first aid kit, flashlight and other routine camping gear should be brought along.

If you find you can't seem to walk a beach without picking up shells, take a plastic bag for hauling treasures. A camera is good, too; Florida sunsets are sensational. Binoculars enhance both bird-watching and beachwatching. And don't, for heaven's sake, forget your copy of *Hidden Florida*.

LODGING

Lodgings in Florida run the gamut from tiny one-room cabins in the woods to glistening highrise condominiums in which every room faces the sea. Bed and breakfasts are relative newcomers to much of Florida, but they are there for the finding. Chain motels line most main thoroughfares and mom-and-pop enterprises still successfully vie for lodgers in every region. Large hotels with names you'd know anywhere appear in most cities of any size. Poshest of all are the upscale resorts. Here one can drop in almost from the sky and never have to leave the grounds. In fact, you can take in all the sports, dining, nightlife, shopping and entertainment needed to make a vacation complete, although you may miss the authentic Florida.

Other Florida lodgings offer more personality, such as historic inns or little hotels where you can eat breakfast with the handful of other guests. And when spending a week at the beach, there's nothing like an old-fashioned beach house, preferably on stilts, where the salt-laden wind blows in off the water and the mockingbirds sing outside in the trees.

Be warned that "waterfront" lodging can mean bay, lake, inlet or even a slough in some cases.

Whatever your preference and budget, you can probably find something to suit your taste with the help of the regional chapters in this book. Remember, rooms are scarce and prices rise in the high season, which is generally summer in the Panhandle and winter to the south. Off-season rates are often drastically reduced in many places, allowing for a week's, or even a month's stay to be a real bargain. Whatever you do, plan ahead and make reservations, especially in the prime tourist seasons.

Accommodations in this book are organized by region and classified according to price. Rates referred to are high-season rates, so if you are looking for low-season bargains, it's good to inquire. *Budget* lodgings generally are less than $50 per night for two people and are satisfactory and clean but modest. *Moderate*-priced lodgings run from $50 to $90; what they have to offer in the way of luxury will depend on their location, but they tend to offer larger rooms and more attractive surroundings. At a *deluxe* hotel or resort you can expect to spend between $90 and $130 for a double; you'll likely find spacious rooms, a fashionable lobby, a restaurant and often a group of shops. *Ultra-deluxe* facilities, priced above $130, are a region's finest, offering all the amenities of a deluxe hotel plus plenty of extras.

If you crave a room facing the surf, be sure to ask specifically. If you are trying to save money, lodgings a block or so from the beach often offer lower rates than those within sight of the waves and, because Florida beaches are public, are often worth the short stroll.

DINING

Eating places in Florida seem to be as numerous as the fish in the sea, and fish is what you will find everywhere. Whether catfish from a river or pompano from the surf, you can almost always count on its being fresh and prepared well. Each region has its specialties, its ethnic influences and its gourmet spots.

Within a particular chapter, restaurants are categorized geographically, with each restaurant entry describing the establishment according to price. Dinner entrées at *budget* restaurants usually cost $8 or less. The ambience is informal, service typically speedy and the crowd often a local one. *Moderately* priced restaurants range between $8 and $16 at dinner; surroundings are casual but pleasant, the menu offers more variety and the pace is usually slower. *Deluxe* establishments tab their entrées from $16 to $24; cuisines may be simple or sophisticated, depending on the location, but the decor is plusher and the service more personalized. *Ultra-deluxe* dining rooms, where entrées begin at $24, are often the gourmet places; here cooking has become a fine art and the service should be impeccable.

Some restaurants change hands often and are occasionally closed in low seasons. Efforts have been made in this book to include places with established reputations for good eating. Breakfast and lunch menus vary less in price from restaurant to restaurant than evening dinners.

TRAVELING WITH CHILDREN

Any state that boasts gentle beaches, developed campgrounds and Mickey Mouse is bound to be a good place to take children. Plenty of family adventures are available in Florida, from manmade attractions to experiences in the wild. A few guidelines will help make travel with children a pleasure.

Book reservations in advance, making sure that the places you stay accept children. If you need a crib or extra cot, arrange for it ahead of time. A travel agent can be of help here, as well as with most other travel plans.

If you are traveling by air, try to reserve bulkhead seats where there is lots of room. Take along extras you may need, such as diapers, changes of clothing, snacks, toys or small games. When traveling by car, take along the extras, too. Make sure you have plenty of water and juices to drink; dehydration can be a subtle problem.

A first-aid kit is a must for any trip. Along with adhesive bandages, antiseptic cream and something to stop itching, include any medicines your pediatrician might recommend to treat allergies, colds, diarrhea or any chronic problems your child may have.

If you plan to spend much time at the beach, take extra care the first few days. Children's skin is usually more tender than adult skin, and severe sunburn can happen before you realize it. A hat is a good idea, along with a reliable sunblock. And be sure to keep a constant eye on children who are near the water.

For parents' night out, many hotels provide a dependable list of baby sitters. In some areas you may find drop-in child care centers; look in the yellow pages for these, and make sure you choose ones that are licensed.

Many towns, parks and attractions offer special activities designed just for children. Consult local newspapers and/or call the numbers in this guide to see what's happening where you're going.

GAY & LESBIAN TRAVELERS

Florida had originally developed as a vacation mecca for the northeastern states. It's not surprising, then, that a number of those areas also flourished into prime gay destinations. Florida's hottest spot is no doubt Miami's South Beach, located on a barrier island off Florida's east coast. In fact, the gay community's involvement was crucial in restoring South Beach's classic art deco architecture. Here you'll find a grand selection of accommodations, eateries, shops and nightclubs catering to gay and lesbian travelers. (See "South Beach Gay Scene" in Chapter Two.)

At the tip of Florida floats the island of Key West, a casual, comfortable getaway from the metropolitan melee of South Beach. The gay community also lent a big hand in reviving the historic district here. Old Town is the center of this gay scene, replete with guesthouses, restaurants, stores and nightspots. (See "Key West Gay Scene" in Chapter Six.)

Sprinkled throughout the state, including a small cluster in Fort Lauderdale, are a number of gay-friendly, gay-owned and/or gay-exclusive establishments.

Numerous resource centers and publications in these areas are ready to help gay and lesbian travelers tap into the local happenings. For a weekly rundown on the trendiest nightspots in Florida, pick up *Contax*, which serves the entire state (and other states, too). ~ 305-757-6333. *Hotspots* covers nightlife and entertainment in South Beach, Fort Lauderdale, Tampa, West Palm Beach and Key West. ~ 305-928-1862.

In Miami, the **Lesbian, Gay & Bisexual Community Center** offers counseling, support groups and bulletin boards loaded with postings and literature. ~ 1335 Alton Road, Miami Beach; 305-531-3666. The **South Beach Business Guild**, the gay chamber of commerce in Miami Beach, is an excellent resource for gays and lesbians. ~ 1205 Drexel Avenue, Miami Beach; 305-672-9100. For a plethora of important phone numbers, call the **Gay, Lesbian, Bisexual Hotline of Greater Miami**. It covers everything from professional services and community groups to nightclubs and publications. ~ 305-759-3661. The weekly *Wire* has information on the vibrant South Beach political and cultural scene. ~ 305-538-3111. *The Fountain*, which comes out monthly, serves the lesbian community here. ~ 305-565-7479.

TWN (*The Weekly News*) focuses on the South Florida scene (including Miami and Fort Lauderdale). In it you'll find news and features pertaining to the gay community. Can't think of anything to do? They also have a comprehensive events listing. ~ 901 Northeast 79th Street, Miami; 305-757-6333.

In Key West, **Helpline, Inc.** is a 24-hour crisis and general information line benefitting the Keys area. ~ 305-296-4357, TDD 305-292-8452. A monthly complete guide to gay Key West, *Southern Exposure* includes a map of Old Town and a calendar of events. ~ 819 Peacock Plaza, Suite 575, Key West; 305-294-6303.

Fort Lauderdale also has some handy resources. Stop by their **Gay/Lesbian Community Center** to pick up brochures and fliers, as well as to see what events and recreational activities they have planned. Closed Sunday. ~ 1164 East Oakland Park Boulevard, Fort Lauderdale; 954-563-9500. For a quick scoop on what's happening in the Miami/Fort Lauderdale area, check out *Scoop Magazine*. This weekly publication features articles and entertainment listings of interest to the gay, lesbian, bisexual and transgender community. ~ 2219 Wilton Drive, Fort Lauderdale; 954-561-9707.

> You'll find more information on services for gay and lesbian travelers by checking out "Gay and lesbian travelers" in the index.

SENIOR TRAVELERS

As millions have discovered, Florida is an ideal place for older vacationers, many of whom turn into part-time or full-time residents. The climate is mild, the terrain level, and many destinations offer significant discounts for seniors. Off-season rates make most areas exceedingly attractive for travelers on limited incomes. Florida residents over 65 can benefit from reduced rates at most state parks,

Text continued on page 24.

Florida Cuisine

With salt water on three sides and rivers, lakes and streams abounding in its interior, seafood and freshwater fish top the list of Florida foods. From the ocean and Gulf come fresh pompano, scamp, grouper, shrimp, yellowfin tuna and mullet—and the list goes on and on. Each region serves up its own special dishes from its particular waters—oysters-on-the-half-shell from Apalachicola Bay in the Panhandle, smoked mullet from the Gulf, conch chowder and fritters in the Keys. Inland, there's nothing tastier than well-fried catfish. Florida lobster, a giant crawfish, gives Maine a run for its money. Alligator tail shows up on Everglades-area menus. Stone crab, available from October to May, is even a humane dish: while you are dining on the claw meat of this accommodating creature, he is busy growing a new claw for the next year.

No matter where you live, you have undoubtedly partaken of Florida citrus fruits and mixed water into a can of Florida concentrated juice. In many areas, in the winter months, you can see oranges, grapefruit, limes and tangelos right alongside the road, both on trees and for sale at inviting roadside stands. Varieties seem endless, with some fruit offering special qualities such as remarkable sweetness or no seeds. A freshly picked, easily peeled tangerine is an entirely different item from its stored-and-transported grocery-store cousin. Late fruits, such as valencia oranges and seedless grapefruit, are available into June and July. Even out of season, you'll find citrus products—marmalades, novelty wines, calamondin and kumquat jellies and lemon candies. Key lime pie is a traditional dessert from the Keys, made originally from the tiny yellow limes that grow there.

Exotic fruits have joined the list of Florida produce, familiar ones such as mangos, avocados and papayas and lesser-known zapotes, lychees and guavas. Coconuts grow in backyards in southern Florida. Swamp cabbage yields up its heart as the chief delicacy in "hearts of palm" salad. Winter vegetables and fruits thrive in the drained Everglades regions, where you can stop and pick strawberries, peppers, tomatoes or whatever else is left over from the great quantities shipped across the United States. In the northern and central regions of the state, pecans and peanuts are popular Florida treats; southern pecan pie is a rich, calorie-laden delicacy. Sugar cane and sorghum are still turned into syrup and molasses in some areas.

Ethnic foods have long influenced Florida cuisine. Throughout the state you will discover Greek dishes and salads originally introduced by the spongefishers of Tarpon Springs. Cuban fare such as *picadillo*, black beans and yellow rice and fried plantains entered southern Florida when travel from the island neighbor was unrestricted. The Minorcan influence around the St. Augustine area reveals itself in pilau, a spicy stew of rice, vegetables, seafood and chicken. Creole cooking is enjoyed in the Panhandle in rich seafood gumbos and jambalayas. In the Everglades area you can try Indian fry breads and mashed cassava roots.

Lately, inventive young chefs have been using local fruits and other tropical ingredients to create a new style of cooking. Seafood, chicken, lamb and beef get tropical treatments, and are often grilled, smoked or blackened. Some call it "tropical fusion" or "nuevo Cubano," while others deem it "new Florida cuisine." Whatever the name, one thing is certain: This brand of cooking is marvelously adventurous. After all, where else can you find Key lime pasta or grilled grouper with mango salsa, plantains and purple potatoes?

Of course, Floridians still relish these down-to-earth comfort foods. Diners and counter-service cafés, which serve mounds of food for a few dollars, are there to be found. And, with about 15,000 ranches statewide, a good barbecued steak is held sacred by many Floridians.

Good old-fashioned Southern cooking and soul food are also an integral part of Florida cuisine, especially in northern and central Florida. Southern fried chicken, though not popular with the cholesterol-conscious, is a beloved delicacy, and fried fish is usually served with a choice of grits or hushpuppies. (The latter are fried balls of cornbread that hunters and fishermen were said to have tossed to their dogs to keep them quiet while supper was being prepared following a successful foray.) In most places, you'll be served breakfast with grits, a true southern dish and a tasty one when eaten with butter.

Winemaking, relatively new to Florida, is becoming serious business. Wild grapes are native to many regions of the state, a good predictor of possible future success. There are wineries in the Panhandle, near Orlando and Fort Myers. These fledgling operations are gaining a reputation for Florida; keep your eye on them.

and the Golden Age Passport, which must be applied for in person, allows discount admission to national parks and monuments for anyone 62 or older.

The **American Association of Retired Persons** (AARP) offers membership to anyone over 50. AARP's benefits include travel discounts. ~ 3200 East Carson Street, Lakewood, CA 90712; 310-496-2277.

Elderhostel offers reasonably priced, all-inclusive educational programs in a variety of Florida locations throughout the year. ~ 75 Federal Street, Boston, MA 02110; 617-426-7788.

Be extra careful about health matters. In addition to the medications you ordinarily use, it's a good idea to bring along the prescriptions for obtaining more. Consider carrying a medical record with you—including your medical history and current medical status as well as your doctor's name, telephone number and address. Make sure that your insurance covers you while away from home.

DISABLED TRAVELERS

Florida is striving to make more and more destinations fully accessible to the disabled. For information on the regions you will be visiting, contact the **Center for Independent Living**, which has branches in Miami at 1335 Northwest 14th Street, 305-547-5444; in Winter Park at 720 North Denning Drive, 407-623-1070; in Gainesville at 1023 Southeast 4th Avenue, 352-378-7474; in Tampa at 12310 North Nebraska Avenue, Suite F, 813-975-6560; in Fort Myers at 3626 Evans Avenue, 941-277-1547; in Tallahassee at 572-C Appleyard Drive, 904-575-9621; and in Pensacola at 513 East Fairfield Drive, 904-435-9343.

There are numerous organizations providing helpful information for disabled travelers. Among them are: **Society for the Advancement of Travel for the Handicapped** at 347 5th Avenue, Suite 610, New York, NY 10016, 212-447-7284; the **Travel Information Service**, 215-329-5715; **Flying Wheels Travel** at P.O. Box 382, Owatonna, MN 55060, 800-535-6790; and **Mobility International** USA at P.O. Box 10767, Eugene, OR 97440, 541-343-1284.

For general travel advice, you can contact **Travelin' Talk**, a networking organization. ~ P.O. Box 3534, Clarksville, TN 37043; 615-552-6670.

Write for more information about **Trout Pond**, a recreation area accessible to the handicapped, located near Tallahassee in the Apalachicola National Forest. ~ Wakulla Ranger District, 1773 Crawfordville Highway, Crawfordville, FL 32327; 904-926-3561.

FOREIGN TRAVELERS

Passports and Visas   Most foreign visitors need a passport and tourist visa to enter the United States. Contact your nearest United States Embassy or Consulate well in advance to obtain a visa and to check on any other entry requirements.

Customs Requirements Foreign travelers are allowed to carry in the following: 200 cigarettes (1 carton), 50 cigars, or 2 kilograms (4.4 pounds) of smoking tobacco; one liter of alcohol for personal use only (you must be 21 years of age to bring in alcohol); and US$100 worth of duty-free gifts that can include an additional quantity of 100 cigars. You may bring in any amount of currency, but must fill out a form if you bring in over US$10,000. Carry any prescription drugs in clearly marked containers. (You may have to produce a written prescription or doctor's statement for the custom's officer.) Meat or meat products, seeds, plants, fruits and narcotics are not allowed to be brought into the United States. Contact the **United States Customs Service** for further information. ~ 1301 Constitution Avenue NW, Washington, DC 20229; 202-927-6724.

Driving If you plan to rent a car, an international driver's license should be obtained before arriving in the United States. Some car rental agencies require both a foreign license and an international driver's license. Many also require a lessee to be at least 25 years of age; all require a major credit card.

Currency United States money is based on the dollar. Bills come in denominations of $1, $5, $10, $20, $50 and $100. Every dollar is divided into 100 cents. Coins are the penny (1 cent), nickel (5 cents), dime (10 cents) and quarter (25 cents). Half-dollar and dollar coins are rarely used. You may not use foreign currency to purchase goods and services in the United States. Consider buying traveler's checks in dollar amounts. You may also use credit cards affiliated with an American company such as Interbank, Barclay Card and American Express.

Electricity Electric outlets use currents of 110 volts, 60 cycles. For appliances made for other electrical systems, you will need a transformer or other adapter.

Weights and Measures The United States uses the English system of weights and measures. American units and their metric equivalents are: 1 inch = 2.5 centimeters; 1 foot (12 inches) = 0.3 meter; 1 yard (3 feet) = 0.9 meter; 1 mile (5280 feet) = 1.6 kilometers; 1 ounce = 28 grams; 1 pound (16 ounces) = 0.45 kilogram; 1 quart (liquid) = 0.9 liter.

Outdoor Adventures

CAMPING

Florida offers a variety of camping opportunities from primitive camping in wilderness areas to recreational vehicle parks that resemble fashionable resorts. For a listing of state parks and recreation areas, send for the *Florida State Parks Guide*. ~ Department of Environmental Protection, Florida Park Service, 3900 Commonwealth Boulevard, Tallahassee, FL 32399; 904-488-9872.

For information on camping in state forests, contact the **Department of Agriculture and Consumer Services**. ~ Division of Forestry,

3125 Conner Boulevard, Tallahassee, FL 32399; 904-488-4274. Information on camping in national forests may be obtained from the **U.S.D.A. Forest Service**. ~ 325 John Knox Road, Building F-100, Tallahassee, FL 32303; 904-942-9300. For information on national parks and seashores, contact the **National Park Service**. ~ Southeast Field Area, 75 Spring Street Southwest, Atlanta, GA 30303; 404-331-4290.

The **Florida Association of RV Parks and Campgrounds** puts out an annual *Florida Camping Directory* of over 200 private campgrounds and RV parks. ~ 1340 Vickers Drive, Tallahassee, FL 32303; 904-562-7151. Also, see the "Beaches & Parks" section in each chapter of this book to discover where camping is available in various areas of the state. An excellent book for visitors planning to camp in the state is *Florida Parks*, by Gerald Grow.

PERMITS

Primitive campsites are provided in certain state parks and recreation areas. You need a permit for wilderness camping away from designated sites in national forests and in certain wilderness areas of national parks and seashores. To obtain permits and information contact individual sites, as found in the "Beaches & Parks" sections of the regional chapters of this book.

The **Florida Trail Association** is creating a hiking trail from Big Cypress Preserve to the Panhandle. Much of it has been completed. By joining the association, you can hike private lands crossed by the trail and obtain maps. ~ P.O. Box 13708, Gainesville, FL 32604; 800-843-1882.

BOATING

From paddle boat to cruise ship, just about every imaginable method of ploughing the waters is available in Florida. You can bring your own boat and travel the Intracoastal Waterway or laze away the day on a quiet lake with a fishing pole. And if you have no boat, you can rent or charter a craft of just about any size or speed. Each chapter in this book offers suggestions on how to go about finding the vessel of your choice. Most marinas and other rental agencies will arm you with maps and advice.

Regional guide packets for boaters and divers may be obtained by contacting the **Florida Sports Foundation**. ~ 1319 Thomaswood Drive, Tallahassee, FL 32312; 904-488-8347. Boating regulations and safety information may be obtained from the **Division of Law Enforcement**. ~ 3900 Commonwealth Boulevard, Mail Station 630, Tallahassee, FL 32399; 904-488-5757.

Canoeing is popular throughout Florida. To obtain the *Florida Recreational Trails System—Canoe Trails* brochure contact the **Office of Greenways and Trails**. ~ 3900 Commonwealth Boulevard, Mail Station 795, Tallahassee, FL 32399; 904-487-4784. *Canoeing the National Forests in Florida* is available from the **U.S.D.A.**

Forest Service. ~ 325 John Knox Road, Building F-100, Talla-hassee, FL 32303; 904-942-9300.

Few places match Florida for the variety of water sports available. Swimming, scuba diving, snorkeling or just basking on a float are options wherever you can get to the shore, spring, lake or river. Surfing is popular on certain ocean and Gulf beaches when the wind is up. Drownings do occur now and then in all these places, but they can be avoided as long as you respect the power of the water, heed appropriate warnings and use good sense.

WATER SAFETY

Wherever you swim, never do it alone. In the ocean or Gulf, if the surf is high, keep your face toward the incoming waves. If you go surfing, learn the proper techniques and dangers from an expert before you start out. Respect signs warning of dangerous currents and undertows. If you get caught in a rip current or any tow that makes you feel out of control, don't try to swim against it. Head across it, paralleling the shore. Exercise caution in the use of floats, inner tubes or rafts: unexpected currents can quickly carry you out to sea.

◆◆◆◆◆◆◆◆◆◆◆◆◆◆◆◆◆◆◆◆

Florida calls itself the "Largemouth Bass Capital of the World" because of the abundance of this freshwater fish, partic-ularly in the north-west.

Jellyfish stings are commonly treated with papain-type meat tenderizers. If you go scalloping, swim in or wade around in murky waters where shellfish dwell, wear canvas shoes to protect your feet.

Remember, you are a guest in the sea. All rights belong to the creatures who dwell there, including sharks. Though they are rarely seen and seldom attack, they should be respected. A wise swimmer who spots a fin simply heads unobtrusively for shore. On the other hand, if dolphins are cavorting in your area, don't worry; they may put on quite a show.

Tragedies occur annually in springs, often to scuba divers who venture into deep caves and become disoriented or swim in off-lim-its areas. Spring diving is not for novices; accomplished divers should accompany every outing. Alligators have been known to drown swimmers or divers who venture into off-limits areas. Pay attention to warning signs; they mean what they say.

Life jackets are a must if you want your boating trip to end happily. This goes for canoes as well as larger and faster craft. And never, never take your eyes off a child who is near the water, no matter how calm conditions may appear. With so much wonder-ful water available in Florida, the best protection is to know how to swim, and to use your good sense.

Over 60 varieties of commercial fish are gathered from Florida wa-ters; shellfish are harvested along all the coasts; and bass and bream almost jump from hook to frying pan beside freshwater

FISHING

streams. Florida is an angler's paradise. How you approach the sport is up to you. You can dangle a hook from a cane pole into a sluggish slough or chase bonefish in the Keys. You can spend the day casting off an abandoned bridge or haul in tarpon from a rollicking charter boat. You can gather scallops with your hands and a bucket in the shallows or catch blue crabs in a net. You may even find yourself casting a seine for mullet along the beach on an autumn morning.

Several species of catfish and members of the sunfish family, such as bluegills, shellcrackers and crappie, abound in large lakes and backroad ponds and canals. Speckled perch are sought out during their spring spawning period, especially in the Lake Okeechobee area. Panfishing season begins with the coming of spring throughout the state and continues through the winter in the far south.

Saltwater fish are varied and abundant in the Gulf and ocean off the shores of the entire state. Common varieties include pompano, bluefish, redfish, snapper, snook, grouper, trout and mackerel. Tarpon, sailfish, marlin and shark challenge sportsfishers eager for a tussle. Crawfish, oysters, stone crabs, clams and scallops may also be harvested in season from the sea.

Salt and freshwater fishing requires a license unless you are fishing from a boat or pier that has its own license. Many bait and tackle shops and sporting goods stores can provide you with the proper documentation. For more information contact a local marina or the **Department of Environmental Protection**. ~ Florida Marine Resources, 3900 Commonwealth Boulevard, Tallahassee, FL 32399; 904-487-3122.

If you'd like to try a kind of fishing that's new to you, you will find guide services available just about everywhere boats are rented and bait sold. Charter fishing is the costliest way to go out to sea; party boats take a crowd but are less expensive and usually great fun. On rivers, lakes and tiny hidden streams, guides can show you the best place to throw a hook or skim a fly.

There are also fish to be viewed in Florida. A face mask, with or without a snorkel, will open up an undersea world of incredible beauty, whether it be in a crystal spring, along the shore or out among the reefs. In fact, colorful tropical fish may well be some of Florida's loveliest hidden treasures.

TWO

Miami

A vibrant city in southeastern Florida, Miami has been viewed for much of this century as America's tropical dream destination. Longing for escape and a large dose of sunshine, visitors have continually sought out the palm-fringed beaches and sapphire waters of this carefree realm.

But like most idyllic locales, Miami and its environs embody far more than postcard-perfect beaches. Intertwined in this 2000-square-mile megalopolis are chic bayside villages, exclusive islands, grand Mediterranean areas and an array of skyscrapers. Across the pancake-flat terrain also lies a maze of bewitching waterways, traffic-choked highways and sprawling residential regions. A close inspection will even reveal a bit of the mangrove wilderness that served as the birthing place of this great resort center.

Miami's story is one of overnight success, a place built so fast and loved so soon that it's easy to forget how young it really is. Little more than a fishing village when it was incorporated in 1896, Miami didn't really evolve as a city until its frenetic 1920s land boom.

Likewise, as late as 1910, that silvery thread of barrier islands called Miami Beach was still awash with avocado and mango plantations. Not until the following decade did the ten miles of coastline finally burst with plush hotels and communities that were immediately frequented by celebrities.

The tale's prologue, however, trickles back to 1513 when Spaniard Ponce de León first set foot on this island strand. He encountered perilous coral reefs and mosquito-infested scrublands that made navigation difficult, even for the Calusa and Tequesta Indians who inhabited the shores.

It wasn't a grand lake, however, that drew railroad magnate Henry Flagler to the state's southern reaches in 1896. Rather, it was a fragrant bouquet of orange blossoms, sent by an astute pioneer named Julia Tuttle. When an unusually harsh freeze killed citrus groves as far south as West Palm Beach, where Flagler had created an elite vacation community, Tuttle dispatched the blooms as proof of warmer climes to the south. Previously skeptical of Miami's treasures, Flagler was at last convinced.

Flagler's railroad fueled progress in the area, bringing curious northern settlers to a land of warm ocean breezes and sunshine. New Jersey businessman John Collins was one of the first to catch a train southward to inspect a yet unseen coconut plantation he had purchased on Miami's barrier islands. Enchanted by the scene, he planted more fruit trees and began constructing a wooden bridge that would link these windswept isles to the mainland.

By 1913, Collins went broke with only half the bridge built and turned to Carl Fisher, inventor of the auto headlight and owner of the Indianapolis Speedway, for help. A shrewd businessman, Fisher finished the bridge in exchange for a swath of island property, then set about molding his new sandspur into beach-rimmed isles with pretty shopping plazas, golf courses, hotels and waterfront homes.

When the 1920s land boom struck, Miami was primed. "Binder boys" stood on street corners hawking real estate for mere pennies, land that turned thousands of investors into overnight millionaires. Dazzled by this newfound investment, wealthy industrialists built fancy oceanfront estates and began shaping the downtown area. To the south, Staten Islander Ralph Munroe formed a quaint bayside village while pioneer George Merrick carved a Mediterranean-style community out of palmetto fronds.

Waves of "tin can tourists" arrived from the frigid north, setting up tents and other makeshift homes along Miami's shores. "Miami or Bust" read the signs that sprinkled highways across the country. Suddenly, Miami Beach was the dream vacation of every red-blooded American.

But the dream was temporarily dashed in 1926 when a perilous hurricane proved that even paradise can go awry. Nearly 400 people were killed and thousands of buildings destroyed or damaged. Then the Depression hit. The area fell into a lull until the mid-1930s, when a new building boom changed the look of southern Miami Beach: art deco architecture began sprouting everywhere. Radiant pastel buildings sporting geometric and streamlined moderne designs—deemed visual metaphors of progress—breathed new life into the area.

During the next two decades, central Miami Beach was a flurry of activity as more glitzy hotels took their places on the sand and posh neighborhoods sprouted along the waterways. At the same time, cultural change was having a major impact on the area. Previously an exclusive niche for the old-money elite, Miami Beach was beginning to attract many Jewish settlers escaping the cold northeastern states or looking for retirement havens. Despite elements of anti-Semitism, half the Miami Beach population was Jewish by 1947.

No doubt Miami's image as a land of promise was also partially responsible for drawing a new group of immigrants between 1960 and 1980. Sparked by Fidel Castro's Cuban revolution in 1959, more than half a million Cubans fled to Miami during subsequent years, searching for political sanctuary and a better life. Yet another large exodus occurred in 1980, when about 125,000 Cuban refugees arrived on Miami's shores by boat.

Eclipsing all previous changes in Miami's history, the arrival of these immigrants ignited a cultural metamorphosis that would dramatically alter this tropical realm. The Latin influence transformed every aspect of Miami's character: language, architecture, fashions, food, music and the media.

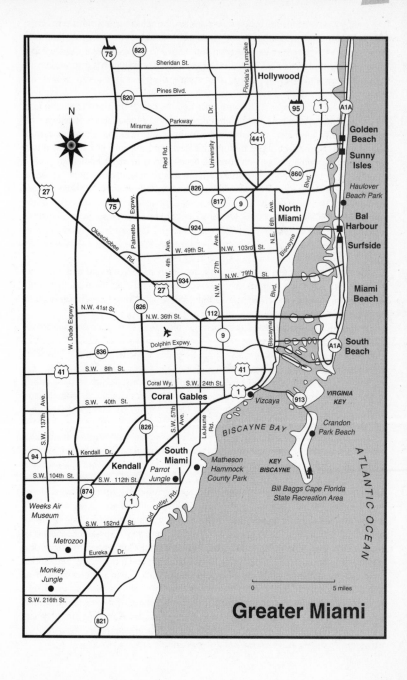

Greater Miami

Today, Central and South Americans are also establishing new lives here. Together with the Cubans, they make up nearly half of Dade County's 1.9 million residents. Spanish billboards dot the metropolis, and sleek Latin financial institutions line the streets of downtown. Throughout the area, Spanish is spoken just as much as English. As in no other major American city, Miami is dominated by Latin politics. Many key area government leaders are Latino, continuing to vie for their piece of political pie. Local elections often center around national and foreign issues dealing with Latin America rather than what's going on in Miami.

In the 1500s, the Tequesta Indians called the swamplands Lake of Mayaime, or "very large" lake, referring to northwestern Lake Okeechobee. The passage of time transformed the words into Miami.

Like virtually every sprawling urban area, Miami is not without big city problems. Healthy crime statistics, racial strife and drug smuggling have not boded well for Miami's vacation image. The city has unique problems as well, like Hurricane Andrew, which struck the coast 25 miles southwest of Miami in August 1992. Packing winds that gusted through Coral Gables at 164 miles per hour, the storm left billions of dollars worth of damage.

But the millions of travelers who come here each year have found much to write home about in the city's sophisticated art, architecture and entertainment, and lovely beaches and parks, as well as in the multifaceted communities that surround Miami in greater Dade County.

Within this culturally varied county lie 27 towns, all basking in a continuously breezy, subtropical climate. While the average temperature hovers splendidly between 70° and 80° Fahrenheit, visitors can expect a few dog-day afternoons when the thermometer climbs to 90° in the summer.

Ethnic diversity is a keynote in the neighborhoods scattered across these balmy environs, where the population includes African-Americans, Asians, Haitians and Jews, as well as numerous Latino cultures. Other groups have found their niches here, too, including gays, artists, trendsetters and aristocrats.

Among the many immigrants who have found permanent sanctuary in Miami are 65,000 Haitians. Fleeing poverty and political turmoil on their island, many settled north of downtown in one of Miami's oldest neighborhoods. There they painted the modest shops and bungalows crayon colors, and fused Caribbean creole flavor into the area. Signs of "Bienvenue!" (Welcome!) greet visitors of Little Haiti.

Miami the city is home to a mere 360,000 people. Its nucleus is a stunning downtown. At night, its skyscrapers form a brilliant skein with glowing bands of colored light twinkling against Biscayne Bay and winking at the Southern Cross so lucid in the sky. Nearby, ships ebb and flow through one of the nation's busiest ports.

Barely two miles across the water rests Miami Beach, a glittering chain of oceanside development that's now enjoying rejuvenation. Still a haven for both the elderly and millions of tourists each year, the area is being renovated by new Latin American settlers who are restoring dilapidated condominiums. Along the southern tip, South Beach is emerging as Miami's shining star, where airy pastel enclaves with streamlined designs draw Europeans, artisans, musicians and actors.

Nestled on the west side of downtown is Little Havana, Miami's Cuban core, which centers around a bustling street flanked by Latin diners, small motels and glitzy nightclubs.

Southerly Virginia Key and Key Biscayne are heady little islands smothered in pine and palm trees and blessed with ribbons of billowy sand and demure waters. Movie stars and presidents have long taken refuge among these shores.

Nearby Coconut Grove is a former hippy harbor that turned trendy in the '80s. Swank shops and galleries, chic discos and eateries dot the bustling streets here, shrouded in towering oak trees.

Coral Gables, touted as the "Miami Riviera," is the area's Mediterranean mecca. Pristine country-club homes mingle with Moorish castles and rows of posh shops. Through the years, these preplanned surroundings have represented the world of Miami's high society.

Across Dade County's southern reaches, sprawling housing developments—desperate for more space—creep through farmlands and back up to the Everglades. On the flip side, northern Dade has already grown beyond its means, a vast parcel of suburbia bursting to the Gold Coast.

Through it all, Miami remains a multifaceted city that continues to struggle for a clear identity, determined to retain its hold as a vacation center while evolving as a Latin American capital. For some, it is a glorious place in the sun, a sphere of heedless days and tropical nights. For others, it signifies a pulsing international center poised on the southeastern tip of the continent.

South Beach

During the post-Depression building boom of the late 1920s and early '30s, South Miami Beach became flush with an architectural rage called streamlined moderne. These geometric, art deco buildings popped up on every street corner and were soon the neighborhood's mainstay. Now, 80 square blocks—bordered roughly by the ocean, Lenox Court, 5th Street and 23rd Street—bulge with more than 800 historic buildings, making this the most concentrated historic district in the nation.

These days, South Beach is experiencing a grand revival of the 1930s and '40s. This oceanside necklace of pastel-coated buildings, breezy alfresco cafés and palm tree–studded sidewalks is foremost a traveler's fairy-tale world.

SIGHTS

Located in the Oceanfront Auditorium, the **Miami Design and Preservation League** can supply maps, information, and biking and walking tours to get you started in the area. ~ 1001 Ocean Drive; 305-672-2014.

To best absorb the deco ambience, stroll **Ocean Drive** between 6th and 23rd streets. Like a decorated candy store, this beachfront roadway brims with sherbet-colored hotels and cafés that snatch continuous ocean breezes.

True to deco style, the powder-blue-and-white **Park Central Hotel** is a three-building study in geometrics. The 1937 beauty is adorned with fluted eaves, octagonal windows and dramatic vertical columns. For a peek at South Beach life in the '30s, check out the black-and-white photographs in the hotel lobby. ~ 640 Ocean Drive; 305-538-1611.

Down at the **Beacon Hotel**, parapets climb the facade and thin racing stripes slip around the sides of the 1936 building. ~ 720 Ocean Drive; 305-531-5891.

The monolithic date and temperature sign at 1001 Ocean Drive still spits out the numbers, as it has since the 1930s. Rooted firmly in the sand next to the **Beach Patrol Station**, the sign is a classic. While you're there, check out the funky lifeguard station, a nautical design that sent girls swooning in those days.

Is it a spaceship or a big awning for the car? The "flying saucer sculptures" at the **Clevelander Hotel** look pretty hokey now, but in 1938 they were the rage. Besides, guests still use them as sunshields. A shady situation, indeed. ~ 1020 Ocean Drive; 305-531-3485.

Typical of the Mediterranean architecture sprinkled throughout the area, the majestic **Amsterdam Palace** is marked by a marble sculpture of "Kneeling Aphrodite." The three-story manor, now an apartment house, is fashioned after the Dominican Republic's Alcazar de Colón, which was home to the son of Christopher Columbus. ~ 1114 Ocean Drive.

With a yellow-and-white art deco exterior somewhat resembling the frosting of a Zinger snackcake, the hotel **Leslie** was built in 1937. ~ 1244 Ocean Drive; 305-531-8800.

The pink-and-peach **Carlyle** forms an impressive series of curves, vertical columns and dramatic circular overhangs called "eyebrows." Built in 1941, the Carlyle was once a bustling hotel but is now empty. ~ 1250 Ocean Drive.

Next door, the **Cardozo Hotel** preens with symmetrical cantilevers and precise strokes of cream paint. Named after 1930s Supreme Court Justice Benjamin Cardozo, the hotel was featured in 1996 film *The Birdcage* with Robin Williams and in the 1959 film *A Hole in the Head* starring Frank Sinatra, who was once a regular around South Beach. ~ 1300 Ocean Drive; 305-535-6500.

Nowadays, the Cardozo and other deco beauties frequently star in television shows and commercials. European modeling firms, also taking advantage of the artsy surroundings, fill up several hotels during the winter months while filming.

Another favorite of film crews is **Española Way** (between Washington and Drexel avenues). Walk this whimsical way and you will discover a Disneyesque vision of peach Mediterranean buildings, colorful striped canopies, wrought-iron balconies and arched windows—all framed by palm trees and gas lamps. Along the way are marvelous vintage clothing nooks, an alfresco café and galleries where you're apt to find artists at work.

Founded in 1922 by settlers who envisioned a Spanish-themed artists' colony, the area never really took off. Locals will tell you, though, how Desi Arnaz started the rumba craze on this very street. Restoration has lent a magical look to the street.

Just around the corner, eye-catching cameo embellishments adorn the entrance of the **Cameo Theatre**. The district's premier theater drew jetsetters to international films when it opened in 1938. As fate would have it, the theater-turned-nightclub with state-of-the-art light shows is the setting for reggae, funk and modern rock concerts. Open weekends. ~ 1445 Washington Avenue; 305-532-0922.

One of the grandest deco buildings, the 1928 **Main Post Office** is crowned by a marble and stained-glass lantern. Inside, light streams in through the glass, reflecting on rich murals and bronze grillwork that creep up a vast rotunda. ~ 1300 Washington Avenue.

Also in the government district, **Old City Hall** asserts its presence with an eight-story neo-classical tower, one of the tallest in these parts. Mediterranean in style, this 1927 building has column-studded corridors that brood with history. ~ 1130 Washington Avenue.

Farther south on Washington Avenue lies a strip that, the city will tell you, is "primed" for redevelopment. In other words, the shops are run down and rows of frame homes haven't seen a coat of fresh paint in years. Still, this area offers a slice of local life. Crusty old Cuban men shoot the breeze on their front porches while dogs laze around the sidewalks. Friendly merchants chat in Spanish to shoppers, pushing specials of the day.

To see neighborhood restoration at its best, head east a block and navigate

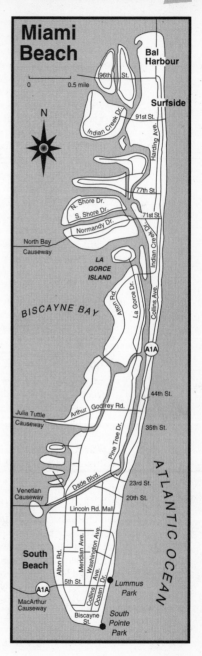

Pennsylvania, Euclid and Jefferson avenues. Quiet and very intimate, these roadways are rimmed with century-old oaks, massive banyans and flourishing seagrapes. The true colors, though, emanate from the charming deco homes and quaint apartment buildings. Distinct strokes of paint—namely, turquoise, pale yellow, salmon and seafoam green—have been carefully applied to cantilevers and parapets, creating a soothing visual effect. For example, try driving by the **Milfred Apartments** (936 Pennsylvania Avenue), **Rosebloom Apartments** (820 Euclid Avenue) and **Murray Apartments** (750 Jefferson Avenue).

A bit farther north, you'll find the **Jackie Gleason Theater of the Performing Arts**, where Miami's favorite entertainer broadcast his national television series. Another deco design, the 2705-seater has a sleek, rounded facade and serves as the venue for Broadway series performances and major ballet and symphony events. ~ 1700 Washington Avenue; 305-673-7300.

If it's a cloudy day, you might stop off at the **Bass Museum of Art**. A streamlined marble motif, the two-story cultural house contains a limited collection of sculptures, period furniture, objets d'art and Old Master paintings, including a Peter Paul Rubens. More interesting, though, are the ever-changing contemporary European and American exhibits as well as historic art from around the world. Closed Monday. Admission. ~ 2121 Park Avenue; 305-673-7530.

LODGING

Despite the decline of many Miami Beach highrise hotels, prices remain at a premium. The trick here is not so much where you stay but when. During the summer months, when temperatures soar, hotel rates plummet as much as 50 percent. One exception is South Beach in South Miami Beach, where a revival of 1930s architecture has spawned small-scale hotels with real character and year-round moderate price tags to match.

The **Colony Hotel** is easily the classiest resting place on the beachfront esplanade. After an 18-month restoration, the art deco

✔ CHECK THESE OUT—UNIQUE SIGHTS

- Delight in the art deco architecture and bustling streetlife as you stroll South Beach's **Ocean Drive**. *page 33*
- Step back to the Renaissance at **Vizcaya Museum and Gardens**, a vast Italianate villa built by farming magnate James Deering. *page 60*
- Sip high tea in the stunning Coral Gables **Biltmore Hotel**, where ceilings are adorned with frescoes and massive chandeliers. *page 79*
- Practice saying "Polly want a cracker?" before visiting the 1000 tropical birds at **Parrot Jungle and Gardens**, a Southern Dade County attraction since 1936. *page 85*

gem reopened in 1991 with lovely results: a tiny lobby area with marble floors and ethereal distressed walls, and 36 contemporary rooms with blonde oak furniture, valance draperies and soothing hues of mauve and pale green. A bustling bistro with a dramatic glass-framed fireplace welcomes guests out front. ~ 736 Ocean Drive; 305-673-0088, 800-226-5669. DELUXE TO ULTRA-DELUXE.

The **Park Central Hotel** evokes a real sense of the area's past. An art deco favorite, this 1937 moderne palace is chock full of wonderful black-and-white photos of old Miami. New life has been breathed into the antique terrazzo floors and mahogany ceiling fans throughout the lobby. Guest rooms—many with ocean views—are far from fancy; restored '30s furniture and spotless white walls display special care. ~ 640 Ocean Drive; 305-538-1611, 800-727-5236. DELUXE TO ULTRA-DELUXE.

Slipped into one of South Beach's hottest beachfront blocks, **Casa Grande** is as soothing as its neighborhood is hopping. Amid the lobby's softly lit recesses are intimate seating areas and soft seagrass mats to cushion your feet. This Mediterranean-style confection has 33 studios and suites with a primitive chic look: rich Indonesian mahogany and teak furnishings, batik-shaded lamps and French- and Italian-tile floors. Full kitchens are an added perk. Casa Grande is sought out by celebrities, so keep out a careful star watch. ~ 834 Ocean Drive; 305-672-7003, 800-688-7678. ULTRA-DELUXE.

A no-frills inn on a congested street, the **Bristol-Deco Hotel** offers 32 clean but sparse rooms. French doors and white ceiling fans give a breezy air to the small lobby of this establishment. There are no views here, but the beach beckons from just a block away. ~ 1340 Collins Avenue; 305-531-3755. MODERATE.

Beautiful European models frequently stay at the **Cavalier** while filming television commercials. This hostelry features a lobby with mirrored walls, green marble fireplace, dramatic ceilings and wrought-iron couches. The 45 oversized rooms and suites contain an interesting combination of period furnishings and high-tech portable phones and VCRs. ~ 1320 Ocean Drive; 305-534-2135, 800-688-7678. DELUXE TO ULTRA-DELUXE.

You'll find a chic crowd at the **Cardozo Hotel**, which is full of high gloss and modern decor. The 1939 design and three floors of sleek cantilevers and delicate strokes of paint are no less than a streamlined heaven. Rooms are bathed in deco blue colors and have shiny lacquer furniture. ~ 1300 Ocean Drive; 305-535-6500, 800-782-6500. DELUXE TO ULTRA-DELUXE.

One of the country's busiest youth hostels has an art deco address and a pretty peach Mediterranean building. At **Hostelling International—Miami Beach,** wrought-iron balconies buzz with people-watchers, and the lobby is a flurry of activity. A 1920 amalgamation of painted cinderblock and dramatic cantilevers, the stopover is two blocks from the ocean and shares quarters with the

Clay Hotel. The hotel offers 100 sparse but tidy rooms, while the hostel has separate dormitories for men and women. Kitchen facilities provided. ~ 1438 Washington Avenue; 305-534-2988, 800-379-2529, fax 305-673-0346. BUDGET.

DINING

To dine in South Beach is to relive the fabulous '30s and '40s. Artfully restored pastel buildings provide fairy-tale enclaves for breezy sidewalk cafés and intimate indoor eateries that stretch for 20 blocks along South Miami Beach.

When **Joe's Stone Crab** opened in 1913, it cornered the market on stone crabs, and little has changed since. The local institution at the southern foot of Miami Beach has infamously long lines. Hungry diners allow bibs to be tied around their necks and subsequently feast on succulent Florida stone crabs dipped in mustard sauce and served with extra-large homemade fries. Miamians insist Joe's serves the best Key lime pie in the United States. Since stone crabs are only available October through May, Joe's might be closed during the summer. ~ 227 Biscayne Street; 305-673-0365. BUDGET TO DELUXE.

Century Restaurant, one of the toniest restaurants below Fifth Street, is known for its bountiful—and grain-chocked—Sunday brunch. The Century's hand-designed stone tables and wrought-iron chairs encircle a pool outside on the patio and continue into the first floor of this small and smartly decorated hotel. The menu leans toward the health conscious and meatless: grilled salmon sautéed in shallot butter and appetizers like grilled shrimp and veggies. The crowd is as stylish as the decor. Three meals a day are served. ~ 140 Ocean Drive; 305-674-8855. MODERATE.

The sidewalk fare at **A Fish Called Avalon** is fresh, imaginative and Floridaish. From its art deco perch in the restored Avalon Hotel, this sleek eatery offers locally caught fish and shellfish fused with tropical fruits and vegetables. There's something new every day, though you're apt to find curried snapper with grilled plantains, chayote and a cool orange sauce served with black-bean salsa or blackened grouper with a papaya relish, sautéed vegetables and herb-roasted potatoes. Chicken and pasta dishes are also tops. White table linens and slip covers on the chairs create a minimalist mood that's appropriately beachy—and positively romantic on a windswept night. Live guitar entertainment nightly. Dinner only. Closed Monday. ~ 700 Ocean Drive; 305-532-1727. DELUXE TO ULTRA-DELUXE.

Foremost among the sidewalk set is the 24-hour **News Café**, where a rather bohemian crowd gathers to sip cappuccino and graze on deli sandwiches and flaky croissants. Serving three meals a day, they also have a full bar, wine list and grill items. The small outdoor wooden tables and wrought-iron chairs create a perfect

people-watching station. ~ 800 Ocean Drive; 305-538-6397. BUD-
GET TO MODERATE.

One of the district's most hip dining addresses, **The Strand**
caters to a mixed bag of artisans and nouveau riche. An arches-and-
mirrors motif establishes a minimalist style, while
the menu offers nouvelle treatments of seafood, pasta
and chicken. For those still waiting to make the big
time, a budget section includes meatloaf and baked
chicken. Closed Monday in the summer. Dinner only. ~
671 Washington Avenue; 305-532-2340. DELUXE.

There's a great news-
stand inside the News
Café which sells cig-
ars, suntan lotions
and the latest novels
on Miami.

In a city where Thai restaurants tend to be average at
best, **Ruen Thai** stands out. The little dining room is stunning with elaborately carved teak tables under glass. The
menu is loaded with ginger and curry dishes (the grouper curry deserves high marks) as well as house specialties such as crispy duck
and a delicious lobster chili paste. Best of all, any dish can be ordered from mild to sizzling hot. Dinner only. ~ 947 Washington
Avenue; 305-534-1504. MODERATE.

Lulu's is the area's tribute to southern dining—an upscale,
down-home place that pushes chicken-fried steak, meatloaf, fried
catfish and collard greens. Old hubcaps and gas station signs are
parked on the walls downstairs, while the second floor is a shrine
to Elvis Presley. Don't miss Elvis' fried peanut butter and banana
sandwich. ~ 1053 Washington Avenue; 305-532-6147. MODERATE.

An annual entry on lists of Miami's best restaurants, **Osteria
Del Teatro** is a bona fide South Beach tradition. Visiting luminaries and local glitterati vie for the dozen tables and feast on salmon
and fennel in orange juice, spinach crêpes and salmon-encircled
eggplant. Reservations are often needed weeks in advance. Dinner
only. Closed Tuesday. ~ 1443 Washington Avenue; 305-538-7850.
DELUXE.

Yuca—the name refers both to the tropical root vegetable and
to the Young Upscale Cuban Americans who adore the restaurant's
inventive cuisine. This mix of new American and Cuban cooking,
or "nuevo Cubano," has produced inspiring dishes such as sweet
plantains stuffed with cured beef, baby back ribs with spicy guava
sauce and braised oxtail in a La Mancha red wine sauce. ~ 501
Lincoln Road; 305-538-9822. DELUXE TO ULTRA-DELUXE.

Grillfish lives up to its name, offering a wide variety of fish
dishes and homemade desserts at reasonable prices. Servers don't
consider attitude a part of the job. Grilled fish is the specialty, but
don't miss the mussels drenched in garlic sauce, the shrimp piccata,
chicken and calamari specials and the ponderous choice of desserts. Dinner only. ~ 1444 Collins Avenue; 305-538-9908. BUDGET.

Gino's Italian Restaurant is one of those refreshing spots with
cozy red booths, plastic grapes and kindly, attentive waiters. Gino's

offers basic Italian fare, such as lasagna, beef *bragiola* and chicken francese. Soft piano music makes you forget about the oceanside hubbub just outside the door. Dinner only. ~ 1906 Collins Avenue; 305-532-6426. MODERATE.

On the quiet southern end of South Beach, **Nemo's** has ultra-mod decor: chairs and tables done in metal geometrics, animal prints and zinc work. The open kitchen churns out lots of sashimi, wok-cooked cuisine and baby lettuce drenched in balsamic vinegar and olive oil. They also have a great baked chicken with cranberry sauce and roasted garlic mashed potatoes. A must. ~ 100 Collins Avenue; 305-532-4550. DELUXE.

SHOPPING   Throughout South Beach, threads of spiffy modern buildings shelter eclectic shops that are perfect for oceanside browsing. Without a doubt, shopping here is sheer entertainment.

Shake off the sand and stroll into **Chocolate,** which bears not candies but chic beach paraphernalia: teeny bikinis, T-shirts and psychedelic painted jewelry. ~ 119 5th Street; 305-674-1906.

Washington Avenue is quickly becoming the place to drop a buck. Vintage clothing and furniture shops and bohemian and ultra-hip boutiques line this noisy thoroughfare.

If you don't like the crazy, 1960s-style fabrics and clothes at **Betsey Johnson,** you'll love the store's decor: Black-and-white checkered floors are accented by hot-pink walls bearing funky art murals. ~ 805 Washington Avenue; 305-673-0023.

A pedestrian center running east and west, **Lincoln Road Mall** was carved out of mangrove swamps back in 1913. For decades a mecca for chic urbanites, the mall now lies nearly deserted much of the time but still possesses a few interesting shops and art galleries. ~ On Lincoln Road between Washington and Alton roads; 305-531-3442.

Immerse yourself in modern art at the increasingly popular **South Florida Art Center,** a collection of galleries spanning three blocks along the mall. About 75 Miami area artists expend their creative energies here. The focus is on contemporary works in all media, although you'll encounter some impressive Renaissance, impressionist, rococo and even exotic Caribbean paintings and sculptures. ~ Along the 800, 900 and 1000 blocks of Lincoln Road Mall; 305-674-8278.

Ete sells hiply understated linen and cotton casual clothes for women and men, shoes, cards, sunglasses and jewelry. ~ 724 Lincoln Road Mall; 305-672-3265.

Lincoln Road Mall has a number of well-stocked furniture and accessory stores packed with one-of-a-kind furniture and haute maintenant knickknacks, but **Details** is the king of Cool Stuff. ~ 1031 Lincoln Road Mall; 305-531-1325.

Pick up a good read at **Books & Books,** a well-stocked mart that stays open until midnight on weekends. ~ 933 Lincoln Road Mall; 305-532-3222.

Formality takes over at **Linda's House of Linen,** where you'll find delicately embroidered linens and towels, as well as fans from all over the world. ~ 612 Lincoln Road Mall; 305-531-3902.

For the hottest nighttime action, head straight to South Beach. This beachside strand is quickly emerging as the heart of Miami's entertainment scene. Here a bohemian mood has spawned blocks of avant-garde clubs as well as breezy sidewalk cafés. Most of the action here is late-night, with many establishments staying open until dawn. The trend is toward alfresco jazz as well as the more unusual "progressive" clubs, which create a smaller rendition of New York City's avant-garde scene.

NIGHTLIFE

On Friday, a happy-hour crowd shows up at **South Point Seafood House and Brewing Company,** where salsa and calypso are played on a waterfront boardwalk. ~ 1 Washington Avenue; 305-673-1708.

Everyone goes to **The Strand** for a drink some time or other. The wavy glass block bar, which is part of a restaurant, is where you relax and soak up South Beach chicness. ~ 671 Washington Avenue; 305-532-2340.

The club with the best-dressed clientele is **Les Bains,** a once Moroccan-style bank refashioned into a Parisian-style, haute fashion club. Eurotourists and cosmopolitan locals frequent this high-tech, strobe-lit dancefloor that is hip to hip by 1 a.m. Beware of the pricey cover charge and burly doormen who double as fashion police. ~ 753 Washington Avenue; 305-532-8768.

Uncle Sam's Music is combined with a small bar that serves beer, soda, etc. The music selection leans heavily toward underground dance music and the crowds don't overwhelm. ~ 1141 Washington Avenue; 305-532-0973.

The dusty jukebox and worn pool tables at the **Irish House Pub** hint that this is one of a dying breed of genuine neighborhood taverns. You can bet the patrons are regulars here. ~ 1430 Alton Road; 305-534-5667.

A hip, brick-and-glass fandango sprawled on the southern tip of Miami Beach, **Penrod's** is a classy sports bar where reggae, jazz and rock-and-roll emanate from various rooms. With a dozen televisions, this place is hot. ~ 1 Ocean Drive; 305-538-1111.

The huge, open-air **Amnesia** on the southernmost end of South Beach is the club favored by tourists, trendoids, the chicer-than-thous and locals who want to dance, dance, dance. The good news: plenty of nearby parking, a dazzling light show, a first-rate sound system and ample outdoor seating and darker, intimate areas. The bad news: the cover charge is a bit daunting and the club is a body jam on weekends. The Sunday afternoon tea dance draws a large gay crowd. Cover. ~ 136 Collins Avenue; 305-531-5535.

THEATER, OPERA, SYMPHONY AND DANCE For four years, Jackie Gleason broadcast his national television series from a Miami Beach theater. Reopened after an extensive facelift, the 2705-seat **Jackie Gleason Theater of the Performing Arts** offers a lineup of Broadway musicals, international and national orchestras, ballet, and Latin and Israeli dance. ~ 1700 Washington Avenue; 305-673-7300.

Built in 1934 by Paramount Studios, the 465-seat **Colony Theater** is a restored art deco beauty that hosts major ballet and symphony performances as well as contemporary dance and theater. ~ 1040 Lincoln Road; 305-674-1026.

To purchase tickets for major productions, call the theaters directly or check with **Ticketmaster** (305-358-5885) outlets.

BEACHES & PARKS

SOUTH POINTE PARK 🏊 🎣 ⚓ Cloaking the tail of South Miami Beach is this slice of close-cropped grass and meandering sidewalks. Situated near the Port of Miami, the park affords scenic views of cruise ship activity but unfortunately has a small beach. The best section leads around a jutting ledge of boulders and a 300-foot pier, where folks come to swim and snorkelers can explore colorful exotic fish. Just be careful of strong currents. Also, cruise ship traffic stirs up the water sometimes. Anglers fish from the pier or rocks for yellowtail, barracuda and snapper. To the north, the strand and highrises of Miami Beach provide an impressive panorama. Facilities include picnic pavilions, restrooms, a general store and an outdoor amphitheater. ~ On the southern tip of Miami Beach, right off of Washington Avenue.

1ST STREET BEACH OR SOUTH BEACH 🚲 🏊 🏄 🎣 There's no official name for this beach, but it's the sand spot in the Miami area. In fact, more people jam onto this one block of southern beach than in the next five blocks combined. A sprawling sports bar spawns all the action, which spills out over a sandy crest and down into the ocean. Volleyball competitions go on continuously, and loud bar music permeates the salty air. Adding a classy touch, a modern boardwalk winds down toward the ocean, where strong tradewinds and currents churn up great bodysurfing waves. It's a good place to swim but it's usually crowded. Bathing suit tops are unofficially optional. ~ At the southernmost block of Miami Beach.

First Street Beach is the *only* place to surf in the Miami area, although it pales in comparison to the waves on Florida's central East Coast.

LUMMUS PARK 🚲 🏊 🎣 Not to be confused with the smaller Lummus Park in downtown Miami, this grassy palm tree plaza wanders along eight blocks of South Miami Beach. Fine

white sand stretches 300 glorious feet to the translucent aquama-
rine ocean. Young Europeans and kite flyers favor this beach, and
the stretch between 12th and 14th streets is very popular with the
gay crowd. The best thing about the park is that South Beach lies
across the street, beckoning beachgoers to its pastel sidewalk cafés.
This beach has good windsurfing and excellent swimming; a sandbar extends about 50 yards out. Facilities include restrooms, lifeguards, a playground, shady park benches, a bandshell, bicycling
and windsurfing rentals, and food and drink vendors. ~ On South
Miami Beach, between 6th and 14th streets; 305-673-7714.

South Beach Gay Scene

As with the revitalization of so many historic communities across America—from
Boston's South End to San Francisco's Cas-
tro District—South Beach owes the success of its amazing comeback to the gay community. Initial efforts to revitalize South Beach
came from a mixed group of gay and straight preservationists who
shared a love of the historic art deco architecture of the area, and
the gay community's contribution had an important impact on the
whole development of South Beach.

For this reason, South Beach is a universally gay-friendly destination where gay men and lesbians are woven into the fabric of
everything that takes place. Ask any hotel if it's gay or gay-friendly
and the man on the other end of the phone will probably laugh
and, in the spirit of the old "I'm not gay, but my boyfriend is" joke,
will respond with "the hotel isn't, but me and the rest of the staff
are." In all seriousness, most if not all the hotels in South Beach are
gay-friendly, as are the restaurants, shops, nightclubs and beaches.

As the community blossomed, the love of aesthetic beauty became the unifying force for many groups of people. The worldwide
fashion industry adopted South Beach as its top shoot location,
and beautiful models are seen everywhere. Even those South Beach
residents who are not officially models are quite gorgeous. Some
are gay, some are straight, but it seems everyone is trying hard to
be beautiful—and most are succeeding!

Contrary to some reports, South Beach is not losing its gay
identity by becoming "the trendiest community in America." It remains a gathering place for lovers of aesthetic beauty, a spot where
the gay traveler can come for a vibrant visit. From staying at its gay
hotels and cruising its fashionable shopping areas to sunning on its
gay beaches and dancing in its nightclubs, South Beach still deserves
its playful reputation as "America's Gay Riviera."

LODGING

For information on gay-friendly hotels and bed and breakfasts,
travelers can contact **South Beach Central**, a gay-owned reservation service. ~ 1688 Meridian Avenue, Suite 106, Miami Beach, FL
33139; 305-538-3616, 800-538-3616, fax 305-538-5858.

Situated five blocks from the beach on a pretty residential street, **European Guesthouse** is a tropical inn for gay men and women. Enveloped in palm trees and painted a sunny yellow, the 1923 wood plank house offers 12 modest rooms with eclectic but inviting decor: checkered floors, bahama fans, reproduction antique furniture and a queen or king size bed. There's plenty of privacy, particularly out back, where wood decks wind through a lush garden punctuated by a whirlpool. Rates include full breakfast. ~ 721 Michigan Avenue; 305-673-6665, fax 305-672-7442. MODERATE.

For bed-and-breakfast accommodations consider the **Jefferson House**, set in a 1929 vintage home. Guests stay in a seven-room building, which is separated from the main house by a lush tropical garden and swimming pool. Each room comes with a private bath and is decorated with handpainted furniture and art deco pieces. A full gourmet breakfast is served on the terrace in the main house. Mostly men, but women are also welcome. ~ 1018 Jefferson Avenue; 305-534-5247, fax 305-534-5953. DELUXE.

To experience the true character of an art deco masterpiece, stay at **The Raleigh Hotel**, a chic 107-room establishment popular with gays and lesbians. Guest rooms combine art deco antiques with the latest technology. Facilities include an award-winning restaurant, a fitness center, a swimming pool, tennis courts, an 18-hole golf course and a beach with water-sport facilities. ~ 1775 Collins Avenue; 305-534-6300, 800-848-1775, fax 305-538-8140. DELUXE TO ULTRA-DELUXE.

Located right in the hub of all the activity is the **Penguin Hotel**, a 44-room establishment that caters to gay men and women. The decor is tropical with a few art deco flourishes. For those of you who wish to spend a longer period of time in South Beach, the hotel also offers two suites with kitchenettes. Guests comingle with local drag queens who make appearances here every afternoon. ~ 1418 Ocean Drive; 305-534-9334, 800-235-6240, fax 305-672-6240. DELUXE TO ULTRA-DELUXE.

For an upscale gay resort, don't miss **Normandy South**. Set in a 1925 Mediterranean deco located at the north end of the art deco district, this men-only guesthouse features eight spacious rooms with private baths. A garden, swimming pool and jacuzzi are among the amenities. Clothing optional. Call ahead for reservations and directions. ~ 305-674-1197. DELUXE TO ULTRA-DELUXE.

DINING

HIDDEN ▶

A gay-operated establishment, **Jeffrey's** is a must. This seafood bistro's candlelight, lace tablecloths and soft music may be the reason many locals consider this the most romantic restaurant in South Beach. Don't miss their signature crab cakes. Dinner only. ~ 1629 Michigan Avenue; 305-673-0690. MODERATE TO DELUXE.

For authentic Italian cuisine, sample the succulent dishes at **Farfalla**, an elegant trattoria that evokes the feeling of an open-air plaza. Selections range from wood-fired pizzas to fresh fish and pasta specials. Although it is not exclusively gay, many gays frequent this popular eatery. ~ 701 Washington Avenue; 305-673-2335. MODERATE.

Don't miss those boisterous all-gay tea dances at Amnesia. This open-air, tropical-style club rocks from 5 p.m. 'til 1 a.m. every Sunday. Cover. ~ 136 Collins Avenue; 305-531-5535.

With a bright blue interior and a large gay clientele, the **Palace Bar & Grill** serves three meals a day at its curvaceous bar. Beachgoers with sand-covered feet sit outside under patio umbrellas and drink chunky fruit smoothies and munch on healthy fare such as pita pockets and veggie melts. At dinner patrons enjoy specials like chicken piccata and lobster linguine marinara. ~ 1200 Ocean Drive; 305-531-9077. MODERATE.

The Front Porch is a casual waterfront restaurant that features healthy homecooked food. At breakfast, there are waffles, omelettes and fresh juices. Lunch features salads, sandwiches and soups. Turkey meat loaf served with homemade mashed potatoes is a dinner favorite. Most diners eat on the patio, which has delightful views of the ocean. ~ 1420 Ocean Drive; 305-531-8300. BUDGET TO MODERATE.

SHOPPING

Although not technically in South Beach, **Lambda Passages Bookstore** has one of the largest selections of gay- and lesbian-oriented books and videos. ~ 7545 Biscayne Boulevard, Miami Beach; 305-754-6900.

GW is a gay and lesbian emporium which features clothes, videos, books, lube and body piercing. ~ 720 Lincoln Road Mall; 305-534-4763.

A casual men's clothing shop, **Whittall and Shon** has a clientele that is 80 percent gay. They stock funky hats, funky clothes and funky underwear. ~ 1319 Washington Avenue; 305-538-2606.

NIGHTLIFE

There's no live entertainment at **Hombre,** but the videos of muscled men leave very little to the imagination. A good 24-hour neighborhood bar. ~ 925 Washington Avenue; 305-538-7883.

One of the beach's best late-night stops, **Twist** boasts no cover charge, a predominantly gay clientele and two floors that include a videobar, pinball machines, a pool table, a small dancefloor and a deejay who spins tunes on weekends. ~ 1057 Washington Avenue; 305-528-9478.

Warsaw Ballroom is one of the hottest gay nightspots in Miami. The giant dance club, which packs thousands of gay men in every weekend, hosts outrageous drag and comedy shows. In between, there's dancing and deejays. Cover. ~ 1450 Collins Avenue; 305-531-4555.

The **West End** is a low-key, dressed-down gay club located in the middle of the Lincoln Road Mall, the strip where locals go to avoid the tourist crush on Ocean Avenue and the trendoid crush on Washington. ~ 942 Lincoln Road; 305-538-9378.

BEACHES & PARKS

12TH STREET BEACH ⚓ This stretch of sand, which is part of Lummus Park, is very popular with the gay crowd. It is a tranquil beach used mostly for bathing and swimming. Facilities include lounge chairs, umbrellas and volleyball nets. Lifeguards are always on duty. One of the park's greatest attractions is that South Beach, with its vibrant cafe scene, lies across the street. ~ On South Miami Beach, between 12th and Ocean Drive; 305-673-7714.

21ST STREET BEACH ⚓ A one-block enclave of granulated sand wedged between highrises, this spot is frequented by gay men and women. The latter frequently shed their tops, making it the area's unofficial topless beach. The city's prized two-mile boardwalk, which offers "unobstructed" ocean views behind formidable skyscrapers, commences here and travels northward along a ridge of sand dunes. Swimming is good at this beach, where there are usually lifeguards. The only other facilities are food vendors. ~ On South Miami Beach at 21st Street; 305-673-7714.

▼▼▼▼▼▼▼▼▼▼▼▼▼▼▼▼
Central Miami Beach

This single stretch of beach—extending generally from 25th Street north to 87th Street—is what put Miami on the big resort map in the 20th century. A drive along the ocean here quickly reveals why. Still the nucleus of Miami's tourism, the area is concentrated with glistening highrise hotels, top-notch restaurants, an unusually wide swath of beach and miles of water on view everywhere.

Though parts of the area had declined during recent decades, a 1990s refurbishment has breathed new life into Central Miami Beach. Today it is quickly gentrifying into something that looks a lot like South Beach. North of the district, Collins Avenue is a virtual wall of freshly painted pastels. Midrise buildings are washed with peach and pink, purple and plum. Streamline moderne eyebrows and balconies decorate their facades, and royal palms accent their feet.

SIGHTS

One neighborhood that's seen little change over the years is the one on **La Gorce Drive.** This one-mile jag, north of Arthur Godfrey Road, serves as the primary address for Miami Beach's old money. Here you'll encounter crisp white palatial homes, Mediterranean estates and loads of big, wispy Australian pine trees.

Down the street lies **The Neighborhood,** seven blocks of beachy stores and apartments flanking Arthur Godfrey Road between Pine Tree Drive and Alton Road. This area also serves as a locus for the Hasidic Jewish community. More recently, young professionals have taken to this area, too, transforming many of the older, dilapidated buildings into quaint bungalows nestled along canals.

For an exceedingly strange experience, especially at night, stand on Collins Avenue, right around 42nd Street, and behold the mastodon before you. There, splashed ten stories high and 120 feet wide, is a mirror image of the **Fontainebleau Hilton**. Behind this clever trompe l'oeil mural, you'll find the real thing, a grandiose beachfront hotel with curving swimming pools and myriads of waterfalls. Though the hotel was built in 1954, the wall wasn't christened until 1986.

Queen of Miami Beach hotels, the Fontainebleau ruled the roost during the glitter days of the 1950s and '60s. With their backs to the street, the twin curved buildings have long promised exclusivity for those within their safe bounds. During the hotel's heyday, Bob Hope and Frank Sinatra frequently performed, and its impressive guest list included Joan Crawford, Joe DiMaggio, John F. Kennedy and Richard Nixon. But today, much of that glamour is gone. Its legendary show club, in fact, is now a cabaret with Las Vegas–style shows. But there's still an edge of opulence and nostalgia that makes visiting the Fontainebleau a must. ~ 4441 Collins Avenue; 305-538-2000.

One especially lovely stretch of Miami Beach, **Indian Creek Drive**, meanders along a spectacular waterway where sparkling luxury houseboats are moored. Get a different perspective of the La Gorce Drive homes across the waterway, their sweeping, well-tended estates flirting with passersby.

Things head downhill here, as "condomania" begins appearing on Collins Avenue along the ocean (but you can't see the water). Blame greedy developers and poor-sighted politicians for this mess along Miami's pristine beach. The reason behind the madness? It provides thousands of people an ocean view while shutting out the rest of the world.

THE CAUSEWAYS   Dazzling by day and stunning at night, Miami's causeways regularly dispense intoxicating views of Biscayne Bay. For beach inhabitants, these eight bridges are lifelines to the mainland, their link to the "real world." For those on the mainland, they act as gateways to pleasure centers of surf and sun.

MacArthur Causeway, which joins South Beach with downtown, offers a worthwhile side trip to **Watson Island**. Here you can watch luxury cruise ships inch their way to and fro in the **Port of Miami**.

In 1913, Miami pioneer John Collins completed the first bridge from downtown to Miami Beach. Now, the gleaming **Venetian Causeway** has taken its place and crosses six islands—San Marino Island, Dilido Island, Biscayne Island, San Marco Island, Belle Isle and Rivo Alto Island. Each with its place in the sun, they lie blanketed with plush residential areas.

The northern causeways, each with a different sumptuous view, are **Julia Tuttle**, **North Bay** (or John F. Kennedy), **Sunny Isles** and **Lehman**.

To the south, **Rickenbacker Causeway** is endowed with two natural spectacles: gorgeous turquoise waters and thin strips of sugary sand. At the end, two more pots of gold await—the smaller, less developed Virginia Key and larger Key Biscayne.

Along the way, you'll encounter seals, Florida manatees, dolphins and a killer whale—but only those living at **Miami Seaquarium**. The 35-acre attraction is flanked by water on three sides and affords a look at local marine and bird life, if you don't mind seeing it in cages and tanks. Get a hug from a sea lion, watch dolphins perform clever tricks and listen to the warbles and chirps of native birds. The place is worth visiting, though overpriced. Admission. ~ 4400 Rickenbacker Causeway; 305-361-5703.

LODGING   Towering hotels and condominiums create a virtual concrete wall eclipsing much of Miami's central coastline. If anyone intended to build a cozy motel along this stretch of beach, they never followed through.

Haute hotelier Ian Shrager's white deco palace by the sea, **The Delano**, is a fantasy fling. An enormous lamp shade hovers over the front desk; a Dali-designed seat with high-heel shoes as feet decorates the "living room" lobby. Outdoors, the "orchard" and "water salon" are Alice in Wonderland places where palm trees parade and grounds are laid with a brass bed, a full-length mirror and a human-sized chess set. Take a seat at the table for two *in* the swimming pool, or at one of the white-cushioned loungers that crowd against its sides. Also on the grounds is Aqua, a rooftop bathhouse where women can indulge in massage, meditation, and other mind- and body-altering therapies. Rooms and suites are all-white affairs—stylish but spare. Go for a spacious poolside bungalow fashioned like those in Beverly Hills. ~ 1685 Collins Avenue; 305-672-2000, 800-555-5001. ULTRA-DELUXE.

A few blocks north of South Beach, you'll find a good buy right on the beach. The **Traymore Hotel** delights with its cream-colored facade and rows of pink ledges that seem to race around the building. Like many area hostelries, the eight-story Traymore has been nicely restored. Shiny terrazzo floors and vast Greek columns grace the lobby, while formica furnishings and pastel schemes accent the modern rooms. Near the beach, a broad clay-tiled loggia surrounds a Mediterranean-style swimming pool and bar. ~ 2445 Collins Avenue; 305-534-7111, 800-445-1512. MODERATE TO DELUXE.

For ocean views at reasonable prices, it's tough to top the **Days Inn Oceanside**. Although it's next to a dingy building, the ten-story hotel saves face with its artsy pink-and-silver lobby and immaculate guest rooms. Amenities include a pool and restaurant. ~ 4299 Collins Avenue; 305-673-1513, 800-356-3017. MODERATE.

Restorations worked wonders for the 1950s-era **Best Western,** a classic Miami Beach highrise with a turquoise-and-white veneer. Things here aren't luxurious, but they are contemporary. Follow the marble floors, clusters of comfy couches and water fountains through the lobby, then take the elevator to any of 250 cheery guest rooms, decorated with modern oak furniture, wall-to-wall carpets and seaside paintings. A concrete pool and two restaurants round out the amenities. ~ 4333 Collins Avenue; 305-532-3311, 800-832-8332. DELUXE TO ULTRA-DELUXE.

Leading the pack of luxury highrises is the **Fontainebleau Hilton,** the signature address of Miami Beach. With 1206 rooms and nearly as many employees, this place is a city unto itself. Three curving, multistory buildings hug a half-mile of beach, creating an alcove for a series of pools with rushing water, hidden rocky caves and palm tree islands. The refurbished lobby, with floor-to-ceiling windows, gigantic crystal chandeliers and magnificent marble staircases, is more opulent than when the hotel opened in 1956. There are 13 restaurants and four bars, but then who's counting? Guest rooms are furnished à la French provincial, but they're far from elaborate. The high-end tab is strictly for service and surroundings. ~ 4441 Collins Avenue; 305-538-2000, 800-548-8886. ULTRA-DELUXE.

Wooden cabañas and miles of poolside concrete harken back to the days when Jackie Gleason was a familiar face at the **Eden Roc.** Perched beachside, the T-shaped, 15-story hotel sports a rooftop fixture resembling a steamship visage. Underground shops and a terrazzo lobby with Moorish columns create a time-worn, campy aura. Expect '50s-style furnishings and extra-large closets in each

✔ **CHECK THESE OUT—UNIQUE LODGING**

- *Budget:* Make new friends and save money for carousing with them when you stay at **Hostelling International—Miami Beach.** *page 37*
- *Moderate to deluxe:* Lounge on the beach in front of Miami Beach's restored **Traymore Hotel,** where Italianate architecture surrounds the alluring swimming pool. *page 48*
- *Deluxe:* Meditate on Miami riverboat traffic from a waterside jacuzzi at the **Occidental Plaza Suite Hotel,** downtown. *page 61*
- *Ultra-deluxe:* Relax in your room's Japanese hot tub at the **Mayfair House,** with its art nouveau decor and sunny atrium. *page 75*

Budget: under $50   Moderate: $50–$90   Deluxe: $90–$130   Ultra-deluxe: over $130

of 350 rooms. ~ 4525 Collins Avenue; 305-531-0000. DELUXE TO ULTRA-DELUXE.

You can easily spot the **Doral Ocean Beach Resort** by its stark white tower set against a wide spread of sand. Built in 1962, the posh complex has kept pace by adding an extensive fitness center, and by refurbishing its 420 guest rooms in plush carpets and pastel colors. There's a heated Olympic-size swimming pool and—for those with bucks to burn—a helicopter pad. ~ 4833 Collins Avenue; 305-532-3600, fax 534-7409. ULTRA-DELUXE.

Another beachfront establishment, **The Alexander Hotel** bears an edge of European refinement. Set in a condo-turned-hotel, the 150 one- and two-bedroom suites are beautifully and individually decorated in styles ranging from classic to modern, and all include full kitchens and wet bars. The private grounds are lush with swirling, boulder-lined pools and myriad flowering plants. ~ 5225 Collins Avenue; 305-865-6500, fax 305-864-8525. ULTRA-DELUXE.

DINING   A palatial Miami institution, **The Forge** has long awed diners with its extravagant rococo designs and reverential Continental cuisine. Massive antique doors, polished brass statues, ten-foot chandeliers and carved wood mantels abound in the restaurant, converted from an actual forge in 1929. Dinner only. ~ 432 Arthur Godfrey Road; 305-538-8533. ULTRA-DELUXE.

Sumptuous-looking kosher health food is found at the colorful **Pineapples**, a cramped store/restaurant combination on shoppers row. Fresh fish, seafood and chicken are prepared with care and panache. Try the grilled salmon teriyaki and exotic fruit salads. Closed on Saturday. ~ 530 Arthur Godfrey Road; 305-532-9731. MODERATE.

Sharing the Delano's chic all-white theme and co-owned by Madonna, the **Blue Door** is also worth writing home about. Its New American cuisine isn't half bad, either, with dishes such as balsamic-basted mahimahi and pan-roasted filet of beef served with artichoke paté heating up the menu. You can also expect sandwiches, vegetarian and pasta dishes, as well as breakfast staples. ~ 1685 Collins Avenue in the Delano; 305-674-6400. ULTRA-DELUXE.

Etched mirrors and art deco pinks and whites set an animated tone at **La Famiglia**. This oceanfront eatery is heavy on Italian with added touches of French. Seafood, poultry, beef and pasta are all well-represented, with specialties like stuffed breast of capon with imported mozzarella, prosciutto and spinach, Mediterranean fish stew and braised veal shanks served with a sauce of tomatoes, garlic, fresh vegetables and black olives. Closed Monday. Dinner only. ~ 2445 Collins Avenue in the Traymore Hotel; 305-534-7111. MODERATE TO DELUXE.

The **Roc Bar** doles out thick, seared burgers and greasy but addicting fries and pizza from its great beachside nook. There's an indoor section, but the best spot is outside where you can dine barefoot at plastic tables right over the sand. Brunch on weekends. ~ 4525 Collins Avenue at the Eden Roc hotel, 305-531-0000. MODERATE.

Romantic candlelit tables overlooking gardens with rushing waterfalls await at **Dominique's**. Local culinary aficionados celebrated when Dominique, owner of a popular Washington, D.C. bistro, brought his talents to this oceanfront address and began lavishing diners with nouvelle delicacies as well as exotics such as diamondback rattlesnake salad and sautéed alligator tail. He serves breakfast, lunch and dinner. ~ 5225 Collins Avenue in the Alexander Hotel; 305-861-5252. ULTRA-DELUXE.

The vast wine cellar at The Forge boasts some rare vintages indeed, with price tags that hit the five-figure range.

MoJazz Bar and Lazy Lizard Grill brings class and one of the city's best jazz venues to mid Beach up on the beach side of the 79th Street Causeway. There are consistently professional and entertaining jazz acts, jam nights with area musicians, and a dessert and breakfast menu. Cover. ~ 928 71st Street; 305-865-2636.

You'll find a mix of Top-40, jazz and blues down the beach at **Brassie's**, where an older crowd sips tropical drinks around a lush garden. ~ 2201 Collins Avenue in the Holiday Inn; 305-534-1511.

Miami's premier Latin cabaret, **Club Tropigala** is a facsimile of a lavish Brazilian samba club. The 650-seat peach-and-white showcase hosts extravagant Las Vegas–style revues as well as orchestra concerts. Cover. ~ 4441 Collins Avenue in the Fontainebleau Hilton; 305-672-7469.

For a panoramic view of the city and beaches, check out **Alfredo's**, an intimate piano bar on the 18th floor of the classy Doral Ocean Beach Resort. ~ 4833 Collins Avenue; 305-532-3600.

The dressy piano bar at **Dominique's** is good for romancing. Three-piece bands play on Sunday. ~ 5225 Collins Avenue in The Alexander; 305-865-6500.

NIGHTLIFE

35TH STREET BEACH ⚓ 🏄 Another one-block respite between highrises, the beach here is narrower than those to the south, and the sand is somewhat shelly. Usually devoid of large crowds and quieter, this site is favored by older people who gather on covered benches along the boardwalk. It's a good place to swim although seaweed sometimes collects near the shore. Facilities include food vendors and lifeguards; many restaurants are nearby. ~ On Miami Beach at 35th Street.

46TH STREET BEACH ⚓ 🏄 Our favorite block of Miami Beach, this niche is strategically adjacent to the Eden Roc and Fontainebleau hotels, putting you in arm's reach of some hoppin' beachside activity. The slightly crested swath of white grains is a hot spot for paddleball players and kite flyers. A calm, shallow

BEACHES & PARKS

ocean shelf makes for excellent swimming. Facilities consist of restrooms, lifeguards, jet ski and sailboat rentals; restaurants are nearby. ~ On Miami Beach at 46th Street.

74TH STREET BEACH You cross a busy roadway and go over a little ridge to reach this one-block recess on Miami Beach. A single row of palms and lush seagrapes flank the shell-studded sand, which stretches for 150 feet out to the ocean. It's a good place for swimming. The best part of being here, though, is the sweeping southern views of Miami Beach. There are restrooms, showers, lifeguards, food vendors and a playground area. ~ On Miami Beach at 74th Street.

NORTH SHORE STATE RECREATION AREA A slice of lush vegetation between skyscrapers, this eight-block locale flourishes with willowy Australian pines, oak trees and sea oats. Best of all, the ginger-colored sand is as clean as a pin and the ocean affords very good swimming. A boardwalk meanders through the foliage, while people laze in grassy coves adjacent to the beach. Facilities include restrooms, a par course and pavilions; restaurants and stores are within walking distance. ~ On Miami Beach between 79th and 87th streets; 305-993-2022.

▼▼▼▼▼▼▼▼▼▼▼▼▼▼
North Miami Beach

Without a doubt, the oceanside towns north of Miami Beach are a separate entity. Set apart geographically but even more detached in spirit, these communities consider themselves a world away from the hustle of their southern neighbor.

Here, along this narrow island strand stretching to the Broward County line, celebrities and other well-to-do residents enjoy a quiet existence within their highly secured condominiums and estates. In fact, two towns—Bal Harbour and Golden Beach—offer no beach access and a minuscule amount of public parking for visitors.

SIGHTS   A 1930s-era settling ground for French Canadians, **Surfside** is only five blocks long and seven blocks wide. You can pick up maps and information at the **Surfside Tourist Board**, a wonderful place for catching up on all the small-town action. The rustic, low-slung complex borders a public swimming pool where old folks lounge under natty green umbrellas and play canasta. On the adjacent beach, you're apt to encounter topless sunbathing—a tradition among the French and German women who vacation here. ~ 9301 Collins Avenue; 305-864-0722.

Cruise down **Harding Avenue**, the main drag where canopied shops and kosher delis nuzzle up to pink sidewalks. Teeming with swimsuit-clad people during the day, the place shuts down at night and resembles a ghost town.

A stone's throw away is the area's poshest point, a 250-acre enclave called **Bal Harbour**. Sculpted lawns, concrete condos and landscaped medians convey a sense of preserved elegance. Center attraction here is the **Bal Harbour Shops**, an open-air collection of designer stores and manicured people. ~ 9700 Collins Avenue; 305-866-0311.

Heading north along the beach, you'll encounter a singular occurrence—a continuous stretch of sand and ocean with nary a building in sight. **Haulover Beach Park** lasts just one and a half miles but affords a peek at natural sand dunes, lush sea oats and unobstructed beach views. ~ 10800 Collins Avenue; 305-947-3525.

Up the road stands the **Newport Beach Pier**, built in 1936 and destroyed three times by hurricanes. Like its predecessors, this latest boardwalk is a hot spot for noisy pelicans and local anglers who ply the ocean waters for mackerel, bluefish and jacks. ~ 16701 Collins Avenue, Sunny Isles; 305-949-1300.

LODGING

Claiming a prime, ten-acre oceanside nest in posh Bal Harbour, the **Sheraton Bal Harbour Beach Resort** boasts a 300-foot beach and elaborate grounds with two freeform pools, rushing waterfalls, tennis courts, underground shops and four restaurants. In this 669-room showplace you'll also find an impressive lobby with a dramatic glass atrium and twirling mobile artwork. Guest rooms lend a tropical flavor, with rattan furniture, wood paneling and jungle prints. ~ 9701 Collins Avenue, Bal Harbour; 305-865-7511, 800-325-3535. ULTRA-DELUXE.

Catering primarily to a Latin and European clientele, **Palms on the Ocean Resort** is a pink-and-aqua anomaly that harkens back to the swinging '60s. Flashing lights, mirrored walls and pink elevator doors make up the lobby of this seven-story building. The 176 rooms offer clean but small accommodations swathed in yet more pink scenes. Locals like to frequent the beachside Olympic-size pool and chickee hut. ~ 9449 Collins Avenue, Surfside; 305-865-3551, 800-327-6644, fax 305-861-6596. ULTRA-DELUXE.

The Coronado Hotel is a rare Miami Beach species, on two accounts. First, it's only two stories tall, and second, the rooms are reasonably priced and clean. The 41-unit hostelry has a heated pool

ENDANGERED RESIDENCES

Dade County's northernmost beach possesses one of Miami's true rarities: oceanfront homes. To see these endangered species, travel northward along Ocean Boulevard through **Golden Beach**, where two miles of palatial, Venetian-style estates blanket the shoreline. The so-called public beach here welcomes only town residents.

and a quiet lobby with a pretty chandelier. Some guest rooms have refrigerators and hot plates. ~ 9501 Collins Avenue, Surfside; 305-866-1625, fax 305-861-1881. MODERATE.

Riu Pan American Ocean Resort is near the swanky Bal Harbour shops and midway between the Miami and Fort Lauderdale airports. Most of the 146 rooms and suites have an ocean view. Also on the grounds is a nine-hole putting green, two restaurants and a poolside grill. ~ 17875 Collins Avenue, Sunny Isles; 305-932-1100, 800-327-5678. ULTRA-DELUXE.

In an area sadly plagued by deteriorating highrise hotels, the **Golden Strand Ocean Villa Resort** is a real gem. The 152-unit resort, a time-share open to the public, is an oceanfront cluster of four- and five-story stucco buildings fashioned in a private, home-like setting. Guests can stroll the beachside boardwalk and tropical gardens that weave about a large pool and tiki hut. Apartments are decorated in contemporary styles with wicker furniture, kitchens and spacious balconies. Three-night minimum. ~ 17901 Collins Avenue, Sunny Isles; 305-931-7000, 800-527-4786. DELUXE TO ULTRA-DELUXE.

DINING

When you're hankering for a thick, juicy, aged steak, go to **Palm Restaurant**. This cozy speakeasy, a clone of the famed Manhattan steakhouse that opened in 1926, is furnished in wood and tin walls tacked with caricatures of local personalities. Besides delicious beef, Palm also excels in seafood such as jumbo Maine lobster. Dinner only. ~ 9650 East Bay Harbor Drive, Bay Harbor; 305-868-7256. ULTRA-DELUXE.

More calorie-laden desserts await at **Coco's Sidewalk Café**. Here you can feast on "death by chocolate," an ultra-indulgent concoction of four chocolates. There are also light meals such as sandwiches and salads. With an indoor decor of striking silver,

◆◆◆

✔ CHECK THESE OUT—UNIQUE DINING

- *Budget:* Settle down to delicious diner fare after braving the lines at **S & S Diner**, a legendary Miami eatery. *page 64*
- *Budget to moderate:* Sample traditional Cuban dishes in the old-style atmosphere of **La Carreta**, where you can follow your entrée with a choice of three dozen desserts. *page 69*
- *Moderate to deluxe:* Gaze down at the the colorful Coconut Grove scene from the windows of **Kaleidoscope**, which serves American nouvelle cuisine in a light, airy atmosphere. *page 76*
- *Deluxe to ultra-deluxe:* Try "tropical fusion" at **Chef Allen's**, owned by Allen Susser of New York's Le Cirque fame. *page 90*

Budget: under $8   Moderate: $8–$16   Deluxe: $16–$24   Ultra-deluxe: over $24

gold and black, Coco's also has outdoor umbrella-covered tables where you can perfectly situate yourself for unashamed people-watching. Breakfast, lunch and dinner. ~ Bal Harbour Shops, 9700 Collins Avenue; 305-864-2626. MODERATE.

To get a good feel for South Florida's outdoors set, spend a weekend afternoon at **Salties**. This bar is perched strategically on the Intracoastal Waterway and features dramatic wooden ceilings and spacious dockside dining. Boaters park their yachts three and four deep, vying for prime dock space. Scantily clad waitresses serve fresh seafood, pasta and hefty burgers and carry extra sun-tan lotion—just in case. Breakfast, lunch and dinner are served every day. ~ 10880 Collins Avenue, Sunny Isles; 305-945-5115. MODERATE TO DELUXE.

Wolfie Cohen's Rascal House Restaurant is legendary in the local Jewish community. Waitresses in white pinafores scurry to and fro, delivering heaping plates of corned beef, chicken in the pot, *kreplaches* and stuffed cabbage to diners chatting in Yiddish. Gaudy aqua booths and scuffed terrazzo floors add to the bustling atmosphere. A series of metal railings keeps the perpetual lines of anxiously waiting patrons in order. Breakfast, lunch and dinner are served. ~ 17190 Collins Avenue, Sunny Isles; 305-947-4581. BUD-GET TO MODERATE.

If you want to indulge—or over-indulge—consider **Prince Hamlet**. This genteel establishment boasts a 62-foot buffet laden with Danish, Jewish and Continental delights. There's beef gou-lash, shrimp, vegetables, cheeses, breads, soups, fruits and salads. Or choose from a menu of duck *à l'orange*, prime rib, kosher sweetbreads and much more. Breakfast and dinner only. ~ 19115 Collins Avenue, Sunny Isles; 305-932-8488. MODERATE TO DELUXE.

Just beyond the mall is Harding Avenue, where a two-block row of colorful canopied shops comprises the heart of tiny Surfside. The 1930s settling place for French Canadians, Harding Avenue mixes the old and new. At **Decor, Inc.** you'll find impressionist paintings framed in ornate brass and incredibly extravagant can-delabra—just a few of the antiques for sale here. ~ 9487 Harding Avenue, Surfside; 305-866-0905.

SHOPPING

Rafe Sweetheart Beauty Salon is one of those wonderful clas-sic salons where women still line up to chat and relax under long rows of hair dryers. Take a peek for old time's sake, or have a shampoo and set for the low price of $8. ~ 9437 Harding Avenue, Surfside; 305-865-9179.

The designer capital of the area, **Bal Harbour Shops** houses such upscale caches as Gucci, Cartier, Fendi and Saks Fifth Avenue. Well-groomed crowds meander two levels of open-air alcoves fes-tooned in tropical foliage, tall palms and waterfalls. ~ 9700 Collins Avenue, Bal Harbour; 305-866-0311.

BEACHES & PARKS

SURFSIDE BEACH 🏖 🏃 Wide sweeps of sand behind small hotels, this area offers a respite from the hustle of Miami Beach. French Canadians, who settled in Surfside during the 1930s and '40s, favor this beach and often shed their bikini tops, raising some local eyebrows. The swimming here is excellent; ocean waves are calm, breaking far in the distance where a sandbar ledge begins. Most days, you'll see some serious card game action under the beach umbrellas. The only facilities are lifeguards; numerous restaurants and stores are nearby. ~ On Collins Avenue in Surfside, between 88th and 96th streets.

HAULOVER BEACH PARK 🏃 🚴 🏖 🎣 🏃 ⚓ 🛥 ⛵ A mile and a half of tropical vegetation with skyscraperless views, this beach got its name in the early 1900s when residents had to "haul" their boats over surrounding swamplands to reach the ocean. During the 1800s, the barefoot mailman traveled this firm-packed shoreline along his South Florida route. Laden with thick carpets of grass, hilly sand dunes and chestnut-colored sand, Haulover is a real beauty and a good place to swim. The jetty is where anglers fish for snapper, grunt, mackerel and yellowtail, and where other folks go to enjoy the southern panorama of Miami Beach. Facilities include picnic tables, restrooms, lifeguards, concession stands and a marina. ~ Along Collins Avenue in south Sunny Isles; 305-947-3525.

SUNNY ISLES BEACH AND NEWPORT BEACH 🏖 🎣 🏃 🏄 ⛵ Extending for two miles in back of condominiums and hotels, these beaches are capped with rocky sand and dotted with small tiki huts. Swimming is the primary activity at Sunny Isles. The rougher surf and perennial winds at Newport Beach draw windsurfers and sailors. The hot spot is in front of the Holiday Inn, where wall-to-wall lounge chairs and pretty people line the beach. For picturesque southerly views, stroll the Newport Pier where anglers regularly gather. Built in 1936, the boardwalk here was destroyed three times by hurricanes but has new life again. Facilities consist of food vendors, and windsurfing, sailboat, parasailing and jet ski rentals near the pier. ~ On Collins Avenue, between 163rd and 192nd streets; 305-949-1300.

▼▼▼▼▼▼▼▼▼▼▼▼
Downtown Miami

More than anything, downtown Miami is an Americanized version of a Latin American city. Two decades of immigration have infused this great core with numerous powerful Latin business centers as well as a government in which the majority of top officials are Latino. Exploring the downtown area, you'll hear more Spanish spoken than English and see many Spanish billboards.

Constantly shaping and reshaping its skyline, downtown is a convolution of ultramodern skyscrapers reflecting against beautiful Biscayne Bay. An expansive yet quite conquerable area, the city is served by the Metromover monorail (305-638-6700), which travels the perimeter of the district, stopping at key points of interest.

Occupying the 27th floor of the sleek Barnett Bank Building, the **Greater Miami Convention and Visitors Bureau** will provide you with sightseeing information as well as a good view of the city. ~ 701 Brickell Avenue; 305-539-3000.

SIGHTS

Slicing through the heart of downtown, **Flagler Street** is the best place to capture urban life. Jammed with taxi cabs and Latin street vendors, this thoroughfare was first brought to life in the 1920s by some of the city's earliest merchants. Nowadays, brick-lined moderne buildings house noisy electronics shops and discount jewelry centers.

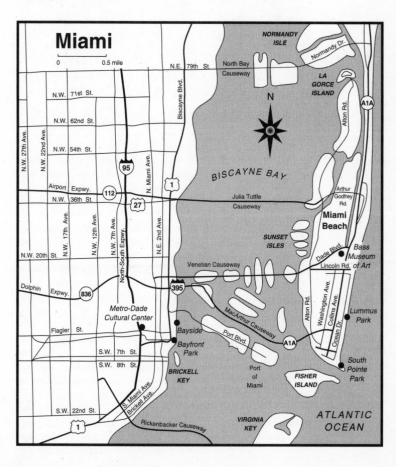

One of the most beautiful buildings downtown, **Gusman Center for the Performing Arts** is a Mediterranean dream world. Built in 1925 for Paramount Studios, the brick-faced theater is wonderfully ornate, resembling an Italian courtyard with twinkling ceiling lights and rolling cloud puffs. It's worth a trip just to experience the surroundings. ~ 174 East Flagler Street; 305-374-2444.

The **Dade County Courthouse** is easily spotted from just about anywhere in the city. A slender building with a striking ziggurat roof, the courthouse is shaped like a rocket poised for lift-off. When it was assembled in 1925, the courthouse was the tallest building south of Washington, D.C., and remained Miami's loftiest structure until the 1970s. Inside, beautiful mosaics swirl across the ceiling and ornate brass designs embellish the doors and wall lamps. You can still see court in session at this granddaddy. ~ 73 West Flagler Street; 305-375-5775.

A couple of blocks to the east beats the cultural pulse of downtown. The three-building **Metro-Dade Cultural Center** is a complex of Mediterranean modernism with broad checkered piazzas. ~ 101 West Flagler Street.

The most enthralling destination here, the **Historical Museum of Southern Florida**, offers a comprehensive, highly entertaining history of the region. Two floors of exhibits span 10,000 years, carrying you through American Indian camps, boom or bust years and Miami's golden years as the nation's playground. Here you can sit in a 19th-century trolley car, don period costumes or relax on the porch of an old cracker home. Better yet, peruse the thousands of snapshots of yesterday's Florida in the extensive photo library. If you love Florida, you'll adore this museum. Admission. ~ 305-375-1492.

Across the piazza, the **Center for the Fine Arts** is a showpiece of Mediterranean style and South Florida's major museum. The center has no permanent collection but hosts more than 15 national and international exhibits annually, including works by such notables as Pablo Picasso and Frank Lloyd Wright. Closed Monday. Admission. ~ 305-375-1700. Rounding out this cultural trio is the four-story **Miami-Dade Public Library**. ~ 305-375-2665.

About four blocks northeast, the **United States Courthouse** is a place where you'll want to spend some time. This stately 1931 building is a masterful work of Spanish Mediterranean revival. Corinthian columns, glass arched doorways and miles of marble floor greet visitors. Around the vine-clad courtyard, artists have taken hold of the hallways, covering them with wild art frescoes. ~ 301 North Miami Avenue; 305-536-4548.

For some more heady scenery, stroll around the corner to the **Ingraham Building**, a 1927 study in Italian Renaissance architecture. Its compass arch entrances, heavy bronze doors and sweeping gold ceilings with hand-painted compartments are overwhelming. The building was named for J. E. Ingraham, Henry Flagler's right-hand man. ~ 25 Southeast 2nd Avenue.

At the east end of 2nd Avenue, the savvy **Bayside Marketplace** rests primly along the bay, luring just as many sightseers as shoppers to its peach enclaves. The sprawling outdoor plaza is a great place to people-watch while enjoying magicians, jugglers and strolling musicians. ~ 401 Biscayne Boulevard; 305-577-3344.

Docked at the Bayside Marketplace is **The Heritage of Miami**, a coastal schooner that offers cruises around Biscayne Bay. The majestic tallship is modeled after the early 1900s schooners that traveled between Miami, Cuba and the Bahamas. Offered several times a day, the two-hour cruise provides excellent views of Vizcaya, Key Biscayne and Miami's skyline. Admission. ~ 401 Biscayne Boulevard; 305-442-9697.

If you need some open space, head next door to **Bayfront Park**, 32 acres of rolling green hills and rock-studded palm tree gardens skirting the bay. This serene fleck of greenery, favored by afterwork joggers, is frequently the site of outdoor concerts. ~ 301 North Biscayne Boulevard; 305-358-7550.

Your most historic stop downtown is several blocks south at the **Lummus Park District**. Here rests Dade County's oldest house, the **Wagner Homestead**. Constructed in 1858 by a struggling pioneer named William Wagner, the simple, four-room pine dwelling has hardly endured hurricanes, wars and the menace of progress. It's not a whole lot to look at, but it signifies a time when this concrete jungle was a mere wilderness. ~ 404 Northwest 3rd Street.

Just south of downtown is Miami's take on Wall Street, a picturesque thoroughfare called **Brickell Avenue**. This impressive collection of ultramodern foreign (and a few domestic) bank buildings juts upward from the roadside, clinging to the skies that rim Biscayne Bay. Along the four-lane road, majestic palm trees and towering oaks create shade and natural sculptures for passing traffic.

Commercial highrises eventually merge with classy residential skyscrapers along this modern roadway. Here you'll spot the cleverly designed **Atlantis** apartment building. The architect built a large square gap into the middle of the building, punctuated the opening with a palm tree and an artsy spiral staircase, and then planted a single, rust-colored triangle atop the building. The Atlantis was completed in the early 1980s to great acclaim from Miami residents. ~ 2025 Brickell Avenue.

In the spirit of competition, the owners of the neighboring **Villa Regina** apartments splashed rainbow colors across their balconies, offsetting them with vertical racing stripes. From Biscayne Bay, the building looks like a painted accordion standing on end. ~ 15815 Brickell Avenue.

The enchantment of **Vizcaya Museum and Gardens** surpasses even all the hype passed out by local promoters. A vast Italian villa perched magnificently on Biscayne Bay, Vizcaya is the mastermind of farming magnate James Deering. A man infatuated with Renaissance styles, Deering hired 1000 people (one-tenth of Miami's population at the time) in 1914 to build the elaborate estate, a project that took two years and more than $15 million. Here you can wind your way through 34 rooms and halls lavishly adorned with priceless European antiques and paintings, oriental carpets, ornate moldings and spectacular architecture. Outside, stroll the botanical gardens, taking in the Great Stone Barge that rests brooding in the bay. Admission. ~ 3251 South Miami Avenue; 305-250-9133.

If you're feeling sleuthy, visit the mock crime scene at the American Police Hall of Fame and Museum and solve a murder. Top detectives are given certificates.

Across the street at the **Miami Museum of Science**, engine parts whir, rainbows dance across a large soap bubble and chattering, wide-eyed children scurry about. This building boasts over 150 creative exhibits for children (and adults too), including an aviary and wildlife center. Admission. ~ 3280 South Miami Avenue; 305-854-4247.

The adjacent **Miami Planetarium**, where you can slink among the dinosaurs and "walk on Mars," hosts laser light and star shows. ~ 3280 South Miami Avenue; cosmic hotline 305-854-2222.

Miami Vice gave you Hollywood's version of local crime-fighting techniques. To see the real stuff, turn in to the **American Police Hall of Fame and Museum**. Distinguished by the patrol car parked across its facade, the museum offers over 10,000 absorbing exhibits that whisk you through the history of villain nabbing. There's a jail cell replica, a real gas chamber and guillotine, and a video crime clock with up-to-the-second statistics. Admission. ~ 3801 Biscayne Boulevard; 305-573-0700.

From Biscayne Boulevard, veer west to Northeast 2nd Avenue and head north. Like a Caribbean island scene, the street is edged with quaint frame buildings and bungalows washed in sunny yellows and sky blues, bright greens and soft pinks. Home to about 65,000 Haitian immigrants, **Little Haiti** (bounded by Biscayne Boulevard, Route 95, Northwest 46th Street and the 79th Street Causeway) is gentrifying into a colorful area rich in Creole cuisine and history.

LODGING   In downtown Miami, ultramodern corporate hotels continue to pop up, helping to shape and reshape the city's skyline. Rates here are deluxe and ultra-deluxe, and they don't fall in the off season. Inland, you'll find sprawling country club resorts and singularly chic addresses intermingled with a few chain motels and even fewer bed and breakfasts.

Conveniently located near the sprawling Bayside shops overlooking the port, the 1926 **Everglades Hotel** has kept pace with time. A restored lobby has attractive darkwood walls and marble floors, while 365 guest rooms are spotlessly decorated with wall-to-wall carpet and rattan furniture. An expansive rooftop pool and bar offer sweeping views. ~ 244 Biscayne Boulevard; 305-379-5461, 800-327-5700, fax 305-577-8390. MODERATE TO DELUXE.

The **Dupont Plaza** is one of those 1950s hotels with underground souvenir shops and pinball arcades. Dwarfed by neighboring highrises, the hotel rests along the Miami River and offers 12 floors of comfortable, spacious rooms done with mauve and beige tones. Breakfast included. ~ 300 Biscayne Boulevard Way; 305-358-2541, 800-327-3480, fax 305-377-4049. DELUXE.

Rising 34 granite floors from Biscayne Bay, the **Hotel Intercontinental** takes on a stark look. Catering largely to a business crowd, the hotel features a lobby with marble walls, a grand piano and a canopy of glass. Guest rooms are cushy, with black lacquer oriental armoires, floral print loveseats and granite tables. ~ 100 Chopin Plaza; 305-577-1000, 800-327-0200. ULTRA-DELUXE.

A definite corporate hotel, the **Hyatt Regency Downtown** has a striking open lobby. The 24-story hostelry is conveniently connected to the Miami Convention Center and offers 615 modernly furnished rooms with contemporary art and good views of the city and river. ~ 400 Southeast 2nd Avenue; 305-358-1234, 800-233-1234. ULTRA-DELUXE.

Perched nicely on the Miami River, the **Occidental Plaza Suite Hotel** is an elegant hotel offering 16 floors of accommodations. Mahogany furnishings and subdued tones of plum and champagne persist throughout the guest rooms, many of which overlook the river. There's also a pool and jacuzzi that rest waterside. ~ 100 Southeast 4th Street; 305-374-5100, fax 305-381-9826. DELUXE.

If it's charming, indigenous lodging you seek, look no further than the **Miami River Inn**. Set in a courtyard of palms, the Victorian bed and breakfast exists in an unlikely area—a neighborhood of fishing companies. But its four early-1900s buildings have been splendidly restored, and its bedrooms individually decorated with antiques, carved wood beds and handmade drapes and quilts. ~ 118 Southwest South River Drive; 305-325-0045, 800-468-3589, fax 305-325-9227. MODERATE TO DELUXE.

◄ **HIDDEN**

DINING

Sadly, there are but a few choice restaurants to be found in Miami's downtown. In a city where nearly half the people are Latino, the most frequently spotted eatery is the Cuban café. These narrow, oftentimes unkempt pit stops almost always have sidewalk takeout windows, where you can listen to Cuban radio stations while picking up some *sopa de pollo* (chicken soup), *papas fritas* (french

Text continued on page 64.

Entrepreneurial Celebrities

The 1980s saw Miami transforming into a pulsing multi-cultural metropolis, attracting slick jetsetters with its sophisticated ambience and tropical beauty. Meanwhile, college and professional sports began to prosper; tourism was also on the rise. It was inevitable: with Miami's growing reputation as a hotspot, the rich and famous couldn't be far behind.

To swanky Miami Beach they came, and many set up permanent residence. Latin singers Gloria Estefan and Julio Iglesias, talk-show diva Oprah Winfrey, Hollywood stars Cher, Sylvester Stallone, Robert DeNiro, Jack Nicholson, Sharon Stone and Mickey Rourke, designers Calvin Klein, Ralph Lauren and Gianni Versace—even Material-turned-Maternal Girl Madonna—all keep homes here.

Many more celebrities are frequent visitors, especially to the refurbished South Beach area, where they enjoy the outré scene. Add to these the resident sports stars who play on (and coach) Miami's teams, as well as royals of several countries, and the continual ebb and flow of high-end models who circulate through the city's increasingly important fashion scene, and you have a fuller picture of how far and wide Miami's celebrity net spreads.

But all these stars need something to *do* in Miami. And what better way to take advantage of the thriving economy and growing tourist industry than to become entrepreneurs? Many of them have done just that: big names are making—or at least investing—big bucks opening restaurants, sports bars and nightclubs with wild abandon. The lure of possibly catching a glimpse of famous figures seems to keep the crowds coming, although more often than not, the patrons are left looking at each other, since most of these star owners rarely make an appearance at their establishments.

Miami's "First Lady" of entertainment, Gloria Estefan, owns two restaurants in town. The first is **Lario's on the Beach**, a casual Cuban eatery. ~ 820 Ocean Drive. MODERATE. Her second venture, farther down Ocean Drive, is **Allioli South Beach Cafe**, serving Spanish fare in an avant-garde Mediterranean setting. Allioli is located in the historic Cardozo Hotel, also owned by Estefan. ~ 1300 Ocean Drive; 305-538-0553. ULTRA-DELUXE.

White rapper Vanilla Ice has opened **To The Extremes**, an outdoor-sports store in the Lincoln Road Mall. A full-service bicycle shop, the store also sells mopeds, snowboards and almost any other adventure equipment you might need. ~ 700 Lincoln Road, Miami Beach; 305-538-1390. Last but certainly not least, perennial pop superstar Madonna is co-owner (with her brother) of the **Blue Door** restaurant in the wildly redesigned Delano Hotel. ~ 1685 Collins Avenue; 305-674-6400. ULTRA-DELUXE.

One-time Madonna spouse Sean Penn runs the trendy nightclub **Bash**, together with Mick Hucknall (of the British rock group Simply Red) and he does tend to show up when in town. Inside, Euro-dance music throbs through the dark, smoky room, while the outdoor patio in back plays reggae and salsa. ~ 655 Washington Avenue, Miami Beach; 305-538-2274.

British actor and longtime London restaurateur Michael Caine has entered the Miami scene with his first American venture, **The South Beach Brasserie**. Managed by his daughter Natasha, the restaurant features "Mediterrasian" cuisine, blending coastal Mediterranean with Asian flavors. ~ 910 Lincoln Road, Miami Beach; 305-534-5511. DELUXE TO ULTRA-DELUXE.

Dolphins quarterback Dan Marino owns a sports bar called—not too surprisingly—**Dan Marino's American Sports Bar & Grill**, where overhead TVs, pool tables and air-hockey games dominate the decor. The menu features pizzas, burgers, pastas and ribs, and the general clientele features college kids, locals, and a healthy dose of celebrity athletes and local sports stars. Yes, this is one spot where sports fans do have a chance at collecting some autographs—if the bigshots aren't all sequestered in the rear VIP lounge. ~ 3015 Grand Avenue, Coconut Grove; 305-567-0013. MODERATE.

Former Dolphins coach Don Shula is also a big business success, operating a hotel and golf club, and two popular restaurants. **Don Shula's Hotel and Golf Club** provides 300 ultra-deluxe-priced rooms in a resort setting, with gardens, golfing greens, and a manmade lagoon. Inside the hotel, **Shula's All-Star Cafe** serves seafood, prime rib, and steak; the lounge and tri-level dining room overlook the gardens and lagoon. ~ 15255 Bull Run Road, Miami Lakes; 305-821-1150, 800-247-4852, fax 305-821-6006. MODERATE TO DELUXE.

Nearby in yet another duffer's paradise, Miami Lakes Golf Resort, is **Shula's Steak House**, where there's no menu—they just wheel a cart to your table and you order as much meat as you can handle. The decor involves dark wood, sports photos and artifacts, and a wall plaque bearing the names of all-star eaters—upon which you too can be immortalized if you're able to conquer the 48-ounce porterhouse! ~ 15400 Northwest 77th Avenue, Miami Lakes; 305-822-2324. MODERATE TO ULTRA-DELUXE.

Finally, if you're really going gaga over the celebrity thing, you may as well hit Miami's **Planet Hollywood**, the ubiquitous celebrity-owned restaurant, which is bound to be just as satisfactory—or unsatisfactory—in Miami as it would be in any other city. Co-owned by a conglomerate of stars, among whom are Sylvester Stallone, Bruce Willis, Arnold Schwarznegger and Demi Moore, Planet Hollywood serves hamburgers, shakes and other diner fare, and enthralls tourists everywhere with its selection of movie-star paraphernalia. ~ Mayfair Shops, Grand Avenue between Virginia and Mary streets, Coconut Grove; 305-445-7277.

fries), *morcillas* (blood sausage) and cold *cervezas* (beer). Stroll the bustling Flagler Street, where Latin street vendors offer *empanadas* (fried meat pies) and *batidos de frutas* (fruit milkshakes).

One sizzling lunch locale is **Granny Feelgood's**, where business types hobnob over clever health food creations. Granny's extensive menu features salads loaded with shrimp and chicken, inventive pastas, steamy vegetable soups and freshly squeezed fruit juices. Choose to eat indoors or out on the terrace. Breakfast and lunch only. Closed weekends. ~ 111 Northwest 1st Street in the Metro-Dade Government Center; 305-579-2104. BUDGET TO MODERATE.

HIDDEN ►   The stained paper sign at **The Big Fish** says it all: "No Shoes, No Shirt, No Suit . . . No Problem. Sit Down." This funky outdoor hideaway, tucked among Miami's drab dockside warehouses, has a tin roof and an array of mismatched wooden and aluminum tables. The menu, a total of five to six daily items posted on a bulletin board, consists of—you guessed it—fresh fish. A friendly owner introduces diners, a mishmash of crusty old folks and neatly dressed attorneys and financiers. ~ 55 Southwest Miami Avenue Road; 305-373-1770. BUDGET.

Ever since *Esquire* magazine named **Las Tapas** one of the best new bars and restaurants of 1987, the Spanish-style eating house has been luring shoppers with its steamy concoctions of beef, chicken, seafood and pork. Glass walls enclose this one-story establishment, rimmed with black iron balconies and painted clay pots. ~ 401 Biscayne Boulevard in Bayside Marketplace; 305-372-2737. MODERATE TO DELUXE.

The ten-page food directory at the Brickell Emporium contains entertaining "deli-talk," with a glossary of eatables.

Perched against the Miami River underneath a bridge, **East Coast Fisheries** has been filling the local fish fix since 1933. The restaurant's fleet of 36 boats deliver fresh catches of the day, which might include grouper, snapper, bluefish, mackerel, kingfish, dolphin, flounder, lobster or stone crabs. For appetizers, the conch fritters are a must; for entrées, try the fried flounder with walnuts and grapes or garlic mahimahi. A casual, uproarious eatery located in a 1918 former shrimp packing house. ~ 360 West Flagler Street; 305-372-1300. MODERATE TO DELUXE.

If the overstuffed bagels and sandwiches at **Brickell Emporium** don't strike any stomach chords, the menu will. Selections include roast pork on garlic bread, cheese blintzes, pizza bagels and more than a dozen fresh salads. Three meals are served on weekdays, breakfast and lunch only on weekends. ~ 1100 Brickell Plaza; 305-377-3354. BUDGET.

Everyone loves **S & S Diner**. The Miami institution, immortalized in Mel Kiser and Corky Irick's movie *Last Night at the S & S Diner*, packs 'em in daily with down-to-earth fare such as meatloaf, roast pork, stuffed cabbage, chopped steak with onions, turkey and dressing, and the best mashed potatoes around. After you've waited in line (and wait you will), you can take one of the 23 seats at the horseshoe counter. Save your appetite: Homespun vittles don't get much better than this. Breakfast, lunch and dinner are served on weekdays, dinner only on Saturday. Closed Sunday. ~ 1757 Northeast 2nd Avenue, just north of downtown; 305-373-4291. BUDGET.

To get a culinary taste of Little Haiti, drive along Northeast 54th Street between Biscayne Boulevard and Miami Avenue. Just west of Miami Avenue, you'll find a gem of a restaurant called **Chez Moy**. The small, immaculate eatery serves creole delicacies (curried goat, spicy steamed fish) that truly makes you feel like you're in the French Caribbean. Dinner only. ~ 1 Northwest 54th Street; 305-757-5056. BUDGET.

SHOPPING

Miami's premier shopping mecca, **Bayside Marketplace** is a study in cool aesthetics. A gay pink plaza hugging sparkling Biscayne Bay, the open-air mall is a labyrinth of giant ferns, palm trees and brick walkways dotted with white flower carts, strolling musicians and mimes. Though it brims with 120 novel stores and restaurants, Bayside is just as much a people-watching spot as a shopping address. **Coastal Cotton Co.** (305-358-2551) has T-shirts, dresses, shorts and much more—all made out of breathable cotton. Men can pick up their *Miami Vice* attire nearby at **Amici Uomo** (305-379-8115). The crisp white European suits and silk ties here carry hefty price tags, though. A flashy address, **Celebrations** (305-539-1515) is jammed with wild art sun visors, postcards, pink flamingos and other Miami-style objects. For a Brazilian flair, **Azteca de Oro** (305-375-0358) has jungle fashions, hand-loomed rugs and large painted parrots. Top it off at **The Hat Attack** (305-373-1428), where you can don baseball caps and all other sports-related crown covers. **Passage to India** (305-375-9504) is where you can pick up fine Indian clothing and bone jewelry. **Geronimo's Trail** (305-375-9504) features American Indian and Southwestern jewelry and clothing. **Baggage Terminal** (305-252-4630) has colorful handbags and wallets made of eelskin, leather and vinyl. ~ 401 Biscayne Boulevard.

Formerly the place to shop downtown, **Omni Mall** has been overshadowed by Bayside and has deteriorated somewhat during recent years. Clustered around the Omni Hotel, the enclosed dual-level center houses about 75 shops—mostly chain stores of all price levels and a few restaurants. The highlight here is not a store but a beautiful Italian carousel that makes kids squeal with delight. ~ 1601 Biscayne Boulevard; 305-374-6664.

For a great selection of bathing suits **Swim 'N' Sport** sells one piecers and mix-and-match bikini tops and bottoms as well as a selection of cover-ups. ~ 1601 Biscayne Boulevard, in the Omni Mall; 305-358-5117.

A bustling urban thoroughfare cutting through the heart of downtown, **Flagler Street** is where some of the city's first merchants set up shop during the 1920s. Today, brick sidewalks are rimmed with Latin street vendors and fronted by noisy electronics marts and discount jewelry centers.

If diamonds are a girl's best friend, then the **Seybold Building** is her dreamland. Herein lies ten floors of stores abounding with those twinkling jewels as well as gold and silver pieces. The name of the game is bargaining, and most merchants are anxious to strike a deal. ~ 39 East Flagler Street.

Don't miss **Burdines Department Store**, a landmark, 1936 streamlined moderne design that adds a touch of nostalgia to the area. ~ 22 East Flagler Street; 305-835-5151.

NIGHTLIFE   **The Oak Room** draws a large business clientele for after-work cocktails. ~ 100 Chopin Plaza in the Intercontinental Hotel; 305-577-1000

Good riverside views can be had at **Currents**, an upbeat, lounge with an eclectic mix of music: Top-40, pop, country, rhythm-and-blues and urban contemporary. ~ 400 Southeast 2nd Avenue in the Hyatt Regency; 305-358-1234.

One of the best bars around, **Tobacco Road** obtained the city's first liquor license back in 1912. An old speakeasy, "The Road" has a secret closet where illegal booze and roulette tables were once stashed. Upstairs, there's always an impressive lineup of rhythm-and-blues bands. Cover on weekends. ~ 626 South Miami Avenue; 305-374-1198.

The garden patio at **Coco Loco** is an after-work roosting place for the suit-and-tie set. Later, you'll find a young Latino crowd dancing to jukebox tunes on weekdays and deejay-spun jazz, reg-

THE SPY WHO LOVED MIAMI

James Bond would have loved Miami. Here he could have shopped to his heart's content from a wide array of espionage toys: thumb-sized cameras for sneaking pictures, eyeglasses that let you see who's creeping up behind you, bugs for eavesdropping on your enemies. Spy shops are sprinkled across Miami, catering to an undercover and security-conscious clientele. In downtown Miami, **Spy Shops International** is like a small department store. ~ 350 Biscayne Boulevard; 305-374-4779. North of downtown, you'll espy **Miami Spy**. ~ 2695 Biscayne Boulevard; 305-573-9999.

gae and disco on weekends. ~ 495 Brickell Avenue in the Sheraton Brickell Point; 305-373-6000.

Bayside Marketplace is the headquarters for outdoor entertainment. Afternoons and evenings, you'll find reggae, jazz, Latin and blues bands playing center stage on the waterfront. ~ 401 Biscayne Boulevard; 305-577-3344.

The **Hard Rock Cafe**, with its blazing neon guitar out front, features rock tunes. ~ Bayside Marketplace, 401 Biscayne Boulevard; 305-377-3110.

Though located in a dicey neighborhood and decorated like a suburban garage, **Churchill's Hideaway** showcases local bands in this no-frills bar. The three pool tables are always crowded and the cost of a beer won't bend your wallet. Grunge rules for fashion here and much of the crowd is tattooed and body pierced, though docile. Cover. ~ 5501 Northeast 2nd Avenue; 305-757-1807.

THEATER, OPERA, SYMPHONY AND DANCE The gorgeous **Gusman Center for the Performing Arts**, an ornate 1709-seat facility, is home to the Florida Philharmonic Orchestra and the New World Symphony. The Gusman also hosts the popular Miami Film Festival. ~ 174 East Flagler Street; 305-374-2444.

Reminiscent of flashy pre-Castro Havana nightclubs, **Les Violins** has strolling violinists and glittering, top-notch Latin floor shows. Cover. ~ 1751 Biscayne Boulevard; 305-371-8668.

The city's prized **Bayfront Park**, which spans 32 acres of waterside palm trees and rolling hills, has a 12,000-person capacity amphitheater for outdoor musical concerts from symphony to rock. ~ 301 Biscayne Boulevard between Northeast 1st and 4th streets; 305-358-7550.

The modern, cylindrical **James L. Knight International Center** is the 5000-seat address of popular Latino, jazz, rock-and-roll and pops concerts. ~ 400 Southeast 2nd Avenue; 305-372-0929.

Larger concerts are held at the 16,500-seat **Miami Arena**, another ultramodern circular facility rimmed with palm trees. ~ 721 Northwest 1st Avenue; 305-530-4400.

Just north of downtown, the **Joseph Caleb Auditorium** presents stellar drama by local artists. The 1001-seat facility is also the site of regional orchestra and Shakespearean performances. ~ 5400 Northwest 22nd Avenue, Brownsville; 305-636-2350.

▼▼▼▼▼▼▼▼▼▼
Little Havana

Despite its name, Little Havana bears little resemblance to the Cuban capital, yet it serves as the core of Miami's Cuban population. The main drag is Southwest 8th Street, known locally as Calle Ocho, stretching just west of downtown from Route 95 to Southwest 35th Avenue. Calle Ocho is really just one long, noisy thoroughfare fringed with discount stores, flashing neon signs, gas stations and great Latin restaurants and nightclubs.

SIGHTS

The best way to soak in the atmosphere here is to park and walk. The street signs, like the restaurant menus, are mainly in Spanish, but it's fairly easy to find someone who can translate. Old Cuban men in *guayaberas* socialize on street corners, while the younger set strolls the sidewalks with radios blasting Spanish music. You'll almost always find a crowd at **Domino Park**, a community center where locals gather for games of chess and dominoes. ~ Southwest 8th Street and Southwest 15th Avenue.

On the roadways flanking **Calle Ocho**, tens of thousands of Cuban immigrants have settled in modest, well-kept neighborhoods. Many residents display the American flag or exhibit bright brass shrines of their favorite patron saint. Every March they hold the country's largest Latino festival, with fabulous food and music and a conga line that continues for blocks.

DINING

Just west of downtown pulses another world. This haven for thousands of Cuban immigrants is also the settling ground for scores of Cuban eateries offering an abundance of food at incredibly cheap prices.

There's a distinct aura of disrepair, of time-worn seediness about **Malaga**. But no matter. This courtyard eatery, barely recognizable from the street, consistently offers some of Miami's foremost Cuban fare at breakfast, lunch and dinner. Quaint wooden tables centered around a tangled mass of trees and vines set the stage for sumptuous pot roast simmered in sausages, spicy fried veal and pork and exceptional paella. ~ 740 Southwest 8th Street; 305-858-4224. MODERATE.

Your Nicaraguan connection can be found at **Guayacan Restaurant**, a modest establishment with counter service and a few tables in the back. You can sample hen soup with meatballs, tripe and vegetables, *salpicón* (marinated beef) and other inexpensive offerings. ~ 1933 Southwest 8th Street; 305-649-2015. BUDGET.

One of the more interesting buildings in Little Havana, **Casa Juancho** depicts Spanish Renaissance architecture. A barrel-tiled roof and tan stucco exterior match the brick pillars and wooden beam ceiling inside. Sacks of garlic and ham hocks hang around the open kitchen, where exceptional seafood and game dishes are whipped up. ~ 2436 Southwest 8th Street; 305-642-2452. DELUXE.

HIDDEN ►

An anomaly in this Latino neighborhood, **Hy-Vong** rightfully takes its place as Miami's best Vietnamese restaurant. With plain white walls and a few wilting plants, the atmosphere is nil, but the food is prepared with great care by one of the owners, a Vietnamese woman who fled Saigon in 1975. The hearty fare includes *thi kho* (pork in coconut milk), *cari tom* (curried shrimp and crab), chicken with jicama and an intriguing squid salad. Dinner only. Closed Monday. ~ 3458 Southwest 8th Street; 305-446-3674. MODERATE.

You'll step back in time when you enter **La Carreta**. Leather-back chairs and heavy wooden chandeliers add a rustic feel to multiple dining rooms, where large color photos of Old Havana adorn the walls. Selections feature traditional Cuban fare such as chicken and yellow rice, pork with black beans and Spanish bean soup. With more than three dozen desserts to choose from, who could resist the final course? ~ 3632 Southwest 8th Street; 305-444-7501. BUDGET TO MODERATE.

The delectable aromas emanating from La Esquina's kitchen may be why President Ronald Reagan visited this diner in 1983.

President Ronald Reagan paid a visit to **La Esquina de Tejas** and turned the nondescript, streetcorner diner into an overnight success. What you'll find here is good standard Cuban food, namely *pollo asado* (baked chicken), *moros* (mixed black beans) and flan. The simple, Western-style decor features red brick floors, wooden paneling and ham hocks hanging in the front windows. Breakfast, lunch and dinner are served. ~ 101 Southwest 12th Avenue; 305-545-5341. BUDGET TO MODERATE.

SHOPPING

Miami's Cuban core offers one long street tagged with discount marts where you'll find not only good buys but an intriguing taste of local ethnic life. Focus on **Southwest 8th Street**, Little Havana's bustling main drag, between Route 95 West and 35th Street.

Over at **Lily's Records**, you can find your favorite Latin tunes. ~ 1260 Southwest 8th Street; 305-856-0536.

España Gift Importers is a cache of everything-Spanish, from frilly dolls and intricate porcelain to elaborate, delicate fans. ~ 1615 Southwest 8th Street; 305-856-4844.

You can pour over hundreds of historic Cuban coins and stamps at **Alvarez Stamp & Coin**. A friendly owner will also show you his collection of pre-Castro documents. ~ 1735 Southwest 8th Street; 305-649-1176.

La Casa de las Piñatas, a second-story shop in the thick of Calle Ocho, Little Havana's main artery is wall-to-wall with piñatas of every size for every occasion, enough candy to send kids everywhere into ecstasy and a genuine example of the cultural bouillabaisse that is Miami. ~ 1756 Southwest 8th Street; 305-649-4711.

For books on international relations, stop by **Librería Universal**, where the topics range from Cuban-American and African-American issues to Caribbean politics. ~ 3090 Southwest 8th Street; 305-642-3234.

NIGHTLIFE

Latino immigrants brought a whole new brand of nightlife to Miami, namely late-night supper clubs with lavish revues. Here on Little Havana's Southwest 8th Street you'll find some of the best.

Centro Vasco is a small, dark club with a heavily Latino crowd and a small stage that features Cuban cabaret and other entertainers on weekends. A little Spanish might be necessary for maximum enjoyment, but the crowds are vibrant and the music is authentically Latino. Cover. ~ 2235 Southwest 8th Street; 305-643-9606.

Several excellent restaurants throw in fiery flamenco and strolling musicians with your meal. Try **Malaga**. ~ 740 Southwest 8th Street; 305-858-4224. **Casa Juancho** is another festive spot. ~ 2436 Southwest 8th Street; 305-642-2452.

You'll see top-name Latin musical and comedy shows at the 255-seat **Teatro de Bellas Artes**. ~ 2173 Southwest 8th Street; 305-325-0515.

West of Little Havana, **Maxim's Restaurant & Night Club** is a classy, elegant affair with an orchestra and piano bar. Latin music is featured nightly. Cover. ~ 7397 Southwest 8th Street; 305-265-4800.

Key Biscayne

▼▼▼▼▼▼▼▼▼▼

Take the undulating Rickenbacker Causeway across the brilliant turquoise water of Biscayne Bay and you'll land on Virginia Key, a speck of an island smothered in immense Australian pines and quiescent beaches. Although the island has remained very much in its natural state, tourism is beginning to leave its mark here.

SIGHTS

Farther down, the larger **Key Biscayne** is a lush flatland dotted with bushy seagrape trees and willowy pines. A historic crossroads, the barrier island was encountered by Ponce de León in 1513, which is when he dubbed it the Cape of Florida.

Crandon Boulevard is the key's main drag, cutting two miles through the length of the island. Quaint strip shopping centers, golf fairways and manicured condos line the boulevard.

Tucked obscurely at the island's tip is the 1825 **Cape Florida Lighthouse,** Florida's oldest remaining lighthouse. Oblivious to noisy beachgoers, the red brick cylinder rises 95 feet from the beach and peers serenely across the Atlantic Ocean, remembering a time when it guided ships through the perilous coastal reefs. Its sturdy walls survived a severe Seminole Indian attack in 1836 as well as an onslaught by Confederate sympathizers during the Civil War. The lighthouse is open every day for tours. Admission. ~ 1200 South Crandon Boulevard in the Bill Baggs Cape Florida State Recreation Area; 305-361-5811.

LODGING

The island has only a smattering of hotels, but thankfully each is nestled on a choice slice of beach. The **Silver Sands**, a traditional, L-shaped motel commanding fantastic views, is a departure from fancy oceanfront highrises. This homey, single-story hostelry surrounds a quiet courtyard with a pool and sandy path snaking its way to the beach. Guest rooms are clean but a little rugged, with exposed electrical cords and natty wall-to-wall carpets. Four wooden cottages are the best accommodations. ~ 301 Ocean Drive; 305-361-5441, fax 305-361-5477. DELUXE TO ULTRA-DELUXE.

The white, pyramid-shaped **Sonesta Beach Resort** sits crossways and purveys a sense of cool island elegance. The lobby is a mesh of Roman tile floors, glass tables and a waterfall plummeting down an abstract wall design. The resort has a palm tree–studded swimming pool and 301 rooms—all with ocean or island views—furnished with modern decor in pastel hues. An extensive children's program draws lots of families. ~ 350 Ocean Drive; 305-361-2021, 800-766-3782, fax 305-365-2082. ULTRA-DELUXE.

DINING

Eating out on Key Biscayne means trysting with cool blue Biscayne Bay. Arguably, the **Rusty Pelican** has cornered the market on views. Poised on the edge of Key Biscayne and surrounded by water on three sides, the Pelican faces sweeping scenes of downtown and glistening Biscayne Bay. The two-story rustic wooden building is set amidst a sea of palm trees and flowering plants. Inside, you'll find brick floors, stone walls and huge fishing nets draped from the ceiling. Atmosphere is the obvious draw here, since the fare—which focuses on seafood, Continental style—is good but overpriced. Try the coconut shrimp, veal saltimbocca (sautéed veal medallions layered with prosciutto and fontina cheese) or Polynesian chicken (charbroiled chicken breast heaped with Polynesian chutney). ~ 3201 Rickenbacker Causeway, Key Biscayne; 305-361-3818. MODERATE TO ULTRA-DELUXE.

Bayside Seafood Hut is known by boaties and windsurfers who frequent the Key. The bar and restaurant is a waterside, casual, mostly outdoor place tucked behind the Miami Marine Stadium and a boatyard. Most of the tables sit under a thatched roof. This is a great place at sunset. The smoked-fish dip is a must and the seafood sandwiches are always good. ~ 3501 Rickenbacker Causeway; 305-361-0808. MODERATE.

If you crave Asian food, you'll love **Two Dragons**. Sit in cozy wicker pagodas and sample traditional Chinese Mandarin and Szechuan cuisine. Black lacquered tables and ornate stained glass accented by palm fronds are found throughout the twin eateries. Dinner only on weekdays, lunch and dinner on weekends. ~ Sonesta Beach Resort, 350 Ocean Drive; 305-361-2021. MODERATE.

Sunday's on the Bay is a popular restaurant and bar. On Sunday a reggae band often plays in the waterfront bar. The Sunday brunch is the best draw here; tables are jammed with more than 50 items. The menu is standard fern bar fare (pastas, burgers, salads, seafood) and the crowd is usually predominantly boaties and folks who celebrate watching sunsets. ~ 5420 Crandon Boulevard; 305-361-6777. MODERATE.

Deliciously fresh pasta keeps the island's chic crowd coming back to **Stefano's**. Winning entrées include linguine in lobster sauce, *agnolotti*, spinach *pappardelle* and snapper in fennel sauce. While there's no glistening bay in sight, pleasant garden surroundings are a acceptable substitute. Dinner only. ~ 24 Crandon Boulevard; 305-361-7007. MODERATE TO ULTRA-DELUXE.

Episodes of Flipper were reportedly filmed around Jimbo's, a ramshackle bar built on the edge of the bay.

Jimbo's, hidden on a Virginia Key backroad, is a behind-the-guidebook kind of place that is pure old Florida. A small bar on the water's edge where the bay trickles into the back areas, the brightly painted Caribbeanesque storefronts that line the area around the bar add to the otherworldliness. A bocce ball court draws a fervid group of regulars. Beer is served out of a cooler and patrons park on an old couch outside the tiny place. The smoked-fish dip, however, made with fresh fish, is sublime. ~ Take the first left after the Miami Marine Stadium on an unmarked street; 305-361-7026. BUDGET.

SHOPPING

Key Biscayne is not known for its shopping and has no malls or upscale shopping streets. Most of the commerce focuses on necessities, and the scant shopping is relegated to a couple of strip centers like **KB Galeria** and the **Square Shopping Center** on Crandon Boulevard, the key's main artery.

In **The Square Shopping Center**, the place for takeout goodies or a cup of coffee is **Saveur** (305-365-9988), which stocks champagne, imported wine, gift baskets and assorted gourmet treats. The **Pretty Boutique** (305-361-8682) is a store that sells islandy-fashion clothes, shoes and accessories for women and children at very reasonable prices. ~ 260 Crandon Boulevard.

For some of the freshest fish in town, visit the docks at the **Crandon Marina** in the late afternoon as the fishers return with the catch of the day. Yellowtail, grouper, snapper and shrimp are sold in the wooden stalls just off Crandon Parkway.

BEACHES & PARKS

HOBIE BEACH 🏊 ⛵ 🚤 A ribbon of fluffy sand along a scenic causeway, this beach gets its name from the hundreds of sailboaters and windsurfers who whiz up and down the coast. Forever windy and spirited, Hobie Beach affords spectacular views of downtown while offering solace under canopies of Australian pines. It's always crowded, especially on weekends, so get here early. When swimming, stay very close to shore. Otherwise, you'll get plowed down by windsurfers and jet skiers. Facilities include sailboard, sailboat, windsurfing and jet ski rentals and food vendors. ~ On the south side of Rickenbacker Causeway.

VIRGINIA KEY BEACH 🏃 🏊 🎣 ⛵ 🚤 Sugar-fine sand rings most of this quiescent island that's smothered in tall pine trees and thick brush. At the eastern tip, where most people can be found, flocks of seagulls scurry about the placid shore, leaving their clawed imprints. But here's the real scoop: If you want seclusion, seek out the key's southwestern rim. Park in lot number one, then backtrack through the wooded areas until you find a series of natural coves. This was once a nude beach, and you'll still see a few birthday suits between these crevices. There's not much sand, but the crystal-clear water is an exceptional place to swim. There are picnic tables, restrooms, lifeguards and wooded trails. ~ Off Rickenbacker Causeway; 305-361-2749.

CRANDON PARK BEACH 🚲 ⚓ Key Biscayne's most popular beach sports a very wide swath of tawny sand edged with clusters of palm trees and a sliver of grassy meadow. A concrete path and spacious grassy areas border the mile-long stretch, which is a popular spot for Latino families. Ocean waves purr gently against a knee-deep sand bar that extends nearly 300 yards out, making this a great place to swim. Facilities consist of picnic areas, restrooms, showers, lifeguards, bike trails, concession stands and botanical gardens. ~ Midway down Key Biscayne off Rickenbacker Causeway; 305-361-5421.

BILL BAGGS CAPE FLORIDA STATE RECREATION AREA ⚓ 🛥 ⚓ 🎣 ⚓ Situated at the pinnacle of Key Biscayne and masked in broad Australian pine trees, the 406-acre park offers scenic drives, broad beaches good for swimming and nine fishing piers. Perched in the sand dunes, an 1825 lighthouse still peers across the horizon. In the distance, several stilt houses—built decades ago by fishermen—are clustered together in the Atlantic Ocean, a peculiar spectacle for beachgoers. Today, anglers fish from the seawall on the Biscayne Bay side for snook, red snapper, yellow tail, jack and grouper. Facilities include picnic tables, restrooms, showers, lifeguards, a restaurant and a boardwalk. Day-use fee, $4. ~ At Key Biscayne's tip, via Rickenbacker Causeway; 305-361-5811.

▼▼▼▼▼▼▼▼▼▼▼
Coconut Grove

South of Miami you'll find Coconut Grove, a turn-of-the-century village and the area's first real winter resort. Long a nest of quiet homes and quaint stores, "The Grove" attracted throngs of hippies during the 1960s and now dances to the trendiness of the 1990s. Although recent crime and deteriorating neighborhoods have caused a mild exodus, the village still remains a hotbed of activity.

SIGHTS

Your first sightseeing opportunity is **Silver Bluff**, an intriguing rock formation extending half a mile along Bayshore Drive between Crystal View and Emathia Street. Carved thousands of years ago by wave action, these knobby white constellations are made of oolitic limestone. Some of the area's first settlers, captured by the beauty of the bluff, built their homes around these rocks overlooking the bay.

Southward around a bend you'll encounter **Miami City Hall**. A two-story gleaming white structure preening on Biscayne Bay, it looks more like a small hotel than a government center. But then, that's typical of Miami. Carvings of little world globes traipse across the facade, hinting that the 1930s building used to be a busy Pan American Airlines seaplane base. ~ 3500 Pan American Drive; 305-250-5300.

The village core lies along **Main Highway** and **Commodore Plaza**, just south of City Hall. Miami's trendiness central, these streets are an experience in contrived aesthetics. Chic shops with bubbled canopies intermingle with towering oaks and nibble at the brick-lined roadways. Fashion-conscious women stroll the sidewalks, laden with perfume and shopping bags.

Coconut Grove founder Ralph Middleton Munroe, a true lover and protector of Florida's natural beauty, would have been heartbroken to see throngs of people and automobiles buzzing around what used to be the world's largest hardwood hammock. Quite aptly, the remaining smidgen of nature here is the **Barnacle State Historic Site**, Munroe's serene five-acre estate overlooking Biscayne Bay. An old buggy trail meanders through a lush hammock to the house. This structure, built in stages between 1891 and 1928, is the oldest Dade County home still located on its original site. Reflecting Munroe's devotion to shipbuilding and the sea, the two-story frame building resembles a barnacle and has a large veranda to catch ocean breezes. Most of the 19th-century furnishings are intact, and Munroe's excellent collection of pioneer photographs adorn the walls. On the grounds is an ancient spring-fed well and a boathouse. Open to the public Friday through Sunday; open Monday through Thursday for reserved tours. Admission. ~ 3485 Main Highway; 305-448-9445.

Another tribute to the area's earlier days, the **Coconut Grove Playhouse** is an inspiring, Spanish-style theater. Constructed in 1926, it was destroyed by the infamous hurricane that year and promptly rebuilt in 1927. Richly ornamented with parapets and twisted columns, the theater now hosts regional and major productions and continues to be a fashionable place to go. ~ 3500 Main Highway; 305-442-4000.

HIDDEN ►

Hidden away from the road in the middle of a private school, the **Pagoda of Ransom-Everglades School** is a real find. The 1902 pine building was the entire school until the campus expanded in the 1940s. Now, strolling back to the pagoda is like taking a trip through time. All around, preppy students laze in the grass or play tennis, while inside the pagoda's dusty walls rest memories of days past: a 1919 typewriter, a 1929 school yearbook, a much-used limestone fireplace. Chances are, you'll be the only sightseer at this historic stop. ~ 3575 Main Highway; 305-460-8800.

One of the area's most unusual hotels, the **Mayfair House** is a work of art. Sculpted mahogany doors, hand-painted tiles and stained-glass panels swirl throughout the small, dark lobby, where guests receive champagne and orange juice upon check-in. The 182 suites, which surround a big, sunlit atrium, are decorated in Viennese art nouveau. Many have baby grand pianos; all have Japanese hot tubs and all-marble baths. ~ 3000 Florida Avenue; 305-441-0000, 800-433-4555. ULTRA-DELUXE.

LODGING

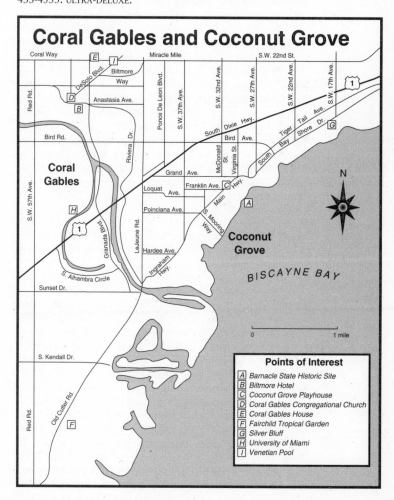

Coral Gables and Coconut Grove

Points of Interest

- A Barnacle State Historic Site
- B Biltmore Hotel
- C Coconut Grove Playhouse
- D Coral Gables Congregational Church
- E Coral Gables House
- F Fairchild Tropical Garden
- G Silver Bluff
- H University of Miami
- I Venetian Pool

A terraced tower overlooking a large yacht basin, the **Double-tree** is a casual but stylish kind of place. White marble tiles, hand-hewn cedar paneling and contemporary works of art adorn the lobby, which spills out onto an airy pool deck overlooking a busy avenue. Some of the 190 guest rooms have wet bars and modern furnishings. ~ 2649 South Bayshore Drive; 305-858-2500, 800-858-5776. DELUXE TO ULTRA-DELUXE.

Beautiful jutting terraces brimming with flowering vines signify that you've reached the **Grand Bay Hotel**, a very ritzy Miami ad-dress. Classical music is piped into a lobby styled with dramatic wood-trimmed glass walls, enormous crystal chandeliers and mir-rored ceilings. Most of the 178 accommodations face the Grove's yacht basin and some are aesthetically furnished with period pieces and sunken marble tubs. All units feature breakfast balconies, minibars and king-sized beds. A pool deck and restaurant are just a few of the amenities. Unmatched for service, the Grand Bay even serves you liquid refreshments when you check in. ~ 2669 South Bayshore Drive; 305-858-9600, 800-327-2788. ULTRA-DELUXE.

Unlike most other regions of Florida, the Miami area has few bed and breakfasts. However, more than 100 families have opened their homes to travelers. The accommodations, most with budget and moderate prices, are sprinkled throughout Dade County and range from chic Coconut Grove homes to horse ranches. For reser-vations, contact **Bed and Breakfast Company for Florida**. ~ P.O. Box 439262, South Miami, FL 33243; phone/fax 305-661-3270; e-mail bedbkfst@icanect.net.

DINING

Green Street Café claims the prime people-watching corner and lavishes its outdoor patrons with tall frozen margaritas and green umbrellas to ward off the blazing sun. Burgers, omelettes, pizza and pasta are good for munching. Breakfast, lunch and dinner. ~ 3468 Main Highway; 305-444-0244. BUDGET TO MODERATE.

Formerly an 1800s caretaker's cottage, **Tuscany's** now indulges a trendy clientele who convene on the outdoor red brick patio to gaze at a diverse group of passersby. The Italian-style menu includes the traditional selection of pastas, salads, soups and desserts. ~ 3484 Main Highway; 305-445-0022. MODERATE TO DELUXE.

The second-floor venue of **Kaleidoscope** provides a bird's-eye view of the street hubbub. This charming, glass-enclosed terrace has white patio furniture, ceiling fans and window box gardens. The cuisine may be American-style, but it's interesting all the same. Try the red snapper with glazed bananas or roast duckling with or-ange chutney and green peppercorns. No lunch on Monday. ~ 3112 Commodore Plaza; 305-446-5010. MODERATE TO DELUXE.

Café Tu Tu Tango is, quite simply, the place to nosh in Coconut Grove. Fashioned after an artist's loft in Barcelona, the wood-floored *tapas* bar is always crowded and always oh-so-good. Graze on an assortment of chips, dips, and fried tidbits such as calamari and alligator, or opt for a gourmet pizza that's brick oven baked. For fare more filling, try the chicken breast stuffed with chorizo (Spanish sausage), spinach and cheese. ~ 3015 Grand Avenue, in the Coco-Walk entertainment plaza; 305-529-2222. BUDGET TO MODERATE.

Go for a Chinese fix at **Mandarin Gardens**, the local headquarters for dependable Hunan, Mandarin and fiery Szechuan cuisine. Nestled along a tree-lined street, the diminutive eatery draws huge lunch crowds who pay homage to the sesame chicken, orange beef and crispy shrimp and broccoli. ~ 3268 Grand Avenue; 305-446-9999. BUDGET TO MODERATE.

Aptly named **Señor Frog's**, this toad-green stucco formation attracts a lively crowd who gulp huge margaritas and feast on gringo food as well as tasty traditional Mexican fare. Sepia photos of Mexican heroes, brick floors and a wooden bar set a casual tone. The extensive menu is quite entertaining, warning against a "boring!" consommé and listing an entrée called *arroa cabezón* but saying, "no translation, just order it!" ~ 3008 Grand Avenue; 305-448-0999. MODERATE.

One of the Grove's most distinguished addresses, the **Mayfair Grill** is situated in the dazzling Mayfair House hotel and purveys a real sense of grandeur. Embellishments of beautiful mahogany, marble and stained glass abound in a subdued, romantic setting. The Australian chef prepares filet of Louisiana ostrich with exotic mushrooms and caramelized shallot demi-glacé, Dutch veal chop with Australian pepperleaf demi-glacé and fire-roasted yellowtail topped with misu beurre blanc. Desserts include luscious lemon myrtle crème brulée and chocolate sin cake. The Mayfair serves three meals a day. ~ 3000 Florida Avenue; 305-441-0000. ULTRA-DELUXE.

Monty Trainer's is a perfect place for a dog-day afternoon. This restaurant plays host to swimsuit-clad locals and tourists who soak up the sun and calypso music. Casual tables overlook an expansive marina. Excellent conch fritters, stone crab and those famous Florida oysters on the half shell are featured. Expect bouillabaisse, lobster, steak and seafood on the dinner menu. ~ 2550 South Bayshore Drive; 305-858-1431. MODERATE TO DELUXE.

For more than a decade, the Grove's vogue shops have been patronized by trendsetters and those who have money to burn. The best part of browsing these shady glass fronts is eyeing the other shoppers, who love to dress up for the occasion.

SHOPPING

The heart of trendiness, **The Streets of Mayfair** has a glass-canopied atrium with savvy written all over it. Shoot up to the second and third floors in glass elevators, or laze around Mexican-tiled waterfalls and ornate marble sculptures. ~ 2911 Grand Avenue; 305-448-1700.

Nearby, watch your necklace being made at **Om Jewelry**, a store and studio featuring gold and silver in freeform and angular designs. ~ 3070 Grand Avenue; 305-445-1865.

Maya Hatcha stocks shoes, women's clothing, purses, jewelry, trinkets, artwork and other cool stuff from Bali, Thailand, Central America and Africa. ~ 3085 Grand Avenue; 305-443-9040.

Just outside the mall, **American Details** proffers an eye-pleasing scheme of handblown vases and perfumers, exotic wooden jewelry boxes and kaleidoscopes. ~ 3107 Grand Avenue; 305-448-6163.

Bask in the past at **Antiques in the Grove**, a marvelous shop where you can sort through flapper beads, jade statues, stunning crystal, antique jewelry, porcelain pieces, housewares and silver tea services. ~ 3168 Commodore Plaza; 305-448-7877.

Mom will find her string bikini at **Ritchie Swimwear**, a colorful collage of neon, print and striped suits for men and women. ~ 3401 Main Highway; 305-443-7919.

NIGHTLIFE   "The Grove" is a hub of nighttime activity. As dusk approaches, the sidewalks teem with shoppers and bar hoppers and a stream of traffic crawls along the village streets.

A shorts-and-flip-flops crowd assembles at **Monty's Raw Bar**, an outdoor, palm-crowned reggae and raw bar overlooking a marina. A live band plays nightly. ~ 2550 South Bayshore Drive; 305-856-3992.

The town's best watering hole is **Tavern in the Grove**, a nontrendy neighborhood spot with a long oak bar and framed Grove art. Pop, blues and folk music resound from a jukebox. ~ 3416 Main Highway; 305-447-3884.

The **Hungry Sailor** is a favorite with reggae fans. This club features live bands every day but Monday and Wednesday, a small

A WALK ON THE STYLED SIDE

The place to be, CocoWalk is a perfect example of the area's trend toward yuppiness. The multi-level shopping and partying extravaganza is a fanciful version of Spanish stucco and coral rock woven with fountains and balconies and walkways. Among the chic CocoWalk shops is **The White House** (305-446-7747), which caters to the woman who loves white. Suits, sportswear, lingerie, parasols and picture frames are available. **Carolyn Lamb** (305-443-4631) keeps the "body conscious" woman in mind with sleek workout suits, lycra dresses and leggings, and other form-fitting getups. ~ 3015 Grand Avenue.

dancefloor, a mellow crowd and a large selection of imported beer. Cover. ~ 3426 Main Highway; 305-444-9359.

The splendid **Coconut Grove Playhouse** showcases major musical and drama productions as well as comedy acts. Built in 1927, the three-story, Spanish-style building is beautifully ornamented with twisted columns and parapets. ~ 3500 Main Highway; 305-442-4000

Built in 1911 as an afternoon teahouse, **Taurus** is now a habitat for trendsetters who mill around its shady pine porch. Live bands play Tuesday through Saturday, featuring blues, rock and jazz sounds. ~ 3540 Main Highway; 305-448-0633.

Tu Tu Tango, a jumping *tapas* eatery, is also popular for its outdoor bar, a second-story perch above the carnival of downtown Coconut Grove. ~ 3015 Grand Avenue, CocoWalk; 305-529-2222.

With a feel of a college bar parked oceanside, **Baja Beach Club** spins Top-40 hits and beach oldies in this crowded, dark bar where waitresses circulate in bikinis. Sunday is host to salsa and merengue sounds. Cover. ~ 3015 Grand Avenue, CocoWalk; 305-445-0278.

▼▼▼▼▼▼▼▼▼▼
Coral Gables

South of Coconut Grove off Route 1, you will find Coral Gables, the dream-come-true city of one George Merrick. In the early 1900s, Merrick looked at these backwoods and envisioned grand things. He cleared citrus groves, laid streets and sidewalks, and brought in Mediterranean architecture, touting the spot as the "Miami Riviera." Those who visited Coral Gables, he promised, would find "endless golden sunlight and bronzed people."

Now this pristine, planned town boasts beautiful Spanish-style architecture and miles of country club living. Largely inhabited by wealthy Latinos, the city is a labyrinth of winding streets that unfortunately can make life difficult for the first-time visitor. Refer to maps and even then, plan to spend some time backtracking.

SIGHTS

Set on 155 acres in the midst of Coral Gables, the **Biltmore Hotel** is a stunning 26-story, 280-room Moorish tower built in the '20s as a replica of the Giralda Tower in Seville, Spain. The lobby boasts vaulted frescoes, massive chandeliers, arched courtyards and the country's largest swimming pool (where Esther Williams swam for some of her films). In 1986, $40 million was spent to restore the hotel to its original grandeur. Weekend tours touch on the hotel's role as the showpiece of Coral Gables—the country's first planned posh community. Consider late-afternoon high tea in the lobby, Sunday brunch in the column-encircled courtyard or a Tuesday night meal in the outdoor café where opera singers serenade the meal. ~ 1200 Anastasia Avenue; 305-445-1926.

Around the time the Biltmore was going up, Merrick donated the land across the street for the **Coral Gables Congregational**

Church. An architectural gem, the city's first church is a Mediterranean revival design with barrel tiles and ornate baroque ornaments. Its bell tower, mirroring the Biltmore's, is nearly as stunning. During the 1920s, University of Miami students—protesting school policies—ran the school's first underground newspaper from the tower. More treasures await inside, where you'll encounter 16th-century furnishings, chandeliers and beautiful pews carved from native pecky cypress. ~ 3010 DeSoto Boulevard; 305-448-7421.

From here, twist your way northeast on DeSoto Boulevard to the **Venetian Pool.** Born out of a rock pit, this Merrick-built retreat is a sprawling lagoon bordered by a Mediterranean villa and the mandatory Miami palm trees. Coral caves, Venetian lampposts and intermittent waterfalls canvas the place, which was the stomping grounds for William Jennings Bryan, Johnny Weissmuller, Esther Williams and other notables. Admission. ~ 2701 DeSoto Boulevard; 305-460-5356.

At the end of DeSoto lies Coral Way, the road where George Merrick spent his boyhood days. The **Coral Gables House,** where Merrick grew up, has been enshrined by locals and is now a museum. Built around the turn of the century, the coral rock structure features a breezy veranda studded with Mediterranean columns and topped with barrel tiles. Open Wednesday and Sunday for tours, or call for an appointment. Admission. ~ 907 Coral Way; 305-460-5361.

Kids won't want to miss the **Miami Youth Museum,** an interesting niche in the Miracle Center mall. The Sea & Me exhibit features an interactive ship, and there are plenty of other activities for youngsters. They can play the role of either receptionist or dentist at Dr. Small's office, or cashier or customer at the grocery store, don a firefighter uniform, or make their own puppets. Admission. ~ 3301 Coral Way, Level U; 305-446-4386.

Travel eastward on DeSoto and you'll uncover a gold mine known as Miracle Mile. This two-block address of swanky shops and brick-lined streets also houses **Coral Gables City Hall,** an imposing limestone structure that integrates circular and square design. Most impressive is a rounded wing with ornate columns and grotesque carvings true to the mannerist style. Stroll through the building and climb the worn, 1920s-era steps to the third and fourth floors. Along the way, you will see antiques and a brilliantly colored mural that spreads across a rotunda. ~ 405 Biltmore Way; 305-446-6800.

An easy place to find, the **University of Miami** is south of downtown Coral Gables. Miami's prestigious university has about 14,000 students and a 260-acre maze of low-slung buildings, twisting canals and shady plazas. ~ 1306 Stanford Drive; 305-284-5500.

Center of activity here is the **Norman A. Whitten University Center,** where crowds of international students mill around game rooms, cafeterias and a large swimming pool. ~ 1306 Stanford Drive; 305-284-5646.

Nearby, student thespians have developed an excellent reputation with performances at the **Ring Theatre**. ~ 1380 Miller Drive; 305-284-3355.

Also on campus is the **Lowe Art Museum**, which features a sizable collection of Renaissance and Baroque paintings, as well as American Indian, tribal African, Asian and pre-Columbian art. Closed Monday. Admission. ~ 1301 Stanford Drive; 305-284-3535.

Perhaps more than anything, Coral Gables is a residential village. Winding through its storybook streets, you'll find clusters of homes with specific architectural designs borrowed from various countries. Called **The Villages**, these 1920s neighborhoods are part of Merrick's scheme to bring in wealthy residents to his model city.

South of Route 1 on Riviera Drive and adjacent streets, **Chinese Village** consists of eight oriental homes styled with carved wooden balconies, curved tiled roofs and a great deal of lattice work.

> Animal sculptures perched atop some houses in Chinese Village are meant to bring good luck to residents.

Just off Riviera on Hardee Road are the **French Country** and **French City Villages**. Country-style estates resemble châteaux, with rounded and square towers and wrought-iron balconies. The city version features snazzy French town homes surrounded by large walls.

The **Dutch South African Village**, on LeJeune Road, is not African at all but mirrors farmhouses of wealthy Dutch colonists. The quaint L-shaped and T-shaped homes are adorned with scroll work, high domed arches and spiraling chimneys.

In the midst of all this gentry is a point lost in time. Abandoned and all but forgotten, the **Pinewood Cemetery** rests in a deserted wooded lot between manicured lawns. Founded in 1855, Dade County's oldest cemetery is overgrown with palmettos and pine trees and sprinkled with pieces of broken headstones. In the center, a single memorial stone pays tribute to more than 200 Miami pioneers buried here. One tombstone that's still intact marks the grave of a Confederate soldier. ~ 47th Avenue just north of Sunset Road.

◀ HIDDEN

For a horticulture treat, travel south on Old Cutler Road to **Fairchild Tropical Garden**. An 83-acre series of quiescent lakes, perfectly formed foliage and carpeted lawn, this place is a quiet reprieve from the surrounding hubbub. Here you get to look and touch. Admission. ~ 10901 Old Cutler Road; 305-667-1651.

Across the street and shrouded among shrubs is a historical marker in front of a **sausage tree**. The tropical tree, born of a seed sent from Egypt in 1907, grows not sausages but rare fruit that looks like a cross between a mango and a papaya. Back in 1926, Miami homesteader Maud Black used the intriguing fruit to make jellies and jams, then sold them from a roadside stand underneath

◀ HIDDEN

the massive tree. If you continue south on Old Cutler Road for a mile, you will see several taller sausage trees on the east side of the street. ~ 10400 Old Cutler Road.

LODGING

HIDDEN ►

A rare find in an urban area, **Place St. Michel** possesses all the charm of a French country inn. A mass of clinging ivy obscures the exterior from passing traffic, while inside awaits an unhurried world of carefully chosen antiques, tiled floors, potted flowers and personal service. Built in 1926, the hotel has 27 bedrooms, warmly decorated with hand-loomed rugs, French shag lamps and high, detailed ceilings. ~ 162 Alcazar Avenue; 305-444-1666, fax 305-529-0074. ULTRA-DELUXE.

Granted, there's not much atmosphere at the **Holiday Inn University of Miami**, located across the street from the University of Miami. But the clean, nicely decorated rooms aren't quite as expensive as others in this pricey town. The three-story, U-shaped building surrounds a standard motel swimming pool. ~ 1350 South Dixie Highway; 305-667-5611, fax 305-669-3153. DELUXE.

The quaint **David William Hotel** offers comfortable accommodations. Slightly camp, with a European flair, the 1965 hostelry has 13 floors of clean, carpeted rooms and a concrete rooftop pool. Continental breakfast included with some rates. ~ 700 Biltmore Way; 305-445-7821, fax 305-445-5585. ULTRA-DELUXE.

The **Hyatt Regency Coral Gables** is one of those ultramodern establishments straining to imitate Old World elegance. Designed with a 14th-century Moorish castle in mind, the hotel features 242 rooms fashioned with impressive ten-foot windows, mini-bars and glass coffee tables. Built in 1987, the 14-story pink-and-white hotel takes up an entire city block and features a pool terrace and a gourmet restaurant. ~ 50 Alhambra Plaza; 305-441-1234, 800-233-1234, fax 305-441-0520. ULTRA-DELUXE.

Al Capone once slept in the great orange Moorish tower of the **Biltmore Hotel**, and Esther Williams performed aquabatics in its enormous swimming pool. Today, celebrities still haunt the 1926 Mediterranean grand dame lavished with old world furnishings, vast arches and columns, handpainted ceiling mosaics, breezeways lined with Italian statuary and perfectly tended gardens and golf greens. The 275 rooms are impeccably adorned—some nearly palatial. The pool is the largest in the country. Two superb restaurants, 10 tennis courts, 18-hole championship golf and a spa and health club make this one of Miami's most desirable resorts. ~ 1200 Anastasia Avenue; 305-445-1926, 800-727-1926. ULTRA-DELUXE.

Another upscale downtown address, the **Omni Colonnade Hotel** is an impressive tribute to Coral Gables' beginnings. In the lobby you'll find enchanting 1920s town photos and corridors of cathedral windows and pink-and-green marble. The 157 accommodations follow suit, providing formal surroundings with hand-blown candelabra, mahogany dressers and intricately painted vases. ~ 180 Aragon Avenue; 305-441-2600, fax 305-445-3929. ULTRA-DELUXE.

A misfit along gourmet row, **House of India** promises two things: to provide some of the area's most exotic food, and to give you lots of it. You'll encounter large portions of dishes such as sweet coconut soup, *navrattan shai korma* (vegetables cooked with spices and cream), curried lamb and an intriguing clay oven–baked bread. Carved wooden dividers create private niches for diners, but the slightly tattered furnishings give a worn look. ~ 22 Merrick Way; 305-444-2348. BUDGET TO MODERATE.

DINING

In a city renowned for its abundance of French restaurants, **John Martin's** is a welcome change of pace. Run by two Irish childhood buddies, the cultured eatery focuses on European cuisine with Gaelic accents. An enormous Waterford chandelier dominates the dining room, a Queen Anne affair with high-back chairs. Try the lamb loin in rosemary mushroom sauce, oak-smoked salmon or Gaelic steak with whiskey-mushroom sauce. ~ 253 Miracle Mile; 305-445-3777. MODERATE TO DELUXE.

You'd sort of expect to find **Restaurant St. Michel** hidden along a hilly road in the French countryside. This splendid little restaurant, situated in a 1926 ivy-clad hotel of the same name, makes you wish the night would linger. Dramatic ceilings, beautiful antiques and elegant draperies punctuated with period furniture create tranquil environs. The New American cuisine is exceptional, with entrées such as sautéed Florida Keys yellowtail with tropical fruit salsa and fried plantains, and crispy Long Island duckling with wild rice and vegetables. Breakfast, lunch and dinner. ~ 162 Alcazar Avenue; 305-444-1666. DELUXE TO ULTRA-DELUXE.

You can order any of the dishes at **Bangkok, Bangkok** with one to five stars, depending on how spicy you like it. Highly regarded by locals, the Thai eatery boasts a full range of fish, beef, seafood and poultry doused in savory and piquant sauces with fruits and vegetables. Two "American" dining rooms are rather plain, but an elaborate Thai balcony has scarlet carpets, redwood walls and carved wood stables with floor cushions. ~ 157 Giralda Avenue; 305-444-2397. MODERATE.

Just east of Coral Gables, a stretch of road called Coral Way offers a handful of reliable neighborhood restaurants. You'll find the same customers day after day at **Villa Italia**, a simple yet intimate neighborhood café that serves Italian cuisine with gusto. This is food like grandma used to make—thick, hearty spaghetti sauces, bubbling cheesy lasagna, pizza loaded with meat and vegetables, and eggplant parmigiana, a house specialty. The prices, many less than $5, are incredible. A place not to miss! ~ 3058 Coral Way; 305-444-0206. BUDGET.

Inhale that wonderful smoky aroma from the **New Hickory Barbecue**, where slabs of pork, beef and chicken are slow-cooked all day over a deep pit filled with hickory chips. The rough stone floors, redwood picnic tables and brick walls give this place a real Deep South feel. ~ 3170 Coral Way; 305-569-0098. BUDGET TO MODERATE.

Scenes of Greek fishing ports are splashed on the walls of **Mykonos**, aptly named for its savory Greek fare. A family-run eatery, this diner gets extra noisy when locals pile in for excellent *dolmadakia* (stuffed grape leaves), *moussaka* (layered beef and eggplant), *spanakopita* (spinach pie) and *pastitsio* (Greek lasagna). A Mediterranean treat. No lunch on Sunday. ~ 1201 Coral Way; 305-856-3140. BUDGET TO MODERATE.

SHOPPING   A bustling Mediterranean-style city with country club pizzazz, Coral Gables boasts two blocks of shops dubbed **Miracle Mile**. ~ Between Douglas and LeJeune roads.

The Estate Wines & Gourmet Foods has shelves stocked with esoteric edibles from around the world as well as a solid selection of wine. ~ 92 Miracle Mile; 305-442-9915.

Albright Jewelers (305-446-2986) carries interesting collectibles such as jewelry and porcelain. In the back, coin and stamp collectors will adore **Gables Coin and Stamp** (305-446-0032). Rows of rare coins and stamps line the shelves of this eclectic spot. ~ 259 Miracle Mile.

At **Rudma Picture Co.** you'll find oils and lithographs from recognized Florida, South American and Cuban artists. ~ 263 Miracle Mile; 305-443-6262.

Satin and lace abound at **Daisy & Tarsi**, an exclusive women's formal wear shop with racks of stunning cocktail gowns and bridal accessories. ~ 311 Miracle Mile; 305-854-5557.

Looking for used and out-of-print books? Check out **Books & Books** for art and design, fiction and poetry. ~ 296 Aragon Avenue; 305-442-4408.

There are more miracles on the east end of Coral Gables in the form of the **Miracle Center**, a futuristic, 31-store mall that includes the Miami Youth Museum. Designed as a shopper's fantasyland, the three-level emporium abounds with purple staircases, white pillars and freeform pools with multiple waterfalls. Step into the elevator, where piped-in music inspires that buying fever. ~ 3301 Coral Way; 305-444-8890.

NIGHTLIFE   A local 1 a.m. bar curfew squelched much of the nighttime action in this posh, largely Latino city. However, sprinkled liberally throughout these well-groomed lawns you'll discover some promising area theater.

Though most of the floor space inside **John Martin's Pub** belongs to the restaurant, the Erin-go-bar downstairs is one of the favored happy-hour stops for much of the Gables business crowd. Irish beer is on tap and Irish newspapers lie on tabletops. The bar has no dancefloor and is overcrowded on Fridays, but the atmosphere is convivial, the bartenders efficient and there's a posse of warmhearted regulars. Expect to jig to Irish bands on Tuesday and Sunday, and rock-and-roll on Saturday. ~ 253 Miracle Mile, 305-445-3777.

The **Alcazaba** in the heart of Coral Gables is best on Fridays when a live salsa band heats up the place. Popular with an older crowd (anyone not considered a Generation X-er), the small dancefloor is full on weekends and Wednesdays when women drink free champagne. ~ Hyatt Regency, 50 Alhambra Plaza; 305-441-1234, ext. 2600.

THEATER, OPERA, SYMPHONY AND DANCE   The 63-seat **New Theatre** hosts both experimental and traditional plays by a resident company. ~ 65 Almeria Avenue; 305-443-5909.

The **University of Miami's Ring Theatre** has cornered a loyal following with quality student-produced musicals, comedy and drama. ~ 1380 Miller Drive; 305-284-3355.

Southern Dade County

Across Dade County's southern reaches lie burgeoning residential developments that—aching for more space—creep through farmlands and citrus groves and back up to the Everglades. Meandering through this extensive spectrum you'll find miles of beautiful old and new homes nestled against pick-it-yourself spots and fruit fields.

The epitome of sprawling suburbia, Kendall is home to several hundred thousand yuppies who navigate the traffic-clogged roadways to downtown each workday. Nearby, Cutler Ridge and Perrine are 1950s neighborhoods originally christened "Big Hunting Ground" by the area's only real natives, the Seminoles. Farther south and seemingly worlds away, Homestead is a congenial farming town where the daily grind takes a back seat to enjoying life.

SIGHTS

Dotted among these expanses are interesting museums along with pockets of historical sights and nature preserves. More than 1000 beautiful but noisy birds reside at **Parrot Jungle and Gardens**, a classic Miami tourist attraction that opened in 1936. Here parrots fly free among 30 acres of tropical foliage and ponds, performing tricks and posing for curious sightseers. Admission. ~ 11000 Southwest 57th Avenue; 305-666-7834.

The bayfront **Charles Deering Estate** offers a sublime look at the area's past. Deering, the half-brother of Vizcaya's James Deering, built the retreat in the 1920s to "escape the hubbub of downtown Miami." Next to a simple, three-story pine homestead built when the town of Old Cutler occupied the site, Deering constructed a spacious stone building to house his art collection. On the grounds are more than 396 acres of virgin pineland, hammock and mangrove areas. There is also a Tequesta Indian burial mound and fossil site. (The estate is currently closed due to hurricane damage and scheduled to reopen in January of 1998. Call ahead.) Admission. ~ 16701 Southwest 72nd Avenue; 305-235-1668.

Scattered throughout the southwest reaches of Dade County lie modern subdivisions, pick-it-yourself produce fields and a few attractions worth the 45-minute drive from Miami.

Metrozoo opened in 1981 and is one of the nation's largest zoos. More than 1000 animals wander about a 290-acre cageless habitat, separated from their spectators by watery moats. Don't miss the adorable Australian koalas and the white Bengal tiger. Also check out the exhibit of Asian river life. Admission. ~ 12400 Southwest 152nd Street; 305-251-0403.

Next door is the interesting but often overlooked **Gold Coast Railroad Museum**. Like a ghost town of train yards, the nearly deserted outpost possesses rows of historic trains. Climb through the fancy Ferdinand Magellan, a 1942 Pullman car built exclusively for U.S. presidents, or the streamlined Silver Crescent, built in 1948 for the California Zephyr. You can also cruise around 68 acres in a steam locomotive. Admission. ~ 12450 Southwest 152nd Street; 305-253-0063.

Go ape at **Monkey Jungle**, a partially cageless primate habitat situated in a lush South Florida hammock. Hundreds of chimpanzees, gorillas, baboons and orangutans swing through trees and perform tricks such as skindiving. ~ 14805 Southwest 216th Street; 305-235-1611.

◆◆◆

FABULOUS FLYING MACHINES

Airplane fanatics will think they've reached heaven at **Weeks Air Museum**. The brainchild of local pilot Kermit Weeks, the museum houses about 30 antique aircraft. The brightly colored machines, poised for takeoff, include an all-plywood DeHavilland and the world's only flyable Grumman Duck, a reconnaissance aircraft used during World War II. Admission. ~ 14710 Southwest 128th Street in Tamiami Airport; 305-233-5197.

Largely a corporate hotel, the **Miami Marriott Dadeland** is situated
along a busy highway but affords picturesque views of downtown
Miami and close proximity to one of the area's largest shopping
malls. The 24-story building houses a spacious seventh-floor pool
deck and guest rooms with large windows, contemporary artwork
and mauve carpets. Marble floors and glass tables give the lobby a
modern edge. Rates include a continental breakfast. ~ 9090 South
Dadeland Boulevard; 305-670-1035, 800-228-9290, fax 305-670-
7540. ULTRA-DELUXE.

LODGING

Sumptuous portions of creative and traditional Japanese fare are in
store at **Kampai**. This venue, which overlooks the inside of the historic Bakery Center, has clusters of shiny wooden tables, a wonderfully fresh sushi bar and an all-Japanese staff. Sample the sashimi,
sunomono, crunchy chicken wings or intriguing grilled *unagi* (eel),
all arranged decoratively in pretty wooden trays. ~ 8745 Sunset
Drive; 305-596-1551. MODERATE TO DELUXE.

DINING

For a taste of bona fide Florida cracker cookin', head for **The
Frog Pond**. The no-frills, family-style eatery, stuck way out on Dade
County's western horizon, pushes frog legs, catfish and alligator,
all crisp-fried and served with hushpuppies, cole slaw and fabulous
french fries. Breakfast is big. No dinner on Sunday. ~ 17690 Southwest 8th Street, 305-553-2725. BUDGET TO MODERATE.

Shorty's has long established a reputation as one of the best
barbecue joints around. The log and brick cabin, which rests along
a buzzing highway, is jammed with rustic wooden tables and decorated with neon beer signs. Folks come here to slurp up Shorty's
scrumptious hickory sauce, which covers smoked ribs, chicken and
beef. The service is extra friendly, but lines tend to be long during
lunch. ~ 9200 South Dixie Highway, Kendall; 305-670-7732. BUD-
GET TO MODERATE.

Shibui is a wonderful place to eat sushi. The shrimp, salmon and
California rolls are outstanding, but best of all, they're served in a
cozy upstairs sushi bar. You can also dine on cushions in a dimly lit
loft or downstairs beneath a high wood ceiling. The regular menu
features delicious tempura, teriyaki, stirfry and sukiyaki. Dinner
only. ~ 10141 Southwest 72nd Street; 305-274-5578. MODERATE.

Although not generally recognized as a shopping destination, the
town of South Miami offers a three-block stretch of eclectic stores
that are worth perusing. You'll find these marts along Sunset Drive,
between Southwest 57th and Southwest 59th avenues.

SHOPPING

Keep an eye out for unusual and traditional antique jewelry at
Five Golden Rings. A solid gold cigar ash preserver, Italian cameos
and intricate Victorian jewels are a few of the finds. ~ 5843 Sunset
Drive; 305-667-3208.

At **Alice's Day Off**, you'll find skimpy neon bikinis, cover-ups and other bright beachwear. ~ 5900 Sunset Drive; 305-284-0301.

Brilliantly blooming azaleas, bromeliads, orchids and begonias beckon from inside **The Garden Gate**. Dainty wicker baskets are also found at this fragrant stop. ~ 5872 Sunset Drive; 305-661-0605.

Lamps in every shade are revealed at **Lightorama**, where you'll discover art deco, Tiffany and contemporary styles. ~ 5832 Sunset Drive; 305-667-8941.

Tucked away in a courtyard, **Antique Maps & Prints** has a marvelous cache of antique maps and charts. Some of the store's world maps date back to the 1500s. ~ 5794 Sunset Drive; 305-665-5070.

Located in a warehouse district, **One Hand Clapping** offers a large collection of 1940s and 1950s art deco items with a tropical flair. You'll also find vintage fabrics and outrageous lamps from the 1950s. Call for an appointment. ~ 7165 Southwest 47th Street, Unit 320; 305-661-6316.

An anomaly in an urban area, **Robert's Western Wear** has an ample stash of geddyup cowboy gear, Indian moccasins and woven blankets. ~ 5854 South Dixie Highway; 305-666-6647.

Along Route 1 near Kendall you'll discover two of the area's most talked-about malls. **Dadeland Mall** is like a city unto itself, with 150 stores and restaurants in a sleek motif of grey, cream and navy blue, glass atriums and ficus trees. Several major department stores as well as chain shops offer everything from chic attire and furnishings to gourmet chocolate and nifty toys. ~ Route 1 and North Kendall Drive; 305-661-7582.

Cascading fountains, rock gardens, breezy gazebos and steep price tags await at **The Falls**, a ritzy collection of more than 50 unique shops and chain stores. This open-air setting is a popular strolling destination, even after the shops have closed at night. ~ Route 1 and Southwest 136th Street; 305-255-4570.

NIGHTLIFE   **Sports Page Pub and Restaurant** is a rowdy, lively bar with line-dancing on Tuesday and Thursday, karaoke on Wednesday and live country and oldies bands on weekends. ~ 113 South Homestead Boulevard, Homestead; 305-246-3633.

BEACHES & PARKS   **MATHESON HAMMOCK COUNTY PARK** 🚶 🚲 ⛵ 🎣 🏊 🚗 🛥️ A coconut plantation in the early 1900s, Matheson Hammock is now the only real "local" beach park left in Dade County. Situated along the shoreline south of Coral Gables, the area is favored by families who picnic, swim and fish. Winding trails crawl through more than 100 acres of thick mangrove hammock that blankets the area. There's not a lot of sand, but a shallow, man-made pond is ideal for shell hunting. There are picnic tables, restrooms, lifeguards, a marina and nature and bike trails. ~ Off old Cutler Road, just south of Coral Gables; 305-667-3035.

LARRY AND PENNY THOMPSON PARK 🚶🚴🛶🎣⛱️⛵ This nucleus of activity is set among the agricultural fields in southern Dade County and offers one of the few large campgrounds around Miami. Here you'll find a crystal clear lake dotted with swimmers, sailboats and skiffs, and 270 acres of crisscrossed jogging paths and rolling green grass. Freshwater fishing is good from lake banks or in boats, and swimming is good year-round. There are picnic areas, restrooms, showers and a store; laundry facilities are provided for campers. ~ At 12451 Southwest 184th Street near Metrozoo; 305-232-1049.

⛺ There are 240 campsites available, offering hook-ups for RVs and vans as well as tent sites; $17 per night.

This wide expanse of suburbia stretches above the head of downtown Miami and serves as the living quarters for more than 150,000 people. Most of the terrain here was developed during the 1940s and '50s and includes an amalgamation of posh estates, yacht-filled canals, gleaming strip shopping centers and crowded highways.

▼▼▼▼▼▼▼▼▼
North Miami

It seems ironic that the single true historic sight in northern Miami is indeed the oldest building in the Western Hemisphere. The **Ancient Spanish Monastery** was originally built under the direction of Cistercian monks in 1141 in Segovia, Spain. In 1925, William Randolph Hearst had the cloister disassembled and carted in more than 10,000 crates across the Atlantic Ocean to Miami. Interestingly, it remained in storage in Brooklyn until 1954, when local developers breathed life back into the grand monastery. Now its rough stone walls, ornate columns and buttressed ceilings rest quietly among palm trees and towering oaks. Carvings of crosses, crescents and stars dance across the stone walls, masons' marks etched by skilled craftsmen who originally constructed the building. Admission. ~ 16711 West Dixie Highway; 305-945-1461.

SIGHTS

Colonial architecture is rarer than snow in these parts, and that's why the **Bay Harbor Inn** is such a wonderful find. Tucked away along the posh Bay Harbor waterways, this charming, restored 1948 hostelry is the pride of the neighborhood. In the main, two-story building, you'll find shiny wooden floors, high beam ceilings, leafy potted plants and turn-of-the century antiques throughout the lobby and suites. A second, 22-unit building offers more modern accommodations—all facing the water. ~ 9660 East Bay Harbor Drive, Bay Harbor Island; 305-868-4141. DELUXE.

LODGING

◄ HIDDEN

If you're wondering where members of Miami's upper crust while away their time, you'll find them at **Turnberry Isle Yacht and Country Club**, a world of multimillion-dollar yachts, spa treatments, Jaguars and celebrities seeking solace. These heady environs consist of 24 tennis courts, two golf courses, five pools, and much more. Hotel suites are cleverly decorated with nouveau art, sleek Italian marble and huge sunken jacuzzis. ~ 19999 West Country Club Drive, Aventura; 305-932-6200, 800-327-7028, fax 305-933-6560. ULTRA-DELUXE.

Best Western On the Bay has one very important thing going for it: water. The no-frills, family-style accommodations overlook beautiful Biscayne Bay and lie five minutes from the beach. A dramatic wooden ceiling and piano add character to the tiny lobby. Guest rooms are rather small, but offer clean, standard furnishings. Some rooms include a refrigerator and microwave. ~ 1819 79th Street Causeway, North Bay Village; 305-865-7100, 800-624-3961, fax 305-868-3483. BUDGET.

DINING

Few restaurants make dining more of an adventure than **Chef Allen's**. Acclaimed South Florida chef Allen Susser, who hails from New York's La Cirque, works his culinary wizardry amid classy art deco surroundings. Neon tubes trace lines around the dining room, washed in a cool grey. The ever-changing menu might feature such extravagances as blackened red snapper with chayote, plantains and orange sauce or *boniato*-crusted chicken breast with tamarind and gingered figs. The food is a tribute to Miami's "tropical fusion" cuisine. Dinner only. ~ 19088 Northeast 29th Avenue, Aventura; 305-935-2900. DELUXE TO ULTRA-DELUXE.

If you're tired of frills, hop over to Biscayne Boulevard and make a pit stop at one of the casual eateries along Miami's main eastern artery. **East Side Mario's** serves giant pizzas and quart-sized beers to hungry shoppers and a late-night local college crowd. High-beam ceilings and polished oak floors give this southern Italian–style bistro a real warehouse feeling. Fresh meats and aged cheeses dangle from above the step-up bar, and restaurant scenes cover an entire wall. ~ 19501 Biscayne Boulevard in the Aventura Mall, Aventura; 305-935-3589. BUDGET TO MODERATE.

Wonderfully imaginative food in an artful setting with black granite and wood-grain paneling make **Mark's Place** one of Miami's best American-style eateries. An open kitchen, loads of greenery and private clusters of tables and booths create intimate yet casual surroundings. Extensive lunch and dinner menus change daily. Innovative selections include potato fritters with caviar and a chive butter sauce, warm lamb salad, oak-grilled baby hen and pistachio-crusted grouper. ~ 2286 Northeast 123rd Street; 305-893-6888. MODERATE TO DELUXE.

Need a health boost? Meander down the block to **Here Comes the Sun**. The health food store/restaurant has an ample selection of salads, sandwiches and hot eats. Try the sunburger, chicken Roma and pasta served with a selection of sauces such as ginger-tamari, orange-sesame or lemon-spice. Heart-studded menu items are fat-, salt- and sugar-free. Closed Sunday. ~ 2188 Northeast 123rd Street; 305-893-5711. BUDGET TO MODERATE.

Across from the noisy highway and rickety train tracks is a tin diner that has all the makings of a truck stop. But don't be deceived. Inside the **Gourmet Diner** awaits a plethora of splendid food—carefully prepared delicacies such as chicken *chasseur*, rack of lamb and seafood au gratin. Check the posted neon chalkboard for more than a dozen daily gastronomic delights. ~ 13951 Biscayne Boulevard; 305-947-2255. BUDGET TO MODERATE.

◄ HIDDEN

Locals developed a craving for Philly steak sandwiches when **Woody's** opened with curbside service in 1956. Now the open-air roadside stop has expanded and serves twice as many of those cheesy steaks on soft, buttery buns. The plastic tables combined with a view of a dirty gas station make for minimal atmosphere, but the place is usually packed. Closed Sunday. ~ 13105 Biscayne Boulevard; 305-891-1451. BUDGET.

Mall shopping—where some serious purchasing gets done—is frequently referred to by Floridians as "malling."

Biscayne Wine Merchants is a simple wine and cheese shop serving fresh, hefty sandwiches and salads to a large lunch time crowd. Pastel table tops, fresh flowers and courteous service greet diners. For dinner, try shrimp dijon, fettuccine carbonara or a special chicken that's stuffed with dill and crabmeat. Closed Sunday. ~ 738 Northeast 125th Street; 305-899-1997. MODERATE.

This area possesses two of Dade County's largest malls, which lure beachgoers away from the sand and into their cool confines.

SHOPPING

Aventura Mall, a modern, two-level enclosed plaza, boasts around 190 shops running the gamut from chic boutiques and furniture stores to jewelry and book marts. Most shops are of the chain variety, and are anchored by several large department stores. ~ 19501 Biscayne Boulevard, Aventura; 305-935-4222.

Just out of whistling distance, **The Mall at 163rd Street** peeks out from underneath a bizarre Teflon-coated fiberglass roof, allowing plenty of light to stream in. More than 150 stores beckon from this location. ~ 1421 Northeast 163rd Street, North Miami Beach; 305-947-9845.

A collection of umbrella-topped tables lining the Intracoastal Waterway, **Shooters** is classic South Florida. People climb from their cushy yachts, parked dockside at the restaurant, to order food and drink. ~ 3969 Northeast 163rd Street; 305-949-2855.

NIGHTLIFE

There's a friendly local crowd at **Delaney Street,** a small dance bar hosting Top-40 and oldies bands. ~ 7353 Fairway Drive, Miami Lakes; 305-823-7555.

Studio One 83 Jazz Room is a great deal: a healthy buffet, happy-hour drinks, a deejay and good live music—jazz and R&B bands—on weekends. Cover. ~ 2860 Northwest 183rd Street, in the Carol City Shopping Plaza, Carol City; 305-621-7295.

Next door, Miami Nights caters to a younger crowd, featuring disco rooms which feature either live music or deejays. Cover on weekends. ~ 2860 Northwest 183rd Street, in the Carol City Shopping Plaza, Carol City; 305-621-2987.

BEACHES & PARKS

OLETA RIVER STATE RECREATION AREA 🏃 🚲 🏊 🛶 ⛱️ 🚣

A real gem, this 880-acre park is nestled at the top of Biscayne Bay near the Intracoastal Waterway and the Oleta River. It bursts with wide open spaces yet shelters dense mangrove preserves. Opossum, raccoons and rabbits can be spotted frequently, along with native birds such as osprey and great blue heron. Though the 1200-foot beach is manmade, the sand consists of white crystals and borders a calm inlet that's ideal for swimming. There's great fishing for snapper, shad and sheepshead from the seawall or dock. Facilities include picnic areas, restrooms, a bike trail and canoe rentals. Day-use fee, $3.25. ~ On Northeast 163rd Street (also State Road 826) and 34th Avenue in North Miami Beach; 305-919-1846.

▼▼▼▼▼▼▼▼▼▼▼▼▼▼

Outdoor Adventures

The Miami area is an outdoor enthusiast's heaven. Those of you who love the water will find plenty to do. From sailing to diving, let the beauty of Miami's waters guide your sensibilities.

SPORT-FISHING

You can wrangle with a sailfish, marlin or even a barracuda when fishing Miami waters.

If you're not afraid to bite off more than you can chew, call The Shark. ~ 10800 Collins Avenue, Sunny Isles; 305-949-2948. Or get out your aquatic aggressions aboard Therapy IV. ~ 10800 Collins Avenue, Sunny Isles; 305-945-1578. Out of Key Biscayne, trawl for big ones with the Carie Ann. ~ Crandon Park Marina, Key Biscayne; 305-361-0117. Be sure to bring your scaling knife aboard The Cutting Edge. ~ 4000 Crandon Boulevard, Key Biscayne; 305-361-9740. In Miami, try fishing with Thomas Flyer. ~ Bayside Marina, Miami; 305-374-4133.

DIVING

You'll find plenty of diving possibilities in the area, especially around nearby coral reefs.

For equipment rentals and/or charters, contact Aquanauts. ~ 880 Southwest 8th Street, Miami; 305-545-9000. Or in Coconut Grove, blow into Bubbles Dive Center. ~ 2671 Southwest 27th Avenue, Coconut Grove; 305-856-0565. Explore the deeps out of Sunny Isles with The Diving Locker. ~ 223 Sunny Isles Boulevard,

Sunny Isles; 305-947-6025. Venture into an underwater Eden with **Diver's Paradise**. ~ 4000 Crandon Boulevard, Key Biscayne; 305-361-3483. In Miami Beach, go with **Scuba Sports**. ~ 16604 Northeast 2nd Avenue, North Miami Beach; 305-940-0926.

It's a windsurfer's heaven around these parts, so grab a board from **Sailboards Miami**. ~ Rickenbacker Causeway; 305-361-7245. In North Miami Beach, look for windsurfing vendors in front of the **Holiday Inn Newport Pier**. ~ 16701 Collins Avenue; 305-949-1300. **WIND-SURFING**

Let the wind guide you around Miami's scenic waters. For sailboat rentals and charters, check out **Florida Yacht**. ~ 1290 5th Street, Miami Beach; 305-532-8600. Also along Miami Beach, look for the sailboat vendors at **46th Street Beach**. ~ Collins Avenue and 46th Street. In Coconut Grove, try **Easy Sailing**. ~ Dinner Key Marina; 305-858-4001. You can also try **Castle Harbor Sailboats**. ~ Dinner Key Marina; 305-858-3212. In North Miami, there's **Gold Coast VIP Services**. ~ 1302 Northwest 188th Terrace; 305-653-0591. **SAILING**

Scenic jogging trails abound in the Miami area, including ones at **Haulover Beach Park**. ~ 10800 Collins Avenue, Sunny Isles; 305-947-3525. In Key Biscayne, try **Crandon Park Beach**. ~ 4000 Crandon Boulevard, Key Biscayne; 305-361-5421. Another is **Matheson Hammock County Park**. ~ 9610 Old Cutler Road, South Dade County; 305-666-6979. In South Dade County, be sure to check out **Larry and Penny Thompson Park**. ~ 12451 Southwest 184th Street, South Dade County; 305-232-1049. In North Miami, try **Greynolds Park**. ~ 17530 West Dixie Highway, North Miami; 305-945-3425. **JOGGING**

You can tee up at numerous public golf courses, including **Bayshore Golf Course**. ~ 2301 Alton Road, Miami Beach; 305-673-1580. **Haulover Beach Golf Course** is a good bet. ~ 10800 Collins **GOLF**

✔ **CHECK THESE OUT—UNIQUE OUTDOOR ADVENTURES**

- Brave the Gulf Coast waters in search of the big fish—marlin or barracuda—on a sportfishing adventure out of Miami. *page 92*
- Commune with denizens of the deep when you sign up for a scuba session with one of the area's several diving outfitters. *page 92*
- Rent a sailboard in Miami Beach and let the gentle Atlantic breeze fill your sail—just make sure no hurricane warning is posted! *page 93*
- Take a two-wheeled tour of beautiful Key Biscayne—opulent residential districts and a county park trail make for scenic cycling. *page 94*

Avenue, Sunny Isles; 305-940-6719. In Miami, try **Bayshore Par Three Golf Course**. ~ 2785 Prairie Avenue, Miami; 305-674-0305. **Fontainebleau Golf Course** is another nice course. ~ 9603 Fontainebleau Boulevard, Miami; 305-221-5181. In Key Biscayne, you'll find **Key Biscayne Golf Course**. ~ 6700 Crandon Boulevard; 305-361-9129. In South Dade County, there's **Palmetto Golf Course**. ~ 9300 Southwest 152nd Street, South Dade County; 305-238-2922. **Golf Club of Miami** hosts a year-round series of championship matches. ~ 6801 Northwest 186th Street, North Miami; 305-829-8449. **Greynolds Park** is available in North Miami. ~ 17530 West Dixie Highway, North Miami; 305-949-1741.

TENNIS

Tennis is the rage around Miami, so not surprisingly there are many top spots for racquet addicts. Try **Flamingo Park Tennis Center**. ~ Corner of 11th Street and Jefferson Avenue, Miami; 305-673-7761. In Miami Beach, don't miss the **North Shore Center**. ~ 350 73rd Street, Miami Beach; 305-993-2022. **Haulover Beach Park** is another good bet. ~ 10800 Collins Avenue, Sunny Isles; 305-947-3525. **Morningside Park** is another good facility. ~ 750 Northeast 55th Terrace, Miami; 305-754-1242. You can also try **Moore Park**. ~ 736 Northwest 36th Street, Miami; 305-635-7459. In Coral Gables, you'll find **Salvadore Park Tennis Center**. ~ 1120 Andalusia Avenue, Coral Gables; 305-460-5333.

BIKING

If island cycling is your bag, you'll love Key Biscayne, where you can cruise through eight miles of shady pines, past sumptuous homes and hidden beach coves. Down in **Matheson Hammock County Park**, a 1.5-mile trail meanders through dense mangroves and along the beaches.

Along **South Miami Beach**, bicyclists take advantage of a wide sidewalk that stretches for more than 20 blocks in South Beach. Farther north, **Haulover Beach** has a 1.5-mile trail along the billowy sand dunes. There are few designated bike paths or lanes on Central Miami Beach, making cycling a little tricky along the crowded, busy streets.

DADE COUNTY BY BICYCLE

Traveling via bike offers a different perspective of the area, but be sure to steer clear of congested downtown. The best bicycle trails are found throughout the suburbs, parks and beaches. For information on area bike routes, call the **Dade County Bicycle and Pedestrian Program**. ~ 305-375-1735.

A 14-mile bike trail exists on **Old Cutler Road** from Coconut Grove southward to Cutler Ridge. Not recommended during rush hour, this route has paths and sidewalks that wind along Biscayne Bay and through the area's remaining agricultural communities.
Bike Rentals   To rent a bike in the Miami area, you can try **Miami Beach Bicycle Center**. ~ 923 West 39th Street, Miami Beach; 305-531-4161. Another good bet is **Key Biscayne Mangrove Bicycle**. ~ 260 Crandon Boulevard; 305-361-5555.

▼▼▼▼▼▼▼▼▼▼
Transportation

If you arrive in Miami by car, you'll find the area laid out in a somewhat orderly fashion, with major highways and thoroughfares easily navigated.

CAR

From the north, **Route 95** runs due south through the city and joins **Route 1**, which continues through Coconut Grove, Coral Gables and south Dade County. **Florida's Turnpike** and **Route 826**, better known as the Palmetto Expressway, head south along the western corridor.

Route 41, also called the Tamiami Trail, will bring you in from Florida's West Coast, and **Route 27** cuts in from Central Florida.

Your main east-west connections through Miami are **Route 836** and **Route 112/195**, which transport you to scenic causeways leading to Miami Beach. **Route A1A** runs north and south along the ocean throughout Miami Beach.

AIR

Miami International Airport (Wilcox Field) brings visitors to the Miami area. Lying eight miles west of downtown, this megaport is served by many domestic/international carriers, including American Airlines, Continental Airlines, Delta Airlines, Northwest Airlines, Trans World Airlines, United Airlines and USAir. There are even more international carriers, including Aerolineas Argentinas, Aeromexico, AeroPeru, Air Canada, Air France, Air Jamaica, ALM, Aviateca, Bahamasair, British Airways, BWIA International, Cayman Airways, El Al, Halisa, Iberia, LAB, Lan Chile, LASCA, Lufthansa, Mexicana, Taca, Varig, Viasa and Virgin Atlantic.

Taxis, limousines and buses wait to take passengers to points all over Dade County. **Super Shuttle** offers transportation via vans to downtown hotels and Miami Beach. ~ 305-871-2000.

BUS

Greyhound Bus Lines (800-231-2222) brings passengers from all over the country to the Miami area. The main Miami terminal is at 4111 Northwest 27th Street, 305-871-1810; in North Miami Beach at 16560 Northeast 6th Avenue, 305-945-0801; and in Homestead at 5 Northeast 3rd Road, 305-247-2040.

If you would like service in Spanish, **Astro Tours** offers daily shuttles between Miami and New York. ~ 2909 Northwest 7th Street; 305-643-6423.

Omnibus La Cubana has daily service between Miami and Virginia, New York and New Jersey. ~ 1101 Northwest 22nd Avenue; 305-541-1700.

TRAIN

Amtrak will bring you into Miami from the northeastern states on its "Silver Star" or "Silver Meteor." From the western United States, there are three trains to Miami by way of Chicago and Washington, D.C. ~ Miami Station, 8303 Northwest 37th Avenue; 800-872-7245.

CAR RENTALS

It's wise to have a car in Miami, even though downtown parking is scarce and expensive.

Several major agencies operate in the airport terminal, including **Avis Rent A Car** (800-331-1212), **Budget Rent A Car** (800-527-0700), **Dollar Rent A Car** (800-800-4000), **Hertz Rent A Car** (800-654-3131) and **National Interrent** (800-227-7368).

Companies with free airport pickup are **Alamo Rent A Car** (800-327-9633), **Biscayne Auto Rentals** (800-688-0721), **Enterprise Rent A Car** (800-325-8007), **Interamerican Car Rental** (800-327-1536), **ABC Rent A Car** (305-871-5050) and **Value Rent A Car** (800-327-2501).

PUBLIC TRANSIT

Although public transportation in Miami is lethargic, you can still get around. The Metropolitan Dade County Transit Authority has about 90 **Metrobus** routes covering about 2000 square miles.

The quickest way to get around is by **Metrorail**, a futuristic train that glides 21 miles along an elevated track between north and south Miami. Downtown, the **Metromover monorail** makes a two-mile radius around the city's perimeter, stopping at major centers and attractions.

For transit maps and a list of schedules, send for the "First Time Rider's Kit" available from the **Metropolitan Dade County Transit Authority**. ~ 360 Northeast 185th Street, Miami Beach, FL 33179; 305-638-6700, fax 305-654-6587.

Tri-Rail is your link to the north, with double-decker trains traveling 67 miles into Dade and Palm Beach counties. ~ 305-728-8445.

For an inexpensive, fun way to see the sights, get on board the **Old Town Trolley**. These shiny trolleys meander through downtown, Coconut Grove and Coral Gables. ~ 401 Biscayne Boulevard, Miami; 305-374-8687.

TAXIS

Many cab companies serve Miami International Airport, including the ubiquitous **Yellow Cab** (305-444-4444) and **Central Cab** (305-532-5555).

THREE

The Gold Coast

Its sparkling hotels, glittering jewels and golden sands would be reason enough to dub this section of southeast Florida "The Gold Coast." But, in fact, it was real gold salvaged from shipwrecks off the coast that earned the area its moniker, which remains applicable more than a century later.

Stretching from the top of Miami up to the Jupiter Inlet, the Gold Coast is anchored by two very different cities. Fort Lauderdale, famed for its inland water ways and fast-paced beach scene, provides the steam that drives the engine of development. Even now, Lauderdale's Broward County is still growing as if no one knew that the Florida land boom was supposed to have been over decades ago. Highway construction seems never-ending, with newer roads leading to residential communities that sprout from former swampland faster that coconuts grow on sandy beaches.

Roughly an hour's drive north, Palm Beach is as private as Fort Lauderdale is public. This island town turns its back on publicity, preferring to bask in its well-entrenched reputation as a playground for the well-to-do. So wealthy are Palm Beach's inhabitants that they occupy many of the town's legendary mansions—estates, really—only a fraction of the year, usually from January until Easter time. (Many shops and restaurants follow suit, closing at least during the summer months.) In the winter, life is a series of charity balls and other high-society gatherings.

Surrounding these two Gold Coast hubs is an enclave of beach towns and tennis and golf resorts. Today's visitor needs only an airline ticket to reach this paradise. But early 19th-century settlers veered into the unknown with little more than guns, machetes and verve.

Fort Lauderdale's beginnings can be traced to at least 1450 A.D., when the aboriginal Tequesta tribe is believed to have begun roaming the area around the New River. After the Spanish "discovered" northern Florida, an increasing tide of colonization forced the Seminole tribe south into the area.

It was during the Seminole Wars in 1837 that one Major William Lauderdale was commissioned to establish the fort—long since crumbled into oblivion—for which the city would one day be named. Even-

Fort Lauderdale sparkles with 250 miles of water-ways, earning it the nickname, "Venice of America."

tually, the fledgling settlement was enhanced by people of vision and skill such as Frank Stranahan. He arrived at the New River in 1893, established a ferry system and opened a trading post with the American Indians. His home as well as those of other early citizens of prominence form the centerpiece of Fort Lauderdale's historic district today.

The Fort Lauderdale area was still mired in swampland when Henry Flagler extended his Florida East Coast Railway to present-day Palm Beach. This town, the legend goes, derived its name from a shipwreck in 1878. A Spanish ship with a full crew and 100 cases of wine aboard washed up on a virtually barren barrier island. They decided to sell their cargo, which included some 20,000 coconuts, to a visionary islander. He, in turn, unloaded the coconuts (at two for a nickel) to his neighbors, who planted them in the sand and created the groves that give Palm Beach its name.

Henry Flagler, who had co-founded Standard Oil with John D. Rockefeller, was apparently quite taken with the Palm Beach setting, so much so that he built the original Breakers Hotel here (it burned down and has since been rebuilt). On his heels came the self-taught architect Addison Mizner, who first visited south Florida for a health cure but soon became inspired to upgrade what he viewed as the inferior architecture of Palm Beach. Mizner's "touch" explains the pseudo-Spanish design of many older mansions in the area.

Yet Palm Beach was only a pit stop to Mizner, who had his sights set on an undeveloped stretch to the south, a place whose Spanish name—Boca Raton—is a vast improvement over the English translation, "rat's mouth." Here Mizner built the most expensive hotel of its time, the 100-room Cloisters Inn, the seed of the present-day Boca Raton Hotel and Club. Mizner worked hard to lure notables like Harold Vanderbilt and Irving Berlin to his paradise-in-the-making. A natural publicity hound, he is said to have declared: "Get the big snobs, and the little ones will follow."

By then, the Roaring '20s were in full swing, and Fort Lauderdale was about to boom. Henry Flagler had extended his railroad there in 1896, but it was a West Virginia developer named Charles Rodes who had the brilliant idea of increasing Fort Lauderdale's available square footage by "finger-islanding," a concept used to create Venice, Italy. He dredged a series of parallel canals from Las Olas to the New River, building up a group of peninsulas that offered waterfront locations to hotels and homes. From then on it was just a matter of time before the rest of the country learned about the "Venice of America."

Today, thousands of vacationers descend on the Gold Coast each year. In parts of Broward and Palm Beach counties, the population swells by as much as one-third during the winter season. In fact, the increase in traffic is almost the only way you can tell it's winter on the Gold Coast. The climate here is amazingly consistent, with a year-round average of about 75°. There are no hills and few lakes to distinguish

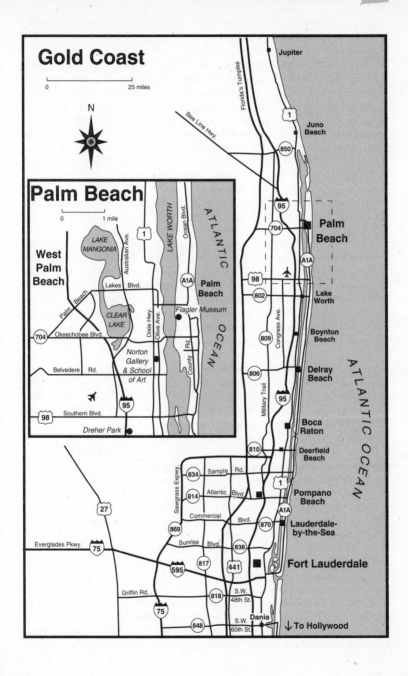

Gold Coast

0   25 miles

N

Jupiter

Florida's Turnpike

Bee Line Hwy.

1

Juno Beach

850

95

704 — **Palm Beach**

A1A

Palm Beach

0   1 mile

LAKE WORTH

ATLANTIC OCEAN

West Palm Beach

LAKE MANGONIA

Australian Ave.

1

Ocean Blvd.

A1A

Palm Beach

Lakes Blvd.

Palm Beach

CLEAR LAKE

704

Okeechobee Blvd.

Dixie Hwy.

Olive Ave.

Flagler Museum

Belvedere Rd.

Norton Gallery & School of Art

County Rd.

95

98   Southern Blvd.

Dreher Park

98

802

Lake Worth

809

Congress Ave.

Boynton Beach

806

Military Trail

95

Delray Beach

Boca Raton

810

Deerfield Beach

834   Sample Rd.

Sawgrass Expwy.

814   Atlantic Blvd.

1

Pompano Beach

Commercial Blvd.

A1A

870

869

Lauderdale-by-the-Sea

Sunrise Blvd.

838

27

817

441

Fort Lauderdale

75

Everglades Pkwy.

595

Griffin Rd.

818

S.W. 48th St.

75

848

Dania

S.W. 60th St.

↓ **To Hollywood**

ATLANTIC OCEAN

one square mile of land from the next. Sand dunes, so well-preserved to the north, are rarely seen here. Slightly inland lie occasional mangrove swamps and hardwood hammocks.

The towns and small cities that have grown up since the 1920s around the hubs of Fort Lauderdale and Palm Beach have their own personalities. Hallandale and Hollywood, for instance, resemble nearby Miami, with their highrise oceanfront condominiums and low-priced motels. Davie, west of Fort Lauderdale, is Florida's version of the Wild West, with farms and horse trails dotting the countryside.

Fort Lauderdale itself remains somewhat popular with college students heading south on spring break, a ritual that brought the city notoriety when portrayed in the 1960 film *Where the Boys Are*. Too much notoriety, it seems, for today the city has taken steps to discourage the hordes, to the delight of year-round residents. Meanwhile, the city's building boom continues unabated.

North of Fort Lauderdale, low-key communities like Lauderdale-by-the-Sea and Pompano Beach exhibit a slower pace, hemmed in by the sea and the Intracoastal Waterway, with no place to grow but up.

Crossing into Palm Beach County, the coast road travels through another series of towns, these with a distinctly different flavor than their cousins to the south. Boca Raton has become a tidy, extremely well-to-do community that attracts large numbers of retirees and golfers as well as an increasing abundance of high-technology companies. It is the site of the liveliest restaurant and nightlife activity in Palm Beach County. Delray Beach is a well-preserved oceanfront enclave for people who can afford Palm Beach prices but eschew the social requirements.

The coast is lined with tiny towns such as Boynton Beach, Lantana and the unsightly burg of Briny Breezes (where most homes are mobile and there is little beach access for visitors). Further north, Lake Worth shows signs of revitalization as an arts and antiques center. And then there's the queen herself, Palm Beach. Pristine and formal to the point of outright intimidation, the grande dame exudes wealth and confidence. Aside from public museums—and a smidgen of beach access—it seems to exist purely to serve itself, with its rows of mansions and abundance of fine shops and limousines.

A few miles north, Singer Island offers a sweep of beautiful beaches, oceanfront hotels and condos. And on the Gold Coast's northern tip lies Jupiter, an underestimated locale favored by celebrities whose names will inevitably come up even during a brief visit.

Wherever visitors choose to go along the Gold Coast, they will find an increased awareness of the area's delicate ecology. Signs admonish speeding boats on waterways that harbor endangered manatees. Alligators, no longer endangered, thrive in the shrinking wilderness; shore birds of all kinds are abundant. The area seems to be devoted to unencumbered pleasurable pursuits, an idyllic getaway for the rest of the country. Deep-sea fishing and scuba diving are challenging tennis and golf as the most prevalent forms of recreation in the region.

Today, gold still washes up on the southeastern Florida beaches, figuratively at least. A stream of blue-sky days interrupted only by hurricane season (August to October), combined with endless recreational opportunities, ensures a gold-plated future for this stretch of the Florida coast.

From Flamingo gardens to jai alai, South Broward County offers another of the Sunshine State's intriguing destinations. Here you

South Broward County

can find American Indian villages and beachfront promenades, pythons and miniature golf courses, as well as Florida's Wild West. Cowboys in Florida? We'll get to that in a bit.

One of the best known towns in this region is Hollywood. This city, home to no movie studios, owes its moniker to one Joseph Young. During the 1920s, Young selected a swath of South Florida swamplands and—dreaming of his beloved Southern California—dubbed it Hollywood.

Today, Hollywood and its southern neighbor, Hallandale, are home to about 160,000 warm-weather loyalists and hard-core beach bums. Set apart from Fort Lauderdale both geographically and in personality, these twin cities exhibit a reserved style of living. The area's many retired residents while away their time on the beach or socializing downtown. Architecture harkens back to the 1950s, with rows of older, highrise condominiums taking center stage throughout the region.

Hollywood's subdued style, together with its colorful beach boardwalk, fine restaurants and quaint motels draw thousands of tourists seeking a pace slower than in Fort Lauderdale.

To get a feel for the area, travel on **Hollywood Boulevard** between Dixie Highway and the Atlantic Ocean. You'll pass through Hollywood's downtown, an area that's enjoying rejuvenation as dilapidated buildings slowly become rows of colorful canopied stores and restaurants. Stroll the brick sidewalks and lush, landscaped medians of this quiet city, then head east toward a scenic stretch of quiescent homes flanked by huge palm trees.

SIGHTS

✔ CHECK THESE OUT—UNIQUE SIGHTS

- Stare in awe as Seminole Indians wrestle alligators and play with pythons at the **Seminole Native Village**. *page 102*
- Cruise the infamous **Fort Lauderdale Strip** where, spring break or not, the action never ends. *page 110*
- Revisit Florida's pioneer days at the **Children's Museum of Boca Raton,** the city's first museum. *page 132*
- Let out a roar at **Lion Country Safari,** where it's the humans who are caged (in their cars) while all manner of exotic animals roam free. *page 143*

The height of activity takes place along the **Broadwalk,** which hugs the beach for over two miles between Simms and Georgia streets. Mom-and-pop motels, beer shacks and souvenir shops crowd along the promenade, creating a mood that's delightfully tacky. It was originally built of coral rock dredged from the Intracoastal Waterway. Long ago it was paved over with asphalt, and today it is peopled with bicyclists, joggers, senior citizens and women in itsy-bitsy bikinis.

The **Art and Culture Center of Hollywood** houses an engaging collection of contemporary paintings and sculptures by South Florida artists. Most fascinating, though, are the ever-changing exhibits such as Florida American Indian and Israeli art, avant-garde works and Czechoslovakia's Minisalon, a collection of sculptural art created by artists under the communist regime. The single-story, airy building also displays an intriguing set of African artifacts. Closed Monday. Admission. ~ 1650 Harrison Street, Hollywood; 954-921-3275.

If your entertainment tastes lean toward the dangerous, don't miss the alligator wrestling and snake shows at the **Seminole Native Village.** Seminole Indians demonstrate their centuries-old technique of chasing and nabbing a man-size alligator. Ever want to pet a python? During the snake show, the Seminoles showcase a python, rattlesnakes and other slithering creatures.

In between the shows, which are held throughout the day, you can tour a wildlife area that's home to bobcats, panthers, crocodiles and otters. Here, children have the opportunity to hold a baby alligator.

An art exhibit displays compelling paintings that trace the history, legends and lifestyles of the Seminoles. The artist, Guy LaBree, is a white man who, as a child, befriended the American Indians and spent weekends on their reservation. He is known across Florida as the "barefoot artist" because—like those early Seminoles—he prefers to live shoeless. Admission. ~ 3551 North State Road 7, Hollywood; 954-961-4519.

The six-story **Hollywood Greyhound Track** is a Gold Coast landmark. During the season (December through May) an average crowd of 5000 racing fans turns out for the evening to watch greyhounds race around the oval track at speeds of up to 40 m.p.h. Admission. ~ Federal Highway and Pembroke Road, Hallandale; 954-454-9400.

Speed comes in another form with the lightning-fast sport of jai alai, played at **Dania Jai Alai.** Evolved from a version of handball played in ancient Basque hillside villages, jai alai is now played by professionals and offers legalized wagering (see "The Exotic Game of Jai Alai" in this chapter). ~ 301 East Dania Beach Boulevard, Dania; 954-426-4330.

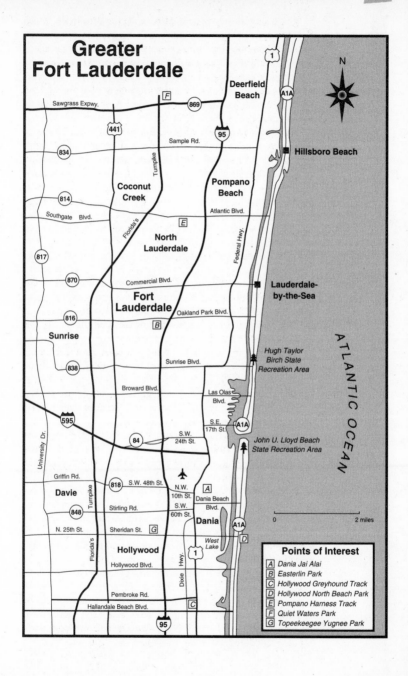

Greater
Fort Lauderdale

N

Sawgrass Expwy.

Deerfield Beach

F

869

1

A1A

441

95

Sample Rd.

834

Hillsboro Beach

Turnpike

Florida's

Coconut
Creek

Pompano
Beach

814

Atlantic Blvd.

Southgate   Blvd.

E

817

North
Lauderdale

Federal Hwy.

870

Commercial Blvd.

Lauderdale-
by-the-Sea

Fort
Lauderdale

816

Oakland Park Blvd.

B

Sunrise

838

Sunrise Blvd.

Hugh Taylor
Birch State
Recreation Area

Broward Blvd.

Las Olas
Blvd.

A T L A N T I C   O C E A N

595

S.E.
17th St.

A1A

University Dr.

84

S.W.
24th St.

John U. Lloyd Beach
State Recreation Area

Griffin Rd.

818

S.W. 48th St.

N.W.
10th St.

A

Davie

Turnpike

Dania Beach
Blvd.

848

Stirling Rd.

S.W.
60th St.

0   2 miles

N. 25th St.

Sheridan St.

G

Dania

A1A

Florida's

West
Lake

D

Hollywood

1

Dixie Hwy.

Hollywood Blvd.

Points of Interest

A Dania Jai Alai
B Easterlin Park
C Hollywood Greyhound Track
D Hollywood North Beach Park
E Pompano Harness Track
F Quiet Waters Park
G Topeekeegee Yugnee Park

Pembroke Rd.

C

Hallandale Beach Blvd.

95

It's easy to find Florida's Wild West. Just head west about six miles inland to **Davie**. This small town seems to have more in common with New Mexico's cattle country than it does with oranges and sandy beaches. Davie country is home to that rare and endangered species, the Florida cowboy, who works the area's cattle and horse ranches in the grand manner. Poking around this region, you'll swear you took a wrong turn somewhere and ended up on the Santa Fe trail.

Flamingo Gardens is a slight misnomer. Small subtropical forest would be more accurate. The best way to get acclimated to the abundance of natural beauty here is to take the one-and-a-half-mile-long tram ride through citrus groves and hammocks of native plants. Bromeliads, orchids, heliconias and ginger plants—among the most beautiful in the country—can be easily spotted. Then there are the trees, especially the two dozen "Champion" trees, the largest of their species in Florida. Parrots, pheasants, flamingos, alligators and more wildlife add to the Fantasy Island feeling. Admission. ~ 3750 Flamingo Road, Davie; 954-473-2955.

LODGING

The only Hollywood hotel on the Intracoastal Waterway is the **Clarion Hotel**. All of the 309 oversized rooms have small balconies with views of a good stretch of the waterway and at least a sliver of ocean. The ambience is nothing to write home about, but the accommodations are spacious and comfortably appointed with contemporary furnishings. One of the best features of this Hilton is its lovely riverside pool and lounge area. ~ 4000 South Ocean Drive, Hollywood; 954-458-1900, 800-252-7466, fax 954-458-7222. ULTRA-DELUXE.

Beneath the brightly painted tower that proclaims a stretch of the Atlantic to be Hallandale, the **Holiday Beach Inn** has 71 oceanfront units in its two-story, peach-colored building. Rooms are smallish and unremarkably decorated. Efficiencies equipped with kitchens are available, and there is an outdoor pool. The price and the location—equidistant between Miami and Fort Lauderdale—are the biggest draws. ~ 4111 South Ocean Drive, Hollywood; 954-457-8000. BUDGET TO MODERATE.

Hallandale and Hollywood are condominium towns, with few hotels; the few motels there and in Dania virtually all require a minimum seven-day booking. Going against the grain is the **Hollywood Beach Resort Hotel**, a pale pink extravaganza of 250 studios and suites. It looms over the beautiful beach and easily outshines the competition. The guest quarters are simply decorated, distinguished by art deco accents, brass track lighting and kitchen facilities. The resort has a pool and a bevy of boutiques, food outlets and movie theaters. ~ 101 North Ocean Drive, Hollywood; 954-921-0990, 800-331-6103, fax 954-920-9480. MODERATE.

With its desert-colored stucco trimmed in brilliant teal awnings, **Sheldon Ocean Resort** stands out on the beach. Inside and
out, the midrise hotel is decorated art deco funky. Terrazzo floors
and a kitschy wall mural accent the lobby, while 42 small but tidy
guest rooms feature ceiling fans, popcorn ceilings and carpeting.
Several efficiencies and one apartment are also offered at this oceanside spot. ~ 1000 North Surf Road, Hollywood Beach; 954-922-
6020, 800-344-6020, fax 954-922-6218. MODERATE TO DELUXE.

Back in the 1930s, Hollywood founder Joseph Young used a
slew of real estate agents to sell his new city. He put them up in a
two-story villa that's now a bed and breakfast called **Maison
Harrison**. Nestled on a palm-lined residential street, the tile-roofed
home has been beautifully renovated with French doors, plush
rugs, period furniture and polished wood floors. The owners used
imagination and attention to detail in the five stylized bedrooms—
two with canopy beds and private wood decks. A lush, secluded
courtyard features an exercise room. Best of all, the rates include a
hearty continental breakfast. ~ 1504 Harrison Street, Hollywood;
954-922-7319. BUDGET TO MODERATE.

DINING

La Concha Beach Club is one of several open-air cafés on the inland side of Broadwalk, the long strip of pavement that runs in
front of the beach. The best time to go is at breakfast, when you
can enjoy eggs, bagels or pancakes while watching strollers and
joggers warming up in the fresh light of day. La Concha is open
throughout the day, serving dishes such as a chicken salad platter.
~ 900 North Broadwalk, Hollywood; 954-921-4190. BUDGET TO
MODERATE.

Marcello's Restaurant has two elegant dining rooms. The one
that fills up first is a high-ceilinged room with tables covered in
linen and an entire trompe l'oeil wall painted to
look like Venetian housefronts. The other is linen-
bedecked as well, but has no mural. But they do
share a menu of homemade gnocchi, tortellini and
other pastas, as well as veal and seafood dishes. Stand-
out entrée: veal scallopine with sambuca and fresh
pears. ~ 1822 South Young Circle, Hollywood; 954-
923-1055. BUDGET TO MODERATE.

The dining rooms of the
Spiced Apple feature col-
lectibles ranging from
antique trumpets to
broom dolls to hand-
made baby cribs.

Once you get past the ornate foyer, an overwrought
fantasy based on the Roman bath concept, **Villa Perone** gets down
to business in two plant-filled, dimly lit dining rooms whose elegance is underscored by tuxedo-clad waiters. The menu is distinguished by several warm appetizers and such main courses as veal
parmesan, chicken, seafood and angel hair pasta with clams. ~ 906
East Hallandale Beach Boulevard, Hallandale; 954-454-8878.
MODERATE TO ULTRA-DELUXE.

HIDDEN ▶ For an informal, inexpensive evening out, a good place to remember is **Mott Street**, a friendly Chinese restaurant with low lights and high spirits. Two aquariums and a sleek lacquered screen dress up this long narrow room, but the point here is the variety of selections such as snapper steamed with ginger, scallions and black beans, orange-peel beef and salt-and-pepper squid. ~ 1295 East Hallandale Beach Boulevard, Hallandale; 954-456-7555. BUDGET TO MODERATE.

Larry and Teddy's Casabella is an outpost of Continental cuisine housed in a converted two-story residence. Each of the seven small rooms is decorated in a different theme. Choose from the Bombay room, the Hunter room, the Flower room, or any of the sun rooms. The menu features osso buco, seafood platters with lobster, prawns, scallops and crabs, and pasta with fresh tomatoes, garlic and basil. ~ 129 North Federal Highway, Dania; 954-923-1000. MODERATE TO DELUXE.

Armadillo Café will endear you to the earthy, seething flavors of the Southwest. Chef couple Eve Montella and Kevin McCarthy combine culinary passions to create delectable dishes spiked with chilis, salsas, pestos and other zesty flavors. Choices might include lobster quesadillas, pan-fried yellowtail with spicy pumpkinseed sauce, or a black-and-white soup that's a fiery combo of black bean and jalapeño jack soups. ~ 4630 Southwest 64th Avenue, Davie; 954-791-5104. MODERATE TO DELUXE.

The Spiced Apple, an old roadside house with six separate dining rooms, appears to have been lifted—rough-sawn cedar, pecky cypress and all—straight from the Blue Ridge Mountains. Country-fried steak, prime rib, roast sirloin with real gravy and Carolina delicacies such as skillet pork chops are among the specialties. There are also a number of seafood dishes on the menu. Between courses, guests may stroll from room to room to check out the unique decor. ~ 3281 Griffin Road, Fort Lauderdale; 954-962-0772. MODERATE TO DELUXE.

The **Rustic Inn Crabhouse** is so far inland that first-time visitors are astonished to find a waterway right out back. It's famous locally for its garlic crab, best eaten over a table covered in newspapers. Fancier fare is also available, including Florida lobster, crab cakes, Key West shrimp and fresh fish. No lunch on Sunday. ~ 4331 Ravenswood Road, Fort Lauderdale; 954-584-1637. MODERATE TO ULTRA-DELUXE.

SHOPPING There's a bevy of boutiques located on **Oceanwalk Mall**. Here you will find offbeat shops such as **Stone Love** (954-925-9374), offering minerals, gems, crystal balls, chimes and other "earthy" items. They also carry New Age books, tapes and videos. For inexpensive gifts and offbeat souvenirs, look into the **Pink Palm Company**

(954-922-2900). Another tropical destination, **Palm Produce** (954-922-2900) carries the very latest in beach attire, including colorful rayon dresses, straw hats, flip-flops and Florida T-shirts that thankfully aren't tacky. ~ Hollywood Beach Resort, 101 North Ocean Drive, Hollywood.

If you feel like slumming it, check out the divey shops along Hollywood's **Broadwalk**. The neon-lit cubbyholes advertise "big sales" and have everything to satisfy the tourist in you. ~ On the ocean between Simms and Georgia streets.

Collectors, browsers and serious antique hunters will all find something to like about **Antique Row**, a cluster of storefronts on Federal Highway in Dania, along Route 1. One of the best and friendliest of the lot is **Rose Antiques**, known for its crystal, china and porcelain by such manufacturers as Royal Vienna and Royal Bayreuth. ~ 17 North Federal Highway, Dania; 954-921-0474.

Dania Antiques District, dubbed the "Antiques Capital of the South," has 80 dealers offering everything from tin to Tiffany. The **Dania Antique Center** houses about two dozen dealers who operate in a line of cubbyholes selling mostly decorative pieces. One to check out is **Linda's Antique Collectibles** (954-920-2030), where you will find memorabilia, books and quilts. ~ One mile south of Fort Lauderdale International Airport on Route 1.

The Captured Image is an eclectic store with jewelry and beautiful collectibles made of pewter, porcelain, brass and lucite. It's also something of a New Age headquarters, selling crystals and incense, as well as 1960s and '70s memorabilia. ~ 611 East Dania Beach Boulevard, Dania; 954-922-8523.

Classy Baskets will custom-design a pretty basket with chocolates, gourmet foods, balloons and other decorative gifts. ~ 7383 Davie Road Extension, Davie; 954-433-4811.

HALLANDALE BEACH 🏊 🐟 🦀 The municipal beach at the northern edge of Hallandale is so tiny that it is easily overcrowded. Soft dark sand extends from a rock outcropping north to the border of Hollywood Beach, which is a short distance indeed. On a typical day, most visitors are teenagers and families with small children. Swimming is good in areas where there are no submerged rocks. Facilities include picnic areas, restrooms, showers, lifeguards and concession stands; restaurants and groceries are nearby. ~ Located at the end of Hallandale Boulevard off Route A1A south of Route 824; 954-457-1450.

BEACHES & PARKS

HOLLYWOOD BEACH 🚴 🏊 🎣 🏄 🦀 ⛵ This five-mile-plus swath of pale sand is larger than some islands. Sprinkled with palm trees, it is one of the most beautiful beaches on the entire Gold Coast. It is also one of the neatest, which, given its immense popularity, is a pleasant surprise. For much of its length, it is bordered by Broadwalk, a wide strip of pavement closed to automobile traffic and open only to bicycles and rollerblades at certain hours. There are also specific areas designated for beach games. The beach itself consists of medium-soft sand, good for walking but a little soft for jogging. Swimming is excellent everywhere along the beach. Surfing is good between Georgia Street and Azalea Terrace and between Mead and Franklin streets. People go surf angling adjacent to and north of Dania Pier. Facilities consist of picnic areas, restrooms, showers, lifeguards, concession stands; restaurants and groceries are on Oceanwalk. ~ There are dozens of access points off Route A1A, from Greenbriar Street to Sherman Street; 954-921-3460, 954-921-3423.

HIDDEN ►   **HOLLYWOOD NORTH BEACH PARK**   It's easy to drive right past this 56-acre park sandwiched between Hollywood Beach and Dania Beach. Much of the park is a greensward planted with 500 species of vegetation, including oak trees and broad-leafed seagrapes. To protect the dunes, several crossovers have been built along the park's mile-long beach access area. You can jog or walk along Broadwalk, the two-mile walkway that extends from Georgia Street to Simms Street. It's an excellent place to swim, and people fish for snapper, jack and snook from the pier on the intracoastal side. A pleasant change from most coastal parks, North Beach also operates a protection and relocation program for sea turtles, which can often be observed in holding tanks. There are many facilities including picnic areas, barbecue pits, play areas, restrooms, showers, lifeguards, concession stands, a 60-foot observation tower, bicycle and rollerblade paths, sports equipment rental and a volleyball court; restaurants and groceries are nearby. ~ At Route A1A and Sheridan Street; 954-926-2444

DANIA BEACH   This half-mile stretch of undeveloped oceanfront enjoys a very special phenomenon: When neighboring beaches erode, much of their sand ends up here. Hence Dania's soft sand has an unusual creamy-silver color. Less hectic than Hollywood Beach, this strand is nicely landscaped with palm trees and vegetation and rimmed with clear, almost-turquoise water. The pier provides excellent fishing: snook, mackerel, snapper, bluefish and more are caught here. A beach campground is scheduled to open in 1997. The only facilities are restrooms, showers and lifeguards; a restaurant is nearby. ~ Off Route A1A at 100 North Beach Road; 954-921-8700.

TOPEEKEEGEE YUGNEE PARK   Scattered around a 40-acre lake, T-Y Park, as it's called locally, is not the most beautiful recreation area on the Gold Coast, but it's an ideal oasis for enjoying a variety of water sports on a hot south

Florida day. You can windsurf, sail, canoe, swim and fish (there's a small fishing island located in the lake). Facilities include picnic areas, restrooms, concession stands, a grocery store, softball and soccer fields, nature trails and bicycle, windsurfing, sailing, paddleboat and canoe rentals. ~ At 3300 North Park Road in Hollywood; 954-985-1980.

▲ There are 12 tent sites and 48 RV hookups; two-week limit. Fees are $18 to $20 per night for tents, $19 to $21 per night for RVs. For information, call 954-985-1979.

Fort Lauderdale's reputation as a spring break haven has sadly led many visitors to overlook some of the splendid sights the city has to offer. Though it boasts 23 miles of balmy beaches, the city's beauty goes well beyond its shoreline. Traveling through the area, you'll quickly discover majestic estates lush with foliage, handsome commercial centers, hardwood hammocks, an impressive maze of clean waterways and a general feeling of the laid-back tropics.

▼▼▼▼▼▼▼▼▼▼▼▼
Fort Lauderdale

Though much of its history barely trickles back 100 years, you'll still find plenty of historical intrigue. Tales of sunken treasure and pirates are interwoven into the architecture and the personalities that gave birth to this carefree locale.

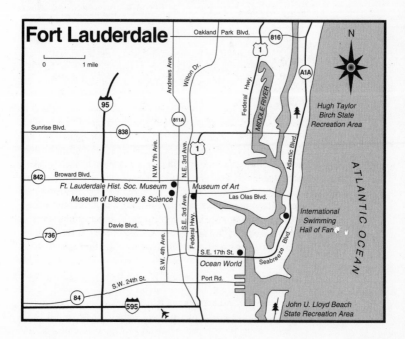

Most of Fort Lauderdale's sights are spread out, so it's essential to navigate by car. The good news is, the roadways are a near-perfect gridwork of east-west and north-south thoroughfares, so it's easy to get around.

SIGHTS   Meander along 17th Street Causeway east to the ocean and then wend your way north along Fort Lauderdale's infamous **Strip**. This five-mile stretch of road, which extends northward to Sunrise Boulevard, pulses with life, as the sidewalks and beach are a constant flurry of activity. Reminiscent of commercial areas along San Francisco's Fisherman's Wharf, the Strip is a series of T-shirt shops, fast-food joints, seedy pool bars and lowrise hotels. This byway seems devised for "cruising," and that's exactly what takes place 24 hours a day. Most nights, traffic is gridlocked along the beach.

This animated stretch of beach—bashed by locals ever since spring break brought it to life—is now nearly void of college vacationers and instead is peopled by a curious mix of families, gays and high school students. In an effort to attract an upscale crowd, city leaders began a massive revitalization of the area. The beach now has a sleek new look. Pretty brick promenades and gas lamps line the street and moorish pillars invite access to the beach. Palm trees divide the roadway and new paint covers several facades.

Fort Lauderdale's former image as Spring Break Capital of the Free World derived, oddly enough, from its popularity among college coaches, who began working out in the area back in the 1930s. Inevitably, word of excellent spring swimming conditions trickled down to underclassmen, who exploded on the scene in the early 1960s. This is one of numerous amazing-but-true facts divulged during a tour of the **International Swimming Hall of Fame**. After expanding and renovating, the museum reopened in early 1993 with computerized exhibits that let you pretend you're an Olympic diver, swimmer or judge. Also on display are artifacts such as wool, turn-of-the-century bathing costumes, sweatshirts that once belonged to such Olympic champions as Mark Spitz and Cynthia Potter, and swim-related works by artists from Honore Daumier to Norman Rockwell. International water buffs will want to tour the Room of Nations, where you can bone up on any swimmer or diver who won an Olympic medal. The Hall of Fame is also home to the Henning Library and Archive, an international center for information on the history of water sports. Admission. ~ 1 Hall of Fame Drive; 954-462-6536.

Some of Fort Lauderdale's original buildings were forged with wood culled from shipwrecks.

For a peek at true Fort Lauderdale living, travel west on **Las Olas Boulevard** and explore the finger islands that protrude from the roadway. These tiny isles provide waterfront berths for thousands of residents and their extravagant yachts. Just west of this area is a row of posh downtown shops where pricey furs and price-less paintings peep from beneath bright awnings. At night the area comes alive with sidewalk cafés and jazz clubs.

Rarely is a traveler able to explore a city on an old-fashioned trolley without spending a dime. The free **Fort Lauderdale trolleys**, painted a brilliant cobalt blue, tool around downtown. Best of all, the trolleys are only ten minutes apart. Free route maps and sched-ules are available on the trolleys, or the Downtown Development Authority. ~ 350 Southeast 2nd Street, Suite 500; 954-463-6574.

Several former private residences in this area are now open for touring. Built in the 1920s as an idyllic family retreat, the charm-ing **Bonnet House** remains an oasis on 35 acres, sheltered from all signs of modern-day urban life. Tours of the beautifully preserved two-story house and various nature trails are open to the public from May through November. The Shell Room, with its inlaid shells and an impressive collection of paired specimens, is worth a trip all by itself. Also not to be missed is the studio of Frederic Bartlett (who built the estate); many of his original paintings remain on dis-play. White swans swim in a peaceful lake, and Brazilian squirrel monkeys cavort in a forest of trees in this enchanting enclave, which also fronts 700 feet of the Atlantic Ocean. Admission. ~ 900 North Birch Road; 954-563-5393.

◀ HIDDEN

For additional information, maps and free brochures, stop by the **Greater Fort Lauderdale Convention and Visitors Bureau**. ~ 200 East Las Olas Boulevard, Suite 1500; 954-765-4466.

The Museum of Art houses pieces from the museum's perma-nent collection of 20th-century American and European paintings and sculpture by Dali, Andy Warhol, Matisse and Picasso, as well as temporary shows. The museum is especially noted for having the largest collection in the United States of artwork from Copenhagen, Brussels and Amsterdam. The museum also houses the largest col-lection in Florida of Primal, pre-Columbian and American Indian art. Admission. ~ 1 East Las Olas Boulevard; 954-763-6464.

Downtown Fort Lauderdale's riverfront, abandoned over recent decades, is experiencing a revival. The city's **Riverwalk** features meandering footpaths, gazebos and manicured gardens and parks. ~ Along the New River between Southeast 2nd Avenue and South-west 7th Avenue.

A real highlight is the **Esplanade Park**, featuring a science ex-hibit complete with giant kaleidoscopes, a rain gauge and sextant, and plaques honoring the world's famous mathematicians and sci-entists. You'll find the park next to the gleaming **Broward Center for the Performing Arts**, a cultural jewel that opened in 1991. ~ 201 Southwest 5th Avenue; 954-462-0222.

The **Fort Lauderdale Historical Society Museum** is the best clearinghouse for information on the city's historic district, which extends roughly from the nearby railroad tracks east of here to 5th

Avenue, and from the New River north to 2nd Street. The exhibits here are not extensive, though nicely done. They include scale models of historic structures and of a Seminole Indian village, complete with arts and crafts from the old days. The museum features an excellent selection of regional books. Admission. ~ 219 Southwest 2nd Avenue; 954-463-4431.

Next door, visitors can tour the **King-Cromartie House**, a 1907 home that now serves as a turn-of-the-century museum furnished with period antiques.

A few blocks away is the **Museum of Discovery & Science**. Chock-full of entertaining and educational exhibits, this is the kind of place where you could spend an entire day (with or without children). Exhibits include a real coral reef with sea creatures and tropical fish, a sound booth inside a "human head" that demonstrates how sound works, a simulated space flight and landing, a demonstration of how running water and electricity work in your home and a gravity-free moon walk. The museum also houses an IMAX theater with a five-story screen on which visitors can view adventure films on such subjects as the Grand Canyon and Antarctica. Admission. ~ 401 Southwest 2nd Street; 954-467-6637.

If you like old-fashioned things, the most attractive building in all of Fort Lauderdale may be the **Stranahan House**. This two-story frame structure was built in 1901 by the city's first citizen, Frank Stranahan, who saw it evolve from a trading post to a family home. Constructed of Dade County pine, the house eventually sprouted bay windows, electric wiring and modern plumbing—all signs of the times—as well as of the Stranahan family's prominence. The house is now restored to the 1915 period, furnished with appropriate examples of Victorian furniture and open to guided tours (except in July when only private tours are given). Admission. ~ Las Olas Boulevard at the New River Tunnel; 954-524-4736.

The best way to see the most beautiful residential areas of Fort Lauderdale is via the city's intricate network of waterways. There are several ways to experience the waterways, but the easiest is simply to call a taxi. A water taxi, that is. **Water Taxi of Fort Lauderdale** possesses a fleet of bright yellow skiffs that—for a moderate fare—shuttle passengers to points along the Intracoastal Waterway and New and Middle rivers. ~ 1900 Southeast 15th Street; 954-467-6677.

If you prefer to travel en masse, try the **Jungle Queen**, a 538-passenger riverboat that meanders through downtown, past Millionaire's Row and up the New River to the **Seminole Indian Village** for a look at native trees and birds. ~ Bahia Mar Yacht Center, 801 Seabreeze Boulevard; 954-462-5596.

There's enough space in west Broward County for a number of "great outdoors" attractions, most notably **Everglades Holiday**

Park. This privately owned facility offers the easiest close-by access point to the vast reaches of the Everglades, which stretches from the middle of the state to the western edge of greater Fort Lauderdale. The reason for driving all the way out here is to hop aboard an airboat that carries large groups out on one-hour tours through tall saw grass and cattails and over low-lying waterplants. Coots, marsh hens and the occasional lone osprey can be easily photographed during frequent stops. Alligators pop up from time to time, sometimes becoming visible as they sun themselves on the banks at the feet of leafy pond apple trees. Included in the fare is a layover at a small replica of a Seminole village for an alligator show. ~ 21940 Griffin Road; 954-434-8111.

LODGING

From Hollywood up to Deerfield Beach, good hotels and quality inns are vastly outnumbered by nondescript motels. In Fort Lauderdale proper, you'll find a number of highrise hotels belonging to major chains, as well as some individually owned facilities on the south end of town. The "strip" of motels, bars and stores along Route A1A, across from the beach, is something of an eyesore, so most of our recommendations are located further afield. Thanks to a local ordinance, there is no construction whatsoever between Route A1A and the heart of the long beach. Since ocean views are a rarity elsewhere, however, it's better to base your lodging selection on other factors.

Graced with a small lagoon on one side and a spectacularly wide semiprivate beach on the other, **Lago Mar** offers a beautiful setting. In fact, with 170 rooms and suites, two swimming pools, tennis courts, a putting green, three restaurants and a lounge, Lago Mar could enter in the resort category. A variety of accommodations are available in buildings designed to catch those gorgeous Gold Coast sunrises. A typical room has soft textured wallpaper, off-white furniture with brass handles, faux stone lamps and accents of rose and forest green throughout. ~ 1700 South Ocean Lane; 954-523-6511. ULTRA-DELUXE.

Pier 66 Crown Resort and Marina looks like a cylindrical spaceship dreamed up by a 1960s sci-fi writer. Topped off with a 17th-floor revolving lounge, it dominates the coastal skyline and offers unsurpassed upper-level views. Spacious accommodations (388 rooms and suites) with subdued tropical color schemes sport small lanais that overlook the Intracoastal Waterway, the city, the ocean and 22 lushly landscaped acres. The amenities include restaurants, tennis courts, a swimming pool, a 40-person jacuzzi, a spa and a health club. ~ 2301 Southeast 17th Street Causeway; 954-525-6666, 800-233-1234. ULTRA-DELUXE.

A great deal—even in season—**The Bermudian Waterfront Motel & Apartments** fronts the Intracoastal and is a block from the ocean. Twenty-four rooms are supplemented with one- and two-bedroom apartments and efficiencies, some with French doors that overlook the pool. Children under 12 stay free. ~ 315 North Birch Road; 954-467-0467. BUDGET.

Two blocks off the beach in a veritable motel ghetto, Fort Lauderdale–style of course, you'll find **Sea Château Motel**. Each room is decorated individually with an eclectic assortment of furniture. Efficiencies are available as well as a pool. ~ 555 North Birch Road; 954-566-8331, 800-726-3732. MODERATE.

Clean, quiet and centrally located, the **Sea View Resort Motel** rests only a football field's length away from the beach. Accommodations with two double beds are available; pastels are the color scheme and there's a pool right outside. Efficiencies are available. ~ 550 North Birch Road; 954-564-3151. MODERATE TO DELUXE.

The gentility is almost palpable at the **Riverside Hotel**. Visitors here find a residential ambience: most of the 109 rooms and suites have comfy beds covered with chenille spreads and solid oak furniture. The views are of tree-lined Las Olas Boulevard, the garden or the boat-bedecked waters of the New River. Coral fireplaces and terra cotta floors add a Spanish flavor. Dining rooms, a bar and a pool round out the amenities. ~ 620 East Las Olas Boulevard; 954-467-0671, 800-325-3280, fax 954-462-2148. DELUXE TO ULTRA-DELUXE.

One of the best values is the two-story **Days Inn**. It has 52 large, well-ventilated, carpeted rooms. Ask for a second-floor room at the back of this motel court, away from Route 1 and the pool, which has thatched-roof lounge areas. ~ 2201 North Federal Highway; 954-564-9636. MODERATE TO DELUXE.

As central Florida continues to be paved over, places like the **Bonaventure Resort and Spa** won't seem so far away. But right

---

✔ CHECK THESE OUT—UNIQUE LODGING

- *Budget:* Sleep cheap a block away from the ocean at **The Bermudian Waterfront Motel & Apartments**, on the Intracoastal Waterway. *page 113*
- *Budget to moderate:* Make **Maison Harrison** your home away from home as you enjoy the courtyard, decks and workout room at this renovated bed and breakfast. *page 105*
- *Moderate to deluxe:* Curl up in the carriage house at **West Palm Beach Bed & Breakfast**, a peaceful hostelry in the historic district. *page 146*
- *Ultra-deluxe:* Relax in the lap of luxury at the beautiful **Boca Raton Resort and Club**, the premier resort on the Atlantic seaboard. *page 133*

Budget: under $50   Moderate: $50–$90   Deluxe: $90–$130   Ultra-deluxe: over $130

now the resort's 1250 acres still seem like they are in the middle of nowhere. The Bonaventure has a reputation for excellent golf and tennis as well as for its extensive spa facilities. Accommodations, spread among nine four-story buildings, do not live up to the quality of the recreational amenities, sad to say. Although large, tidy and more than serviceable, rooms and suites have none of the pizzazz you'd expect of such a resort. There are pools, however. ~ 250 Racquet Club Road; 954-389-3300. ULTRA-DELUXE.

Marriott's Harbor Beach Resort sits on 16 prime oceanfront acres. All rooms have balconies; the priciest overlook the ocean. Fountains and lush landscaping make this resort feel as deluxe as it is. The beach has a water sports concession and cabanas. Five restaurants on the premises range from formal to no shoes required. The swimming pool is a massive 8000 square feet. ~ 3030 Holiday Drive; 954-525-4000, 800-222-6543, fax 954-766-6193. DELUXE.

Galt Ocean Mile is a well-known location in north Fort Lauderdale, consisting of one long phalanx of condominiums and other highrises. One of the few places open to the public is **Ocean Manor Resort**, an 11-story, 75-room beachfront structure with a mix of shapes, sizes and styles from which to choose. Contemporary furnishings and views of either ocean or city add an extra dimension to otherwise unexciting accommodations. Suites with full kitchens are available and there's also a pool. ~ 4040 Galt Ocean Drive; 954-566-7500, 800-955-0444, fax 954-564-3075. ULTRA-DELUXE.

If you're looking for something a little less upscale, try the **Hostelling International—International House.** Close to the beach, this hostel features 94 bunk beds in single-sex dormitories and a few private rooms for couples and families. The hostel is located in an old motel and comes complete with outdoor pool, courtyard and garden area. ~ 3811 North Ocean Boulevard; 954-568-1615, 800-444-6111. BUDGET.

GAY LODGING   Nestled on a finger island in one of Fort Lauderdale's most desirable neighborhoods, **Admiral's Court** is absolutely charming. The two-story, clay-tiled Mediterranean buildings hug a swimming pool and gardens dotted with sculptures and fountains. Out back, there's a second pool and a canal lined with yachts and sailboats. Eclecticism reigns in the 37 efficiencies and motel rooms. Some rooms have ceramic tile or cobblestone floors and formica furniture; others have carpeting and wicker. All units in this gay-friendly establishment are clean and comfortable. ~ 21 Hendricks Isle; 954-462-5072, 800-248-6669, fax 954-763-8863. MODERATE.

For gay men only, **The Blue Dolphin** rests in the prettiest of pink buildings just two blocks from the ocean. The rooms in this U-shaped motel are adorned with pale blue carpets, colorful bedspreads and modern appliances. One-bedroom apartments, efficiencies and spacious motel rooms are available. There's a heated swimming pool on the grounds, and grocery stores nearby for do-it-yourselfers. A large fence surrounds the grounds, ensuring privacy for the guests. ~ 725 North Birch Road; 954-565-8437, 800-893-2583, fax 954-565-6015. MODERATE TO DELUXE.

Expect plush accommodations at **The Royal Palms**, which earned and received *Out & About's* 1996 palm rating. This men-only establishment outfits its contemporary-styled rooms with king- or queen-sized beds, tasteful artwork and ceiling fans. You'll also find refrigerators, VCRs and CD players at your disposal. Four suites boast even more luxurious amenities—full kitchens, separate dining areas and private decks. All this in a tropical setting just two blocks from the beach, complete with palm trees and myriad exotic plants, a pool and a sundeck. Complimentary continental breakfast is included. Three-night minimum stay required during the peak season. ~ 2901 Terramar Street; 954-564-6444, 800-237-7256, fax 954-564-6443. ~ ULTRA-DELUXE.

Fashioned in tropical Key West style, **Big Ruby's Guesthouse** offers surroundings so private it's easy to miss the place. The ivory clapboard building is adorned with Christmas lights, flower boxes and lacy gingerbread, and enveloped by jungle gardens. Ten comfortable guest rooms offer Bahamas fans, soft carpets, microwaves and refrigerators. Out front, there's a swimming pool, waterfall and spacious wood deck for sunning in the buff. A real retreat for gay men. ~ 908 Northeast 15th Avenue; 954-523-7829, 888-244-7829. MODERATE TO DELUXE.

DINING

Burt & Jack's stands alone on a point of land overlooking the Intracoastal Waterway. The setting and the star power of one owner—Burt Reynolds—may have something to do with the popularity of this place, which looks like a Mediterranean villa. The menu has a macho side—lots of lamb and steaks—but also some popular seafood selections such as sea scallops and Maine lobster. Dinner only; jackets for gentlemen and reservations recommended. ~ Berth 23, Port Everglades; 954-522-5225. DELUXE TO ULTRA-DELUXE.

HIDDEN ►

Insiders know that the place to go for succulent, explosively hot barbecue is **Ernie's Bar B Que and Lounge**. A plain building with few adornments in the one high-ceilinged dining room, Ernie's relies on a dynamite sauce for its draw. Meat choices include chicken, pork and ribs, each of which can be accompanied by corn on the cob, cole slaw and gallons of iced tea. ~ 1843 South Federal Highway; 954-523-8636. BUDGET TO MODERATE.

An upscale waterfront bistro in the California style, **California Café** is an absolutely delightful spot. Everything on the Caribbean and Mediterranean influenced menu seems to be successful, from homemade pasta to delicate seafood dishes. Spacious dining areas are staggered, affording views of the marina action beyond. ~ At Pier 66 Resort and Marina, 2301 Southeast 17th Street; 954-525-6666. MODERATE TO DELUXE.

Food and drink are finally allowed in Fort Lauderdale's main library—if you get them from Charcuterie Too, that is.

It's difficult to get reservations at the **15th Street Fisheries,** but locals swear it's always worth the trouble. This out-of-the-way waterfront restaurant offers excellent views and two levels of dining, both literally and figuratively. Go for the upstairs, where weathered wood walls are festooned with shrimp nets and small tables are covered with marble-colored tablecloths. Seafood is king here: blackened tuna, grouper, dolphin and snapper are usually available, but veal and steak dishes are, too. ~ 1900 Southeast 15th Street; 954-763-2777. MODERATE TO ULTRA-DELUXE.

The hip way to arrive at the **Southport Raw Bar** is via private boat, but it's acceptable to come by land as well. This dockside joint is mighty lively, with loyal patrons sliding down oysters and clams, conch salad, excellent clam chowder, crisp crab cakes and fried shrimp. A great place to drop by for a snack in mid-afternoon. ~ 1536 Cordova Road; 954-525-2526. BUDGET.

Tucked away in the back of **The Chemist Shop** is a corner coffee shop worth investigating. Shopkeepers from the neighborhood flock to this little nook, with only a counter and a few tables, to enjoy good cheap food such as sirloin burgers and old-fashioned sandwiches like cream-cheese-and-olive and peanut-butter-and-bacon. For dessert, there are soda-shop goodies concocted with an extra-rich ice cream and homemade bittersweet chocolate sauce. ~ 817 East Las Olas Boulevard; 954-463-8981. BUDGET.

◄ HIDDEN

In the heart of the Las Olas shopping district, **La Bonne Crêpe** provides a refined oasis from the commercial bustle. A small restaurant with a slightly worn carpet and about a dozen tables clothed in lace, this is a local favorite famous for its authentic crêpes, cooked on a special grill imported from La Belle, France. The repertoire includes some 50 crêpes, including ones made with sausage, ratatouille and Swiss cheese, as well as a variety of dessert crêpes. Reservations are suggested. ~ 815 East Las Olas Boulevard; 954-761-1515. MODERATE TO DELUXE.

Across the New River from the Las Olas shopping district, **Shirttail Charlie's Restaurant** is a multilevel, multipurpose restaurant and bar. It's wonderful for an al fresco dockside luncheon of seafood salad, grilled fish or kebabs of steak, chicken, shrimp or fish. At night, dinners are served indoors in the upstairs dining room overlooking the river. A rather interesting menu lists a variety of fresh seafood, including conch, along with steaks, chicken

and alligator. ~ 400 Southwest 3rd Avenue; 954-463-3474. MOD-
ERATE TO DELUXE.

One of downtown Fort Lauderdale's best-kept secrets is a
delightful French café located in, of all places, the main library.
HIDDEN ► **Charcuterie Too** is an artsy breakfast and lunch niche. Gastronomic delights such as chicken *pommery*, crab-stuffed potatoes,
pasta primavera and *torte rustica* (flaky pastry rolled with ham,
spinach and artichoke hearts) are displayed cafeteria-style, presenting a row of sheer visual delicacies. The surroundings are pure
Miami Vice, with pink ceramic palm trees and white marble tabletops. Power lunchers know this is a prime place to nosh. No dinner. Closed Saturday and Sunday. ~ 100 South Andrews Avenue;
954-463-9578. BUDGET.

HIDDEN ► From the outside, **Siam Cuisine** looks like little more than a
roadside diner. Pity those who drive by and miss the sumptuous
feast waiting inside. One of the better Thai restaurants to grace
Broward County, Siam Cuisine offers sizzling fare such as *panang
nua* (beef with coconut milk, curry and peanut sauce), *tom yum
koong* (sour shrimp soup), *kanom gheeb* (steamed dumplings) and
squid salad. Mirrored walls and only 17 wooden tables give a
quaint, homey feel to the interior. ~ 2010 Wilton Drive, Wilton
Manors; 954-564-3411. BUDGET TO MODERATE.

If there's ever an award for prettiest restaurant in Broward
County, it should go to **Victoria Park Restaurant**. The basic palette
is sunrise-in-the-Caribbean—pink, white, yellow and blue; enchanting artwork underscores the concept. The food is French Caribbean. On a typical night, the menu might list filet mignon in red
wine, calf's liver Provençal and fresh fish, either grilled or sautéed,
embellished with a special spicy creole sauce. The choices are limited, but they change frequently in this upbeat setting. Seating is
also limited, so reservations are advised. Dinner only. Closed Sunday; also closed Monday from June until October. ~ 900 Northeast
20th Avenue; 954-764-6868. MODERATE TO DELUXE.

Acclaimed for the best and biggest pizzas in town, **Big Louie's**
lists 21 toppings, including Canadian bacon, fresh garlic, walnuts
and spinach. Also popular are several versions of calzone, stuffed
with cheeses, meats and vegetables. A wall of mirrors reflects
Tiffany-style chandeliers and wooden tables trimmed in red and
green in this friendly, casual pizzeria. ~ 1990 East Sunrise Boulevard; 954-467-1166. BUDGET TO MODERATE.

HIDDEN ► **Croissan'Time** is one of those wonderfully hidden eateries that
depends on word-of-mouth advertising. Judging by the perpetual
mobs, everyone's talking. The bright French café and bakery, decorated with checkerboard floors, mirrors and a handful of tiny
tables, offers pâtés, quiches, french bread pizzas and croissants
stuffed with meats and cheeses. Desserts are the kind you can't pass

up. No dinner. Closed Monday. ~ 1201 North Federal Highway; 954-565-8555. BUDGET.

Now it can be told where those lovely older coffee shop waitresses get their start: as lovely younger coffee shop waitresses at **The Egg and You**. This is a classic, where blue leatherette booths and counter stools are carefully coordinated with blue-and-white wallpaper. The joint is jammed for weekend breakfasts because nearly everyone in town knows about the fresh ingredients and home-style cooking here. Open all day, The Egg and You serves deli-style sandwiches and homemade soups from lunchtime on. Typical dinner offerings are veal patties and dishes involving ground beef or chicken. ~ 2621 North Federal Highway; 954-564-2045. BUDGET.

Shooter's Restaurant is an extremely popular eatery, with an outdoor dining room right on the Intracoastal Waterway. Here several dozen umbrella-topped tables offer views of the passing flotilla of motorboats and luxury yachts. Appetizers (shrimp, nachos and chicken quesadillas) by far outnumber entrées such as grilled fish, New York strip steak and pasta dishes. There is also lighter fare here, salads and sandwiches perfect for noshing outdoors. Lunch, dinner and Sunday brunch are served. ~ 3033 Northeast 32nd Avenue; 954-566-2855. MODERATE.

One of the Fort Lauderdale area's best restaurants would seem to have two strikes against it. **By Word of Mouth** is very hard to find and does no advertising. But word of mouth has, indeed, worked very well. And no wonder, given the quality and variety of its gourmet Continental cuisine. The setting is as fresh as the concept: ceiling fans cool the two airy rooms rimmed by windows and white lace curtains. A typical day's offerings include Key West lobster with artichokes, poblano-stuffed chicken and pasta roulade with spinach and pinenuts, to name only a few. Lunch Monday through Friday, dinner Wednesday through Saturday. Reservations are suggested for dinner. ~ 3200 Northeast 12th Avenue, Oakland Park; 954-564-3663. DELUXE.

◄ HIDDEN

Down Under may be Fort Lauderdale's best-known restaurant, famous for Continental cuisine in a semiformal setting facing the Intracoastal Waterway. The decor—dark wood, dimly lit—is not to my taste, but the food and service are virtually impeccable. Numerous seafood dishes include options from Maine lobster to Idaho trout to local snapper and pompano. Preparation is imaginative and consistent whether you're ordering chicken curry, beef Wellington or various veal or lamb dishes. ~ 3000 East Oakland Park Boulevard; 954-563-4123. DELUXE TO ULTRA-DELUXE.

Housed in a cavernous building at a busy intersection, **Who-Song & Larry's Restaurant and Cantina** is the kind of rollicking joint where everyone seems to be having a grand old time. A thoroughly south-of-the-border menu offers some twists on old standards, including lobster fajitas. ~ 3100 North Federal Highway; 954-566-9771. BUDGET TO MODERATE.

Fort Lauderdale's answer to Hawaii's most lavish restaurants, the **Mai-Kai** has gone one better and added an extensive garden out back, complete with walkways and waterfalls. For a romantic dinner à deux, reserve table number 185, which has a nook all its own in the gardens. Otherwise, join the fun-loving crowd inside for Peking duck, Cantonese dishes, scallops with oysters and ginger, or a variety of meats roasted in Chinese wood-burning ovens. Try the tasty lobster *pango-pango*—it's very popular. The setting is a South Seas fantasy, complete with carved sculptures and grass skirts, but the effect is rather irresistible. ~ 3599 North Federal Highway; 954-563-3272. DELUXE TO ULTRA-DELUXE.

SHOPPING

Despite the advance of malls into seemingly every neighborhood on the Gold Coast, the best-known shopping address in Fort Lauderdale is **Las Olas Boulevard**. This tree-lined street in a residential area is home to a wide variety of stores, mostly one-of-a-kind boutiques.

Braided rugs, silky quilts and earthenware vessels are just some of the homespun handiworks you'll find at **Country Collection**. The sweet-smelling emporium also sells potpourri, candles and women's clothing. ~ 808 East Las Olas Boulevard; 954-462-6205.

It seems ironic that one of Broward County's biggest commercial centers—Sawgrass Mills—was built next to its greatest natural treasure—the Everglades.

Audace caters primarily to the gay man who likes his undergarments soft, clingy and pricey. T-shirts, belts and jewelry round out the accessories here. ~ 813 East Las Olas Boulevard; 954-522-7503.

South by Southwest is a visual delight. Handbags too beautiful to use and other wearable art are the mainstay. But true to its name, this boutique stocks string ties, elaborate leather belts, silver jewelry, framed southwestern artwork and fantasy sculpture like bandanna-clad coyotes howling in silence. There's even a neon cactus! ~ 833 East Las Olas Boulevard; 954-761-1196.

One local attention-getter, **Apropos Art Gallery**, carries modern pieces by artists such as Michael Parks, Jurgen Gorg and Sheri Brush. Works here span a variety of media. You'll find paintings, sculptures and drawings as well as unique furniture. ~ 1016 East Las Olas Boulevard; 954-524-2100.

Within **The Galleria** are 150 shops and restaurants, anchored by several major department stores and dozens of chain outlets specializing in best sellers, polo shirts, safari clothing and imported soaps. ~ On East Sunrise Boulevard between Ocean Boulevard and Federal Highway; 954-564-1015.

Sightseeing on the Gold Coast leads to some interesting finds such as the **Explore Store**. The store, located at the Museum of Discovery & Science, spills over with kites, kaleidoscopes and treasures like inexpensive magnifying glasses, tops, books, games and playing cards depicting endangered species. ~ 401 Southwest 2nd Street; 954-467-6637.

The Seminole Indian Reservation, located in west Fort Lauderdale is home to a few shops with American Indian crafts. At the **Anhinga Indian Museum and Art Gallery** you'll find a large stock of clothing (much of it fringed), turquoise and silver jewelry, woven rugs, beaded dolls and potholders in traditional Seminole patchwork designs. ~ 5791 South State Road 7; 954-581-0416.

In the same little complex, the **Flying Bird Gift Shop** sells jewelry, pottery, dolls and woven rugs. ~ 954-894-9641.

The 87-acre **Swap Shop** is a great discount haven where more than 2000 vendors ply clothing, kitchen items, hardware, jewelry and much more. ~ 3291 West Sunrise Boulevard; 954-791-7927.

Sawgrass Mills, billed as the world's largest outlet mall, sprawls right on the edge of the Everglades—that fragile, mystical river of sawgrass. Opened in 1990, the retail extravaganza houses over 200 discount stores in a variety of architectural styles, including Mediterranean and Caribbean, contemporary and art deco. Many brand-name and designer stores are here, including a **Spiegel** (954-846-1276) outlet. The mall's real highlight, though, is the indoor lake filled with fake alligators and flamingos that talk. ~ At West Sunrise Boulevard and Flamingo Road, Sunrise; 954-846-2350.

Riverwatch Lounge has a small dancefloor. Reflected in the club's glass-and-brass fixtures, patrons dance to live jazz, blues and rock. ~ Fort Lauderdale Marina Marriott, 1881 Southeast 17th Street; 954-463-4000.

NIGHTLIFE

The bars that best epitomize Fort Lauderdale's casual outdoor nightscene are clustered along the roadways flanking the Oakland Park Boulevard Bridge. Here half a dozen clubs and restaurant bars hug the Intracoastal Waterway, drawing lofty yachts that vie for prime dock space.

With its stylish tropical motif and splendid dockside location, **Mombasa Bay** is the place to kick back, Florida-style. There is live entertainment nightly featuring reggae. Cover on weekends. ~ 3051 Northeast 32nd Avenue; 954-565-7441.

You'll find a super-casual crowd at **Shooters**, a popular indoor-outdoor spot with umbrella tables and dockside benches. ~ 3033 Northeast 32nd Avenue; 954-566-2855.

Bootleggers is another laid-back habitat where all the action centers around a swimming pool and live bands on the weekends. ~ 3003 Northeast 32nd Avenue; 954-563-4337.

The topnotch house band at **September's**, a fixture for several years, plays to a faithful local following that crowds the place Wednesday through Sunday. The classy club, loaded with silk plants and lined with carpeted walls, caters to a over-30 crowd. Cover on weekends. ~ 2975 North Federal Highway; 954-563-4331.

The bi-level danceclub **Roxy** features two dancefloors and a huge wall of 30 televisions. Here you dance to a mix of current Top-40 and oldies. ~ 4000 North Federal Highway; 954-565-3555.

Squeeze has black walls, black lights and a new wave attitude. The music is progressive, the crowd hip. This club has live music on Wednesday and Friday; there's an open mike on Sunday. Cover. ~ 2 South New River Drive; 954-522-2068.

Of course Fort Lauderdale would have a waterborne nightclub. **Discovery Cruises** offers a variety of evening cruises with dancing to bands and deejays. There's also the Captain's Club Gala Dinner cruise. Cover. ~ Pier 4, Port Everglades; 954-525-8400.

Jazz, reggae, rhythm-and-blues and even occasional rock-and-roll concerts are presented at the **Musician's Exchange**. This is the spot to hear both regional bands and nationally known artists in a comfortable lounge setting. Cover. ~ 729 West Sunrise Boulevard; 954-764-1905.

THEATER, OPERA, SYMPHONY AND DANCE   Broadway shows, including some performed by nationally known actors, are the main fare at the **Parker Playhouse**. Plan to reserve tickets well in advance. ~ 707 Northeast 8th Street; 954-764-0700.

The Gold Coast's newest cultural gem, **Broward Center for the Performing Arts** has an impressive dependable lineup of Broadway plays, regional opera and drama, and Afro-Caribbean dance. ~ 201 Southwest 5th Avenue; 954-462-0222.

One of the most promising area theaters, **Brian C. Smith's Off Broadway at East 26th Street** stages an excellent lineup of major drama and avant-garde productions in a 300-seat former film house. ~ 1444 Northeast 26th Street, Wilton Manors; 954-566-0554.

GAY SCENE   Fort Lauderdale is a popular destination for gays. As more move into the area, more businesses, like those listed below, open to serve this growing segment of the visiting and resident populace. While there is no single gathering spot, certain beaches (such as the middle part of both John U. Lloyd Beach State Recreation Area in north Hollywood and Fort Lauderdale's strip), restaurants, hotels and nightclubs cater to a gay clientele.

For over a decade, **The Copa** has been the city's most popular gay bar. Cool, clean and rambling, it features numerous rooms and a sprawling Key West–style patio bar strung with tiny lights. The extravagant entertainment runs till 4 a.m. Cover. ~ 624 Southeast 28th Street; 954-463-1507.

Billed as a preppie video bar, **Club Cathode Ray** is gay-friendly and best known for its nightly drink specials. ~ 1105 East Las Olas Boulevard; 954-462-8611.

A sort of compound of gay entertainment, the **Stud** is a one-stop place with plenty of entertainment choices. It features a video bar, a patio and a dancehall with a large dancefloor. If that's not enough, add the male dancers, a gift shop with leather items and artwork, a loyal crowd and an often raucous atmosphere. Cover on weekends. ~ 1000 West State Road 84; 954-525-7883.

When a live band isn't playing, deejay mixes are guaranteed to bring the primarily lesbian crowd at **Otherside of Fort Lauderdale** to its feet. The full bar serves up two-for-one drink specials on Wednesday while the boutique proffers jewelry and other goodies. There's an assortment of games and Sunday football to tackle as well. Cover occasionally. ~ 2283 Wilton Drive; 954-565-5538.

JOHN U. LLOYD BEACH STATE RECREATION AREA

BEACHES & PARKS

As soon as we passed the guard station to this park, we could feel it was something special. A mile-long, tree-lined road leads past several beach access areas, each with its own personality. A narrow white sand beach extends 11,500 feet up to a jetty, the tip of which offers a sweeping view of the oceanfront to the south. Most beachgoers make a little nest between the high-water mark and the seagrass, which gives them a proprietary feeling that is one of the park's greatest appeals. Within these 244 acres is a self-guided nature trail meandering through a semitropical coastal hammock that takes about 45 minutes roundtrip. Bird life is abundant and manatees are spotted in the shallows of Whiskey Creek. The gentle surf makes swimming a pleasure. Fishing is excellent off the jetty at the north end of the park; you can also try the Intracoastal Waterway. Facilities include picnic areas, barbecue grills, restrooms, showers, lifeguards, canoe rentals and concession stands; restaurants and grocery stores are a short drive away. ~ North of the intersection of Dania Beach Boulevard and North Ocean Drive; 954-923-2833.

FORT LAUDERDALE BEACH

Many movie-goers of a certain age got their first impressions of Fort Lauderdale from the 1960 film *Where the Boys Are*, which prominently featured the glorious palm-fringed beach. The same film also started a trend among college students, who descended upon the beach-front every year for spring break. The city is discouraging these hordes, but Route A1A in Fort Lauderdale remains one of the most developed strips on the Gold Coast. Since hotel construction is limited to the inland side of the highway roughly from Las Olas Boulevard to Northeast 18th Street, most of the three-and-a half-mile beach of crushed shells and slightly coarse beige sand lies in

HIDDEN ► full view. There is a promenade wall where beachgoers walk, bike and rollerblade. The least-crowded area is **South Beach Park**. It's not well-known, thus its relative peacefulness. Plus, it's an excellent place to swim. Surf angling is allowed from sunset to sunrise. To the north, the highrises along Galt Ocean Mile shade the narrow beach, which offers little public access anyway. Facilities consist of showers and lifeguards; restaurants and groceries are across the highway. ~ Located in front of the major hotels south of South Route A1A. Major access street ends are Sunrise Boulevard and Oakland Park Boulevard; 954-468-1595.

HUGH TAYLOR BIRCH STATE RECREATION AREA 🚶 🚲 ⛵
🎣 ⛱ Within sight of highrise condominiums lie 180 protected acres of green trees and fresh water. The facility includes a coastal hammock, mangroves, freshwater lagoons and underground access to a pristine stretch of beach. The long, narrow park occupies an almost rectangular portion of barrier island between the Atlantic Ocean and the Intracoastal Waterway. Established in 1942, when Fort Lauderdale was still a small city, this peaceful sanctuary still offers visitors a glimpse of old Florida in its natural state. The swimming is wonderful and saltwater angling on the Intracoastal Waterway is often rewarding. Surfers try the waves just north of the park. Facilities include picnic areas, barbecue grills, restrooms, a concession stand, a nature trail, canoe rentals and an exercise course; restaurants and groceries are nearby. ~ At 3109 East Sunrise Boulevard, Fort Lauderdale; 954-564-4521.

▼▼▼▼▼▼▼▼▼▼▼▼▼▼▼▼
North Broward County

No doubt North Broward County—particularly along the Atlantic Ocean—provides some of the most attractive scenery in the entire Fort Lauderdale area. The necklace of beach towns that extends to Palm Beach County are generally quiet and family-oriented, offering a reflective look at tropical living.

Along the north coast, towns such as tiny Lauderdale-by-the-Sea and Hillsboro Beach long ago developed to capacity and now continue to maintain and renovate what's already there. To the northwest, Coral Springs and Coconut Creek explode with new commercial centers and neighborhoods, providing housing for young professionals and a large retired population. It's here, out West, that you'll still find a few natural habitats and wonderfully dense hammocks.

SIGHTS Pompano Beach is a small town with few formal sightseeing attractions. However, the **Pompano Harness Track** is the only place on the Gold Coast where you can see highly trained horses and their drivers in intense professional competition. Admission. ~ On Powerline Road south of Atlantic Boulevard; 954-972-2000.

Perhaps the most scenic stretch of Broward County coastline lies from Deerfield Beach north to the Palm Beach County border. Here, a picturesque little town called **Hillsboro Beach** possesses a rare South Florida species: oceanfront estates. To take a peek (and that's as much as you'll ever get), drive along Route A1A north of Hillsboro Boulevard for about two miles. This thin strip of road is flanked on the west by the Intracoastal Waterway and on the east by majestic estates situated on manmade hills and shrouded by lush vegetation.

LODGING

In South Florida, the word "villa" means a cluster of accommodations, not a grand estate in the Mediterranean tradition. A case in point is **Villas-by-the-Sea**. A total of 149 units are spread among eight buildings marching back from the beach. Every room was recently given a fresh look, with decorum that's light and contemporary: ceramic tile floors, wicker and formica furniture and modern amenities. The grounds are manicured and palmy, and feature heated swimming pools, a jacuzzi and barbecue grills. Efficiencies, suites and large apartments are also available. ~ 4456 El Mar Drive, Lauderdale-by-the-Sea; 954-772-3550, 800-247-8963, fax 954-772-3835. DELUXE TO ULTRA-DELUXE.

Somewhat cozier than the average beach town motel, the **Sea Spray Inn** has only six units on its two floors. This inn is decked out in blue and mauve color combinations. Sparkling clean rooms all have kitchen facilities (tucked discreetly behind a partial wall) and breakfast tables. Across the street from the beach and within walking distance of shops and restaurants, the Sea Spray offers excellent value. ~ 4245 El Mar Drive, Lauderdale-by-the-Sea; 954-776-1311, fax 954-772-3178. MODERATE.

Blue Seas Courtyard is a 12-room, two-story hotel in a quiet neighborhood. The smartly decorated tiled rooms have Haitian

••

FLUTTER WORLD

We hadn't thought much about the lifespan of butterflies until we took the spellbinding tour at **Butterfly World**. Protected in this paradise for flying insects, some of the 2000 specimens often survive here for as long as 14 days—twice their normal lifespan in the wild. The iridescent blue-banded eggfly, the Ecuadorian metalmark, and more than 100 other types of butterflies and moths flutter amid three acres landscaped with beautiful nectar-producing plants. The Tropical Rain Forest, an 8000-square-foot screened structure, houses specimens from all over the world. Admission. ~ Tradewinds Park South, 3600 West Sample Road, Coconut Creek; 954-977-4400.

art, Peruvian wall hangings and brilliantly patterned rugs. ~ 4525 El Mar Drive, Lauderdale-by-the-Sea; 954-772-3336. BUDGET.

The **Pier Pointe Resort** is a sleek and glossy complex with 98 accommodations clustered in various villas. Pristine rooms are painted in pastels and carpeted in earthtones. With ceiling fans, rattan furniture and contemporary window coverings, this place evokes an atmosphere similar to that of some of the better inns in the Caribbean. Masterful poolside landscaping and a beachfront location near the pier add up to very good value. Efficiencies are available. ~ 4324 El Mar Drive, Lauderdale-by-the-Sea; 954-776-5121, 800-331-6384, fax 954-491-9284. DELUXE TO ULTRA-DELUXE.

A brightly colored balcony rims the second story of **The Rainbow on the Ocean**, an attractive motel fronting a narrow sand beach. The 25 units are well-kept and larger than average. Furniture is a hodgepodge of pseudo-French provincial and nondescript rattan. They have one efficiency. ~ 1231 Route A1A, Hillsboro Beach; 954-426-2525. MODERATE TO DELUXE.

In an area of interchangeable motels, **Hansel and Gretel's Tropical Guest House** stands out as a congenial spot with an excellent location. The storybook motif is pretty much limited to lawn statuary in the shapes of dwarves and mushrooms, but who'd want to sleep in a gingerbread house anyway? Accommodations at this glorified motel court are quite modern. Each room is decorated according to a different theme such as tropical and German-style; there are also efficiencies and apartments. The pool is a bonus. ~ 97 South Route A1A, Deerfield Beach; 954-427-4381, 954-427-5979. MODERATE.

Accommodations in the seven-story **Embassy Suites** are characteristic of this chain's reputation for spacious, well-appointed rooms. What's unusual here is the hotel's prime beachfront location (plus its being the only sizable facility in town). The design should win awards: rooms are well laid-out, beautifully decorated in tropical colors cool enough to soothe a sunburn, and furnished with comfortable beds, sofas and a slew of glass-and-brass tables. The elegant lobby and pool setting are reminiscent of better offshore resorts. Cocktails and a continental breakfast are complimentary. ~ 950 Southeast 20th Avenue, Deerfield Beach; 954-426-0478, 800-362-2779. ULTRA-DELUXE.

DINING   If you fancy spectacular sunrises, don't miss the **Pier Coffeeshop**. This no-frills eatery rests right on the Commercial Boulevard Pier, offering a few indoor tables and five outdoor booths suspended over the sand and peering across the ocean. The breakfast and lunch menus (no dinner) are scrawled on a rustic wooden sign. Choices are standard budget eats: bacon and eggs, pancakes, patty melts and frothy milkshakes. ~ 2 East Commercial Boulevard, Lauderdale-by-the-Sea; 954-776-1690. BUDGET.

◄ HIDDEN

The hours just prior to sundown are the most beautiful at **Sea Watch**, one of the very few oceanfront restaurants on the Gold Coast. Hidden between condominium buildings, Sea Watch offers fabulous views of Jade Beach. You can stave off hunger pangs with seafood appetizers while you peruse a varied menu of fish, scampi, chicken and beef dishes. Rough wood and an expanse of glass add to the romantic atmosphere. ~ 6002 North Ocean Boulevard, Fort Lauderdale; 954-781-2200. MODERATE TO ULTRA-DELUXE.

If you dine at only one Broward County restaurant, make it **Café Max**. The little art deco gem, tucked in a strip shopping center, is widely known for its fabulous food artistry that tastes as good as it looks. Celebrated young chef Oliver Saucy, who cooks to rock-and-roll music in his open kitchen, uses the freshest ingredients to craft each day's menu. For appetizers, there might be caviar pie or "bumble bee" striped Florida lobster raviolis. For entrées, sweet onion–crusted yellowtail snapper or pistachio-crusted rack of lamb with raisin coconut couscous. Before dinner, visit the splendid wine bar. ~ 2601 East Atlantic Boulevard, Pompano Beach; 954-782-0606. MODERATE TO ULTRA-DELUXE.

The Pelican Pub would be wonderful if it were located on the Intracoastal Waterway, and not just near it. Still, it's comforting to be greeted by the sight of a fish case filled with pompano and snapper plucked from the sea that very morning. This casual, open-air restaurant casts a wide net, featuring lobster from Maine, scrod from Boston, crab from Alaska and conch from the Keys. ~ 2635 North Riverside Drive, Pompano Beach; 954-785-8550. MODERATE TO DELUXE.

You can appraise artifacts from the days of illegal gambling at the Riverview Restaurant. Some of the items on display: antique slot machines and ancient poker chips embedded into table tops.

It's easy to get lost on the way to **Cap's Place Island Restaurant and Bar**. First you have to find the right two-lane road. When that dead-ends at the water, you board a motorboat that is the sole means of transport to this unique destination. You will be following in the wake of Winston Churchill, John F. Kennedy and Marilyn Monroe, all of whom visited this local legend (though not at the same time, according to one chatty bartender). The food plays second fiddle to the rum-running, gambling-den atmosphere of this ramshackle restaurant. A highlight is stone crab, served warm or cold in season. Delicate snapper and other seafood round out a menu that includes a sprinkling of chicken, pasta and steak dishes. Not to be missed is the salad made with fresh hearts of palm, still soft and sweet after the trip from a Lake Okeechobee palm farm. Since everything is cooked to order, you can take time to wander from room to room to view faded photographs and read old newspaper clippings about the area and the history of this one-of-a-kind gem. Call for directions. ~ Cap's Island off Lighthouse Point; 954-941-0418. MODERATE TO DELUXE.

The restaurant reputed to have the best Continental food in Deerfield Beach also has the most seats. In fact, with room for nearly 300 diners, **Brooks Restaurant** seems almost too large, as the menu is better suited to an intimate setting. Still, the interior is a smooth medley of light pinks and blues, with candlelight reflected in mirrors and polished formal dining chairs. Appetizers, especially several with seafood, could constitute a meal. Among the main courses are Gulf shrimp, rack of lamb, duckling and fettuccine, as well as half-a-dozen grilled meat choices. Dinner only. ~ 500 South Federal Highway, Deerfield Beach; 954-427-9302. ULTRA-DELUXE.

Formerly a hideaway casino for the cognoscenti, the **Riverview Restaurant** has cleaned up its act. Diners in three low-ceilinged waterfront rooms can analyze a lengthy menu, and choose from such seafood items as stone crabs, pompano, lobster or scallops. Or they may try "good things other than seafood," such as roast beef, veal, country ham or chicken. ~ 1741 East Riverview Road, Deerfield Beach; 954-428-3463. MODERATE TO DELUXE.

SHOPPING   When it comes to inexpensive Florida souvenirs, an excellent source is **Bill's 5 & 10**. If the object has oranges, palm trees or flamingos on it, you can find it at this well-stocked, old-fashioned dime store. ~ 26 North Ocean Boulevard, Pompano Beach; 954-941-5994.

NIGHTLIFE   Reminiscent of a cozy, northern-style bar, **Raindancer** is adorned in dark woods and set off by a fireplace that never stops roaring. The recorded jazz and folk tunes and friendly bartender only add to the romance of this unexpected spot. ~ 3031 East Commercial Boulevard, Fort Lauderdale; 954-772-0337.

Fisherman's Wharf Lounge is one of those places where you can kick back under the stars. The beachfront patio stages live rock on weekends and draws a curious mix of people. ~ 222 North Pompano Beach Boulevard, Pompano Beach; 954-941-5522.

Cool breezes flow with live mellow rock and Jamaican steel drum music on Sunday at **The Cove**, a casual but classy bar and restaurant perched along the Intracoastal Waterway. ~ 1754 Southeast 3rd Court, Deerfield Beach; 954-421-9272.

BEACHES & PARKS   EASTERLIN PARK 🚶🚲⛵🛶 Peacocks pose and strut in the shade of Royal Palms and pine trees, vying with squirrels and rabbits for handouts. This lovely grove, which includes 250-year-old cypress trees as well as ferns and wild coffee plants, is a family park. It's pleasant, though not spectacular, with low-key facilities such as picnic areas, a playground, a small kidney-shaped lake, a nature trail and volleyball and shuffleboard courts. There are also restrooms and showers; restaurants and grocery stores are nearby.

Day-use fee on weekends, $1. ~ At 1000 Northwest 38th Street, Oakland Park; 954-938-0610.

▲ There are 55 campsites, 45 with RV hookups; $17 to $22 per night.

MARKHAM PARK Sprawling over 665 acres west of Fort Lauderdale, Markham Park probably offers more recreational diversity than any other public facility on the Gold Coast. Trees and picnic shelters and canoe rides and green-swards offer relief from the heat. In cooler weather, there's plenty of room for kite flying and football. You can also play volleyball on the court, take in the sights from the observatory tower or go fishing (a license is required for the lake and the lagoon. To the east is a model-airplane field, and to the north two target ranges. In short, something for just about everyone. Other facilities include restrooms, showers, a boat ramp and a concession stand. Day-use fee, $1. ~ At 16001 West State Road 84 in Sunrise; 954-389-2000.

▲ There are 84 sites, 8 with RV hookups; $18 to $19 per night.

LAUDERDALE-BY-THE-SEA BEACH Less glamorous than its namesake to the south, this is more of a community beach. The shoreline stretches about one mile in front of motels and private residences. Fringed by palm trees, the sand is the same coarse mixture as that on Fort Lauderdale Beach. It's a very good place to swim, and if you head over to Anglin's Pier, it's also a fine place to fish. Surfing is fair north of the pier. Facilities are limited to restrooms and showers; restaurants and groceries are located nearby. ~ Located between Codrington Drive and Pine Avenue off Route A1A; 954-776-0576.

POMPANO BEACH Another segment of the beach that extends nearly the entire length of Broward County, Pompano has about three miles of coarse sand on which to romp. It lacks some of the allure of Fort Lauderdale Beach because most of it is obscured by concrete buildings between the ocean and Route A1A. The pier has been extended to more than 1000 feet, making it the longest one on the Gold Coast, and it's perfect for casting a line. Swimming is very good here. Facilities include picnic areas, restrooms, showers, lifeguards, concessions; groceries and restaurants are located nearby. ~ Located in Pompano Beach off Route A1A between Southeast 14th Street and the Hillsboro Inlet, with numerous access points; 954-786-4191.

QUIET WATERS PARK The lake waters in this 427-acre park are indeed quiet, even though water skiing is allowed. That's because no powerboats are involved; skiers are towed around the lake via cable. Bike paths and wide paved roads give this park an open feel. It is quite popular with families, especially on weekends and holidays. Bass, bream and catfish angling is allowed everywhere except in the swimming and waterskiing areas. You may only swim in designated lake areas. There are picnic areas, pavilion rentals, restrooms, a playground, lifeguards, a concession stand, a miniature golf course and boat and bike rentals; restaurants and grocery stores are nearby. ~ Located at 6601 North Powerline Road in Pompano Beach; 954-360-1315.

▲ There are 23 sites; no RVs are allowed; $17 to $25 per night.

DEERFIELD BEACH This 5700-foot undeveloped beach is one of the few places on the Gold Coast where shells can be collected. The sand is soft and deep and studded with boulders. The southern part is more serene than the other sections, though farther away from shops and restaurants. You can fish from the pier and swim between the pier and 10th Street. Surfing is allowed north of the fishing pier. Facilities include picnic areas, restrooms, showers and lifeguards; restaurants and groceries are nearby. ~ Located in Deerfield Beach between Southeast 10th Street and Northeast 4th Street off 21st Avenue; 954-480-4425.

DEERFIELD ISLAND PARK Accessible only by water, this 55-acre park is a remarkable wilderness area with two fascinating trails. Mangrove Trail is a 1500-foot raised boardwalk leading through eight acres of red, white and black mangroves, a stunning swamp where light trickles through the leaves and shorebirds can be seen cruising above the Royal Palm Waterway and the Hillsboro Canal. On the other side of the island, Coquina Trail proceeds toward the Intracoastal Waterway, where there is a rocky overlook. Keep an eye out for raccoons, tortoises and armadillos. Allow at least two hours to enjoy this unique wonderland. There are regularly scheduled nature walks and birdwatching expeditions. Facilities are limited to picnic areas and restrooms. ~ Access is by private boat or via the free boat transportation (reservation only) from the dock on Riverview Road, Deerfield Beach; 954-360-1320.

▼▼▼▼▼▼▼▼▼
Boca Raton & Delray Beach

Driving north on Route A1A from Deerfield Beach into Boca Raton—and from Broward County into Palm Beach County—lends credence to the adage that "the grass is always greener on the other side." A sense of order, of serenity, of the wherewithal to hire full-time gardeners is unmistakable as one crosses the county line. The well-kept condominiums one hasn't seen since Hallandale appear once again, this time with bright green manicured lawns.

SIGHTS

Boca Raton has become a tidy, extremely well-to-do community that attracts large numbers of retirees and golfers as well as an increasing abundance of high-technology companies. It is the site of the liveliest restaurant and nightlife activity in Palm Beach County. Delray Beach is a well-preserved oceanfront enclave for people who can afford Palm Beach's lofty prices but eschew the social requirements.

The bustle that characterizes the areas to the south is largely absent here; serenity has been preserved—or established—in a number of places. The **Gumbo-Limbo Nature Center,** for example, has been set up to protect the area's West Indian hardwood hammocks. The free educational facility, run by the county school system, features an ocean research center, biology lab, and naturalist exhibits that allow visitors to touch the skin of a snake or the pelts of small animals. Four saltwater aquariums showcase brilliant fish, stingrays, crabs, shrimp and other ocean wonders. Visitors can poke their hand into one tank and pet a live conch, sea urchin or

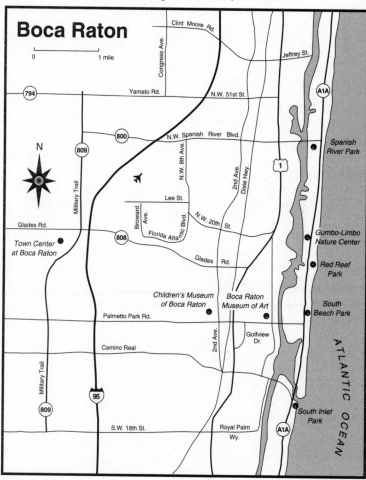

horseshoe crab. From here, a wide boardwalk leads through a shady glen to an observation tower where you can scan much of the 67-acre park as well as the beach nearby. ~ 1801 North Ocean Boulevard, Boca Raton; 561-338-1473.

Part of the fun of touring Boca Raton is the chance to look at the Spanish influence in architecture that distinguishes many homes as well as shopping centers. Stop by the **Historical Society** to pick up their brochure highlighting the town's historic buildings. ~ 71 North Federal Highway, Boca Raton; 561-395-6766.

Boca Raton's first museum is the **Children's Museum of Boca Raton**. The house itself, said to be the oldest unaltered woodframe building in the city, is as interesting as the exhibits inside. A "Florida cracker cottage" constructed, in part, of Dade County pine floors and timber found on the beach, it was moved in 1976 to its present hideaway location. The museum focuses on Victoriana and pioneer Florida memorabilia, including a kitchen that's equipped with an ancient stove, a vintage Singer sewing machine and an old-fashioned telephone. Creative exhibits for children include marvelous antique toys and a minibank where kids can write checks and withdraw money and a minimarket where they can spend their newfound cash. Admission. ~ 498 Crawford Boulevard; 561-368-6875.

The **Boca Raton Museum of Art** has three galleries, one of which houses the permanent collection of late 19th- and early 20th-century works by such artists as Picasso, Degas and Matisse. The other two galleries display temporary exhibits ranging from one-person shows of oil paintings to collections of photography to annual presentations of African artworks. ~ 801 West Palmetto Park Road, Boca Raton; 561-392-2500.

A PACIFIC PRESERVE

An atmosphere of peace envelops the **Morikami Museum and Japanese Gardens**. The centerpiece of this 200-acre pine forest preserve is the museum, which is devoted to the Japanese folk arts and stands in tribute to the Japanese Yamato colony that existed here early in this century. A Shinto sanctuary, with harmonious proportions typical of 16th- and 17th-century architecture is housed here. There are displays on Japanese baths and tea ceremonies and hands-on exhibits of obi tying, origami and musical instruments. Also of note is a two-acre, Japanese-style garden with a koi pond and a bonsai garden in the back. Guided tours are available. Admission. ~ 4000 Morikami Park Road, Delray Beach; 561-495-0233.

In recent years, Palm Beach County and polo have become inextricably linked. The winter season lasts from January through April at the **Royal Palm Polo Sports Club**. Polo is a difficult game to grasp, what with thundering hooves and swinging mallets. But the game's speed and complicated rules make this a fascinating sport to watch, and a rewarding one to master. Admission. ~ 6300 Old Clint Moore Road, Boca Raton; 561-994-1876.

As you follow Route A1A out of Boca Raton toward Delray Beach, the ocean disappears behind trimmed hedges that border beachfront mansions one can only imagine visiting. **Delray Beach** is a vital town, with a real "Main Street" (Atlantic Avenue) and a sense of life-beyond-tourism.

The ambience at **The Boca Raton Radisson Bridge Resort** evokes the serenity of the unruffled 1950s. In keeping with the genteel feel, the style and decor of the 121 accommodations employs a contemporary palette of pastel colors throughout the rooms. Private balconies, especially on the upper floors, offer stupendous views of the Intracoastal Waterway. A health spa and pool are provided. ~ 999 East Camino Real, Boca Raton; 561-368-9500, 800-333-3333, fax 561-362-0492. ULTRA-DELUXE.

LODGING

One of the most famous, most beautiful and—at the time it was constructed—most expensive hotels on the Gold Coast is the **Boca Raton Resort and Club**. Designed in 1926 as the Cloister Inn by eccentric architect Addison Mizner, the property has become an extensive world-class resort. The original hotel, which exudes Old World charm, has been expanded to 327 guest rooms, all exquisitely decorated with floral print fabrics and lustrous mahogany furniture. Another 775 rooms have been added; they range from golf villas to modern hotel rooms in a 27-story tower and in the more casual Beach Club located nearby. The hotel, perched on the Intracoastal Waterway, has a full-service marina. Golf, tennis, pools and restaurants round out the amenities. ~ 501 East Camino Real, Boca Raton; 561-395-3000, 800-327-0130, fax 561-447-5870. ULTRA-DELUXE.

You could bounce a quarter off the neat-as-a-pin beds at the **Shore Edge Motel**, a low-slung structure surrounding a little pool and manicured courtyard. The rooms are on the small side, though chrome-framed artwork and attractive patterned curtains add a fillip of freshness. Spanking clean bathrooms are tiled in festive south Florida colors such as aqua and pink. A few dollars more nets a large efficiency unit, with a separate dining area. ~ 425 North Route A1A, Boca Raton; 561-395-4491, 800-262-2786. DELUXE.

An impressive colonial facade distinguishes **Wright-by-the-Sea**, one of the more agreeable oceanfront inns in southern Palm Beach County. Within, 28 sizable units are arranged in two two-story structures facing a neatly landscaped lawn that has a heated pool as its centerpiece. A tiki hut on the private beach is a gathering spot for barbecues, and there's also croquet and shuffleboard courts for the guests' enjoyment. The studios as well as one- and two-bedroom apartments have full kitchens and plenty of windows for cross-ventilation. Typical decor includes elegant window valances and high-quality cane furniture that underscores the residential tone. ~ 1901 South Ocean Boulevard, Delray Beach; 561-278-3355, fax 561-278-2871. ULTRA-DELUXE.

Royal palms soar to the second story of the 15-unit **Huntingdon Resort**, located one block from the beach. The deluxe-priced one-bedroom accommodations are vast affairs, with all-electric kitchens and fairly attractive furnishings, though nothing matches. Small efficiencies and studios go for moderate prices. All accommodations can be rented by the week or the month and there's also a pool for use. ~ 82 Gleason Street, Delray Beach; 561-278-1700. MODERATE TO DELUXE.

The Seagate Hotel and Beach Club has a private beach and is a nice combination of motel and resort with an excellent location midway between Fort Lauderdale and Palm Beach. Two buildings house 70 accommodations that face either a garden or one of two pools. A typical room has peach-colored furnishings with green accents in the floral chintz upholstery, ceiling fans and wall-to-wall carpeting. Efficiencies are available. ~ 400 South Ocean Boulevard, Delray Beach; 561-276-2421, 800-233-3581, fax 561-243-4714. ULTRA-DELUXE.

One of the prettiest seaside inns on the central Gold Coast is **Dover House**. In the off season, rates begin in the moderate range but skyrocket to ultra-deluxe in the winter. Accommodations are spacious, sporting attractive wallpaper, contemporary furnishings, ceiling fans and full kitchens. Dover House comprises 41 units spread over two floors in three buildings, all sporting snappy awning-shaded, furnished semi-private balconies. ~ 110 South Ocean Boulevard, Delray Beach; 561-276-0309, fax 561-276-7364. MODERATE TO ULTRA-DELUXE.

Pastel colors, ceiling fans and blond furniture suit the ocean-view location of the **Bermuda Inn**. Wall-to-wall carpeting and a dining table compensate for the small size of the accommodations at this two-story motel across the street from a public beach. A pool, however, is right on the grounds if you don't want to make the short trek. Efficiencies cost a bit more. ~ 64 South Ocean Boulevard, Delray Beach; 561-276-5288. MODERATE TO DELUXE.

Riviera Palms Motel is a clean but no-frills 34-room place. No phones in rooms, but the rooms are large and the swimming pool is the place to hang out. ~ 3960 North Ocean Boulevard, Delray Beach; 561-276-3032. BUDGET.

Top of the Bridge is the kind of standby supported by locals and tourists alike. Adorned in a classic color scheme of forest green and salmon and furnished with sturdy club chairs and high-backed banquettes, the huge room manages to be interesting but not stimulating. So it is with the menu, a collection of local seafood, veal, beef, lobster and pasta dishes. It's a comforting choice for people who can afford the tariff but are not in the mood to sample exotic culinary trends, thank you very much. Dinner only and Sunday brunch. Closed Monday. ~ Bridge Hotel, 999 East Camino Real, Boca Raton; 561-368-9500. DELUXE TO ULTRA-DELUXE.

Certain restaurants tend to show up on everyone's Top Ten list. A case in point is **La Vieille Maison**. The people who founded this restaurant used a formula they developed in Fort Lauderdale: an old house, lots of antiques, dark floral carpeting and an expensive menu devoted almost exclusively to Continental cuisine. La Vieille Maison features an eye-catching entrance through wrought-iron gates and a jungle of a garden. Florida seafood gets French treatment in dishes such as the *pavé de merou rôti au maïs bleu* (roasted grouper steak coated with blue cornmeal), served on a bed of leeks with sherry wine. Other specials include quail, lamb, veal and venison. Dining is a leisurely affair here, and the earlier of two nightly seatings is recommended. ~ 770 East Palmetto Park Road, Boca Raton; 561-391-6701. DELUXE TO ULTRA-DELUXE.

Tom's Place is a local favorite secure in its niche as the king of the barbecue hill. This is no place to linger; you come here when you want good food and you want it fast. There's beef stew, fried chicken, generous "fixin's" and, of course, ribs, chicken and pork swimming in a legendary secret sauce. Closed Sunday and Monday. ~ 7251 North Federal Highway, Boca Raton; 561-997-0920. BUDGET TO MODERATE.

They named this tiny roadside eatery **Basil Garden**, but the place is so redolent of garlic they should call it the "stinking rose" garden. Yet this is the kind of warm, neighborhood *ristorante* to which patrons return time and again for seafood and such Italian dishes as pasta and veal specialties including saltimbocca and osso buco. Dinner only. Closed Sunday and Monday. ~ 5837 North Federal Highway, Boca Raton; 561-994-2554. MODERATE TO DELUXE.

The **Seafood Connection Restaurant** is where local diners come when they want to eat well in an attractive setting without breaking the family budget. Lots of green plants, ceiling fans and rattan light fixtures enliven two separate dining rooms. A variety of seafood is prepared in a variety of ways, from unusual combination platters to more elegant dishes such as salmon Wellington. ~ 6998 North Federal Highway, Boca Raton; 561-997-5562. BUDGET TO MODERATE.

Displaced Bostonians aren't the only travelers who'll feel at ease at **Boston's on the Beach**. There's an anything-goes atmosphere at this beach town eatery just across the highway from the surf. Go for a table on the covered porch, as indoor seating is nothing special. Hot entrées include sole, shrimp, lobster, fried clams and a "Cape Cod" broiled platter. ~ 40 South Route A1A, Delray Beach; 561-278-3364. MODERATE TO ULTRA-DELUXE.

The **Fifth Avenue Grill** is an unabashed homage to beef with a handful of seafood and chicken dishes thrown onto the menu as well. Patrons rave about the banana grouper *almondine* (a slab of fresh fish ladled with banana butter sauce) and the Louisiana bread pudding with rum and caramel sauce. The interior feels like a French country inn. ~ 821 South Federal Highway, Delray Beach; 561-265-0122. MODERATE TO DELUXE.

Parked on a corner of Atlantic Avenue, Delray's historic and renovated strolling street, **The Green Owl** is the kind of place where the waitresses call you honey when they take your order. The menu is middle-American lunchtime fare: sandwiches, burgers, soups and salads. This down-home eatery is a popular lunch and breakfast spot. ~ 330 East Atlantic Avenue, Delray Beach; 561-272-7766. BUDGET.

A shining example of the casual dockside hangout, the convivial **Banana Boat Restaurant** has a wooden deck with tables so close to the water that diners can recognize friends cruising the Intracoastal Waterway. The food is good and the setting ideal for a late lunch or hot entrées such as fresh fish, shrimp or teriyaki steak. ~ 739 East Ocean Avenue, Boynton Beach; 561-732-9400. MODERATE TO DELUXE.

SHOPPING   The bubble-gum pink facade and red tile roofs of the **Royal Palm Plaza** make this landmark Boca Raton shopping center easy to spot. It contains shops such as **Maus & Hoffman** (561-368-9983), a branch of the well-known menswear shop featuring a large selection of suits, sportshirts, shoes, ties (many by Hermès) and lightweight hats ideal for the Gold Coast climate. This Spanish-style plaza also houses gift boutiques such as the **Crystal Bowl** (561-391-3678), filled to the brim with decanters, vases, bowls and candlesticks. ~ Located between Palmetto Park Road and Camino Real off Route 1, Boca Raton.

Just north of Royal Palm Plaza is the city's newest shopping gem. Fashioned like a little Mediterranean village, **Mizner Park** is a delightful place. Here you'll find palm-lined stone streets, fountains and tiny pools, as well as peach sandstone buildings decorated with curved balconies, vivid awnings and dozens of clever shops and eateries. There's everything from jewelry stores and high-fashion swimwear to an Israeli art gallery and a large bookstore. But even if you don't buy, strolling here is sheer entertainment. Among the notable stores here are **Swim 'n' Sport** (561-391-3990), which features contemporary swimwear, and **Christy Taylor Gallery** (561-750-7302), where you can find delicate blown-glass sculptures of modern design. ~ Federal Highway, two blocks north of Palmetto Park Road, Boca Raton.

The **Town Center at Boca Raton** is home to a variety of fine shops as well as chain stores. The people who turn out collectibles they call "tomorrow's heirlooms" have a retail outlet at **The Franklin Mint Gallery** (561-392-4144). In this store you will find an array of specialty items such as wildlife prints, porcelain figurines and Rolls Royce models. **Maraolo** (561-391-7001) is a purveyor of elegant shoes and glamorous accessories in leather and exotic fabrics. **Bentley's Luggage** (561-395-2380) stocks national-brand suitcases as well as leather goods, travel accessories and gift items. Town Center also has a place in its heart for larger-size women's fashions: **August Max** (561-392-7494) has casual clothes as well as career ensembles. ~ 6000 West Glades Road, Boca Raton.

Browsing the handful of shops at **Crocker Center** provides a pleasant change from shopping in a full-scale mall. Decorating your home? Stop in **Lois Collection** (561-750-1288) and scan the murals, silk flower arrangements, wood furnishings and china. ~ 5050 Town Center Circle, Boca Raton.

The local branch of Maine's **Snappy Turtle of Kennebunkport** brims with clever clothes and accessories for women and children. ~ 1038 East Atlantic Avenue, Delray Beach; 561-276-8088.

In downtown Delray Beach, **Penelope's Breads and Threads** is a one-of-a-kind mix of handicrafts (mostly woven) and fresh-from-the-oven baked goods. ~ 520 East Atlantic Avenue, Delray Beach; 561-272-1000.

The **Plaza del Mar Shopping Center** (561-585-3311) looks like a bit of Cape Cod with its lowrise, grey-shingled facade. One of the best shops here is **Straw and Substance**. Distinctive gift items include offbeat walking canes (some topped with duck heads), crystal objets d'art and potpourri. ~ Located at the intersection of South Ocean Boulevard and Ocean Avenue, Manalapan.

Atop an 11-story hotel, the **Top of the Bridge Lounge** offers romantic views of the Intracoastal Waterway. You'll find a variety of bands playing jazz and swing Tuesday through Saturday. ~ 999 Camino Real, Boca Raton; 561-368-9500.

NIGHTLIFE

Club Boca is a high-decibel nightclub with a central bar and two dancefloors in back. A big hit with young urban professionals, it offers patio seating in the rear for cooling off after tearing it up to the latest progressive dance music, reggae and disco. Cover. ~ 7000 West Palmetto Park Road, Boca Raton; 561-368-3333.

A large replica of a three-masted schooner makes an unusual centerpiece at **Club Asia**. Every Friday and Saturday night there is dancing to Top-40; on other nights they'll be playing '70s funk, house or alternative music. Cover. ~ Holiday Inn, 1950 Glades Road, Boca Raton; 561-391-4488.

THEATER, OPERA, SYMPHONY AND DANCE   Broadway reproductions, occasionally with guest stars, are the main fare at the **Royal Palm Dinner Theatre**. ~ 303 Southeast Mizner Boulevard, Boca Raton; 561-392-3755.

The **Caldwell Theatre Company** offers a mix of popular comedy and dramatic stage productions during their summer and winter seasons. ~ 7873 North Federal Highway, Boca Raton; 561-241-7432.

BEACHES & PARKS

HIDDEN ►

SOUTH INLET PARK   The least-known beach in Boca Raton, South Inlet Park has 850 feet of soft clean sand. Since it is so small, it is often less crowded than its neighbors to the north and is therefore an especially good choice on weekdays. Swimming and surf angling are very good here. Facilities include picnic areas, restrooms, showers and lifeguards; restaurants and groceries are a short drive away. Day-use fee, $2 to $4. ~ Off South Route A1A, at 1298 South Ocean Boulevard, directly south of Boca Inlet; 561-964-4420.

SOUTH BEACH PARK   The dense tropical growth that characterizes Boca Raton's sand dunes is one of South Beach's greatest charms. In fact, one almost despairs of finding the beach at all, but rest assured, it lies on the other side, accessible via three walkways. This pristine—if rather narrow—swath of semicoarse sand disappears beyond curve after curve of coastline. There's good swimming and snorkeling. You'll find restrooms, showers and lifeguards; restaurants and groceries are a short drive away. ~ 400 North State Road A1A, Boca Raton; 561-393-7810, 561-393-7989.

RED REEF PARK   Touted as a local favorite, the developed beach at Red Reef Park is nearly a mile long and roughly 80 acres in size. A very long boardwalk leads through a veritable forest of seagrapes, palmettos, Australian pine and palm trees before descending to the pristine beach itself, which is composed of pale, loosely packed sand. On the inland side is the Gumbo-Limbo Nature Center. There's excellent surf angling in designated areas. Swimming is very good and snorkeling is good in spots. Facilities include picnic areas, restrooms, showers and lifeguards; restaurants and grocery stores are a short drive away. Day-use fee, $8 to $10. ~ 1400 North State Road A1A, Boca Raton; 561-393-7974.

SPANISH RIVER PARK 🏃 🚲 🏊 🎣 👫 🚤 ⛵ This is really Boca Raton's crowning glory, offering forest shade, sunswept beach and more facilities than any other local park. Perhaps there is a well-enforced city ordinance declaring that all Boca beaches be kept sparkling clean; that would explain the almost primitive look of this wide, oyster-shell-white apron of sand. Within the 93-acre park are dozens of spots for picnicking, including a sheltered area on a lagoon off the Intracoastal Waterway. Swimming is excellent on the beach and you can fish in the Intracoastal Waterway. Facilities consist of picnic areas, restrooms, showers, lifeguards, a boat lagoon, a playground, a pavilion, volleyball courts, a nature trail and bicycle trails. ~ 3001 North State Road A1A, Boca Raton; 561-393-7840, 561-393-7815.

ATLANTIC DUNES PARK 🏊 🎣 Only the eagle-eyed traveler will spot the sign for Atlantic Dunes Park on the first pass. The entrance is nearly invisible, thanks to stands of Australian pines. The soft pale sand beach is so small—the park is only seven acres in all—that it has almost a clubby feel. The beach is fairly narrow and the waves do not break right for bodysurfing, but it's wonderful for strolling and sunbathing away from urban development. Restrooms, showers and a lifeguard are the only facilities. ~ Located off South Route A1A, one mile south of Delray Municipal Beach across from Azalea Avenue. Parking is on the west side of Route A1A; 561-243-7250.

◀ *HIDDEN*

DELRAY MUNICIPAL BEACH 🏊 🎣 Some 7000 feet of very soft light-brown sand fronts the city of Delray Beach. There's something irresistible about a beautiful beach, strewn with shells, that's easy to find, easy to reach and easy to love. Low dunes covered with seagrapes are interspersed with foot paths leading down from the parking area. On crystal-clear days, the Gulf Stream, less than five miles offshore, is visible as a strip of darker blue, often with some wave action to distinguish it. Swimming is outstanding here; bodysurfing is good. Facilities include restrooms, showers, lifeguards and concession stands for cabanas and umbrellas; restaurants and groceries are nearby. ~ Located on Route A1A, with numerous access points from Casuarina Road up to Vista del Mar; 561-243-7250.

GULF STREAM COUNTY PARK 🏊 Since beach access is highly restricted in the posh enclave of Gulf Stream, it's especially satisfying to find this little gem. It's a public park that looks like a private resort landscaped with palmettos, Australian pines and tall seagrapes. A long boardwalk leads to a 600-foot ribbon of white sand. A manmade reef attracts snorkeling enthusiasts. The sole drawback to this beach is some rocks that are submerged at high tide.

Swimming is good at low tide. There are picnic areas, barbecue grills, restrooms, showers and a lifeguard; restaurants and groceries are nearby. ~ At 4489 North Ocean Boulevard south of Briny Breezes; 561-930-5116.

BOYNTON PUBLIC BEACH 🏊 🚶 ⚓ A 1000-foot wooden boardwalk extends the length of the beautifully landscaped park fronting Boynton Beach. From there, dune walkovers lead to a narrow beach, where medium-hard sand slopes deeply to the water's edge. Parking is at a premium so early—or late—arrival is recommended. Swimming is good here. You'll find picnic areas, restrooms, showers, concession stands and lifeguards; restaurants and grocery stores are a short drive away. ~ Off Route A1A one block north of Ocean Boulevard; 561-737-4540.

LANTANA MUNICIPAL BEACH 🏊 🚶 ⚓ Distinguished by abundant shrubbery, including seagrapes as high as palm trees, the approach to Lantana Beach is as attractive as the beach itself. Several boardwalks lead over tall sand dunes to a 746-foot-long strip of dark sand that narrows to as little as ten feet at high tide. Accordingly, the beach has a secluded feel with none of the grandeur of wider, more open stretches of coastline. Facilities include picnic areas, restrooms, showers and lifeguards; restaurants and grocery stores are a short drive away. ~ At Ocean Avenue and Route A1A, Lantana; 561-586-0217, 561-582-9094.

▼▼▼▼▼▼▼▼▼▼▼▼▼
Palm Beach & West Palm Beach

Palm Beach is a town imbued with sheer extravagance and social formalities—daily spa treatments, elegant balls, winsome polo matches—not to mention a certain magic that emanates from all this prosperity. By contrast, West Palm Beach exists as the area's major metropolitan center, a stretch of flat, tropical earth with a sizable downtown area and sprawling residential developments.

Downtown West Palm Beach has two completely different faces. Skirting its eastern boundary is Flagler Street, a three-mile strip of picturesque roadways flanked by rows of massive palm trees and estates. But on the west side of town lies a poorer economic stratum and buildings in need of repair. Around the city are breezy tropical neighborhoods inhabited largely by young professionals who are renovating older homes, as well as retirement centers for wealthy northeasterners.

Lying in the southern shadow of these two communities is Lake Worth, a turn-of-the-century town situated around a beautiful lake. Its historic beachfront is a hot spot for locals and tourists alike.

Unlike southern Miami and Fort Lauderdale, the West Palm Beach area virtually shuts down during the summer months. Hotels offer rates that are 50 to 70 percent off winter prices, and many

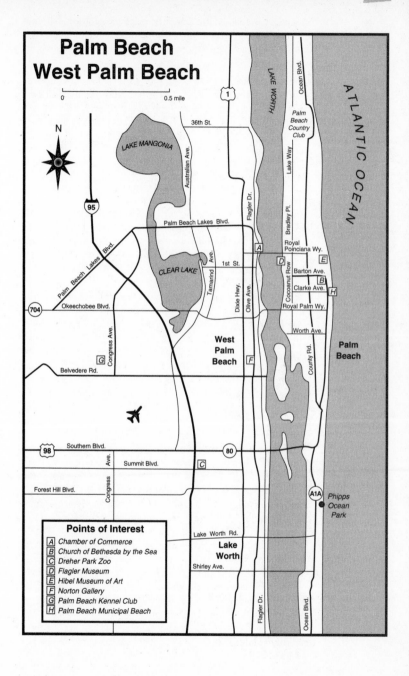

Palm Beach
West Palm Beach

0   0.5 mile

West Palm Beach

Palm Beach

Lake Worth

Points of Interest

A Chamber of Commerce
B Church of Bethesda by the Sea
C Dreher Park Zoo
D Flagler Museum
E Hibel Museum of Art
F Norton Gallery
G Palm Beach Kennel Club
H Palm Beach Municipal Beach

restaurants and shops close completely. That means the beaches are less crowded (yes, you might even find yourself alone on a long stretch of sand) and the universal mood is quite placid.

SIGHTS

As visitors approach the city of Palm Beach, they usually keep an eye out for the **elegant homes** the town is noted for. Along Route A1A south of the city, many mansions are hidden behind tall hedges and looming walls. You'll have better luck in two other places: the blocks between Route A1A and Lake Worth (the Intracoastal Waterway) south of town, and along Ocean Boulevard north of the Breakers Hotel.

HIDDEN ►   The **Church of Bethesda by the Sea** makes for a refreshing pause between more intense sightseeing stops. The walls of the clerestory have stained-glass windows representing the saints of various Christian countries such as St. George of England and St. Joan of France. Hidden behind the church, beyond the flagstone courtyard, is a lovely formal setting known as **Cluett Gardens**. Fountains, benches and unusual botanical species combine with a tiled pond to create a serene retreat. ~ 141 South County Road at Barton Avenue, Palm Beach; 561-655-4554.

The **Society of Four Arts Garden** is a beautifully kept landscape with high walls, decorative fencing and myriad details such as a lichen-covered stone bench. Tiny walkways lead past ponds filled with gold fish to clusters of trees and flowering shrubs and, finally, to an expansive lawned area. Here in the **Philip Hulitar Sculpture Garden** stands a variety of outdoor pieces, ranging from some classic animal forms to more whimsical items such as a six-foot-tall curve of black steel sculpted to form a question mark and bearing a humorous inscription. Closed on weekends from May through November. ~ Off Royal Palm Way one block east of the Intracoastal Waterway, Palm Beach; 561-655-7226.

Additional sightseeing information can be obtained from the **Palm Beach Chamber of Commerce**. ~ 45 Cocoanut Row, Palm Beach; 561-655-3282. Plenty of tourism tips can be obtained at the **Chamber of Commerce of the Palm Beaches**. ~ 401 North Flagler Drive, West Palm Beach; 561-833-3711. The **Palm Beach County Convention and Visitors Bureau** can also be of service. ~ 1555 Palm Beach Lakes Boulevard, West Palm Beach; 561-471-3995.

Also in Palm Beach are some very unusual points of interest. The **Hibel Museum of Art** is a love-it-or-hate-it kind of place devoted to the works of Edna Hibel. As such, it claims to be the only nonprofit art museum in the United States consisting solely of the works of a living female artist. There are ten rooms of paintings, lithographs and drawings, all lovingly displayed in good light. The guides here will tell you all you ever wanted to know, perhaps even more, about Edna Hibel. ~ 150 Royal Poinciana Plaza, Palm Beach; 561-833-6870.

For an instructive lesson on how to spend lots of money, and spend it well, visit the **Henry M. Flagler Museum**. Commanding a close-up view of Lake Worth (the Intracoastal Waterway), Whitehall was built in 1901 by Flagler, the king of the Florida East Coast Railroad and the man credited with putting Palm Beach on the map. The 55-room mansion is a monument to the Gilded Age: period rooms, vast collections of porcelains, paintings and silver. There is so much to see that it's advisable to sign up with a guide who knows which furniture actually belonged to Flagler and which decorative pieces were added later. Allow time to tour The Rambler, the rail car that Flagler himself used. Built in 1886, it was restored with carefully reproduced carpeting, upholstery and window coverings. Admission. ~ Cocoanut Row and Whitehall Way, Palm Beach; 561-655-0868.

Looking at the papered ceiling, inlaid wood, tulip chandeliers and brass flourishes of the Rambler rail car at the Flagler Museum, one wonders if things get any better than this on the Orient Express.

West Palm Beach is a hodgepodge of one-way streets and resuscitated downtown neighborhoods. But there are some gems for the determined visitor. Especially in light of its relatively small size, the **Norton Gallery and School of Art** has an extraordinarily impressive collection. Buddhist sculptures, jade carvings and ceramics can be found in the Chinese collection, and a good selection of paintings by Bonnard, Dufy, Monet, Pissarro, Gauguin and Renoir can be found in the French section. The Norton is famed for its 20th-century American art holdings as well. ~ 1451 South Olive Avenue, West Palm Beach; 561-832-5194.

Far west of the glittering arcades of Palm Beach lies another manmade wonder, the 500-acre wildlife enclave at **Lion Country Safari**. Here, some 63 species of animals roam almost free, while humans, caged in their automobiles with windows rolled up for security, tour the park on paved roads. When Lion Country Safari opened in 1967, it was the first attempt at "cageless zoos" in the United States. While it is a far cry from the Serengeti Plain in Africa, the park is unsurpassed in affording Florida travelers a chance to go eyeball to eyeball with exotic animals—lions, zebras, ostriches, elephants—which they can photograph in a seminatural setting. The attraction also offers a petting zoo, featuring both domestic species and a variety of animals of African and Asian stock. The driving tour takes anywhere from 45 to 60 minutes and can be followed with amusement rides, paddleboat excursions or other diversions. Admission. ~ 2003 Lion Country Road off Route 80, West Palm Beach; 561-793-1084.

The **Dreher Park Zoo** may not be the world's finest, but it has some distinctive features. There is a petting zoo and a special place for South American animals such as the impressive capybara (at about four feet and 100 pounds, the world's largest rodent) and the common rhea, a two-legged feather duster that closely resembles an ostrich. Admission. ~ 1301 Summit Boulevard, West Palm Beach; 561-533-0887.

Dreher Park is also home to the **South Florida Science Museum**, an outstanding facility with compelling experimental exhibits that teach visitors about optical illusions and other scientific phenomena. The **Aldrin Planetarium** has a regular schedule of entertainment, including laser light shows on Saturday nights, while the **Gibson Observatory** is open for stargazing on Friday evenings from dusk until 10 p.m. when skies are clear. Admission. ~ 4801 Dreher Trail North, West Palm Beach; 561-832-1348.

The season in Palm Beach would not be complete without attending a polo match. The most prestigious place to watch the ponies in action is the **Palm Beach Polo**, not only because of its world-class facilities but because its name is linked with that of England's Prince Charles, who has played a few chukkers here. Matches are scheduled every Sunday afternoon from early January until mid-April. Admission. ~ 13420 South Shore Boulevard, West Palm Beach; 561-793-1440.

If you're not interested in watching polo matches, there's always the races—dog races that is. Anyone who's watched horse races will likely be intrigued by greyhound racing. These high-bred dogs run around the track at speeds of up to 40 miles per hour. The place in Palm Beach County to see the action is the **Palm Beach Kennel Club**. There are both day and night races and, of course, plenty of wagering windows. The club also features simulcasting of jai alai. Admission. ~ Belvedere Road and Congress Avenue, West Palm Beach; 561-683-2222.

Palm Beach County has its own point of access to the Everglades, located off a grim stretch of state road far to the west of frontóns and polo fields: the **Arthur R. Marshall Loxahatchee National Wildlife Refuge**. This 145,000-acre refuge is home to a wide variety of reptiles, mammals and waterfowl. The highly endangered Everglade kite feeds here, along with various snakes such as the Everglade indigo snake and yellow rat snake. A haven for wildlife, it is less hospitable to humans, who must hike two trails to explore the refuge's sawgrass ridges, sloughs, wet prairies and tree islands. Before venturing into the region, check out the visitors center located at the park's entrance. Admission. ~ Route 441 and Lee Road, Boynton Beach; 561-734-8303.

LODGING   This is the land of grande dame hotels, dignified resorts of the old school that attract the same well-heeled clientele year in and year out. But smaller, less expensive facilities here also offer access to the same magnificent beaches, marvelous shopping and myriad restaurants.

There's not much besides palm trees and salt air to remind one of the islands at the **Palm Beach Hawaiian Ocean Inn**. A long two-story building contains a variety of accommodations, from standards rooms (each with two double beds) to oceanfront suites on a private beach. Amenities include a pool, restaurant and bar. ~ 3550 South Ocean Boulevard, South Palm Beach; 561-582-5631, 800-457-5631, fax 561-582-5631. DELUXE TO ULTRA-DELUXE.

Several one and two-story buildings are scattered between Ocean Boulevard and the water at the **Beachcomber Sea Cay Motor Apartments**. Furniture in the 50 mid-sized accommodations is distinctive, if a little worn. Fabric vertical blinds and pastel-tiled baths help spiff things up. There are efficiencies available and a pool. ~ 3024 South Ocean Boulevard, Palm Beach; 561-585-4646. DELUXE TO ULTRA-DELUXE.

The decidedly unglamorous **Sea Lord Hotel** has 40 clean apartment suites and rooms and a hideaway feel. Some rooms overlook Lake Worth, all come equipped with fridges and most were refurbished in 1991. ~ 2315 South Ocean Boulevard, Palm Beach; 561-582-1461, 800-638-6127. DELUXE TO ULTRA-DELUXE.

The **Plaza Inn** calls itself Palm Beach's finest bed and breakfast, but it feels more like a charming hotel. Washed a pale pink, the three-story art deco house has been restored so that its wood floors and carved ceilings positively gleam. Each of the 50 rooms offer cozy touches such as handmade comforters and lace draperies, and four-poster beds are offered in the deluxe suites. Amenities include a heated swimming pool and jacuzzi. Bountiful breakfasts are served in a cypress dining room. The ocean is just one block away. ~ 215 Brazilian Avenue, Palm Beach; 561-832-8666, 800-233-2632, fax 561-835-8776. DELUXE TO ULTRA-DELUXE.

The queen of the Palm Beach landscape, the **Breakers Hotel** has been holding court high above the ocean since 1926, when the ceilings of its great public rooms were hand-painted by European artists. Fifteenth-century Flemish tapestries, bronze and crystal chandeliers, and 20-foot-high windows facing courtyard gardens and fountains make this palatial resort one of the most distinctive hotels on the Gold Coast. About 1100 staff members—that's roughly two per guest room—knock themselves out to keep things running smoothly. Accommodations are large and done mostly in seafoam green and sunrise pink. The hotel offers a variety of restaurants, golf courses, tennis courts and an extensive beach club. ~ 1 South County Road, Palm Beach; 561-655-6611, 888-273-2537, fax 561-659-8403. ULTRA-DELUXE.

The **Heart of Palm Beach Hotel** manages to be charming and   ◄ HIDDEN
congenial almost to the point of intimacy, in spite of having 88 accommodations. Rooms are decked out simply in light colors, glass-topped tables and summer-cottage fabrics. Some have tiny lanais near the heated pool out back. In a town that can turn a cold shoulder to travelers, this is that rarity: a home away from home (in a great location to boot, midway between Worth Avenue shops and

the public beach). ~ 160 Royal Palm Way, Palm Beach; 561-655-5600, 800-523-5377, fax 561-832-1201. DELUXE TO ULTRA-DELUXE.

The **Brazilian Court** is the kind of luxury residential-style hotel that appeals to long-term visitors. The 100 accommodations, located in several buildings interspersed with courtyards, are liberally decorated in sunny colors. The Brazilian Court has enjoyed a reputation for excellent service and European ambience since the days it hosted such dashing guests as Errol Flynn, Gary Cooper and Cary Grant. ~ 301 Australian Avenue, Palm Beach; 561-655-7740, 800-552-0335, fax 561-655-0801. ULTRA-DELUXE.

Two of the island's most popular activities—shopping and beaching-it—are easy to pursue from the **Colony Hotel**. Only one-half block from the ocean and a short stroll to posh boutiques, the six-story white complex hugs a Florida-shaped pool and a tiki bar. The 91 cool white guest rooms are styled with floral-print draperies and bedspreads. ~ 155 Hammon Avenue, Palm Beach; 561-655-5430, 800-521-5525, fax 561-659-8104. ULTRA-DELUXE.

HIDDEN ►   Bed and breakfasts are a rare commodity in South Florida, and that makes **Hibiscus House** an incredible find. Tucked discreetly in a historic manicured neighborhood and shrouded in lush vegetation, the charming frame hostelry was built in 1921 as the home of a West Palm Beach mayor. Distinctive period furniture, Oriental rugs and glossy oak floors decorate the sitting rooms and seven bedrooms of the two-story building. Also available at higher rates are a balconied suite and a poolside cottage. Outside you'll find a quaint courtyard where a swimming pool is surrounded by wood decking and vine-covered trellises. All rooms have private baths, trellises and ceiling fans and include a full breakfast. ~ 501 30th Street, West Palm Beach; 561-863-5633, 800-203-4927, fax 561-863-5633. MODERATE.

The **West Palm Beach Bed & Breakfast** has quiet guest rooms in a ten-block historic district about a mile north of downtown. All rooms have private baths and are decorated with white wicker furniture. The best bet is the carriage house with its own entrance and a set of French doors that overlook the swimming pool. This lodging is gay- and lesbian-friendly. ~ 419 32nd Street, West Palm Beach; 561-848-4064, 800-736-4064, fax 561-848-2422. MODERATE TO DELUXE.

Far from the madding crowd at the beach, sequestered on 2200 acres, the **Palm Beach Polo and Country Club** is a world unto itself. This sports mecca attracts tennis buffs and golf and polo players (from Prince Charles down to rank beginners) to some of the finest facilities in Florida. Decor in the one- and two-story condominiums is typically a refined blend of pale colors, fine furnishings and handsome artwork. They also provide pools. ~ 11809 Polo Club Road, West Palm Beach; 561-798-7000, fax 561-798-7345. ULTRA-DELUXE.

It's hard to miss **John G's**—just look for the perpetual lines of customers that stretch around the corner. Revered by locals, who pack the place for succulent fresh fish, John G's is a nautical-style diner that serves hearty portions. For breakfast, try the cinnamon-nut french toast or stuffed croissant; lunch specialties include rainbow trout, fish and chips, and an assortment of sandwiches, soups and salads. ~ 10 South Ocean Boulevard, Lake Worth; 561-585-9860. BUDGET TO MODERATE.

A wee bit of Ireland in Palm Beach, **Dempsey's** is run by a George Dempsey, a retired Florida horse rancher. The place is boisterous, especially during pro football games, and chicken hash Dempsey is the favorite entrée, concocted with sherry as one of the primary seasonings. The crab soup has a drop of scotch. ~ 50 Cocoanut Nut Row, Palm Beach; 407-835-0400. MODERATE.

Only in Palm Beach. Where else would you find women dressed to the hilt in a cheap burger joint? Of course, **Hamburger Heaven** isn't just any burger dive. Since 1945, the local coffee shop has been dealing out famously delicious hamburgers oozing with juice and cheese. Terrazzo floors, a U-shaped bar and the constant clang of dishes create a friendly, unpretentious mood. But if you're feeling slightly pretentious, go for the steak tartar or pot roast. During the summer the restaurant serves only breakfast and lunch. ~ 314 South County Road, Palm Beach; 561-655-5277. BUDGET TO MODERATE.

No socialite worth his or her caviar would consider a visit to Palm Beach complete without a meal at **Café L'Europe**. Sequestered on the upper floor of The Esplanade shopping arcade, this is a very formal restaurant in the Continental style, with acres of polished wood floors and yards of pink linen tablecloths topped with diminutive lamps and lots of fresh flowers. Typical entrées include pecan-crusted salmon, roast duckling and sautéed veal. To one side

---

✔ CHECK THESE OUT—UNIQUE DINING

- *Budget:* Dine on delicious deli food—sandwiches, soups and hearty breakfasts—at **The Egg and You**, a classic booth-and-counter coffee shop. *page 119*
- *Budget to moderate:* Hunker down to some genuine Southern cooking, including flapjacks, catfish and baby back ribs, at the **Log Cabin**, which really is in a log cabin. *page 156*
- *Moderate to deluxe:* Board a boat for **Cap's Place Island Restaurant and Bar,** a legendary locale accessible only by water. *page 127*
- *Deluxe to ultra-deluxe:* Make a selection from an array of mouthwatering Continental dishes at the elegant **La Vieille Maison**. *page 135*

Budget: under $8   Moderate: $8–$16   Deluxe: $16–$24   Ultra-deluxe: over $24

is a "caviar bar" for light seafood dishes and gourmet coffees. ~ 331 South County Road, Palm Beach; 561-655-4020. DELUXE TO ULTRA-DELUXE.

French and Italian are the dominant culinary influences at **Renato's**. Specialties range from pâté and escargot to veal and grilled fish. The setting is French country, with lots of glass and rich Provençal fabrics. Patio seating available during the high season. ~ 87 Via Mizner, Palm Beach; 561-655-9752. DELUXE TO ULTRA-DELUXE.

It's almost impossible to visit Palm Beach without being referred to **Chuck & Harold's Café**. Unfortunately, securing one of the sidewalk tables requires expert timing (or a friendship with the staff). If the bar is noisy, head for the rear of the restaurant, where tables are arranged around the rim of a circular room with a tropical motif. The extensive menu can be confusing; stick to seafood, house-made pastas or barbecued anything and you'll probably be happy. ~ 207 Royal Poinciana Way, Palm Beach; 561-659-1440. MODERATE TO DELUXE.

HIDDEN ▶   Several Palm Beach restaurants inspire unswerving loyalty; a prime example is **Toojay's**. The deli section up front is usually crowded with people in tennis togs ordering take-out; beyond that is a large room that looks out to a courtyard. Toojay's is particularly notable for its elaborate salads, but the dinner menu also includes such hot entrées as crab cakes, lasagna and meat loaf. ~ 313 Poinciana Plaza, Palm Beach; 561-659-7232. BUDGET TO MODERATE.

E. R. Bradley's Saloon started life in the 1920s as a casino and has now evolved into a watering-hole-cum-kitchen especially beloved by the younger crowd. A limited menu relies heavily on salads, steaks, pastas and enormous burgers, which can be enjoyed in either of two small dining rooms or on a side patio. Bradley's is at peak form at brunch, when the chef turns out offbeat dishes such as Cajun eggs and sausage with hollandaise sauce. ~ 111 Bradley Place, Palm Beach; 561-833-3520. BUDGET TO MODERATE.

One of the most affordable Thai restaurants on the Gold Coast is **Wattana Thai**. Curried sea scallops, crisp-fried frog legs and "Volcano Jumbo Shrimp" are among the intriguing listings. Mirrored walls and glass-topped tables reflect the few oriental-red wall decorations in this small restaurant. ~ 7201 South Dixie Highway, West Palm Beach; 561-588-9383. BUDGET TO MODERATE.

"Cooked in sight, must be right," declares the sign outside **Howley's**, a landmark coffee shop outfitted with formica tables, spindly houseplants and windows overlooking the busy street. This is the place to go for homecooked stomach warmers such as a barbecued pork sandwich, meat loaf with brown gravy and roast pork with dressing. Burgers are big, as are the breakfasts. ~ 4700 South Dixie Highway, West Palm Beach; 561-833-5691. BUDGET.

The **Rhythm Café** is a pit stop with real soul. Lingering unob- ◄ *HIDDEN*
trusively along a busy highway, the funky eatery sports dusty
black-and-white checkered floors, '50s and '60s antiques and a bar
top that looks like a piano keyboard. Not the kind of place you'd
expect to dine on gourmet cuisine such as pistachio-crusted yellowtail snapper, caramelized-onion-and-goat-cheese pie, and grilled
filet mignon. The one-page menu, which changes daily, spells pure
gastronomic delight. Dinner only. Closed Sunday and Monday. ~
3238 South Dixie Highway, West Palm Beach; 561-833-3406. MOD-
ERATE TO DELUXE.

Bimini Bay Café is a stop for hipsters after work who hang out
on the outdoor deck gazing across the Intracoastal to Palm Beach.
Great munchies to accompany the high-octane drinks. The best
entrée selections are the grilled fish dishes. Live tunes on weekends.
~ 104 Clematis Street, West Palm Beach; 561-833-9554. MODER-
ATE TO DELUXE.

SHOPPING

Not many people view Lake Worth as a mecca of merchandise, but
in fact Lake Avenue is becoming known for its antique shops,
among other things. At **Carousel Antique Center**, a group of small
dealers has joined forces to offer a wide variety of oldies but goodies. ~ 815 Lake Avenue; 561-533-0678.

A fine literary alcove, **Two On A Shelf** stocks 50,000-plus
books on art, Florida architecture and history and much more. ~
2521 North Dixie Highway, Lake Worth; 561-582-0067.

A stone's throw from Lake Avenue, top-notch paintings and
sculptures by local artists grace the walls of **Lake Avenue Gallery**,
which specializes in contemporary American craftwork, including
some fine jewelry. ~ 709 Lucerne Avenue just off of Lake Avenue,
Lake Worth; 561-585-0003.

West of Lake Worth and worth a special trip is **Hoffman's
Chocolate Shoppe**, a chocolate "shoppe" with a dizzying assortment of fruits and handmade chocolates (some sugar-free) that can
be boxed on the spot or shipped anywhere. While you're trying to
make up your mind, you can watch chocolate-making through big
glass windows or stroll the small but lovely gardens outside. ~
5190 Lake Worth Road, Greenacres; 561-433-4438.

CHIC AVENUE

No visit to Palm Beach is complete without at least a window-shopping
stroll down **Worth Avenue**, which runs from the ocean inland for several
blocks of merchandising paradise. Of particular interest are the small
"vias" tucked away beyond archways leading from Worth Avenue
into tiny courtyards lined with fine boutiques and chic restaurants.

The best-known shopping street on the Gold Coast—if not in all of Florida—is **Worth Avenue** in Palm Beach, a boulevard of chic boutiques that qualifies as a tourist attraction in its own right. A mere few blocks are lined with some 200 stores, ranging from homegrown enterprises to the royalty of internationally known merchant princes.

You will come across many familiar names of designer stores—Cartier, Hermès, Chanel and Sara Fredericks, to name a few—but you can also stop at unique places such as **The Meissen Shop**, which offers an outstanding collection of antique porcelain Meissen figures and dinnerware from the 18th, 19th and early 20th century. You'll also find rare collectors' items by the great Meissen masters. The only store of its kind in the United States, this exquisite shop qualifies as a small museum. ~ 329 Worth Avenue, Palm Beach; 561-832-2504.

HIDDEN ►

On a corner of Worth Avenue, **Cloud 10** will dress little girls in dreamy thousand-dollar dresses—and more affordable ones as well. For little boys, there are hand-painted sneakers, designer jeans and snazzy three-piece suits. ~ 450 South County Road; 561-835-9110.

One bizarre "via" sidetrip is **Gallery Via Veneto**, where a courtyard is sprinkled with bigger-than-life bronze and onyx sculptures. ~ 250 Worth Avenue, Suite 1; 561-835-1399.

On the south side of Worth Avenue, between branches of world-class shops you will find less ubiquitous merchants. Lovers of linen will be elated to discover **Pratesi**, renowned for its luxurious bedsheets. ~ 324 Worth Avenue; 561-655-4414.

Kassatly's, Inc. has been a local favorite for linens (including a marvelous array of handkerchiefs), lingerie and sportswear for men and women since 1923. ~ 250 Worth Avenue; 561-655-5655.

Falling somewhere between an art gallery and a clothing store, **Salvatore Ferragamo** displays its signature silk scarves as if they were valuable paintings. Also on hand are stunning evening bags, dresses, suits and shoes for women, as well as clothing and luggage for men. ~ 200 Worth Avenue; 561-659-0602.

Within the confines of the two-story **Esplanade** you'll find a bevy of famous designer stores as well as one-of-a-kind shops. If time is tight, make a beeline for the **Purple Turtle**, which stocks a high-fashion line of children's clothes with an emphasis on European manufacturers. ~ 150 Worth Avenue; 561-655-1625.

West Palm Beach's shopping thunder is stolen by the tony boutiques across the bridge in Palm Beach, but along Dixie Highway (Route 1) south of Southern Boulevard, is the city's Antique Row, an assortment of dozens of antique stores. On the corner of Roseland and Dixie, look for the Heart of Antique Row, a cozy strip center of seven antique stores like **James and Jeffrey** with collectibles of furniture, dishes, postcards and artwork. ~ 3703-A South Dixie Highway; 561-832-1760.

In the old, restored downtown section of West Palm Beach, the storefronts of Clematis Street have been renovated and the area is becoming an artsy, funky shopping destination. **Last Resort** sells linen and cotton clothes for men and women in a chic, industrial interior. ~ 311 Clematis Street; 561-833-8861.

In an elegant supper-club setting appropriate for Palm Beach, the lounge at the **Colony Hotel** features sophisticated nightcaps and weekend dancing to jazz and big-band sounds 'til the wee hours. ~ 155 Hammon Avenue, Palm Beach; 561-655-5430.

NIGHTLIFE

With its big and brassy bar, Corinthian columns and pink balloon draperies, **Au Bar** looks like a place for celebrities. Little wonder, since the bar made it big the night William Kennedy Smith and his uncle, Senator Ted Kennedy, met a young woman here. (The woman left with Smith and later charged him with rape—but the verdict was in Smith's favor.) Ever since, curious tourists have been pouring in to Au Bar—which responded by charging a $10 weekend cover. Dance music, spun by a deejay, ranges from heavy metal to Viennese waltzes. ~ 336 Royal Poinciana Way, Palm Beach; 561-832-4800.

Illusion Lounge is a hip-hop and reggae club with a young, hip, twenty-something crowd. ~ 4340 Forest Hill Boulevard, Palm Beach; 561-965-0597.

A funky habitat with a warehouse feel, **Respectable Street Café** is smack in the middle of downtown but incredibly easy to miss. A late-night local crowd mingles in cozy booths and listens to live reggae. Also featured is a deejay playing progressive and house music. Cover on weekends and for live shows. ~ 518 Clematis Street, West Palm Beach; 561-832-9999.

One of the hottest area nighttime destinations is **Waterway Café**, an expansive club that rests waterside. Crowds jam the inside bars and spill across a bridge to a floating tiki bar festooned with life preservers. Most nights there are bands playing reggae or rock. ~ 2300 PGA Boulevard, West Palm Beach; 561-694-1700.

THEATER, OPERA, SYMPHONY AND DANCE   The **Raymond F. Kravis Center for Performing Arts** is the venue for a variety of programs, including symphony concerts, musicals, classical concerts and ballet performances. ~ 701 Okeechobee Boulevard, West Palm Beach; 561-832-7469. This is also the site of productions by the **Palm Beach Opera**, which stages performances of major operas between December and March. ~ 561-833-7888.

GAY SCENE   **HeartBreaker**, decorated in grey and mauve and glass block, has the look of a small palladium. Laser lights and recorded house music get feet moving in this popular weekend club for gay men and women. Cover on weekends. ~ 2677 Forest Hill Boulevard, West Palm Beach; 561-966-1590.

H. G. Rooster's is a prime example of a friendly, high-class bar. Ceramic tile, faux finished walls and soft lights give it a stylized ambience, while videos and Top-40 music provide entertainment for its gay clientele. ~ 823 Belvedere Road, West Palm Beach; 561-832-9119.

BEACHES & PARKS

LAKE WORTH MUNICIPAL BEACH 🏊 🏖 ⛵ A forbidding jumble of squat concrete buildings diminishes the charm of this 1200-foot-long public beach. Intended as a casino, the main structure houses an office and a couple of shops. Next door is a large freshwater public pool. Soft cream-colored sand and substantial surf action nevertheless make this one of the prettiest beaches in the area. For a good view of the beach, walk out onto the long fishing pier. There's pier or surf fishing. The swimming here is first-rate and the surfing is very good south of the pier. Facilities include picnic areas, barbecue grills, a playground, restrooms, showers, lifeguards and concession stands. ~ Routes 802 and A1A (South Ocean Boulevard); 561-533-7367.

JOHN PRINCE PARK 🏃 🚴 🏊 ⛵ 🏖 🛶 🚤 ⛴ Located on the shores of Lake Osborne, John Prince Park devotes more than 600 acres of its 1000 acres to recreational facilities. Graced with grassy picnic areas and lake views and dotted with trees, the park is a very relaxing place to spend an entire day. You may engage in freshwater fishing. There are picnic areas, restrooms, a nature trail, a softball field, a bicycle path, a par course, a wheelchair course and tennis courts; restaurants and grocery stores are nearby. ~ 2700 6th Avenue South, Lake Worth; 561-966-6600.

▲ There are 265 sites for tents and RVs; hookups available; $14 to $17.50 per night.

PHIPPS OCEAN PARK 🏊 🏖 🏄 One of the few public beaches in the vicinity of Palm Beach, this low-profile park is easily overlooked. The sand is soft and pale on this 1300-foot beach. Otherwise, it is unremarkable. Swimmers should note that there is quite a drop-off just beyond the high-water mark. Facilities include picnic areas, restrooms, showers and lifeguards; restaurants and grocery stores are nearby. ~ Located one and a half miles north of Lake Worth Pier in Palm Beach; 561-585-9203.

PALM BEACH MUNICIPAL BEACH 🏊 🏖 🏄 Though mostly invisible from the highway, there is over a mile of public beach on the other side of the seawall along South Route A1A. The pale, pink-tinged sand virtually disappears at points, but a good place to set up camp is at **Clarke Avenue Beach** at the foot of Clarke Avenue. The lifeguards at the main city beach can warn you against places where obstructions lie beneath the mint-green seawater (there are no lifeguards at Clarke Avenue Beach; proceed with caution). Given how much of Palm Beach is strictly private property, one gets an almost giddy feeling about enjoying this long stretch of public beach. Swimming is excellent and you'll find great waves at the end of Hammon Avenue. Facilities are limited to lifeguards; restaurants are nearby. ~ Major access points are between Hammon Avenue and Barton Avenue; 561-838-5485.

▼▼▼▼▼▼▼▼▼▼▼▼
Northern Palm Beach County

This northern ledge of the Gold Coast is arguably one of its most scenic. The frenetic development that blankets Fort Lauderdale and much of Palm Beach County has barely brushed these windswept shores. In an effort to preserve what nature has bestowed upon them, Jupiter residents have long restricted new construction and thus protected their beaches from highrise buildings. Life is still quiet in these reaches, unhindered by the fast-paced social set of Palm Beach and void of any real industry except tourism.

SIGHTS

A boat ride on the Intracoastal Waterway is a stressless way to tour northern Palm Beach County. *The Star of Palm Beach*, a replica of a Mississippi River paddlewheeler, cruises out of **Star Landing**. The boat accommodates 300 passengers on an enclosed lower main deck and a promenade deck above. The captain will undoubtedly deliver a spiel laced with gossip, tall tales and some actual facts as you putt-putt past the glorious mansions lining the Intracoastal Waterway between Singer Island and Palm Beach. Luncheon, brunch and dinner-dance cruises are currently available. Admission. ~ Phil Foster Park, under the Blue Heron Bridge, Riviera Beach; 561-842-0882.

Heading north from Palm Beach, Route A1A merges occasionally with Route 1 as its heads toward Juno Beach. There's not much traditional sightseeing in this town, but ◆◆◆◆◆◆◆◆◆◆◆◆◆◆◆◆◆◆◆◆◆◆
what's here tends to be outdoors-oriented. The **Marinelife Center of Juno Beach** forms the centerpiece of Loggerhead Park. A small but enthusiastic and knowledgeable staff explains the ecology of sea turtles and shows specimens. Various marine organisms and other small displays fill the remainder of this small but engaging science museum. During the summer, the museum conducts "turtle walks" along a nearby beach. ~ 1200 Route 1; 561-627-8280.

Be forewarned: the complex waterways around Jupiter pose a challenge to the driving visitor. You may make several passes before finding a particular attraction.

Be sure to look for the picturesque **Dubois House**, built in the late 1890s by Harry Dubois. His new bride wanted a water view, and she apparently got it: the house is set atop a 20-foot-high, 90-foot-long American Indian shell mound (bits of which the family allegedly sold over the years). Aside from a coat of paint over previously plain cypress walls and the construction of a coquina rock fireplace, the house is said to look much as it did in the early part of the century. Period furnishings include the old Dubois dining set and a piano, and other objects donated later such as a treadle sewing machine and a food safe. Open on Wednesday afternoon only. ~ Dubois Park, Jupiter; 561-747-6639.

The **Loxahatchee Historical Museum**, housed in a re-created Florida cracker-style building, is a one-room exhibit hall that tracks local history for the past 10,000 years. In addition to pre-historic American Indian displays, you'll find artifacts galore, all packed wall-to-wall in this tiny but intriguing showplace. The museum also has a traveling-exhibit room that features exhibits from the Smithsonian and the Florida History Museum. The museum store sells books, cards and other gift shop items. Admission. ~ Burt Reynolds Park, 805 North Route 1, Jupiter; 561-747-6639.

The oldest existing structure in Palm Beach County is the **Jupiter Inlet Lighthouse**. This red brick landmark, constructed by the U.S. Lighthouse Service in 1860, has a small museum at its base featuring historical artifacts and other memorabilia related to the area. Open Sunday afternoon only. Tours of the Jupiter Inlet Lighthouse are arranged by the Loxahatchee Historical Museum. ~ Jupiter Inlet; 561-747-6639.

LODGING   The **Tahiti on the Ocean** is a two-story, 52-unit structure that stretches from the highway all the way to the sands of Singer Island. Moderately priced motel rooms have two double beds and fully tiled baths, but not much in the way of frills. Furnishings are a mixture of dark veneer and provincial designs. On site you'll find two pools, a croquet court and a putting green. Efficiencies containing a bedroom, bath and kitchen are available. Both one- and two-bedroom apartments are also available. ~ 3920 North Ocean Drive, Riviera Beach; 561-848-9767, fax 561-881-2116. MODERATE TO DELUXE.

HIDDEN ►   Exceptional value lies beyond the unassuming exterior of **Bellatrix**. It looks like just another roadside motel, but a typical room features high ceilings, one entire wall made of mirrors, and queen-sized sleeper sofas. This 14-unit motel, with efficiencies and one-bedroom apartments, offers dockage at the back door on the Intracoastal Waterway. Pool, barbecue and free laundry facilities are provided. ~ 1000 East Blue Heron Boulevard, Singer Island; 561-848-4815. MODERATE TO DELUXE.

The place to stay in Jupiter is the **Jupiter Beach Resort**. The rooms are so endearingly decorated with rattan and wicker and floral fabrics that most guests would never guess the hotel's size— 186 rooms. Standard rooms with two double beds are a bit cramped, but there is a balcony with a view of the splendid beach. They also have a pool. ~ Route A1A and Indiantown Road, Jupiter; 561-746-2511, 800-228-8810, fax 561-744-1741. ULTRA-DELUXE.

The Exotic Game
of Jai Alai

They call it the fastest game on two feet, and it's one of the oldest ball games in the world, yet jai alai remains a mystery to most Americans. That's probably because there are only ten places to play the game in the United States. Of those, six are located in Florida. On the Gold Coast, there are *frontóns*—large arenas with indoor courts built especially for jai alai—at **Dania Jai Alai**. ~ 301 East Dania Beach Boulevard, Dania; 954-426-4330.

The best way to learn how jai alai is played is to observe a few games. But it does help to know a little bit about how the sport developed and what is happening on the court. Since the ball frequently travels at 150 miles per hour, there is a great deal of action.

Jai alai (pronounced hi-li) originated in the Pyrenees Mountains of northern Spain during the 15th century. Basque villagers decided the game of handball would be considerably enhanced if they used a breadbasket to catch and sling the ball. Eventually, the basket evolved into the curved *cesta* used today. The *pelota* developed into a ball smaller than a baseball but as hard as a golf ball.

In many ways, jai alai resembles the game of handball. The game is played on a three-walled court called a *cancha*, normally 175 feet long. A wire fence on the fourth side of the court protects spectators from the action. To their right is the *frontis* (front wall), usually made of granite to resist the force of the *pelota*. In both singles and doubles, the point is to hurl the ball against the front wall with such finesse that it cannot be hit by the opposition. The agility of professional jai alai players is astounding to watch, especially since it's nearly impossible for spectators to anticipate where the ball is going to rebound from the wall.

A typical evening of jai alai (a Basque term meaning "merry festival") includes 14 games, each lasting approximately 15 minutes with 10-minute intermissions. Spectators are allowed to place a wide variety of bets: win, place, show, daily doubles, quiniela doubles, quinielas, perfectas, superfectas, trifectas, trisuper and Pick 3.

It takes a while to get the hang of it, but the more you know the particulars (or the more money you have riding on the outcome), the more exciting you will find this fast-paced sport.

DINING

HIDDEN ►

Tucked under the Blue Heron Bridge like some genial troll, the **Crab Pot** doubles as a time machine taking patrons back to simpler, lazier days on the river. Start your meal with a cool drink at the chickee bar (*chickee* being Seminole for thatched roof) while you take time to adjust to the relaxed, easy-does-it ambience. Then try something from the raw bar or a full seafood dinner of stone crab claws, stuffed flounder, scallops, shrimp, or the trademark platter of three different versions of fresh crab. Somehow everything tastes better when eaten in an open-air waterfront setting. ~ 386 East Blue Heron Boulevard, Riviera Beach; 561-844-2722. MODERATE TO DELUXE.

Sinclair's American Grill benefits from its sophisticated tropical decor, a blend of light woods, luxuriant foliage and muted color combinations. The kitchen seems to do best with grilled meats; seafood dishes and more elaborate concoctions can be a disappointment. With restrained expectations, Sinclair's can offer an extremely pleasant experience. ~ Jupiter Beach Resort, Indiantown Road and Route A1A, Jupiter; 561-746-2511. MODERATE TO DELUXE.

HIDDEN ►

At the top of our list of reasons for visiting the Gold Coast is the opportunity to dine outdoors on balmy evenings. A fabulous place to indulge in this sensuous experience is **Crab House**. Some regulars do prefer the large, casual dining room with its knotty pine, wooden trellises and replicas of marine animals, but nothing compares with the outside tables, in full view of the scenic Jupiter Inlet and the lighthouse across the way. (If you're going for breakfast, try to arrive in time to watch the sunrise.) The menu lists Maryland blue crabs, pan-fried trout, chicken and beef. ~ 1065 North Route A1A, Jupiter; 561-744-1300. MODERATE TO DELUXE.

The **Log Cabin** looks as though it should be nestled against some hazy Carolina mountain. This true find is a real log cabin, wonderfully furnished with country antiques and permeated with rough hewn oak floors, cedar paneling and vaulted beam ceilings. The hearty fare is strictly Southern, with specialties such as baby

BURT REYNOLDS RANCH

Nestled out in the rural part of Jupiter is the **Burt Reynolds Ranch**. Burt fans will recognize the area (which doubles as a film studio) from a number of his movies, including *Smokey and the Bandit* and *The Man From Left Field*. A tour is given daily of the grounds and the museum, which displays a collection of movie memorabilia. A kiddie petting zoo, with emus, goats and horses, is a side attraction. The gift shop is the best spot to stock up on Burt paraphernalia. Admission. ~ 16133 Jupiter Farms Road, Jupiter; 561-744-2230.

back ribs, fried Okeechobee catfish, Brunswick stew and flapjacks blanketed in hot syrup. With such a scrumptious lineup, who could resist this place? ~ 631 North A1A, Jupiter; 561-746-6877. BUDGET TO MODERATE.

Tucked into an innocuous strip shopping center, **Thaicoon** serves consistently good Thai food at different spice levels for reasonable prices. Take-out is also available. ~ 450 North Lake Boulevard, North Palm Beach; 561-848-8538. MODERATE.

The outstanding shopping possibilities dwindle north of Palm Beach itself. For a last-ditch effort at toting back souvenirs, comb through **Sea Shell City**, noted for its assortment of shells, collected from all over the world. ~ 2100 Broadway, Riviera Beach; 561-844-2576.

SHOPPING

Cadazzle is chockablock with swimsuits, cover-ups and beachy accessories. ~ 2442 PGA Boulevard, Palm Beach Gardens; 561-775-7441.

Singer Island's **Ocean Mall**, a cluster of low-slung beachfront buildings and modules, does offer some interesting window shopping as well as unusual stores. Brightly painted wooden birds peek out from **Singer Island Boutique**, a beachy shop filled with unique and handpainted clothes as well as unusual gifts. ~ 2419 Ocean Avenue, Singer Island; 561-842-7177.

Walking into **Club Safari** is like stepping into an Indiana Jones film. Webbed with vines and spidery trees, this faux jungle has idols, bulls and other Disneylike characters that sing and blow smoke. Bring your dancing shoes—everyone jams to energized acid, house and techno music, spun by a deejay. Cover on weekends. ~ 8000 RCA Boulevard, in the Marriott Hotel, Palm Beach Gardens; 561-622-7024.

NIGHTLIFE

Jox Sports Club is guaranteed to satisfy the "upscale jock" in the crowd. Shoot a game of hoops or pool, or jam on the big dancefloor, mesmerized by 50 video monitors. Top-40 music is compliments of a deejay. Cover on Saturdays. ~ 200 North Route 1, Jupiter; 561-744-6600.

RIVIERA BEACH MUNICIPAL BEACH 🏊 🎣 This is a picture-postcard beach, replete with hard-packed powder-white sand. Backed by numerous highrise hotels and condominiums, it is still wide enough to remain in full sun most of the day. It is an outstanding beach for strolling or jogging, as well as swimming in mild surf. There are restrooms, showers and lifeguards; restaurants and groceries are nearby. ~ Located due east of the Blue Heron Boulevard Bridge off Route A1A, Singer Island; 561-845-4079.

BEACHES & PARKS

OCEAN REEF PARK 🏊 🎣 Sandwiched between hotels, Ocean Reef Park is landscaped with Australian pines, seagrapes and numerous palm trees. With grey squirrels darting through the underbrush and picnic areas scattered far apart, it is a very pleasant place for a midday stop. Wooden dune crossovers lead to a wide dark-sand beach. There's good swimming here. Facilities include picnic areas, a playground, restrooms, showers and lifeguards; restaurants and grocery stores are nearby. ~ Located about three-fourths of a mile north of the Blue Heron Boulevard Bridge off North Route A1A.

HIDDEN ► **JOHN D. MACARTHUR BEACH STATE PARK** 🏃 ⛵ 🛶 🎣 👣 When you want to get away from it all, head up Route A1A on Singer Island. From the parking lot you can take a tram or walk the quarter-mile-long boardwalk to the beach. On the other side of a tall sand dune is a completely undeveloped beach of soft mocha-colored sand. If you walk north, you'll soon be completely out of sight of the oceanfront hotels. It's a Robinson Crusoe kind of place, where you have to take everything you need. The surf is mild here. Swimming is excellent at the first beach. As for skindiving, this beach has one of the best shoreside limestone reefs in this part of Florida. Facilities consist of picnic areas, restrooms, showers, nature trails and a nature center. Day-use fee, $3.50. ~ 10900 South Route A1A, Singer Island, North Palm Beach; 561-624-6950.

HIDDEN ► **JUNO BEACH** ⛵ 🎣 👣 This unmarked stretch of oceanfront lies nearly out of sight of the bluff-top highway. A narrow band of soft dark sand extends some 2600 feet on this underpopulated part of the coast. Roadside parking is at a minimum, and it takes a bit of ingenuity to find your way down to the beach. There's first-rate swimming here, and surf fishing is permitted. Facilities include a picnic area, restrooms, showers and a playground. ~ Located in Juno Beach off Route A1A approximately three-fourths of a mile north of Donald Ross Road; 561-966-6600.

LOGGERHEAD PARK 🏃 ⛵ Extending from Route 1 east and encompassing some 900 feet of beach, this public park contains an observatory tower, recreational offices and the Marinelife Center of Juno Beach. Swimming is permitted. There are restrooms, picnic areas, a playground, tennis courts, a nature trail and a lifeguard. ~ 1200 Route 1, Juno Beach; 561-627-8280.

CARLIN PARK ⛵ 🛶 🎣 👣 This developed park fronts 3000 feet of rock-strewn beach, accessible via boardwalk. Rimmed with Australian pines and seagrapes, the dark, soft sand beach is rather narrow. Across the street is a softball diamond, six tennis courts lit for night play, a parcourse and a duck pond. You'll find great swimming and surf angling here. Other facilities are picnic areas, restrooms, showers, lifeguards, concession stands. ~ Off Route A1A in Jupiter, south of Indiantown Road; 561-966-6600.

JUPITER BEACH PARK 🏊 ⛵ 🎣 ⚓ This developed beach extends 1700 feet south of the Jupiter Inlet. The sand is grainy and chocolate-colored, and rocky outcroppings lie near the high-water mark. It's a good beach for walking and for watching boats cruise in and out of Jupiter Inlet. Swimming and surf fishing are also pretty good here. Facilities include picnic areas, restrooms, showers and lifeguards; restaurants and groceries are a short drive away. ~ On Jupiter Beach Road off Route A1A, Jupiter; 561-966-6600.

BLOWING ROCKS PRESERVE 🚶 🏊 This wild area of coastline would look more appropriate in the Galapagos Islands than in Florida. What makes it intriguing are the extensive rock formations that comprise most of the beach. Only 4000 feet long, Blowing Rocks has a wild, windswept appearance, though much salt-tolerant vegetation manages to survive on the dunes. Try to arrive at high tide, when the surf occasionally blows water through holes in the outcroppings. Guided tours are offered on Wednesday and Sunday, or you can stroll the nature trails on your own. Swimming is good in the summer. ~ Off Route A1A, a mile south of the Martin County line; 561-747-3113.

◄ *HIDDEN*

Deep-sea fishing for marlin, shark, dolphin and sailfish is one of the most popular sports on the Gold Coast, and there seems to be no end to charter outfits in the area.

▼▼▼▼▼▼▼▼▼▼▼▼
Outdoor Adventures

SPORT-FISHING

For sportfishing outfits, contact **Flamingo Fishing**. ~ 801 Seabreeze Boulevard in the Bahia Mar Yacht Basin, Fort Lauderdale; 954-462-9194. Another one is **Captain Bill's**. ~ Bahia Mar Yacht Basin, Fort Lauderdale; 954-522-1333. In Boynton Beach, the place to call is **Drift Boat Two Georges**. ~ 728 Casa Loma Boulevard, Boynton Beach; 561-732-4411. In the Jupiter area, try your luck with **Blue Water Sportfishing**. ~ 1095 North Route A1A, Jupiter; 561-743-6942.

The most economical approach, clearly, is to pay the nominal fee to fish off **Anglin's Fishing Pier**. You can rent equipment, buy bait and fish to your heart's content 24 hours a day. ~ 2 Commercial Boulevard, Lauderdale-by-the-Sea; 954-491-9403.

BOATING

Fort Lauderdale, dubbed "The Venice of America" for its extensive canal system, is a boater's paradise. The Intracoastal Waterway, which extends the length of the Gold Coast, can be explored via sailboat or motorboat.

You can charter a sailboat or rent powerboats at **American Boat Rental**. ~ 1005 Seabreeze Boulevard, Fort Lauderdale; 954-761-8845. If you can handle a Hobie Cat, contact **Radical Surf & Sail**. ~ 615 Ocean Drive, Pompano Beach; 954-781-0033. **Fun**

Boards offers lessons and rents a variety of sailboats. ~ 500 South Ocean Boulevard, Delray; 561-272-3036.

The ubiquitous **Club Nautico** has several locations for renting powerboats. One is in Fort Lauderdale. ~ Pier 66; 954-523-0033. The other is in Pompano Beach. ~ 101 North Riverside Drive, in the Sand's Harbor Resort Marina; 954-942-3270.

Renting a boat near Jupiter provides easy access to both Palm Beach county waters and the intriguing waterways of the Treasure Coast to the north. **Jupiter Hills Lighthouse and Marina** rents pontoon boats and powerboats. ~ 18261 Southeast Federal Highway, Tequesta; 561-744-0727.

DIVING

The clear waters along the Gold Coast create sensational conditions for a variety of water sports. Coral reefs, sunken wrecks and abundant marine life off the 23-mile coastline of Broward County, in particular, afford almost limitless scuba diving and snorkeling opportunities.

One of the most highly respected dive shops is **Pro Dive**, which offers daily reef and wreck dives as well as basic, open-water and advanced certification classes. ~ Bahia Mar Yachting Center, Fort Lauderdale; 954-761-3413. Also in Fort Lauderdale is the **Lauderdale Diver**. ~ 1334 Southeast 17th Street, Fort Lauderdale; 954-467-2822.

Similar services are available through **Divers Unlimited**. ~ 6023 Hollywood Boulevard, Hollywood; 954-981-0156. In Boynton Beach, try **Dive Shop II**. ~ 700 Casa Loma Boulevard; 561-734-5566. For dive rentals and charters in West Palm Beach, contact **Dixie Divers**. ~ 1401 South Military Trail; 561-969-6688.

Force E has outlets in Fort Lauderdale at 2160 West Oakland Park Boulevard, 954-735-6227; in Pompano Beach at 2700 East Atlantic Boulevard, 954-943-3483; and in Boca Raton at 877 East Palmetto Park Road, 561-368-0555.

SURFING & WIND-SURFING

Surfers and windsurfers will find an endless summer on the Fort Lauderdale waters. In Fort Lauderdale, surfboards, boogie boards and skin boards can be rented from BC **Surf & Sport**. ~ 1495 North Federal Highway; 954-564-0202. Windsurf boards can be rented at **Fun Boards**. ~ 500 South Ocean Boulevard, Delray; 561-272-3036.

WATER-SKIING

In Fort Lauderdale, you can rent boats, as well as waverunners, at **Bill Sunrise Watersports**. They offer professional instruction. ~ 2025 East Sunrise Boulevard; 954-761-1672.

Waverunners—like two-person jet skis, only more stable—are also available in Fort Lauderdale at **Surf Water Sports**. ~ On the beach in front of the Marriott Harbor Beach Hotel; 954-462-7245.

Instruction is available at **McGinnis Ski School.** ~ 2421 Southwest 46th Avenue, Fort Lauderdale; 954-584-9007. Also try **Lyle Lee's Ski School.** ~ 3701 Northwest 9th Avenue, Pompano Beach; 954-943-7766.

An unusual twist is waterskiing without a boat, something you can try at **Ski River.** A contraption known as Ski Rixen involves a cable that pulls skiers around a lake. ~ 6601 North Powerline Road at Quiet Waters Park, Pompano Beach; 954-429-0215.

PARA-SAILING

On a clear day, one of the loveliest sights in Fort Lauderdale is parasailors soaring above the ocean. Call **Surf Water Sports.** ~ Located on the beach in front of the Marriott Harbor Beach Hotel; 954-462-7245.

GOLF

The Gold Coast climate is ideal for such sports as golf. Dozens of courses dot the Greater Fort Lauderdale area, including many semiprivate clubs that welcome nonmembers.

Robert Trent Jones designed the 18-hole course at the **American Golfers Club.** ~ 3850 North Federal Highway, Fort Lauderdale; 954-564-8760. **Bonaventure Country Club** also has a challenging course. ~ 200 Bonaventure Boulevard, Fort Lauderdale; 954-389-2100. In Deerfield Beach, try **Deer Creek Golf Club.** ~ 2801 Deer Creek Country Club Boulevard, Deerfield Beach; 954-421-5550. **Grand Palms Golf Country Club** is another option. ~ 110 Grand Palms Drive, Pembroke Pines; 954-431-8800. **City of Lauderhill Municipal Golf Course** is a duffer's delight. ~ 4141 Northwest 16th Street, Lauderhill; 954-730-2990.

In Delray Beach, visitors may play a few holes at **Delray Beach Golf Club.** ~ 2200 Highland Avenue; 561-243-7380. Also in Delray Beach is **Kings Point Par Three.** ~ 7000 West Atlantic Avenue; 561-499-0140.

✔ CHECK THESE OUT—UNIQUE OUTDOOR ADVENTURES

- Fly high above the Fort Lauderdale coastline as you join the increasing number of vacationers who sign up for a parasailing adventure. *page 161*
- Whizz across the water on waterskis, tethered to a boat in front of you—or to a Ski Rixen!—as you experience the sport for which Florida is famous. *page 160*
- Stay on terra firma—or not so firma, depending on your skill—rent rollerblades and cruise the region's level bike paths. *page 162*
- Explore the canals of the Intracoastal Waterway in a boat; lessons and a variety of craft can be had throughout the area. *page 159*

If you're in Boynton Beach, tee off at **Cypress Creek Country Club**. ~ 9400 South Military Trail; 561-732-4202. **Boynton Beach Municipal Golf Course** is another choice. ~ 8020 Jog Road; 561-969-2200.

There are also many courses in Palm Beach County that are open to the public. **Boca Raton Municipal Golf Course** is one. ~ 8111 Golf Road, Boca Raton; 561-483-6100. Another one worth checking out is **Red Reef Executive Golf Course**. ~ 1111 North Ocean Boulevard, Boca Raton; 561-391-5014. If you can take a break from the action in Palm Beach, head to **North Palm Beach Country Club**. ~ 951 Route 1, North Palm Beach; 561-626-4343. There's also **West Palm Beach Country Club**. ~ 7001 Parker Avenue; 561-582-2019.

TENNIS

The tennis courts of south Florida have produced such champions as Chris Evert Lloyd. We can't guarantee your backhand will improve, but we can guarantee enough courts to go around.

Courts and instruction are available at **George English Park**. ~ 1101 Bayview Drive, Fort Lauderdale; 954-396-3620. Give **Holiday Park** a try. ~ 701 Northeast 12th Avenue, Fort Lauderdale; 954-761-5378. In Hollywood, there's **West Lake Park**. ~ 751 Sheridan Street, Hollywood; 954-926-2410. The City of Boca Raton offers instruction at **Memorial Park**. ~ 271 Northwest 2nd Avenue; 561-393-7978. The **Palm Beach Parks and Recreation Department** can direct out-of-towners to courts in their vicinity. ~ 561-964-4420. In Lake Worth, there are courts at **John Prince Park**. ~ 2700 Sixth Avenue South, Lake Worth; 561-964-4420. Practice your serve at **Lake Worth Racquet and Swim Club**. ~ 4090 Cocoanut Road, Lake Worth; 561-967-3900.

ROLLER-BLADING

Florida's flat terrain and abundance of bike paths make rollerblading very popular. You can rent rollerblades at several places.

A good place to try is the **International Bike Shop**. ~ 1900 East Sunrise Boulevard, Fort Lauderdale; 954-764-8800. **Palm Beach Bicycle Trail Shop** also rents 'blades. ~ 223 Sunrise Avenue, Palm Beach; 561-659-4583.

BIKING

Since southeast Florida is almost entirely level, bicycling is an easy way to get around. The best places to ride in the Fort Lauderdale area are along the wide paved roads on the west side of the city, such as **Nob Hill Road** north of Broward Boulevard and **Atlantic Boulevard** (which parallels Route A1A on the east side).

In Dania, the smooth road inside **John U. Lloyd State Park** is a good cycling route (four miles round trip). In this area, group rides are organized by **Mike's Cyclery**. ~ 5429 North Federal Highway, Fort Lauderdale; 954-493-5277. Rides are also set by **Big Wheel**. ~ 6847 Taft Street, Hollywood; 954-962-7857.

For scenic routes, it's hard to beat the one that parallels the **Intracoastal Waterway** on the west side of Palm Beach. The paved trail begins just north of the Flagler Bridge and runs nearly to the tip of the island. Cycling is also the best way (short of a personal invitation) to see the mansions in Palm Beach, on both the narrow interior streets and the wider avenues such as **Ocean Boulevard**, which runs north of Royal Poinciana Way to the northern tip of the island.

A trail runs along the west side of **Route A1A** between Deerfield Beach and Boca Raton, adjacent towns on the Broward/Palm Beach county line.

To join the Saturday morning 38-mile group ride from Boca Raton to the Lake Worth pier and back, call **Boca Schwinn**. ~ 3150 North Federal Highway, Boca Raton; 561-391-0800.

Bike Rentals   You can rent bicycles in Fort Lauderdale from **International Bike Shop**. ~ 1900 East Sunrise Boulevard, Fort Lauderdale; 954-764-8800. Another rental outlet is **Palm Beach Bicycle Trail Shop**. ~ 223 Sunrise Avenue, Palm Beach; 561-659-4583.

Thanks to its completely flat landscape and year-round high temperatures, the Gold Coast is not known for its hiking trails. The best places to hike range from the beaches—where the pack is hard enough—to various parks and nature preserves. All distances for hiking trails are one way unless otherwise noted. Few places allow overnight camping.

HIKING

SOUTH BROWARD COUNTY   Though not really a hiking trail, a good walk uninterrupted by traffic lights can be enjoyed at **Broadwalk** (1.5 miles), the paved path, closed to automobiles, that runs beside Hollywood Beach.

FORT LAUDERDALE   In **Hugh Taylor Birch State Recreation Area** there is a paved hiking trail through much of the 180 acres of coastal hammock and other plant communities.

Two trails lead through different parts of the Secret Woods Nature Center (954-791-1030) in Fort Lauderdale. **Laurel Oaks** is a short, 1200-foot wood-chip trail where you may spot birds and squirrels rustling among fall leaves. This makes a good combination walk with **New River Trail**, a 3200-foot-long boardwalk leading through various habitats: a raised portion leads to a stand of pond apple and mangrove trees along the south fork of the New River. There is a self-guiding trail book, and this trail is wheelchair accessible.

NORTH BROWARD COUNTY   The Fern Forest Nature Center (954-970-0150) in Pompano Beach has three trails. **Cypress Creek Trail** (.5 mile) is a boardwalk excursion; ask for a self-guiding trail booklet and the arboretum guide booklet. **Prairie Overlook Trail** (1 mile) loops past an open prairie, providing eye-level views of oak-cabbage palm communities. **Maple Walk** (.3 mile) runs through a red maple swamp that is often quite wet during the late summer rainy season.

A good hike is available on Saturday mornings at Deerfield Island Park (Deerfield Beach), accessible by boat only from the dock on Riverview Road, near the Riverview Restaurant. The 1500-foot **Mangrove Trail** boardwalk is an entrancing exploration through eight acres of red, white and black mangrove. **Coquina Trail** is a slightly rocky path that leads to a lookout over the Intracoastal Waterway. Guided nature tours offer information on the varied plant life of this secluded island.

DELRAY BEACH   Within Delray Beach's **Morikami Japanese Park** is a path (1.5 miles) through a peaceful pine forest.

PALM BEACH AND WEST PALM BEACH   A bike path (5 miles) in **John Prince Park** in Lake Worth provides lakeside hiking opportunities. There is also a nature trail in this urban park.

▼▼▼▼▼▼▼▼▼▼▼
Transportation
CAR

Route 95 is the major north-south artery on the Gold Coast. Closer to the ocean, **Route 1** (Federal Highway) is used largely for local traffic. On the coast itself, **Route A1A** parallels the Atlantic almost the entire distance from Hollywood to Jupiter.

AIR

Two airports are located on the Gold Coast: Fort Lauderdale Airport and Palm Beach International Airport. Also convenient is Miami International Airport, about an hour's drive southwest of Fort Lauderdale (see the "Transportation" section in Chapter Two).

The **Fort Lauderdale Airport** has regularly scheduled service by Air Canada, Continental Airlines, Delta Airlines, Northwest Airlines, Trans World Airlines, United Airlines and USAir.

Located in West Palm Beach, the **Palm Beach International Airport** is served by American Airlines, Continental Airlines, Delta Airlines, Northwest Airlines, Trans World Airlines, United Airlines and USAir.

In Fort Lauderdale, **Broward County Transit** has bus service between the airport and its main terminal at Northwest 1st Avenue and Broward Boulevard. ~ 954-357-8400.

Palm Beach Transportation services the Palm Beach International Airport. ~ 561-684-9900.

Transportation between Boca Raton and the Palm Beach International Airport is provided by **Boyce-Transportation, Inc.** ~ 561-391-4762.

BUS

Greyhound Bus Lines (800-231-2222) has extensive service throughout the Gold Coast. In addition to bus stops, there are terminals in the Fort Lauderdale area in Hollywood at 1707 Tyler Street, 954-922-8228; and in Fort Lauderdale at 513 Northeast 3rd Street, 954-764-6551;

In the Palm Beach area, Greyhound has terminals in Delray Beach at 402 Southeast 6th Avenue, 561-272-6447; and in West Palm Beach at 100 1st Street, 561-833-8534.

For train aficionados, **Amtrak** offers service via the "Palmetto," "Silver Star" and "Silver Meteor" to the West Palm Beach station. ~ 201 South Tamarind Avenue; 800-872-7245.

TRAIN

Among the major firms located in or near the terminal at Fort Lauderdale Airport are:

Alamo Rent A Car (800-327-9633), **Avis Rent A Car** (800-831-2847), **Budget and Sears Car and Truck Rental** (800-527-0700), **Dollar Rent A Car** (800-800-4000) and **Hertz Rent A Car** (800-654-3131).

Car-rental agencies at the Palm Beach International Airport include **Avis Rent A Car** (800-831-2847), **Budget and Sears Car and Truck Rental** (800-527-0700), **Dollar Rent A Car** (800-800-4000) and **National Interrent** (800-227-7368).

CAR RENTALS

Bus service throughout Broward County is provided by **Broward County Transit**. Public libraries, chamber of commerce offices and many beachfront hotels and motels sell weekly Transpasses, which entitle the buyer to unlimited use of the bus system for seven days. ~ 954-357-8400.

In the Palm Beach area, regularly scheduled bus service on a variety of routes is offered by **Co Tran**. ~ 561-233-1111.

TRI-RAIL is a commuter rail system operating throughout the Gold Coast, with 67 miles of track between Miami International Airport and Palm Beach. ~ 954-728-8445.

PUBLIC TRANSIT

Service at the Fort Lauderdale airport is available from **Friendly Checker** (954-923-2302) and **Yellow Cab** (954-565-5400). In Palm Beach, taxi service is provided by **Yellow Cab** (561-689-4222). For limousine service, call the airport location of **Yellow Cab** (561-689-9900).

TAXIS

FOUR

The East Coast

Florida's East Coast stretches more than 300 miles, from the glittering edge of the Gold Coast up to the genteel environs bordering the Georgia state line. For that entire distance, the Atlantic Ocean alternately laps and crashes against a seemingly endless stretch of beach.

Those who rush through the state along the fast-moving inland interstates rarely realize that virtually all of this coast is separated from the ocean by a series of lovely barrier islands. Between these islands and the mainland is the Intracoastal Waterway (called a river in some locales), where calmer inland waters provide safe passage for pleasure craft everywhere on the coast. Most of the fun, a lot of the area's history, and even a glimpse into the future can be found on the islands.

This chapter leads the Florida visitor from south to north, but the state, and its East Coast, was originally developed north to south. The first known visitor to Florida was the Spanish explorer Ponce de León, who landed in 1513 near present-day St. Augustine. By 1562, the French were making inroads near the mouth of the St. Johns River. While the land itself was not considered particularly valuable—no precious metals and little fertile land had been found—the peninsula was deemed strategic for the safe passage of Spanish ships, laden with treasure from the south and bound for the mother country. King Philip II's determination to rout the French from northeast Florida led to a series of encounters so brutal that the bay at St. Augustine (now Matanzas Bay) became known as "The Bay of Slaughter."

There were more struggles in the early 1600s against the British, and later against English colonists from the north who succeeded in establishing Florida's northern boundary at the St. Marys River in 1742. Still to come were lengthy wars with the Seminoles, the American Indians who resisted displacement by American settlers, and the American Civil War, which divided Florida between Union and Confederate control.

By the late 19th century, however, the smoke had cleared and guidebooks to the state were drawing visitors eager to escape the northern winters. In the 1880s Florida lured its most important tourist since Ponce de León. His name was Henry Flagler, and he had a vision of Florida's East Coast as one long stretch of luxury resorts. Frustrated by the lack of transportation, the former Standard Oil executive established the Florida East Coast Railway and extended it from Jacksonville all the way to Miami. Thus began the state's big boom. With each few miles of railway, another wintertime playground was established, frequently by Flagler himself, who built such legendary resorts as the Flagler Hotel in St. Augustine and the Breakers in Palm Beach.

Over the years, various settlers arrived on the East Coast for varied reasons. The French Huguenots, for instance, driven from the North by the Spanish, were the first Europeans to invade what had been the territory of the Tomoka Indians. Indigo and sugar plantations and orange groves were established around Daytona Beach, but, as elsewhere on the coast, the population explosion ultimately arrived via Flagler's train cars. As a result, the East Coast has a hodge-podge history, as outposts were built years before an adequate transportation system that would assure stability.

Today, no single focal point highlights the region, but it is united by one sensibility—an overwhelming consciousness of the ocean's proximity. The salt air, the casual atmosphere, the emphasis on water sports and the abundance of exquisite seafood provide constant reminders.

If a common thread can be identified, it is the threat of overdevelopment along the coast. The ocean, which as late as 1980 was visible for miles at a stretch, has been disappearing behind a phalanx of condominiums—and, in Daytona Beach especially—has largely become the exclusive visual domain of oceanfront hotel guests. The good news is that virtually every square foot of East Coast beach is open to the public.

The geography in this region is fairly consistent: flat sandy beaches fringed with palm trees and imported Australian pines (not true pines, by the way). The climate is another matter. Winter can be quite chilly in the north, for instance, and sweaters are often necessary in January as far south as Cocoa Beach. But the climate is on the whole temperate. On the central East Coast, temperatures range from an average low of 50° in January to an average high of 89° in July. In the northeast, nighttime temperatures dip to an average of 47° in winter and rise to an average of 89° in summer.

Oddly enough, the best sightseeing route in eastern Florida has evolved into almost "hidden" status. It is possible—and recommended—for visitors to drive the entire East Coast along Route A1A. This beach-hugging road lopes through resort towns and retirement enclaves and villages not much bigger than intersections. Route A1A runs through the barrier islands, often within earshot of the surf.

Except in the bigger towns, A1A has a sleepy quality to it, especially when it narrows to two lanes. This route runs through "Old Florida," a land of fishing camps, marinas and waterfront shanties with some of the freshest, most inexpensive seafood in the state.

Along the way is a string of towns and cities, many of them quite distinct. Fort Pierce, for example, more closely resembles a 19th-century fishing village than it does the glossy brochure image of Florida beach resort towns. Established in 1838 as a United States Army post to fend off the Seminole Indians, the fort developed as a distribution center for beef, citrus and vegetables raised in the surrounding agricultural areas. The waterways from Stuart up to Vero Beach have gained acclaim as prime sportfishing ports, yet there is no trace of self-importance among natives.

North of Vero Beach, Fort Pierce's fancier neighbor, is a particularly beautiful stretch of road; at points, you can see the ocean on one side and the Intracoastal Waterway on the other. It is off this part of the coast that many Spanish cargo ships were wrecked in past centuries. To this day, pieces of eight still wash up on the beaches after major storms. Hence the nickname of the region, the Treasure Coast.

Indialantic and Satellite Beach are so small that they could be missed were it not for roadside signs. The next real city up the road is Cocoa Beach. Established at the end of the 19th century, the town is said to be named for the coco plum, which once flourished here along with citrus groves.

Since NASA established a space center here in the 1960s, the town has turned into something of a bedroom community for scientists, astronauts and support staff. A beautiful stretch of beach offers sensational viewing points for space launches. Sharing nearby Merritt Island with the Kennedy Space Center is the 140,000-acre Merritt Island National Wildlife Refuge and the Canaveral National Seashore, expanses of pristine wilderness that provide a safe habitat for hundreds of species of mammals, reptiles, amphibians, birds and fish.

The most developed of east Florida's resort towns is Daytona Beach. Here automobile traffic is still tolerated on the beach, but professional racing has been removed inland to the tracks at the Daytona Beach Speedway. In fact all beach driving is hotly disputed and may end soon, as environmentalists argue that the cars interfere with Mother Nature, especially the sea turtles who come up to lay their eggs on Florida's beaches in the early summer.

St. Augustine has attracted visitors ever since Ponce de León stepped ashore, allegedly in search of the mythical Fountain of Youth. Established in 1565 by Pedro Menéndez de Aviles for the king of Spain, it is the oldest city in the country, a fact pounded home at virtually every old house and tourist attraction. This is a quaint city of narrow streets and considerable charm. It was envisioned by Henry Flagler as the first in a string of resort towns. But as the railroad took more and more tourists and settlers to the south, St. Augustine faded from prominence. Thus, its downtown area looks much the way it has for centuries.

Forty miles north of St. Augustine, Jacksonville is more a working-class city, a sprawling megalopolis that may one day rival Atlanta as the industrial hub of the South. Several years ago this city began reviving its downtown area and rehabilitating some of the lovely old neighborhoods. Nearby lie the towns of Atlantic Beach and Jacksonville Beach, which, although they have their share of motels, still remain largely residential and far more low-key than Daytona Beach.

Tucked away in the northeast corner of the state, within sight of Georgia's coast, Amelia Island is virtually a hidden destination in itself. The south end of the island has largely been appropriated for golf courses and condominiums, while Fernandina Beach, on the north end, has the monopoly on historic sites. While there is not as

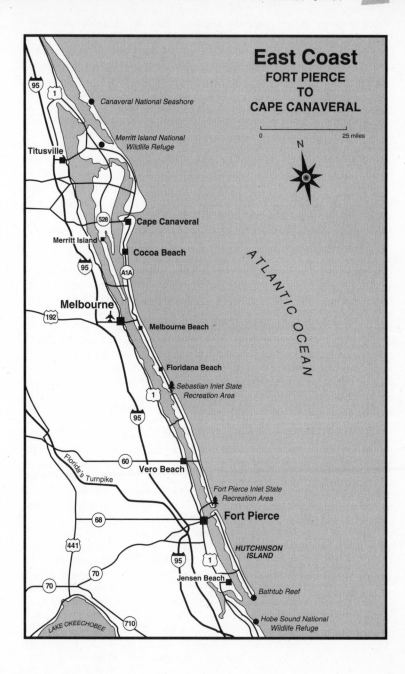

East Coast
FORT PIERCE
TO
CAPE CANAVERAL

0   25 miles

N

ATLANTIC OCEAN

Canaveral National Seashore

Merritt Island National
Wildlife Refuge

Titusville

Cape Canaveral

Merritt Island

Cocoa Beach

Melbourne

Melbourne Beach

Floridana Beach

Sebastian Inlet State
Recreation Area

Florida's Turnpike

Vero Beach

Fort Pierce Inlet State
Recreation Area

Fort Pierce

HUTCHINSON
ISLAND

Jensen Beach

Bathtub Reef

Hobe Sound National
Wildlife Refuge

LAKE OKEECHOBEE

much to see here as in St. Augustine, Amelia Island has an even more complex military history, having existed under eight different flags since 1562: French, Spanish, English, Spanish again, Patriots (a local group that overthrew the Spaniards), the Green Cross of Florida, Mexican, American, Confederate and then American again.

From Spanish conquerors to time-share condominiums, the East Coast of Florida has remained one of the most enticing destinations in the country.

▼▼▼▼▼▼▼▼▼▼▼▼
Fort Pierce Area

If anything could be said to unify the disparate communities from Jensen Beach to Sebastian Inlet, it would be the sleepy quality of this string of small riverfront cities and little beach towns. Vero Beach is something of an exception, with its posh shops and chic restaurants, but for the most part it seems the 20th century has yet to make its presence known. Route 1 serves as the major inland artery, while Route A1A zigzags from mainland to oceanside, over bridges connecting the Intracoastal Waterway to the slim barrier islands of South Hutchinson and North Hutchinson.

The same temperate climate that has made Indian River citrus famous for quality has also made the Fort Pierce area a mecca for sports lovers. The calm inland waterways provide bountiful opportunities for fishing, as do offshore currents. But in centuries past, the ocean also spelled doom for Spanish galleons and other ships caught in storms or unexpectedly rough waters, and the bounty salvaged from these wrecks inspired a new nomenclature for the region. Sandwiched between the Gold Coast and the Space Coast (as the Cape Canaveral area has been dubbed), this part of the world now calls itself the Treasure Coast.

SIGHTS

This area's approach to tourism is so low key that travelers must use some initiative to spot several points of interest. The **Environmental Studies Center,** for instance, looks like a small-town elementary school. But this 1930s-era WPA building houses an intriguing array of natural science exhibits, including a display of manatee and dolphin skeletons and a wet lab where you can observe captive loggerheads, sharks and other marine life. Closed weekends. ~ 2900 Northeast Indian River Drive, Jensen Beach; 561-334-1262.

HIDDEN ►

Gilbert's Bar House of Refuge was built in the 1870s as a haven for sailors shipwrecked in nearby waters. Standing on a slim strand only yards from the ocean, the green clapboard house, said to be the oldest structure in the area, has several ground floor rooms furnished much as they were when stranded sailors stayed here. There is a small museum displaying marine artifacts and antiquated lifesaving equipment. Also on view is a small aquarium with seasonal fish. Closed Monday. Admission. ~ 301 Southeast MacArthur Boulevard, Stuart; 561-225-1875.

Dominating a curve of road north of Gilbert's Bar, the **Elliott Museum** is easily recognized by gracious white columns that complement its pink exterior. The museum, named after American inventor Sterling Elliott, houses collections of almost Smithsonian scope. Most curious is an old-fashioned apothecary shop that recreates a turn-of-the-century commercial establishment. You'll also find local history displays, including American Indian artifacts, as well as a hodgepodge that ranges from a baseball museum and antique photographic equipment to an old-fashioned Victorian parlor. The museum's crowning glory is its lineup of classic automobiles, motorcycles and bicycles, a fantasy garage that illustrates the history of automotive engineering. Admission. ~ 825 Northeast Ocean Boulevard, Stuart; 561-225-1961.

From here north to Fort Pierce and beyond, some of the best sightseeing can be done from a car, driving either on Route A1A or on **Indian River Drive**, the narrow winding road that parallels ◄ HIDDEN the west bank of the Indian River. Shaded, peaceful and traveled mostly by locals, the drive passes between the river and gracious homes, some so large they have names instead of numbers.

Be sure to stop by **Heathcote Botanical Gardens**, a three-and- ◄ HIDDEN a-half-acre public garden thick with mature trees, blooming flowers and radiant foliage. Don't miss the palm walk, the tropical orchid house or the native plant and Japanese bonsai exhibits. Closed Monday; closed Sunday in the summer. Admission. ~ Savannah Road, one-and-a-half blocks east of Route 1, Fort Pierce; 561-464-4672.

Indian River Drive leads north into Fort Pierce, where you can find South Route A1A (Seaway Drive) and cross the causeway heading east. You can stop at the **St. Lucie County Historical Museum**, which specializes in artifacts from the 1715 wreck of a Spanish treasure fleet bound from Spain. A glass-encased exhibit

---

✔ CHECK THESE OUT—UNIQUE SIGHTS

- Learn the basics of blasting off at the **Kennedy Space Center's Visitors Center**, where you can stroll in the Rocket Garden and tour the Gallery of Space Flight. *page 181*
- Tear down the track at **Daytona International Speedway**—in a tour bus—while attempting to fulfill Speed Racer fantasies. *page 192*
- Board a **Sightseeing Train** for a seven-mile narrated tour of the nation's oldest city, St. Augustine. *page 202*
- Have lunch under the cooling spray of the 120-foot-high **Friendship Fountain** near Jacksonville's inviting Riverwalk. *page 211*

shows how divers locate the many wreck sites off this stretch of coastline. Also educational are a reconstructed Seminole Indian encampment, a 1919 American LaFrance fire engine and the 1907 Gardner House next door. Closed Monday. Admission. ~ 414 Seaway Drive, Fort Pierce; 561-462-1795.

The **St. Lucie County Chamber of Commerce** can provide more information on the historic sights. ~ 2200 Virginia Avenue, Fort Pierce; 561-461-2700.

Fort Pierce Jai Alai is a huge frontón where you can watch the fast-action sport of jai alai, originally developed by Basque peasants in the Pyrenees Mountains. Closed Tuesday. Admission. ~ 1750 South King's Highway, Fort Pierce; 561-464-7500.

Even nondivers will find much of interest at the circular little **UDT-SEAL Museum**. Located on a World War II beach training site, the museum honors the Underwater Demolition Teams (UDTs) and Sea, Air and Land Teams (SEALs) with military exhibits, documents, photographs and paintings from several wars. The small weapons and other artifacts collected from North Vietnamese soldiers alone warrant a visit. Closed Monday. Admission. ~ 3300 North Route A1A at Pepper Park, Fort Pierce; 561-462-3597.

The **Center for the Arts** is the local showcase for artwork. Programs include a lecture series for children, galleries with children's work, a gallery for Florida artists as well as performances and workshops by visiting artists and musicians. ~ 3001 Riverside Park Drive, Vero Beach; 561-231-0707.

The **McLarty Treasure Museum** displays relics salvaged from the 1715 shipwreck off the nearby coast. A narrated slide show illustrates the history of the shipwreck and modern-day salvaging, and rangers are often on hand to answer questions about such topics. After the show, step out onto the observation deck to watch those salvagers at work. Admission. ~ Route A1A, 14 miles north of Vero Beach; 561-589-2147.

LODGING   The coast from Stuart to Vero Beach is better known for citrus and sailfishing than for its posh accommodations. Condominiums outnumber hotel rooms; the best motels are along the inlet in Fort Pierce itself and near the ocean in Vero Beach.

The **Indian River Plantation Resort** makes a stunning first impression when approached via Route A1A from the west. The 200-acre resort stretches from the Indian River Intracoastal Waterway to the Atlantic Ocean, with 306 guest accommodations ranging from condominium suites to luxurious hotel rooms decorated in soft colors and outfitted with handsome, well-made contemporary furnishings. The plantation is a sports-lover's dream: golf courses meandering beside waterways, tennis courts, swimming pools, jacuzzis and access to myriad water sports. ~ 555 Northeast Ocean

Boulevard, Stuart; 561-225-3700, 800-444-3389, fax 561-225-0003. ULTRA-DELUXE.

River's Edge Motel seems to be the only motel in this entire area located directly on the Indian River. The accommodations are spacious at this tan-and-brown two-story complex of 18 two-room suites. The decor, however, is almost nonexistent, and kitchenettes seem to have been squeezed in as an afterthought. ~ 2625 Northeast Indian River Drive, Jensen Beach; 561-334-4759. MODERATE.

The **Harbor Light Inn** is by far the smartest of the little lodging spots along Seaway, the southern route to the beaches. Painted a cheery Mediterranean blue and white, with flourishing tropical plants flanking a blue-tiled pool (complete with built-in spa and a gazebo), this 20-room inn proves that accommodations don't have to be rustic to fit right in with the relaxing pace of riverside life. Rooms are spacious, well lit and equipped with a refrigerator and wet bar. The best ones have furnished balconies where guests can view sea birds and fishing boats. And when the sun begins to set, the place to appreciate it is on one of the inn's private docks. ~ 1160 Seaway Drive, Fort Pierce; 561-468-3555. MODERATE TO DELUXE.

The **Caribbean Apartments and Motel** offers 12 spacious ground-floor guest rooms hugging a large waterfront courtyard. Kitchenettes available. ~ 1502 Seaway Drive, Fort Pierce; 561-461-5628. BUDGET.

The accommodations at the **Surf and Sand Oceanfront Resort** are quite a deal. Each room is decorated in a different color scheme; some rooms have ocean views and kitchenettes. The motel features a small pool and proximity to the beach, shops and restaurants. ~ 1516 South Ocean Drive, Vero Beach; 561-231-5700, fax 561-231-9386. MODERATE TO DELUXE.

True to its name, the **Aquarius Oceanfront Resort** sits right on the beach. Fringed with palm trees, sea oats and tiki huts, the two-story complex features a heated pool and shuffleboard courts. Most of the 27 guest rooms have kitchenettes, and all offer wall-

GREASING THE GEARS

Standard Oil executive Henry Flagler built the **Ormond Hotel** in Ormond Beach, paving the way for scores of prosperous families from the Northeast (the Astors, Rockefellers and Vanderbilts among them) to discover the pleasures of Daytona Beach. When the beach was found suitable for automobile traffic, the race was on, assuring this city its place in world land-speed record books.

to-wall carpets and tropical decor. ~ 1526 South Ocean Drive, Vero Beach; 561-231-5218. MODERATE TO DELUXE.

Doubletree Guest Suites is the beachside deluxe hotel of choice with 55 suites that include mini-fridges and coffeemakers. Stamped out of a standard mold, the resort lacks individuality but makes up for it in comfort and reliability. ~ 3500 Ocean Drive, Vero Beach; 561-231-5666, 800-841-5666, fax 561-234-4866. ULTRA-DELUXE.

DINING

The poshest restaurant on Hutchinson Island is **Scalawags**. French country furniture, fine linens and a tasteful color scheme of green and rose warm up this 140-seat restaurant. Two walls of glass provide an expansive view of the marina and the Intracoastal Waterway. Seafood and beef receive imaginative treatment here, as do pasta dishes. Dinner only. Champagne brunch on Sunday; seafood buffet on Wednesday. ~ 555 Northeast Ocean Boulevard in the Indian River Plantation Resort, Stuart; 561-225-6818. DELUXE TO ULTRA-DELUXE.

HIDDEN ►

Conchy Joe's Seafood Restaurant sports a thatched roof and an island-inspired decor that make it look suspiciously like a tourist trap, yet it's anything but. You'll almost always find a crowd of regulars in the delightful open-air dining room perched over the Indian River. At lunch, they'll usually be snacking on conch meat in some guise (fritters, burgers, etc.), or something from the raw bar. But there's also a full menu featuring specialties such as soft shell crab and seafood pasta dishes. ~ 3945 North Indian River Drive, Jensen Beach; 561-334-1130. MODERATE TO DELUXE.

Cooled off by pastel walls and plenty of fans suspended from high ceilings, the **Captain's Galley** is place to go for an imaginative breakfast: pigs in a blanket, pork chops with eggs, pecan pancakes or granola. You can order breakfast any time of day, but then you'd miss the hearty conch chowder, seafood salads, chicken dishes and the catch-of-the-day served for lunch and dinner. ~ 825 North Indian River Drive, Fort Pierce; 561-466-8495. BUDGET TO MODERATE.

Few restaurants make as much of their setting as does **Mangrove Mattie's**, where bare wood and tropical prints look wonderful against the backdrop of Fort Pierce Inlet. Ask to be seated on the veranda and order a cup of conch chowder, a throat-warming concoction with tomatoes and spices. Also recommended are almost any dishes made with the sweet local shrimp. ~ 1640 Seaway Drive, Fort Pierce; 561-466-1044. MODERATE TO DELUXE.

HIDDEN ►

It's worth going out of your way to find **Out of Bounds Steak & Grill**, an odd combination of good, creative food served in a spacious dining room festooned with tennis racquets and hockey sticks. The sports-inspired list of dishes includes the "Jack Nicklaus" (battered and pan-fried fish topped with hollandaise sauce) and the "Jennifer Capriati" (snails with spinach). But the chef turns serious in the kitchen, creating such daily specials as lobster and beef tenderloin sautéed with garlic, mushrooms, onions and macadamia nuts then flambéed with Jack Daniels. Dinner served nightly; lunch on weekends only. ~ 2838 South U.S. 1, Fort Pierce; 561-468-4363. MODERATE.

A small, nine-booth café festooned with piñatas and sombreros, **Enriqo's Mexican Restaurant** is known for its innovative approach to south-of-the-border standbys such as *chile rellenos*, fajitas and *pollo asada*. Closed Sunday. ~ 3215 South Route 1, Fort Pierce; 561-465-1608. BUDGET.

Route 1 is blessed with a number of ethnic restaurants that offer great food. Located right on the highway, **Chunbo Restaurant** has the short, squat look of a fast-food joint. In fact, it's a hospitable place with an impressively long menu. Pork and seafood predominate at this Szechuan-style restaurant. ~ 3211 South Route 1, Fort Pierce; 561-465-0570. MODERATE.

One of the many ethnic restaurants located in shopping centers, **Italia in Boca** pays homage to the mother country with ceiling lamps in the green, white and red color scheme of Italy's flag. So much for decor. In addition to pizzas, this modest place features veal, shrimp and pasta dishes. ~ 2509 South Route 1, Fort Pierce; 561-461-0065. MODERATE.

The station wagons with Florida license tags that fill the large parking lot at **Norris's Famous Place for Ribs** provide evidence that locals often patronize this lively family-style restaurant. Big tables are set for big appetites. Beef is the major draw here—everything from barbecued ribs to french dip to old-fashioned hamburgers. Then there's chicken, seafood and side dishes like corn on the cob and Texas-style chili. ~ 3080 North Route 1, North Fort Pierce; 561-464-4000. BUDGET TO MODERATE.

P. V. Martin's Beach Café is a large, single-story clapboard structure in a beautiful oceanfront location where sea oats graze the windows. Far from being ramshackle, the dimly lit dining rooms are graced with elegant touches such as tables topped with Mexican blue tiles. The menu includes alligator tails and soft shell crab as well as more conventional beef and chicken dishes. And local connoisseurs consistently recommend P. V. Martin's Sunday brunch. Dinner nightly. ~ 5150 North Route A1A, Fort Pierce; 561-465-7300. DELUXE TO ULTRA-DELUXE.

The most compelling feature of **Vero Beach Inn Restaurant** is its atrium setting overlooking a pool. Open for breakfast, lunch and dinner in the winter months (breakfast and dinner only in the summer), this restaurant capably serves up hamburgers, sandwiches and baby back ribs. The island-inspired furnishings and waterside setting give this café a serene, enchanting atmosphere. ~ 4700 North Route A1A, Vero Beach; 561-231-1600. BUDGET TO MODERATE.

It's a little disconcerting to find a pool at the front door of **Chez Yannick**, but that's only one distinguishing feature of this interesting restaurant. Understated in its decor and ingeniously designed with freestanding room dividers, Chez Yannick offers a *très Français* menu highlighting duck *à l'orange*, filet mignon béarnaise and other sophisticated fare. Dinner only. ~ 1601 South Ocean Drive, Vero Beach; 561-234-4115. MODERATE TO DELUXE.

The Beachside Restaurant is a welcome respite from the pricier establishments in this oceanfront neighborhood. Breakfast foods, salads, sandwiches and delicacies like crabmeat quiche are served at neat tables covered with white tablecloths and topped with glass. No greasy spoons here. Breakfast, lunch and dinner. ~ 3125 Ocean Drive, Vero Beach; 561-234-4477. BUDGET.

Black Pearl is not on the ocean, but it does ride the wave of haute cuisine sweeping the area. A comely restaurant with salmon-colored walls, floral drapes and outdoor seating, it has come up with offerings such as grilled Jamaican jerk shrimp, local fish in parchment and Cajun pasta dishes. No lunch on weekends. ~ 2855 Ocean Drive, Vero Beach; 561-234-4426. DELUXE.

It's easy to guess that Waldo Sexton, the local legend behind the nearby Driftwood Resort, had a hand in creating the **Ocean Grill**, a weathered-wood wonder that appears ready to fall into the sea with the next big wave. The basic surf 'n' turf menu is spiced with coquilles St. Jacques, crab au gratin and the catch of the day. Lunch served on weekdays only. ~ 1050 Sexton Plaza, Vero Beach; 561-231-5409. MODERATE TO ULTRA-DELUXE.

SHOPPING   Not surprisingly, in light of the fierce sun and heat, the preferred habitat of the southeast Florida shopper is the fully air-conditioned mall. In second place is one of the many shopping centers and strips that line Route 1 from Stuart all the way to Vero Beach. High-priced boutiques are a dime a dozen in the finer hotels, but other than those, there isn't much retail action at the beach.

Sequestered in a semi-forested setting, **Treasure Coast Square** exudes sleek elegance in and out. Marble-clad lobbies decorated with fancy trees and skylights enhance the fantasy image of this stunning structure. Nationally and internationally known chains such as **Waldenbooks** (561-692-9615) make this their address in Jensen Beach. You'll find a variety of Florida jams and jellies, salad dressings, local cookbooks and gourmet coffees at **Lechters** (561-692-2838). This kitchen shop also offers wreaths, dried flower arrangements and baskets, as well as a wide range of utensils, bakeware and cookware. A contemporary shop offering both men's sportswear and dresswear, **J. Riggings** (561-692-0161) is also a good place to look for accessories. ~ Route 1 and Jensen Beach Boulevard, Jensen Beach.

For an area specialty, try smoked food at **Mrs. Peter's,** where the motto is "We Smoke Everything But Mermaids." Since 1931 Mrs. Peter's has offered hand-smoked kingfish, amberjack, turkey and mullet. ~ Stuart Heritage Museum, 161 North Flagler Avenue, Stuart, 407-220-4600; and 1500 Route 707, Jensen Beach, 561-334-2184.

Chocoholics unite, and untie a gift box of hand-dipped chocolates (dietetic or regular strength) from **Bruno's House of Chocolates.** The people at Bruno's give tours of the "factory" (really a candy kitchen), where they create candies and novelties using loving hands and no preservatives. ~ 2650 North Route 1, North Fort Pierce; 561-461-3229.

A four-block stretch along Ocean Drive in Vero Beach is a trove of delightful discoveries. The biggest sparkler is **Bottalico Gallery,** a gallery/studio for the highly original work of Glen Bottalico. Colorful trompe l'oeil scenes cover screens, boxes and canvases. Whimsical shells, butterflies and flowers are painted on baskets and candlesticks. And the prices seem quite moderate when you consider these are all collector's items. ~ 3121 Ocean Drive, Vero Beach; 561-231-0414.

◄ *HIDDEN*

A must-see, especially for women looking for that special something to wear to a nice Vero Beach restaurant, is **Orchid Island Trading Co.** Here you'll find fine dresses, beach wear and accessories that make excellent gifts. ~ 3143 Ocean Drive, Vero Beach; 561-231-0620.

In the airy bleached stucco **Portales de Vero Shopping Arcade,** ground-floor merchants include **The Art Works** (561-231-4688), a contemporary gallery; and the **Artist Guild Gallery** (561-231-4551), a cooperative art gallery. Toward the back, **Roundabout** (561-231-3323) overflows with small gifts and stationery items. What a selection: personalized writing paper and invitations; sophisticated wrapping paper and festive bags; children's writing materials; and oodles of small items at dime-store prices. ~ 2855 Ocean Drive, Vero Beach.

Scalawag's Lounge in the Indian River Plantation is an elegant little place upstairs and inside the nicest resort in the region. The views are bucolic and there's entertainment (usually a duo performing Top-40 hits) Tuesday through Saturday. ~ 555 Northeast Ocean Boulevard, Stuart; 561-225-6818.

NIGHTLIFE

Café Coconuts is three bars in one: the downstairs bar is full of televisions most often tuned to sporting events, a second patio bar is for nuzzling and conversing and the third upstairs alfresco bar is beachy. On weekends, the cafe features live music without a cover. ~ 4304 Northeast Ocean Boulevard, Hutchinson Island; 561-225-6006.

The 633-seat **Riverside Theatre** presents half a dozen performances by the Acting Company of Riverside each year, such as Broadway musicals, comedies and dramas, in addition to a classical music concert series. ~ 3250 Riverside Park Drive, Vero Beach; 561-231-6990.

BEACHES & PARKS

HOBE SOUND NATIONAL WILDLIFE REFUGE
Hobe Sound Refuge consists of more than three miles of beach, sand dunes and mangroves plus a sand pine scrub forest. So abundant is the wildlife in this refuge that an appealing sign has been posted admonishing visitors not to "aggravate, harass, irritate, molest, bother, beleaguer" or otherwise annoy the animals. Thus protected, scrub jays and other songbirds survive in peace in the mainland forest, and several varieties of sea turtles struggle to shore to lay their eggs on the island portion of the park. Saltwater fishing is allowed off the beach and along the Intracoastal Waterway. There is good ocean swimming off of North Beach Road. Surfing is also good. Facilities include restrooms, an interpretive museum and a nature trail. Day-use fee, $4. ~ Located off Route 1 several miles north of Jupiter; 561-546-6141.

JONATHAN DICKINSON STATE PARK
This inland park undulates through 13,000 acres topped by Hobe Mountain, at 86 feet the closest thing to a real mountain in south Florida. A variety of plant communities including sand pine scrub, mangrove and river swamp support a great deal of animal life. Deer and rabbit are common sights, but there are also otter, snakes, fish and birds. The park is a refuge for nearly extinct species such as southern bald eagles and Florida scrub jays, which live in the portions of the Loxahatchee River where salt water has made an intrusion. Within the park are a picnic area, canoe rentals, a concession stand and nature and bike trails; guided boat tours up the wild Loxahatchee are offered. There is both salt and freshwater angling. Day-use fee, $3.25. ~ Located five miles north of Jupiter off Route 1; 561-546-2771.

One of the most successful sea turtle nesting areas in the country is Hobe Sound National Wildlife Refuge.

▲ There are 135 sites, most with RV hookups, electricity, water and dump stations; $14 to $17 per night. Moderately priced cabins are also available (reservations required); information, 561-746-1466.

BATHTUB REEF PARK An offshore reef near the southern tip of Hutchinson Island forms a bathtub-calm shallow area that attracts snorkelers, swimmers and anglers. This sandy, undeveloped beach extends for 1100 feet just north of St. Lucie Inlet. There are restrooms, showers and lifeguards; groceries and restaurants are nearby. ~ Follow Route A1A south to the end of Hutchinson Island.

STUART BEACH 🏊 🚶 ⛵ This oceanfront stretch of Martin   ◄ HIDDEN
County is one of the loveliest developed beaches around Fort Pierce. Stuart Beach is accessible via a boardwalk shaded by several stands of Australian pines. Dune crossovers lead to a smooth, light-brown beach, extremely popular with locals. Swimming is good here, but waves break close to beach. Surfing is only fair. There is surf fishing in front of boardwalk. Facilities include picnic areas, restrooms, showers, lifeguards, a playground, volleyball courts, basketball courts and a concession stand. There are undeveloped beaches both north and south of this park. ~ On MacArthur Boulevard, Hutchinson Island; 561-288-5690.

SAVANNAS RECREATION AREA 🚶 🚴 ⛵ 🚤 Fort Pierce has the distinction of having a 550-acre wilderness park located within its city limits. A delicate ecosystem of marsh and uplands, the park features freshwater lagoons and creeks banked with lily pads and soft marsh grasses, home to a number of waterfowl and wading birds. You can fish for bass and compatible freshwater game fish. There are picnic areas, restrooms, showers, a concession stand and canoe and boat rentals. Day-use fee, $1. ~ Located off Route 707-A (Midway Road) between Route 1 and the Indian River; 561-464-7855.

▲ There are 65 sites, all with RV hookups, electricity, water and dump stations; $10 to $16 per night.

FREDERICK DOUGLASS MEMORIAL PARK 🏇 🏊 Of the ten or   ◄ HIDDEN
so public access points on Hutchinson Island, this minimally developed park is one of the most stunning. A narrow strip of clean, creamy sand stretches for more than 1000 feet. Fringed by delicate Australian pines, the beach is one of the prettiest in this area. It's an excellent place to swim. The park has a picnic area, restrooms, showers and lifeguards in the summer; grocery and restaurants are nearby. ~ On Route A1A four miles south of Fort Pierce Inlet; 561-462-1521.

FORT PIERCE INLET STATE RECREATION AREA 🚴 🏊 🐟 🚶 🚤 ⛵ Covering 420 acres directly north of the inlet, the park includes a coastal hammock, dunes and a pristine swath of hard sand known as North Jetty Beach. This beach and others to the north have better waves than those on the south side of the inlet, thanks to the creation of a rock jetty that affects the wave patterns. Here you'll find some of the county's best surfing. Swimming is excellent at North Jetty Beach and snorkeling is pretty good near the rocks. The most popular spot for fishing is off the jetty. Dynamite Point, on the inlet, is the best place in the area for observing the shorebirds that feed and nest along the waterfront. There is also some beachfront along the inlet itself. Within the recreation area are picnic areas, restrooms, showers and lifeguards in the summer; groceries and restaurants are nearby. Day-use fee, $3.25. ~ 905 Shore Winds Drive in Fort Pierce; 561-468-3985.

PEPPER PARK ⬥ Wooden walkways cross tall sand dunes dotted with seagrapes to a 2000-foot stretch of hard sand beach. This simple and pristine spot is ideal for picnicking. It's also a choice spot for swimming. Surfing, however, is not the best. Facilities include a playground, tennis and volleyball courts, showers restrooms and lifeguards; restaurants and grocery stores are located nearby. ~ On North Route A1A north of Fort Pierce Inlet, Fort Pierce; 561-462-1521.

HIDDEN ▶ **JACK ISLAND STATE PRESERVE** 🚶 Even people who have heard of Jack Island have trouble finding it and may drive past the narrow access road several times before making the correct turn. At the end of a glorified driveway, invisible from the highway, a footbridge leads across the water to a 631-acre mangrove island. Nature trails lead visitors to several excellent vantage points for observing the waterfowl and other birds that flourish in this sanctuary. Mangroves, seagrapes and a coastal hammock add to the allure. Jack Island is a good place to fish. There are no facilities. ~ Located two and a half miles north of Fort Pierce Inlet off Route A1A; 561-468-3985.

SEBASTIAN INLET STATE RECREATION AREA 🏊 🛶 🚶 ⬥ Sebastian is a name well known to surfers who love to ride the six-foot waves that pound the northside beach next to the jetty. But the beautiful 600-acre recreation area also attracts swimmers, walkers, anglers, birdwatchers and boaters. Fishing and shrimping are good off the catwalks under the inlet bridge. Surf angling is best north of the jetty. Swimming is best north of the fishing and surfing beaches. The park, less than a mile across at its widest point, is divided by a manmade inlet. Pristine white sand beaches on either side of the inlet stretch off into the horizon. On the inlet's north side, a good-sized lagoon offers calm, warm, shallow waters. Beachcombing is excellent; gold coins from offshore wrecks are occasionally washed on shore by storms. There are picnic areas, restrooms, showers, lifeguards in summer, bait and concession stands, and eco-boat tours around the inlet. The marina has canoe and boat rentals. Day-use fee, $3.25. ~ Located 16 miles north of Vero Beach on Route A1A; 407-984-4852.

▲ There are 51 sites with RV hookups, electricity, water and dump stations; $15 to $17 per night; information, 561-589-9659. Reservations recommended in the winter.

Scenic Route A1A hugs the shoreline on its way ▼▼▼▼▼▼▼▼▼▼▼▼▼▼▼
north from the to Cape Canaveral. Except for a **Cape Canaveral Area**
few condominium complexes, virtually nothing
lies between the roadway and the beach as the two-lane highway
cuts through small residential communities such as Indialantic and
Melbourne Beach. The biggest city in the region is Melbourne, a
landlocked harbor on the Intracoastal Waterway, but Cocoa
Beach, basically a company town for NASA and the Kennedy Space
Center, is better located for sightseeing.

Melbourne boasts several art galleries and one major museum de-   **SIGHTS**
voted to the arts. Located in a beautifully landscaped setting overlooking the Intracoastal Waterway, the **Brevard Museum of Art &**
Science rotates displays of its permanent collection of modern art,
African primitive works and pre-Columbian art. This sleek, contemporary museum also hosts touring art exhibitions from around
the country. The science museum is a great place for kids (and
adults!) to garner hands-on experience. Closed Monday. Admission. ~ 1463 North Highland Avenue, Melbourne; 407-242-0737.

Mother Nature and the trappings of the space age exist side by
side in the Cape Canaveral area. Every time a space shuttle blasts
off in a cloud of steam and smoke, the waterfowl and other wildlife
on surrounding Merritt Island are momentarily disturbed before
returning to the peaceful routine established by their kind over the
centuries.

You can recapture the history of America's space exploration—
plus glimpse its future—at the **Kennedy Space Center's Visitors**
Center. This fascinating complex is an absolute must-see and one
of the greatest values in Florida, especially since most of the attractions are free. You should begin with a walk in the *Rocket Gar-*
den, where you can find rockets from each stage of America's space
program. Established in 1958, NASA is nearby Cape Canaveral,
and is still the site of weather and communications satellite launchings. By 1964, what had become known as the NASA Kennedy Space
Center was relocated to adjacent Merritt Island.

Inside the *Gallery of Space Flight* are full-sized models of a
lunar rover and the Viking Mars Lander, along with actual spacecraft. One of the most eye-opening displays is the one-tenth scale
model of the rocket that propelled the Apollo 11 astronauts to the
moon; it's amazing to see how small the capsule was compared
with the size of the entire spacecraft.

The *Galaxy Center* houses an exhibit of space-related art and
two theaters. The Galaxy Theater screens multimedia presentations on various space topics. But for sheer exhilaration, you simply cannot top the films shown on 70-foot-wide screens in the two
IMAX Theaters (admission). The sound system is so extraordinary

that the entire theater shudders when a shuttle is launched into space. The films consist of spectacular footage shot by astronauts in the course of various missions. You will feel almost as if you, too, are looking down on the planet earth from outer space, practicing emergency evacuations and conducting experiments in weightlessness.

You should make reservations as soon as you arrive for this show as well as for the two-hour **Bus Tour** (admission) of outlying attractions inaccessible by private vehicle. Double-decker buses depart from the visitor center every 15 minutes all day long and take visitors to the 52-story Vehicle Assembly Building, a replica of a control room that lies within good snapshot distance of one of the two launch pads near the ocean. ~ Route 405, Merritt Island; 407-452-2121.

Also on Merritt Island are the offices of the **Cocoa Beach Tourism and Convention Council**, a good place to pick up maps and brochures. ~ 400 Fortenberry Road, Merritt Island; 407-452-4390.

The remainder of Merritt Island, north of the Kennedy Space Center, is largely devoted to the **Merritt Island National Wildlife Refuge** and the Canaveral National Seashore (see the "Beaches & Parks" section below). Within Merritt Island Refuge, an auto tour route guides visitors to prime viewing sites. ~ 407-861-0667. The **Black Point Wildlife Drive** leads into habitats for such unusual species as the anhinga, a bird that swims in the canals with only its snakelike head visible above the water.

HIDDEN ▶

Florida's greatest natural resource, sunshine, is the main attraction at the **Florida Solar Energy Center**. This unusual site, located on the University of Central Florida campus in Cocoa (which shares the grounds with Brevard Community College), has a visitors center filled with informative exhibits. Closed weekends. ~ 1679 Clearlake Road, Cocoa; 407-638-1000.

The **Astronaut Memorial Planetarium & Observatory** at Brevard Community College offers several perspectives on natural history and the space age. The comfortable theaters here screen a changing roster of educational skyscape shows and full-dome motion pictures. The huge planetarium boasts the largest telescope available to the public in the entire state. and a lobby filled with space memorabilia. Admission. ~ 1519 Clearlake Road, Cocoa; 407-634-3732.

A short drive away on the same campus, the **Brevard Museum of History and Natural Science** takes visitors back in time through exhibits of early settler furniture, American Indian tools and pottery, and the remains of extinct animals. As for natural history, the museum maintains an extensive shell collection and 22 acres of nature trails. Closed Monday. Admission. ~ 2201 Michigan Avenue, Cocoa; 407-632-1830.

The wildlife that inhabits the upper reaches of the St. Johns River is best viewed from a boat. Half-hour airboat rides at the **Lone Cabbage Fish Camp** cruise the inland marshes for a close-up look at exotic flora and fauna. (See "On the Wild Side: Sea Turtles and Alligators" in this chapter.) ~ 8199 Route 520, four miles west of Route 95, Cocoa; 407-632-4199.

◀ *HIDDEN*

LODGING

Most of the accommodations in the area are near the ocean, and the better ones can be found in Cocoa Beach. The city of Cocoa, separated from the beach by the Banana River, Merritt Island and the Intracoastal Waterway, is a few miles closer to the Kennedy Space Center.

The **Pelican Landing Resort** is a find—a beachfront hotel with 11 rooms; all are efficiencies with equipped kitchens. Behind the hotel is a deck you can lounge on before traipsing down the boardwalks that lead to the beach and the endless stretch of the Atlantic. Reservations strongly advised from January through March. ~ 1201 South Atlantic Avenue, Cocoa Beach; 407-783-7197. MODERATE.

One of the biggest surprises in Cocoa Beach is the **Howard Johnson Plaza-Hotel**. Forget the image of screaming orange and blue so familiar to highway travelers—this is a different Howard Johnson's. Take the lobby, for instance: a gleam of marble and sparkling tile with wicker settees and a high ceiling. Upstairs, lux-

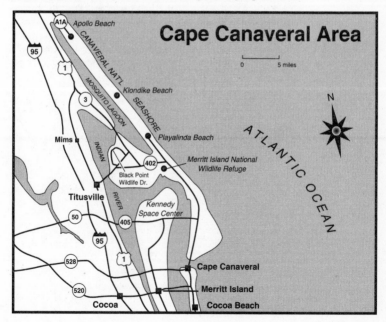

Cape Canaveral Area

urious rooms are sleekly furnished in pale woods and come in peaches-and-cream or aqua-and-turquoise colors. ~ 2080 North Atlantic Avenue, Cocoa Beach; 407-783-9222, 800-552-3224, fax 407-799-3234. DELUXE TO ULTRA-DELUXE.

The **Days Inn Oceanfront** is a bargain only if you insist on a second-story guest room facing the courtyard. Otherwise, your door will open onto either a pathway to the ocean or an unattractive parking lot. Peach and seafoam green decor is contemporary in a bare-bones kind of way. Eight units are equipped with modest cooking facilities. ~ 5600 North Atlantic Avenue, Cocoa Beach; 407-783-7621, 800-962-0028, fax 407-799-4576. MODERATE TO DELUXE.

The **Inn at Cocoa Beach** offers the best of everything. All the rooms in this T-shaped inn are beautifully decorated with fine furniture, plush carpeting and little touches like throw pillows, stools and framed artwork. Attractive drapes cover sliding glass doors that open onto private patios and balconies. There are gorgeous views of the ocean right out front, and it's possible to witness space launches from the third-floor observation deck. This place has a residential charm all too rare in an area dominated by chain hotels. ~ 4300 Ocean Beach Boulevard, Cocoa Beach; 407-799-3460, 800-343-5307, fax 407-784-8632. DELUXE TO ULTRA-DELUXE.

Within easy walking distance of the Cocoa Beach Pier, the **Ocean Suite Hotel** makes up in room size what it lacks in proximity to the ocean. Variations of beige and rose give the rooms a streamlined look that compensates for the rather bulky appearance of the building itself. ~ 5500 Ocean Beach Boulevard, Cocoa Beach; 407-784-4343, 800-367-1223, fax 407-783-6514. MODERATE TO ULTRA-DELUXE.

- -

✔ CHECK THESE OUT—UNIQUE LODGING

- *Budget:* Lounge on the beach in front of the **Day Star Motel**—clean rooms with full kitchens and a heated pool add up to a great deal. *page 196*
- *Moderate:* Slip into Southern comfort at the **House on Cherry Street;** you'll sleep in a canopy bed at the water's edge and wake to a full breakfast. *page 212*
- *Moderate to deluxe:* Head home to the **Harbor Light Inn,** an airy riverside accommodation with an oasis atmosphere. *page 173*
- *Deluxe to ultra-deluxe:* Choose between views of the ocean or space shuttle launches when you stay at the **Inn at Cocoa Beach**, a charming beachside hotel. *page 184*

Budget: under $50 Moderate: $50–$90 Deluxe: $90–$130 Ultra-deluxe: over $130

Nannie Lee's Strawberry Mansion is just about impossible to miss. Inside this pink Victorian confection, tables are set in practically every room, upstairs and down, within a homey setting of stained glass and floral wallpaper. The menu lists elaborate dishes such as pecan-crusted mahimahi along with seafood, veal, pasta dishes, chicken dinners and steaks considered the best in town. Dinner only. Closed Monday. ~ 1218 East New Haven Avenue, Melbourne; 407-724-8627. MODERATE TO DELUXE.

Cheek-by-jowl with the decorous Nannie Lee's, **Mister Beaujeans** shares its brick courtyard entry but not much else. Waffles, omelettes and unusual breakfast offerings like eggs and cheese in a pita pocket are served all day in a small L-shaped room gleaming with polished wood. After the sun warms the courtyard, it's fun to enjoy luncheon offerings such as BLTs, cheeseburgers with guacamole, grouper sandwich or conch fritters at one of the glass-topped tables outside complemented by wrought-iron furniture. The dinner menu consists of pasta, chicken, grouper and steak platters. No dinner on Monday. ~ 1218 East New Haven Avenue, Melbourne; 407-984-3121. BUDGET.

◄ HIDDEN

Peking Garden is an attractive establishment with dark Chinese-red furnishings and lace-curtained booths. Among the two dozen chef's specialties are hot-and-spicy pork and beef dishes, and versions of sweet-and-sour chicken and pork that appeal to children's palates. ~ 155 East Route 520, Merritt Island; 407-459-2999. BUDGET.

It's a good idea to tuck a meal under your belt before setting out for the Kennedy Space Center. Cheap and convenient is the **Kountry Kitchen**. In this big, friendly joint, an honest country breakfast of bacon, eggs, grits and biscuits is laid out as early as 6 a.m. Or on the way back, stop in for homestyle dinners: spareribs, salmon patties, chicken and dumplings, chicken-fried steaks and other hearty meals. ~ 1115 North Courtenay Parkway, Merritt Island; 407-459-3457. BUDGET.

◄ HIDDEN

On the main thoroughfare leading to the Kennedy Space Center is **Victoria's Family Restaurant**. The exterior won't remind you much of Greece, but within the brick-and-wood interior you will find moussaka and its country cousins, as well as seafood and chops. Breakfast, lunch and dinner are cooked up daily, but there's no dinner on Sunday. ~ 370 North Courtenay Parkway, Merritt Island; 407-459-1656. BUDGET TO MODERATE.

Most towns have one restaurant revered as a local institution. On the Space Coast, that place is **Bernard's Surf**. It's been on the same corner since the 1940s, boasting the freshest crab, lobster and fish in the county. Bernard's is divided into three parts: a raw bar; a formal, dimly lit dining room; and a bar and grill rimmed by red leatherette booths. An oversized menu is required to list the steak, rib and chicken offerings as well as dozens of seafood dishes, all in a variety of combinations. You'll also find such delicacies as Cajun-fried alligator tail, caviar and escargot. Dinner only. ~ 2 South Atlantic Avenue, Cocoa Beach; 407-783-2401. MODERATE TO ULTRA-DELUXE.

An exterior of glass and neon announces that **Herbie K's Diner** is an updated version of the all-American '50s diner; inside, black-and-white tiles, counter seating and tabletop jukeboxes and dancing servers set the mood for burgers, fries, shakes, malts, sandwiches and much more. Open for breakfast, lunch and dinner. ~ 2080 North Atlantic Avenue, Cocoa Beach; 407-783-6740. BUDGET.

The urge to splurge can be satisfied at **Carlyle's**, a formal, airy restaurant. Seated on hand-carved chairs upholstered in tapestry fabric, diners peruse a diverse menu that includes an oriental combination of shrimp stir-fry and rice, and nightly specials such as filet *au poivre* (coated with peppercorns, flamed with brandy and topped with a bordelaise sauce) and grouper sautéed with artichoke hearts, mushrooms and capers. In a what may be a concession to more plebian tastes, the lunch menu also lists hamburgers and sandwiches, but they seem out of place in such an elegant setting. Brunch is served on Sunday. ~ 2080 North Atlantic Avenue in the Howard Johnson Plaza-Hotel, Cocoa Beach; 407-783-9222. MODERATE.

The St. John River is one the of the few North American rivers that runs south to north.

Desperadoes serves up south-of-the-border fare like tostadas, *quesadillas* and *sopapillas* in a casual, rough-wood setting. You'll also find steak, chicken and other dishes on the menu to feast on inside or on the outdoor patio of the beachfront cantina. ~ 301 North Atlantic Avenue, Cocoa Beach; 407-784-3363. BUDGET TO MODERATE.

The most interesting restaurant in Cocoa Beach is **The Mango Tree**. Food doesn't get much better than this, nor does interior design. The restaurant is an artist's concept of Caribbean dining, with orchids and trees growing through the ceiling. An added greenhouse dining area enhances the tropical ambience. A spirited and obviously well-to-do crowd patronizes The Mango Tree for unusual appetizers such as seafood *en croûte* and dinner entrées developed from classic Continental cuisine: Dover sole, veal piccata, sweetbreads in bordelaise sauce, steak *au poivre*. Dinner only. Closed Monday. ~ 118 North Atlantic Avenue, Cocoa Beach; 407-799-0513. MODERATE TO DELUXE.

Alma's Seafood & Italian Restaurant offers a menu ranging from seafood and veal to pizza, and boasts a wine cellar of 200 vintages. A maze of small rooms makes this old-fashioned Italian eatery warm and inviting. Dinner only. ~ 306 North Orlando Avenue, Cocoa Beach; 407-783-1981. MODERATE TO DELUXE.

Coconuts on the Beach has a stucco exterior that belies its laid-back ambience. Although you can order full seafood entrées and dine indoors, most of the action is outside, where tables are filled with casually dressed beachgoers enjoying appetizers such as nachos or sweet-potato fries. ~ 2 Minuteman Causeway, Cocoa Beach; 407-784-1422. BUDGET TO MODERATE.

On the mainland, lunch in quaint little Cocoa Village can be as fancy as a meal in a French restaurant or as simple as a homemade sandwich and an ice cream cone at the **Village Ice Cream and Sandwich Shop**, a hole-in-the-wall located near some of the best boutiques in the neighborhood. No dinner. ~ 120-B Harrison Street, Cocoa; 407-632-2311. BUDGET.

The best-known spot to eat in Cocoa Village is the **Black Tulip**. For lunch you can choose from items such as quiche or crab cakes, and for dinner you can take advantage of local seafood dishes: grouper with shrimp in hollandaise or the catch-of-the-day with bananas in lemon butter. Service is formal in this cozy spot. Closed Sunday. ~ 207 Brevard Avenue, Cocoa; 407-631-1133. MODERATE TO DELUXE.

For an intimate lunch or dinner amid New Orleans–style decor, stop in at **Café Margeaux**. The menu offers entrées such as Caribbean duckling in coconut sauce, filet mignon and Dover sole. Closed Tuesday. ~ 220 Brevard Avenue, Cocoa; 407-639-8343. MODERATE TO DELUXE.

Between Cocoa and the Merritt Island Wildlife Refuge, a pleasant mainland stop near Route 1 is **Dixie Crossroads**. Despite its ◄ HIDDEN size (about 400 seats), this family-style favorite makes you feel right at home, with waitresses refilling your glass of iced tea every time they pass by the table. And everything edible that swims in nearby waters can be found here, in plentiful helpings. Don't miss the rock shrimp, succulent and tasty thumb-size delicacies that go well with a little red rice. Shellfish can be ordered in servings of one dozen, two dozen or all-you-can-eat. Dinners include soup, salad, a side dish and light, bite-sized corn fritters. ~ 1475 Garden Street, Titusville; 407-268-5000. MODERATE.

The **Lone Cabbage Fish Camp** is the spot on the St. Johns ◄ HIDDEN River for canoeing, airboat rides and a menu that is true Florida: catfish, alligator, turtle and country ham. A listing little wooden waterside building, the Lone Cabbage is funky and fun and way off the tourist itinerary. ~ 8199 Route 520, nine miles north of Cocoa and four miles west of Route 95; 407-632-4199. BUDGET TO MODERATE.

In the city of Melbourne, **East New Haven Avenue** is a quaint **SHOPPING** neighborhood of antique stores and art galleries with a smattering of clothing shops.

Ron Jon Surf Shop almost qualifies as a tourist destination. This warehouse-size store consists of two floors awash with swim wear, beach gear and equipment for all manner of watersports (including an extensive rental department). ~ 4151 North Route A1A, Cocoa Beach; 407-799-8888.

Brick walkways, cobblestone patios and an abundance of shade trees play up the historic atmosphere of **Cocoa Village** in downtown Cocoa. Some 50 shops are interspersed with restaurants and service establishments over approximately 15 city blocks. Mostly housed in restored lowrise buildings dating from the turn of the century, the retail shops range from hardware stores to purveyors of antique jewelry. ~ Bounded by Riveredge Boulevard, King Street, Florida Avenue and Derby Street, Cocoa.

Annie's Toy Chest offers a impressive selection of dolls and old-fashioned wooden train sets. ~ 405 Brevard Avenue, Cocoa; 407-632-5890.

Typical of the homey atmosphere in Cocoa Village, **Handwerk House** features figurines, dollhouses and collectibles. ~ 401 Brevard Avenue, Cocoa; 407-631-6367.

The Gourmet Experience devotes its large corner location to kitchenware, Australian, South African and Californian wines (relatively hard to find in this part of the world) and accessories such as baskets and gourmet foods. ~ 316 Brevard Avenue, Cocoa; 407-636-5480.

On the rim of Cocoa Village, **SunRay T-Shirts** could be mistaken for a loading dock, but it's actually a place that manufactures specialty T-shirts, notably ones for the Kennedy Space Center. ~ 105 Brevard Avenue, Cocoa; 407-632-6666.

You wouldn't dare eat off the dinnerware at **Village Plate Collector**, which carries beautifully etched china, miniatures, bells and figurines as well as lithographs, dolls and other collectibles. ~ 120 Forest Avenue, Cocoa; 407-636-6914.

HIDDEN ►

Not many travelers are in the market for hardware, but that's no reason to bypass **S. F. Travis Company**. Established in 1885, ten years before Cocoa made the map, this is the kind of place where you can buy a single nail or screw. Or simply tour the 35,000-square-foot premises, where barges used to dock out back before the space was landfilled. This low-key legend has the most authentically historic atmosphere in all of Cocoa Village. ~ 300 Delannoy Avenue, Cocoa; 407-636-1441.

You can observe artist Harry Guthrie Philips in progress at **Harry Guthrie Philips—Sculptor**, a charming one-room outlet accessible through a tiny palm-fringed courtyard. In this tropical oasis, Harry fashions sculptures of tropical fish and birds. He also sells pottery made by local residents. ~ 116-B Harrison Street, Cocoa; 407-636-4160.

Jus' Clownin Around With Balloons and Baskets offers gag gifts, baskets decorated and stuffed for all occasions, imported food and party supplies and gourmet candy. ~ 110 North Tropical Trail, Cocoa; 407-453-8161.

Popular with the gay and lesbian crowd, **Cold Keg** is a 4000-square-foot dance bar located in a pastel-colored building. Inside you'll find two bars, mirrors and ceiling fans. A variety of events will keep you entertained: female impersonators perform once a week, and "trash night," a strip show and contest on Thursday nights, is always popular. Cover charge on Thursday. ~ 4060 West New Haven Avenue, Melbourne; 407-724-1510.

NIGHTLIFE

"Your dime, my time" is how folks at **Bumper's Dance Bar** answer the phone. Besides peppy employees, the bebopping, skirt-swirling joint features '50s and '60s decor and music to match. ~ 2080 North Atlantic Avenue in Herbie K's Diner, Cocoa Beach; 407-783-6740.

Weekends are the best time to drop by **Desperadoes**, a casual, rough-hewn spot that features live soloists and bands. ~ 301 North Atlantic Avenue, Cocoa Beach; 407-784-3363.

Cocoa Beach nightlife isn't all rock-and-roll; it just seems that way. A dependable spot to relax after dark is **Dino's Jazz Piano Bar**. In this dark room lined with bookshelves and furnished with a bevy of cocktail tables, there's usually a combo playing on a small platform. Cover occasionally. ~ 315 West Route 520, Cocoa Beach; 407-799-4677.

Techno tunes, progressive and house music are the soundtrack at **Marz**, a club catering to a younger clientele. Weekends sport guest deejays. Open until sunrise. Weekend cover charge. ~ 507 North Orlando Avenue, Cocoa; 407-799-0600.

CANAVERAL NATIONAL SEASHORE It took an act of Congress to set aside the last 25-mile stretch of undeveloped beach in eastern Florida. In 1975, the government acted to preserve some 60,000 acres of water and wilderness stretching north from the Kennedy Space Center. In this pristine setting, alligators, turtles and manatees can be seen in some of the shallow lagoons; some 300 species of birds have been observed at the seashore, including the brown pelican and the threatened bald eagle. The barrier island, consisting mostly of pure quartz sand, was formed more than a million years ago. Evidence of ancient residents has been found stacked into a number of mounds, most notably Turtle Mound, a 35-foot-tall pile of oyster shells assembled by the Surreque Indians sometime between 600 and 1200 A.D. Vegetation has covered the mound, but it's still possible to climb up for a view of the surrounding terrain.

BEACHES & PARKS

Klondike Beach 🚶🏇 This is the central of three distinct beaches at Canaveral National Seashore. Klondike is a totally undeveloped area at the end of a hike through saw palmettos and Spanish bayonets. Angel wings, sand dollars, and smooth rounded moon snails are among the many shells found on all three beaches. (The other two beaches, Playalinda and Apollo, are described below.)

Playalinda Beach 🏊🎣🏖️ Though primitive, Playalinda is Cape Canaveral's most developed beach and its most accessible. Five miles of pristine white sand form a narrow ribbon between the high-water line and the delicate sand dunes. Within sight of NASA's launch pads, Playalinda is usually closed for days prior to a launch. This is an excellent place to swim; the waves are big enough for surfing but currents can be strong. It's a good beach for surf angling. The only facilities here are portable toilets. ~ Located east of Titusville off Route 402; 407-267-1110.

Apollo Beach 🏊🎣🏖️ Located at the north end of Cape Canaveral Seashore, this beach is accessible by dune walkovers. Like Playalinda, it is a long strip of white quartz sand. Not surprisingly, the swimming here is excellent; surfing is good; and there's surf and pier angling. Restrooms and a visitors center on the north end are the only facilities. ~ Take Route A1A south from New Smyrna Beach; 407-267-1110.

MERRITT ISLAND NATIONAL WILDLIFE REFUGE 🚶 Egrets, herons, gulls and terns form a welcoming committee on this 140,000-acre preserve north of the John F. Kennedy Space Center. A diverse habitat includes salty estuaries, dense marshes, pine flatwoods and hammocks of hardwood where armadillos are as common as grey squirrels. The portions of the refuge that are not marsh consist of dense vegetation that helps protect such exotic species as air plants and indigo snakes. The best times to visit are spring, fall and winter. Several species of migratory waterfowl retreat here during the coldest months of the year, making this one of Florida's prime birdwatching areas. There's fishing in both fresh and saltwater. Restrooms, marked walking trails and an auto tour route are among the amenities; visitors center. ~ On Merritt Island along Route 402, east of Titusville; 407-861-0667.

TOSOHATCHEE STATE RESERVE 🚶🚴🏇🏖️ Here woodlands and wetlands comprise 28,800 acres of eastern Orange County along the St. Johns River. This spacious park boasts two natural wonders: a rare virgin cypress swamp and Florida's largest stand of virgin slash pine. Activity is kept low key here. Hiking trails are extensive and fishing for crappie, catfish and bass is popular. There are no facilities. Groceries and restaurants are nearby. ~ Between Route 50 and Route 520 near Christmas; 407-568-5893.

▲ Primitive camping is available for backpackers and horseback trail riders only; $3 per night.

The best-known resort town on the central East Coast, Daytona Beach is famous for its 23-mile-long beach, a marvel of sparkling sand packed so hard you can easily drive a car on it. And that's what people began to do in the early 1900s, gradually developing the beach into a natural race track where speed records were set as early as 1903.

▼▼▼▼▼▼▼▼▼▼▼▼▼▼
Daytona Beach Area

Today, automobile racing and sunshine are still the paramount attractions up and down the strip of sand that stretches from Ponce Inlet north to Flagler Beach. There is history here, too, in archaeological remains and the ruins of old plantations.

The marshlands around Turnbull Creek provide a serene setting for the **Atlantic Center for the Arts**, an unusual multicultural facility devoted to the arts. Writers, dancers, painters, composers and other artists from around the world come here to teach and create. Single-story grey wooden buildings scattered over some 67 acres give the property the appearance of a low-key resort. In fact, they are used as galleries, performance spaces and lodging for the resident artists. Closed Sunday. ~ 1414 Art Center Avenue, New Smyrna Beach; 904-427-6975.

SIGHTS

Poised near the inlet separating New Smyrna Beach from Daytona Beach, the second-tallest brick lighthouse in the United States, the 173-foot-tall **Ponce de León Inlet Lighthouse** affords a breathtaking view of the inlet as well as the surrounding communities. Built in 1887, the so-called "Light Station at Mosquito Inlet" is still in service, and the entire facility, including the keeper's cottages (which were converted into museums), is open to the public. Admission. ~ South Peninsula Drive, Ponce Inlet; 904-761-1821.

Appropriately, **Daytona Beach Convention and Visitors Bureau** is centrally located, the better to offer guidance and tips to visitors. ~ 126 East Orange Avenue, Daytona Beach; 904-255-0415.

Another way to get your bearings in Daytona Beach and the nearby communities is by leaving the driving to someone else. Such as a riverboat captain. The 90-foot **Sea Critter** sails the inlet and the Atlantic. ~ 800-338-0850. **Coastal Cruise Lines** maneuvers on the Indian River and offers lunch, dinner and sunset cruises. There are also cruises that set out to view space shuttle launchings. ~ 800-881-2628. **Tiny Cruise Line** plies the Halifax River and offers waterview cruises of riverfront estates and the Intracoastal. ~ 904-226-2343.

Housed in a former bank that is Daytona Beach's finest example of Beaux-Arts design, the **Halifax Historical Museum** is best known for the six murals depicting local attractions such as the Ponce de León Inlet Lighthouse. But more fascinating is a highly detailed wood-carved model of the Boardwalk area circa 1938, with hundreds of thumb-sized people filling the bandshell. This elegant museum's historical displays range from artifacts retrieved from nearby plantation ruins to a smattering of memorabilia from the early days of car racing. Closed Sunday and Monday. Admission. ~ 252 South Beach Street, Daytona Beach; 904-255-6976.

A single stretch of International Speedway Boulevard near the Daytona Beach Municipal Airport constitutes a sporting paradise in itself, with three major attractions within sight of each other. Most famous is the **Daytona International Speedway**, which replaced the beach as the prime racing locale in 1959. You too can travel the banked, 2.5-mile tri-oval race track that drivers like Cale Yarborough and Richard Petty helped put on the map. Unless you're a qualified racer, however, you won't be driving, but riding in a tour bus. The most renowned of many events hosted here is the Daytona 500, which attracts hundreds of thousands of visitors each February. Admission. ~ 1801 West International Speedway Boulevard, Daytona Beach; 904-253-7223.

Next door at the **Daytona Beach Kennel Club** you can wager on the greyhounds circling the track. This clean, well-lit facility attracts a crowd of families and older couples, particularly for its matinee races. Admission. ~ 2201 West International Speedway Boulevard, Daytona Beach; 904-252-6484.

Things in Daytona Beach didn't always move so fast, as you can see at one of the city's most interesting museums, where a giant sloth is displayed next to contemporary Florida artworks. Far from the beaten track, in a forested setting in Tuscawilla Park, the **Museum of Arts and Science** boasts an eclectic collection including 19th-century drawings and one of the largest displays of Cuban artwork in the United States. It shows off African and Chinese art as well. In the same facility you will find a planetarium and a natural science exhibit. Closed Monday. Admission. ~ 1040 Museum Boulevard, Daytona Beach; 904-255-0285.

Among the more impressive riverfront sights in neighboring Ormond Beach is **The Casements**, a 1912 mansion that was once the winter retreat of John D. Rockefeller. (Legend has it that Rockefeller, in a fit of spite, purchased the eight-acre estate for a pittance after discovering that the nearby Ormond Hotel was charging him more than another guest for the same accommodations.) Exhibits of Hungarian folk art and Boy Scout memorabilia are displayed within the house; regional and national artwork is exhibited in the gallery and in the great octagonal atrium. There are tours of the building Monday through Saturday. Closed Sunday. ~ 25 Riverside Drive, Ormond Beach; 904-676-3216.

The setting is as appealing as the artwork at the **Ormond Memorial Art Museum**. Lush tropical gardens filled with palms, shrubbery, flowers, fish ponds, walkways, benches and a small gazebo provide an oasis only steps away from Granada Avenue traffic. Founded to display the highly symbolic religious paintings

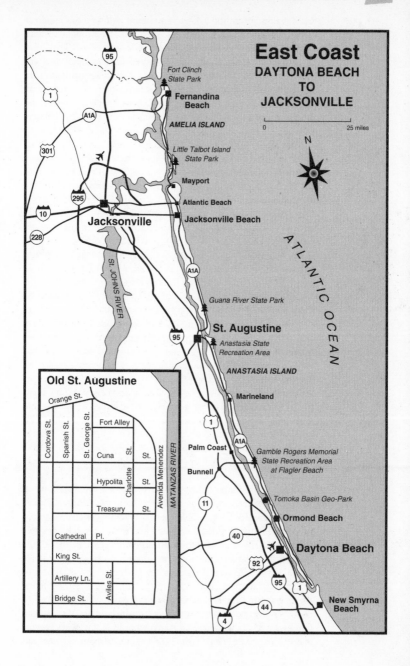

East Coast
DAYTONA BEACH
TO
JACKSONVILLE

0 — 25 miles

N

95

1

Fort Clinch
State Park

Fernandina
Beach

A1A

AMELIA ISLAND

301

Little Talbot Island
State Park

Mayport

295

Atlantic Beach

Jacksonville

10

Jacksonville Beach

228

ST. JOHNS RIVER

A1A

ATLANTIC OCEAN

Guana River State Park

95

St. Augustine

Anastasia State
Recreation Area

ANASTASIA ISLAND

Marineland

Old St. Augustine

Orange St.

Cordova St.

Spanish St.

St. George St.

Fort Alley

Cuna St.

St.

Charlotte St.

Avenida Menendez

MATANZAS RIVER

Hypolita St.

Treasury St.

Cathedral Pl.

King St.

Artillery Ln.

Aviles St.

Bridge St.

1

Palm Coast

A1A

Gamble Rogers Memorial
State Recreation Area
at Flagler Beach

Bunnell

11

Tomoka Basin Geo-Park

40

Ormond Beach

Daytona Beach

92

95

1

44

New Smyrna
Beach

4

of Malcolm Fraser, the five-room museum also serves as a gallery, with visiting exhibits by Florida artists and sculptors. ~ 78 East Granada Avenue, Ormond Beach; 904-676-3347.

Racing artifacts can also be found at the **Birthplace of Speed Museum**, which covers the years 1902 to 1958. Only aficionados of the sport, however, will find much of interest in this small museum, where the main exhibits are photographs of cars and drivers. Admission. ~ 160 East Granada Boulevard, Ormond Beach; 904-677-0311.

HIDDEN ▶   For a step into the more recent past, drive north of Ormond Beach to **Bulow Plantation Ruins State Historic Site**. A mile-long unpaved road leads through dense undergrowth to a picnic area; the ruins lie another quarter-mile away to the left. Looming out of the jungle like a movie prop from *Raiders of the Lost Ark* is a series of crumbling coquina shell ruins, all that remains of an 18th-century sugar mill. An interpretive center nearby tells the story of the plantation's development by slave labor, its prosperous production of sugar cane, cotton, rice and indigo, and its ultimate destruction by the Seminole Indians who burned plantations in anger over being displaced by settlers. Bring your lunch and enjoy the picnic area. Admission. ~ Off King's Road north of the Old Dixie Highway, Bunnell; 904-517-2084.

Nearly midway between Daytona Beach and St. Augustine is one of the coast's best-kept secrets, **Washington Oaks State Gardens**. This 400-acre park provides a sublime sanctuary where nature has been largely left alone. A half-mile trail leads through a coastal hammock of magnolia, hickory, oak and shore juniper along the Matanzas River. Equally lovely are the ornamental manmade gardens, a delightful arrangement of flowering plants and shrubs such as azaleas and camellias interspersed with small reflecting ponds and enhanced by the sounds of songbirds. There's also a beach with coquina rock formations. Admission. ~ 6400 North Oceanshore Boulevard, Palm Coast; 904-446-6780.

HIDDEN ▶

About 40 miles north of Daytona, Route A1A runs right through **Marineland**, a roadside attraction since it was built in 1938 to facilitate underwater filming. Newer oceanariums have since surpassed it in scope, but there's something endearing about this seaside complex, despite fading paint and a somewhat confusing layout. The most enduring feature is the dolphin show, performed several times a day by well-trained sea mammals in an oceanview amphitheater. There is almost always entertainment of some kind, whether it's a special-effects film called *Sea Dream* or divers hand-feeding sharks in a huge tank sporting hundreds of portholes for underwater viewing. Marineland also boasts an impressive 35,000-gallon re-creation of a Florida freshwater spring, and wildlife exhibits featuring live alligators, caimans, iguanas and other reptiles. Admission. ~ 9507 Oceanshore Boulevard, Marine-land; 904-471-1111.

Its temperate climate and 23-mile-long beach have made this area among the hottest destinations in Florida. Route A1A is one long canyon of hotels and motels that try to differentiate themselves with decorative themes ranging from Polynesian to Mayan. In fact, many of them are very much alike on the inside, and almost all are equidistant from the beach. The places below have been selected for value, individuality and location.

LODGING

South of Daytona Beach, the town of New Smyrna Beach is so sleepy as to be nearly yawn-inducing. The perfect place to take advantage of this back-to-the-19th-century feeling is the **Riverview Hotel**. You truly can't miss this place. It presides over the Intra-coastal Waterway in a sparkling coat of bright pink-colored paint, its cheery white balconies gleaming in the sun. Built as a two-story house, this former bridge tender's residence grew into a three-story hotel in the early 1900s. The rooms are decorated with reproduc-tion antiques, including four-poster beds. Louvered French doors lead to a balcony, a patio or the pool deck. Continental breakfast is included. ~ 103 Flagler Avenue, New Smyrna Beach; 904-428-5858, 800-945-7416, fax 904-423-8927. MODERATE TO ULTRA-DELUXE.

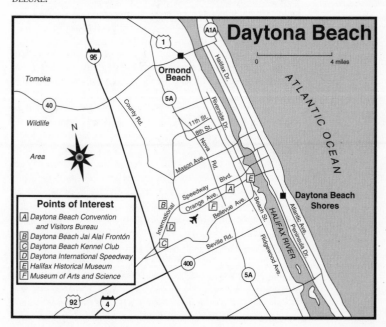

Daytona Beach

0 ——————— 4 miles

ATLANTIC OCEAN

Tomoka

Ormond Beach

Wildlife

Area

N

Daytona Beach Shores

HALIFAX RIVER

Points of Interest
- A Daytona Beach Convention and Visitors Bureau
- B Daytona Beach Jai Alai Frontón
- C Daytona Beach Kennel Club
- D Daytona International Speedway
- E Halifax Historical Museum
- F Museum of Arts and Science

A few stoplights south of the frantic midtown action, the beach has the same sun, the same clean sand, but fewer people. In front of the **Day Star Motel,** you can at least find a square of sand to call your own. For reasonable prices, you get two double beds and a full kitchen. For a little more, you can get a large oceanfront efficiency. Also on the grounds is a heated pool. These accommodations aren't beautiful, but they are clean and well maintained. ~ 3811 South Atlantic Avenue, Daytona Beach; 904-767-3780, 800-506-5505. BUDGET.

The aroma of potpourri greets the visitor at **Captain's Quarters Inn,** a five-story all-suite inn. Country provincial patterns, oak dressers and plump pillows piled up on the sofa give these suites a homey touch. The country style extends to private balconies furnished with rocking chairs. ~ 3711 South Atlantic Avenue, Daytona Beach; 904-767-3119, 800-332-3119, fax 904-767-0883. DELUXE.

One of the most unusual hotel configurations I've ever seen belongs to **Perry's Ocean-Edge,** a complex of 206 units. Once you make up your mind whether to rent an oceanfront motel room, enclosed garden room, apartment suite or garden efficiency, you then must decide which of three pools to enjoy. The huge solar-heated one is sheltered from the fierce Florida sun by soaring shade trees, plus a retractable roof. There's plenty of room poolside for lounge chairs, tables and a whirlpool. ~ 2209 South Atlantic Avenue, Daytona Beach; 904-255-0581, 800-447-0002, fax 904-258-7315. MODERATE TO DELUXE.

Its prime beach location, the generous size of its rooms and the tasteful decor make the highrise **Nautilus Inn** a good stopping place. Pastel patterns blend in perfectly with the beach palette visible from every private balcony. Evening cocktails and a continental breakfast are served in a bright oceanfront room. An outdoor spa bubbles away between pool and beach. Kitchenettes available. ~ 1515 South Atlantic Avenue, Daytona Beach; 904-254-8600, 800-254-0560, fax 904-254-8427. MODERATE TO DELUXE.

It's hard to beat a hostel for low prices, and the **Daytona Beach International Youth Hostel** is no exception. Odds are you'll find long-haired youngsters watching television or playing pool in the lobby. If you don't mind sharing a room and sleeping in a bunk bed (lockers are available for a fee), this centrally located, 180-bed hostel is a deal. Hostel rooms include TV and private bath, as do the private motel rooms. ~ 140 South Atlantic Avenue, Daytona Beach; 904-258-6937, fax 904-258-6541. BUDGET TO DELUXE.

The **Sea Brazil Motel** offers a good location and motel rooms in typical color combinations of blue and brown. Amenities here include cable television and kitchenettes. ~ 39 South Ocean Avenue, Daytona Beach; 904-238-0054, fax 904-238-1234. BUDGET.

Just west of the Halifax River sits the gay-friendly **Coquina Inn Bed & Breakfast**. Each of the four rooms (Azalea, Jasmine, Hibiscus and Magnolia) is individually and elegantly appointed with ceiling fans, French doors, balconies and canopied four-poster beds. Guests may use bicycles gratis. The breakfasts are gourmet, buffet-style affairs. Along with choice of beverage, fruit and breads, daily entrées may include quiche lorraine or country ham and creamy egg custard in a home-fried potato crust. Ever-present classical music sets the mood. ~ 544 South Palmetto Avenue, Daytona Beach; phone/fax 904-254-4969, 800-805-7533. MODERATE TO DELUXE.

Anyone who has ever wanted to sleep in a room named for Christopher Columbus, Queen Isabella, King Juan Carlos or Marco Polo can do so at **The Villa**. This gay-friendly, Spanish-style mansion is set on three acres with a pool and hot tub. It's one block from the Halifax River and four blocks from the beach. Guests sleep in a four-poster bed or in a nautically themed room where Columbus would feel right at home. Baroque furniture, a library and formal dining room make it a best buy. ~ 801 North Peninsula Drive, Daytona Beach; phone/fax 904-248-2020. DELUXE.

Indigo Lakes Holiday Inn is an oasis of velvet green fairways, grounds sprinkled with lakes, ponds and trees, all-weather tennis courts and an Olympic-size pool, all capturing the subdued ambience of a country club. This self-contained resort also harbors a fitness trail and shuffleboard and volleyball courts. The focus here is on the outdoors; the rooms are spacious, very comfortable and equipped with a private patio or balcony. Kitchenettes are available. Guests will have to drive about 15 minutes to the beach. ~ 2620 West International Speedway Boulevard, Daytona Beach; 904-258-6333, fax 904-254-3698. DELUXE TO ULTRA-DELUXE.

The gay-friendly **Buccaneer Motel** offers 15 quiet rooms as well as five suites in an adjacent Spanish-style home with a tile roof. Across the street from the beach, this complex has six kitchenettes and a pool. Carpeted rooms have a tropical motif and ceiling fans. Second floor units offer an ocean view. ~ 2301 North Atlantic Avenue, Daytona Beach; 904-253-9678, 800-972-6056, fax 904-255-3946. BUDGET TO MODERATE.

Directly north of Daytona Beach is Ormond Beach, a quieter, more residential neighborhood. Here the **Mainsail Motel** lives up to its name; everything is done in bright whites and sky blues. Rooms are sparkling and spacious, with a railed balcony and a view of palm trees and the oceanside pool. There is also a sauna and exercise room. ~ 281 South Atlantic Avenue, Ormond Beach; 904-677-2131, 800-843-5142. MODERATE TO DELUXE.

South of St. Augustine in Marineland, there's only one game in town, and that's the **Marineland Ocean Resort**, an unprepossessing set of concrete blocks that separate Route A1A from the beach. The best thing to be said about the 122 clean, no-frills rooms is that they all have some kind of ocean view. The vistas from the upstairs balconies in the older building make rooms in that section preferable. ~ 9507 Ocean Shore Boulevard, Marineland; 904-471-1222, 800-824-4218, fax 904-471-3352. MODERATE TO ULTRA-DELUXE.

DINING

A brick courtyard embellished with wrought iron makes a lovely entrance to **Riverview Charlie's**. True to its waterfront location, this glass-walled restaurant does best with its seafood, including local shellfish as well as Boston scrod and mahimahi. Chicken, pastas, sirloin and salads are also available. ~ 101 Flagler Avenue, New Smyrna Beach; 904-428-1865. MODERATE TO DELUXE.

The **China American Garden Restaurant** is staffed with tuxedo-clad servers who bring you Chinese food prepared in a variety of styles. Occupying a tiny corner of a shopping strip, this family-style establishment serves spicy Szechuan dishes as well as even spicier Hunan cuisine. ~ 2516 South Atlantic Avenue, Daytona Beach Shores; 904-788-6269. BUDGET TO MODERATE.

The **St. Regis Hotel and Restaurant** stands out as one of the most elegant dining rooms in town. Hardwood floors, mirrors and attractive paintings create an exquisite dining spot within this historic hotel. Scallops, crab, shrimp and other seafood courses are executed with the same flair as the veal and beef dishes. Service is cordial but professional. Closed Sunday and Monday. ~ 509 Seabreeze Boulevard, Daytona Beach; 904-252-8743. MODERATE TO DELUXE.

It seems that every beach town has a restaurant called the **Chart House**, but this one is grander than most. Tables are grouped for

✔ **CHECK THESE OUT—UNIQUE DINING**

- *Budget:* Feast on a hearty sandwich at **The Monk's Vineyard**, brought to you by a real monk—or at least someone dressed like one. *page 207*
- *Budget to moderate:* Snuggle up to a soft shell crab at **Snug Harbor**—large portions of fresh seafood keep the locals coming back. *page 217*
- *Moderate to deluxe:* Drop into **The Mango Tree** and delight in the delicious improvisations on Continental cuisine. *page 186*
- *Ultra-deluxe:* Make the effort to find the tucked-away **La Crêpe en Haut,** and you'll be rewarded with elegant cuisine in a luxurious yet relaxed atmosphere. *page 199*

Budget: under $8   Moderate: $8–$16   Deluxe: $16–$24   Ultra-deluxe: over $24

intimacy and arranged in semicircular tiers; lots of bare wood, glass, foliage and a view of the Halifax River give the place a distinctly pleasant personality. Steaks are big, juicy and properly cooked to order, but the fresh fish dishes are the real stars. They also have a delicious salad bar. Dinner only. ~ 1100 Marina Point Drive, Daytona Beach; 904-255-9022. MODERATE TO DELUXE.

A popular family-style eatery, **Delta Restaurant** rest across from the ocean and supplies fine views from its glass-enclosed atrium. Prime rib, seafood, gyros and *souvlaki* are a few of the American and Greek-style offerings. Open for breakfast, lunch and dinner. ~ 790 South Atlantic Avenue, Ormond Beach; 904-672-3140. MODERATE.

Easily identifiable by its deeply pitched roof, **Julian's Dining Room and Lounge** is a spacious, dimly lit restaurant specializing in charbroiled steaks, chops, chicken and seafood. Dinner only. ~ 88 South Atlantic Avenue, Ormond Beach; 904-677-6767. MODERATE TO ULTRA-DELUXE.

If you want some of the best food in the area, you'll have to work hard at finding **La Crêpe en Haut**. Located on the upper floor of a courtyard mall called Fountain Square, it has an atmosphere akin to a rather swank living room decorated with fine furniture and serene colors. Lamb, seafood, sweetbreads and elegant beef dishes are only a few of the items on a serious, multicourse menu. Lunch served on weekdays. Closed Monday. ~ 142 East Granada Boulevard, Ormond Beach; 904-673-1999. ULTRA-DELUXE.

SHOPPING

You could fill a book with a list of Florida's shopping malls, but the **Daytona Beach Outlet Mall** warrants singling out. Forget to pack a particular item of clothing? You could outfit the entire family at some of the 40 factory outlets here and pay maybe one-half what you would in a department store. A little larger than a boutique, **Bon Worth** (904-760-4794) manufactures its own line of upscale women's sportswear, from trendy slacks and shorts to blazers and skirts. ~ 2400 South Ridgewood Avenue, South Daytona.

Discount shopping is something of a specialty in Daytona Beach. Women's clothing can be bought direct from the factory at **Frayne Fashions**. ~ 2675 North Atlantic Avenue in Bel Air Plaza, Daytona Beach; 904-673-3489.

The **Daytona Beach Flea Market**, running Friday through Sunday, is one of the largest in the state selling the usual range of knickknacks, produce and funky stuff. Some antiques also and great kitschy souvenirs for the ones left back home. ~ Intersection of Routes 4 and 92.

Take your credit cards along to **The Lucille Leigh Collection**, the most beautiful store on this part of the coast. The merchandise here is somewhere between museum and department store quality.

◄ *HIDDEN*

Essentially high-fashion accessories for the home, the selection includes exquisite candle holders, silk tassel pulls, cloisonné vases and glass objets d'art. ~ 162 Vining Court, Ormond Beach; 904-673-2042.

NIGHTLIFE A good place to start the evening, before going on to the dance palaces, is the **Oyster Pub**. All comers to this convivial corner saloon are greeted with a powerful aroma of salt—that's from the raw oysters. A sea of cocktail tables surrounds an enormous horseshoe bar; the music is loud, the vibes very, very casual. ~ 555 Seabreeze Boulevard, Daytona Beach; 904-255-6348.

Razzles features the latest light, video and sound equipment. Once the crowd—a mix of sizes, shapes and ages, but all trying to be cool—deigns to step onto the dancefloor to the beat of high-energy music, this cavernous disco can be the liveliest place in town, and it's tops for people-watching. Wednesday and Friday are Ladies' Night. Cover. ~ 611 Seabreeze Boulevard, Daytona Beach; 904-257-6236.

When the surf's up, head for **Point Break**, a brightly colored lounge featuring beach logos on the walls and surfboards hanging from the ceiling. They offer music most nights, provided by live bands or deejays. ~ 600 North Atlantic Avenue in the Holiday Inn Sunspree Resort, Daytona Beach; 904-255-4471.

Finally, if you simply must dance to "Louie, Louie" one more time, get on down to the **Ocean Deck**, the local favorite for late-night raw bar snacking. You'll recognize it by the booming sound system that always seems as if it's about to raise the roof. Reggae and Caribbean bands hit the stage every night except on Sunday, when a rock-and-roll band is in the spotlight. ~ 127 South Ocean Avenue, Daytona Beach; 904-253-5224.

THEATER, OPERA, SYMPHONY AND DANCE The **Seaside Music Theater** has a somewhat split personality. In the summer months, the repertory company of performers and musicians stage light opera, Broadway fare and other productions at the **Daytona Beach Community College Theater Center**. ~ 1200 West International Speedway Boulevard, Daytona Beach. In the winter they perform at the **Ormond Beach Performing Arts Center**. ~ 399 North U.S. 1, Ormond Beach; 904-252-6200.

The Daytona Playhouse hosts various theater productions from September through June. ~ 100 Jessamine Boulevard, Daytona Beach; 904-255-2431.

GAY SCENE **Beachside Club** is known for its female impersonation shows Thursday through Sunday, and for its drink specials at a 34-foot bar. A deejay plays danceable music and a little jazz. Sunday through Tuesday are karaoke nights. ~ 415 Main Street, Daytona Beach; 904-252-5465.

Located in a red-and-white brick building, **769 Club Restaurant and Lounge** is a popular women's club that features American cuisine. You can relax at the U-shaped bar and listen to tunes from the jukebox. Pool tables and an outdoor volleyball court add to the fun. Although the crowd is predominantly lesbian, men are also welcome. ~ 769 Alabama Street, Daytona Beach; 904-253-4361.

LIGHTHOUSE POINT COUNTY PARK   When the locals tire of the crowds in central Daytona Beach, they head south to a less well-known beach. Bypassed by Route A1A, Ponce Inlet Park is often overlooked except by travelers in search of the Ponce de León Inlet Lighthouse. The southern portion of the park is a tree-shaded greensward where you can enjoy a picnic while watching the fishing boats in the marina. To the east is a particularly beautiful stretch of pale sandy beach where it's possible to take long walks in relative peace and quiet. This is a good place to swim and surf fish. There are five boardwalks, one of which leads to the jetty. Facilities are limited to a picnic area, nature trails and restrooms; grocery stores and restaurants are nearby. Day-use fee, $3. ~ At the end of Atlantic Avenue south of Daytona Beach; 904-756-7488.

BEACHES & PARKS

◄ *HIDDEN*

DAYTONA BEACH   The promotional brochures proclaim 23 miles of hard sand beach, but technically only four miles of that lie within the city limits of Daytona Beach. To the south is Daytona Beach Shores, to the north, Ormond Beach, both virtually indistinguishable from Daytona Beach. Aside from the expanse of clean beige sand (500 feet wide at low tide), the most striking aspect of the beach is the presence of automobiles. Motorists are required to park perpendicular to the ocean, in single file, and to restrict their beach driving to poorly marked "lanes." A speed limit of 10 mph is enforced, but it is still distracting to have to look both ways before proceeding into the surf. Nonetheless, this is an excellent place to swim; surfing is good at the north end; and there's both surf and pier angling. Facilities include picnic areas, restrooms, showers and lifeguards; grocery stores and restaurants are nearby. ~ Located between Ocean Dunes Road and Plaza Boulevard off Route A1A.

TOMOKA BASIN GEO-PARK   The scenic approach to this 2000-acre preserve is along a driveway worthy of an antebellum plantation (which it once was), with magnolia trees and moss-draped oaks threatening to overtake the road. Flanked by the Halifax and Tomoka rivers, Tomoka Basin Geo-Park has coastal hammocks dense with shrubs and trees. Picnicking, saltwater fishing and canoeing are the primary activities. Facilities include an interpretive center, canoe rentals, restrooms and showers;

◄ *HIDDEN*

grocery stores and restaurants are nearby. Day-use fee, $3.25. ~ At 2099 North Beach Street in Ormond Beach; 904-676-4050.

▲ There are 100 sites with RV hookups; $8 to $17 per night.

GAMBLE ROGERS MEMORIAL STATE RECREATION AREA AT FLAGLER BEACH 🏃 🚲 ⛵ 🎣 ⛴ 🚤 ⛽ Named after the country-and-western singer who drowned while attempting to save another swimmer, this windswept park offers close encounters with a variety of wildlife. With frontage on the ocean as well as on the Intracoastal Waterway, a nature trail winds through taller sand dunes, where scrub oaks and shrubs make an excellent habitat for the Florida scrub jay. On the inland side of the park, fiddler crabs and wading birds wander through the marsh grasses and shallow waters near the boat basin. On the ocean side, sea turtles lay their eggs (in early summer) in the rough coquina-shell sand above the high water mark on this narrow, undeveloped beach. Swimming is excellent here. Pompano and whiting are common surf-casting fish. Flounder and speckled trout can be caught in the Intracoastal Waterway. There are pavilions, restrooms, showers, picnic areas and a boat launch; groceries and restaurants are nearby. Day-use fee, $2. ~ 3100 South Route A1A, Flagler Beach; 904-517-2086.

▲ There are 34 sites with RV hookups, water and electricity; $17 to $19 per night.

▼▼▼▼▼▼▼▼▼▼
St. Augustine

The oldest city in the United States is a singular blend of narrow lanes and wide sweeping beaches, overhanging balconies and grand old homes. Founded in 1565 by Pedro Menéndez de Aviles, the Spanish settlement was looted in 1586 by Sir Francis Drake and eventually taken by the British two centuries later. Over the centuries it has been the jewel in the crown of Florida, a prize for which several nations have fought.

With more than 400 years of history behind it, St. Augustine today offers more sightseeing spots than any other city on Florida's east coast, especially along the narrow streets in the heart of the old town.

SIGHTS

The picturesque Bridge of Lions spans the Intracoastal Waterway to link Anastasia Island with St. Augustine. Here, since many of the city's numerous attractions charge nominal admission fees, the economical and efficient way to tour is via **Sightseeing Trains**, which offer narrated seven-mile tours with stop-off privileges at major points of interest. Passengers may disembark at will and take any later train they wish. ~ 170 San Marco Avenue; 904-829-6545.

It is at **Fort Matanzas National Monument** that visitors get their first glimpse of St. Augustine's history. Actually, the crumbling fort, built in 1742 near the sites of bloody 16th-century battles between the French and Spanish, sits across the Matanzas

River on Rattlesnake Island and is accessible by a small ferry that docks at the visitors center. ~ Southern end of Anastasia Island; 904-471-0116.

The candy-striped tower visible from 20 miles away makes it easy to find the **Lighthouse Museum of St. Augustine**. Florida's first lighthouse is still used, and off-limits, but the partially burned out, two-story Victorian lighthouse keeper's home has been restored as a coastal museum with exhibits on the area's history, a period room and a theater that screens a half-hour video on lightkeepers. Admission. ~ 81 Lighthouse Avenue, Anastasia Island; 904-829-0745.

The St. Augustine Visitors Information Center offers brochures, maps of the historic district and even an introductory video for visitors. ~ 10 Castillo Drive; 904-825-1000.

The most imposing structure in old St. Augustine is **Castillo de San Marcos National Monument**, a massive, symmetrical 17th-century structure built by the Spanish from coquina shell rock. Visitors enter near the **Old City Gate** via a drawbridge across the moat and proceed into a grassy courtyard. Some of the surrounding ground-floor rooms have been furnished to reflect various aspects of garrison life throughout the fort's extensive history; others serve as museums with exhibits on military history. Visitors should appreciate the view from atop the 35-foot-high ramparts. And make sure to take a walk around the outside grounds, a setting so pastoral it's hard to envision the carnage that took place beyond the gates of this never-conquered fort. Admission. ~ 1 South Castillo Drive; 904-829-6506.

Close to the center of town, **St. George Street** is closed to automobile traffic from Orange Street south to Cathedral Place. This district, restored to evoke a late 18th-century atmosphere, is lined with coquina stone houses converted into shops. Among these buildings are such interesting attractions as the **Oldest Wooden Schoolhouse**, used by the Spanish during the 18th century. Today it exhibits educational artifacts from that period. Admission. ~ 14 St. George Street; 904-824-0192.

Nearby, **St. Augustine's Spanish Quarter Museum** is a reconstructed Spanish village where craftspeople in period costumes demonstrate blacksmithing, woodworking and other daily-life activities. Admission. ~ 29 St. George Street; 904-825-6830.

Through a door off the main thoroughfare, persistent visitors will find the **St. Photios Shrine**, a tiny building with an altar surrounded by stunning frescoes, religious icons painted directly onto the walls and domes. Also here is an enlightening display relating to Greek-American history, plus a small gift shop with exquisite postcards of the chapel interiors as well as souvenirs and Greek-made clothing. ~ 41 St. George Street; 904-829-8205.

◄ HIDDEN

For further glimpses into Florida's past, stop by the **Dr. Peck House**, a 19th-century home decorated in early antebellum style.

Closed Sunday in the summer. Admission. ~ 143 St. George Street; 904-829-5064.

Another impressive landmark, the **Cathedral Basilica of St. Augustine** dates to 1797. Built to replace a church that was demolished when the area was under British rule, it is open for daily tours. ~ 38 Cathedral Place; 904-824-2806.

Elsewhere in the historic part of town is the **Oldest House**, occupied as early as 1727 and now headquarters for the local historical society. On the property are both the **Webb Museum**, devoted to St. Augustine's past, and the **Tovar House**, which houses an army museum. Admission. ~ 14 St. Francis Street; 904-824-2872.

Diverting but of dubious authenticity is the so-called **Oldest Store Museum**, where the atmosphere of a 19th-century general store is somewhat diluted by the inclusion of a 1927 Model T Ford truck and the like. Admission. ~ 4 Artillery Lane; 904-829-9729.

In a city of so many "oldests," it comes as no surprise that **Potter's Wax Museum** claims to be the first of its genre in the United States. Guide yourself past more than 170 exceptionally well-crafted likenesses of such notables as John F. Kennedy, plus composers, artists, noblemen and other historic figures. Admission. ~ 17 King Street; 904-829-9056.

The very impressive **Lightner Museum** packs a double wallop. First, it occupies the site of the former Alcazar Hotel, part of Henry Flagler's legacy of elegant Florida resorts. Second, the museum comprises three floors of exquisite possessions displayed with matching good taste. The Lightners' collection of cut glass, Victorian art glass and the stained-glass creations of Louis Tiffany could serve as a graduate course in the history of this painstaking craft. Other decorative arts, furnishings and costumes evoke America's Gilded Age, but the best spot is the Music Box Room, where tour guides demonstrate the features of these delicate antiques. Admission. ~ City Hall Complex, King and Cordova streets; 904-824-2874.

Venturing out along San Marco Avenue, you will happen upon the **Old Jail and Florida Heritage Museum**. Tours of the jail are

CROSS PURPOSES

Near the Fountain of Youth Discovery Park, the **Mission of Nombre de Dios** is easily sighted by the Great Cross that soars 208 feet above the easternmost point of the mission. It's believed to be the site of the first Roman Catholic mass ever celebrated in the United States. ~ 27 Ocean Avenue; 904-824-2809.

offered by guides in period costume, and the museum features exhibits on the history and accomplishments of Henry Flagler, as well as replicas of American Indian villages. Separate admission. ~ 167 San Marco Avenue; 904-829-3800.

The **Old Sugar Mill** houses a museum displaying 19th-century milling tools. ~ 254 San Marco Avenue; 904-829-6545.

Ripley's Believe It Or Not Museum is one of several similar exhibits in the country. Here are a dizzying three floors filled with testimony to the weird, odd, compulsive, inventive and misshapen people and things of this world, from the Tower of London fashioned from some 264,345 toothpicks to the stuffed body of a two-headed calf, complete with exclamation points following every description! Admission. ~ 19 San Marco Avenue; 904-824-1606.

Although it seems kind of hokey, the **Fountain of Youth Discovery Park** is as irresistible to most tourists as the concept of youth-giving waters must have been to Ponce de León, who is believed to have set foot near here in 1513. You might skip sampling from the fountain and go straight to the Historical Discovery Globe, representing a view of earth from outer space, and the planetarium, where the skies are set to look as they would have from the deck of Ponce de León's galleon. Take note of Magnolia Avenue, a glorious archway formed by oak trees. Admission. ~ 11 Magnolia Avenue; 904-829-3168.

LODGING

Small inns are not everyone's cup of afternoon tea, yet they are most simpatico with the intimate atmosphere of historic St. Augustine. Other than these, the most prevalent type of lodging is the moderate-priced motel, both in town and near the beach.

The Mediterranean revival–style **Casa de la Paz** makes a nice counterpoint to St. Augustine's Victorian bed and breakfast inns. The smooth stucco exterior would be austere were it not for the barrel-tile roofing and molded sills. Here the best views of Matanzas Bay belong to a suite that occupies the entire third floor. The other rooms also have their charms, and each its own bath, but for extra privacy book one of the veranda rooms, which have their own entrances. Every guest can enjoy the seclusion of a Spanish walled courtyard and sunporch. ~ 22 Avenida Menéndez; 904-829-2915, 800-929-2915. MODERATE TO ULTRA-DELUXE.

No one is going to turn down your bed at the **Monson Bayfront Resort**, a pseudo-Spanish-style motel that delivers surprising value. Rooms are spacious enough to accommodate a couple of imitation-leather reading chairs and louvered dividers between bedroom and dressing room. The tiled baths are also nice. ~ 32 Avenida Menéndez; 904-829-2277. MODERATE.

Absolutely free for the taking is one of St. Augustine's finest attractions: the sweeping view of Matanzas Bay. This bonanza can be easily appreciated from one of the three porches that embellish the **Westcott House**. A Victorian concoction of pale peach and blue with carved white trim, this bed and breakfast inn is resplendent with antiques, lush carpeting and lustrous pine floors. All eight rooms have private baths, some with clawfoot tubs, and a distinctive color scheme; almost every inch of the ground-floor Menéndez Suite, for instance, is painted eggshell blue. Some might object to the Westcott's overstylized decor; everything is just too-too. However, that's easy to overlook when you consider the pluses: verandas furnished with perfect white wicker and a brick courtyard for enjoying breakfast alfresco. ~ 146 Avenida Menéndez; phone/fax 904-824-4301. DELUXE TO ULTRA-DELUXE.

HIDDEN ►

Unlike some of the more formal bed and breakfasts in this quaint town, the **Kenwood Inn** has that definite lived-in feeling. In 14 one-of-a-kind guest rooms, the Kenwood mixes antiques and lace curtains with fresh touches such as hand-stenciled walls. The large parlor, a comfortable gathering place for guests, is transformed into a dining room for breakfast. The graceful pecan tree partially shading the brick-lined patio may well have been planted when this house was built more than a century ago. But the pool—a rare amenity in St. Augustine—is contemporary. ~ 38 Marine Street; 904-824-2116, fax 904-824-1689. MODERATE TO ULTRA-DELUXE.

The **St. Francis Inn**, a public guest house since 1845, is a comfortable three-story warren of individually decorated accommodations ranging from single rooms to three-room suites with kitchenettes. Original fireplaces and attractive wainscoting imbue this cozy coquina inn with much charm, as do the courtyard and tropical gardens. In the courtyard is a two-bedroom, two-bath cottage and a pool. ~ 279 St. George Street; 904-824-6068, 800-824-6062, fax 904-810-5525. MODERATE TO ULTRA-DELUXE.

In the heart of the well-preserved historic district, two very different bed and breakfasts sit cattycornered. **The Victorian House** offers accommodations in the main house and a four-room carriage house. Both are painted a soft vanilla with pewter-blue trim and are connected with a spiffy white picket fence. Built as a boarding house in 1890, the renovated version plays up its past with canopied beds, handwoven coverlets and hand-hooked rugs on heartpine floors. ~ 11 Cadiz Street; 904-824-5214. MODERATE TO DELUXE.

You can't beat the **St. Augustine Hostel** for clean, well-priced accommodations. Situated in the historic downtown district, the hostel features five dormitories and two couple/family rooms. Guests can hang out in the living room or relax on the rooftop garden. The kitchen is also available for use. ~ 32 Treasury Street; phone/fax 904-829-6163. BUDGET.

Casa de Solana is geared toward travelers who like everything just so and don't mind adhering to a rigid timetable. For example, breakfast is served at a ten-foot-long mahogany table in the formal dining room at 8:30 on the dot. Of course, the reward is a classic southern breakfast. Four suites are decorated with antiques; each has either a fireplace, a view of Matanzas Bay or a balcony overlooking a large garden. ~ 21 Aviles Street; 904-824-3555, 800-760-3556, fax 904-824-3316. DELUXE.

North of the historic district, accommodations are available at the **Ramada Inn**. This five-story motel has clean, decent rooms with views of the pool or the parking lot, but we wouldn't recommend staying here except for the convenient location. ~ 116 San Marco Avenue; 904-824-4352, 800-575-5289, fax 904-824-2745. MODERATE.

Across Matanzas Bay on Anastasia Island, the **Conch House Marina Resort** looks as if it had been lifted, thatched roof and all, directly from a South Seas island. Most rooms are spacious—even the studio apartments have two double beds—and have wallpaper, contemporary furnishings and drapes covering sliding glass doors. The best views, however, are not from the rooms but from the pool, the small riverside beach and a number of multilevel outdoor bars that help give this resort its extremely relaxed ambience. ~ 57 Comares Avenue; 904-829-8646, 800-940-6256, fax 904-829-5414. MODERATE TO DELUXE.

DINING

Bunches of plastic grapes droop from the ceiling of **The Monk's Vineyard**, a funky, stained-glass grotto where waiters pad around in monk's robes and sandals. Loaded sandwiches are the highlight, with specials like "the Abbott" (roast beef, mushrooms, Swiss cheese and horseradish sauce). Also available is a wide selection of California vintages. No dinner. Closed Wednesday. ~ 56 St. George Street; 904-824-5888. BUDGET.

With its stucco facade, archways, tiled walls and fountains, The **Columbia Restaurant St. Augustine** looks as though it might have been shipped over from Spain. The cuisine is in keeping: paella, chicken with yellow rice, *boliche* (Cuban rump roast with chorizo sausage). ~ 98 St. George Street; 904-824-3341. MODERATE.

Scarlett O'Hara's is a convivial restaurant used as a watering hole by hordes of locals. Located in a renovated residence on a shady side street, it is a convenient spot for affordable lunches of soup, salad and sandwiches. In the evenings, finger food such as clams, shrimp and raw oysters can be enjoyed inside the lounge or out on the front porch where you can watch the passing scene. ~ 70 Hypolita Street; 904-824-6535. BUDGET.

As if St. Augustine didn't claim enough "oldests" and "firsts," it also has what could be the world's only café located in a (nowempty) swimming pool. The **Café Alcazar**, hidden away in the mall of antique shops behind the Lightner Museum, is well worth the effort required to find it. Crêpes, "croissandwiches" and imagina-

◄ HIDDEN

tive salads combine to create one of the most innovative menus in town. No dinner. ~ 25 Granada Street; 904-824-7813. BUDGET.

Le Pavillon serves hearty European food like roast rack of lamb, duckling, schnitzel and bouillabaisse in a small turn-of-the-century house with French country decor. ~ 45 San Marco Avenue; 904-824-6202. MODERATE TO DELUXE.

One look at **Raintree Restaurant** tells you this place must have been a private home, and indeed it was. Built in 1879, it features a formal dining room with antiques and huge historic paintings, a garden terrace and upstairs seating on weekends. The fare is elaborate: veal Oscar, rack of lamb, seafood and various duck, chicken and beef dishes. Dinner only. ~ 102 San Marco Avenue; 904-824-7211. MODERATE TO DELUXE.

Local legend says that Henry Flagler and some of the moneyed Vanderbilts used to eat oysters at **Oscar's Old Florida Grill**, an authentically Florida kind of place housed in a 90-year-old roadhouse with a tin ceiling. On Wednesday and Thursday nights live bluegrass bands serenade the patrons who dock here to eat buckets of steamed oysters, crab patties and fresh fish catches of the day—all accompanied by homemade cole slaw and hush puppies as big as Ping-Pong balls. For dessert, the sweet potato pie is sublime. Lunch served only on Friday through Sunday. Closed Monday and Tuesday. ~ 614 Euclid Avenue; 904-829-3794. BUDGET TO MODERATE.

The **Gypsy Cab Company** has a casual, café atmosphere that transcends bare floors and a view of the highway. The standard menu of fresh fish and steaks is spiced up with such offbeat selections as chicken stuffed with garlic butter and Swiss cheese, and Cajun shrimp. No lunch on Tuesday. ~ 828 Anastasia Boulevard; 904-824-8244. MODERATE.

SHOPPING   Souvenir buying is a snap in St. Augustine; most of the 40-plus attractions in the country's oldest city stock all manner of mementos. The best shopping is along historic **St. George Street**, where pubs and points of interest rub shoulders with an intriguing medley of shops.

The cozy **Colonial Shop** specializes in early Americana and country wares, including nostalgia items such as metal piggy banks and ragdolls. ~ 8 St. George Street; 904-824-8974.

The Museum Store is great fun to tour. Blue Zoo ceramics from Chile and Mexican "worry stones" are a few of the items imported from around the world. The store also carries a wide selection of books and educational tools. ~ 33 St. George Street; 904-825-5040.

Among the handmade goods at **San Agustin Imports** are Panama hats, the real thing from Ecuador. ~ 46 St. George Street; 904-829-0032.

Finding seashells in Florida is like shooting fish in a barrel, but **The Shell Shop** is known for its good-looking glass-bottomed lamps filled with beautiful specimens. ~ 148 St. George Street; 904-824-8778.

A block from St. George Street, **Casa Italia** stocks hundreds of colorful porcelain dolls and clowns. Collectors will discover both common and rare dolls measuring from a tiny two inches to three feet in size. ~ 12 Cathedral Place; 904-824-1961.

In a city as old as St. Augustine, you'd expect to find antiques. The place to go is the **Lightner Antique Mall**, where you'll find a wide range of collectibles, including antique linens and moderately priced pieces of china. ~ King and Granada streets, behind the Lightner Museum; 904-824-2874.

St. Augustine will never be ranked with the great nightlife cities of the world. This is a daytime town but, true to its tradition of southern hospitality, it does offer a little bit for almost every visitor with energy left over from a full day of sightseeing.

NIGHTLIFE

Right in the historic district, the **Monson Bayfront Resort** features a pianist Thursday through Sunday. He plays a variety of music, including show tunes, from the '50s and '60s. ~ 32 Avenida Menéndez, in the Monson Lodge; 904-829-2277.

After dark, **Scarlett O'Hara's** undergoes a subtle metamorphosis from restaurant to Happy Hour hangout to dance bar. It features blues and rhythm-and-blues bands most evenings except Sunday and Monday, when karaoke reigns. Cover on weekends. ~ 70 Hypolita Street; 904-824-6535.

The **Conch House Marina Lounge** is a convivial spot where the atmosphere is enhanced by the riverfront setting and the plucking of a lone guitarist. ~ 57 Comares Avenue; 904-829-8646.

Scores is a sports bar with 16 TVs for your viewing pleasure. ~ Holiday Inn, 860 A1A Beach Boulevard; 904-471-2555.

ST. AUGUSTINE BEACH This is a simple beach—just a few thousand square feet of hard sand topped with a little powder and nudged by an endless series of small waves. It's an excellent place to swim and there's good fishing off the pier. The only drawback to this paradise is that automobile traffic is allowed on the beach. Facilities include picnic areas, restrooms and lifeguards; restaurants and grocery stores are nearby. ~ There are eight access points to this beach, all located between Ocean Trace Road and Pope Road, off Route A1A, south of St. Augustine; 904-471-1596.

BEACHES & PARKS

ANASTASIA STATE RECREATION AREA Within this 1722-acre park are four distinct plant communities: sand dunes, salt marsh, coastal scrub and coastal hammock. Gulls, pelicans and sandpipers swoop along the broad beach, while the lagoon and tidal marshes to the west harbor herons, egrets and other wading birds. Salt Run Lagoon, an area popular with windsurfers, offers shelter from the waves, high winds, and large crowds that spill onto this two-mile swath of white sand south of the St. Augustine Inlet. Swimming is exceptional here and surfing is fair. Angler fish in the surf and the lagoon. There are restrooms, showers, picnic areas, lifeguards and a concession stand. ~ Located at 5 Anastasia Park Drive, St. Augustine; 904-461-2033.

Jacksonville Area

The military fortifications that played such a strategic role in Florida's early history add a special dimension to sightseeing in the northeast corner of the state, especially on Amelia Island. In Jacksonville, the presence of several fine arts museums and renovated old neighborhoods reflect that city's increasing sophistication.

The largest city by area in the contiguous United States, Jacksonville is also one of the oldest cities in Florida. Resting along the St. Johns River it combines a highrise cityscape with the lazy ambience of the Old South.

SIGHTS

For tourism information, drop by the **Jacksonville Chamber of Commerce.** ~ 3 Independent Drive, Jacksonville; 904-366-6600.

The **Beaches Chamber and Visitors Center** can also be of assistance. ~ 1101 Beach Boulevard, Jacksonville Beach; 904-249-3868.

The **Fort Caroline National Memorial** covers 134 acres along the St. Johns River. A reconstructed version of the original 16th-century fort is located at the end of a quarter-mile path beyond the visitor center, where displays help interpret the conflicts between the original French settlers and the Spanish soldiers who followed. ~ 12713 Fort Caroline Road, near the junction with Monument Road, Jacksonville; 904-641-7155.

The **Jacksonville Museum of Contemporary Art,** the oldest museum in the city, features rotating exhibits on arts related to the city's history. In addition to pre-Columbian artifacts and contemporary works of art, the museum also offers classes, concerts and lectures. Closed Mondays. ~ 4160 Boulevard Center Drive, Jacksonville; 904-398-8336.

The **Jacksonville Museum of Science and History** has both permanent and changing exhibits on natural history, American Indian cultures and ancient Egypt as well as shows on physical science. The planetarium in this vast building is known for its powerful projector, capable of showing the night sky as it would be seen from any location in the world. Admission. ~ 1025 Museum Circle, Jacksonville; 904-396-7061.

The fountain is lit at night, providing a beautiful focal point for nearby **Riverwalk**, a 20-foot wide cement boardwalk bordering the south bank of the St. Johns River. Several pavilions feature daytime entertainment for joggers, walkers and office workers taking a break to enjoy the view of north Jacksonville from the comfort of a park bench. Built of weathered wood to resemble an old-fashioned pier, Riverwalk features arching lampposts that echo the form of the bridges at either end.

The **Cummer Museum of Arts and Gardens** is known for its displays of decorative and fine art, notably its collection of Japanese *netsuke* (small carved figurines of jade, ivory and wood) and Chinese snuff bottles fashioned from semi-precious stones or porcelain. An entire room is devoted to 18th-century Meissen porcelain tableware, believed to be the largest collection in the world open to the public. A formal Florentine-style garden, a series of plants, trees, brick walkways and reflecting pools, extends from the mansion down to the river's edge. Closed Monday. Admission. ~ 829 Riverside Avenue, Jacksonville; 904-356-6857.

Located in front of the Museum of Science and History, the spectacular Friendship Fountain sprays 17,000 gallons of water per minute 120 feet into the air.

The **Jacksonville Zoological Gardens** features some unusual innovations, such as separating some of its 700 animals by moats rather than cage bars. The Birds of Prey Aviary has tall trees and even a waterfall; the Wetlands Discovery features an elevated walkway above a natural swamp. Hop on the train for an adventurous ride around the zoo. Admission. ~ One mile east of Heckscher Drive, Jacksonville; 904-757-4462.

Guided and self-guided tours are offered at the **Anheuser-Busch Brewery**. Enveloped in a constant aroma of brewing beers, this enormous facility features huge windows overlooking the floor where the long brewing process is conducted. There is also a tasting room. Closed Sunday. ~ 111 Busch Drive near the airport, Jacksonville; 904-751-8116.

There's almost always a greyhound race to be found somewhere in greater Jacksonville, but the track closest to downtown is the **Jacksonville Kennel Club**. Closed Tuesday. Admission. ~ 1440 North McDuff Avenue, Jacksonville; 904-646-0001.

North of the ferry docks on Fort George Island, the **Kingsley Plantation** affords an unsettling glimpse into history. One of the oldest plantations in the state, it was purchased in 1813 by Zephaniah Kingsley, who lived on the plantation with his wife, an African woman he purchased as a slave and later freed. A two-mile oyster-shell road, under the canopy of subtropical forest, leads to the riverfront buildings where Kingsley and his wife and slaves once lived. Visitors may tour the house, kitchen, barn and what's left of the slave quarters. ~ 11676 Palmetto Avenue, Jacksonville; 904-251-3537.

◄ HIDDEN

In sleepy little Mayport, an old schoolhouse has been transformed into the low-key, highly informative **Marine Science Education Center**. Essentially a facility for local schoolchildren, it also welcomes curious visitors. There is an outstanding display of regional shells, exhibits on the formation of beaches and specimens of marine life ranging from shark jaws to live turtles and alligators. Also of interest is the hands-on "Wet Lab." Closed weekends. ~ 1347 Palmer Street, Mayport; 904-247-5973.

LODGING   For a city of its mind-boggling size, Jacksonville has surprisingly few non-chain hotels, especially in the downtown area. The most notable exception is the elegant **Omni Hotel**. Pale, polished wood columns and walls swathed in rose and beige fabrics seem the epitome of refinement compared to the concrete jungle outside. Expect to pay for beautiful rooms, fine service and amenities such as a gorgeous restaurant and lounge. ~ 245 Water Street, Jacksonville; 904-355-6664, 800-843-6664, fax 904-355-7415. ULTRA-DELUXE.

On the river, **House on Cherry Street** offers southern comfort. This four-room Georgian Colonial home features beautiful Pennsylvania antiques, a big screen porch and large yard reaching down to the water's edge. Spend the night in a canopy bed and wake up to a full breakfast featuring homemade muffins. Be sure to check out the duck decoy collection. ~ 1844 Cherry Street, Jacksonville; 904-384-1999, fax 904-384-5013. MODERATE.

If you want to stay in a one- or two-bedroom condominium on the water, consider the **Beachcombers**. Decorated with bamboo furniture, this white stucco condo provides full kitchens and private balconies. Units are rented for a minimum of two nights. ~ 411 South 1st Street, Jacksonville Beach; phone/fax 904-249-2663. DELUXE TO ULTRA-DELUXE.

The **Sea Turtle Inn** is built so that every room has a view of at least a slice of ocean, so close you can almost smell it. But not quite: all the room windows are sealed. Other than that, the place is delightful, with comfortable dual double beds and endless vistas of the sand stretching into the horizon. ~ 1 Ocean Boulevard, Atlantic Beach; 904-249-7402, 800-874-6000, fax 904-247-1517. DELUXE.

RAZE THE FLAG

The history of northeastern Florida—which existed under eight different flags over four centuries—is a story of confrontations, military skirmishes and fleeting triumphs on a par with the more Byzantine plots concocted by Hollywood adventure-movie writers. For a glimpse of it, check out the carefully arranged maps, charts, pictures and memorabilia at the **Amelia Island Museum of History**. Call ahead if you'd like one of the excellent guided tours (by reservation only) of the museum and/or of the historic district. Closed Sunday. Admission. ~ 233 South 3rd Street, Fernandina Beach; 904-261-7378.

On Amelia Island, the best-known destination is the **Amelia Island Plantation**, a first-rate resort that sprawls over 1240 acres between pristine beach and carefully preserved tidal marshlands. The plantation (a word commonly used on Florida's East Coast to describe residential resort communities) is known for the quality and quantity of its villas, available in one- to three-bedroom sizes. Fashioned of pale stucco and built in clusters around swimming pools, these luxurious accommodations are nestled in the semi-shade of ancient oak trees and graceful palmettos. The decor is sophisticated: top-quality chairs and sofas, sparkling kitchens, attractive drapes. In addition to 45 holes of golf, 25 tennis courts and a full-service health center, recreational opportunities include bicycle and horseback riding, boating, fishing and nature trails that curve along the golden marshes. Not to mention four miles of beachfront so clean that the shells look as if they had been polished by hand. ~ Route A1A, Amelia Island; 904-261-6161, 800-874-6878, fax 904-277-5945. ULTRA-DELUXE.

An oceanfront inn right out of a 1940s romantic movie provides most visitors with their first glimpse of Fernandina Beach's charm. Clapboard-covered and unpretentious, the **Seaside Inn** is a wayfarer's delight, a renovated hotel, restaurant and lounge on the very lip of the Atlantic. Second-floor oceanside rooms are decorated in the simple fashion of a well-worn summer home, with pastel walls, ceiling fans and double beds topped with fluffy comforters. ~ 1998 South Fletcher Avenue, Fernandina Beach; 904-261-0954. MODERATE.

Ever fantasized about your very own lighthouse? A uniquely romantic conception, the **Lighthouse** never really served as one, but feels as if it did. Four circular rooms are stacked one on top of another, with sea oats brushing against the shuttered windows and the surf only feet away. Old lacquered charts cover the walls of the circular stairway. In the kitchen, tables and seats are suspended from the beamed ceiling. The top floor of this two-bedroom delight is an empty room surrounded by a railed deck with a 360 view. For the price you get the entire complex and breakfast delivered in a basket. ~ 748 South Fletcher Avenue, Fernandina Beach; 904-261-5878, 800-872-8531, fax 904-261-2900. ULTRA-DELUXE.

The cozy **1735 House**, built of tongue-and-groove Georgia pine in 1928, has five rooms whose names (Patriots, Captain's Cabin, etc.) refer to Amelia Island's seagoing history. In fact, ten more yards to the east and the inn itself would be seagoing. All ocean-view rooms are outfitted with a dining table, rather funky baths, small refrigerators (some have efficiency kitchens) and sitting areas decorated in rattan with rose fabrics that complement the patterned bedcovers. Continental breakfast is included. ~ 584 South Fletcher Avenue, Fernandina Beach; 904-261-5878, 800-872-8531, fax 904-261-2900. ULTRA-DELUXE.

The **Captain's House** would fit right in on old Cape Cod, with its pale grey clapboard exterior trimmed in white. Nine comfortably furnished apartments extend along the length of this three-story building, fronted by sliding glass doors that open onto a patio. ~ 268 South Fletcher Avenue, Fernandina Beach; 904-261-5878, 800-872-8531, fax 904-261-2900. ULTRA-DELUXE.

HIDDEN ▶

Off the beach in downtown Fernandina Beach, the spacious **Amelia Island Williams House** makes you wonder what it would have been like to grow up amid 7000 square feet of floor space—and another 1300 square feet of covered porch. This pre-Civil War, two-story taupe-and-cream bed and breakfast has eight rooms upstairs, all sporting a balcony underlooking a centuries-old oak tree. The house is resplendent in beautiful antiques, many of them museum pieces dating back to the 16th century. The rear courtyard offers a Victorian fountain and a formal English walking garden. ~ 103 South 9th Street, Amelia Island; 904-277-2328, 800-414-9257. ULTRA-DELUXE.

The **Bailey House** is a traditional Victorian building with turrets, gables, peaks and bay windows, a wide staircase and spacious parlors decorated with assorted antiques, including an old organ in working condition. Five spacious guest rooms are furnished in antique beds, clawfoot tubs and fringed lamp shades. ~ 28 South 7th Street, Fernandina Beach; 904-261-5390, 800-251-5390, fax 904-321-0103. MODERATE TO DELUXE.

DINING

Pale taupe walls, pink napkins, fresh flowers, lace curtains and moss green carpet set the tone for **Sterling's Café**. European specialties include wild mushroom pasta, grilled swordfish and salmon baked with ginger and fresh ground pepper served on a celeryroot purée bed with a cabernet buerre rouge. ~ 3551 St. Johns Avenue, Jacksonville; 904-387-0700. DELUXE.

With its gazebo-like interior and white trellises, the **Yum Yum Tree** is well suited to its upscale Avondale surroundings. This is where shoppers stop for gourmet sandwiches, quiches, crêpes and other light luncheon items. No dinner. Closed Sunday. ~ 3566 St. Johns Avenue, Jacksonville; 904-388-9007. BUDGET.

The **Mozzarella Cafe** commands a sweeping view of the St. Johns River from its deck tables. Inside, a long narrow room is festooned with paintings and posters. The menu features pizza, pasta, steaks and fresh fish, plus a lot of small dishes suitable for a late lunch or early dinner. Chicken appetizers come barbecued, herbed or Cajun-level spicy and go well with creamy potato-cheese soup, deep-dish quiche or a hearty salad. ~ Jacksonville Landing, 2 East Independent Drive, Jacksonville; 904-353-4503. MODERATE.

Juliette's is an expansive, elegant restaurant. You can enjoy fresh fish cooked to order, bouillabaisse, fresh shrimp, sirloin filet or other steak dishes in the formal dining room with its low lighting and tapestried booths, or at tables set in the plant-rimmed atrium. Breakfast, lunch and dinner are served daily. ~ 245 Water Street, in the Omni Hotel, Jacksonville; 904-355-6664. DELUXE.

When we finally spotted **Crawdaddy's** behind a phalanx of office towers, we thought the building had burned; but no, that's the way it's supposed to look, sort of like an abandoned warehouse. The interior is equally distinctive: several whimsically decorated rooms scattered over numerous levels, where nothing matches except a handful of carved wooden chairs. In this one-of-a-kind setting, specialties range from alligator and Cajun dishes to seafood, chicken and prime rib. ~ 1643 Prudential Drive, Jacksonville; 904-396-3546. MODERATE TO DELUXE.

The restaurants in the revitalized San Marco district attract a lot of young people who have discovered the European flavor of the neighborhood. **The Café Carmon** exudes cosmopolitan intimacy, with a choice of seating at café tables located out front or along a brick wall hung with impressionist prints. An inspired mix of salads, such as goat cheese with sun-dried tomatoes, or won ton salad with poached chicken, water chestnuts, beans and celery, complement a menu of steak, fish, chicken and freshmade pasta. It's an excellent choice for late-night dining. There is also a Sunday brunch. ~ 1986 San Marco Boulevard, Jacksonville; 904-399-4488. MODERATE.

The beachfront **Crab Pot Restaurant** is a landmark located across from the Flag Pavilion. Cavernous and kind of corny with its plastic bibs and a flashy T-shirt display in the lobby, the Crab Pot prints a long menu of local and imported fresh bounty from the sea: shrimp, scampi, steamed blue crabs, tuna salad, conch fritters, seafood creole, catfish parmesan, peel 'em yourself shrimp and a variety of mixed platters. ~ 12 North Oceanfront Drive, Jacksonville Beach; 904-241-4188. MODERATE.

A tasty all-you-care-to-eat barbecue buffet makes **Chiang's Mongolian Bar-B-Q** a terrific value, especially since it includes beef, pork, chicken and vegetables. Other than that, Chiang's is standard shopping-strip Asian, a big, brightly lit room with typical red and gold decor. You can also order à la carte from a sizable list of such standbys as lemon chicken, wonton soup, chow mein and teriyaki chicken. Service is prompt and friendly and portions are large at this family-oriented restaurant. ~ 1504 North 3rd Street, Jacksonville Beach; 904-241-3075. BUDGET TO MODERATE.

G'day. At the tin-roofed **Outback Steakhouse** you'll find boomerangs and kangaroo pictures on the wall, safari clad waitpeople and some of the zestiest food in town. This down under theme, designed to make any Australian feel at home, is an ideal steak house setting. If you're not hungry for prime rib, filet or porterhouse, try the ribs, chicken, shrimp, pork or fish of the day. Even the appetizers have a kick. Dinner only. ~ 3760 South 3rd Street, Jacksonville Beach; 904-247-7888. MODERATE.

A tiered dining room on the ocean, **First Street Grille** is a picture-window perfect place to enjoy fresh seafood and steaks. Done in Key West style with flowers and painted birds on the walls, the dining room is complemented by a spacious deck complete with a tiki bar where you can enjoy steel drum and jazz bands. ~ 807 North 1st Street, Jacksonville Beach; 904-246-6555. MODERATE.

Sprouting huge awnings and a spiffy picket fence, the **Homestead** has long been a roadside favorite for deep South home-style cooking. The atmosphere is cozy despite plastic tablecloths and wrought-iron chairs. Who cares, when they can be eating all kinds of seafood and chicken dishes, including a special called "lizards"—a combination of chicken liver and gizzards served with rice. Dinner only. ~ 1712 Beach Boulevard, Jacksonville Beach; 904-249-5240. MODERATE.

Ragtime Tavern and Taproom is a hot nightspot for jazz and blues (see "Nightlife" listing) and for dining. The menu, atmosphere and music all follow a New Orleans theme. Try the po' boy sandwich, a couple of beignets with your coffee or the Sunday brunch. Pasta, salads and fajitas also show up on the menu. ~ 207 Atlantic Avenue, Atlantic Beach; 904-241-7877. MODERATE.

HIDDEN ► Head to Amelia Island and you will find restaurants serving everything from flounder to fettuccine. **Southern Tip**, located at the shopping/dining complex called Palmetto Walk, could easily be mistaken for a French country home. Paintings, mirrors and flowers appoint this gracious two-story dining room featuring a full bar. Specialties include lamb, pasta, beef and the catch of the day. Among the popular appetizers are black-eyed pea cakes and stuffed artichoke hearts. ~ 4802 First Coast Highway, Amelia Island; 904-261-6184. MODERATE TO DELUXE.

The Sandbar is an out-of-the-way institution on the west side of Amelia Island. Billboards with large red arrows lead diners to this marshfront family-style restaurant, where dark wood and low ceilings enhance the hideaway feeling. Half the items on the menu—oysters, shrimp and crab served fried, broiled, fresh or raw in the shell—probably were caught within half a mile of the Sandbar. Chicken and steaks are also available. Dinner only. Closed Monday. ~ 1220 Sandbar Place, Fernandina Beach; 904-261-4185. MODERATE.

The prettiest restaurant in the town of Fernandina Beach is unquestionably **Brett's Waterway Café**. With an elegant feel, this waterfront eatery offers both indoor and outdoor dining during lunch. The menu is equally sumptuous—a mix of Continental cuisine, fresh seafood and beef dishes. ~ 1 South Front Street, Fernandina Beach; 904-261-2660. MODERATE TO DELUXE.

If you're looking for elegant seafood dishes, consider **Surf Restaurant**. Across the street from the beach, this unpretentious establishment with a teal and white color scheme, overhead fans and plants, has a deck open for lunch and a dining room open for dinner. The Surf is known for its fried seafood, as well as charcoal-grilled fish and steaks. ~ 3199 Fletcher Avenue, Fernandina Beach; 904-261-5711. MODERATE TO DELUXE.

The **1878 Steak House** specializes in local seafood and steak sold by the ounce. The decor is rather florid, giving this second-floor restaurant the atmosphere of a Wild West hotel. Downstairs has a bar and courtyard. ~ 12 North 2nd Street, Fernandina Beach; 904-261-4049. MODERATE TO DELUXE.

The **Marina Restaurant** is so close to the docks that fishermen could probably toss their catches from the boat decks into the frying pan. Except for a few nautical artifacts like a miniature lighthouse, the decor is plain, letting the fantail shrimp and plump flounder carry the day. Also on the menu are chicken dishes and burgers. You'll find large portions. Open for breakfast, lunch and dinner. ~ 101 Centre Street, Fernandina Beach; 904-261-5310. BUDGET TO MODERATE.

Slider's Restaurant, named after the Louisiana slang word for oysters, is the quintessential beach town hangout. No table linens, no decoration, no pretensions; just a short, simple menu dominated by raw oysters, fried shrimp and broiled fish. Lunch on weekends only. ~ 1998 South Fletcher Avenue at the Seaside Inn, Fernandina Beach; 904-261-0954. MODERATE.

Snug Harbor is one of half-a-dozen restaurants clustered around Centre Street, the main shopping artery. The back porch here is often occupied with locals waiting in line for some soft shell crabs, baked grouper or fresh Florida lobster. The lunch specials are large enough to keep a fisherman going all day. ~ 201 Alachua Street, Fernandina Beach; 904-261-8031. BUDGET TO MODERATE.

SHOPPING

Sprawling over 841 square miles, the city of Jacksonville has plenty of room for vast suburban malls such as **Regency Square**. The stores here cover a wide range. The general department store is **Dillard's** (904-721-9166). **Victoria's Secret** (904-721-2161) is a local branch of the national lingerie chain. ~ 9501 Arlington Expressway, Jacksonville.

Something of a magnet for the credit card–carrying public, the two-story **Jacksonville Landing** dominates the north bank of the St. Johns River just west of the Main Street Bridge. You could easily spend a day here, stopping for nourishment at any of half a dozen restaurants or sipping espresso while watching the passing parade of river traffic. Instead of the giant department stores and hole-in-the-wall T-shirt shops found in so many malls, most of the retailers here are medium-sized concerns specializing in quality goods. At **Laura Ashley** (904-358-7548) you'll find an array of dresses and fabrics sporting floral prints inspired by the English countryside. ~ 2 Independent Drive, Jacksonville.

Neighborhoods like Five Points and San Marco offer an eclectic mix of boutiques, but the grande dame of residential retailing is unquestionably Avondale. Dubbed "Little Landing" by locals making a comparison to the much bigger Jacksonville Landing, **Avondale** is located between 3000 and 4000 St. Johns Avenue. For a good selection of children's clothing, check **The Hobby Horse**. ~ 3550 St. Johns Avenue, Jacksonville; 904-389-7992.

White's Bookstore, which has a number of outlets in the area, is represented here with a large, well-lit room full of fiction, nonfiction, magazines and book-related gifts. ~ 3563 St. Johns Avenue, Jacksonville; 904-387-9288.

For contemporary gifts, one of the best shops in all of Jacksonville is **The Jade Tree**. Elegant picture frames, antique porcelain, glass and crystal objets d'art, chic coffee mugs and picnic baskets are available in almost every price range. ~ 3600 St. Johns Avenue, Jacksonville; 904-384-7287.

Shops such as **Miz Lucy** reflect the tax bracket of the surrounding neighborhood of mansions and sweeping lawns. This small store is known for its tasteful fashions for women. ~ 3637 St. Johns Avenue, Jacksonville; 904-387-1231.

A variety of toys and gourmet kitchenware can be had at **Khakis**. ~ 3643 St. Johns Avenue, Jacksonville; 904-384-2712.

A good place to browse for somebody's heirlooms is **Canterbury House Antiques**. ~ 1776 Canterbury Street, Jacksonville; 904-387-1776.

In the Jacksonville Beach area, **Costa Verde Shopping Center** is one of the smaller and nicer clusters of shops to be found on or near Route A1A. China and crystal vases galore sparkle in the windows at the **Pineapple Post** (904-249-7477), which also carries an array of less fragile gift items. Next door, the latest fashions from Milan and Paris are the stock-in-trade at **Barton/Sligh's** (904-246-9436), a name known to career women, who frequent the downtown location of this upscale boutique. ~ 2403 South 3rd Street, Jacksonville Beach.

Get a feel for Florida's northern neighbor at **China Cat Antiques**, where old Georgia pine and pecan furnishings are among the lovely antiques. ~ 226 4th Avenue South, Jacksonville Beach; 904-241-0344.

For a look at some original local artwork, try **Sunshine Frames**. This small gallery also sells engravings and lithographs. ~ 1315 North 3rd Street, Jacksonville Beach; 904-246-7133.

Several shops are near the intersection of Route A1A and the ocean. **The Crabapple Tree** is a sweetheart of a store laden with teddy bears, Christmas ornaments, fudge and Crabtree & Evelyn toiletries. ~ 40 Ocean Boulevard, Atlantic Beach; 904-249-5182.

If you just have to take a gift home and can't think of anything, you'll get help at both **Shorelines**, which has inexpensive casual jewelry, T-shirts and gifts. ~ 109 1st Street, Neptune Beach; 904-246-9133.

On Amelia Island a couple of miles north of the Amelia Island Plantation, **Palmetto Walk** consists of several residential-type buildings that house a number of boutiques and restaurants. The sportswear for men and women at **Heron's Sportswear Inc.** (904-261-3677) wears labels such as Polo/Ralph Lauren and is eminently suitable for resort life. Exquisite antique furniture, silver frames and needlepoint pillows make **The Plantation Shop** (904-261-2030) look like someone's lovingly decorated parlor. ~ 4800 Route A1A, Amelia Island.

The pride and joy of Fernandina Beach's restored district is **Centre Street**, which extends inland several blocks from the City Docks. The slow pace of island life can be felt here even in the busiest shops that share the street with restaurants and service establishments catering to locals.

The best of several women's clothing shops is **Personalities**. This comfortably chic boutique sells beach togs, walking shorts and T-shirts. ~ 118 Centre Street, Fernandina Beach; 904-277-3319.

For material on the state's history and tourist attractions, as well as a good assortment of Florida-based fiction, check out the **Book Loft**. ~ 214 Centre Street, Fernandina Beach; 904-261-8991.

If you want to take a little bit of Dixie home with you, you should dawdle in **Southern Touch**, purveyors of basketry and other country handcrafts. ~ 301 Centre Street, Fernandina Beach; 904-261-5377.

A couple of blocks off Centre Street, **Helen D'Agnese** sells works of art in a variety of media (and claims former president Jimmy Carter as a collector). Her specialties include bronze and limestone sculptures and oil paintings in the Latin American primitive style. ~ 14-1/2 North 4th Street, Fernandina Beach; 904-261-0433.

If shopping centers had existed at the turn of the century, they would have looked like **C House Colony**, a ramshackle string of clapboard buildings. At **Jeff Steel Jewelers** (904-277-3830) artisans

can often be seen at work fashioning pieces of jewelry out of gold.
~ South 9th and Beach streets, Fernandina Beach.

NIGHTLIFE   **Club Carousel** is an all-ages affair for danceaholics. The 30,000
square feet of space includes a 4000-square-foot dancefloor, a revolving stage and an intergalactic laser light system. Deejays play
the hippest house and techno around. Open Friday, Saturday and
Sunday. Cover. ~ 8550 Arlington Expressway, Jacksonville; 904-
725-2582.

The lounge at **Crawdaddy's** is one of the area's more unusual
nightclubs. A sizable bar and dancefloor are the focal points of a
barnlike main room where the decor is half the fun. The musical
fare on Thursday is reggae, Friday is a mixed bag and Saturday has
R&B. Cover charge on Saturday. ~ 1643 Prudential Drive, Jacksonville; 904-396-3546.

An outpost of restaurants and clubs makes Baymeadows Road,
between downtown Jacksonville and the beaches, something of an
after-dark mecca. There's usually a sizable crowd at the **Bombay
Bicycle Club**. This high-profile restaurant/ lounge complex rocks
to Top-40 tunes nightly until the wee hours. ~ 8909 Baymeadows
Road, Jacksonville; 904-737-9555.

The southern music tradition is alive at **57 Heaven**. This roadside joint is a sentimentalist's dream, with dance music from the
'50s to the '80s. Cover on weekends. ~ 8136 Atlantic Boulevard,
Jacksonville; 904-721-5757.

As you might expect, **Einstein-A-GoGo** attracts a collegiate
crowd, but you'll also find a mix of much older and somewhat
younger fans dancing to live and deejay music Thursday through
Sunday nights at this easygoing nightclub. Cover. ~ 327 North 1st
Street, Jacksonville Beach; 904-249-4646.

The music isn't always live, but the patrons certainly are at
Bukkets Baha. Disc jockeys spin alternative and rock music Tuesday through Saturday, except on Wednesday when a reggae band
takes the stage. ~ 222 Ocean Front Boulevard,
Jacksonville Beach; 904-246-7701.

Built in 1878, the Palace
Saloon in Fernandina
Beach is believed to be
the oldest bar in
Florida.

In the midst of a popular bar-hopping stretch of the
beach, **Ragtime Tavern and Taproom** brews its own
beer (in its microbrewery on the premises) and has live
jazz and blues bands Thursday through Sunday
evenings. ~ 207 Atlantic Avenue, Atlantic Beach; 904-
241-7877.

Out in the Amelia Island area you'll find several prime night
spots. **The Palace Saloon**, built in 1878 and believed to be the oldest bar in Florida, should be on your must-see list. A large, high-
ceilinged room with memorabilia from the early days, it's the prime
local gathering spot from happy hour into the wee hours. Rock

bands play Thursday through Saturday. Cover on weekends. ~ 113 Centre Street, Fernandina Beach; 904-261-6320.

Downstairs at the 1878 Steak House, the brick-walled **Brass Rail Bar** has live entertainment Friday and Saturday evenings. ~ 12 North 2nd Street, Fernandina Beach; 904-261-4049.

The liveliest spot on Amelia Island is **Slider's Lounge,** an easy-going nightclub that features a changing line-up of homegrown and visiting bands six nights a week. Thursday is disco night. ~ 1998 South Fletcher Avenue at the Seaside Inn, Fernandina Beach; 904-261-0954.

THEATER, OPERA, SYMPHONY AND DANCE   Broadway musicals and comedies are the stock in trade at the **Alhambra Dinner Theatre.** Buffet dinners are available before evening performances. ~ 12000 Beach Boulevard, Jacksonville; 904-641-1212.

Jacksonville's oldest continually producing theater company, **Theatre Jacksonville,** also claims to have been entertaining audiences longer than any other community theater in the country. ~ 2032 San Marco Boulevard, Jacksonville; 904-396-4425.

The **Florida Ballet** offers an array of programs from classical ballet to contemporary works. ~ 123 East Forsyth Street, Jacksonville; 904-353-7518.

The **Jacksonville Symphony** schedules more than 100 performances each year. The sizable regional orchestra and its various ensembles play in pops concerts at the Florida Theater and elsewhere. ~ 33 South Hogan Street, Suite 400, Jacksonville; 904-354-5547.

GAY SCENE   A red-brick building decorated with a train motif, **Junction** is a popular gay bar. If you wander in on a Wednesday or a weekend night, don't be surprised to find a comedy act going on or country-and-western singers performing. ~ 1261 King Street, Jacksonville; 904-388-3434.

The only gay bar and nightclub on the beach, **Bo's Coral Reef** is a mauve cinderblock building accommodating crowds up to 1000. This mirrored club has a big dancefloor, video monitors and pool tables. Deejays play progressive, high-energy music Wednesday through Sunday. On Thursday's amateur nights you can show off your talents. Cover on Saturday. ~ 201 5th Avenue North, Jacksonville Beach; 904-246-9874.

GUANA RIVER STATE PARK   Of four beaches between St. Augustine and Jacksonville, this one is the most special. There is a wild, untamed feeling to this grainy sand beach laden with thousands of shells. From the parking lot, follow one of the boardwalks to a breathtaking expanse of uncrowded oceanfront. Swimming varies from fair to very good because of a big dropoff at certain tide levels. There's surf fishing,

BEACHES & PARKS

◄ *HIDDEN*

as well as freshwater fishing in Guana Lake and River. You'll find restrooms by the dam. ~ About five miles north of St. Augustine on Route A1A; 904-825-5071.

JACKSONVILLE BEACH The southernmost of the three urban beaches east of downtown, Jacksonville Beach encompasses some 2400 feet of hard sand. It is extremely popular with locals and tends to be more crowded on the weekends than either Neptune or Atlantic beaches to the north. Fishing is good everywhere on the beach and fishing is best off the pier. Facilities include a seawalk, a pavilion, concession stands and lifeguards. Restrooms and showers are found at the north end; restaurants and groceries are nearby. ~ Located near Route A1A between J. Turner Butler and Beach boulevards; the beach can be reached at the end of any of 64 streets that cross North 1st Street in Jacksonville.

HANNA PARK One of the best-marked and best-maintained parks in northern Florida, this spot has 450 variegated acres, with freshwater lakes, hiking trails, a nature preserve, well-preserved sand dunes and more than a mile of clean hard-sand beach. Swimming is fine along the entire beachfront but is most popular in front of Pelican Plaza. The best waves for surfing are at the north end off Dolphin Plaza. Surf and freshwater angling is consistently good. There are picnic areas, restrooms, showers and lifeguards; restaurants are in nearby Mayport and Atlantic Beach. ~ At 500 Wonderwood Drive in Atlantic Beach; 904-249-4700.

▲ There are 300 camping sites, all with RV hookups; $10 to $14 per night.

LITTLE TALBOT ISLAND STATE PARK Actually an entire 2500-acre barrier island north of the mouth of the Fort George River, this long, narrow strip of land offers a diverse landscape that changes continually from the effects of wind and water. In this nearly pristine environment, it's possible to see what Florida looked like before the coming of condominiums. A series of seaward dunes, interspersed with low-lying troughs, are in many places lush with low-growing plants such as flowering morning-glories and held in place with taller sea oats. Five miles of glistening white sand beach are accessible by dune crossovers, one at the south end of the island and one near the middle. Inland estuaries support abundant marsh life; oysters, crab, fish, turtles and migrating seabirds are common sights. The central portion of this wild island harbors a hammock of oak, holly and magnolia trees. This is a good place for surfing and bodysurfing. Anglers try for speckled trout, striped bass, bluefish, redfish, flounder, mullet, sheepshead and whiting in the Atlantic, the Fort George River and

Myrtle and Simpson creeks. Facilities include picnic areas, restrooms and showers. ~ Located northeast of Jacksonville on Route A1A; 904-251-2320.

▲ There are 40 sites, all with RV hookups; $16 to $18 per night.

FERNANDINA BEACH ![icons] The ◄ HIDDEN
southernmost section of this barrier island is arguably the most beautiful in east Florida. The sand is fine, dark and firmly packed; small, perfectly formed shells appear to have been arranged by hand in orderly patterns. A secondary ridge of sand dunes, behind the eroded line of beachfront dunes, forms a pretty backdrop with sea oats and other salt-resistant plants. Part of the beach fronts Amelia Island Plantation, which the public may not walk through, but you will find easy public access north of the resort. Fernandina Beach is an excellent place for swimming, and surf fishing is quite good. The beach is equipped with restrooms, picnic areas, concession stands and lifeguards. ~ Located north of Nassau Sound off Route A1A, near Amelia City. Major access points at Peters Point, South Fletcher Avenue, Scott Road and Sadler Road.

FORT CLINCH STATE PARK ![icons] Located at the northern tip of Amelia Island, this 1100-acre park has both natural and historic attractions. Bounded by the Amelia River on the west, Cumberland Sound on the north, and the Atlantic on the east, the park's many natural features include a coastal hardwood hammock, huge sand dunes, a sandy beach and a salt marsh. Alligators, wading birds and small animals can be sighted along a nature trail. You can fish for striped bass and speckled trout; they're plentiful off the long pier on the east side of the park. Swimming is excellent on the ocean side. There are picnic areas, restrooms and showers; restaurants and grocery stores are nearby. ~ Located at 2601 Atlantic Avenue in Fernandina Beach; 904-277-7274.

▲ There are 62 sites, all with RV hookups, electricity and water; $19 to $21 per night.

FORT PIERCE AREA For a deep-sea fishing tour, contact **Happy Hooker Charter Boats**. ~ 201 Fisherman's Wharf, Fort Pierce; 561-489-2180.

▼▼▼▼▼▼▼▼▼▼▼▼▼▼
Outdoor Adventures

SPORT-FISHING

CAPE CANAVERAL AREA Most of the charter fishing boats in the are docked at Port Canaveral for easy access to an ocean teeming with snapper, grouper and shark, to name a few of the common fish. **Miss Cape Canaveral** is an 85-foot party boat that takes day and nighttime excursions. ~ 407-783-5274. At 95 feet, the **Pelican Princess** is said to be the largest fiberglass party boat in the country; at least it's large enough to contain a sundeck and a galley. ~ 407-784-3474.

DAYTONA BEACH AREA   Full-day or half-day fishing excursions are among the most popular sports in this area; some boats take anglers as far out as the Gulf Stream. A number of charter outfits are located within a short drive from major Daytona Beach hotels, including **Sea Love Marina**. ~ 4884 Front Street, Ponce Inlet; 904-767-3406.

ST. AUGUSTINE AREA   Tarpon, king fish and shark are common in the waters off St. Augustine. Fishing boats can be chartered at **Conch House Marina Resort**. ~ 57 Comares Avenue, Anastasia Island; 904-824-4347.

Another choice is **Sea Love Charters**. ~ 250 Vilano Road, St. Augustine; 904-824-3328. **Lighthouse Charters, Inc.** offers fishing and sailing charters. ~ 3074 Harbor Drive, St. Augustine; 904-825-1985, 800-333-8750.

JACKSONVILLE AREA   There are myriad opportunities to fish in the surf or off piers along the East Coast of Florida, but offshore angling is a completely different experience. Charter boats can be hired at **King Neptune Deep-Sea Fishing**, a short drive north from Atlantic Beach. ~ Monty's Marina, 4378 Ocean Street, Mayport; 904-246-7575. On Amelia Island, you can sign on for either fishing or sightseeing aboard a boat from **Tradewinds**. ~ 1 South Front Street, Fernandina Beach; 904-261-9486. The same options are offered by **Amelia Angler Charter Boat Association**. ~ 3 South Front Street, Amelia Island; 904-261-2870.

BOATING   **FORT PIERCE AREA**   To cruise the Intracoastal Waterway under your own power, you can rent a variety of craft and waterskis from **Rosemeyer's Boat Rental**. ~ 3281 Northeast Indian River Drive, Jensen Beach; 561-334-1000. For renting pontoons, powerboats, sailboats and waverunners, try **U.S.A. Watersports**. ~ 4000 Northeast Ocean Boulevard, Stuart; 561-225-2158.

DAYTONA BEACH AREA   Sailboats are the specialty at **Marina Port Orange**. ~ 3537 Halifax Drive, Port Orange; 904-767-6408.

ST. AUGUSTINE   Sailboat rentals and lessons can be had at **St. Augustine Sailing, Inc.** ~ 3076 Harbor Drive, St. Augustine; 904-829-0648, 800-683-7245.

SURFING & WIND-SURFING   **FORT PIERCE AREA**   Windsurfing can be ventured either in the surf or on the smoother waters of the Intracoastal Waterway. Lessons and rentals are available at **Windsurfing Treasure Coast**, which also rents surfboards. ~ 2659 Northeast Dixie Highway, Jensen Beach; 561-334-6722. Another place where you can rent the right stuff for surfing the big waves is **Island Watersports**. They also give lessons. ~ 3291 Northeast Indian River Drive, Jensen Beach; 561-334-1999. At Vero Beach, try **Deep 6 Dive & Watersports**. ~ 416 Miracle Mile Extension, Vero Beach; 561-562-2883.

CAPE CANAVERAL AREA For the widest array of surfing equipment and accessories in the Cape Canaveral area, and possibly on the entire East Coast, surfers pay their respects to the **Ron Jon Surf Shop**. This warehouse-size store also stocks clothing and equipment for a wide variety of other watersports. ~ 4151 North Route A1A, Cocoa Beach; 407-799-8888. The smooth waters of the Banana River are at the doorstep of **Calema Boardsailing**. ~ 2755 North Banana River Drive, Cocoa Beach; 407-453-3223.

DAYTONA BEACH AREA Several shops in this area rent surfboards including **Daytona Beach Surf Shop**. ~ 520 Seabreeze Boulevard, Daytona Beach; 904-253-3366. For windsurfing and kayak rentals and lessons, **Sandy Point Progressive Sports** is conveniently located on the Intracoastal Waterway. ~ 3109 South Ridgewood Avenue, South Daytona Beach; 904-756-7564.

ST. AUGUSTINE AREA Certain stretches of the beaches around St. Augustine are specially designated for surfers and windsurfers. If you left your board at home, you can rent one at **Blue Sky Surf Shop**. ~ 517 Anastasia Boulevard, St. Augustine; 904-824-2734. Another source for surfing necessities is the **Surf Station**. ~ 1020 Anastasia Boulevard, St. Augustine; 904-471-9463.

JACKSONVILLE AREA The long expanse of uncluttered beaches east of Jacksonville have become very popular with surfers and windsurfers. Several outfits in the area rent surfboards, boogie boards and even skates. Try calling **Aqua East Surf Shop** to see what they have available. ~ 696 Atlantic Boulevard, Neptune Beach; 904-246-2550. Aqua East also maintains a **hotline** with recorded information on surfing and sailing conditions. ~ 904-246-9744.

A variety of reefs and wrecks make the waters off the Treasure Coast exceptional for diving. For trips or lessons, contact **Dixie Divers**. ~ 1717 South Route 1, Fort Pierce; 561-461-4488. Or try **Deep 6 Dive & Watersports**. ~ 416 Miracle Mile Extension, Vero Beach; 561-562-2883. To hook up with other divers and snorkelers, or to rent gear, try **American Divers International**. ~ 691 North Courtenay Parkway, Merritt Island; 407-453-0600.

DIVING

FORT PIERCE AREA Several semiprivate clubs offer golfing privileges to the public. Try **Indian Hills Country Club**. ~ 1600 South 3rd Street, Fort Pierce; 561-461-9620. Another option is **Gator Trace Golf and Country Club**. ~ 4302 Gator Trace Drive, Fort Pierce; 561-464-7442. The 18-hole championship course at **Dodger Pines Country Club** is also open to the public. ~ 4600 26th Avenue, Vero Beach; 561-569-9606. Another public access course is **Sebastian Municipal Golf Course**. ~ 101 East Airport Drive, Sebastian; 561-589-6800.

GOLF

Text continued on page 228.

On the Wild Side: Sea Turtles and Alligators

An odd ritual can be observed on summer nights along Florida's barrier islands. A group of people, usually dressed in raincoats to protect against a gentle rainfall, walk slowly in front of the sand dunes, peering down at the ground in the moonlight. Occasionally, they will spot huge tracks, like something a tractor might make, leading from the water's edge to the dunes and back again. These are the tracks of sea turtles, which come out of the water to lay their precious eggs in the sand above the high water mark. The people are there to help protect the eggs from poachers and other animals of prey. When the eggs—perhaps 120 or more per female—do hatch, the tiny turtles will make the precarious way to the ocean, where more predators, such as sharks, reduce the survival rate to as little as one in a thousand.

For more than 100 million years, sea turtles have been roaming the earth's waters, though relatively few people ever get a chance to see them. For a few weeks each year, however, it is possible along Florida's East Coast to spot one of these enormous creatures, which often grow as long as five feet and weigh 500 pounds or more. Depending on the locale, loggerhead and greenback turtles can be spotted sometime between June and October.

Sea turtles, hunted for centuries for their meat, are now protected by the Endangered Species Act. To ensure their survival, regulatory agencies carefully oversee their habitat, which includes the beaches. From Jensen Beach to Amelia Island, however, park rangers and other authorized groups sponsor "Turtle Watches" that allow people to witness the giant reptiles laboring to crawl the 40 or 50 yards from the sea to the safety of the sand dunes and using their flippers to dig out a nest. Some turtle eggs may be scooped up by rangers, to be released later. The rest are guarded until the hatchlings appear and begin their instinctive but treacherous journey to the open water. No one knows where the turtles spend their first year or how they navigate the oceans, but the females will ultimately return to the original beach to build their own nests.

Turtle walks are sponsored at the Sebastian Inlet State Park and at Jensen Beach. Call the appropriate chambers of commerce for information about reservations.

Turtles, of course, are not the stuff of legends, which are spun about Florida's other big reptiles. Some people call them alligators, some call them crocodiles, but Floridians refer to those long, scary-looking creatures with big teeth and equally big appetites simply as 'gators. (Actually, American alligators are technically one family of Crocodilia; they share ancestors with the dinosaur.) Like sharks, alligators have remained relatively unchanged over millions of years and, also like sharks, they are among the most feared marine predators in the world. So feared, in fact, and so valued for their meat and leatherlike hides that they were placed on the Endangered Species List until 1977. Now, as any visitor to Florida can tell you, there seems to be no shortage.

Mangrove swamps such as those on Merritt Island are favorite habitats of the alligator, as are the marshes along rivers such as the St. John's, which runs north from around Melbourne all the way to Jacksonville. Alligators, which are typically seven to eight feet long, are cold-blooded predators that often seize their prey under water. They can and do, however, also seize small animals from the banks of ponds.

In places such as the Merritt Island National Wildlife Refuge, the best vantage point for observing alligators is from an automobile. It is also possible to see alligators from an airboat such as the one operated by the **Lone Cabbage Fish Camp** west of Cocoa. These and similar craft cruise the shallow waterways, often passing 'gators sunning themselves on the banks or slithering in the tall grass. The alligator's eyes and nostrils jut above its head so that it can swim with little of its scaly body exposed yet still breathe and see its surroundings. This quirk makes it easy to spot alligators in the water; just look for a pair of protruding eyes. ~ 407-632-4199.

The best place to see alligators is at the **St. Augustine Alligator Farm**, where the 'gator has been the star attraction for nearly a century. Here is the oldest and largest collection of alligators existing in a controlled environment, a natural center for continuing research on this still-mysterious species. Wooden decks spanning the habitats create ideal viewing conditions while offering total safety for the curious public. Carved out of 30 acres of forest, this clean and well-run facility provides a chillingly close, open-air encounter with enough of these forbidding creatures to populate several nightmares. To round things out, there are water birds, tortoises, turtles and, for children to pet and feed, sheep, goats and deer. Admission. ~ Route A1A, two miles south of the Bridge of Lions, Anastasia Island; 904-824-3337.

CAPE CANAVERAL AREA Though not as popular here as elsewhere, golf is a growing sport in this area. Several courses are open to the public. Try **Cocoa Beach Municipal**. ~ Tom Warriner Boulevard, Cocoa Beach; 407-868-3351. Or try **Turtle Creek**. ~ 1278 Admiralty Boulevard, Rockledge; 407-632-2520.

DAYTONA BEACH AREA The best-known course is probably **Indigo Lakes**, which is rated the eighth best in Florida. ~ Route 92 at Route 95, Daytona Beach; 904-254-3607. Another choice is **Daytona Beach Golf and Country Club**. ~ 600 Wilder Boulevard, Daytona Beach; 904-258-3119. Or try **New Smyrna Beach Municipal Golf Course**. ~ 1000 Wayne Avenue, New Smyrna Beach; 904-424-2190. Another is the **Tomoka Oaks Country Club**. ~ Route 1 and Nova Road, Ormond Beach; 904-677-7117.

JACKSONVILLE AREA Golf courses are sprinkled around Jacksonville from the airport to the beach. Public links include **Pine Lakes Golf Club**. ~ Main Street near Pecan Park Road, Jacksonville; 904-757-0318. Another one is **Jacksonville Beach Golf Course**. ~ South Penman Road, Jacksonville Beach; 904-247-6184. Most of the courses on Amelia Island are open only to resort guests. An exception is the **City of Fernandina Beach Golf Course**. ~ 2800 Bill Melton Road, Fernandina Beach; 904-277-7370.

TENNIS

FORT PIERCE AREA The best places to play are the courts protected from strong ocean winds. In Fort Pierce, try the **Lawnwood Recreation Complex**. ~ 1302 Virginia Avenue; 561-462-1521. You can make reservations in Vero Beach at the **Riverside Tennis & Racquet Club**. ~ 350 Dahlia Lane; 561-231-4787.

CAPE CANAVERAL AREA If you're staying in this area, there's a number of public courts nearby. **Cape Canaveral Recreation Com-**

✔ **CHECK THESE OUT—UNIQUE OUTDOOR ADVENTURES**

- Get out into the Gulf Stream and drop a line for shark with a sportfishing expedition from one of Florida's east coast towns. *page 223*
- Grab a board and sail and try windsurfing on the calm waters of the Intracoastal Waterway—or, if you dare, out in the surf. *page 224*
- Saddle up on Amelia Island and enjoy a romantic canter along the beach when you sign up for a horseback riding excursion at the stables here. *page 229*
- Hike among the mangroves along the Loxahatchee River, where you can choose anything from a ranger-guided tour to a primitive backpacking trip. *page 230*

plex is one. ~ 7300 North Atlantic Avenue, Cape Canaveral; 407-868-1226. Another public facility is **Cocoa Beach Recreation Complex**. ~ Tom Warriner Boulevard, Cocoa Beach; 407-868-3333. There's also **Kiwanis Island Park**. ~ Route 520 on Merritt Island; 407-455-1380.

DAYTONA BEACH AREA   Just north of Daytona Beach in Ormond Beach, there are courts at the semiprivate **Tomoka Oaks Country Club**. ~ 20 Tomoka Oaks Boulevard; 904-672-3397. The beautifully landscaped **Ormond Beach Racquet Club** accepts reservations. ~ 38 East Granada Boulevard; 904-676-3285.

JACKSONVILLE AREA   You can play tennis comfortably almost all year round in northern Florida, with the exception of the dead of winter. The Jacksonville area has a number of public tennis courts including **Boone Park**. ~ 3730 Park Street, Jacksonville; 904-384-8687. **Huguenot Park** is another one. ~ 200 16th Avenue South, Jacksonville Beach, 904-249-9407.

RIDING STABLES

One of the most romantic activities is horseback riding on the beach, but there are few places on Florida's East Coast where this is possible. One exception is on Amelia Island, where **Sea Horse Stables** has horses and guides available to the public. ~ 7500 First Coast Highway, Amelia Island; 904-261-4878.

BIKING

Bicycling in Florida means never having to pedal uphill. In the Fort Pierce area, a good north-south route is along **Route A1A**, which is often in sight of either the ocean or the Intracoastal Waterway. **Indian River Drive** is another scenic two-lane road that parallels the Intracoastal Waterway on its west bank from Jensen Beach north to Fort Pierce. The views include the river as well as the lovely waterfront homes.

In the Cape Canaveral area, one trail option lies slightly inland. To reach the **South Tropical Trail**, which follows the Banana River; head west from Indian Harbor Beach over the Mathers Bridge; there is no bike path, but many experienced cyclists do ride the road all the way up to the intersection with Route 520 on Merritt Island.

Cyclists in the know recommend the **Ormond Scenic Loop,** which travels up and down John Anderson Drive and runs north of Ormond Bridge along the east bank of the Intracoastal Waterway. On the west side of the water is **Beach Street**, which leads through residential areas up to Tomoka State Park.

St. Augustine's historic district is an excellent place to bicycle, the better to appreciate the old homes, gardens and other sights.

In Jacksonville, the people at **Champion Schwinn** conduct guided 15-to 30-mile bicycle tours. ~ 1025 Arlington Road; 904-

724-4922. Some of the smoothest cycling is at the beach, or on it. First Street is good for bicycling and is close to the ocean. On Amelia Island, the 30-block historic district in downtown Fernandina Beach is a good place to sightsee from a bicycle seat.

Bike Rentals **Mac's Bike Shop** rents children's and adult's bicycles as well as baby seats and bike carriers for the car. ~ 3472 Northeast Savannah Road, Jensen Beach; 561-334-4343. In Vero Beach, try **Vero Beach Cycling and Fitness** for parts, service and rentals. ~ 1865 14th Avenue, Vero Beach; 561-562-2781. Beach bikes can be rented from **Ron Jon's Surf Shop**. ~ 4151 North Route A1A, Cocoa Beach; 407-799-8888. In the Daytona Beach area, **The Bicycle Co.** rents bicycles. ~ 201 East Granada Boulevard in the Granada Plaza, Ormond Beach; 904-676-2453.

Bicycles are available for rent in Jacksonville Beach at the **American Bicycle Company**. The store rents bikes and conducts evening and weekend-morning group rides. ~ 1404 South 3rd Street, Jacksonville Beach; 904-246-4433. On Amelia Island, bikes can be rented at the **Village Store**. ~ Amelia Island Plantation; 904-261-4428. Or try **Fernandina Beach Cycling and Fitness**. ~ 11 South 8th Street, Fernandina Beach; 904-277-3227.

HIKING

FORT PIERCE AREA Designated hiking trails are few and far between along the Treasure Coast, unless you count the vast stretches of beach that make up 22-mile-long Hutchinson Island. All distances for hiking trails are one way unless otherwise noted. Four suggested trails can be found on protected state property:

The **Sand Pine Scrub Nature Trail** (.25 mile) winds over a sandy ridge bordering the Intracoastal Waterway. Sand pine trees, scrub oak, wild rosemary and wildlife such as opossum, raccoon and the occasional armadillo provide a changing landscape.

NORTHERN PALM BEACH COUNTY Within **Jonathan Dickinson State Park** (9.3 miles) is a trail that leads to primitive backpacking sites. Several nature trails can be found in this 13,000-acre Hobe Sound Park, which consists of mangrove, river swamp, sand pine scrub, pine flatwoods and a portion of the Loxahatchee River. Ranger-guided tours are available on Sunday morning throughout the year.

Unless you go by boat, reaching **St. Lucie Inlet State Preserve** requires a six-mile hike from the U.S. Department of the Interior Wildlife Refuge at the north end of Jupiter Island. Additional trails lie within the 360-acre park.

Within the 600-acre refuge that comprises Jack Island, the **Marsh Rabbit Run Trail** (4 miles) is named for the dark-brown, short-eared animal often visible in the shrubs or even in the water. Walkways lead through red, white and black mangroves, into a tropical beach hammock.

CAPE CANAVERAL AREA   The best-known trails in the region lie on Merritt Island, whose northern portion is dominated by a vast wilderness refuge, though shorter nature trails can be found on the mainland.

The fully paved **Dent Smith Trail** (1 mile) makes a convenient tour through 30 acres on the campus of the Florida Institute of Technology in Melbourne. Some 200 varieties of tropical ferns, palms and other lush flora flourish within this shade-filled botanical garden.

Running from Melbourne Beach to Sebastian Inlet, South Beaches Trail, a paved "family" trail, connects up with many oceanfront parks to stop at along the way.

The **Brevard Museum Nature Center** (25 acres) has three short trails (one paved) that meander through three distinct ecosystems: a pine sandhill community, a hardwood hammock and a freshwater marsh.

Within the Merritt Island National Wildlife Refuge are several hiking trails. The **Black Point Wildlife Drive** (7 miles) is so poorly paved that it's better to hike it. The path borders coastal salt marshes harboring abundant wildlife—mammals, amphibians, reptiles and fish. Hundreds of species of birds nest in or near the refuge; the best times for birdwatching are early morning and early evening.

The **Allan Cruickshank Memorial Trail** (5 miles) begins at Stop 8 on the Black Point Wildlife Drive and loops around a shallow saltwater marsh. There is an observation tower overlooking the marsh as well as a photo blind, located near the parking lot.

Southeast of these two trails is the **Oak Hammock Trail** (.5 mile), which runs through a subtropical forest where the ecology of the hammock plant community is explained in interpretive signs. The **Palm Hammock Trail** (2.5 miles), which shares a parking lot with the Oak Hammock Trail, leads through cabbage palm hammocks, hardwood forest and open marsh.

One of the most unusual trails on Florida's East Coast is the **Sand Road Trail** (13 miles), which runs north from Playalinda Beach to Apollo Beach. Actually a two-rut road, it offers a close encounter with the vegetation that grows on and behind the coastal dunes. The path also runs directly beneath the Atlantic Flyway, where hundreds of thousands of migratory birds fly back and forth on their annual journeys.

The **Beach Trail** (24 miles) is any beachcomber's dream, starting at Playalinda Beach and ending up at Apollo Beach. The Canaveral National Seashore is virtually unmatched as a long stretch of publicly owned beach in Florida, and this trail is completely undeveloped.

The **Tosohatchee Recreational Trail** (10 miles) provides an easy to moderate tour of woods, hardwood hammocks, marshes and swamps. Hikers can see diverse wildlife, as the grey fox, hawk, bobcat, owl and turkey all call the preserve home.

DAYTONA BEACH AREA   Few marked trails exist on this part of Florida's east coast, though the hard sand beach is excellent for hiking.

The trailhead for the **Bulow Woods Hiking Trail** (4 miles) is located deep in the woods near the Bulow Plantation Ruins. It leads into an ancient hammock of live oak and hardwood trees, following the former plantation road across a stream to an island before looping back.

The **Washington Oaks State Gardens Nature Trail** (.5 mile) borders the scenic tidal marshes of the Matanzas River. An excellent habitat for wading birds and waterfowl, the trail is especially recommended at sunset.

JACKSONVILLE AREA   Although there are short nature trails within a couple of parks, the best hiking in the area can be found north of the Jacksonville city limits.

The **Island Hiking Trail** (4.1 miles) is laid out in a loop on Little Talbot Island. It leads north from near the entrance station through a maritime hammock believed to be the oldest part of the island. Besides the extensive barrier island vegetation, the best feature of this trail is the number of shorebirds and migrating waterfowl that can be viewed. The well-marked trail passes near huge sand dunes before emerging at the beach. From this point, it is a one-and-seven-tenths-mile hike south toward the trailhead.

▼▼▼▼▼▼▼▼▼▼▼
Transportation

CAR

Route 1, which runs from Stuart to Jacksonville, is the main highway on the East Coast. To the east of Route 1, **Route A1A** runs along the Atlantic Ocean wherever possible, crossing bridges between barrier islands or curling slightly inland, often dovetailing with Route 1. To the west of Route 1 is **Route 95**, the interstate that extends the length of Florida.

AIR

Three major airports serve this part of Florida: Melbourne International Airport, Daytona Beach Regional Airport and Jacksonville International Airport. In addition, it is possible to reach the southern portion of the East Coast via Palm Beach International Airport, the closest major airport to Fort Pierce. (See Chapter Three for information about Palm Beach International Airport.)

The **Melbourne Regional Airport** has regular service by American Eagle, Continental Airlines, Delta Airlines and USAir.

A number of major airlines provide scheduled service into **Daytona Beach Regional Airport**. Among them are Continental Airlines, Delta Airlines and USAir.

Jacksonville International Airport is presently served by most national carriers. There is regularly scheduled service via American Airlines, Continental Airlines, Delta Airlines, Northwest Airlines, TWA, United Airlines and USAir.

In addition to taxis, there is scheduled service to and from the Daytona Beach airport via the Daytona Orlando Transit Service, or DOTS, with home and hotel pick-ups available. ~ 904-257-5411. At Jacksonville International Airport, Gator City Taxi provides service to and from Amelia Island. ~ 904-355-8294.

Greyhound Bus Lines (800-231-2222) has several locations on the East Coast. They are in Cocoa at 302 Main Street, 407-636-6531; in Melbourne at 460 South Harbor City, 407-723-4323; in the Daytona Beach terminal at 138 South Ridgewood Avenue; in St. Augustine at 100 Malaga Street, 904-829-6401; and in Jacksonville at 10 North Pearl Street.

BUS

Jacksonville is a busy hub for both interstate and intrastate service by Amtrak. ~ 3570 Clifford Lane; 904-766-5110. Amtrak also stops in West Palm Beach, the closest station to Fort Pierce. ~ 201 South Tamarind Avenue; 561-832-6169.

TRAIN

Arriving at the Melbourne International Airport, you will find well-known car rental agencies such as Alamo Rent A Car (800-327-9633), Avis Rent A Car (800-331-1212) and Hertz Rent A Car (800-654-3131).

CAR RENTALS

Car-rental agencies providing service to the Daytona Beach Regional Airport include Alamo Rent A Car (800-327-9633), Avis Rent A Car (800-331-1212), Budget Rent A Car (800-527-0700) and Hertz Rent A Car (800-654-3131).

Alamo Rent A Car (800-327-9633), Avis Rent A Car (800-331-1212), Hertz Rent A Car (800-654-3131) and National Interrent (800-227-7368) all have rental agencies in the vicinity of Jacksonville International Airport.

Getting around the East Coast without a car is not easy, but it is possible. In the Cape Canaveral area, limited bus service is available via Space Coast Area Transit. ~ 407-633-1878.

PUBLIC TRANSIT

The Volusia County Transit Authority, or VOTRANS, provides extensive bus service throughout the Daytona Beach area. VOTRANS also operates a trolley that runs up and down Route A1A near the beach. ~ 904-761-7700.

Jacksonville Transit Authority has bus service both within the city and between downtown Jacksonville and the beaches. ~ 904-630-3100.

TAXIS   From the Melbourne International Airport, taxi service into Cocoa Beach and other Space Coast locales is available through **Beach Yellow Cab** (407-773-2500).

Service to Jacksonville International Airport is provided by **Yellow Cab** (904-260-1111) and **Checker Cabs** (904-764-2472).

FIVE

Central Florida

Central Florida is a land of many faces. At last count, at least five separate personalities could be spotted in its crazy-quilt character. One minute you might notice the youthful spirit of its green, rolling hills. Then, in a flash, you're dealing with sophisticated six-lane interstates buzzing between rollercoasters, mouse ears, acrobatic whales and discount outlet malls. The next minute, a soft jolt returns you to a quieter time when steamboats puffed along lazy rivers toward destinations studded with Victorian mansions.

One enchanting aspect of central Florida was around long before the steamboats—the area's countless springs, lakes and rivers. This part of the state boasts waters of crystal-ball clarity, waters that gush and gurgle and teem with fish, waters that have given life to fertile agricultural lands. Those acres have produced still another side of central Florida—rows of citrus trees that lie like neatly plaited hair, as well as farms of winter vegetables and miles of cattle scrub.

Central Florida's past is as multifaceted as its landscape. The mouse-eared character now most associated with the area lives only in the short-term memory of central Florida history. Evidence found at mid-Florida archaeological sites reveal an era of prehistoric American Indian tribes and, deeper still into the memory banks, of ancient seas covering the land.

Recorded history here begins with the invasion of the Spanish in the 16th century. Oddly enough, their greatest contribution to central Florida's future was the herd of cattle they brought to the New World. The conquistadors eventually left, but the cows remained. The herds adapted to scrubland pasture, multiplied and became the foundation of lucrative ranches.

During the early ranching era, the word "cracker" first came into use to describe this region's inhabitants. The word got its origin from the whips used on cattle drives through the Florida scrubland. In later years, "cracker" came to describe the common lifestyle of inland Floridians. Although it sometimes carries a negative tone today, the term actually defined earthy, hard-working folks who strove to make a living off the *ocali*, as they called the scrubland. Much of this cracker scrubland later became the Ocala National Forest, named after the old American Indian word borrowed by the crackers.

Citrus fruit, one of the crackers' earliest commercial crops, eventually helped give birth to Florida's tourist trade. Union soldiers returning from Florida after the Civil War told great tales of the land where oranges flourished and water clear as gin bubbled from the bowels of the earth.

Soon the dawning of Florida's golden age of steamboats fueled both tourism and agricultural enterprise. Rumors that a fountain of youth lay at DeLeon Springs near DeLand, and word of the incredibly warm and colorful waters at Silver Springs, kept river traffic at a full head of steam. Glamorous steamers, carrying produce and freight below, often boasted fabulous staterooms and salons on upper decks. They carried the wealthy and powerful on sightseeing tours of Florida's interior. In 1882, one such steamer, the *DeBary*, took President Chester Arthur up the St. Johns River.

Today remnants of that era can be found in the glorious mansions these rich visitors left in their wake, in styles ranging from spiffed-up cracker to Victorian Gothic. By the 1800s, railroads had replaced steamships as the principal mode of transportation, and tourism flourished.

Life in this area during the 20th century generally rolled along at a steamboat pace. Then, in 1971, central Florida was given a solid shake. That's the year a quiet little town named Orlando had its environs invaded by a mouse, the year Walt Disney World was born. The Orlando area has never been the same since.

The 27,400-acre park actually lies in a community called Lake Buena Vista. But both Kissimmee and Orlando have been set ablaze by Disney's precedent-setting attraction. All the hoopla has metamorphed sleepy little Orlando into the world's number one tourist destination. This gives the entire area a cosmopolitan flavor. Shops, restaurants and attractions have responded with imported wares, international cuisine and multilingual service.

Fortunately the city has handled its newfound fame well. While other Florida resort areas have fallen victim to haphazard development, Orlando and Kissimmee have retained their natural beauty and have held fast to their cowtown roots.

Away from Orlando, farther into Florida's interior, you'll find the area's history hiding. Northeast of the city, the towns of Sanford and DeLand remember the steamship era with architectural monuments and riverboat attractions. Sand pine forest and spring waters still refresh travelers tired of resort hubbub. The magic number 72 is the temperature these springs maintain, as well as the average temperature of upper central Florida.

State parks and national forests in this area also offer refuge to the crowd-weary, and to alligators, Florida panthers, deer, wild turkeys and migratory birds. Here fishing camps take the place of towering hotels, and fried catfish pushes steak *au poivre* off the plate.

At the northern reaches of central Florida, the city of Gainesville remains relatively untouched by tourism. The University of Florida here focuses on horticulture and veterinary sciences and has gained fame for developing the sports drink Gatorade, named for the school mascot.

Neighboring Cross Creek is best known for a former resident, Pulitzer Prize–winner Margaret Kinnan Rawlings, who named a collection of short stories and a cook-

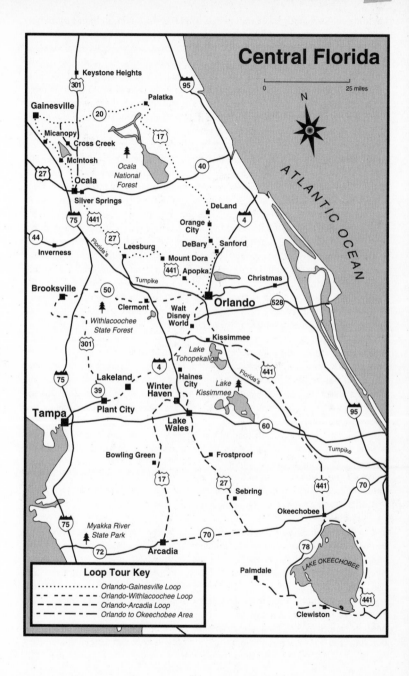

Central Florida

0   25 miles

N

ATLANTIC OCEAN

Keystone Heights

301

95

Gainesville

20

Palatka

Micanopy

17

Cross Creek

McIntosh

27

Ocala

Ocala National Forest

40

Silver Springs

75   441

DeLand

44

27

Orange City

4

Inverness

Florida's

Leesburg

DeBary

Sanford

Mount Dora

441

Apopka

Christmas

Turnpike

Brooksville

50

Clermont

Walt Disney World

Orlando

528

Withlacoochee State Forest

Kissimmee

301

Lake Tohopekaliga

75

4

Haines City

Lake Kissimmee

Florida's

Lakeland

39

Winter Haven

95

Tampa

Plant City

Lake Wales

60

Bowling Green

Frostproof

Turnpike

17

27

Sebring

441

70

75

Okeechobee

Myakka River State Park

70

Palmdale

78

72

Arcadia

LAKE OKEECHOBEE

441

Clewiston

Loop Tour Key

.... Orlando-Gainesville Loop

– – – – – Orlando-Withlacoochee Loop

— — — Orlando-Arcadia Loop

—·—·— Orlando to Okeechobee Area

book after the town. Sadly, the film *Cross Creek* has brought hordes of tourists to the town, disrupting its rural lifestyle. The nearby villages of Micanopy and McIntosh have had no such misfortune and retain their quiet ways, enlivened somewhat by art and antique shopping districts.

Southwest of the Gainesville area, Ocala borders a national forest of the same name. In the past few decades, the city has become synonymous with thoroughbred horse breeding. Here, sleek Arabians and Morgans adorn the scenery as they graze beneath trees heavy with Spanish moss. Numerous springs surround the Ocala National Forest. Among them, Silver Springs, which produces a billion gallons of water a day, is thought to be the world's largest formation of artesian springs.

Between Ocala and the western coastline, Florida remains mostly rural. The Withlacoochee River winds toward the Gulf above a state forest bearing the same name. Nearby in Brooksville, a historic marker commemorates a tragic event in Florida history. On December 28, 1835, a tribe of angry Seminole Indians massacred 139 U.S. soldiers, reopening a barely healed scar and igniting the second Seminole War.

Citrus still reigns in the hills south of Orlando. Here temperatures average in the high 70s and the climate is generally rainier than along the coast. Blossom-scented tranquility settles in between pretty little towns named either for the many nearby lakes or for the escape from cold they offer: Winter Haven, Lakeland, Lake Alfred, Frostproof, Lake Wales.

Arcadia's name comes from the Greek word for bucolic pleasures. Once an important railroad stop, today it is known mainly for its rural riverside orientation, cowboy population and annual rodeo.

Lake Okeechobee, whose name means "big water" in the Seminole language, forms a thumbhole in the palette of Florida landscape. After the lake overflowed during a 1928 hurricane, destroying crops and costing lives, President Herbert Hoover mandated that it be dammed. The resulting dikes created rich soils where crops could flourish. The lake and its waterways, which lead to both coasts as well as the Everglades, were once an important transportation route for American Indians and early settlers. Today it serves as an agricultural center surrounded by Indian reservations, sugar cane fields and small towns whose population changes with the seasons of crop harvesting. It is the most hidden of central Florida's personalities—the last face visitors usually get to know.

In the inner areas of central Florida, visitors can find the state's true character, hidden behind Florida's sparkling mask of sand and sophistication. By unraveling the different personalities of this area, you can come to understand the real depth of that character.

To explore multifaceted central Florida, we have divided the area into several loops (see map at the beginning of this chapter). The listings begin with the **Orlando and Disney World** area—the first destination for most visitors who arrive in central Florida. From there you'll find several sidetrips looping between Orlando and outlying areas: The **Orlando–Gainesville Loop** heads north and encompasses the Ocala region. The **Orlando–Withlacoochee Loop** leads north and west of Orlando, to the Withlacoochee State Forest and back through the Lakeland area. Heading south and west of Orlando is the **Orlando–Arcadia Loop**, which includes Myakka River State Park near the West Coast. The final route out of the city is a straight shot south and is labeled **Orlando to Okeechobee Area**.

Almost everyone, no matter how reclusive, regardless of age, creed or religion, inevitably visits Walt Disney World. Cynics—

who snicker at its fantasy formula, orderliness, ultracleanliness, cornball humor and conservative overtones—nevertheless seem to be swept away by the pure joy of Uncle Walt's fertile imagination.

Here you are in amusement park heaven. This rollicking tour must begin where the history of Florida theme parks took its first Peter Pan–like leap: **Walt Disney World**. Before you visit, it's wise to plan ahead how you will spend your time among attractions too numerous to see in a week. Admission. ~ Lake Buena Vista, Orlando; 407-934-7639.

SIGHTS

For comprehensive information on all the theme parks of Orlando you can pick up a copy of *Disney World and Beyond: The Ultimate Family Guidebook*.

If at all possible, plan your Disney World visit to avoid holidays and peak seasons. Huge crowds mean long waiting lines. In any case, it's a good idea to arrive as the park opens so you can be among the first wave of visitors fanning out into the park's many theme lands.

The wonderful world of Disney à la Florida encompasses 29,900 acres that include the Magic Kingdom, EPCOT Center, Disney World Village, Disney-MGM Studios, resorts, playgrounds and camping facilities. First here was the **Magic Kingdom**, claiming almost 107 of those acres. You board this trip to never-never land right on *Main Street* in the Town Square, which sports turn-of-the-century shops and other buildings. But this is no ordinary main street, you soon discover. Hedges are trimmed to look like mouse ears and animals, and not a speck of litter is to be seen.

And then, straight ahead, you spot a sight that makes even adult hearts leap: Cinderella's Castle rising in the distance. You

✔ **CHECK THESE OUT—UNIQUE SIGHTS**

- Take a break from the fantasy and watch real animals cavort amidst live plants at Walt Disney World's **Discovery Island**. *page 242*
- Take to the skies in a flamingo-shaped **hot-air balloon** and you'll get (and give others) an unforgettable view of Orlando. *page 257*
- Investigate **Silver Springs**, a spot that has attracted the likes of Mary Todd Lincoln and Harriet Beecher Stowe with its crystalline waters and exotic animals. *page 268*
- Find the crowning glory of the found-art world at **King Solomon's Castle** in Zolfo Springs, a three-story castle made of junk by artist Howard Solomon, the "DaVinci of Debris." *page 288*

expect Tinkerbell to sprinkle stardust any minute now—some sort of magic must be used, for this place transforms even the most cynical theme-park critic into a kid.

Several subkingdoms lie within the Magic Kingdom. In *Adventureland*, "Pirates of the Caribbean" is one of the most popular animated exhibits. As with the other favorites, it is best to schedule this swashbuckling boat trip late in the afternoon or early evening hours to avoid crowds.

In *Frontierland*, all the world's a raucous gold-rush town. The big draw here is "Splash Mountain," a watery ride that drops you five stories into the Briar Patch. And if you like rollercoasters, don't miss "Big Thunder Mountain Railroad," a wild and rowdy ride.

Liberty Square's crowd-pleasers are the "Haunted Mansion," with its stretching room and hitchhiking ghosts, and the "Hall of Presidents," with its audio-animatronic heads of state.

In *Fantasyland*, amusement park rides with the Snow White and Dumbo themes are best enjoyed before too much cotton candy, soda pop and hot dogs are ingested. Lines form continuously for the ever-popular "Legend of the Lion King" show and the terminally cute "It's A Small World."

Mickey's Starland opened on the mouse's 60th birthday in 1988. Mickey and friends greet visitors to this playground/petting farm.

"Space Mountain" in *New Tomorrowland* builds up suspense with sound effects, signs warning heart patients against undue excitement, and long lines. You are then wheeled into the dark and whizzed through galaxies with no idea when the bottom is going to drop out. You do know for sure that it will happen—and it eventually does, to the thrill of strong-stomached joyriders. Also in New Tomorrowland, "The ExtraTERRORestrial Alien Encounter" brings you frighteningly close to an alien beast.

In the Experimental Prototype Community of Tomorrow, better known as EPCOT, the world is divided merely in two: *Future World* and *World Showcase*. As you enter, you'll pass beneath the spherical trademark of EPCOT, which rises 17 stories. If you plan to eat dinner at one of the international theme restaurants in World Showcase, your first stop ought to be at Guest Relations, where computer video screens take your reservations. The more popular restaurants fill as early as 10 a.m. in the winter season, so take care of this piece of business first.

World Showcase opens late in the morning, usually at 11 a.m., so you'll spend the first half of your day in Future World. You'll want to hit the most popular attractions first since they fill up early and stay that way through early evening. Don't miss the rowdiest ride at EPCOT, "Body Wars," a mind trip through the human body. Another popular Future World attraction is "Honey, I Shrunk the Kids," a 3D show with brilliant special effects. A favorite among younger children, "Journey Into Imagination" is a soothing glide hosted by characters Dreamfinder and Figment. One of our preferred attractions is called "The Image Works," where big kids as well as little ones are invited to play a series of games involving art, music, electronics and filmmaking.

Gene Kelly personally inspected his robot look-alike for Disney-MGM's "The Great Movie Ride."

The scenic bridge from Future World to World Showcase seems to create a time warp: On one side lies Future World's metal and mirror scenery, on the other, a skyline etched with ancient pyramids, painted pagodas and the Eiffel Tower. While World Showcase is not a realistic tour of the 11 nations it visits (and it undoubtedly lacks the animated sophistication of Future World and the Magic Kingdom), it nonetheless adds culture and class to the world of Disney. The different countries are represented in this circular tour by films and live street shows as well as structures, wares and foods demonstrating heritage and customs.

For instance, a CircleVision film takes you on a dizzying tour of Canada. The United Kingdom exhibit features a pub and food shops. In France, the focus is on cuisine and the Eiffel Tower model, re-created from original blueprints. Moroccan streets are lined with aromatic shops while pagodas and bonsai welcome you to Japan.

For a World Showcase tour of the United States, "American Adventure" presents a 30-minute audio-animatronics show tracing the history of the nation in a colonial theater setting. Your hosts: Ben Franklin and Mark Twain. Then you can visit the bridges and gondolas of Venice, followed by a large, continent-wide step to a Bavarian village. The CircleVision film in the China exhibit whisks you away on an impressive journey beyond the Great Wall. From Norway take an adventure sail into the land of the midnight sun aboard the *Maelstrom*. Last stop: Mexico for a boat ride, some animated theatrics and a quick burrito. Who said you couldn't make it around the world in 80 minutes?

Disney World visitors can play Swiss Family Robinson on a tropical island at **Typhoon Lagoon** (separate admission). At this aquatic park you can snorkel among creatures of the Caribbean, such as baby sharks and parrotfish. Or you can get wet on any of the many water slides and rapids, or float a tube down a 100-foot artificial mountain.

In 1995, Disney opened **Blizzard Beach** (separate admission), a "snowy" version of Typhoon Lagoon. Here you can ride Disney's (and some say the world's) fastest water slide, Summit Plummet. How does freefalling 120 feet at 55 mph sound? If you prefer less excitement, consider trying the tamer water slides or reclining on a chair beside the wave pool.

Another water theme park, **River Country** (separate admission), is laid out in a woodsy setting at the Fort Wilderness Campground Resort. Heated swimming pool, water slides and whitewater tubing provide wet fun.

Also at Disney World, **Discovery Island** (separate admission) takes a nonanimated look at nature. The island zoo features more than 120 animal and 250 plant species, including exotic animals such as the Galapagos tortoise.

Another attraction on these 27,400 acres is the **Disney-MGM Studios** (separate admission). Here visitors can dabble in acting and tour animation production facilities, sound stages and street scenes where Disney and Touchstone films will be shot. Rides and shows are also an important part of the Disney-MGM experience. The "Twilight Zone Tower of Terror," undoubtedly one of the park's most popular rides, drops your elevator cage car from the top of the Hollywood Tower Hotel (twice!). Paying tribute to the spirit of moviemaking, "The Great Movie Ride" transports you to scenes from many Hollywood classics. "Jim Henson's Muppet-Vision 3D" is a rambunctious adventure with an astonishing array of special effects. These are just a few of the highlights.

Second only to the Disney attractions in popularity is **Sea World**. Here the famous killer whale Shamu is the star of the sea show. Sea lions, otters, a walrus, dolphins and myriad street performers and dancers perform. Going to a polar extreme at Sea World, the Penguin Encounter has created a natural environment for over 200 of the tuxedoed birds. The 160,000-gallon Tropical Reef, a waterski show and the "Terrors of the Deep" tunnel are added attractions at this splashy park. Admission. ~ 7007 Sea World Drive, Orlando; 407-351-3600.

Covering 200 acres and spotlighting more than 20 shows and major exhibits, Sea World literally provides a world of experiences, as well as a playground for the kids. When you're ready to depart terra firma you can enter the 400-foot Sky Tower and survey the world's most popular marine-life theme park.

Lying just north of International Drive, **Mystery Fun House** is a glorified combination of a house of mirrors and spook house. They've thrown in moving floors and other special effects, as well as a shooting arcade, miniature golf course and Enchanted Forest. Admission. ~ 5767 Major Boulevard, Orlando; 407-351-3355.

With so much waterfront in Florida, the current wave of man-made water parks seems redundant. They remain popular, nonetheless. One in this area, **Wet 'n Wild**, includes the typical aquatic adventures of these places—water slides, flumes, tubing chutes and wave pools. Admission. ~ 6200 International Drive, Orlando; 407-351-3200.

Fun 'n Wheels is a small park by Orlando's standards. Its yellow-and-white striped awnings herald kiddy automotive fun in the form of bumper cars, go-carts and other carnival rides such as a Ferris wheel. Admission. ~ 6739 Sand Lake Road at International Drive, Orlando; 407-351-5651.

When you've experienced enough disasters, go a round with a big ape—King Kong, that is—at **Universal Studios**. Located about 20 miles north of Disney World, the Florida rendition of California's Universal Studios Tour whisks you through "Jaws" shark attacks, "Ghostbuster" raids, "Psycho" shower scenes and other memorable movie encounters. Admission. ~ 1000 Universal Studios Plaza, Orlando; 407-363-8000.

For more information on Orlando's sights, visit the **Orlando/ Orange County Convention & Visitors Bureau, Inc.** ~ 8445 International Drive, Orlando; 407-363-5871.

EAST OF WALT DISNEY WORLD   Route 192 leads you into downtown **Kissimmee** along a trail of flashing billboards and high-tech signs with ten-foot letters, all trying to persuade you to feed an alligator, watch a medieval joust, get wet, ride an airboat, buy oranges or T-shirts and eat seafood. This stretch is "Tourist Trap Trail," also known as Irlo Bronson Memorial Highway or Spacecoast Parkway.

One of the first super attractions you will encounter is **Old Town**, a nostalgic extravaganza of more than 70 shops and restaurants, with a Ferris wheel, carousel, go-cart track, haunted house and cobbled streets. A classic auto cruise, complete with live rock-and-roll band, commences every Saturday night. ~ 5770 West Route 192, Kissimmee; 407-396-4888.

Eight acres of wild animals, reptiles and alligators are the draw at **Jungleland**, where over 500 exotic animals keep the Florida natives company. Admission. ~ 4580 West Route 192, Kissimmee; 407-396-1012.

Despite its whirlwind tourist reputation, Kissimmee manages to maintain the flavor of its humble cattle town beginnings. When you reach this town at the end of the road, you will find a total change from the maelstrom behind you. Little has changed in the

MONUMENT OF STATES

Located near the lakefront in downtown Kissimmee, the **Monument of States** is built of stones from every state in the nation, plus 21 foreign countries. Built in 1943 by the townspeople, it stands as a 70-foot monument to tourism. Somewhat disheveled in appearance, it appeals to rock-hounds with its impressive gathering of flint, alabaster, coquina, meteors, stalagmites, marble, petrified teeth, lava and other specimens. ~ Monument Avenue, Lakefront Park.

heart of the city since its founding in 1878. Many original buildings remain, including the courthouse and **Makinson's Hardware Store**, purported to be the state's first retail hardware store. ~ 308 East Broadway, Kissimmee; 407-847-2100.

A weekly event recalls the town's beef and dairy industry roots: every Wednesday visitors can sit in on the town's cattle auction at the **Kissimmee Livestock Market**. ~ 805 East Donegan Avenue, Kissimmee; 407-847-3521.

Lakefront Park lies at the end of Monument Avenue. This city park skirts Tohopekaliga Lake (called Lake Toho for short), where fishing, canoeing and bicycling are popular sports.

HIDDEN ▶ Another hint of Kissimmee's noncontrived lifestyle can be found in the 50-mile-long **Kissimmee Chain-of-Lakes** resort area. This string of lakes—of which Lake Toho is the largest—provides seclusion to its visitors. Houseboating, motorboating, sailing, bass fishing and bird watching are among the water activities offered here. Follow Route 525 out of Kissimmee for a scenic oak-tunnel drive around the big lake. ~ 407-847-3174.

For more information on the area, stop in at, call or write the **Kissimmee-St. Cloud Convention and Visitors Bureau**. ~ 1925 East Irlo Bronson Memorial Highway; P.O. Box 422007, Kissimmee, FL 34742; 407-847-5000.

NORTH OF KISSIMMEE   On Route 441, you will find a pair of giant alligator jaws beckoning you to enter **Gatorland**. Here over 5000 Florida alligators and crocodiles can be viewed, along with exotic snakes, birds and monkeys. Not as much a tourist trap as it sounds, this refuge maintains a natural cypress swamp setting, carpeted with ferns and brightened with orchids. Scenes from *Indiana Jones and the Temple of Doom* were filmed in this jungle atmosphere. Admission. ~ Route 441, Orlando; 407-855-5496.

LODGING   With the dawning of Walt Disney World, hotels began to bud more profusely than orange blossoms in the area. It has taken a while for the demand to catch up with the supply of slapped-up chain lodgings. Consequently, you can find some deals here, especially in the off-season (from May 1 until December 15).

Lodging at Walt Disney World is not your least expensive option, but if personality is important to you, you'll find plenty of it here. Room rates reflect the glamour and convenience of staying in fantasyland. The properties are family-oriented and provide free transportation to and from the Magic Kingdom. In season, booking a year in advance is not considered overpreparation. Accommodations at all Disney properties can be booked through the **Walt Disney World Central Reservations Office**. ~ Box 10100, Lake Buena Vista, FL 32830; 407-934-7639.

Contemporary Resort has the least amount of personality of the Disney properties. Meant to look futuristic with a monorail through the lobby, lots of glass and a 11-story atrium housing shops and restaurants, the place actually comes off as stark and sterile. Of its 1053 spacious rooms, those facing the Magic Kingdom offer the best view. ~ 4600 North World Drive, Lake Buena Vista; 407-824-1000. ULTRA-DELUXE.

The 899-room **Grand Floridian Beach Resort** is the grande dame of the Disney resort area. Though relatively new, it has a look and feel of old elegance that recalls the privileged style of Florida's 19th-century railroad tycoons. Victorian verandas, red gabled roofs and brick chimneys lend the exterior its grand appearance. Inside, Florida's belle epoch is re-created using fine detail work: stained-glass domes, crystal chandeliers and ornate balustrades. ~ 4401 Floridian Way, Lake Buena Vista; 407-824-3000. ULTRA-DELUXE.

Polynesian Resort creates a South Pacific ambience. The two-story longhouses lie on South Seas Lagoon and its sandy, tropical beaches. In typical Disney fashion, the common areas feature a bit of manufactured Polynesia, complete with volcanic rock fountains and rain forests. The 853 rooms accommodate up to five people each. ~ 1600 Seven Seas Drive, Lake Buena Vista; 407-824-2000. ULTRA-DELUXE.

The accommodations at **The Caribbean Beach Resort** are named and color-coded for the different islands: peach for Barbados, purple for Aruba, red for Martinique, etc. A centrally located street market with Caribbean food and wares contributes to the theme. The 2112 units surround a 42-acre lake, with a marina and beach. Each "island" has its own pool. ~ 900 Cayman Way, Lake Buena Vista; 407-934-3400. DELUXE.

The least expensive Disney lodging is the new **Disney's All-Star Sports Resort**. The hotel features five major sport themes: football, baseball, basketball, tennis and surfing. Bright colors, basketballs five feet in diameter, huge football helmets and pennants of popular college teams decorate the grounds and the 1920 rooms. Inventive landscaping and architecture make this a unique—if somewhat overwhelming—hostelry. ~ 1704 West Buena Vista Drive, Lake Buena Vista; 407-939-5000. MODERATE.

The **Wilderness Lodge Resort** resembles a magnificent multi-storied log cabin, complete with two towering totem poles and a massive stone fireplace gracing the grandiose lobby. Designed in an attempt to recreate a rustic wilderness retreat, the lodge features western and American Indian artwork and detailing. Outdoor hot springs, pools, streams and geysers all help to create a wilderness atmosphere. The 728 rooms are decorated in shades of brown and green and most have balconies overlooking the courtyards, the lake or the surrounding woods. The resort offers three restaurants. ~ 901 West Timberline Drive, Lake Buena Vista; 407-824-3200. ULTRA-DELUXE.

Other resorts in the mega-park, although called "official" Disney hotels, are not owned by Disney World, which means slightly lower rates. Most offer free transportation and restaurant reservation privileges. You can also reserve rooms at these hotels through the Walt Disney World Central Reservations Office.

Tennis players with generous vacationing budgets might like **Vistana Resort**. With nearly 1000 units available, the resort can accommodate large groups in their spacious designer villas and town houses, all with full kitchens. Thirteen tennis courts are framed in 135 acres of lush landscaping. Swimming pools, jacuzzis and fitness centers are other extras. ~ 8800 Vistana Center Drive, Lake Buena Vista; 407-239-3100, 800-877-8787, fax 407-239-3062. ULTRA-DELUXE.

For a taste of old England, try **Grosvenor Resort**. Its 630 rooms are pleasantly decorated in a modern style with British flair and are equipped with a refrigerator and VCR. Guests have access to a game room, tennis courts, two pools, and volleyball and basketball courts. ~ 1850 Hotel Plaza Boulevard, Lake Buena Vista; 407-828-4444, fax 407-828-8192. MODERATE TO ULTRA-DELUXE.

The **Hotel Royal Plaza** plays the other side of the street. Modern with Spanish highlights, this 396-room facility is decorated in contemporary style and offers its guests a restaurant, a lounge, tennis courts, a sauna and a swimming pool. The hotel's boast is its celebrity rooms: one two-bedroom suite with memorabilia from Burt Reynolds, the other with Barbara Mandrell's personal belongings and family portrait. ~ 1905 Hotel Plaza Boulevard, Lake Buena Vista; 407-828-2828. ULTRA-DELUXE.

To top that, the **Buena Vista Palace** houses 1028 rooms and even trendier decor. The interior is lavish and sleek, featuring a sky-high atrium topped with stained glass. The rooms are modern affairs with private balconies. ~ 1900 Buena Vista Drive, Lake Buena Vista; 407-827-2727, 800-327-2990, fax 407-827-3472. ULTRA-DELUXE.

Few hotels anywhere cater to families like the **Holiday Inn Sunspree—Lake Buena Vista**. Kids even have their own restaurant (sorry, no parents allowed). The 507 rooms come with microwave ovens, refrigerators, VCRs and oversize bathrooms. Outside, there is a swimming pool, while inside next to the lobby is Max's Magic Castle—an enormous child-care center where kids can enjoy movies, puppet shows and magicians. The best news is, kids under 12 eat free (in their restaurant). ~ 13351 Route 535, Lake Buena Vista; 407-239-4500, 800-366-6299, fax 407-239-7713. DELUXE.

Besides its distinction as one of Florida's largest hotels, **Marriott's Orlando World Center** is also one of the most dramatic. The 143,000-square-foot resort rests on 200 acres adorned with swimming pools and fountains, rock grottoes, golf greens and ponds filled with neon fish. The main building is a series of tiered towers that unite in a dazzling atrium lobby with marble floors, waterfalls and Chinese artifacts. At night, braids of light trace the hotel's tiers and are striking from miles away. The 1503 guest rooms, decorated in soft pastels, feel relaxed and airy. Included in the myriad of amenities are a health club, four swimming pools (including one indoor), eight tennis courts, a basketball court, a miniature golf course, 13 restaurants and lounges and the Lollipop Lounge babysitting service. ~ 1 World Center Drive, Orlando; 407-239-4200, 800-621-0638, fax 407-238-8948. ULTRA-DELUXE.

For a luxury Orlando vacation no one can touch, experience the **Hyatt Regency Grand Cypress**. This full-service resort trolleys you to all the many available activities: jogging trails, a 45-acre Audubon nature preserve, golf courses, a tri-level fantasy swimming pool cascading with waterfalls and spanned by a suspension bridge, horseback riding, tennis courts, boat rentals, bicycling trails, sand beach, racquetball courts—there's not much you *can't* do at Grand Cypress. Inside the hotel, the lobby exalts in flowing streams and flourishing tropical flora. The guest rooms are furnished with special touches such as wicker settees, love seats and floral color schemes. ~ 1 Grand Cypress Boulevard, Orlando; 407-239-1234, 800-233-1234, fax 407-239-3800. ULTRA-DELUXE.

Lodging on or near International Drive south of Orlando offers proximity to the area's attractions, plus a solid dose of character. These hotels are generally more upscale than the ones found on Route 192 near Disney World.

The personality of **Country Hearts Inn** is southern Victorian. Its 150 guest rooms are done in lacy curtains, quilted bed covers and paddle fans. The lobby is a vision of wainscot, floral wallpaper, stretch windows and antique chandeliers. ~ 9861 International Drive, Orlando; 407-352-0008, 800-447-1890, fax 407-352-5449. MODERATE TO DELUXE.

Dozens more motels and hotels beckon to travelers. By far the most luxurious, **The Peabody Orlando** is distinguished by the profile of a duck on its tower. Inside, five real mallard ducks parade across a red carpet rolled out for their processions to the pond. Guests gather for the twice-daily event in the lobby, an elegant, soaring space filled with sunlight, marble and vigorous plantings of orchids, ferns and bromeliads. There's a Mallard Lounge and the outstanding Dux Restaurant (but no duck on the menu). The hotel's 891 rooms are extra large and plushly adorned; the service, exceptional. On the fourth floor you'll find lighted tennis courts; a heated, double-size Olympic pool; a health club and beauty salon; and a "duck palace" where the feathered guys spend their evenings. ~ 9801 International Drive, Orlando; 407-352-4000, 800-732-2639, fax 407-351-0073. ULTRA-DELUXE.

MIC **Lakefront Inn** is a modern 164-room facility sitting on the edge of a small lake across from the Wet 'n Wild theme park. The attractions include a large and inviting rooms, a polished lobby, a lovely pool area and a trendy bar. ~ 6500 International Drive, Orlando; 407-345-5340. MODERATE TO DELUXE.

EAST OF WALT DISNEY WORLD   For the most reasonable prices near Disney World, head to the string of chains on Route 192. The two-story brickfront **Golden Link Motel** sits on Lake Cecile. A heated swimming pool and fishing pier come with 84 clean and adequate rooms. ~ 4914 Route 192, Kissimmee; 407-396-0555, 800-654-3957, fax 407-396-6531. MODERATE.

Arches and red-brick trim lend **Gemini Motel** a touch of Mediterranean flavor. Eighty large, modern rooms are complemented by a swimming pool. ~ 4624 Route 192, Kissimmee; 407-396-2151, 800-648-4148, fax 407-396-7418. BUDGET.

One hotel that deserves mention along this route is the **Casa Rosa Inn**. The 55 rooms offer quiet rest and a small pool. The motel itself shows a little character with its blushing Iberian facade. The rooms are thankfully clean and not gimmicky. ~ 4600 West Route 192, Kissimmee; 407-396-2020, 800-432-0665. BUDGET TO MODERATE.

Dull but reliable, **Ramada Inn** decorates its 114 rooms in neutral tones and offers family convenience. Some rooms include kitchenettes, and the inn also has a restaurant. Swimming pool and playground are kid-pleasers. ~ 4559 Route 192, Kissimmee; 407-396-1212, 800-446-5669, fax 407-396-7926. BUDGET.

DINING   Critics have acclaimed the restaurants at EPCOT's **"World Showcase"** in Walt Disney World for some of the finest ethnic and Continental cuisine in the state. During the winter season, the most popular ones are difficult to get into. Same-day reservations can be made at one of Disney's World Key Information Centers; if you are staying at a Disney resort you can book further in advance by calling 407-824-8800.

At EPCOT's **Rose & Crown Dining Room**, serving wenches deliver simple English pub fare such as fish and chips, Scotch eggs or steak-and-kidney pie. You can dine indoors or on the patio at the edge of the lagoon. MODERATE TO DELUXE.

The most talked-about of EPCOT's restaurants, **Les Chefs de France** boasts superb cuisine, with French classics such as braised beef burgundy and roasted red snapper in puff pastry with a lobster crème sauce. Some find the imported French service staff a bit snobby, but that was never my experience. The only problem I found was overcrowding. DELUXE TO ULTRA-DELUXE.

L'Originale Alfredo di Roma Ristorante comes a close second to the French restaurant in popularity at EPCOT. Fine Italian dishes such as fettuccine Alfredo (whose inventor the restaurant is named for), veal piccata and plenty of pasta are featured. MODERATE TO DELUXE.

For Mexican food, try EPCOT's candlelit, romantic **San Angel Inn**. Mexican-American courses include stuffed Baja lobster, chicken mole, red snapper in peppers and onions, and the incredi-

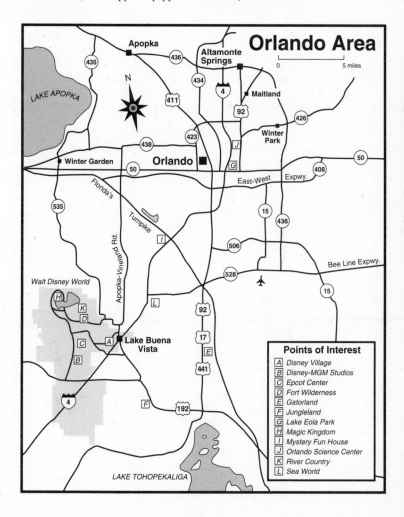

Orlando Area

0   5 miles

Apopka

Altamonte Springs

Maitland

LAKE APOPKA

Winter Garden

Orlando

Winter Park

East-West Expwy.

Florida's Turnpike

Apopka-Vineland Rd.

Bee Line Expwy.

Walt Disney World

Lake Buena Vista

LAKE TOHOPEKALIGA

Points of Interest

A	Disney Village
B	Disney-MGM Studios
C	Epcot Center
D	Fort Wilderness
E	Gatorland
F	Jungleland
G	Lake Eola Park
H	Magic Kingdom
I	Mystery Fun House
J	Orlando Science Center
K	River Country
L	Sea World

ble margaritas and chocolate Kahlua mousse pie. MODERATE TO DELUXE.

Couscous and *bastila* are some of the exotic-sounding dishes served at the **Restaurant Marrakesh** in EPCOT. The first consists of tiny seminola grains served with a vegetable stew; the second is spicy pork, almonds, saffron and cinnamon layered with phyllo. The atmosphere is properly North African, featuring belly dancers and musicians. MODERATE TO DELUXE.

The Norwegian buffet-style smorgasbord at **Akershush**, also in EPCOT, includes an array of cold meats and fine cheeses as well as salmon, herring, lamb, venison and poultry; salad is available for the health-conscious. MODERATE TO DELUXE.

Because of keen competition between hotels, many of the area's best restaurants can be found in its resorts. At the Grand Floridian Beach Resort, **Victoria & Albert's** does a prix-fixe menu served by folks dressed as maids and butlers. The restaurant offers fish, fowl, veal, beef and lamb dinners, often followed by their famous dessert soufflés. Dress code. Two seatings nightly. ~ Disney World Village, Lake Buena Vista; 407-824-3000. ULTRA-DELUXE.

The Outback, located in Disney's Buena Vista Palace Hotel, takes its guests down under. Australian-style food is prepared on grills in the middle of the dining room. Rack of lamb, lobster tail and a wide selection of domestic and imported beers are served by waiters in safari suits. To arrive at the restaurant, guests ride a glass elevator car through a waterfall. ~ 1900 Buena Vista Drive, Lake Buena Vista; 407-827-3430. MODERATE.

In the same hotel, the elegant **Arthur's 27** dazzles with primo cuisine and breathtaking views of the Magic Kingdom in lights. Caviar and grilled shrimp with asparagus head up imaginative specialties including lobster bisque in a flaky pastry bowl and filet of tenderloin. Four- or six-course meals are prix fixe. ~ 407-827-3450. ULTRA-DELUXE.

Nearby, in the Hilton Hotel, **Finn's Grill** serves steaks, seafood and tropical drinks in a Key West setting. You can begin your meal with the "Aw, Shucks" appetizer—a selection of oyster, crab and seafood from the raw bar. Dinner specials include chilled Florida stone crab claws. ~ 1751 Hotel Plaza Boulevard, Lake Buena Vista; 407-827-4000. DELUXE.

The Grand Cypress' **La Coquina** does it all with perfection, from the spotless table linen and glimmering chandeliers, to the nouvelle Continental cuisine and artistic pastries, to the single rose for the lady upon departure. The menu dabbles in seafood, poultry, lamb and delightful sauces. ~ 1 Grand Cypress Boulevard, Orlando; 407-239-1234. DELUXE TO ULTRA-DELUXE.

In almost every Florida city, one finds a restaurant named for Ernest Hemingway, and Orlando is no exception. This **Heming-**

way's conforms to the Key West style preferred by most of these restaurants, with a casual atmosphere and seafood cuisine. Orlando's version also offers an elevated poolside location and a woodsy ambience. The menu swims with grouper, squid, conch, shrimp and other salty creatures, plus a steak or two. ~ Grand Cypress Resort; 407-239-1234. DELUXE TO ULTRA-DELUXE.

Creativity is the main ingredient at the Peabody Hotel's **Dux Restaurant**. Madeira raisin sauce tops pheasant; steamed salmon and sole are braided together; grilled veal loin is served with a sage corn sauce. The marble and crystal grandeur is as impressive as the menu. ~ 9801 International Drive, Orlando; 407-352-4000. ULTRA-DELUXE.

At **Capriccio**, also in the Peabody, Italian goes to California. Besides innovative dishes of Italian descent, pizza is the pièce de résistance here. No ordinary pizza, mind you; these are topped with such ingredients as sun-dried tomatoes, deli cheeses and fresh herbs, then cooked in wood-burning ovens. Among the other delicacies prepared here are grilled mahimahi with vermicelli, risotto and white beans, and grilled chicken with mushrooms and pancetta in a white wine sauce—all served in an atmosphere of polished black marble. ~ 9801 International Drive, Orlando; 407-352-4000. DELUXE.

Fashioned as a Spanish artist's loft with distressed yellow walls, original artwork and worn wood floors, tables and booths, **Cafe Tu Tu Tango** offers "food for the starving artist." A branch of the tapas bars in Miami and Atlanta, this restaurant has an uproarious bar and serves Mediterranean nouvelle offerings: brick-oven pizzas, grilled swordfish, chicken and shrimp orzo paella and alligator niblets, each served in an appetizer-size portion. The hungrier you are the more you will undoubtedly order. ~ 8625 International Drive, adjoining The Castle hotel, Orlando; 407-248-2222. BUDGET TO DELUXE.

For inexpensive meals with an exotic flair, check out the international food pavilion at **Mercado Shopping Village**. You'll have a choice of fast foods from Greece, Latin America, Mexico, Italy and the United States. We tried **The Greek Place** (407-352-6930) and enjoyed Greek salad and lemon soup that rated well above the average mall food. The counter menu also offers *moussaka*, gyro sandwiches, dolmades and other authentically prepared Greek specialties. ~ 8445 International Drive, Orlando. BUDGET.

Orlandoites will point to **Ran-Getsu** as your best bet for authentic Japanese food. The sushi bar whips around like a dragon's tail, and floor tables overlook a bonsai garden and pond. Besides sushi, the restaurant offers sukiyaki, *kushiyaki*, alligator meatballs and other Japanese-Floridian crossbreeds. ~ 8400 International Drive, Orlando; 407-345-0044. DELUXE TO ULTRA-DELUXE.

Local couples and families are the main patrons of **Donato's**, located near Universal Studios. The wood-floored Italian deli and eatery, stashed away in a strip shopping center, serves huge portions of delicious veal, chicken, spaghetti and other saucy pasta dishes. There's also pizza and fresh seafood. Best of all, its boisterous, homestyle atmosphere makes it an anomaly in this gimmicky theme park area. ~ 5159 International Drive, Orlando; 407-363-5959. BUDGET TO MODERATE.

In a simple setting, **Christini's** creates a formal atmosphere and imaginative Italian cuisine. The pasta is made fresh on the premises and served with fish, shrimp, lamb, lobster, clam and veal specialties, seasoned with herbs from the owner's garden. ~ 7600 Dr. Phillips Boulevard, Orlando; 407-345-8770. DELUXE.

The Stouffer Renaissance Resort's **Atlantis** serves elegant Mediterranean cuisine on tables surrounded by nicely appointed furnishings and art. The menu emphasizes seafood and contains such pleasures as poached Maine lobster with risotto, yellowfin tuna with soy truffle vinaigrette, and rack of lamb with garlic rosemary sauce. ~ 6677 Sea Harbor Drive, Orlando; 407-351-5555. DELUXE TO ULTRA-DELUXE.

The Stouffer Renaissance Resort's less formal **Tradewinds** offers fancy sandwiches and salads as well as nouvelle preparations such as rainbow trout with pine nuts, dill and lime meunière. ~ 6677 Sea Harbor Drive, Orlando; 407-351-5555. MODERATE TO DELUXE.

EAST OF WALT DISNEY WORLD   An old island atmosphere is created with wooden fanback chairs painted in pastels, a tropical beach mural on the wall and casual attitudes at **Key Largo Steaks & Seafood**. The menu mixes steak with grouper, mahimahi, scallops and lobster entrées. ~ 5770 West Route 192, Kissimmee; 407-397-7610. MODERATE TO DELUXE.

SHOPPING   At **Walt Disney World**, you will find many ways to spend your shopping dollars. Within the Magic Kingdom and EPCOT, shops offering exotic and fantasy souvenirs abound. ~ Lake Buena Vista; 407-824-4321.

Walt Disney World Village Marketplace is a gathering of more shops, in case you have any money left. You will find unique gifts and souvenirs in all of these shops, but you are better off concentrating on rides and shows while at Disney World, and looking around the Orlando area for gifts. Many of the nearby shopping centers carry the same items at better prices. ~ 407-828-3058.

If you are intent upon an authentic Disney World memento, however, here are a few places to check out:

Sea chest goodies are buried in **House of Treasure** (Adventureland, Magic Kingdom). Buy your pirate souvenirs here. **Frontier-**

land Trading Post (Frontier land, Magic Kingdom) offers gifts and leather goods in a western, American Indian and Mexican vein.

Pringle of Scotland (United Kingdom, World Showcase, EPCOT) deals in wools, tartan, kilts and other Scottish wear. American Indian and Eskimo crafts, moccasins and such are stocked at Northwest Mercantile (Canada, World Showcase, EPCOT). Tangier Traders (Morocco, World Showcase, EPCOT) carries genuine goods from Morocco—clothing, leather goods and accessories. German giftware, such as cuckoo clocks and beer steins can be found at Volkskunst (Germany, World Showcase, EPCOT). The Puffin's Roost (Norway, World Showcase, EPCOT) sells authentic Norwegian souvenirs made of glass, pewter and wood.

If the cowboy bug bites, mosey on over to Great Western Boot Co. to get outfitted in one of their 5000 pairs of boots. ~ 5597 International Drive, Orlando; 407-345-8103.

At Mercado Shopping Village, shoppers are entertained while they browse the brick streets and Mediterranean-style storefronts full of ethnic shops. The Conch Republic (407-363-0227) sells Key West aloe lotions and singer Jimmy Buffet's line of tropical clothing and jewelry. Coral Reef (407-351-0100) carries unique artwork including Oriental *chokin* items and some remarkable pieces by a Gainesville artist working with crushed pecan shell and powder. Spiffy clothing and gifts for the car enthusiast await at One For the Road (407-345-0120). ~ 8445 International Drive, Orlando.

One of the largest gatherings of factory outlets is Belz Factory Outlet World. Over 180 stores sell discounted books, jewelry, electronics, clothing and dinnerware. One shop at Belz called Everything But Water (407-363-9752) sells swimwear and a variety of accessories. ~ 5401 West Oakridge Road, Orlando.

Florida Mall, although conventional, stands out because of its size. Housing more than 150 retailers, its anchors include several department stores. ~ 8001 South Orange Blossom Trail, Orlando; 407-851-6255.

EAST OF WALT DISNEY WORLD   Old Town is a tourist-belt shopping center offering specialty wares and trendy items in an old-fashioned ambience. Brick-lined streets re-create a nostalgic atmosphere of nickel colas, merry-go-rounds, ice cream parlors and city squares. Swinging Things (407-396-7238) carries imported hammocks, hammock chairs and wind chimes. At the same location, A Shop Called Mango (407-396-1336) deals in T-shirts, cotton fashions, straw hats and other items with Caribbean soul. Racing World (407-396-6994) is a car-lover's mecca, carrying mugs, T-shirts and even toilet paper emblazoned with car names. Old Town Magic Shop (407-396-6884) carries an enticing collection of tricks and magic books, with a free lesson for every trick purchase. ~ 5770 West Route 192, Kissimmee.

NIGHTLIFE　The Disney area, so resplendent with sightseeing gimmickry, has debuted its own brand of dining entertainment. Area restaurants take dinner theater a step further, to "dinner arena." The entertainment is usually more noteworthy than the food at these extravaganzas. Most require advance reservations, especially on weekends. I have included most of the major dinner attractions here, along with a sampling of more low-key gathering spots and watering holes.

This new wave of dinner theater was no doubt born at Disney World, where revue theater abounds. Most popular is **Hoop-Dee-Doo Musical Revue**, where the Pioneer Hall Players crack corn in an Old West setting with appropriate chow. ~ Fort Wilderness Resort, Walt Disney World, Lake Buena Vista; 407-934-7639.

At **Polynesian Luau** and **Mickey's Tropical Luau**, two different shows appeal to children and adults with an outdoor South Seas motif. Hula dancers and fire jugglers entertain while diners enjoy barbecue fare. ~ Polynesian Resort, Walt Disney World, 1600 Seas Drive, Lake Buena Vista; 407-824-8000.

Aside from the revues, Walt Disney World offers a few other forms of lively evening entertainment. **The Biergarten** at EPCOT inspires good times with a Bavarian beer garden atmosphere. An oom-pah-pah band and yodelers entertain the crowd.

The **IllumiNations Laser Show** at EPCOT is a must-see. This grand finale could easily be the highlight of your Disney visit. Staged at 9 or 10 p.m. nightly over the lagoon at World Showcase, the program features laser projections choreographed with classical and modern music. The illuminations go much further than most laser shows, creating powerful images across shooting streams of water, the Spaceship Earth globe and EPCOT's international buildings.

With typical Disney extravagance, **Pleasure Island** combines, in a single complex, seven themed nightclubs catering to every musical taste, a comedy club, a teen dance club, restaurants, lounges and a ten-screen movie house. A single cover charge allows entrance into all this nightlife palace has to offer.

Also in the vicinity, **The Giraffe Lounge** is a splashy, crowded dance spot featuring video screens and Top-40 music. ~ Hotel Royal Plaza, Walt Disney World Village, Lake Buena Vista; 407-828-2828.

Nearby, **Laughing Kookaburra Good Time Bar** lists 99 varieties of beer and features live dance music in an Australian-theme setting. ~ Buena Vista Palace, Walt Disney World Village, Lake Buena Vista; 407-827-2727.

The entertainment at **Mark Two Dinner Theater** features local troupes performing a variety of Broadway classics. ~ 3376 Edgewater Drive, Orlando; 407-843-6275.

Studio 70, in the Delta Orlando Resort, is an Orlando favorite offering a big-screen TV and karaoke nights. Occasional live music is featured. ~ 5715 Major Boulevard, Orlando; 407-351-3340.

For yukmeisters, the **Comedy Zone** in the Holiday Inn features comedians who've appeared on Letterman, Leno and Showtime. Cover. ~ 6515 International Drive, Orlando; 407-262-1451.

EAST OF WALT DISNEY WORLD   The **Arabian Nights** dinner attraction features chariot races, Arabian horse dancing and white Lippizaner horse shows. ~ 6225 West Route 192, Kissimmee; 407-239-9223.

Another dining novelty, **Medieval Times** brings back the Middle Ages. Here you eat fowl with your fingers and watch jousting tableside. ~ 4510 Route 192, Kissimmee; 407-396-1518.

Fried chicken and cowboy shenanigans are served up at another dinner attraction called **Wild Bill's**. ~ 4510 East Route 192, Kissimmee; 407-351-5151.

FORT WILDERNESS RESORT 🚶🚴🐎⛵⛺ This 740-acre woodland area lies along Bay Lake at the northern extremity of Walt Disney World. Streams and smaller lakes facilitate canoeing and other water activities including swimming. Overnight campers are afforded the added bonus of free bus transportation to and from the Magic Kingdom and EPCOT amusement areas. There are restrooms, showers, lifeguards and canoe rentals; groceries and restaurants nearby. ~ Located on Vista Drive in Walt Disney World; 407-824-2900.

▲ There are 784 sites, all with RV hookups; $38 to $49 per night.

PARKS

SOUTHPORT PARK 🚶⛵⛺🚤 A natural recreational refuge on Lake Tohopekaliga's south shore, this facility is years away from metro mania. The difficult-to-find spot is maintained as a prime fishing area and secluded park. Carpets of grass and live oak hammocks make the grounds comfortable and attractive. This is a good place for swimming. The park has a picnic area, restrooms, showers and groceries; restaurants are a few miles away in Kissimmee. ~ Located on Southport Road, east of Route 531 and about 20 miles south of Kissimmee; 407-933-5822.

◄ **HIDDEN**

▲ There are 53 sites, most with RV hookups; $10 to $13 per night.

TURKEY LAKE PARK 🚶🚴⛵🚤 A large, natural city park that centers around a lake known as the headwaters of the Everglades. Designed for family pleasure, the park features two sandy stretches along the lake (although swimming is not allowed), a swimming pool, bike trails and natural flora that thrive here in the midst of the metropolis. Children will enjoy the re-created cracker farm and the petting zoo. You can also cast for panfish off the pier. The park features picnic areas, restrooms, showers, a playground, an observation deck and nature trails; groceries and restaurants are nearby. ~ 3401 South Hiawassee Road in Orlando; 407-299-5594.

▲ There are 32 sites, all with RV hookups, and a primitive campground; $6.55 to $16.50 per night.

HIDDEN ▶   **MOSS PARK** 🏃 🚣 🎣 ⛺ 🏊 🚤 ⛵ Moss Park is a 1551-acre county park sandwiched between two lovely lakes. Shadiness and a nice sand beach give this metropolitan fringe park its oasis feel. Much of its acreage remains in a natural, undeveloped state. It's not well-advertised, but the locals know it well. Swimming is good here and anglers try for perch, bass and other local freshwater fish. Facilities at the park include picnic areas, restrooms, pavilions, a playground, tennis courts, horseshoe pits and a nature trail; groceries and restaurants are nearby. ~ Located off Route 15A on Moss Park Road, southeast of Orlando's Route 528; 407-273-2327.

▲ There are 44 sites, 16 with RV hookups, and a primitive campground; $7 to $14 per night.

▼▼▼▼▼▼▼▼▼▼
Downtown and
North Orlando

There was, once upon a time, a snoozing, full-of-character little town known as Orlando. Today the character we associate with Orlando wears mouse ears. The city woke up with a jolt and became one of the fastest-growing centers of tourism in the world. But away from the theme parks that bring travelers to Orlando's door still beats the heart of a real city. Downtown Orlando boasts character even today: museums, galleries, renovated shops and restaurants, turn-of-the-century architecture, science centers, tropical gardens and parks.

SIGHTS   The city's mix of historic and modern architecture finds a pretty reflection in the many lakes of downtown Orlando. In the town's center is Lake Eola, whose **Centennial Fountain** was built to commemorate the city's 100th anniversary in 1975. When the Centennial Fountain was dedicated, waters were added from fountains in Spain, England, the Confederacy, France and the U.S.—all nations that have ruled Florida. It features a modern-sculpture design and a rainbow of lights at night. A lovely lakeside park, with moss-covered oaks and an Oriental pagoda, provides a spectacular view of the fountain. The Orlando neighborhood known as Loch Haven Park offers three fine museums. The **Orlando Museum of Art** spotlights 19th- and 20th-century American works, pre-Columbian artifacts, African art and rotating exhibits from around the world. ~ 2416 North Mills Avenue, Orlando; 407-896-4231.

The **Orange County Historical Museum** travels back 10,000 years with the display of a Timucuan Indian canoe, then takes visitors to the Florida frontier days and finally rolls into the early

20th-century era of boom and depression. An old firehouse station at the back door recalls the days of bucket brigade firefighting. Admission. ~ 812 East Rollins Street, Orlando; 407-897-6350.

Facts are flavored with fun at the **Orlando Science Center**. Here you can touch amphibians and reptiles (including three baby alligators) in the Nature Works section of the museum, while in the Tunnel of Discovery section you can enjoy many different types of hands-on exhibits. You can even explore a simulated space craft. Daily planetarium shows run in an adjoining facility. Temporary exhibits spotlight phenomena such as black holes and electricity. Admission. ~ 810 East Rollins Street, Orlando; 407-896-7151.

Sightseeing takes a natural turn at **Leu Gardens**. Bordering one of the many lakes that turned Orlando into a wet and wild playground, the gardens include over 50 acres of trees, orchids, roses, camellias and other flowering flora. A home on the property showcases the lifestyle of a wealthy turn-of-the-century family. Admission. ~ 1920 North Forest Avenue, Orlando; 407-246-2620.

Interested in touring Orlando from the clouds? Try one of the ballooning enterprises in the area. Try a champagne excursion in a flamingo-shaped balloon at **Rise & Float Balloon Tours** for an overview of this colorful city. ~ 5767 Major Boulevard, Orlando; 407-352-8191. **Aerial Adventures** includes a champagne toast after you land. ~ 3529 Edgewater Drive, Orlando; 407-841-8787.

Right outside Orlando on Route 426, the town of **Winter Park** delights visitors with its tree-lined avenues and a lovely old-time **Central Park** complete with benches, fountains and a stage. In recent years, a sinkhole that gobbled up a few buildings has gained the town's notice.

Rollins College, with its Mediterranean design, is the cultural center of Winter Park. At the entrance of the lakeside campus, the Walk of Fame is lined by 800 inscribed stones from the homes of luminaries such as Charles Dickens and Mary Queen of Scots. ~ 1000 Holt Avenue, Winter Park; 407-646-2000.

◆◆

THE LEGEND OF ORLANDO REEVES

No one knows for sure how Orlando got its name, but many believe it comes from a brave but ill-fated soldier named Orlando Reeves. In 1835, Reeves joined a posse scouting for central Florida Indians. He was on sentinel duty one night when some Indians, disguised as pine tree logs, snuck into the soldiers' camp. Reeves spotted the intruders, fired his gun and saved his companions. Unfortunately, he was pierced by an arrow and died on the spot. Soon people started calling the town Orlando, and eventually that became the official name.

The **Charles Hosmer Morse Museum of American Art** features turn-of-the-century functional and decorative art. Blown glass, pottery and paintings make up the large collection. Most impressive is the priceless display of Tiffany stained glass and lamps. Closed Monday. Admission. ~ 445 Park Avenue North, Winter Park; 407-645-5311.

HIDDEN ► **Scenic Boat Tours** takes you on a peaceful one-hour tour of Winter Park's extensive lakes and canals. Here you can relax amid the migratory birds and waterfowl—Florida nature at its undisturbed best. ~ 312 East Morse Boulevard, Winter Park; 407-644-4056.

HIDDEN ► The work of internationally acclaimed realist artist Albin Polasek is preserved at the **Polasek Foundation**. The facility served as home to the sculptor/painter for his final 16 years, and many of his original works, as well as replicas, are kept there for public viewing. Closed July and August. ~ 633 Osceola Avenue, Winter Park; 407-647-6294.

The **Maitland Art Center** displays contemporary art in a Mayan-Aztec–motif complex of buildings and tranquil gardens designed as a retreat for avant-garde artists. The lovely Garden Chapel on the grounds has become a popular spot for weddings. ~ 231 West Packwood Avenue, Maitland; 407-539-2181.

The **Florida Audubon Society State Headquarters** concentrates, as one would suspect, on bird life. It includes a gift shop and a huge aviary. ~ 1101 Audubon Way, Maitland; 407-645-3826.

LODGING Overlooking Lake Eola Park from across the street, the **Orlando International Youth Hostel** provides uncommon hostel accommodations. Housed in an old stucco, Mediterranean-style home in an upscale downtown neighborhood, the Plantation Manor features a lobby fireplace and piano and a generous, breezy front porch with a view of the lake. There are 33 dormitory-style rooms in the historic building, plus 11 more in a motel building behind it. ~ 227 North Eola Drive, Orlando; 407-843-8888, fax 407-841-8867. BUDGET.

The **Courtyard at Lake Lucerne** offers 22 suites in three lovely homes. One building, the Norment-Parry Inn, is the oldest existing home in Orlando. Sitting on Lake Lucerne, it offers guests loveliness indoors and out. Ornate Victorian embellishments are complemented with American and English antiques throughout the seven character-filled guest suites, parlor and other rooms. ~ 211 North Lucerne Circle East, Orlando; 407-648-5188. MODERATE TO ULTRA-DELUXE.

Parliament House offers 120 carpeted rooms and efficiencies at very affordable prices. The motel has a pleasant beach on Roc Lake where guests can go sailing, an Olympic-size pool and a restaurant that is open 24 hours on Friday and Saturday. Rooms in this gay-friendly motel feature Florida scenes and balconies with views of the lake, pool or a pecan grove. ~ 410 North Orange Blossom Trail, Orlando; 407-425-7571, fax 407-425-5881. BUDGET.

A find for the crowd-escapee is **Park Plaza Hotel**. This 27-room hotel oozes old-fashioned southern charm. Wicker and antique furniture, fern-decked balconies, brass accents and seclusion are the perfect antidotes to a whirlwind trip through the Orlando area. Amenities include a restaurant and bar. ~ 307 Park Avenue South, Winter Park; 407-647-1072, 800-647-0961, fax 407-647-4081. MODERATE TO ULTRA-DELUXE.

Just off Park Avenue, the **Langford Resort Hotel** offers 220 guest rooms, dressed up simply and offering a hint of hotel days gone by. The lobby boasts a Seminole Indian decor with art, cypress tables, terra-cotta floors and jungle vegetation. A sauna, whirlpool, swimming pool and restaurant with live entertainment complete a one-of-a-kind lodging package. ~ 300 East New England Avenue, Winter Park; 407-644-3400, fax 407-628-1952. MODERATE TO DELUXE.

DINING

Lili Marlene's Aviator Pub in Church Street Station serves steaks and seafood in an atmosphere of an English pub with an antique airplane theme. ~ 129 West Church Street, Orlando; 407-422-2434. MODERATE TO DELUXE.

Número Uno holds high regard among Orlando residents for its Cuban cuisine. The facility offers simple decor and a menu of standard Cuban specialties such as rice and beans, roast pork, paella and bean soup. ~ 2499 South Orange Avenue, Orlando; 407-841-3840. BUDGET TO MODERATE.

Unpretentious surroundings and dependably fine French fare draw the locals to **Coq au Vin**. One of the best values and best restaurants in central Florida, the seasonal and regional menu changes every two months and features such favorites as eggplant *bayou têche*, with fresh crab, shrimp and a Cajun hollandaise sauce. ~ 4800 South Orange Avenue, Orlando; 407-851-6980. MODERATE TO DELUXE.

Haute cuisine graces the tables at **La Normandie**. In six different rooms, handmade Norman chairs and other French furniture and tableware bestow an air of elegance. Delicacies such as filet mignon with béarnaise sauce, roast duckling with oranges, salmon and rack of lamb with garlic sauce please the palate. For dessert, try the classic Grand Marnier soufflé. ~ 2021 East Colonial Drive, Orlando; 407-896-9976. MODERATE TO DELUXE.

Chinese food is served by waiters pushing carts at **4-5-6**. Entrées such as steamed sea bass and chicken with snow peas are well-prepared in an ultracasual atmosphere. ~ 657 North Primrose Drive, Orlando; 407-898-1899. BUDGET TO MODERATE.

If you're hankering to quietly eat a steak away from tourist crowds, **Cattle Ranch Family Steak House** is your place. Thick cuts are tossed onto a blazing orangewood fire for extraordinary flavor. Fried shrimp, grilled chicken breast and crisp salads balance the menu. Cowpoke elegance describes the ambience; down-home good describes the food. Closed Sunday and Monday. ~ 6129 Old Winter Garden Road, Orlando; 407-298-7334. MODERATE.

The place to go in ritzy Winter Park is **Park Plaza Gardens**. Here the lunch menu includes innovations like curry chicken salad; dinner emphasis is on veal and seafood (try the West Indian salmon with a horseradish crust, served with hearty garlic potatoes). The charmingly elegant dining room is filled with plants and lit with candles for romance. Closed Sunday from June through August. ~ 319 Park Avenue South, Winter Park; 407-645-2475. DELUXE TO ULTRA-DELUXE.

The stylish **Park Avenue Grille** is decorated with marble tables, maroon-and-grey trappings, rows of tall cross-hatched windows and—the Avenue's trademark—lots of plants. Seafood—with a few landlubber specialties thrown in—is served broiled, blackened, fried, steamed. You choose the method. ~ 358 North Park Avenue, Winter Park; 407-647-4556. MODERATE.

Ask any local where to go for fun as well as haute cuisine and they'll likely direct you to **Pebbles**. Here imaginative food is served in a trendy but warm setting: snug booths and tables topped with mini potted palms and pepper mills. Try the goat cheese tomato concassé, chicken Vesuvio, nutty cheesy salad or honey-roasted spareribs. ~ 2516 Aloma Avenue, Winter Park; 407-678-7001. MODERATE TO DELUXE.

If authentic Mexican food in a packed *casa* is your style, try the homemade guacamole and refried beans, burritos and more at **Paco's**. Closed Sunday. ~ 1801 West Fairbanks Avenue, Winter Park; 407-629-0149. BUDGET.

Maison & Jardin is named for its homey, garden atmosphere. Highly accomplished in local gourmet cuisine, this dressy restaurant features a variable Continental menu that includes traditional dishes such as beef Wellington and rack of lamb, and the more innovative snapper *maison*. Outside, showy flower beds frame Mediterranean villa architecture. On the inside, windows and a glassed gazebo give diners a view of the seven-acre grounds. ~ 430 South Wymore Road, Altamonte Springs; 407-862-4410. DELUXE TO ULTRA-DELUXE.

SHOPPING   **Church Street Station** is a cobblestone and wrought-iron complex of saloons, restaurants and shops. Within the Station, the **Church Street Exchange** is filled with specialty shops; an immense game room comprises one floor. In the Station's Bumby Building, the

Buffalo Trading Co. (407-841-8472) sells jewelry and western clothing, in keeping with the shoot-'em-up theme of the mall. In the same building, the **Bumby Gift Shop** (407-422-2434) deals in gift items and Church Street souvenirs. ~ 129 West Church Street, Orlando.

Caribbean One Stop offers Jamaican take-out, groceries, records and accessories. ~ 2117 West Colonial Drive, Orlando; 407-423-7552.

Catering to Orlando's gay and lesbian community, **Out and About Books** sells T-shirts, jewelry, books, cards and small gifts. In the back of the store an art gallery showcases the paintings of local artists. After selecting a good read, settle down with a frothy cappuccino at the café next door. ~ 930 North Mills Avenue, Orlando; 407-896-0204.

Madge Elaine's World has been an Orlando fixture since the mid-'70s. Wigs, stage and theatrical makeup, gag gifts and novelty items are sold here for thespians or the merely curious and costume-inclined. ~ 5150 East Colonial Drive, Orlando; 407-281-9333.

For the chic, **Park Avenue** in Winter Park lines up designer-name shops, antique boutiques and restaurants. Here, fern bar trendiness is taken to the streets, where rows of greenery hang from wrought-iron balconies.

Also on the Avenue, **The Black Sheep** specializes in hand-painted needlepoint canvases, imported wools, silks, fabrics and accessories. ~ 128 Park Avenue South, Winter Park; 407-644-0122.

Winter Park Stamps stocks several hundred thousand stamps, some dating back to the 1840s. ~ 199 East Welborn Street, Winter Park; 407-628-1120.

The bulk of Orlando's nightlife falls into two categories—country-and-western dance halls and comedy clubs.

NIGHTLIFE

You can dance to live country-and-western music Wednesday through Saturday at the down-home **Sullivan's Entertainment Complex**. Cover. ~ 1108 South Orange Blossom Trail, Orlando; 407-843-2934.

Downtown Orlando is pulsating with evening activity. Venture to Orange Avenue and Church Street, where you'll encounter 15 lively establishments within a five-block area. To mention a few of the most popular: **Chapter's Café and Coffee House** is a mellow place for reading, conversation, light food and coffee. ~ 113 South Orange Avenue; 407-426-8365. Daiquiris and beer reign at **Fat Tuesday**. ~ 41 West Church Street; 407-843-6104. If you're in the mood for Irish folk music and imported beer, the place to be is **Mulvaney's Irish Pub**. ~ 27 West Church Street; 407-872-3296. Also here is **Dekkos**, which looks like something from *Star Wars* with its multilevel dancefloor, state-of-the-art, high-tech light show and indoor pyrotechnics. House, progressive and new-wave tunes are featured. ~ 46 North Orange Avenue; 407-648-8363. Weekend cover at all clubs.

For an update on children's entertainment and events around Orlando, call 407-740-6500 and press 2118 (touch tone phone only).

Church Street Station houses several clubs. The most famous is **Rosie O'Grady's**, which features bawdy Dixieland entertainment: cancan dancers, Dixie bands, tap dancers and vaudeville acts. For disco fanatics, **Phineas Phogg's Balloon Works** blares out contemporary tunes. At **Cheyenne Saloon**, a lot of strummin', pickin' and foot stompin' goes on in a huge former opera house. The **Orchid Garden** hosts a live rock-and-roll band that plays classics from the '50s to the '90s. ~ 129 West Church Street, Orlando; 407-422-2434.

Dramatic ceilings, beautiful artwork and mellow music make **Pebbles Downtown** a classy spot for a drink. ~ 17 West Church Street, Orlando; 407-839-0892.

HIDDEN ►

For a cozy pub atmosphere, go to **Bull & Bush**, have a Guinness and play some darts. ~ 2408 East Robinson Street, Orlando; 407-896-7546.

Deejay-spun Top-40 tops the charts at **Frat House**. ~ 11599 East Colonial Drive, Orlando; 407-273-9600.

The Mill serves up just-brewed beer, relaxing jazz, occasional shots of "alternative rock" and acoustic guitar. ~ 330 West Fairbanks Avenue, Winter Park; 407-644-1544.

THEATER, OPERA, SYMPHONY AND DANCE   For a taste of culture, be sure to check out what's happening on stage at the **Bob Carr Performing Arts Center**. This community theater produces a different play each month. ~ 401 West Livingston Street, Orlando; 407-849-2577.

Rollins College's **Annie Russell Theatre** hosts theater performances October through May. ~ 1000 Holt Avenue, Winter Park; 407-646-2501.

GAY SCENE   **Parliament House Nightclub** offers five venues popular with the gay crowd. In the show bar there are female impersonators and a variety of reviews and contests. Another possibility is the horseshoe-shaped piano bar. The parquet floor in the nicely lit disco is ideal for dancing. The vast lounge bar includes a variety of video games. ~ 410 North Orange Blossom Trail, Orlando; 407-425-7571.

Faces is the only lesbian bar in Orlando. It features low lighting inside, live entertainment on weekends, dancefloor with deejay and an outside patio. On Friday night there is a buffet; on Sunday the mike is open. Cover on weekends. ~ 4910 Edgewater Drive, Orlando; 407-291-7571.

Since most central Florida vacations begin in Orlando, we will take you on a series of loops to outlying areas, tours that can be accomplished in a day or two. The first loop heads west toward Gainesville, via DeLand and Palatka—a tour featuring the riverside vistas and lively springs of central Florida. We return through Ocala, known for its thoroughbreds and the nearby Silver Springs and Ocala National Forest.

Orlando–Gainesville Loop

Right outside Orlando, the **Bradlee-McIntyre House** exemplifies the mansions that heralded the golden days of steamships. Built in 1885 in Altamonte Springs, it was moved to its present location in the early 1970s. The architecture and appointments have been restored to Queen Anne style. ~ 133 West Warren Street, Longwood; 407-332-6920.

SIGHTS

At **Big Tree Park**, a 128-foot-high knobby growth marks the largest bald cypress tree in the United States. With a diameter of over 17 feet, the "Senator" has been estimated to be 3500 years old. ~ General Hutchinson Parkway, north of Longwood; 407-323-9615.

The old steamboat town of **Sanford** is today known as the "Celery Capital of the World." Still retaining its riverside personality, Sanford also blends agricultural, historic and metropolitan characteristics.

The **Museum of Seminole County History** depicts the town's diversity with exhibits covering the citrus industry, cattle ranching and vegetable farming. Railroad and steamboat memorabilia, as well as furnished rooms of a typical steamboat-era mansion are also featured. ~ 300 Bush Boulevard, Sanford; 407-321-2489.

For a narrated tour of St. Johns River wildlife and a peek at its great steamboat days, ride aboard **St. John's River Cruises and Tours**. Alligators, osprey, manatees and bald eagles will greet your passage as they did a century ago. It's wise to call a few days in advance because the trips often fill up. Admission. ~ Sanford Boat Works Marina, Route 415, Sanford; 407-330-1612.

Rivership Romance leaves out of Monroe Harbor Marina on a popular river sightseeing trip aboard a 110-foot catamaran. The Friday and Saturday evening cruise includes dinner and dancing. Admission. ~ 433 North Palmetto Avenue, Sanford; 407-321-5091.

More information on the Celery Capital awaits at the **Greater Sanford Chamber of Commerce**. ~ 400 East First Street, Sanford; 407-322-2212.

As you follow Route 1792 out of Sanford along glistening Lake Monroe, you will come to the **Central Florida Zoological Park**, a

110-acre zoo and picnic area with thatched-roof shelters. Llamas, ostriches and 400 other exotic animals are on display here. Admission. ~ 3755 Route 1792, Lake Monroe; 407-323-4450.

An interesting sidetrip en route to DeLand takes you into the

HIDDEN ► city of **Cassadaga**, a community begun by spiritualists. Psychics meet here in the winter months, and palm readers abound year-round in this shady, eccentric little village.

DeLand once was an important steamboat stop on the St. Johns River. Today, it is home to Florida's oldest private university, named for the cowboy hat that funded it: Stetson University (Woodland Boulevard). On campus, you will find the **Gillespie Museum of Minerals**. This collection of over 25,000 specimens includes Florida coral rock, fluorescents and meteorites. ~ Michigan and Amelia avenues, DeLand; 904-822-7330.

Even if you're reluctant to try it, you may want to watch folks skydiving, a sport popular in the DeLand area. Both lessons and

HIDDEN ► shows are offered at **Skydive DeLand**. ~ 1600 Flight Line Boulevard, DeLand; 904-738-3539.

For more information, and a self-guided tour of the DeLand area, see the folks at the **DeLand Area Chamber of Commerce and Visitors Center**. ~ 336 North Woodland Boulevard, DeLand; 904-734-4331.

At **Barberville**, you can visit a folk museum for demonstrations of the lifestyles of early settlers. The **Pioneer Settlement for the Creative Arts** features a bridge house, log cabin, country store, caboose and train depot as they appeared at the turn of the century. Admission. ~ 1776 Lightfoot Lane, Barberville; 904-749-2959.

Up **Palatka** way, the St. Johns River thickens, scoring deep folds in the hills in its way. The **Ravine State Gardens** takes you down into the lush world of moss, ferns, palms, jasmine, mimosa, azalea, and banana trees. Two deep ravines create a cool refuge and a dreamy mood filled with butterflies and songbirds. ~ 1600 Twigg Street, Palatka; 904-329-3721.

The area of central Florida west of Palatka was made famous by writer Marjorie Kinnan Rawlings. Best known for her Pulitzer Prize–winning novel, *The Yearling*, Rawlings moved to this part of cracker Florida to write and manage a citrus grove. In her autobiography *Cross Creek*, Rawlings documented the simple lifestyles of her central Florida neighbors. In *Cross Creek Cookery*, she compiled recipes and food lore of the region. The **Marjorie Kinnan Rawlings State Historic Site** faithfully preserves the author's rambling cracker home as it appeared when she lived there. An antique typewriter sits on a screened-in porch, tinned goods and dried herbs stock kitchen shelves, and bottles of Appleton Rum and a carton of Lucky Strikes sit by the parlor fireplace. All this tells the story of a woman who called herself "part man," and who endured the hardship of bare-bones backwoods living. Tours are given to a limited number of visitors (it's best to go early or late in the day) by a woman who dresses and plays the part of Rawlings. Admission. ~ South County Road 352, Cross Creek; 352-466-3672.

Our tour next leads to **Gainesville**, known primarily as a university town. Away from big-city contact, life in this town remains quiet, arty and liberal. These qualities are immediately evident in the downtown area, where sidewalk cafés, restored storefronts and cobblestoned plazas add character.

Southwest of Palatka lies the small town of Cross Creek, which also serves as the title of Marjorie Kinnan Rawlings' autobiography.

The **Gainesville Area Chamber of Commerce** distributes information nearby. ~ 300 East University Avenue, Gainesville; 352-334-7100.

Gainesville's premier attraction re-creates the area's rich prehistory. The **Florida Museum of Natural History** displays a Mayan palace, Florida cave, Sioux Indian exhibit, fossil study center and a superb collection of rare seashells. ~ University of Florida, Newell Drive and Museum Road, Gainesville; 352-392-1721.

You can step back even further in time at **Devil's Millhopper State Geological Site**, where the discovery of fossilized sharks' teeth and other artifacts proved that the state was once covered by the sea. Here a five-acre sinkhole plunges 120 feet deep and shelters wildlife peculiar to the area. The temperature seems to drop ten degrees as you follow the boardwalk from pines to splashy waterfalls and furry ferns. Admission. ~ 4732 Millhopper Road, Gainesville; 352-955-2008.

Jungle and safari life have come to Gainesville at the unusual **Fred Bear Museum**. Bear founded the museum with artifacts from his worldwide career hunting with a bow, which he touts as good sportsmanship. Along with the buffalo, wolves, caribou and elephant Bear has felled, visitors can view archery exhibits and relics from American Indian, Eskimo and African civilizations. Closed Monday and Tuesday. Admission. ~ Fred Bear Drive at Archer Road, Gainesville; 352-376-2411.

◄ HIDDEN

After Gainesville, this looping tour heads back south on its return to Orlando. Along the way via Route 441, you encounter the town of **Micanopy**, listed on the National Register of Historic Districts. It is the picturesque headquarters of artisans and antiquarians in the Gainesville area.

Farther along, **McIntosh** sits as content as a purring cat on the shores of Orange Lake. The quiet village is half Victorian homes of the early 1900s, half RV fish camp of midcentury making. One would not be surprised to meet a horse-drawn carriage traipsing McIntosh streets, one of which was designed to run on either side of an old tree, rather than plowing it down.

Text continued on page 268.

Central Florida's Grapefruit League

In Florida, spring fever arrives early. And it hits at a fever pitch—the speed of a sizzling fastball. For this is the site of the Grapefruit League, where baseball pros turn the flab of winter into the muscle of spring. Across the Sunshine State, the month of March means hot dogs, line drives and the crack of a bat. It means baseball training season.

Grapefruit League training is serious business. Over a million fans attend the Florida games each year, bringing millions of dollars into local economies. Cities and counties vie to be chosen as spring training sites, each pitching fancy enticements to team owners. And few areas pursue the sport more aggressively than central Florida.

The most grandiose temptation was Polk County's creation of an entire city for the Kansas City Royals, which had played for years in Fort Myers. Orlando-based publishing giant Harcourt Brace Jovanovich wooed the team by building the magnificent 7000-seat **Baseball City Stadium**, which opened in time for the 1988 season. Then, to sweeten the deal, the company built a $15-million, 43-acre baseball complex with six full-size fields, indoor batting tunnels, a minor league clubhouse and a player dorm. ~ Route 27 at Route 4, Baseball City; 941-424-2424.

The Houston Astros are kept happy at the **Osceola County Stadium and Sports Complex**. This top-of-the-line facility boasts four practice fields and a two-story clubhouse with conference rooms, kitchen and locker rooms. ~ 1000 Bill Beck Boulevard, Kissimmee; 407-933-5400.

Lakeland has managed to keep the Detroit Tigers on home turf for more than 50 years at **Joker Marchant Stadium**. ~ 2301 Lakeland Hills Boulevard, Lakeland; 941-499-8229. Little Plant City staged a ninth-inning coup when it stole the Cincinnati Reds from urban Tampa, just 15 miles to the west. Now, thousands of fans show up for practice and exhibition games at the **Cincinnati Reds Spring Training Complex**. ~ 1900 South Park Road, Plant City; 813-752-1878.

Not to be stuck out in left field, Fort Myers lured the Minnesota Twins from Orlando with promises of a state-of-the-art facility. The $15 million **Lee County Sports Complex** features a 7500-seat stadium for the Twins as well as several training and community fields. ~ Corner of Six Mile Parkway and Daniels Parkway, Fort Myers; 941-768-4200.

A southern agricultural neighbor of Miami, Homestead has built a premier $20 million, 6500-seat complex. It is still unclear which pro team will claim it as their spring training site, but the stadium draws international sports teams throughout the year. **The Homestead Sports Complex** has 17 skyboxes, an electronic press box and parking for 3000. ~ 1601 Southeast 48th Avenue, Homestead; 305-247-1801, extension 6100.

Northward on the Gold Coast, the Baltimore Orioles call **Fort Lauderdale Stadium** home during the spring. ~ 5301 Northwest 12th Avenue, Fort Lauderdale; 305-938-4980. The Atlanta Braves and Montreal Expos share the **West Palm Beach Municipal Stadium**. ~ 715 Hank Aaron Drive, West Palm Beach; 407-683-6100 for the Braves; 407-684-6801 for the Expos.

Along Florida's East Coast, catch the New York Mets at the **St. Lucie County Sports Complex**. ~ 525 Northwest Peacock Boulevard, Port St. Lucie; 561-871-2100. Or see the Los Angeles Dodgers at **Holman Stadium** in Vero Beach. ~ 4101 26th Street; 407-569-4900. The Florida Marlins, baseball's newest team, warms up at the **Brevard County Manatees**. ~ 5800 Stadium Parkway, Melbourne; 407-633-9200.

Over on the West Coast the Texas Rangers play at **Charlotte County Stadium**. ~ 2300 El Jobean Road, Port Charlotte; 941-627-1628. The Sarasota Red Sox are at **Ed Smith Stadium**. ~ 2700 12th Street; 941-954-4101. The Pittsburg Pirates wind up at Bradenton's **McKechnie Field**. ~ 17th Avenue and 9th Street West, Bradenton; 813-747-3031. The St. Louis Cardinals play ball at St. Petersburg's **Al Lang Stadium**. ~ 180 2nd Avenue Southeast, St. Petersburg; 813-822-3384. The Philadelphia Phillies show up at **Jack Russell Stadium** in Clearwater. ~ 800 Phillies Drive, Clearwater; 813-441-8638. A short pitch north, **Dunedin Stadium at Grant Field** is home to the Toronto Blue Jays. ~ 373 Douglas Avenue, Dunedin; 813-733-9302.

Catch Florida's brand of spring fever. If you're like most fans, you'll find spring training action more intimate and even more exciting than regular season games. Call well in advance for tickets or plan to arrive around 10 a.m. for practice time. Most parks feature amateur baseball games when the big leaguers aren't around.

Parimutuel betters enjoy following the fast-paced game of jai alai at the **Ocala Jai Alai Frontón**. Admission. ~ 4601 Northwest Route 318, Reddick; 352-591-2345.

Ocala is known for its thoroughbreds and stately homes. The city has worked hard to re-establish an old-fashioned flavor. At its center sits the **town square park**, with its reproduced, domed Victorian gazebo. The downtown area is called "Brick City" because it was rebuilt with red brick following a devastating fire in 1883. ~ Northeast 8th Avenue and Silver Springs Boulevard.

A few blocks away, another **historic district** stretches along Fort King Avenue between 3rd and 13th streets. Here the era of early tourism and steamboat mansions is remembered in over 200 homes built in styles ranging from Gothic to colonial Italianate to Queen Anne revival.

The **Appleton Museum of Art** houses exotic and unusual treasures collected by Arthur Appleton, Chicago industrialist and local thoroughbred trainer. Within this marble palace you'll find earthenware from 12th-century Persia, Oriental vases, 1st-century Peruvian art, a Mexican effigy vessel, a Napoleonic sword and 19th-century paintings. In short, it's a varied and rich collection of art spanning 5000 years of culture. Admission. ~ 4333 East Silver Springs Boulevard, Ocala; 352-236-7100.

Ocala's outlying area is a land of gurgling springs, oaks covered with hanging moss, pine scents, white-fenced ranches and muscular thoroughbreds sleek with sweat. A few decades ago, breeders discovered that Ocala's healthful combination of sunshine, mineral spring water and fertile soil was as good for race horses as it was for the visitors who had discovered the area's many fountains of youth a century before.

Today, this lush area of coastal backyards is dotted with **thoroughbred farms** that make you think you've arrived in Kentucky, but for the occasional sabal palm towering above low-slung ranch homes. Many of these bluegrass farms can be seen off routes 441 and 301; the greatest concentration roll along Route 200. Some of the ranches welcome visitors. The best way to arrange a tour is through the **Ocala/Marion County Chamber of Commerce**. ~ 110 East Silver Springs Boulevard, Ocala; 904-629-8051.

A different sort of racing is the focus at **Don Garlits' Museum of Drag Racing**. Displays here trace the history of the sport back to its California infancy in the 1950s. Vehicles raced by the museum's founder and namesake, King of Speed "Big Daddy" Don Garlits, are exhibited along with other unusual four-wheel forms of transportation. Admission. ~ Exit 67 off Route 75, Ocala; 904-245-8661.

One of the best known bubbling spring fountains in the state is **Silver Springs**, which has attracted touring nature lovers since first lady Mary Todd Lincoln and author Harriet Beecher Stowe came here in the 1880s. It's the largest limestone artesian spring formation in the world, with an average output of 800 million gallons of water a day. The teeming life visible through the springs' pure waters inspired the invention of the glass-bottom boat by a Silver Springs resident. This is still a favored mode of seeing what lies above and below the waters here. Admission. ~ 5656 East Silver Springs Boulevard, Silver Springs; 904-236-2121.

Within the 360 acres, those who can take their eyes off what lies underwater will spot giraffes, ostrich, monkeys, llamas and other exotic animals. If you feel as though you're in a Tarzan movie, you're not far from the truth. The jungle setting of Silver Springs was often used for making these jungle films. There's also a petting zoo and daily animal shows.

Continuing on Route 40, you will travel into the extensive wild lands of **Ocala National Forest** (see the "Beaches & Parks" section below). A good route for exploring this area is a loop that begins north on Route 314, then south on Route 19 out of the forest toward Mount Dora. Or, you can follow Route 42 west to Route 27-441 for an unpopulated inspection of the forest and the cracker way of life it once bred. Along this twisty road you'll see a hidden cross-section of Central Florida: cracker shacks, horse and cattle farms, rolling hills, spring waters and citrus groves.

One of the prettiest towns in Florida, **Mount Dora** is a storybook village of gingerbread mansions, lakeside inns and 19th-century ambience. The downtown sector boasts brick and wrought-iron structures, New England touches, one of the state's proudest antique store districts and a mountainous Florida elevation of 184 feet. Stop in at the **Mount Dora Area Chamber of Commerce**, housed in a restored railroad station, for a guide to the area's antique shops and historic homes. ~ 341 Alexander Street, Mount Dora; 352-383-2165.

Housed downtown in the old city firehouse and jailblock, **Royellou Museum** features historic photographs as well as tempo-

MASONS IN MANSIONS

Among the showiest of Mount Dora's regally preserved mansions is the **Donnelly House**, an ornate fantasy castle in Steamboat Gothic style, accented with stained glass and hand-carved trim. Built in 1893 for one of the city's founders, it is now used as a Masonic Lodge. Across the street, shady Donnelly Park offers visitors shuffleboard and tennis courts. ~ Donnelly Street between 5th and 6th avenues, Mount Dora.

rary exhibits. ~ 450 Royellou Lane between 5th and 4th avenues off Baker Street, Mount Dora; 352-383-0006.

The **Miss Dora** takes tours out of Gator Inlet Marina into the Dora Canal, the channel that runs between Lake Dora and Lake Eustis. These lovely cypress-studded waters have been preserved from logging to provide refuge for various waterfowl and migratory birds. Admission. ~ 1505 Route 441, Tavares; 904-343-0200.

HIDDEN ▶ **Florida Cactus, Inc.** will change any preconceived notions about cactus being merely green prickly plants that grow in desert wastelands. Visitors here can see the amazing plants growing across the United States: a 6-by-4-foot map of the country is made of cacti, a different variety representing each state. Red, yellow and pink cacti, cacti that form a 6-foot-circumference electric clock, small cacti, gigantic cacti—Florida Cactus does more with cacti than you ever cared to imagine. ~ 2542 South Peterson Road, Plymouth; 407-886-1833.

LODGING A cute little row motel, **DeBary Motel** rents 12 units with kitchenettes. Clunky wooden chairs and potted plants in front of each room give this unfancy place a cozy feel. ~ 101 Route 1792, DeBary; 407-668-5230. BUDGET.

The historic **Sprague House Inn** houses a collection of stained-glass windows that trace the history of the area's steamboat days. This restored facility offers bed-and-breakfast hospitality in a turn-of-the-century building. The six guest rooms each include a sitting room and private bath. The three offering lake views are irresistible. A gourmet restaurant serving Continental and American cuisine is a draw for locals and visitors. ~ 125 Central Avenue, Crescent City; 904-698-2430. MODERATE TO DELUXE.

For a smidgen of New England hospitality, stay at **Cape Cod Inn,** a 40-room facility at the southern end of town. The ambience

---

✔ CHECK THESE OUT—UNIQUE LODGING

- *Budget:* Row a boat out onto the clear lake that laps at your door when you retreat to the peaceful **Lake Brentwood Motel** in Avon Park. *page 289*
- *Moderate:* Cheer for the home team at **Disney's All-Star Sports Resort**—sports fans will love the athletically oriented architecture. *page 245*
- *Deluxe to ultra-deluxe:* Relax in sororal splendor at Ocala's **Seven Sisters Inn,** with its eight lavish Victorian guest rooms, private baths and scrumptious breakfasts. *page 271*
- *Ultra-deluxe:* Spend your entire vacation at **Grenelefe Golf and Tennis Resort** on the wooded shores of Lake Marion; boating, hiking, golf and tennis will keep you busy. *page 289*

Budget: under $50   Moderate: $50–$90   Deluxe: $90–$130   Ultra-deluxe: over $130

here is colonial with a tropical flavor. Broyhill furniture and pastel shell bedspreads decorate the rooms. Exterior architectural design makes this roadside motel look like a country inn. ~ 3820 Southwest 13th Street, Gainesville; 352-371-2500, fax 352-373-5829. BUDGET.

Sitting among a row of impressive old Florida homes and renovated store fronts, the **Herlong Mansion** is a stately affair in Greek revival style. Set in a historic village, this old-fashioned bed and breakfast has 12 guest rooms and suites. Ten fireplaces warm the 15-room mansion, which once was a humble home. Now a three-story palace, it boasts 12-foot ceilings, carefully reworked wood and antiques of many periods. ~ 402 Northeast Cholakka Boulevard, Micanopy; 352-466-3322, phone/fax 800-437-5664. MODERATE TO DELUXE.

◀ HIDDEN

Merrily Bed & Breakfast is a perfectly charming place to stay. Oak-shaded grounds, a home the color of butter, tin peaked roofs, a porch swing, banana muffins at the breakfast table and afternoon tea instill the proper ingredients into this experience. Built in 1888, the inn houses three guest rooms, two with baths. ~ Avenue G and 6th Street, McIntosh; 352-591-1180. MODERATE.

◀ HIDDEN

A handful of cinderblock cabins with full kitchens dot the lake shores at **Orange Lake Fish Camp**. You can rent boats at this peaceful haven fringed with cypress. ~ Lake Road, Orange Lake; 352-591-1870. BUDGET.

Seven Sisters Inn takes you back to the 19th century with style and good taste. The eight restored guest rooms are lavishly furnished with antiques, king-sized beds, hand-stitched linen and private baths. Victorian grace is remembered in the architecture of the three-story mansion with its wraparound porch. Breakfast, served in the garden room, includes scrumptious dishes such as fresh fruit in cream and blueberry french toast cobbler. ~ 820 Southeast Fort King Street, Ocala; 352-867-1170, 800-250-3496, fax 352-867-5266. DELUXE TO ULTRA-DELUXE.

The **Days Inn Ocala** is a gracious 100-room facility with boastful grounds. The guest rooms are touched with luxury, each with either a balcony or patio. Units are reasonably priced. There's also a pool, a lounge and a restaurant. ~ 3620 West Silver Springs Boulevard, Ocala; 352-629-0091, 800-329-7466, fax 352-867-8399. BUDGET TO MODERATE.

In the Victorian city of Mount Dora, **Lakeside Inn** preserves a feeling of old-fashioned hospitality graced with natural outdoor beauty and perfect period appointments. Like a clutch of southern belles, the inn's five pale and pretty buildings sit shaded in plantation ambience and vegetation. Modern amenities complementing the natural beauty include a swimming pool, tennis courts, lawn bowling, gourmet restaurant and lounge. A boardwalk leads to a wildlife picnic island while a sandy beach fringes the lake. The 88 restored rooms are done à la Laura Ashley and heavy on the romance. ~ 100 North Alexander Street, Mount Dora; 352-383-4101, 800-556-5016, fax 352-735-2642. DELUXE TO ULTRA-DELUXE.

DINING

Old whiskey stills, washing machines and studio cameras—all copper of course—establish the theme at **Copper Cove**. Set against a wooded glen, this eatery dishes up home-cooked vittles like grilled ham steak and fried chicken, biscuits and gravy, and french toast. Closed Monday. ~ 201 Cassadaga Road, Lake Helen; 904-228-3400. BUDGET.

Pondo's serves Continental versions of pasta, prime rib, steak, duckling and veal in the gracious, comfortable setting of a two-story 1920s home. The place has an air of old elegance, dressed up in crisp tablecloths in varying pastels. A beautiful fireplace and oak antiques greet guests at the restaurant's entrance. ~ 1915 Old New York Avenue, DeLand; 904-734-1995. DELUXE TO ULTRA-DELUXE.

One of Florida's oldest destinations for travelers, Silver Springs attracted such luminaries as writers William Cullen Bryant and Harriet Beecher Stowe in the 1880s.

The homestyle cooking at **Original Holiday House** has drawn crowds since the late 1950s. Guests serve themselves buffet-style in this well-preserved old home. Choices include leg of lamb, fish, roast beef and salad. ~ 704 North Woodland Boulevard, DeLand; 904-734-6319. BUDGET.

Amid Far East trappings, **Won Lee** specializes in Cantonese cooking and also offers the usual Chinese dishes. ~ 1329 North Woodland Boulevard, DeLand; 904-734-0904. BUDGET.

One of the most interesting breakfast spots you'll come across is **Old Spanish Sugar Mill Restaurant**, inside DeLeon Springs State Recreation Area. Here, the tables have built-in griddles so you can create your own flapjacks with various batters and toppings. Sandwiches and salads are on the lunch menu. ~ 601 Ponce de León Boulevard, DeLeon Springs; 904-985-5644. BUDGET.

Continental goes from Old World to nouvelle at **Karlings Inn**, set in a converted home. Roasted duck with black bing–cherry sauce, blue crab cakes drizzled with spicy apricot sauce, and heavenly Hungarian apple strudel with cinnamon ice cream and caramel sauce will delight your senses. Closed Sunday and Monday. ~ 4640 North Route 17, DeLeon Springs; 904-985-5535. MODERATE.

The **Sprague House Inn** serves lunch and dinner in its Victorian steamboat-age dining room. The menu covers prime rib, shrimp, fresh fish, vegetarian pasta and chicken specialties. ~ 125 Central Avenue, Crescent City; 904-698-2430. MODERATE.

The **Wine and Cheese Gallery** serves hefty, cheesy sandwiches and imaginative salads in an umbrellaed courtyard behind a bistro and wine shop. The Big Cheese, for example, stacks Havarti, Jarlsberg and Danish Caraway cheeses on homemade French bread.

The menu also offers seafood stew, chicken and pasta entrées, as well as over 100 brands of import beer and a wide selection of wine. ~ 113 North Main Street, Gainesville; 352-372-8446. BUDGET.

If you enter **Sovereign Restaurant** on the garden side, you will walk down a narrow alley that feels like New Orleans' French Quarter. White-painted brick walls hung with carriage lanterns lead to a glass-encased patio fringed in greenery. Inside, the restaurant sits in an old, high-ceilinged warehouse, where an extensive menu offers rack of lamb, seafood Newburg, duckling, "scabalone" (scallops and abalone) and other dishes of European descent. ~ 12 Southeast 2nd Avenue, Gainesville; 352-378-6307. DELUXE.

Along Gainesville's downtown streets, lovely sidewalk cafés add a European charm. One such place is **Emiliano's Café and Bakery**. Named for a master baker whose grandchildren revived his Puerto Rican fame in America, Emiliano's specializes in Caribbean pleasures. Chicken breasts in a passion fruit sauce, swordfish *escabeche* and Caribbean pork roast star here. Seating is both indoors and out. Closed Sunday and Monday. ~ 7 Southeast 1st Avenue, Gainesville; 352-375-7381. MODERATE TO DELUXE.

Joe's Deli may be the most perpetually mobbed eatery for miles around. It's the place to be before and after college football games, late at night and almost any other time. Expect generous, meaty subs and great people-watching. ~ 1802 West University Avenue, Gainesville; 352-373-4026. BUDGET.

Intimate and diminutive, **Petite Jardin** resides in an airy storefront setting of white linens and fresh flowers. The bill of fare is Continental-American, with goodies like lobster Newburg, prime sirloin *au poivre flambé* and sautéed soft shell crab. The wine list includes 80 labels, most from California. Dinner only. Closed Sunday. ~ 2209 East Silver Springs Boulevard, Ocala; 352-351-4140. MODERATE TO DELUXE.

The German Kitchen, across from the Econo Lodge, is a small, family-run restaurant that serves German-American entrées for lunch and dinner. ~ 5340 East Silver Springs Boulevard, Ocala; 352-236-3055. MODERATE.

The accent is on Florida at the Ocala Hilton's **Arthur's**. Pastel colors complement an atmosphere both open and intimate. The regional cuisine favors hometown favorites such as lobster bisque, plus other American dishes like prime rib, snapper and filet mignon. Breakfast and lunch buffets are offered, as well as a sumptuous Sunday brunch. ~ 3600 Southwest 36th Avenue, Ocala; 904-854-1400. MODERATE TO DELUXE.

Rocking chairs sit on the wide front porch of Lakeside Inn's **Beauclair Dining Room**. Formal elegance reigns inside, where heavy valanced curtains are tied back around windows overlooking the pastoral inn grounds. The menu offers nouvelle entrées such as roast Long Island duckling with raspberry-orange *coulis*, and filet mignon topped with blue cheese and port sauce. ~ 100 North Alexander Street, Mount Dora; 352-383-4101. MODERATE TO DELUXE.

Behind a picket fence, **The Gables** serves meals in a quaint but elegant setting. Recommended appetizers include escargot in puff pastry, blackened sea scallops and pan-seared tomato topped with jumbo shrimp; for your main course, shrimp, scallops and salmon in Cajun cream sauce, and roasted duck with mandarin sauce and wild berry juice. Closed Monday. ~ 322 Alexander Street, Mount Dora; 904-383-8993. MODERATE TO DELUXE.

For a respite from the antique shopping Mount Dora is known for, the **Windsor Rose Tea Room and Garden Shop** is a little slice of British repose. A small tea room with indoor and outdoor tables, the chintz-covered tables and quietly genteel atmosphere make this a civilized late-afternoon stop for full English tea. You can also order Scottish eggs, sausage rolls, soup, steak and mushroom pies. ~ 144 West Fourth Avenue, Mount Dora; 904-735-2551. MODERATE.

Perched on a rising hill outside Orlando, **Townsend Plantation** enables diners to view grazing horses, white picket fences, restored Queen Anne buildings, a pond and floral gardens from the main dining room. The three-story building has several other dining areas—the Victorian-style McBride Room, the memorabilia-filled War Room and a third whose theme is a child's rumpus room. Southern-style food is served by the bowlful. House specialties include Cajun alligator tail and chicken with garden herbs (grown right outside the door). Closed Monday through Thursday; open every day November 24 to January 1. ~ 604 East Main Street, Apopka; 407-880-1313. MODERATE TO DELUXE.

SHOPPING   In Sanford, the **Magnolia Mall** is an outdoor downtown renewal project that adds a little flash to this rural community. In the mall, **Delightful Finds** (407-323-3995) gathers antiques, Wedgwood china, Depression-era glass and other collectibles and gifts. ~ 1st Street and Magnolia Avenue.

Flea World-Fun World peddles everything you can imagine, from oranges to automobiles within a 100-acre enclosed flea market. It also features an amusement park for the kids. ~ 433 North Palmetto Avenue, Sanford; 407-321-1792.

Jabberwocky sells unusual old-fashioned gifts and children's books. ~ 113 West Rich Avenue, DeLand; 904-738-3210.

Gainesville reflects the sort of downtown shopping our cities used to offer before urban sprawl and mega-malls took over. Behind restored storefronts lie the boutiques, natural food restaurants and quirky shops typical of older university villages.

Persona is an interesting little costume shop that rents and sells masks, costumes and antique clothes, hats and jewelry. ~ 1023 West University Avenue, Gainesville; 352-372-0455.

Gainesville is known for its artists and craftsmen. A collection of their creations can be found at **Gainesville's Artisans' Guild**. ~ 806 West University Avenue, Gainesville; 352-378-1383.

For mall-lovers, **Gainesville Mall** features big and small shops alike. ~ 2564 Northwest 13th Street, Gainesville; 352-372-9615.

The small gift shop at **Fred Bear Museum** carries big treasure. Rare American Indian and Eskimo art, archery equipment and other articles reflect the museum's emphasis on bow-hunting and safari life. ~ Fred Bear Drive at Archer Road, Gainesville; 352-376-2411.

North of Gainesville, **Wisteria Corner** is a treasure trove of antique objects such as oak furniture, linens, teddy bears and farm tools. Check the old barns out back for great bargains. ~ 225 North Main Street, High Springs; 352-454-3555.

For the adventurer, **The Great Outdoors Trading Co.** supplies kayaks, backpacks, sleeping bags and other roughing-it necessities. ~ 65 North Main Street, High Springs; 352-454-2900.

Paddock Mall is the area's largest enclosed shopping center. Taking its name from Ocala's horse-farming tradition, it features a striking equestrian sculpture at the mall's center, around which cluster some 80 specialty and department stores. ~ 3100 College Road, Ocala; 352-237-1221.

Antique shops are scattered throughout the antique-looking downtown area, and found en masse at **Renningers Twin Markets**. ~ South Route 441, Mount Dora; 352-383-8393.

Karen's Gift Shoppe sells gifts of distinction such as antique picture frames, jewelry and decorative lamps. ~ 120 East 4th Avenue, Mount Dora; 352-735-0660.

In Sanford, **The Barn** is a huge dancehall that offers free dance **NIGHTLIFE** lessons and live tunes Thursday through Saturday. Cover. ~ 1200 South French Avenue, Sanford; 407-330-4978.

Western entertainment is presented at **Wild Turkey Saloon** at the Holiday Inn. A live country band plays on weekends. ~ 350 International Speedway Boulevard, DeLand; 904-738-5200.

The collegiate crowd frequents **BW-3 Establishment**, a sports pub with a jukebox. ~ 1 West University Avenue and Main Street, Gainesville; 352-372-4293.

Reggae music finds an enthusiastic audience in Gainesville. Try **Maui Beach Club** for live reggae and other types of music. Cover. ~ 201 West University Avenue, Gainesville; 352-374-8002.

Lillian's Music Store is a jazzed-up urban saloon where live bands play Top-40 and '60s music. Jazz on Sunday. ~ 112 Southeast 1st Street, Gainesville; 352-372-1010.

You'll find 50-cent pitchers of beer on Thursday, pool tables, and DJs spinning house and techno at **Players Billiards & Sports Club**. ~ 1611 Southwest 13th Street, Gainesville; 352-378-1599.

The Days Inn has two places to check out for evening entertainment. **Wings N' Curls** is popular with locals and tourists for its karaoke nights and deejay-driven dance nights. Next door, the **Locker Room** is a sports bar where patrons pay rapt attention to the Sports Event of the Moment. ~ 3620 West Silver Springs Boulevard, Ocala; 352-629-0091.

THEATER, OPERA, SYMPHONY AND DANCE Cultural entertainment can be found at **Seminole Community College**, where concerts, plays and poetry readings are staged. ~ 100 Weldon Boulevard, Sanford; 407-323-1450.

Various music and dance acts perform at the **Florida Theater**. ~ 233 West University Avenue, Gainesville; 352-375-7361.

The old, impressively preserved **Hippodrome State Theater** stars a professional cast of thespians performing contemporary theater. ~ 25 Southeast 2nd Place, Gainesville; 352-375-4477.

The **Ocala Civic Center** hosts a variety of touring musical and dramatic productions, as well as the Marion County Performing Ballet. ~ 4337 East Silver Springs Boulevard, Ocala; 352-236-2851.

The Icehouse Players stage theatrical performances throughout the year. ~ 11th and Unser streets, Mount Dora; 904-383-4616.

PARKS

With the exception of the Everglades, this segment of Florida gives the best view of what the state looked like before the Europeans arrived. It also contains one of the state's largest concentrations of outdoor recreational areas. Springs, lakes, forests and rolling hills provide an endless playground for sportsfolk.

LAKE MONROE PARK 🏃 🚣 ⛴ 🎣 🚽 🛥 ⛽ At the spot where the St. Johns River bulges into a lake, this county park maintains unsophisticated charm beneath tunnels of spreading oak. Used mostly for boating and fishing by locals, you will find it quiet and secluded. There are picnic areas, restrooms and showers; groceries and restaurants are nearby in Lake Monroe or DeBary. ~ On Route 17-92 between Sanford and DeBary; 407-668-6522. The ferry landing is located at 2309 Riverridge Road near DeLand.

▲ There are 44 sites with RV hookups (ten accommodate tents); $8 to $11 per night.

BLUE SPRING STATE PARK 🏃 🚣 🎣 🚽 🛥 ⛽ Winter home of Florida's cherished manatee, this park's river shores once served as a steamboat landing. The year-round 72° waters offer refuge for St. Johns River's population of lovable one-ton sea mammals. The manatees can be seen from observation platforms built along Blue Spring Run. At certain times during the manatees' winter stay, the waters actually become crowded with the huge mammals. A two-hour boat ride affords more opportunity to observe them. Or you can view them when snorkeling. This state park also affords good swimming and anglers often get lucky with largemouth bass, bream, blue gill and crappie. A visitors center is located at the park's entrance. Other facilities include a picnic area, restrooms, showers, lifeguards, hiking trails, canoe rentals (904-775-6888) and a snack bar; limited groceries are sold in the park, restaurants are a few miles away in DeLand or Orange City. ~ Located at 2100 West French Avenue in Orange City; 904-775-3663.

▲ There are 51 sites, 25 with RV hookups; $15 to $17 per night. A hike-in camp is also available for backpackers; $2 to $3 per night. Six cabins are available for groups of four(reservations can be made up to a year in advance and are recommended); $55 per night.

HONTOON ISLAND STATE PARK 🚶 🚲 ⛵ 🛶 ⛴ 🚤 🎣 At this facility you'll see Indian mounds, bald eagles and cypress trees—all viewable from an 80-foot observation tower—and a replica of a Timucuan Indian totem that was found here. But no cars or motorcycles: this 1650-acre spit of land lies in the middle of St. Johns River and requires boat transportation to reach. A ferry comes here daily. Fishing is good for bass, crappie and other freshwater panfish. Facilities on the island include a picnic area, restrooms, a playground, bike trails and a hiking trail; groceries and restaurants are several miles away in DeLand. ~ The ferry landing is at 2309 River Ridge Road near DeLand; 904-736-5309.

▲ There are 12 tent sites; $8 per night. Also available are six rustic cabins, each accommodating up to six people; $20 to $25 per night. Overnight boat camping is also available; $10 to $12 (water and electric hookups included). Reservations required.

DELEON SPRINGS STATE RECREATION AREA 🚶 🚲 ⛵ 🛶 ⛴ 🚤 🎣 This park promised a fountain of youth to wintering visitors as far back as the 1890s and was named for the original seeker of anti-aging waters. A great deal of wildlife can be spotted along the nature trails here. Remains of an old Spanish sugar mill stand near the spring, a favorite local swimming hole. Fishing is also a popular activity here. There are picnic areas, restrooms, a pool and a restaurant; groceries are a few miles away. ~ Located off of Route 17, six miles north of DeLand; 904-985-4212.

GOLD HEAD BRANCH STATE PARK 🚶 🚲 🛶 🚤 🎣 This 1561-acre park claims diverse terrains, including a dramatic ravine where waters gush and the rare needle palm grows. Remains of a dam and cotton gin are visible along a nature trail. Four lakes and a marsh habitat support fox, gophers, squirrels and the rare black bear. The ravine is cool and lush, with a verdant carpet of ferns growing beneath turkey oaks and other hardwoods. This is a good place to swim; anglers frequent the area and try for bass, crappie and bream. The park has a picnic area, restrooms, showers, backpack trails and canoe rentals; restaurants and grocery stores are about six miles away in Keystone Heights. ~ Located off Route 21, about six miles northeast of Keystone Heights; 352-473-4701.

▲ There are 74 sites, 37 with RV hookups; $10 to $12 per night. Primitive, hike-in camping allowed; $3 per night. Also available are 14 fully equipped cabins; $40 to $50 per night. Reservations required.

SAN FELASCO HAMMOCK STATE PRESERVE 🏃 A mosaic of hilly, woodsy, swampy terrain covered with sinkholes, caves, lakes, ponds, ravines and American Indian sites. This preserve provides an excellent example of Florida's precarious honeycombed underground. Along the nature trail you'll see springs being sucked out of sight, only to bubble up to the surface here and there and disappear again. The park is named for its outstanding groves of trees, representing over 150 species. Other than the nature trail, there are no facilities. ~ Located on Route 232, four miles northwest of Gainesville; 352-466-3397.

PAYNE'S PRAIRIE STATE PRESERVE 🏃 🚲 🏊 🛶 ⛵ 🚤 This is a park that combines history and recreation. A visitors center unreels the area's past from 10,000 B.C., the date of its oldest American Indian artifacts, through the 1600s, when the land served as the largest Spanish cattle ranch in Florida. Flora here consist mostly of the sort of spooky marshes that recall horror movies. Visitors can see the park from an observation tower or on guided tours. Lake Wauberg is edged by a grassy beach; fishing is permitted but swimming is not. Bird life of all sorts abounds. Facilities include picnic areas, restrooms, showers, a playground and hiking trails; groceries and restaurants are nearby in Micanopy. ~ The entrance is located on Route 441 near Micanopy; 904-466-3397.

▲ There are 50 sites, 30 with RV hookups; $10 to $12 per night.

O'LENO STATE PARK 🏃 🚲 🛶 ⛵ A riverside park encompassing a variety of Florida landscapes. The Santa Fe River goes underground at a pool and then returns to the surface three miles downstream. Sinkholes, hardwood hammocks, a river swamp and sandhill communities provide diversified sightseeing along nature and bike trails. People also enjoy fishing and swimming here. There are picnic areas, restrooms and showers; grocery stores and restaurants are located five miles away in High Springs. ~ Located on Route 441 near the junction of Route 27; 904-454-1853.

▲ There are 61 sites, all with RV hookups; $11 to $13 per night. A backpacking campground is also available; $3 per night.

OCALA NATIONAL FOREST

The southernmost national forest in the continental United States, this 400,000-acre, pristine terrain combines the invigorating scent of pine woods with the exotic warmth of clean spring waters. The forest's recreation areas invite bass fishermen, snorkelers, sunbathers, hikers, swimmers, campers, wildlife lovers, hunters and canoers. Deer, squirrels, raccoons and alligators dwell among the sand pine. Within the forest, several different recreational areas cluster around separate springs. For more information on the area, stop in at the Visitor Information Center. ~ Located on Route 40, east of Ocala; 352-625-7470.

> The terrain most associated with Ocala is the hot, dry lands known as The Big Scrub, which was made famous by Marjorie Kinnan Rawlings in *The Yearling*.

▲ There are many primitive and developed campgrounds throughout the forests; prices range from no charge (backpacking camps) to $14 per night (RV hookups). Some of the developed areas include Juniper Springs, Alexander Springs and Salt Springs.

ALEXANDER SPRINGS

The springs here maintain a perfectly swimmable 72° year-round and are among the largest in the area. A clean, sandy beach skirts these fertile springs, which produce over 75 million gallons of fresh water daily. One of the largest deer herds in the state also headquarters among the sand pine. It's a great place for diving and many instructors certify students here. If you're on your own, you must show a certification card to the official on duty. Nature trails and canoe runs take visitors back to unspoiled Florida. Fishing is great for bass and other freshwater fish. Facilities include picnic areas, restrooms, showers and canoe rentals; groceries and snack bar are in the park. ~ Located in Ocala National Forest off Route 445; 352-669-3522.

▲ There are 67 sites, no hookups; $10 per night.

JUNIPER SPRINGS

Another natural bubbler, Juniper Springs pumps out 20 million gallons of water a day and provides recreational facilities for the outdoor enthusiast. This particularly lovely spot features an old wheel-powered stone mill that sits at the edge of the springs. The waters are so clear you can takes pictures fish darting among the lily pads. The only pool where swimming is allowed is Juniper Springs. The park has a spring-fed cement pool edged in sandy beach. There are picnic areas, restrooms, showers and canoe rentals; groceries and snack bars are in the park. ~ Located in Ocala National Forest on Route 40; 352-625-3147.

▲ 79 sites, 60 with RV access; no hookups; $11 to $13 per night.

SALT SPRINGS CAMPGROUND

The springs here flow into Lake George, Florida's second largest lake. The warm springs have helped to create the most tropical environment in the

Ocala area, with palms and vibrant flora. This is a good spot for swimming and fishing (common catches are striped and large-mouth bass, catfish, bream, mullet and crappie). Facilities here include picnic areas, restrooms, showers, groceries and canoe and boat rentals. Day-use fee, $2. ~ Located in Ocala National Forest on Route 19; 352-685-2048.

▲ There are 208 sites, 135 with RV hookups; $10 to $12 per night. Primitive camping is available.

HIDDEN ▶ **FARLES PRAIRIE** 🏃 Visitors who want to escape the crowds at the major Ocala campgrounds should check this one out. It is one of several lightly developed sites designed for more primitive camping. The area, sheltered in pines and cleared for easy access, makes an ideal spot for campers who like to rough it a bit. The only facilities are pit toilets; groceries and restaurants are several miles away. ~ Located in Ocala National Forest on Route 595; 904-669-3153.

▲ Permitted; no fee.

HIDDEN ▶ **BIG SCRUB** A true cracker experience for hardcore escapists, this campsite is even more remote than Farles Prairie. Rolling dunes of sand provide the only shade from the scrub's aridity. Midday, you'll find even the lizards snuggled below ground, away from the desertlike heat. The only facilities are restrooms; groceries and restaurants several miles away. ~ Located in Ocala National Forest at the intersection of Routes F88 and F79; 352-625-7470.

▲ Permitted; no fee.

LAKE GRIFFIN STATE RECREATION AREA 🏃 ⌐ ⚓ ⛵ ⛴ ⌐
A natural boating and fishing haven on the shores of a large lake. Bass and bream are common catches. Much of the park is marshy and swimming is not allowed. Locals will tell you this is the place to see "floating islands," a phenomenon caused by chunks of shoreline breaking away into the lake. Facilities include a picnic area, restrooms, canoe rentals and a nature trail; groceries and restaurants are nearby in Fruitland Park. Day-use fee, $3.25. ~ Located on Route 27 about four miles south of Fruitland Park; 904-787-7402.

▲ There are 40 sites, all with hookups; $8 to $10 per night.

HIDDEN ▶ **TRIMBLE PARK** 🏃 ⌐ ⚓ ⛵ ⛴ ⌐ This bird sanctuary and county recreational area lies on a peninsula jutting into Lake Beauclair. The lake, known principally to locals, is huge and beautifully trimmed in mossy oaks and cypress. You'll have to watch closely for a sign on Route 441 that signals the turnoff for the park, which takes you down a winding scenic road. Mainly a fishermen's mecca, this park is also a satisfying find for privacy-seeking campers. The park has a picnic area, restrooms, showers, pavilions, a playground and nature trails; groceries and restaurants are several miles away in Mount Dora. ~ Located at 5802 Trimble Park Road off Earlwood Road near Mount Dora; 904-383-1993.

▲ There are 15 sites, all with RV hookups; $11 to $14 per night. Discounts available for seniors.

KELLY PARK 🚶🏊 This 200-acre county park features the highly productive clearwater Rock Spring, that has created a large pool which is excellent for swimming. The park shows off some of the area's loveliest natural attire of oaks and palm trees. Boardwalks have been built on some of the nature trails. Other facilities are a picnic area, restrooms and a playground; grocery stores and restaurants are a few miles away. Day-use fee, $1. ~ Located on Kelly Park Drive, one-half mile off Route 435 near Apopka; 407-889-4179.

▲ There are 23 sites, most with RV hookups; $11 to $14 per night.

WEKIWA SPRINGS STATE PARK 🚶🚴🏇🎣🏊🛶🎣 Here you'll find sand pine forest and wetlands on an extensive springs system. These spring-warmed waters have created a popular swimming spot for Orlando refugees. The area around the spring swimming pool is cemented, with a wooden bridge that crosses the crystalline waters and leads to a nature trail. Trails take you through wet forests along the springs, and to various other plant communities. Angling is good for catfish and other freshwater fish. Because of the marshes, you must fish from a boat. The park features many facilities: a picnic area, restrooms, showers, a playground, hiking trails, horse trails, canoe rentals and a snack bar; groceries and restaurants are a few miles away (one nearby restaurant can be reached by canoe). Day-use fee, $3.25. ~ Located off Wekiva Springs Road between Apopka and Route 4; from Route 434 take Exit 49 (Longwood); 407-884-2009.

▲ There are 60 sites, all with RV hookups; $15 to 17 per night. Primitive camping allowed; $3 per night.

▼▼▼▼▼▼▼▼▼▼▼▼▼▼▼
Orlando–Withlacoochee Loop

To explore the section of inland Florida west of Orlando, head out of town northbound, to begin a looping route that skirts the West Coast and Tampa, and returns to Orlando from the southwest. This area is known as the Green Swamp and is an important underground aquifer system in Central Florida. Typical Green Swamp terrain includes cypress marshes, sandhills, pine forests and hardwood hammocks.

SIGHTS

The loop tour begins at the **Florida Citrus Tower**, which offers a sweeping view of miles of fruit groves. A tram tour keeps acrophobics closer to the ground to view the same area. There's also a citrus packing plant, an ice cream shop, a candy kitchen, a restaurant and gift shops. Admission. ~ 141 North Route 27, Clermont; 352-394-4061.

HIDDEN ► View one of Florida's most recent enterprises—winemaking—at **Lakeridge Winery & Vineyards**. The winery opened in 1989 and uses all Florida-grown grapes. Over 40 acres of grapes have been planted for future use. Tours and samplings are offered daily. ~ 19239 Route 27 North, Clermont; 352-394-8627.

If you go west to **Bushnell**, you can view the site where the Second Seminole War began at the **Dade Battlefield State Historic Site**. The museum and nature trail here commemorate December 28, 1835, when a tribe of American Indians ambushed troops under Major Francis L. Dade. The Dade Massacre began seven more years of bloody and costly battles in Florida. ~ South Battlefield Drive, off State Road 476, Bushnell; 352-793-4781.

From there you can explore the **Withlacoochee State Forest**, which lies between Inverness and Brooksville (see the "Beaches & Parks" section below). Stop at the **Hernando County Chamber of Commerce** to find out more about the area. ~ 31178 Cortez Boulevard, Brooksville; 352-683-3700.

> The Florida Southern College campus boasts the largest concentration of Frank Lloyd Wright's architecture in the world.

Many towns in central Florida's garden belt claim a crop for their identity. In **Plant City**, the strawberry is king with its own mid-winter Strawberry Festival. Plant City, named for Florida developer Henry Plant, is also home to the Cincinnati Reds baseball training camp (see "Central Florida's Grapefruit League" in this chapter).

Nearby, the city of **Lakeland** is most famous for the Frank Lloyd Wright architecture at **Florida Southern College**. The campus sits on one of the town's 13 lakes and is open to the public. Twelve buildings here were designed by Wright, including a chapel with a unique steeple and the spectacular science building with its planetarium. The renowned architect built the structures of steel, sand and glass with an eye for blending his structures into the grove and lake surroundings. For a self-guided tour map of the campus, stop at the administration building. ~ 111 Lake Hollingsworth Drive, Lakeland; 941-680-4111.

On Lake Morton in Lakeland, the **Polk Museum of Art** presents a dynamic world of contemporary and classic art. Closed Monday. ~ 800 East Palmetto Street, Lakeland; 941-688-7743.

The **Lakeland Area Chamber of Commerce** distributes information on the city and its environs. Closed weekends. ~ 35 Lake Morton Drive, Lakeland; 941-688-8551.

LODGING **Mission Inn Golf and Tennis Resort** offers modern-day amenities with a taste of Florida's heritage. The architecture of the 188-room facility is Spanish, the vintage of the golf course is Roaring '20s,

the river yacht's design is the '30s, and the concept behind the ja-
cuzzi, marina, tennis courts and exercise room is definitely the '80s.
The resort is especially known for its hilly (in Florida!) golf course.
You'll also hear boasts about the multitude of bass in Lake Harris.
~ Howey-in-the-Hills; 352-324-3101, 800-874-9053, fax 352-
324-2636. ULTRA-DELUXE.

To find the most inexpensive lodging in central Florida, try one
of the down-to-earth fish camps that dot nearly every lake. Some
offer only RV facilities, but many rent cabins or cottages. One such
place is **Riverside Lodge**, east of town on the Withlacoochee River.
Nine cinderblock cabins are equipped with full kitchens and
screened porches. Three-day minimum. ~ 12561 East Gulf to Lake
Highway, Inverness; 352-726-2002. BUDGET TO MODERATE.

The Crown Hotel gets its name from the collection of repli-
cated British crown jewels it displays in its resplendent lobby of
brass, wood and gold-edged mirrors. To complete the regal spell, a
sword collection sits against a blue velvet background, and royalty
portraiture adorns the wall of the sweeping staircase. The Crown
houses 34 rooms, an English pub and restaurant, and a pool in the
backyard. The cozy rooms are small but lavishly decorated with
tasseled drapery and carriage lamp accents. ~ 109 North Seminole
Avenue, Inverness; 352-344-5555, fax 352-726-4040. MODERATE.

Lakeland has its share of chain motels and roadhouses. One
you will find tidy and pleasant is the **Bradley Motel**. Its 18 rooms
come with a kitchenette. ~ 3208 Route 92 East, Lakeland; 941-
665-4065. BUDGET.

DINING

El Conquistador matches the Spanish flavor of the Mission Inn resort, where it is located. The menu is as simple as the surroundings
are elegant. The featured dishes include steak with béarnaise or
green peppercorn sauce and grilled tuna steak with an orange,
pineapple and teriyaki marinade. ~ Howey-in-the-Hills; 352-324-
3101. DELUXE.

Complete elegance graces the atmosphere at **Churchill's Grill** in
the fabulous Crown Hotel. Classic British and American fare is
served in Victorian surroundings. Floral wallpaper and lace curtains are set off with brass fixtures and crystal chandeliers. The
menu features grilled seafood, meat and poultry dishes. ~ 109
North Seminole Avenue, Inverness; 352-344-5555. MODERATE TO
DELUXE.

The best deal around town is found at a little cornflower blue
cottage with white trim known as the **Blueberry Patch Tea Room**.
Inside, the color scheme continues, complemented with white
wicker, an antique stove, a grandfather clock, an old phonograph
and other unusual pieces. You get homemade dinners with a gourmet flair at a price that's a terrific value. Crab soufflés, quiches,
seafood creole, salads and diet-breaking desserts such as silk and

pecan pies are some of the specialties. As for the name: you get blueberry muffins with every meal, and a different vintage teapot sits upon each table. ~ 414 East Liberty Street, Brooksville; 352-796-6005. BUDGET.

HIDDEN ► **Bayport Inn** is an out-of-the-way roadhouse that serves good food. There's a warmth to the place, with its fireplace, but what really attracts the locals is the downright good catfish, 'gator and frogs' legs. Be sure to take advantage of the "all-you-can-eat fishfry." ~ 4835 Cortez Boulevard, Springfield; 352-596-1088. MODERATE.

HIDDEN ► One of the joys of visiting this part of Florida is taking a trip to **Buddy Freddy's**. Here you'll happily discover the foods of home: fried chicken with whipped potatoes, thick-sauced chicken and dumplings, gooey macaroni and cheese and stewed lima beans. Thank Freddy for the wonderful eats, and brother Buddy (who plays host) for the friendly, neighborly ambience. ~ 1101 Goldfinch Drive, Plant City; 813-754-5120. BUDGET TO MODERATE.

HIDDEN ► If you love steak—or even sort of like it—head for **The Red Barn**. Still hidden to many locals, this down-home gem has earned a reputation as one of Florida's premier steakhouses. Lodged in a no-frills, 1930s dairy barn, it features a cold case piled with just-cut beef. Order from here or from the menu that also lists chicken, seafood and ham (what else?) steak. ~ 6150 New Tampa Highway, Lakeland; 941-686-2754. ULTRA-DELUXE.

SHOPPING   Only those completely lacking in curiosity can pass up **Chez Funk**. It attracts customers with outrageous signs advertising "world famous 'tourist trap' art." Inside you'll find an array of used and antique glad rags. ~ 661 Route 41, Brooksville; 352-799-8658.

Brooke Pottery Inc. provides an ample selection of jewelry, woodworking and functional and decorative pottery. ~ 223 North Kentucky Avenue, Lakeland; 941-688-6844.

Lakeland Square is the area's largest enclosed mall. Among its 120 stores and shops are counted several major department stores. ~ 3800 Route 98 North, Lakeland; 941-859-5411.

NIGHTLIFE   There's live country music entertainment three nights a week at **Brass Rail Saloon**. ~ 1065 South Vineland Road, Winter Garden; 407-656-8300.

In quiet lakeside Inverness, nightlife begins and ends at the town hub, the Crown Hotel. **The Fox and Hounds Pub** within provides warm surroundings for a glass of ale or a nightcap. ~ 109 North Seminole Avenue, Inverness; 352-344-5555.

Roy's Green Parrot is predominantly a gay club with a mixed gay and lesbian crowd on weekends. It provides a small dancefloor, occasional drag shows and a friendly crowd of unpretentious regulars. ~ 1030 East Main Street, Lakeland; 941-683-6021.

Zimmerman's is a favorite of local college students, visiting Detroit Tiger baseball players and reporters from the local paper. Posters cover the ceiling; the wallpaper has seen better days, but the unpretentious decor is overlooked by the ace bartender and the amiable crowd. Live bands on weekends during the school year. Cover. ~ 1015 South Florida Avenue, Lakeland; 941-682-9078.

THEATER, OPERA, SYMPHONY AND DANCE   The cultural center of Lakeland is **Florida Southern College**. Call the school to find out about upcoming concerts and dance performances. ~ 111 Lake Hollingsworth Drive, Lakeland; 941-680-4116.

The **Polk Museum of Art** hosts orchestras and performing artists. ~ 800 East Palmetto Street, Lakeland; 941-688-7743.

PARKS

LAKE LOUISA STATE PARK 🚲🏇🏊🚣 A preserved segment of Green Swamp, this area is an important underground aquifer system in central Florida. The park lies on the shores of Lake Louisa and also encompasses Bear Lake. Typical Green Swamp terrain is found here: cypress marshes, sandhills, pine forests and hardwood hammocks. There are good spots for swimming and fishing. Trails are available for equestrians. The only facilities within the park are picnic areas and restrooms; grocery stores and restaurants are a few miles away in Clermont. ~ Located off Route 561 south of Clermont off Lake Nellie Road; 352-394-3969.

WITHLACOOCHEE STATE FOREST 🥾🚲🏇⛴🛥🚣 This is the second largest state forest in Florida. Within its 130,000 acres are several separate tracts, including Forest Headquarters, Croom, Richloam, Citrus and Jumper Creek. These are subdivided into various recreation areas and forestry stations. The park focuses on the Withlacoochee and Little Withlacoochee rivers, which flow through a variety of indigenous Florida landscapes. Hiking trails penetrate the forest in several areas, allowing visitors a look at the region's diverse flora and fauna. Fishing for catfish and panfish is recommended. Facilities include picnic areas and restrooms; grocery stores and restaurants are located in Inverness and Brooksville. ~ The park, which spreads through five counties, has its main entrance off Route 75 near Brooksville; 352-754-6777.

▲ There are three main campgrounds (hookups available); $8 to $10 per night. Primitive camping is allowed off the hiking trails.

FORT COOPER STATE PARK 🏃🚣⛱🛥🚤 The sandy lake beach here may not be the kind you see touted in Florida vacation brochures, but it is one of the nicest freshwater beaches of central Florida. The Old Military Trail on the edge of Lake Holathlikaha leads you down the path of history, where wounded soldiers once recuperated at a hastily built fort during the Seminole wars. Vegetation includes sweetgums, hickories and magnolias among the area's typical oak and longleaf pines. This park offers good fishing, canoeing and swimming. There are also volleyball courts, a playground, horseshoes, a nature trail, picnic area, restrooms, showers, canoe and boat rentals; groceries and restaurants a few miles away in Inverness. Day-use fee, $2. ~ Located at 3100 South Old Floral City Road, south of Inverness; 352-726-0315.

▲ There are two primitive campsites; $3 per adult, $2 per child.

SADDLE CREEK PARK 🏃 ⛵ ⛵ 🚣 A 734-acre county park with a sand beach bordering the creek, Saddle Creek has good places for swimming and well-maintained camping and picnicking facilities. But because of development there's little left of nature here, and not much seclusion. Facilities include a picnic area, restrooms, a playground and a nature trail; groceries and restaurants are a few miles away. ~ Located on Fish Hatchery Road off Route 92 between Lakeland and Auburndale; 941-499-2613, 941-534-4340.

▲ There are 40 sites, half with RV hookups; $9 to $11 per night.

▼▼▼▼▼▼▼▼▼▼▼▼ Orlando–Arcadia Loop

For a pleasant drive into rural Central Florida, take alternate Route 27, which veers off Route 4 south of Orlando. Here in the heartland, citrus scents the air with its blossoms in spring, its ripe juices in winter. Known as the Highlands area, this section lies along Florida's central ridge.

SIGHTS

The quirkiness of **Lake Wales** can be seen by its main attractions: an eccentric dollhouse-like country inn, a singing tower and a "spooked" hill. Start exploring the area north of town at the first

HIDDEN ▶

of these, **Chalet Suzanne Inn Village**, and have a peek at the quaint Old World restaurant, inn, gift shops and ceramics studio. Tours can be arranged through the soup cannery, where the restaurant's trademark dishes are canned. Its signature romaine soup was sent to space with Apollo 16. In the tiny ceramics studio in the midst of the meandering cobblestone village, you can watch craftspeople making dishware and personalized gifts. ~ Chalet Suzanne Road, Lake Wales; 941-676-6011.

HIDDEN ▶

A trip to **Bok Tower Gardens** is a treat for the senses: exotic blossoms scent leaf-paved paths and squirrels chatter atop towering oaks. Here, in 1928, Dutch immigrant Edward Bok built a 200-foot carillon tower of Georgia marble and St. Augustine coquina stone to show his appreciation for the beauty he felt America had brought into his life. He planted the 128 acres around the "singing tower" in magnolias, azaleas and plants from the Orient to create an atmosphere of peace. The carillon, a registered historic structure, rings out classic harmonies every half hour to add a special magic to this place. Admission. ~ 1151 Tower Boulevard, Lake Wales; 941-676-1408.

Lake Wales itself is a pretty little town that lassoes a lake. For a scenic view of the water and its lakeside mansions and park, follow **Lakeshore Boulevard.** The history of the area, including the building of the railroad that settled inland Florida, can be seen at **Lake Wales Depot Museum.** The museum, housed in the Atlantic Coastline Depot, sits next to a historic railroad car. ~ 325 South Scenic Highway, Lake Wales; 941-678-4209.

Also surrounded by lovely lakes, Avon Park offers a single formal attraction, the **Avon Park Museum.** An old Seaboard Coast Lines railroad depot houses a homely little museum containing memorabilia of the area's development. ~ 3 North Museum Avenue, Avon Park; 941-453-3525.

Sebring is best known for its **Sebring International Raceway,** where the 12-Hour Endurance Race is held each March. Aside from the roar of engines, this is a pretty lake-mottled town blending a sense of heritage, a touch of sophistication and an outdoors orientation. ~ 113 Midway Drive; 941-655-1442. For more information, stop at the **Greater Sebring Chamber of Commerce.** ~ 309 South Circle, Sebring; 941-385-8448.

At the crossroads of Routes 27 and 70, head west toward Arcadia. As you approach the city, you'll probably notice an increase in pickup trucks. This town is the center for area ranchers. The state's oldest rodeo, the **All-Florida Championship Rodeo,** has been held in Arcadia since 1929. ~ 941-494-2014.

Downtown Arcadia has been restored to its railroad days. **The Depot** was redone to house museum items, photos and train paraphernalia. A small collection of shops is also housed there. Stop in and ask for a tour. ~ 4 West Oak Street.

For a lovely sidetrip into Florida's deeper past, visit **Myakka River State Park,** which remains virtually the same as it did before the state was settled. ~ 13207 State Road, east of Sarasota; 813-361-6511. To tour this massive region of pristine lakes, rivers, marshes and forest, **Myakka Wildlife Tours** takes tram safaris and airboat tours into the woods and swamps. ~ 813-365-0100.

Following Route 17 back north out of Arcadia, you will catch glimpses of the aptly named Peace River. This shallow waterway offers an off-the-civilized-path view of backwoods Florida as the American Indians knew it, via canoe. The river trip reveals nature in the raw. Cypress knees and alligator snouts break the surface of the calm waters. Armadillos and deer scurry alongside the banks, while cranes and herons pick minnows from the shallows. Live oaks tower, supporting their own mini-forests of air plants, epiphytes, mistletoe and Spanish moss. **Canoe Outpost–Peace River** will arrange equipment and transportation for any length trip you have in mind, all the way up to Fort Mead. ~ Two miles west of Arcadia via Route 70; 941-494-1215.

Pioneer Park is a modest preservation-recreational area that features board-and-batten structures from the area's frontier days. Located on the Peace River, it is also a popular canoeing and fishing spot. ~ Routes 64 and 17, Zolfo Springs; 813-735-0330.

For an entirely unusual sidetrip to a bizarre kingdom, visit **King Solomon's Castle**, west of Zolfo Springs off Route 665. It's hard to say which entertains more, the three-story castle built of offset-press plates and other articles scavenged from the junk yard, the creekside natural trail, or artist Howard Solomon—the self-proclaimed ruler in this world removed from reality. Once dubbed the "DaVinci of Debris," Solomon has created imaginative stained-glass and second-life works that are truly inspired. He has also built a restaurant called The Boat in the Moat. Closed July through September. Admission. ~ Take Route 75 to Route 64, then take County Road 665 to Solomon's Road, Lily; 813-494-6077.

One of Florida's oldest and most popular destinations for travelers is **Cypress Gardens**, where you can literally lose yourself in vast botanical gardens. Visitors can stroll through the gardens or board canal boats, while Kodak's "Island in the Sky" takes you on a ride to a world towering 16 stories above the botanical gardens. On the grounds you'll also find an old Southern town that harks back to the antebellum era, and **Lake Eloise** where a world-famous waterski revue is staged. The park's **Plantation Gardens** includes "Wings of Wonder," a 5500-square-foot Victorian-style butterfly conservatory where you can mingle with a thousand of these free-flying insects. There are also four seasonal flower festivals. This precursor of modern amusement parks offers at least a day's worth of entertainment. Admission. ~ Route 540, Winter Haven; 941-324-2111.

HIDDEN ▶   An unusual museum found in Winter Haven is the **Water Ski Museum and Hall of Fame**. The memorabilia, photos and literature here trace the development of waterskiing from 1922, when the sport was born at Lake Pepin, Minnesota, to modern times. ~ 799 Overlook Drive, Winter Haven; 941-324-2472.

◆◆

SPOOK OR FLUKE?

The thing we found spookiest about **Spook Hill** was the convoluted route you must take to get there if you follow the signs. To make it simpler, take a left on North Avenue when returning to town from Bok Gardens. At the bottom of the hill, you must turn around to experience the mystery here: "spooks" power your car back up the hill. A legend accompanies the mystery. ~ North Avenue and 5th Street, Lake Wales.

The prestigious **Grenelefe Golf and Tennis Resort** offers an entire   **LODGING**
vacation on its grounds. Hidden among Florida highland hills, its
woodsy 1000 acres cling to the shores of ample Lake Marion. The
resort takes its Robin Hood theme from the lake's name, with
roads dubbed Nottingham Way and Robyn Lane and a café called
Camelot's Patio. Three golf courses, 20 tennis courts, four swimming pools, nature trails, two restaurants, a lounge, a marina
stocked with rental boats and fishing guides keep guests active. The
resort holds 950 modern, roomy suites and villas. ~ 3200 State
Road 546, Grenelefe; 941-422-7511, 800-422-5333, fax 941-421-
5025. ULTRA-DELUXE.

Old World eclecticism reigns at quirky **Chalet Suzanne Country
Inn**. Squeezed in among hills of citrus groves, the inn features 30
rooms personalized with a mix of Scandinavian and Mediterranean styles. Red-brick and wrought-iron architecture is accented
by cobblestone walkways in the courtyard. A pool, specialty shops
and private lake are added attractions. ~ 3800 Chalet Suzanne
Drive, Lake Wales; 941-676-6011. DELUXE TO ULTRA-DELUXE.

Guests can have a Western-style vacation at **River Ranch**. Dude
ranch activities include a bridle path and hayrides, and the facility
features tennis, horseshoes, badminton, golf and a fitness center.
Accommodations range from budget-to-moderate-priced RV sites
and efficiencies to deluxe-to-ultra-deluxe-priced suites and luxury
cottages. Outdoor barbecues, wild west saloons and rodeo shows
complete this new concept in Florida vacationing. ~ Route 60,
Lake Wales; 941-692-1321, 800-785-2102, fax 941-692-1303.
BUDGET TO ULTRA-DELUXE.

For something less ostentatious, try the **Big Oak Motel**. This
15-unit row motel puts its back to Lake Starr; the end room has a
view of the lake. The rooms and efficiencies have friendly little
touches here and there. All have kitchenettes. ~ 3618 Alternate
Route 27 North, Lake Wales; 941-676-7427. BUDGET.

You don't even have to sleep to feel rested at **Lake Brentwood
Motel**. A calm and clear lake laps at the 14-unit property's back
door, and rowboats sit in waiting for guests to use free of charge.
Generous trees shade lawn chairs that induce an immediate drop
in blood pressure. ~ 2060 Route 27 North, Avon Park; 941-453-
4358. BUDGET.

Back again by popular demand, the **Kenilworth Lodge** is a restored Sebring landmark. This time around it's been reincarnated
as an imposing bed and breakfast of 137 rooms. Its distinctive dou-
ble-towered face overlooks Lake Jackson across the street. The
enormous lobby shows its age with a grand blackened-brick fireplace, a majestic staircase and a potbelly stove. Modern touches include rattan and floral furnishings and dhurrie rugs. Room decor
also blends old and new. A swimming pool, a restaurant (serving
an unexpected combination of Greek, American and Italian cui-

sine) and an old-time sitting porch complete the amenities of this historic inn. ~ 836 Southeast Lakeview Drive, Sebring; 941-385-0111, 800-423-5939, fax 941-385-4686. BUDGET TO MODERATE.

The **Santa Rosa Inn** is a restored three-story brick building with palpable character on one of the town's main roads. The front yard is lined with oaks laced with Spanish moss and the inn's lobby is decorated with a Christmas tree that sits vigil year round. The 25 rooms have high ceilings, post-colonial Americana furniture and a definite proclivity for chintz. ~ 509 Ridgewood Drive, Sebring; 941-385-0641. MODERATE.

Lake Roy Motor Lodge is not only down the street from its hometown attraction, Cypress Gardens, it also has a white sand beach to brag about. The rooms are carpeted and paneled in dark, less-than-modern shades and textures. But you can't beat the view of the lake. Most of the 34 units are apartments with full kitchens. Watercraft of every variety can be rented on the premises to take full advantage of the chain of lakes the lodge borders. ~ 1823 Cypress Gardens, Winter Haven; 941-324-6320. MODERATE.

DINING

Chalet Suzanne Restaurant is legendary for its fine cuisine, served in a Swiss-style chalet. Its signature romaine soup is canned on the premises as are other soups bearing the Chalet Suzanne label. The tables, set with fine European china, offer either a stunning overlook of the lake or seclusion behind stained-glass windows. Chicken Suzanne, curried shrimp, shad roe and lobster Newburg are among the proffered entrées. ~ 3800 Chalet Suzanne Drive, Lake Wales; 813-676-6011. ULTRA-DELUXE.

One of the loveliest places to eat in all of Florida is on the patio of the **Garden Café** at Bok Tower Gardens. Here, with a view of the chiming pink monument and its surrounding green-and-floral

---

✔ **CHECK THESE OUT—UNIQUE DINING**

- *Budget:* Dine to the chimes of Lake Wales' Bok Tower on the patio of the **Garden Café**; this pastoral setting can't be beat. *page 290*
- *Moderate:* Try the roasted duck with black bing–cherry sauce at **Karlings Inn** in DeLeon Springs, and finish up with Hungarian apple strudel topped with cinnamon ice cream. *page 272*
- *Moderate to deluxe:* Toss tips to belly dancers while dining on North African cuisine at EPCOT's **Restaurant Marrakesh**. *page 250*
- *Deluxe to ultra-deluxe:* Keep up with the Joneses in Winter Park by dining at **Park Plaza Gardens**, where the cuisine is gourmet and the setting elegant. *page 260*

Budget: under $8 Moderate: $8–$16 Deluxe: $16–$24 Ultra-deluxe: over $24

al fresco decor, you feel cut off from modern tempos. The fare is nothing more than counter-service sandwiches, salads, soup and hot dogs, but the pastoral ambience and serenades from Bok Tower can't be beat by the swankiest restaurant. ~ 1151 Tower Boulevard, Lake Wales; 941-676-1355. BUDGET.

A spot of great local repute, the **Olympic Restaurant** seems to serve the entire town at lunchtime. The dining area is a couple of sprawling rooms with some Greek pictures on the wall. The food is plain good eating: country-fried chicken, fried seafood platter, barbecue spare ribs, Alaskan king crab and sandwiches. ~ 504 Route 27 North, Avon Park; 941-452-2700. BUDGET TO MODERATE.

To eat where the locals do in Arcadia, get over to **Wheeler's Goody Café**. This side-street spot features typical diner decor—a formica counter with wooden stools, and china plates on the walls. The menu is covered with denim and offers cracker dishes such as country-fried steak, catfish dinners, baked sausage and rice, hot roast beef sandwiches and ten different varieties of homemade pies. ~ 13 South Monroe Avenue, Arcadia; 941-494-3909. BUDGET.

Tasty seafood and prime steaks have given **Christy's Sundown** its top billing with locals and critics. Antiques and works of art combine to create a Mediterranean mood. The fare runs from lobster, stone crab, and shish kebab to Kansas City steaks. ~ Route 17 South, Winter Haven; 941-293-0069. MODERATE.

SHOPPING

In Chalet Suzanne Restaurant's **Gift Shop**, you can buy gift packages of assorted Chalet Suzanne soups, homemade bottled sauces and sets of the restaurant's special dishware. Also within the village at Chalet Suzanne, the **Antique Chapel** sells elegant antique glass and china. ~ Chalet Suzanne Road, Lake Wales; 941-676-6011.

The **Bok Tower Gardens Gift Shop** offers a unique selection of giftware relating to the singing tower and its gardens: recorded carillon and classical music, bells and chimes, nature books and floral crafts. ~ 1151 Tower Boulevard; Lake Wales; 941-678-1159.

Among the barrage of citrus and souvenir shops in central Florida, the **Fruitree** is king of the heap. In one stop you can buy all the bagged oranges, bottled jellies, cypress clocks and "I was here" gifts you could possibly need. ~ Highway 27 South at Route 542, Dundee; 941-439-1396.

In Arcadia, buy your cowboy boots at the **American Shoe Shop**. ~ 112 West Oak Street, Arcadia; 941-494-3911. One of Arcadia's many antique dealers is **Townsend Antiques**. ~ 5 East Oak Street, Arcadia; 941-494-2137.

NIGHTLIFE

Lake Wales Little Theater stages community theater performances. ~ 411 3rd Street North, Lake Wales; 941-676-1266.

Afternoon cultural events are regularly hosted at **Bok Tower Gardens**, including recitals and special gala events that celebrate the blossoming of certain flowers. ~ Route 17A, Lake Wales; 941-676-1408.

PARKS

LAKE KISSIMMEE STATE PARK 🚶 🚲 ⚓ 🛶 🚤 🛥 ⛴ A 5000-acre lakeland that features a reconstructed cow camp of the 1870s. Two other lakes named Tiger and Rosalie keep the great Kissimmee company in this out-of-the-way wildlife haven. A trail along the park's scrubland features scenes and exhibitions of life in the year 1876, when cowboys herded scrub cows here. History comes alive here as cattle herders re-enact their 19th-century ways. The park also features hiking trails and an observation deck overlooking Lake Kissimmee, and it's a good place to spot the area's rich wildlife. Bald eagles are relatively common here, keeping company with squirrels, quail, ospreys, sandhill cranes, alligators and white-tailed deer. Bream and bass are often caught by anglers, and there's a fishing pier that accommodates the disabled. Facilities include picnic areas, restrooms and showers; restaurants and grocery stores are several miles away in Lake Wales. Day-use fee, $3.25. ~ Located at 14248 Camp Mack Road, 15 miles east of Lake Wales; 941-696-1112.

▲ There are 60 campsites, half with RV hookups; $8 to $14 per night.

HIDDEN ►

LAKE ARBUCKLE PARK ⚓ 🛥 A secluded, rustic fishing and camping haven sitting on Lake Arbuckle. The park's seven acres feature cypress- and oak-studded grounds. Common catches here include crappie, bass and bream. The only facilities are a picnic area and restrooms; groceries and restaurants are several miles away. ~ Located eight miles off Lake Reedy Boulevard east of Frostproof; 941-635-2811.

▲ There are 38 sites, 11 with RV hookups; $6.50 to $11 per night.

HIGHLANDS HAMMOCK STATE PARK 🚶 🚲 🐎 Alligators and orchids can be seen from a "trackless train" that tours the cypress swamps and semitropical jungles in this popular park. Hiking trails also travel some of its 4500 acres, and a paved bicycling loop traverses the hammock. The park is named for the high, forested terrain found on Florida's central ridge. White-tailed deer herd here, and otters, Florida scrub jays, red-shouldered hawks and bobcats plus an occasional bald eagle and Florida panther can be found. Besides the abundant wildlife, another big draw for visitors is the State of Florida Civilian Conservation Corps Museum, where a considerable array of memorabilia from FDR's Depression-era experiment is showcased. The park also has 11 miles of equestrian trails and picnic areas, restrooms, playgrounds and bike rentals. Day-use fee, $3.25. ~ Located west of Sebring off Route 27 at the end of Hammock Road (County Road 234); 941-386-6094.

▲ There are 138 campsites, 113 with RV hookups; $8 to $15 per night.

MYAKKA RIVER STATE PARK 🚶🚴🏊🛶🚤🛥️ A large recreational and wildlife refuge area bordering both river and lake. This beautiful, pristine park of 28,875 acres includes mossy laurel oaks along the river, butterfly orchids, saw palmettos and pop ash. Log cabin structures serve as picnic pavilions. Deer, turkey, wood storks, sandhill cranes, owls and sapsuckers populate the forest. A wilderness preserve of 7500 acres restricts the number of visitors who enter this area of pure old Florida panoramas. Popular activities include fishing (for bass, bream and catfish), canoeing, biking and hiking. The park has a picnic area, an interpretive center, pavilions, excursion airboat and tram tours (941-365-0100), canoe and boat rentals, bicycle rentals, nature trails, a snack bar and groceries. Day-use fee, $4. ~ The main entrance is located at 13207 Route 72, about 17 miles east of Sarasota. A north entrance on Route 780 is open only on weekends and holidays; 941-361-6511.

▲ There are 76 sites, half with RV hookups; $11 to $17 per night. There are also five cabins (with electricity and running water); $55 per night.

▼▼▼▼▼▼▼▼▼▼▼▼

Orlando to Okeechobee Area

This final route leaving Orlando takes you to Florida's most secluded areas, south toward the Everglades and the southwest Gulf Coast.

Heading south out of Orlando, Route 441 is part of the Florida Cracker Trail. The names of towns along the way sound cowboy-inspired: Holopaw and Yeehaw Junction. Okeechobee, the town that borrows its name from Lake Okeechobee, is known as the speckled perch (more commonly known as crappie) capital of the world.

The lake itself, the second largest freshwater lake within United States boundaries, covers 750 square miles. With most of the region's waterways flowing into it, Lake Okeechobee in turn serves as a major source of water for southern Florida.

SIGHTS

The city of **Clewiston** perches on the southwest edge of Lake Okeechobee like a fisherman on the high seat of a bass boat—something you see much of in this famous fishing mecca. Surrounding the lake is a skirt of fertile mucklands, which Clewiston puts to use sweetening its economy with sugar cane. The city pays homage to the crop that has lifted it above the poverty of neighboring towns. Besides the Sugarland Highway and a football arena called Cane Field, there are local shops selling stalks of cane and other sweet souvenirs.

West of Clewiston a fork in the road gives you a choice between staying on Route 27 to explore the wildlife and unusual attractions of Fisheating Creek, or heading to the town of **LaBelle**, known for its annual Swamp Cabbage Festival. This mid-winter event honors the state tree, the sabal palm, whose insides are now known at trendy delis as hearts of palm, but which old crackers simply called swamp cabbage. The festival features displays of Seminole Indian arts and food, clogging shows and stewed swamp cabbage. If you opt to head north, near the little town of **Palmdale** you'll find two unusual attractions that represent the endurance of cracker life. The **Cypress Knee Museum** displays nature's best sculptured masterpieces. Given such titles as "Mother and Child," "FDR" and "Flipper," cypress knees are the knobby protuberances that allow the submerged roots of the cypress tree to breathe. In the center of the museum grows the world's largest transplanted cypress. A cypress swamp and an oak and palm hammock lie along a boardwalk. ~ Routes 27 and 29, Palmdale; 941-675-2951.

> The name Lake Okeechobee is of American Indian invention and means "big water," an apt title for the state's largest inland body of water.

Gatorama celebrates one of Florida's oldest natives in the way they did it before the big parks came along. Looking like so many other exploitative roadside attractions, this one is low-key, soft-sell. You see 'gators, of course, and crocodiles, bobcats, ostriches, deer, raccoons and peacocks—all in their natural habitat. That's all. No Ferris wheels. No animation. Admission. ~ Route 27, Palmdale; 941-675-0623.

Also near Palmdale, **Babcock Wilderness Adventures** combines a nature tour with a history lesson of the 90,000-acre Babcock Ranch. Visitors board a swamp buggy, penetrate secluded cypress swamp and hear about the area's ranching efforts. Along the way you'll likely see a herd of bison, cougars, alligators, deer, turkeys and wildlife. Admission. ~ 8000 Route 31, Punta Gorda; 919-489-3911, 800-500-5583.

LODGING The town of Clewiston actually defines itself by the colonial, pillared **Clewiston Inn Hotel**, rebuilt in 1937 after fire destroyed it. Painted sugar white and sporting wildlife murals, the inn on Lake Okeechobee tells the town's history—where once the Everglades encroached, now sugarcane fields flourish. The 53 rooms are simple and comfortable. A restaurant and bar are located within. Complimentary breakfast is included with lodging. ~ 109 Royal Palm Avenue, Clewiston; 941-983-8151, 800-749-4466, fax 941-983-4602. MODERATE.

DINING The **Clewiston Inn Restaurant** in the Clewiston Inn is set back in the hotel's sugarcane heyday of 1926. Shuttered windows, sugar-white linen and ladderback chairs create a colonial ambience. The menu includes 'gator tail, fresh catfish, steaks and chicken. ~ 108 Royal Palm Avenue, Clewiston; 941-983-8151. MODERATE.

You can't miss **Old South Bar-B-Q.** The forest of wooden Burma Shave–style signs promise the type of good food one expects from a barbecue joint. As much a tourist attraction as a food service, the restaurant is a veritable museum of frontier Florida artifacts. You can get your fill of barbecued vittles, catfish, 'gator tails, hushpuppies and hot apple pie. ~ 602 East Sugarland Highway, Clewiston; 941-983-7756. BUDGET TO MODERATE.

Country Touch carries baskets, potpourri, stuffed animals and other pretty gifts. ~ 450 Highway Labelle, Labelle; 941-675-7770.

The **Cypress Knee Museum** includes a gift shop where you can purchase peeled cypress knees (an early Florida art form), a glass table with a cypress base and many other related articles. ~ Routes 27 and 29, Palmdale; 941-675-2951.

SHOPPING

The **Everglades Lounge** in the Clewiston Inn features a wildlife mural and old-fashioned socializing. ~ 108 Royal Palm Avenue, Clewiston; 941-983-8151.

Another good place for a cold brew in Clewiston is **The Pub.** ~ 210 West Sugarland Highway, Clewiston; 941-983-9511.

NIGHTLIFE

PRAIRIE LAKES REFUGE Eight thousand acres of well-protected wet forest and grasslands shelter diverse animal species here. The endangered sandhill crane favors the area's habitat, as do alligators, deer and a variety of migratory birds. Two five-mile loop trails traverse the park. Three lakes border the park: Kissimmee, Jackson and Marian. The preserve's principal purpose is protecting animal life; however, fishing is allowed. Facilities are geared toward the backpacker and are purposely sparse: picnic areas, pit toilets, nature trails. Groceries and restaurants are several miles away in Kenansville. ~ Located on Route 523, 11 miles northwest of Kenansville; 941-732-1225 or 407-436-1818.

PARKS

◄ HIDDEN

▲ Permitted in three primitive campgrounds; free. Permit and two-week advance reservation are required. Bring potable water.

OKEE-TANTEE RECREATION AREA Basically an RV park on Lake Okeechobee, the state's largest inland body of water is known for its large fish population and good fishing. The lake is the big attraction here; the rest of the terrain is virtually arid grasslands. A security fence fails to add much to the ambience. Facilities include a picnic area, restrooms, showers, boat rentals, groceries and a restaurant. ~ Located at 10430 Route 78 West, south of Okeechobee; 941-763-2622.

▲ There are 280 campsites, most with RV hookups; $25 to $29 per night.

PAHOKEE MARINA AND CAMPGROUND 🚣 🏊 🛥 ⛵ A small preserve on a strip of shoreline at Florida's mammoth Lake Okeechobee, this is the geological center of a fertile agricultural area. Camping sites fall along the lake's shoreline, which has been dammed to prevent flooding. The marina is a good fishing spot for the area's boast—speckled perch. The vegetation consists mostly of Australian pines. There are boat tours (561-924-8113), restrooms, showers, washers/dryers and phones; groceries and restaurants are nearby. ~ On Route 441 at Pahokee; 561-924-7832.

▲ There are 86 sites, all with hookups; $10 to $12 per night.

LOXAHATCHEE NATIONAL WILDLIFE REFUGE 🏃 🏊 🛥 🚤 ⛵ The northernmost introduction to Everglades territory and its unique ecosystem, this is alligator and panther homeland comprises 146,000 acres. Visitors will learn about the fragile world that thrives within the life-giving swamp waters of the Everglades. Mangroves, sawgrass, cattails and some cypress grow in this animal refuge. The highly endangered Everglade kite nests here, along with various snakes such as the Everglades racer and yellow rat snake. Fishing is good here, especially for bass. Facilities include restrooms, an interpretive center, walking tours and nature trails; groceries and restaurants several miles from the entrances. ~ There are three entrances. A boat ramp lies off Route 441 near the town of Loxahatchee. The southern end can be reached from Lox Road north of Hillsboro Boulevard near Delray Beach. Park headquarters are located off Lee Road between Boynton and Delray beaches; 561-734-8303.

▼▼▼▼▼▼▼▼▼▼▼▼▼ Outdoor Adventures

SPORT-FISHING

Visitors staying near Disney World can hook up with a fishing excursion through **Fort Wilderness Campground**. ~ 4510 North Fort Wilderness Trail; 407-824-2900. Also in the Orlando area, **Bass Bustin' Guide** guarantees fish. ~ 5935 Swoffield Drive, Orlando; 407-281-0845. **Chuck Matthews** takes bass fishing charters into the Kissimmee-area Chain of Lakes. ~ St. Cloud; 941-892-7184. A long-time fishing guide on Lake Okeechobee, **Eddie Clay** specializes in catching bass. ~ Okeechobee; 941-763-2785.

BOATING

See the "real" Florida as pilot of your own airboat at **Airboat Rentals U-Drives**. ~ 4266 Vine Street, Kissimmee; 407-847-3672. **Sanford Boat Rentals** rents houseboats and pontoons. ~ 4370 Carraway Place, Sanford; 407-321-5906. The **Rusty Anchor** also rents motorboats and runs tours on the lakes. ~ 400 West Fourth Avenue, Mount Dora; 352-383-3933.

Along the St. Johns River, houseboating is a popular pastime that combines sightseeing with lodging. Houseboat arrangements can be made at **Sanford Boat Rentals**. ~ 4370 Carraway Place, Sanford; 407-321-5906. You can also rent houseboats at **Hontoon Landing Marina**. ~ 2317 River Ridge Road, DeLand; 352-734-2474.

HOUSE-BOATING

Orange Lake Watersports takes you waterskiing and rents jet skis in Florida's land of lakes. ~ 8505 West Route 192, Kissimmee; 407-239-4444. You can be schooled in windsurfing, parasailing, waterskiing and jet skiing at **Splash-N-Ski**. ~ 10000 Turkey Lake Road, Orlando; 407-352-1494.

WATER SPORTS

Central Florida waterways provide prime canoeing.

CANOEING

WALT DISNEY WORLD AREA   In the Disney area, canoes can be rented at **Fort Wilderness Campground**. ~ North Fort Wilderness Trail, Walt Disney World, Lake Buena Vista; 407-824-2900.

ORLANDO–GAINESVILLE LOOP   Northwest of Orlando, there's **King's Landing**. ~ 5714 Baptist Camp Road, Apopka; 407-886-0859. Near Sanford, **Katie's Wekiva River Landing** provides livery and equipment service for canoeing trips. ~ 190 Katie's Cove, Sanford; 407-322-4470. **Santa Fe Canoe Outpost** outfits canoers for trips on the Santa Fe River. ~ Route 441, High Springs; 904-454-2050.

More than 45 miles of canoe runs have been established in Ocala National Forest (Route 40, Ocala). Canoes can be rented at **Alexander Springs Recreation Area**. ~ 352-669-3522. You can also try **Juniper Springs Recreation Area**. ~ 352-625-2808. **Salt Springs Recreation Area** is another rental option. ~ 904-685-2048. **Oklawaha Outpost** rents canoes, kayaks and equipment, and provides livery service for trips on the Oklawaha River in Ocala National Forest. ~ Off Route 316, four miles from Fort McCoy in Eureka; 352-236-4606.

ORLANDO–WITHLACOOCHEE LOOP   The **Withlacoochee River RV Park** rents canoes for paddling trips in the area. ~ State Road 575, Withlacoochee; 352-583-4778. The **Nobleton Canoe Outpost** arranges trips on the Withlacoochee River ranging from two hours to one week in length. ~ Route 476, Nobleton; 352-796-4343.

ORLANDO–ARCADIA LOOP   Canoe **Outpost–Peace River** is an excellent canoe outfitter. You can choose from a number of trips on the shallow Peace River, ranging from day trips to overnighters requiring up to 30 hours of paddling. ~ 2816 Northwest County Road 661, Arcadia; 813-494-1215.

You can rent canoes at **Myakka River State Park**, famous for the great canoeing possibilities along the river and in its lakes. ~ 13207 State Road 72, east of Sarasota; 813-361-6511.

GOLF

Walt Disney World boasts five championship golf courses. ~ Lake Buena Vista; 407-824-2270. Nearby **Poinciana Golf & Racquet Club** allows public play. ~ 500 Cypress Parkway, Kissimmee; 407-933-5300. In Sanford, you can golf at the **Mayfair Country Club**. ~ Country Club Road, near Highway 46A; 407-322-2531. **Golden Ocala Golf Course** is famous for its replication of eight internationally known holes, including the St. Andrew's 1, the first hole ever played. ~ 7300 Highway 27, Ocala; 352-622-0198. In Lakeland, **Skyview Golf Course** has 18 holes. ~ 1100 Skyview Boulevard; 352-665-4005. **Sebring Shore Golf and Country Club** is open to the public. ~ 603 Lake Sebring Drive, Sebring; 941-385-7113. **Haine City's Sun Air Golf and Country Club** welcomes area golfers. ~ 50 Sun Air Boulevard East; 813-439-1576. In the Lake Okeechobee area, tee off at **Clewiston Golf Course**. ~ 1200 San Luiz, Clewiston; 813-983-1448.

TENNIS

In the Orlando area, try the **Orange Lake Country Club Resort**. ~ 8505 Route 192, Kissimmee; 407-239-0000. The courts at **Oak Street Park** feature tennis, racquetball and lighted facilities. ~ Oak Street, Kissimmee. **Mount Dora** has public courts. ~ 6th and Donnelly streets; 11th and Unser streets. Public tennis courts lie within **Dade Battlefield State Historic Site**. ~ Off County Road 476, Bushnell; 352-793-4781. In Lakeland, eight courts are open to the public at **Scott Kelly Recreation Complex**. ~ 404 Imperial Boulevard; 941-499-8235.

RIDING STABLES

Horseback riding provides a unique and popular mode for experiencing inland forests. Many state parks in this area have blazed bridle paths, but you must bring your own mount. Following are some places you can rent horses.

Poinciana Horse World rents horses. ~ 3705 Poinciana Boulevard, Kissimmee; 407-847-4343. In Ocala's fertile horse farming country, you can jump into the saddle at **Oakview Stable**. ~ Southwest 27th Avenue, Ocala; 352-237-8844. **Myakka Valley Campground and Stables, Inc.** rents horses to ride on its trails and provides tent sites and showers for equestrian campers. ~ 7220 Myakka Valley Trail, east of Sarasota; 813-924-8435.

BIKING

The best biking in the Orlando area is at **Walt Disney World**. There are no bicycle paths, but the roads are safe for scenic rides along lakes and forests outside the hustle and bustle of Magic Kingdom and EPCOT.

Bike paths weave around many of Orlando's lakes, such as at **Turkey Lake Park**. ~ 3401 Hiawassee Road; 407-299-5594. Bike paths also circle many of the lakes and parks in the Kissimmee area, and in Winter Park, Sanford and Lake Wales.

The university area of Gainesville provides special lanes and paths for cyclists. **Highlands Hammock State Park** has bicycle trails as well as rentals. ~ Hammock Road, Sebring; 813-386-6094. **Myakka River State Park** allows biking on its many backwoods roads. ~ 13207 Route 72, east of Sarasota; 941-361-6511.

Bike Rentals   The **Fort Wilderness Bike Barn** at the Disney campground rents bikes. ~ Walt Disney World, Lake Buena Vista; 407-824-2742. **Bikes and More** services bike renters in the Gainesville area. ~ 2133 Northwest 6th Street; 352-373-6574. Bicycles can be rented at **Highlands Hammock State Park**. ~ Hammock Road, Sebring; 941-386-6094. Rental bikes are also available at **Myakka River State Park**. ~ 13207 Route 72, Sarasota; 941-361-6511.

HIKING

Florida hiking approaches its finest here in the land of lakes, springs and forests. Over 200 miles of the statewide **Florida National Scenic Trail** zigzag through this primeval belt, augmented by a smorgasbord of short jaunts in the area's many state, county and city parks. All distances for hiking are one way unless otherwise noted.

WALT DISNEY WORLD AREA   **Turkey Lake Park** (7 miles) provides a moderate hike inside Orlando. The system of nature trails here borders Turkey Lake with its live oak hammocks and cattail marshes.

ORLANDO–GAINESVILLE LOOP   **Blue Spring State Park Trail** (8 miles) winds gently through hardwood hammocks, swamp marsh, sand pine scrub and flatwoods, ending at the park's primitive campground. The easy trail views mostly vegetation, although an occasional squirrel or raccoon can be seen.

Gold Head Branch State Park (3 miles) comprises a section of the Florida National Scenic Trail. The habitat is sand pine scrub, except for the park's outstanding ravine, which allows 1.4 miles of

✦✦

✔ CHECK THESE OUT—UNIQUE OUTDOOR ADVENTURES

- Forget those overpriced waterfront hotels—stay *on* the water when you cruise the St. John's River aboard your own houseboat. *page 297*
- Hike across a natural bridge over a submerged river and follow the route of the first telegraph wires in O'Leno State Park. *page 300*
- Cycle through some unusual manmade scenery as you take to the wide, safe roads of Walt Disney World on a bike. *page 298*
- Find inner serenity as you paddle a canoe on the shallow waters of the Peace River. *page 297*

cool respite. The trail also skirts around the swimming area on Lake Johnson.

The **Natural Bridge Hiking Trail** (13 miles) winds through O'Leno State Park north of High Springs. It crosses the natural land bridge known as River Sink, where the Sante Fe river flows subterraneously, and the River Rise, where it reappears. The whole gamut of northern Florida wildlife lies along this path.

A portion of the Natural Bridge Hiking Trail takes historic paths, such as the one along Wire Road where the first telegraph lines were strung.

The **Ocala Trail** (67 miles), a portion of the 1300-mile-long Florida National Scenic Trail, travels the length of the Ocala National Forest. It is the largest continuous trail on public property in the state. White-tailed deer are the stars of the animal show here, appearing in abundance. The forest is also home to the endangered red-cockaded woodpecker.

Hikers are also allowed to use the **Ocala One-Hundred Mile Horse Trail**, which is divided into three sections: the 40-mile Prairie Trail, the 40-mile Flatwoods Trail and the 20-mile Baptist Lake Trail. These are all loop trails for which the trailheads are located off Route 19, about two miles north of Altoona.

The **Timucuan Indian Trail** (1.8 miles), in Ocala Forest's Alexander Springs Recreation Area, takes you on a self-guided tour of the lives of Florida's ancient American Indian tribes. The trail skirts the springs pool, then loops back through marsh and hardwood vegetation.

The **Wekiwa Springs** (13.5 miles) section of the Florida National Scenic Trail traverses the state park located along the springs. Hikers can enjoy the wet world of limestone cavern springs; they can also spot black bear, cranes, herons and owls as well as the threatened gopher tortoise and indigo snake.

ORLANDO–WITHLACOOCHEE LOOP   The **Croom Hiking Trail** (31 miles) in the Withlacoochee State Forest traverses abandoned rock mines, prairies and ravines. The easy terrain follows the Withlacoochee River and then loops off into different paths.

At **Richloam Tract** (31 miles) a looping trail takes you through a low-lying, more densely timbered section of the Withlacoochee. The moderate-to-difficult trail runs along the Withlacoochee River and its little brother and crosses various streams and creeks. Hikers will see a great deal of wildlife on this trail.

McKethan Lake Nature Trail (2 miles) is a less ambitious Withlacoochee hike that circles a small fishing lake. It lies within the Forest Headquarters Tract of the state forest, located between Brooksville and Inverness. Don't be fooled by its shortness. Hikers still get an eyeful of various lovely terrains: bottomlands, hardwood hammocks and pinelands brightened by wildflowers and magnolias.

ORLANDO–ARCADIA LOOP Lake Kissimmee State Park's (12.5 miles) contribution to the Florida National Scenic Trail consists of double loops. The first travels through the pine and scrubby flat-woods of Buster Island. Along the north loop, hikers can view the remains of an old cemetery and turpentine-producing operation.

The **Caloosa Nature Trail** at Babson Park Audubon Center, north of Babson Park, is a self-guided hike that points out differ-ent species of indigenous plant life, such as the papaw, golden rod and muscadine grape. Abundant animal life includes fox, rabbits, gopher tortoises and various birds. ~ 200 Crooked Lake Road, off Route 27A; 941-638-1355.

In **Myakka State Park** (38 miles), the Florida Trail Association has created a network of scenic footpaths divided into four loops. The landscape ranges from high and dry to low and marshy, the trail difficulty from easy to moderate. Many native species find refuge here, including alligators, otters, bald eagles and sandhill cranes.

▼▼▼▼▼▼▼▼▼▼

Transportation

Orlando is the Rome of central Florida. Since the major-ity of Florida vacations begin here, all roads seem to lead to Orlando, and away from it to coastal lands or heart-land lake resorts and parks.

CAR

Route 4, which runs from Daytona Beach to Tampa, is the major artery through Orlando. Forming an X with Route 4, the **Florida Turnpike** traverses mid-Florida from Miami in the south-east to Route 75 northwest of Orlando. **Route 75** and parallel **Route 441** skewer Ocala and Gainesville.

Bisecting all of central Florida and running west of Orlando is **Route 27**, which threads its way south of Gainesville, through Ocala, Lake Wales and Sebring, to Lake Okeechobee and the Ever-glades. **Route 17** shoots off 27 at Haines City to reach the quiet towns of Bartow, Wauchula and Arcadia.

AIR

The **Orlando International Airport** receives direct flights from over 50 cities in the United States. Major domestic airlines serving the area include American Airlines, Continental Airlines, Delta Air Lines, Northwest Airlines, Trans World Airlines, United Airlines and USAir. International service is provided by Air Canada, British Airways, Icelandair and KLM Royal Dutch Airlines.

Inexpensive ground transportation to the Disney World area is provided by **Mears Motor Shuttle.** ~ 407-423-5566. Ground trans-portation in the Orlando area is provided by **Airport Limousine Service of Orlando.** ~ 407-422-4561. Also serving Orlando is **Kis-simmee Checker Cab.** ~ 407-847-4867. **Airport Passenger Express** provides scheduled service between the Orlando airport and Ocala daily. ~ 352-622-2292.

The **Gainesville Airport** is serviced by Delta Air Lines and USAir Express.

Lake Limo provides ground transportation to and from the airport. ~ 352-378-8975. So does the **Gainesville Cab Company.** ~ 352-371-1515.

BUS

Greyhound Bus Lines (800-231-2222) has a number of stations in central Florida. They are located in Orlando at 555 North Magruder Street; in Ocala at 512 North Magnolia Avenue, 352-732-2677; and in DeLand at 224 East Ohio Avenue, 904-734-2747.

TRAIN

Amtrak (800-872-7245) makes stops up and down central Florida. Amtrak trains stop in Orlando at 1400 Sligh Boulevard; in Kissimmee at 111 Dakin Street; in DeLand at 2491 Old New York Avenue; and in Palatka at 220 North 11th Street at Reid Street.

If you are traveling to the Orlando area from the New York City area, consider Amtrak's **Auto-train.** You can board your car at Lorton, Virginia, four hours from New York, and drive it off less than 25 miles east of Orlando at Sanford. ~ 600 Persimmon Avenue.

CAR RENTALS

Car rental companies located at the Orlando airport include **Avis Rent A Car** (800-331-1212), **Budget Rent A Car** (800-327-0700), **Dollar Rent A Car** (800-800-4000), **Hertz Rent A Car** (800-654-3131) and **National Interrent** (800-227-7368). Need free airport pickup service? Call **Enterprise Rent A Car** (800-325-8007).

A & A Rent A Car supplies used rental cars. ~ Kissimmee; 407-847-5599.

At the Gainesville Airport you can rent from **Avis Rent A Car** (800-331-1212), **Hertz Rent A Car** (800-654-3131) or **National Interrent** (800-227-7368); **Enterprise Rent A Car** (800-325-8007) offers free pickup service.

PUBLIC TRANSIT

Limited city bus service covers the main drags in Kissimmee and Orlando. For schedules in Orange, Osceola and Seminole counties, call the LYNX **Transit Authority** information office. ~ 407-841-8240.

Regional Transit System runs throughout Gainesville. ~ 352-334-2600.

AERIAL TOURS

If you're flying to Fort Lauderdale or Key West, you can flash back to the 1940s on **Vintage Air Tours.** The charter air tour, owned by British entrepreneur Richard Branson, offers flights aboard restored DC-3s with huge picture windows (great for viewing the coral reefs and Everglades) and flight attendants who dress and act like it's the '40s. ~ 407-932-1400.

SIX

The Everglades and the Keys

 At the tip of Florida lie two of the state's greatest treasures, the Everglades and the Florida Keys. Technically, the former is a great, broad and shallow life-giving river flowing from Lake Okeechobee through thousands of acres of marshland. The latter are a chain of lush subtropical islands floating like an emerald necklace that marks the meeting of the Atlantic Ocean and the Gulf of Mexico.

To last century's dreamers and speculators, the Everglades loomed as a useless, mosquito-ridden swamp that might one day be drained and tamed and put to good use. The Keys harbored tales of pirate treasure and fortunes gleaned from ships tossed to bits on the shallow coral reefs that lay to the east in the Atlantic Ocean. At least one man envisioned these islands as a playground for wealthy sportsmen and a natural gateway to Cuba and Central America.

An understanding and appreciation of the Everglades has come only in recent decades, far too long after the waters that spilled out of Lake Okeechobee and gently fed this region were diked and rechanneled. Developers and farmers were both unaware and unconcerned about the devastating effects of so drastically changing the natural world of South Florida.

Then, in 1947, Marjorie Stoneman Douglas wrote a book that acclaimed the unique value of this subtropical wilderness, once inhabited by American Indians and now home to myriad creatures and plants found nowhere else in the United States. She also struck at the conscience of those who had ignored the irreparable damage being done to this important natural region whose existence contributes to the ecological life of the whole peninsula. "There are no other Everglades in the world," she began in *The Everglades: River of Grass*. Her words held both truth and warning.

The year that remarkable book was published, President Truman dedicated 2000 square miles of the southernmost Everglades as a national park. UNESCO declared the region a World Heritage Site in recognition of its value as a critical natural wonder of the world. In this preserved area visitors can begin to experience what Douglas described almost half a century ago. Here they can admire the hidden beauty and learn of the fragility of the *pa-hay-okee* or "grassy water," as the American Indians called this vast, beautiful region.

Each entrance to the park shows a different side of the Everglades' rich character. In the northeastern region, Shark Valley offers a tour into sawgrass prairie, rich in birdlife and alligators. The northwest gateway is at Everglades City, jumping-off place to the Ten Thousand Islands, a Gulf Coast mangrove archipelago popular with fisherfolk and vacationers. The main entrance, southwest of Homestead, leads visitors along a 38-mile park road that meanders through sawgrass prairie, hardwood hammock, cypress swamps and lake regions, ending at Flamingo on the edge of Florida Bay.

Winter is the time to visit the Everglades, the only season when mosquitoes won't eat you alive. In winter you can leave your car, walk the trails, canoe the streams and contemplate the subtle beauty of the place. There are no breathtaking panoramas in this region, where the altitude seldom rises above three feet, but rich rewards await those who take the time to explore. Slumbering alligators lie like half-sunken logs in shallow ponds. Comical anhingas gather on low branches, hanging their wings out to dry after fishing forays. Bird populations are spectacular and diverse, including such easily recognized favorites as roseate spoonbills, osprey, brown pelicans and bald eagles. Endangered and rare animals such as the shy manatee, the Florida panther and the American crocodile, though seldom seen, reside deep within the watery world of the Everglades.

Though the signs explain where to go and how to get there, the Everglades is a region of hidden treasures waiting to be discovered by those who quietly search, wait and watch. And everywhere within the park rings the message that the Everglades is still a fragile region whose water supply is controlled from the outside by those who turn the valves and try to balance the needs of humans with those of this crucial, life-giving place.

In 1912, developer Henry Flagler completed his greatest project—a railroad from Florida City to Key West. He was spurred by dreams of carrying sportsmen to luxurious fishing camps and freight to ships sailing from Key West to Cuba and Central America. The remarkable rail line crossed three dozen islands and spanned bridges from less than 50 feet in length to one seven miles long. The state's worst recorded hurricane destroyed the railroad in 1935, but the sturdy bridges and trestles became the links for what would become the Overseas Highway, which still follows or parallels the original rail route.

Some of the Keys are so narrow that you can watch the sunrise over the Atlantic and see it set into the Gulf of Mexico only by strolling across the road. To the east lie the continental United States' only living coral reefs, popular with divers, snorkelers and passengers in glass-bottom boats. Because of these protective reefs, there is little surf and hence few sandy beaches in the Keys, a fact which surprises to most visitors.

Time, folks claim, means very little in the Keys. Visitors quickly discover that slowing down is both easy and essential, especially when the weather is too good to pass up (which it is most of the time). Winters are wonderfully mild, with average temperature highs around 77° and lows around 60°. Summer highs average about 89°, but sea breezes help keep life pleasant.

The Keys are basically vacation and retirement havens these days, now that wrecked sailing ships no longer yield up their booty on the rocky reefs, the sponge beds are gone and the commercial fishing industry has greatly dwindled. Romantics call these spots "America's Caribbean islands" or "the islands you can drive to." Accommodations run from crowded RV and trailer parks to motels with a boat dock for each room to luxurious resorts. Dining runs the gamut from shrimp-boils on a pier to gourmet feasting in sedate surroundings. The basic fare, of course, is seafood.

Fishing, boating and diving are the main sports of the Keys. Marinas lie on both sides of many of the islands; game fishing can be accomplished from rickety bridges as well as from classy yachts. Each population center claims to be "the best" of something, whether it be fishing, diving, relaxing, eating or partying.

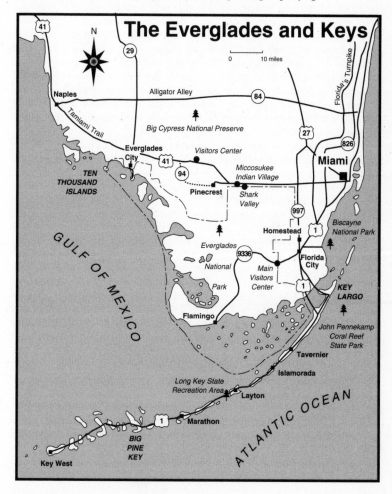

The Everglades and Keys

Note: Addresses and directions throughout the Florida Keys are usually given in "Mile Markers" (MM). Each mile along Route 1 is marked on a small green sign with white numbers, beginning with MM 126, one mile south of Florida City, and ending with MM 0 in Key West.

Largest of all the islands, Key Largo is the gateway to the Keys and the beginning of the 113-mile journey to Key West. As Route 1 meanders out to sea, it passes through populated areas that could be anywhere in the country, with chain motels, restaurants, little shopping centers and ever-increasing development. But that's where the similarity ends, for this is a water-borne highway heading into magnificent sunsets, bordered by sea or mangroves or marinas and even bits of surviving jungle-like hammocks. Alongside it runs the vital viaduct, a huge pipe carrying water from the mainland to sustain the residents and visitors to these dependent islands that, though surrounded by the sea, offer nothing but rainwater for drinking.

As the closest key to John Pennekamp Coral Reef State Park, Key Largo is the area's premier diving site. Less than 20 miles farther along, Islamorada, on Upper Matecumbe Key, is the centerpiece of a group known as the "purple isles," thanks to an explorer who probably named them for the violet sea snails that thrived there. The region is famous for sportfishing and was once the prosperous headquarters for wreckers and salvagers. The next good-sized center of population is the town of Marathon on Vaca Key. The whole area is a popular winter resort and choice fishing spot.

Crossing the famous Seven Mile Bridge, Route 1 enters the Lower Keys, whose population center is Big Pine Key. The flora and fauna are different here from much of the rest of the Keys, and one of the few fine beaches is found in the Lower Keys. Big Pine is also home to the endangered tiny Key deer. From here on, the population thins out considerably until one approaches Key West, the nation's southernmost city and nearly the outermost region of the state. Only the Dry Tortugas, 68 miles out to sea, lie beyond.

Key West offers visitors just about everything the rest of the Keys do, and much, much more. The main tourist center, Old Town, swings with nightlife, sightseeing trips, diving, fishing, arts events, festivals and a nightly sunset celebration. Following in the footsteps of former residents Ernest Hemingway and Tennessee Williams, artists and writers have gathered in Key West for decades. It's also the site of a large gay community. There is history here, too, evidenced especially in the grand collection of historic old Victorian and Bahamian-style houses and the tales of famous folk who have lived and visited here. Key West has become one of the nation's chief traveler destinations. Some claim it is the only city in the United States that has never had a frost.

One might suspect that the Keys, being such a narrow chain of islands, could not provide any "hidden" sites to explore. But the hidden spots are there for the finding—little pockets of natural wilderness, small restaurants away from the highway, quiet lodgings on out-of-the-way islands, bits of history and treasure out to sea. Since winter is the chief tourist season in the Keys, rates are considerably lower in the summer.

Last century's dreamers and speculators might be surprised at what Florida has made of or, some might say, done to its southernmost treasures, the Everglades and the Florida Keys. For travelers, the area is rich indeed.

The Everglades region is so vast it would take many weeks to experience its many subtle, hidden offerings. At first glance, much of it appears to be an endless prairie, dotted here and there with bits of forest. But first glances are misleading. The "prairie" is actually a slowly flowing river, its "forests" often island hammocks or little stands of dwarf cypress. Travelers who take time to search out the Everglades' treasures will be rewarded with views of exotic wildlife and plant life, from the abundant alligator to jewel-like snails, from gumbo-limbo trees to delicately blooming marsh grasses.

Everglades Area

The auto traveler has several options; for a broad introduction to the Everglades, consider trying both the routes suggested here. We have included wilderness regions as well as coastal sights.

WESTWARD FROM MIAMI   Heading westward from Miami, Route 41, known as the Tamiami Trail, provides an almost straight shot from the Atlantic to the Gulf Coast. It plunges through the heart of the Everglades, skirting the northern edge of **Everglades National Park** and cutting through the southern portion of the **Big Cypress National Preserve**. Though not wildly scenic, it is an intriguing road, traveling through miles and miles of what the American Indians called *pa-hay-okee*, or "grassy water." Sometimes the narrow highway is paralleled by canals, their banks busy with people fishing with cane poles. But mostly the landscape is sawgrass prairie, with the great, wide—almost hidden—life-giving river running imperceptibly through it. Drivers are instructed to travel this road with lights on at all times, a safeguard against possible tedium and the strange effect the region seems to have on one's depth perception when contemplating passing.

SIGHTS

Although the Miccosukee Indians trace their ancestry back to centuries before the United States became a nation, they were not recognized as a tribe by the federal government until 1962. About 500 of them now live on a reservation along Route 1. They are descendants of a group which successfully hid in the Everglades during the period when Florida's American Indians were being captured and forcibly sent west. You can visit the designed-for-tourists **Miccosukee Indian Village** for a guided or self-guided tour that includes a museum, cooking and living chickees (palm-thatched native houses), a nature walk, craft areas and an arena where you can watch alligator shows. Admission. ~ Route 41, about 25 miles west of Florida's Turnpike; 305-223-8388. Also in the Indian village, the **Miccosukee Airboat Rides** offer noisy, environmentally questionable trips over the sawgrass deeper into the Everglades. It includes a stop at an old hammock-style American Indian camp.

The 15-mile, two-hour tram tours offered in the **Shark Valley** section of the Everglades National Park acquaint visitors with the heart of the sawgrass region. Stops are made along the way to spot birds or alligators, and for lessons on the park's hydrology, geology, vegetation and wildlife. Time is also allowed for climbing the 65-foot observation tower, which provides excellent views of the vast wetlands. Sightseers may also travel the tram road on foot or bicycles, which are rented at the entrance. Admission. ~ Route 41, about 25 miles west of Florida's Turnpike; 305-221-8455.

Believe it or not, the Everglades is really a river running 50 miles wide and a few inches deep. A close look into the tall sawgrass reveals the area's true nature.

Where Route 41 veers northwestward, you can head straight and take a scenic detour on **Route 94**, which meanders deep into cypress and pineland backcountry on its way out toward Pinecrest. This is called the "loop road," but unless you have a four-wheel-drive vehicle, you would do best to turn back when the road begins to deteriorate (about eight miles in), near an interpretive center.

Back on Route 41, slow down as you come up to the microscopic community of **Ochopee**, or you might miss "the smallest and most photographed post office in North America." You'll know it by the American flag, the blue letter box, the sign that reads **Post Office, Ochopee, FL** and all the tour buses disgorging passengers so that they can go into the tiny frame building and get their letters stamped. ~ 941-695-4131.

HIDDEN ►

Soon you will enter **Big Cypress National Preserve**, 716,000 acres of subtropical Florida swampland vital to the preservation of the Everglades. To get an idea of Big Cypress' beauty and importance, stop at the **Oasis Visitors Center** and see the excellent audiovisual introduction to this crucial region. ~ 941-695-4111.

Though not encouraged by the National Park folks because of their noise and impact on the fragile environment, airboats and swamp buggies are popular with tourists. **Wooten's** offers these rides all day long, every day, carrying visitors away from the highway into the deeper regions of the Everglades. You may observe alligators at the animal sanctuary. A number of private individuals also offer rides; you'll see their signs along the road. Admission. ~ Route 41, Ochopee; 941-695-2781.

Not far past Wooten's, take the turnoff leading south on Route 29 that leads to **Everglades City**, the western edge of the Everglades National Park. You can stop at the **Everglades City Chamber of Commerce** to procure information about this little town and the neighboring region. ~ 32016 Tamiami Trail East, Everglades City; 941-695-3941.

At the privately owned **Eden of the Everglades** you can ride a quiet jungle boat or airboat to observe some of the flora and fauna of the area in a natural setting. Admission. ~ Route 29, two miles south of Route 41, Everglades City; 941-695-2800.

Continue south to the **Everglades National Park Visitors Center**. Here you can obtain information about the western regions of the park, including the **Ten Thousand Islands** area, the largest mangrove forest in the world. ~ Gulf Coast Ranger Station, Route 29, south of Everglades City; 941-695-3311.

The **Everglades National Park Boat Tours** cover portions of this territory on the Gulf of Mexico, informing visitors how the mangrove islands are formed and acquainting them with the resident wildlife, especially shore and wading birds like the roseate spoonbill. American bald eagles, gentle manatees and playful dolphins often reward the sharp-eyed explorer. Some of the tours make stops on a small Gulf island for shelling and a guided walk. ~ Ranger Station; 941-695-2591, 800-445-7724.

Nature trips by boat into the Ten Thousand Islands area are offered by **Captain Dan**. ~ Chokoloskee Island; 941-695-4573. **Chokoloskee Island Charters** offers nature trips especially geared to photographers and birdwatchers. ~ Chokoloskee Island; 941-695-2286.

Chokoloskee, a small island filled with motor homes, cottages and little motels, is a popular spot for visitors wishing to fish the Ten Thousand Islands region. It also has the distinction of being built on a gigantic shell mound created by early American Indians. ~ Route 29, across the causeway south of Everglades City.

◄ HIDDEN

After you leave the park's western area, you can travel seven miles east of Route 29 on Route 41 to get to **Fakahatchee Strand State Preserve**, the major drainage slough of the Big Cypress Swamp (see the "Beaches & Parks" section below). You can walk the boardwalk through the tall, dense, swamp forest of royal palm and bald cypress and admire the numerous orchidlike air plants that are said to grow only here. From November through February rangers conduct weekend "wet" walks into the swamp to see other rare plant life. ~ 941-695-4593.

SOUTHWARD FROM MIAMI The Florida City/Homestead communities serve as a gateway to both the Everglades and the Florida Keys. For information on this area, you might begin at the very fine **Tropical Everglades Visitors Association** in Florida City. Here you can obtain information about the main public portion of Everglades National Park as well as a number of other places to see and things to do in the Florida City/Homestead area. ~ 160 Route 1, Florida City; 305-245-9180.

There is a lot to be seen off the Atlantic coast east of Florida City in **Biscayne National Park**, most of it underwater (see the "Beaches & Parks" section below). But even if you are not a snorkeler or scuba diver, you can get an excellent view of the nearby coral reef from the **glass-bottom boat** that departs from park headquarters at Convoy Point. Daily trips to the reef, with occasional island cruises in the winter, are offered by **Biscayne National Underwater Park Tours Inc.** ~ Biscayne National Park Headquarters, end of 328th Street, east of Florida City; 305-230-1100.

Florida City is the hub of the most southern farming area in the continental United States. A drive northward on Krome Avenue or along any side road in the area will take you through vast truck gardens where you may see—and even pick from—great fields of tomatoes, corn, strawberries, okra, peppers and other fruits and vegetables. Large areas are also devoted to avocados, limes, mangos and papayas.

HIDDEN ►

You can get an idea of how the early settlers lived in this fertile, challenging region between the eastern edge of the Everglades and the sea by visiting the **Florida Pioneer Museum**. The downhome collection consists mainly of fine old photographs and items from Florida family attics, and is housed in a caboose—a reconstructed railway station and an agent's house left over from the days of Henry Flagler's "railroad that went to the sea." Open October through April. Admission. ~ 826 North Krome Avenue, Florida City; 305-246-9531.

The **Coral Castle** is a strange place; some claim it's almost mystical. According to legend, this curious limestone mansion was built, between 1923 and 1940, because of an unrequited love. Its creator, a Latvian immigrant, claimed to know the secret of the construction of the pyramids. Perhaps he did, for he was able to move multi-ton pieces of local coral rock to the site and construct towers, massive stone furnishings, a nine-ton gate that swings open to the touch, a 5000-pound valentine heart and myriad other strange symbols of devotion to his mysterious lost love. Supposedly, no one has ever figured out the builder's secret, but you can go and give it a try, and marvel at this historic curiosity. Take the 35-minute self-guided audio tour in English, Spanish, French or German. Admission. ~ 28655 Route 1, Homestead; 305-248-6344.

North of Homestead, the **Preston B. Bird & Mary Heinlein Fruit & Spice Park** is a 30-acre random grove planted with over 500 varieties of fruit, spices and herbs from around the world. Visitors are invited to stop by the giftshop and stroll among the citrus, banana, lychee, mango, starfruit and other tropical trees. ~ 24801 Southwest 187th Avenue, Homestead; 305-247-5727.

EVERGLADES NATIONAL PARK South of Homestead, the cultivation suddenly stops—and Everglades National Park begins, almost like a boundary of uneasy truce between man and nature. You quickly forget that Miami is just up the road a piece or that tended gardens lie behind you. Before you lies the mysterious world of what some call "the real Florida," the home of the alligator, the panther, the royal palm and the flamingo.

There are a number of ways to tackle this area of the park. For help in designing your plan, stop at the **Main Visitors Center**. Here park staff members will provide you with all sorts of helpful information, including weather, trail and insect conditions and listings of the season's varied and informative ranger-guided tours. A fine audiovisual presentation and a wide assortment of books provide good introductions to the area. ~ 40001 State Road 9336, 10 miles southwest of Homestead; 305-242-7700.

Once you have paid your admission and entered the park, you are on the single park road that will eventually arrive at **Flamingo**, 38 miles away, at the tip of the state on the edge of Florida Bay. This winding, lonely road traverses the heart of the park, meandering among tall pines, through seemingly endless expanses of sawgrass prairie and alongside mysterious dark ponds. Off this road lie a number of paths, trails, boardwalks and waterways designed to give the visitor as wide an Everglades experience as possible. Some of the trails require only short strolls of half a mile or less, but they reward with close-up views of a great range of environments and inhabitants. Because so much of the terrain is submerged in water, it is wise to stick to the paths provided unless you go exploring with a park ranger.

About four miles inside the park entrance, watch for signs to the **Royal Palm Visitor Center** on your left. Even if you have already spent a good amount of time at the main center, you should take a stroll down each of the two half-mile trails that begin here. Close together but very different, each plunges into a distinctive Everglades environment. Interpretive signs help you notice things you might otherwise miss, such as how the strangler fig got its name or why alligators are so vital to the survival of the region.

The **Anhinga Trail** travels a boardwalk across Taylor Slough, a marshy pool that attracts winter birds and other wildlife that assemble with apparent unconcern for the season's thousands of visitors with cameras and zoom lenses. This is a perfect spot for viewing alligators and numerous water birds. Here, too, you can gaze across broad vistas of sawgrass prairie.

✔ **CHECK THESE OUT—UNIQUE SIGHTS**

• Stop by the **Miccosukee Indian Village** in Everglades National Park, where you'll see chickees (palm-thatched houses), a crafts area, a museum and an alligator show. *page 307*

• Swim with dolphins and take a "bottomless" boat ride at **Theatre of the Sea**, one of the oldest marine parks in the world. *page 330*

• Join the throngs of sun-worshippers who gather at **Mallory Square** each sunset to bid farewell to Ol' Sol for the night. *page 356*

• Ride an airboat through the beautiful cypress swamps at **Big Cypress National Preserve**, after catching the audio-visual show at the Visitors Center. *page 308*

Nearby, the **Gumbo-Limbo Trail** leads through a jungly tropical hardwood hammock rich in gumbo-limbo, strangler fig, wild coffee, royal palms and other tropical trees as well as numerous orchids and ferns. Air plants and butterflies often add to the beauty of this spot; interpretive signs help visitors get acquainted with tropical flora that will appear again and again throughout the park.

At some point during its existence, enterprising residents of the area that is now the Flamingo Visitors Center produced moonshine whiskey and gathered bird plumes for ladies fashionwear.

About six miles from the main entrance, the half-mile **Pinelands Trail**, near a camping area at Long Pine Key, circles through a section of slash pine forest. Here the ground is dry; occasional fires keep undergrowth in check so the pines can thrive without competition. This is a good place to get a look at the rock and solution holes formed in the shallow bed of limestone that lies under South Florida. Or just to picnic beside a quiet lake. For a view of pinelands closer to the park road, stop at the **Pinelands** sign about a mile farther on.

As you continue down the park road and gaze across the sawgrass prairie, you'll notice stands of stunted trees that, during winter, appear dead or dying, since they are hung with moss from ghostlike grey branches. These are bald cypress, which thrive in watery terrain but remain dwarfed due to the peculiar conditions of the Everglades. In spring they put out lovely green needles. Some, though dwarfed, have been growing here for over a century.

About six miles beyond the Pinelands, you come to the **Pa-hay-okee Overlook**, named for the American Indian word for Everglades, meaning "grassy waters." Walk the short boardwalk and climb the observation tower for a wonderful panorama of the sawgrass prairie dotted with collections of ancient dwarf cypress and small island hammocks of hardwoods. This is one of the best overviews in the park; it's a great place for birdwatching.

Some park rangers refer to hammocks as the "bedrooms of the Everglades," the places where so many wild creatures, large and small, find dry ground and shade from the tropical sun. About seven miles from Pa-hay-okee, you can explore one of these magnificent "highlands" that thrive just above the waterlines. The half-mile **Mahogany Hammock Trail** enters the cool, dark, jungly environment of a typical hardwood hammock, where you'll find rare paurotis palms and large mahogany trees, including one said to be the largest mahogany in the United States. Look and listen closely— barred owls, golden orb spiders, colorful *Liguus* tree snails and many other creatures make their homes in this humid "bedroom."

From Mahogany Hammock the park road heads due south through stands of pine and cypress and across more sawgrass prairie. You are now nearing the coast and will begin to see the first mangrove trees, evidence of the mixing of salt water from Florida

Bay with the freshwater that flows from the north. You will pass several canoe-access spots along the road here, including the one at West Lake, about 11 miles from Mahogany Hammock.

Stop at the **West Lake Trail** for a good close-up look at mangroves. You can walk among the three varieties that thrive here along the half-mile boardwalk trail. With practice you will be able to identify them all—the predominant red mangroves with their arched, spidery prop roofs, black mangroves sending up fingerlike breathing tubes called "pneumatophores" from the mud and white mangroves and buttonwood on the higher, dryer shores of the swampy areas. The West Lake shoreline is one of many important spawning grounds for fish and shellfish that in turn attract raccoons and other wildlife who come to feed. You may see a gourmet diner or two if you walk quietly and keep your eyes open.

As you near the end of the park road, you will pass **Mzarek Pond**, another lovely birdwatching spot, especially rewarding during the winter months. Roseate spoonbills often come to this quiet, glassy pond to feed, along with many other common and exotic waterfowl.

The road ends at the **Flamingo Visitors Center**, where a remote fishing village once stood. Early settlers could reach the area only by boat, and along with fishing, farming and the making of charcoal, all sorts of other activity, legal and not—went on here. The town is gone now, replaced by a marina, concessions, a motel and cabins, and a shop and visitors center. At Flamingo you can select from a variety of sightseeing opportunities, such as ranger-guided walks, wilderness canoe trips, a tram ride, campfire programs and hands-on activities. Offerings vary with the seasons; check at the visitors center for a schedule. ~ 38 miles from the main entrance; 941-695-3101, ext. 182.

Sightseeing by boat is particularly enjoyable. Most boat tours in this region, including some backcountry explorations, are available year-round. Sunset cruises are a delight, offering views of spectacular skies as well as allowing close-ups of a wide variety of birds winging their way to shore. In winter, pelicans ride the gentle waves, and gulls soar up and around the boat. Some boat trips will take you to **Cape Sable**, the farthest-out point of southwestern Florida, where the Gulf of Mexico laps a broad, sandy beach.

◄ HIDDEN

For more birdwatching, especially in winter, take a short stroll from the visitors center to nearby **Eco Pond**. At dusk you may see ibis, egrets and other water birds winging in for the night to nest in nearby trees.

LODGING

If you prefer to stay close to the western park area, try the **Captain's Table Lodge and Villas**. This large resort offers hotel rooms and suites in its main lodge and one-bedroom villas, some featuring screened decks. There is a large pool and a boat ramp. Boat tours of the Ten Thousand Islands are available; good beaches are only five miles away—by boat. ~ Route 29, Everglades City; 941-695-4211, 800-741-6430, fax 941-695-2633. MODERATE.

HIDDEN ▶ The **Rod and Gun Club**, a 1920s-era hunting and fishing club, no longer rents rooms in the lodge itself. You *can* sit on its airy screened porch or admire the mounted game fish and red cypress paneling of the massive old lobby. And you can stay in the rather ordinary cottages on the grounds, swim in the screened-in pool, play tennis and feast on the large waterfront veranda. Complete docking facilities alongside attract some pretty impressive boats. ~ 200 Riverside Drive, Everglades City; 941-695-2101. MODERATE TO DELUXE.

Ivey House Bed and Breakfast is a shotgun-style residence built in 1929 with a large living room and library and twin- to queen-bedded rooms furnished in southern pine. You can also rent a two-bedroom cottage with a bath, a kitchen and a screened porch. Have a continental breakfast on one of the comfortable porches. There are daily guided fishing, seashelling (excellent here) and canoeing/kayaking excursions; half-day or overnight camping trips are offered. Complimentary bicycles are available for touring on your own. ~ 107 Camellia Street, Everglades City; summer, 860-739-0791; winter, 941-695-3299, fax 941-695-4155; e-mail: NACT1@aol.com. MODERATE.

The usual chain motels line Route 1 in Homestead and Florida City. If you are looking for less expensive lodging, head into the downtown areas where you'll find rows of mom-and-pop motels along Krome Avenue. The **Super 8 Motel** is near several restaurants and offers plain but clean and roomy accommodations. A swimming pool, coconut palms and other tropical plants set this one somewhat apart. ~ 1202 North Krome Avenue, Florida City; 305-245-0311, 800-800-8000, fax 305-247-9136. BUDGET.

The **Hampton Inn** offers comfortable accommodations within easy reach of both Biscayne and Everglades national parks. The 123-unit facility is clean and modern, and has the obligatory swimming pool. A rarity for chain hotels, there's no charge for the continental breakfast and local calls. ~ 124 East Palm Drive, Florida City; 305-247-8833, 800-426-7866, fax 305-247-6456. MODERATE.

To really experience the Everglades, stay at least a couple of nights in the **Flamingo Lodge**. This, the only accommodation in the park, is a plain old motel with window air-conditioners and jalousies that can be opened to let in the intriguing watery smells of the 'glades and the shallow bay. Far from city lights and surrounded by jungle sounds, Flamingo Lodge lies in the heart of the Everglades. It offers a beautiful pool circled by tropical plants. Flamingo also offers rustic cottages with fully equipped kitchens and all motel amenities. ~ 1 Flamingo Road, in the Everglades National

Park; 941-695-3101, 800-600-3813, fax 941-695-3921. DELUXE
TO ULTRA-DELUXE.

DINING

◄ HIDDEN

The **Miccosukee Restaurant** is a typical roadside restaurant with
fried-fish fare. But the local American Indians who own and operate this place add their own special dishes to the menu—good
things such as pumpkin bread, chili and fry bread, Miccosukee
burgers and tacos, and hushpuppies and Everglades-caught catfish.
It's the best place to eat while traveling the Tamiami Trail. ~ Route
41, Miccosukee Indian Village; 305-223-8380. MODERATE.

Along with steak, chicken and the usual fried and broiled
seafood, you can try grilled pompano and such delicacies as 'gator
tail, cooter (freshwater soft shell terrapin) and lobster tail at the
Oyster House. Ships' wheels and other nautical paraphernalia create a very pleasant, informal seaside atmosphere. ~ Route 29, Everglades City; 941-695-2073. MODERATE TO DELUXE.

The menu at the **Rod and Gun Club**, like so many area eateries, features frogs' legs, stone crab claws and native fish in season,
but the ambience is unlike any other in far South Florida. You may
dine in the massive, dark, cypress-paneled dining hall of this once-
elegant old hunting and fishing lodge or be seated on the large, airy
veranda where you can have a splendid view of the yachts and
other fine boats that dock a stone's throw away. The selection of
seafood, steak and chicken is small, but well prepared. ~ 200 Riverside Drive, Everglades City; 941-695-2101. MODERATE TO DELUXE.

If you wonder what happens to all those good vegetables that
grow around Homestead, you'll find bunches of them in hefty servings at **Potlikker**. A barbecue pit smokes away on the premises,
preparing succulent ribs that are part of the down-home southern
assortment of items including steak, chicken pot pie and Cajun
breaded catfish. The freshly carved turkey and all-you-can-eat
shrimp are favorites. The place boasts at least 11 vegetables daily,
ranging from mustard greens to okra-and-tomatoes. This friendly,
family-type eatery is located in a frame, country-style building. ~
591 Washington Avenue, Homestead; 305-248-0835. BUDGET TO
MODERATE.

What does Homestead have in common with Paris? The right
answer is **La Soupière**, a French-style café that specializes in traditional soups. The soup du jour ranges from cream of broccoli to
French onion, and a creamy fish chowder is served every Friday.
Don't miss the sandwiches made on fresh baguettes and the rich
desserts. Dinner served Friday and Saturday only. Closed Sunday.
~ 30360 Old Dixie Highway, Homestead; 305-246-1633. BUDGET
TO MODERATE.

The Mexican fare at the light and airy **Casita Tejas** includes
such Tex-Mex favorites as fajitas and chimichangas but also features

genuine south-of-the-border dishes like *carne guisada* (spicy stewed beef and potatoes) and shrimp à la Mexicana (grilled shrimp with tomatoes, jalapeños and onions). The setting is fun and cheery, styled with wooden floors, woven blankets and glass tables. ~ 20 North Krome Avenue, Homestead; 305-248-8224. BUDGET TO MODERATE.

Although it's the only place to dine in the Everglades National Park, the **Flamingo Lodge Restaurant** is surprisingly good. The small but satisfactory menu features chicken and beef dishes. Located on the second floor of a small complex, the multilevel restaurant presents pretty views of Florida Bay. Tropical plants within and the dark night without remind you that while the menu is routine, the setting is quite exotic. ~ 1 Flamingo Road, in the Everglades National Park; 941-695-3101. MODERATE.

SHOPPING   Along with the usual souvenirs, you will find handcrafted baskets, beaded jewelry and the intricate, colorful patchwork clothing for which the Miccosukee Indian women are famous, at the **Miccosukee Indian Village Gift Shop**. ~ Route 41, 25 miles west of Florida's Turnpike; 305-223-8388.

HIDDEN ►   If you've about given up on finding a souvenir of Florida that's truly Floridian and a work of art to boot, stop in at **Big Cypress Gallery**, where Clyde Butcher, photographer extraordinaire, produces and displays amazing black-and-white scenes of Florida, particularly its wetlands. Take home a wall-size limited-edition print, a poster or maybe even a T-shirt you might sooner frame than wear. Clyde's wife, Niki, shoots black-and-white landscapes. The gallery's wilderness setting alone is worth the trip (45 miles west of the Turnpike and about 60 miles east of Naples) and mosquitoes are not a problem in the summer. ~ 52388 Tamiami Trail, Ochopee; 941-695-2428.

If you are a souvenir hound, stop at **Wooten's** and you'll never have to go anywhere else for those plastic flamingos and vinyl alligators. ~ Route 41, Ochopee; 813-695-2781.

Cauley Square has a Miami address, but Homestead claims it, too. This restored area of historic homes and buildings encompasses a variety of shops, including an art gallery selling south Florida and Bahamian art, a Christmas store, a Guatemala shop and the Cauley Square Tearoom. ~ 22400 Old Dixie Highway, Goulds; 305-258-3543.

The **Redland Fruit & Spice Park Gift Shop** is located on the grounds of the Preston B. Bird & Mary Heinlein Fruit & Spice Park. Here you can browse among shelves of imported and domestic dried and canned exotic fruits, unusual spices and seeds, and out-of-the-ordinary juices, jellies and jams. There's a good selection of cookbooks and reference books on tropical fruits. ~ 24801 Southwest 187th Avenue, Homestead; 305-247-5727.

On your drive to the main entrance of Everglades National Park, you'll pass a large, tacky, ramshackle produce stand known as **Robert Is Here**. Robert has fresh fruit such as mangos, lychees, monstera, tamarind and star fruit, and he has added sweet onions, cabbage, broccoli and cauliflower to the array. His U-Pick service for strawberries and snapdragons lasts the growing season (Thanksgiving to Easter). He serves up Key lime milkshakes and pies and sells jellies and preserves "made by his own mother." ~ 19200 Southwest 344th Street, Homestead; 305-246-1592.

While the **Gift Shop at Flamingo Resort** has lots of the usual Florida souvenirs, they also have some interesting books on the Everglades, along with high-quality shirts and stationery. Open November through April. ~ 1 Flamingo Road, in the Everglades National Park; 941-695-3101.

NIGHTLIFE

Folks in search of serious nightlife in the Everglades City area go to Naples. From the Florida City/Homestead area, it is less than an hour's drive to the bright lights of Miami and Miami Beach.

"The Glassroom" at the **Oyster House** is great for private parties. The main bar of this father-and-son establishment has sports trophies on the wall, a jukebox and a pool table, all beside an 80-foot observation tower—the highest in the Everglades. There is dancing to live bands in the winter. ~ Route 29, Everglades City; 941-695-2073.

In Homestead and Florida City, there is an assortment of roadside taverns, and some of the motels keep their lounges open and provide occasional entertainment for late-night socializers. But most folks will tell you that the sidewalks roll up early around here.

If you spend any nights in Flamingo, deep in the Everglades, take time to walk outside (providing it's not mosquito time) away from the lights of the lodge and marina. On a moonless night, you'll experience a darkness that is ultimate and hear sounds made nowhere else in the United States as the subtropical jungle creatures begin their night-long serenades.

PARKS

EVERGLADES NATIONAL PARK 🚶 🚲 ⛴ 🛥 ⛵ With an area of 1.5 million acres, this protected section of Florida's Everglades covers the southwestern end of the state and a vast section of shallow Florida Bay dotted with tiny keys. There is no other park like it in the world. Geologically and climatically unique, the Everglades is a 50-mile-wide subtropical "river of grass" flowing almost imperceptibly from Lake Okeechobee to the sea. To fully appreciate it, one needs to spend time here, for it does not overwhelm with spectacular scenery. Rather, its gently waving grasses dotted with stunted bald cypress, its clear ponds, its hardwood hammocks and pinelands are home to plant and animal life native to both the Caribbean Islands and the temperate United States. Inhabitants such as roseate spoonbills, wood storks, crocodiles and alligators, green sea turtles, southern bald eagles and manatees can be discovered by walking the trails, canoeing the waters and exploring with park rangers. Fishing is excellent in inland waters, especially for largemouth bass, and in coastal waters for snook, snapper, redfish and trout. Swimming is not recommended except on certain island locations accessible only by boat. Winter is the most comfortable time to visit, unless one is well-equipped to do battle with mosquitoes. Facilities in Flamingo, the main area, include picnic areas, restrooms, a restaurant, a motel, cabins, a grocery, a marina, interpretive trails, boat tours and boat rentals, a pool and canoe and bike rentals. In Shark Valley there are restrooms, hiking and biking trails, bicycle rentals and tram rides. In Everglades City you will find restrooms, a visitors center, boat tours and canoe rentals. Some of the facilities are closed from May 1 to October 31.

> The Big Cypress National Preserve exists to protect the watershed as well as the abundant wildlife living in the Everglades.

There are three main accesses to Everglades National Park, with shuttle service to each. On the northern boundary, Shark Valley (305-221-8776) is a day-use area; the entrance is off Route 41, 35 miles west of downtown Miami. Everglades City (941-695-3311), on the western side, offers access to the Ten Thousand Islands region; the entrance is on Route 29 off Route 41. The main park area (305-242-7700) for visitors encompasses the southern tip of the Florida mainland; the entrance is off Route 9336, ten miles southwest of Florida City.

▲ There are 225 tent/RV sites (no hookups); $10 per night. There are also 61 walk-in tent sites; $10 per night. There are four group camping sites. Wilderness camping is allowed, with a permit, in the main area and Everglades City area; no fee. There are also many privately owned campgrounds throughout the park.

BIG CYPRESS NATIONAL PRESERVE 🏃 🚲 🛶 ⛵ A 729,000-acre area of subtropical Florida known as Big Cypress Swamp makes up this preserve. Its establishment reflected a serious concern for the state's dwindling wetlands and watersheds, especially those affecting the Everglades National Park. Established in 1974, this preserved wilderness area of wet and dry prairies, coastal plains, marshes, mangrove forests, sandy pine woods and mixed hardwood hammocks has few facilities for visitors. There are picnic tables at several roadside parks, restrooms at the visitors center, bike trails and a hiking trail. ~ The visitors center is on Route 41 between Shark Valley and Everglades City; 941-695-4111.

▲ Primitive camping allowed; several campgrounds have sites for RVs, but there are no hookups; no fee except at Bona Park.

FAKAHATCHEE STRAND STATE PRESERVE 🚲 ⛵ This strand, the drainage slough for the Big Cypress Swamp, is the largest and

most interesting of these natural channels cut by the flow of water into the limestone plain. The slough's tall, dense, swamp forest stands out on the horizon in contrast to the open terrain and saw-grass plain around it. Its forest of royal palms, bald cypress trees and air plants is said to be unique on earth. Approximately 20 miles long and three to five miles wide, the preserve offers visitors views of some of its rare plant life, including 44 varieties of orchids—the largest concentration in the United States. From November through April, rangers conduct weekend "wet" walks into the swamp to see other unusual and endangered plant life. The only facilities are an interpretive trail and a boardwalk leading into the swamp. ~ On Route 29, seven miles northwest of Everglades City; 941-695-4593.

CHEKIKA RECREATION AREA 🏃 🚣 🛶 This 640-acre park allows easy exploration of some of the many Everglades terrains, including a tropical hammock, tree islands and the grassy waters flowing over honeycombed limestone surface rock. There's pleasant swimming and fishing in a natural lagoon. However, this was one of the areas in Everglades National Park hit hardest by Hurricane Andrew. Fallen trees still litter the park, but all the paths have been cleared. The small campground is located in the hardwood hammock, providing a pleasant and protected wilderness experience within an easy drive of Miami. Alligators make their home in the park and are to be respected. Facilities include a picnic area, restrooms, showers, a nature trail and a boardwalk; groceries and restaurants in Homestead. ~ Off Krome Avenue, 15 miles from Homestead; 305-242-7700.

▲ There are 20 sites, some accommodate RVs (no hookups); $14 per night.

BISCAYNE NATIONAL PARK 🏃 🚣 ⛵ 🐟 🛶 This 181,500-acre marine park is one of the largest of its kind in the National Park system, but most of it is hidden from the average traveler since it lies beneath the waters of Biscayne Bay and the Atlantic Ocean. The park includes a small area of mangrove shoreline (which was hit hard by Hurricane Andrew), part of the bay, a line of narrow islands of the northern Florida Keys and the northern part of John Pennekamp Coral Reef. Brown pelicans, little blue herons, snowy egrets and a few exotic fish can be seen by even the most casual stroller from the mainland jetty, but to fully appreciate the beauty of this unusual park you should take a glass-bottom boat tour or go snorkeling or scuba diving around the colorful reef. The park may also be explored by canoe or with a ranger on a guided trip. The little mangrove-fringed keys allow discovery of such tropical flora as gumbo-limbo trees, strangler fig and devil's potato. Birdlife abounds. This park features excellent saltwater fishing in open waters; fishing, however, is prohibited in harbors.

Lobster may be taken east of the islands in season. Swimming is not recommended except on the tiny beaches of Elliott and Sands keys where care must be taken to avoid sharp coral rock and spiny sea urchins. Picnic areas, restrooms, showers, canoe rentals and boat tours can be found here. ~ Park headquarters are at Convoy Point, nine miles east of Homestead. The rest of the park is accessible by boat from Convoy Point; 305-230-7275.

▲ Primitive camping is allowed on Elliott Key in about 30 sites, boat access only; no fee. Prepare for mosquitoes.

HOMESTEAD BAYFRONT PARK This is a next-door neighbor to the mainland part of Biscayne National Park (see above). It's a very popular spot enhanced by a small manmade beach, grassy areas and some shade offered by pines and palms. Entrance to the park is through a dense grove of mangroves, allowing a close look at these amazing island-building trees. There's good shore fishing for snapper. Swimming is pleasant and facilities include picnic areas, a playground, restrooms, showers and a marina. Day-use fee, $3.50. ~ Follow signs at Biscayne National Park (see above); 305-230-3034.

▼▼▼▼▼▼▼▼▼▼▼
Key Largo Area

Key Largo is the first of the Keys you will reach along the Great Overseas Highway, Route 1, when you head south from Florida City. Motels, resorts and campgrounds abound through much of this, the largest of the Keys. The center of population is the town of Key Largo, where you'll pass dozens of dive shops, for directly to the east of this long key lies the only living coral reef in the continental United States. This underwater paradise is rich in both marine life and interesting shipwrecks, some centuries old.

SIGHTS

For lots of good information on the Key Largo area, stop at the **Key Largo Chamber of Commerce.** ~ MM 106; 305-451-1414, 800-822-1088.

Caribbean Cigar Shop and Factory is where Cuban master cigar rollers ply their craft, and the air is redolent as a result. A visit to the "humidor," the back room where the air is kept a constant 70 degrees, refreshes the weary and keeps expensive stogies—each one lying in state in its own little sarcophagus—in peak condition. The factory's own brands, "West Indies Vanilla" and "Rum Runners," produce the greatest olfactory pleasure. ~ In the Pink Plaza, MM 103.4, Key Largo; 305-453-4014.

Slow down as you approach the short bridge that crosses the **Marvin D. Adams Waterway,** a manmade cut that creates a channel all the way across a narrow section of Key Largo. The banks on either side of the cut are the one place you can really get a good look at the geological makeup of the Upper Keys. There are fine

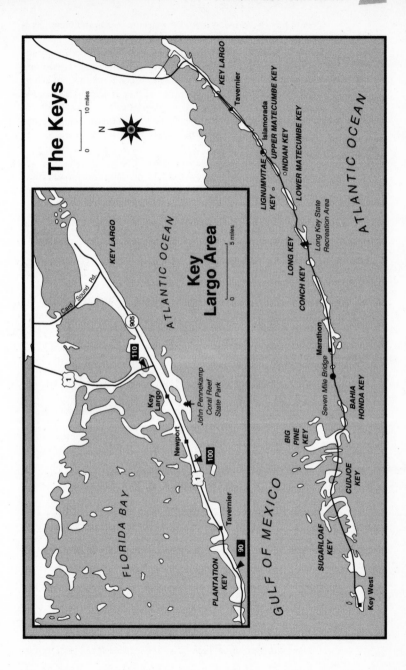

examples of petrified staghorn coral, coral heads and other pieces of the ancient coral reef on which the islands are built. ~ MM 103.

To observe treasures recovered from Florida's reefs, visit the **Maritime Museum of the Florida Keys**. Resembling a 15th-century castle, the "treasure castle" contains historical exhibits and glittering riches. The spoils on display include a jewel-studded gold medallion, Chinese "blue and white" porcelain, a collection of sea-salvaged coins and rotating exhibits of treasures from shipwrecked Spanish galleons in the Caribbean. If they are very strong, visitors may lift an 80-pound silver bar. Closed Thursday. Admission. ~ MM 102.6, Key Largo; 305-451-6444.

Whether or not you're a snorkeler or scuba diver, **John Pennekamp Coral Reef State Park** offers many ways to enjoy this underwater treasure (see the "Beaches & Parks" section below). An excellent visitors center features a giant reconstruction of a living patch reef in a circular aquarium and other exhibits of the undersea world, mangrove swamps and hardwood hammocks. Admission. ~ Route 1, MM 102.5, Key Largo; 305-451-1202. Glass-bottom boat tours, as well as scuba and snorkeling tours, are offered daily. ~ 305-451-1621.

Glass-bottom boat cruises to the reef are also available on the **Key Largo Princess**, which sails to Molasses Reef in the National Marine Sanctuary. Choose from daily public cruises as well as sunset cruises with underwater lights. ~ MM 100, Holiday Inn docks, Key Largo; 305-451-4655.

Atlantic bottle-nosed dolphins can often be spotted swimming and cavorting in Key Largo area waters, especially on the bay side. For a closer experience with these delightful and intelligent sea mammals, make an appointment to visit **Dolphins Plus**, one of several places in the Keys where you can actually swim with dolphins (although you must be at least ten years old to swim). Basically a research center, Dolphins Plus studies how dolphins relate to human beings. They are also researching the dolphin's role in "zoo-therapy" with disabled individuals. Admission. ~ MM 100, Key Largo; 305-451-1993.

BOGIE'S BOAT

If you want a very small bit of nostalgia, you can usually see the original *African Queen* (the little boat in which Humphrey Bogart and Katharine Hepburn battled the jungle and found romance) on display at the Holiday Inn docks. If the ship's gone for the day, you can have a look at the *Thayer IV*, the boat seen in the Hepburn film *On Golden Pond*. ~ MM 100, Key Largo.

The little town of **Tavernier** boasts a bit of history that local folks are hanging onto as best they can. Along with the Old Methodist Church on Route 1, a few **old frame houses** with big shutters for protection against hurricanes remain, mementos of the farming days before pizza parlors and gas stations. You can see them if you wander the few side streets and peer into the dense grove of tropical trees. ~ Around MM 92.

◄ *HIDDEN*

Watch for an unobtrusive entrance just south of Key Largo on the bay side. **Florida Keys Wild Bird Rehabilitation Center** is a nonprofit organization—it started with one caring woman and continues to grow with the help of some dedicated volunteers—that cares for ailing avians. Stop by and get close up and personal with wild birds that you would usually see only from very far away. You'll find it somewhat heartrending when you realize that much of the damage is done by man's inhumanity to his fellow creatures, but heartwarming at the same time to find that there are still many people who care deeply. ~ MM 93.6; 305-852-4486.

◄ *HIDDEN*

For Everglades airboat rides and sightseeing tours, contact **Captain Ray Cramer** (said to be one of the best authorities on the region), an excellent guide and spinner of regional tales. He'll make arrangements to meet you. ~ Key Largo; 305-852-5339.

Accommodations are numerous in the Keys, from small motels to condominiums to chain hotels to luxurious resorts. Almost all offer something special, from a dock for snorkeling to extensive dive and fishing charters. Lodging information may be obtained from the **Florida Keys Visitors Bureau**. ~ Key West; 800-352-5397.

LODGING

Calling itself the "best little dive resort in Key Largo," **Kelly's Motel & the Aqua-Nuts Dive Resort** offers Caribbean-style charm where diving enthusiasts can almost roll out of bed and into the water. Kelly's is located on the sunset side of Key Largo, has 32 comfortably furnished rooms and efficiencies, a dive center, a pool, a 42-foot dive boat and both PADI and NAUI scuba courses. Breakfast is included. ~ MM 104.2, Key Largo; 305-451-1622, 800-226-0415, fax 305-451-4623. MODERATE TO ULTRA-DELUXE.

Opened in summer 1993 as the Keys' latest getaway resort, **Marriott Key Largo Bay Beach Resort** impresses with its rambling four-story sun-washed buildings, embellished with white wrought iron and coral rock pillars, and looking across a great sweep of shimmering bay. Along the bay is more fantasy design, including a suspension bridge and numerous peak-roofed gazebos, a swimming pool and a manmade beach with attendant lounge chairs. Only ten of the 153 rooms do not command a bay view; all rooms feature plush surroundings that include white-washed oak and vibrant tropical patterns, as well as spacious balconies. Amenities include a restaurant, café, tiki bar, dive shop and exercise room. ~

MM 103.5, Key Largo; 305-453-9393, 800-932-9332, fax 305-453-0093. ULTRA-DELUXE.

HIDDEN ► **Jules' Undersea Lodge** is so hidden that you can't even see it when you get there because it's 22 feet below the surface of a tropical lagoon. You don't have to be an advanced scuba diver to get into your air-conditioned quarters (there are two rooms for guests and an entertainment room); the staff will give you lessons. The reward is a unique underwater experience—with fish swimming by your 42-inch windows, no noise except the comforting reminder of the air support system and the knowledge that you are staying in the only underwater hotel in the world! ~ 51 Shoreland Drive, near MM 103.2, Key Largo; 305-451-2353, fax 305-451-4789. ULTRA-DELUXE.

Tropical trees, dense foliage, ibis in the yard and a nice little bayside beach reinforce the claim at **Largo Lodge** that "paradise can be reasonable." For the reasonable price you get one of six very nice, roomy apartments with a kitchen, a living room and a big screened porch with space for lots of diving gear. The place is beautifully maintained and the owner is delightful. ~ MM 101.5, Key Largo; 305-451-0424. DELUXE.

Marina del Mar Resort is one of those places with everything—lodging, marina, restaurant and nightclub, tennis courts, fitness center, pool and diving services. On the oceanside of the island, it is convenient to the popular nearby diving waters. The one- to three-bedroom suites are spacious and airy with tile floors and whirlpool tubs; there are also studios with full kitchens. ~ MM 100, Key Largo; 305-451-4107, 800-451-3483, fax 305-451-1891. DELUXE TO ULTRA-DELUXE.

The **Sunset Cove Motel** is really a complex of small, old-time, plain but neat rooms and apartments. This modest spot has a real old Keys feel. It's set among life-sized carved panthers and pelicans

---

✔ CHECK THESE OUT—UNIQUE LODGING

- *Budget:* Congratulate yourself when you check into the **Key West Hostel**—here, you can sleep, cook and store your stuff—and save money. *page 362*
- *Moderate:* Swim in the clear ocean or fresh- and saltwater pools at Islamorada's **Islander Motel**, set amid 24 acres of tropical foliage. *page 332*
- *Deluxe to ultra-deluxe:* Lounge in the pool, surrounded by tropical plants, at the **Flamingo Lodge**, the only accommodation in Everglades National Park. *page 314*
- *Ultra-deluxe:* Fish swim by your windows in a lagoon at Key Largo's **Jules' Undersea Lodge**, the world's only undersea hotel. *page 324*

Budget: under $50   Moderate: $50–$90   Deluxe: $90–$130   Ultra-deluxe: over $130

and enhanced with talking parrots and wonderful, relaxing Jamaican swings in the shade of thatched chickees huts. Guests may play the jukebox, watch the pelicans and use their glass-bottom paddleboat and canoes. ~ MM 99.5, Key Largo; 305-451-0705. MODERATE.

Here is a resort that reminds one of what the Keys used to look like. The **Sheraton Key Largo**, obscured as it is in hardwood hammock, offers a glimpse of a natural habitat. Footpaths wend along the property, and signs point to wild coffee plants and a mahogany tree—surely one of the few remaining in the Upper Keys. The 200 balconied rooms are far from woodsy, offering luxuries such as marble vanities with theater lighting, cushy carpets and coffee makers. Fourth-floor rooms, with views of the bay instead of the forest, are most coveted. Another plus: twin swimming pools—one for families, the other for adults. ~ MM 97, Key Largo; 305-852-5553, 800-826-1006, fax 305-852-8669. ULTRA-DELUXE.

At the **Stone Ledge Resort** you'll have access to a nice dock, a small bayside beach, a shady yard and a pleasant motel room, efficiency or studio apartment in the long, low cream-colored stucco building. Typical of many of the area's mom-and-pop motels, this one is quite pleasant. Ask for a unit away from the highway. ~ MM 95.3, Key Largo; 305-852-8114. MODERATE.

The innovative seafood dishes at **Sundowner's** won't disappoint. It's a casual but classy place, with friendly waiters who call you by name. The glasswalled dining room faces the bay for splendid sunset gazing. There are steak, pasta and chicken dishes, but best are the nightly fish specials such as crabmeat-stuffed yellowtail with béarnaise sauce, fresh Florida lobster tail and grilled or blackened mahimahi. ~ MM 103.9, Key Largo; 305-451-4502. MODERATE TO DELUXE.

DINING

Within Marriott's Key Largo Bay Beach Resort, **Gus' Grille** appears as a large, airy space with natural woods, coral-rock walls and a wood-burning pizza oven. Window walls overlook Florida Bay for a spectacular show each evening as the setting sun turns the waters crimson and gold. The food is as gorgeously presented as the view, but, alas, lacks character. But the pizza from the aforementioned traditional oven is outstanding. Outdoors, by the pool, you can sip a piña colada while watching the dive boats come and go. ~ MM 103.8, Key Largo; 305-453-0000. DELUXE.

South of the Border, while purporting to refer to the land of tacos and tequila, really seems to mean the Dade-Monroe county line. Owned by the same restaurateurs who have long pleased customers at Mrs. Mac's Kitchen, the menu is an eclectic mix of the same down-home favorites enjoyed there and just enough Mexican specialities to justify the name (try the fajitas). The ambience, too, is slightly confused, but the overall effect is pleasant. ~ In the Pink Plaza, MM 103.4, Key Largo; 305-451-3307. BUDGET TO MODERATE.

The fresh fish at **Makoto** is far from Keys-standard: It's served raw and wrapped in seaweed, with rice and cucumber and various other accompaniments. The only place for sushi until Key West, Makoto is surprisingly good. Located in a yellow-awninged building with a glass wall facing the ocean, it's adorned with Japanese prints and paper lanterns. Choose from sushi and sashimi combos, tempura, teriyaki, sukiyaki or interesting appetizers such as soft shell crab with teriyaki sauce. ~ MM 101.6, Key Largo; 305-451-7083. MODERATE.

HIDDEN ► Turn toward the ocean side at MM 100 and follow side streets until you come to the **Pilot House**. It may be a little tricky to find, but if you enjoy a low-key atmosphere with a "waterfront" view, an outdoor bar and friendly waitstaff, you'll love this place where locals come for Harvey's fish sandwich (praised in *Keys Cuisine*), hazelnut yellowtail and filet mignon. The view is less than stunning, but it's fun to watch the boats come and go. ~ 13 Seagate Boulevard, Key Largo; 305-451-3142. MODERATE TO DELUXE.

Hidden within a small grove of large coconut palms is the lilac canopy that leads to **Snook's Bayside**, a French country–style place with high-backed chairs and displays of family antiques and fine china. This is an intimate spot for fine dining on seafood, Angus beef, veal and chicken inside or out on the patio. Roast beef is the specialty every Friday and a waterfront, Southern, all-you-can-eat brunch buffet rounds out the week on Sunday. Closed Monday from August through October. MM 99.9, Key Largo; 305-453-3799. MODERATE TO DELUXE.

Sushi Nami is a terrific sushi bar that has a tatami room where you can curl up barefoot on big, satiny cushions. Enjoy traditional fare such as teriyaki, tempura, soba noodles and sashimi. The mounted fish on the walls help you remember you're in the Keys. No lunch served on the weekend. ~ MM 99.5, Key Largo; 305-453-9798. MODERATE.

Cafe Largo serves good Italian food—all the traditional pasta, chicken and veal dishes plus excellent daily specials using yellowtail and dolphin, stone crabs, lobster and other local seafood. The Mediterranean setting is indoors and typical of family-style Italian places. Dinner only. ~ 305-451-4885. On the same property, connected by a walkway, is the **Bayside Grill**. Diners enjoy steak and seafood dishes in the glass-enclosed dining room situated on the waterfront. Along with lunch and dinner, they also serve Sunday brunch. ~ MM 99.5, Key Largo; 305-451-3380. MODERATE TO DELUXE.

If you tire of seafood or want a little down-home mainland food, stop at **Mrs. Mac's Kitchen**. This shack-style eatery has about the best chili east of Texas and pita bread concoctions almost too fat to bite down on. The chefs cook up huge breakfasts, broil delicious steaks and feature different theme specials (Italian, meat, seafood, etc.) for dinner every night. The place is small, with more varieties of beers than seats, so it's noisy and fun. Closed Sunday. ~ MM 99.4, Key Largo; 305-451-3722. BUDGET TO MODERATE.

Ballyhoo's has the best breakfast in the Upper Keys: mashed potato omelets and Swedish oatmeal pancakes, seafood omelets with hollandaise and good bloody marys and mimosas. Atmosphere is pure Keys: funky tables and chairs, a wall-unit air-conditioner grumbling and a view of the highway through windows filmed with coral rock dust. Breakfast, lunch and dinner are served daily. ~ MM 98, Key Largo; 305-852-0822. MODERATE TO DELUXE.

Humphrey Bogart and Lauren Bacall made the town famous in their spellbinding movie *Key Largo*. You'll still hear about the film today; a few places claim to have had a part in its making.

Old Tavernier Restaurant grew so popular it had to relocate to a bigger spot just to accommodate the nightly mobs. Now, between the spacious dining room and outdoor veranda along a mangrove canal, there's plenty of room to enjoy what Old Tavernier does best: huge portions of sauce-drenched pastas that arrive bubbling at your table. Nightly specials often depart from pasta with such dishes as rack of lamb, grilled veal chops and fresh fish. ~ MM 90, Tavernier; 305-852-6012. MODERATE.

Key Largo is the main spot for Upper Keys shoppers, so there are shopping centers, groceries and all the functional kinds of stores you might need, as well as tacky souvenir and T-shirt shops.

SHOPPING

The **Pink Plaza** is one-stop shopping, Keys-style. Among the noteworthy shops are **Cudawear** (305-453-0210), for fine silk-screened clothing for women and boating wear for men, with accessories from deck shoes to fishing poles. **Fundora Art Gallery** (305-451-2200) specializes in oils, prints and watercolors. The **Caribbean Cigar Shop and Factory** (305-453-4014) features cigars rolled by Cuban masters. ~ MM 103.4.

A well-known underwater photographer offers all the necessary equipment—for sale or for rent—for capturing your diving and snorkeling adventures on still or video film at **Stephen Frink Photographic**. He will also process and enlarge your slides. ~ MM 102.5, Key Largo; 305-451-3737.

The Book Nook has a large variety of books about the area and Florida in general, as well as maps and charts for divers. They also keep a good selection of classics as well as plenty of recent bestsellers, magazines and newspapers (British and German, too) to keep you busy when you've had too much sun, and "island" music to relax to. ~ MM 100, Waldorf Plaza, Key Largo; 305-451-1468.

Junk is about the last thing you'll find at **Josie's Junk Alley**. Small but unique, this consignment store sells deco, vintage and modern clothing, jewelry and those special "one-of-a-kind" items. ~ MM 99.5, Key Largo; 305-451-1995.

The neighboring **Pink Junktique** specializes in unusual, artsy, funky, high-quality "everything," from clothing, jewelry and furniture to baskets, books and bowls—all priced to sell. ~ MM 99.5, Key Largo; 305-451-4347.

In a little Quonset hut housing **Island Feet**, you'll step into the largest selection of sandals—Birkenstock, Reef Rider, Teva, Rainbow and Kino's—in the Keys. ~ MM 94, Tavernier; 305-852-5691.

Several places in the Keys specialize in embossed and handpainted handbags, some ready-made, many with nautical designs, and others done to suit your own special wishes. You can find them at the **Florida Keys Handbag Factory**, where they also sell T-shirts and "island" clothing. ~ MM 91.5, Tavernier; 305-852-8690.

NIGHTLIFE

If you're willing to experience a raunchy sort of bikers' beach bar in exchange for some possible nostalgia, stop at the **Caribbean Club**. It is claimed that some parts of the movie *Key Largo* were filmed here, and it just may be true. Even if it's not, the sunsets from the deck are terrific. The joint is open from 7 a.m. to 4 a.m. and offers live rock, blues and reggae bands several nights a week. ~ MM 104, Key Largo; 305-451-9970.

Coconuts is a waterfront spot with live entertainment every night ranging from Top-40 to reggae. Inside, the huge dancefloor has a classy light show; outside, you can enjoy a drink on the canopied deck overlooking a canal with boats. Ladies night on Wednesday. ~ MM 100 at Marina del Mar, Key Largo; 305-453-9794.

At **Snook's Bayside**, the natives gather by car or by boat to watch the sunset and enjoy a friendly drink at the outdoor bar. There is dining seating inside, with live entertainment weekends in the summer and every evening during the season—usually classical and easy-listening music. ~ MM 99.9, Key Largo; 305-453-3799.

BEACHES & PARKS

JOHN PENNEKAMP CORAL REEF STATE PARK This remarkable place is the first underwater state park in the United States. Together with the adjacent **Key Largo Coral Reef National Marine Sanctuary** (305-451-1644), the park encompasses an area of about 178 nautical square miles, most of which lies out in the Atlantic Ocean north and east of Key Largo. Most visitors come to see the coral formations, seagrass beds and spectacular marine life of the reefs, either by scuba diving, snorkeling or taking a glass-bottom boat tour. Fishing is another popular activity. It's allowed in the mangroves (for mangrove snapper, trout, sheepshead and snook) and in the Atlantic (for gamefish such as kingfish, mackerel and yellowtail). Tropical fish, however, are protected. There are also two small manmade swimming beaches with a "sunken ship" offshore. The land section of the park acquaints visitors with mangrove swamps, numerous shore birds and a tropical hammock with many varieties of indigenous plant life. An excellent visitors center, featuring a replication of a patch reef complete with marine life in a 30,000-gallon aquarium, allows even those who prefer staying on dry land to experience a bit of the underwater world. Other facilities include picnic areas, restrooms, a bathhouse, showers, nature trails, an observation tower, a snack bar, a gift shop, a dive shop, a marina and docks. Day-use fee, $4. ~ Entrance at MM 102.5 on Route 1, in Key Largo. Much of the park is accessible only by boat; 305-451-1202.

▲ There are 47 sites, all with electricity and water, at the state park; $24 per night for tent sites, $26 per night for hookups. Private RV and tent campgrounds are nearby. **Key Largo Kampground and Marina** has 38 tent sites and 60 RV sites; $18 to $20 per night for tent sites, $33 to $38 per night for RV sites. ~ MM 101.5, Key Largo; 305-451-1431. **Calusa Camp Resort** has 36 tent sites and 340 RV sites; $25 to $31 per night. The grounds tend to be cramped but offer functional places for divers to stay. ~ MM 101.5, Key Largo; 305-451-0232.

HARRY HARRIS PARK   This county park is one of the few public parks in the area for spending a day beside the ocean. It is spacious, with broad grassy areas and scattered trees. The beach isn't much, but the water is clear and full of fish. You can fish off the jetties; the water, however, is shallow. Swimming is also good here. Facilities include picnic areas, restrooms, playgrounds and shuffleboard. ~ Take Burton Drive at MM 92.5 in Tavernier; it's about a quarter of a mile to the park.

Islamorada (pronounced *eye-lah-mor-ah-dah*) was named by Spanish explorers and means "purple isles," perhaps for the way the land appeared on the horizon,

▼▼▼▼▼▼▼▼▼▼▼▼
Islamorada Area

perhaps for the abundant violet snail shells or the brilliant flowering plants found there when the islands were wild.

The Islamorada area begins at Windley Key (MM 85) and runs through Long Key (below MM 68). The community of Islamorada, on Upper Matecumbe Key, is its center of population. The area's brief ventures have included shipbuilding, tropical fruit and vegetable farming, turtling, sponging and the immensely prosperous business of salvaging shipwrecks. Fishing has always been especially fine in this area, and today tourism is the chief enterprise here.

The town is a collection of businesses that provide local folk with essentials while inviting visitors to "stay here," "eat here," "party here" and "buy here." Holiday Isle, a gigantic resort and entertainment complex, dominates Windley Key with the latest in youthful party hype.

SIGHTS

As with the other parts of the Keys, much of what Islamorada has to offer is out to sea. You'll see signs along Route 1 for boat rentals, diving cruises and fishing charters. Stop at the red caboose that houses the **Islamorada Chamber of Commerce** for information about both land and sea areas. ~ MM 82.5; 305-664-4503, 800-322-5397.

If you are traveling with your boat, you'll like knowing about **Bud N' Mary's Marina and Dive Center**, especially if you enjoy being in the middle of such sea-related activities as diving, snorkeling, backcountry fishing, and glass-bottom and deep-sea boating. Even without your own vessel in tow, you can still enjoy Bud N' Mary's occasional boat cruises that go out to the lighthouse at Alligator Reef, named for one of the ships that ran aground here. Along the way you'll have a chance to do a little snorkeling. ~ MM 79.8; 305-664-2211, 800-344-7352 (dive center); 305-664-2461, 800-742-7945 (marina).

For a nice, friendly marine show where, if you're lucky, you might get to hold a hoop for a jumping dolphin or get a kiss from a seal, stop at **Theatre of the Sea**, one of the oldest marine parks in the world. It may now have fancier, more sophisticated competitors, but this place is still fun and quite personal. There are myriad sea creatures that can be touched, wild dolphins that join visitors for a "bottomless" boat trip and beautiful tropical grounds to explore. Visitors can also swim with dolphins here by reservation (ages 13 and up). Admission. ~ MM 84.5, Islamorada; 305-664-2431.

HIDDEN ►

After a three-hour boat trip to **Indian Key State Historic Site** you'll be presented with the remarkable story of the ten-acre island that was once the prosperous seat of Dade County. Beneath the nearby, usually calm waters of the Atlantic lie the most treacherous reefs off the Florida coast. The reefs were a source of income for Indians and then for Americans, who turned "salvaging" wrecked ships into profitable businesses. At that time the island town was a bustling place and boasted a grand hotel with a large ballroom, a bar and bowling alleys. One famous hotel guest was naturalist John James Audubon, who stayed over on his way to the Lower Keys. He filed one of the first complaints on record—the incessant dancing and partying made it hard for him to concentrate. Today, there is little sign of the merriment that had the bird man grinding his teeth. The town was destroyed in a grisly Indian attack in 1840. Rangers now guide visitors down reconstructed village "streets" among the tall century plants and other tropical growth. Admission. ~ 305-664-4815.

HIDDEN ►

It's another three-hour trip to **Lignumvitae Key State Botanical Site**. This key encompasses 280 acres; its virgin tropical forest is a reminder of how all the Keys probably appeared before people came in numbers. Ranger-guided walks through this rare environment introduce such unusual trees as the gumbo-limbo, mastic and poisonwood. The restored Matheson House, built in 1919, has survived hurricane and time; it demonstrates how island dwellers managed in the early days of Keys settlement, dependent on wind power, rainwater and food from the sea. Indian Key and Lignumvitae Key are accessible by private boat only. (Check the boating listing at the end of the chapter under "Outdoor Adventures.") Admission. ~ 305-644-4815.

The **Layton Nature Trail** is an almost-hidden loop trail from highway to bay, winding through a dense hammock of carefully marked tropical plants, such as pigeon plum, wild coffee and gumbo-limbo, that are unique to the Keys. For travelers in a hurry, the 20-minute walk provides a good introduction to the flora that once covered most of the Keys. ~ Near MM 66.

◄ *HIDDEN*

Located 18 feet below the surface of the Atlantic Ocean, the **San Pedro Underwater Archaeological Preserve** welcomes divers, snorkelers and observers in glass-bottom boats. The *San Pedro* was a 287-ton, Dutch-built galleon in the New Spain fleet that left Havana harbor on Friday, July 13, 1733, and met its doom when hurricane winds drove it onto the reefs. The shipwreck park, dedicated in 1989, features an underwater nature trail where one can view a variety of fish, crustaceans, mollusks and corals. Original anchors, ballast stones, bricks from the ship's galley and concrete cannon replicas enhance the park. ~ 1.3 nautical miles south of Indian Key; P.O. Box 776, Long Key, FL 33001; 305-664-4815.

◄ *HIDDEN*

A **historical marker** west of Layton marks the site of Long Key Fishing Club, established in 1906 by Flagler's East Coast Hotel Company. One aim of the group was to stop the wholesale destruction of gamefish in this mecca for saltwater anglers. The president

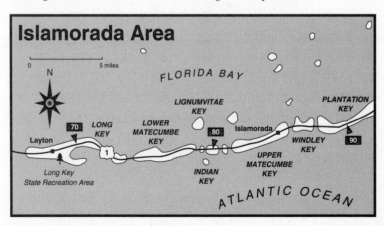

Islamorada Area

of the club, which fell victim to the 1935 hurricane, was American author Zane Grey. ~ Near MM 66.

LODGING

The Islamorada business area includes another piece of Route 1 lined with mom-and-pop and various chain motels. If you prefer renting a home, condo or townhouse for a week, or even months, contact **Freewheeler Realty**. ~ 85960 Overseas Highway, Islamorada; 305-664-2075.

Folks who enjoy being where the action is choose to stay at **Holiday Isle Resorts and Marina**, a great complex of lodgings, swimming pools, bars, restaurants and shops strung out along a stretch of Atlantic beach. The six-story main hotel and its three-story neighbor offer oceanfront rooms, efficiencies, apartments and suites with a peach and teal theme. Some are ordinary motel-type rooms; others are luxury apartments with kitchens, bars and wraparound balconies overlooking the ocean. ~ MM 84, Islamorada; 305-664-2321, 800-327-7070, fax 305-664-2703. DELUXE TO ULTRA-DELUXE.

If you want the glitz and fervor of Holiday Isle for lower rates, go a mile back up the road to **Harbor Lights** for moderate motel rooms and deluxe-priced efficiencies. Owned by Holiday Isle, this place operates a free trolley to take guests to the bustling center of things. ~ MM 85, Islamorada; 305-664-3611, 800-327-7070, fax 305-664-2703. MODERATE TO DELUXE.

At **The Islander Motel** you can snorkel in the clear ocean water off the fishing pier or swim in the freshwater and saltwater pools. The Islander offers pleasant hotel rooms (some with kitchenettes) and fully equipped villas with screened porches. The 24-acre oceanside resort is rich in tropical plants and features shuffleboard. This is a popular place for families. ~ MM 82.1, Islamorada; 305-664-2031. MODERATE.

Vacationers in search of sheer luxury have been coming to **Cheeca Lodge** for over half a century. Perched on the edge of the Atlantic Ocean, this four-story hotel received a massive facelift in 1989. Much of the original wood remains in the updated lodge, which has classy lobby areas, spacious rooms, freshwater and salt-

A NATURAL TRAGEDY

Stop for a minute at the **Hurricane Monument** to meditate on the terrible storm of Labor Day, 1935. Before the anemometer blew away, winds were recorded at 200 mph; the barometer fell to 26.35, one of the lowest pressures ever recorded in the Western Hemisphere. This slightly neglected but nevertheless moving monument was dedicated in 1937 to the memory of the 423 people who died in that storm. ~ MM 81.5, Islamorada.

water pools, indoor and outdoor dining, tennis courts and a nine-hole golf course. White-and-blue villas are scattered around grounds shaded by a variety of tropical trees. A fine, long pier invites fishing and serves as a take-off point for scuba divers and snorkelers. ~ MM 82.5, Islamorada; 305-664-4651, 800-327-2888, fax 305-664-2893. ULTRA-DELUXE.

The quiet, unadorned, oldish **Gamefish Resort** offers motel rooms, efficiency apartments or combinations for families needing suites. The place is very plain, with tropical plantings, chickee huts and a clear tidal salt pool complete with lobsters and stone crabs in the rocks. It's very popular with families and retired folk who like the quiet and easy access to fishing and who feel comfortable with the new but old-style furnishings. ~ MM 75.5; 305-664-5568. MODERATE TO DELUXE.

DINING

The restaurant with the reputation is **Marker 88**, whose Continental cuisine has garnered raves from some of the nation's top culinary magazines. Entrées include fish Martinique topped with tomato concassé and sliced grilled bananas, and rice colonial Bombay—a magic mélange of beef and veal slices, curry, shrimp, scallops, pineapple, banana, pimento and scallions. Nestled beside Florida Bay and shaded by waving palms, Marker 88 is informally elegant and intimate with a rich tropical ambience. The wine list is as impressive as the creative menu. Closed Monday. ~ MM 88, Islamorada; 305-852-9315. DELUXE TO ULTRA-DELUXE.

Of the many places to eat at Holiday Isle Resort, the classiest is the **Horizon Restaurant** atop the five-story main hotel. You can get fine views of the bay and the ocean while enjoying Keys seafood prepared in a variety of fashions including traditional broiled or fried, and meunière or almondine styles. Cajun-style dolphinfish fillets, tuna *au poivre*, and grilled lamb chops find their way onto the menu. The chef also does a variety of things with Caribbean queen conch, an old-time Keys shellfish now protected locally. ~ MM 84, Islamorada; 305-664-2321. DELUXE TO ULTRA-DELUXE.

You have two choices at the red-and-white-awninged **Coral Grill**. You can gorge at the sumptuous dinner buffet upstairs, which features country staples like fried fish, roast turkey and chicken and dumplings, or you can stay downstairs and control your intake. Native fish are treated several ways; especially tasty is the "Matecumbe" style, sautéed with scallions, pimento, black olives, butter and lime. Except for all the sparkling lights in the trees out front, the place appears undistinguished, but the very affordable menu makes it good for families. ~ MM 83.5, Islamorada; 305-664-4803. MODERATE.

The shimmering mermaid on the wall of the **Lorelei** may catch your eye, but it's the trellises, ceiling fans and handblown light fixtures that give this yacht-basin restaurant a nice "early Keys" feel.

They do all sorts of things with the catch of the day here—broil, blacken, coconut-fry and serve it with Creole or meunière sauces. There are traditional conch chowder and fritters, daily blackboard specials and a devastating chocolate-chip Kahlua cheesecake for dessert. ~ MM 82, Islamorada; 305-664-4656. MODERATE TO DELUXE.

Just before President George Bush was inaugurated in 1989, he went bonefishing in Islamorada and had dinner at Cheeca Lodge's main dining room, the **Atlantic's Edge Restaurant**. The appetizer was stone-crab pie with scallions and tomatoes, a sublime sample of the excellent gourmet dining available in this elegant restaurant. Sea scallops are prepared with fresh mixed greens, candied walnuts and strawberry vinaigrette; coho salmon is seared and served with leeks, potatoes and a rich tomato butter; and lobster fritters are seasoned with Key lime–roasted aioli. As if the food weren't enough, there's also a fine wine list. ~ MM 82, Islamorada; 305-664-4651. DELUXE TO ULTRA-DELUXE.

HIDDEN ▶

Set back on the old highway that runs beside the main thoroughfare is a deeply shaded, Easter egg–colored conch-style building. **Grove Park Cafe**, with brightly cushioned and handpainted Bentwood chairs, is a fine-dining restaurant with a wine and espresso bar. The menu features such dishes as chicken Matecumbe (with prosciutto, sage and snow peas in a light cream sauce) and yellowtail tropicale (sautéed snapper in a macadamia-nut crust served over rice with mango-papaya salsa). You can also order box lunches or picnic baskets to go. Lunch features *panini* sandwiches on home-baked *focaccia*. There is a single umbrella-topped table in the garden (for smokers) and the resident kitty is too well fed to beg at your table. ~ MM 81.7, Islamorada; 305-664-0116. MODERATE TO DELUXE.

✔ CHECK THESE OUT—UNIQUE DINING

- *Budget to moderate:* Catch some Cuban flavors at Marathon's **Don Pedro**, where entrées of roast pork or *picadillo* come with fried bananas and black beans. *page 341*
- *Moderate:* Dine inside or on the veranda at Key Largo's **Old Tavernier Restaurant**, known for hearty pasta dishes and varied sauces. *page 327*
- *Deluxe:* Sip tasty conch bisque while enjoying the serene Gulf view and soft piano music at Key West's **Pier House Restaurant**. *page 363*
- *Deluxe to ultra-deluxe:* Informal elegance and nationally acclaimed Continental cuisine await you Islamorada's **Marker 88**. *page 333*

Budget: under $8   Moderate: $8–$16   Deluxe: $16–$24   Ultra-deluxe: over $24

Manny and Isa's Kitchen is a very delightful, very plain little place where chatter among the staff is Spanish and food is tops. A number of authentic Cuban dishes such as *picadillo*, *ropa vieja* and *palomilla* steak with black beans and rice make a very ample meal. Regular Keys seafood and other American items extend into the moderate range. With 24 hours notice, Manny and Isa will prepare a special Spanish paella dinner for two or more. ~ MM 81.6, Islamorada; 305-664-5019. BUDGET TO MODERATE.

The **Green Turtle Inn** has been a Keys tradition since 1947, and although the dark, clubby atmosphere shows its age, diners still flock here and go away happy after filling up on the famous turtle or conch chowder, alligator or conch steak, stone crabs (in season) and the ubiquitous seafood, steaks and chops. And no meal is considered complete without Key lime pie. You can also take home canned chowders or Key lime pie filling. Closed Monday. ~ MM 81.5, Islamorada; 305-664-9031. MODERATE TO DELUXE.

In a weathered old house overlooking Tea Table Relief, **Papa Joe's Landmark Restaurant** really is a landmark, with battered wood floors, pecky cypress walls and ancient air-conditioners that chase away the island heat. Papa Joe's does fresh fish seven different ways, including coconut-fried, Oscar and meunière. They will also cook your catch for a slightly lower price. They also serve many steak entrées and have a good early-bird menu. The adjoining waterfront bar is a scenic place to meet local characters. ~ MM 79.7, Islamorada; 305-664-8109. MODERATE.

Little Italy is about as rustic as can be, with shell lamps and wine bottles lining the windows. The food is terrific and plentiful. Bowls come to your table brimming with Sicilian-style seafood like sautéed snapper heaped with fresh tomatoes, black olives, mushrooms, shrimp and scallops in a sherry and lemon butter sauce. There are also many chicken and veal entrées, and traditional favorites such as ravioli and lasagna. ~ MM 68.5, Layton; 305-664-4472. MODERATE.

A long, two-story aqua restaurant with a panoramic ocean view, **Chef Mark's Paradise Restaurant** serves good, tasty Italian food reminiscent of a homemade meal. Try the *braciola*, a rolled and baked steak stuffed with four cheeses, raisins and pine nuts, served with Marsala wine sauce. Or try the Maryland crab bomb, jumbled together with capers and dressing and served with garlic sauce on toast. A local favorite. ~ MM 68.5, Layton; 305-664-4900. MODERATE TO DELUXE.

The Rain Barrel is a store full of top-quality crafts and much more. Many of the craftspeople create their wares right in this tropical setting that resembles a village more than a store. There are glass blowers, jewelers, leather workers, fine artists and potters, whom

SHOPPING

you can often see working at their crafts. ~ MM 86.7, Plantation Key; 305-852-3084.

A faux castle with a mammoth faux lobster out front, **Treasure Village** is a collection of unique little gift and artisan shops plus one department-sized store. The latter, **Treasure Harbor Trading** (305-852-0511), features fashionable gifts with environmental themes, from clothing to cassettes to massage potions. ~ MM 86.7, Islamorada.

For trendy sporting goods and clothing, as well as fishing tackle that includes handmade rods, gaffs, flies and trolling lures and reels, stop at **H. T. Chittum & Co.** ~ MM 82.7, Islamorada; 305-664-4421.

NIGHTLIFE   There's live entertainment on the weekend in the restaurant/lounge at **Plantation Yacht Harbor Resort,** a pleasant spot overlooking Florida Bay. It's all blues music here, usually featuring a single performer but occasionally a top touring band. ~ MM 87, Islamorada; 305-852-2381.

Nightlife begins in the daytime at **Holiday Isles Resort,** with a host of party areas sporting such names as Jaws Raw Bar, Wreck Bar and the World Famous Tiki Bar. Signs also point you to "Kokomo," a beach bar named after the fact for the Beach Boys' famous song. There's canned and live music to suit a variety of tastes throughout the days and nights. Up in **Horizon,** atop the five-story main hotel, there are fine views of the ocean with quieter live entertainment for listening and dancing. ~ MM 84, Islamorada; 305-664-2321.

Next to the "all-you-can-eat" restaurant at Whale Harbor, the **Harbor Bar** features live rock music and a raw bar. Come early enough to watch the fishing boats come in. Some consider this place to be a mellow alternative to the area's late-night teen haunts. ~ MM 83.5, Islamorada; 305-664-9888.

You can enjoy a quiet drink at a table overlooking the Atlantic in Cheeca Lodge's elegant **Light Tackle Lounge.** There's also deck seating available. ~ MM 82.5, Islamorada; 305-664-4651.

In 1960, Hurricane Donna blew what is now the **Cabaña Bar** out to sea. After it was towed back, the place became a mellow bayside lounge. Live musicians perform reggae and easy-listening "sunset music" nightly. ~ MM 82, Islamorada; 305-664-4338.

PARKS   **LONG KEY STATE RECREATION AREA**   Like the key on which it is located, this park is long and narrow—its shoreline of shallow flats, thin beaches and mangrove lagoons all shaped by the usually gentle Atlantic waters. Mahogany, Jamaica dogwood, gumbo-limbo and other tropical trees inhabit the tangled hammocks that, along with the mangrove swamps, can be crossed on boardwalks and viewed from an observation tower. Even though the traffic of Route 1 is closer than you might wish, you can actually camp right next to the ocean, shaded by tall Australian pines. This is a good place for children to wade or swim, and saltwater fishing is excellent adjacent to the park and in deep Gulf Stream waters of the Atlantic. Facilities include picnic areas, restrooms, a nature trail, a canoe trail, showers, an observation tower and canoe rentals; groceries are nearby in Layton. Day-use fee, $3.20. ~ The recreation area is located on the ocean side of Route 1 at MM 67.5; 305-664-4815.

▲ There are 60 sites, including 30 with RV hookups, and six primitive sites; $24 per night, $26 for hookups.

▼▼▼▼▼▼▼▼▼▼
Marathon Area

The Marathon area actually encompasses a collection of islands from Conch Key (below MM 65) to the beginning of the Seven Mile Bridge (MM 47) and includes far more than the bustling, traffic-filled, friendly metropolis and its occasional suburbs and resorts. Just before the outskirts of the city lies the oceanfront community of Key Colony Beach, a designed village where even the smallest houses seem to have their own boat docks. And here and there among these islands and from their bridges you'll encounter open spaces and fine views of the ocean and Gulf.

SIGHTS

One of those views hits visitors immediately upon entering the Marathon area via **Long Key Bridge**. If you have not yet been overwhelmed by the realization that when you travel the Keys you're really heading out to sea, get ready. You'll certainly feel the impact after you leave Layton and cross the beautiful bridge over the point where the Atlantic Ocean meets the Gulf of Mexico between Long Key and the first little Conch Key. On most days, this meeting is calm and gentle. The horizon stretches blue on all sides as sea and sky meld. Travelers often stop at the little pull-offs on either end of this bridge—the second longest in the Keys—to take in the vastness of the water and the handsome bridge. Because the shore is sandy here, you will see people wading out in the shallow water or trying out their snorkeling and scuba gear.

After leaving the beautiful scenes at the Long Key Bridge, Route 1 continues through several small Keys, including Duck Key, once site of a salt-making enterprise and now inhabited by showy homes and a large resort, Hawk's Cay. Nearby **Grassy Key** is home of the **Dolphin Research Center**, where you can play and swim with the friendly creatures (reservations are required and you must be at least 12 years old). There are also five daily walking tours. Your money goes, in part, to the center's program of providing rest and recreation for dolphins who have become stressed-out from long years of performance and the crowded conditions of captivity. (Like humans, dolphins can suffer from ulcers and loss of appetite.) Closed Tuesday morning. Admission. ~ MM 59; 305-289-1121.

Continuing on Route 1, you will encounter population pockets and empty spaces, skirt the residential and vacation village of Key Colony Beach, and arrive finally at **Marathon**, the last good-sized town before the famous Seven Mile Bridge. Stop at the **Greater Marathon Chamber of Commerce** for information on this bustling area, which boasts shopping malls, a modern airport, commercial boat yards and lots of facilities for travelers. ~ MM 53.5; 305-743-5417, 800-262-7284.

HIDDEN ►   Hidden from the casual observer, though actually located in the heart of Marathon, is **Crane Point Hammock**, headquarters of Florida Keys Land and Sea Trust. Considered by many to be the most environmentally and historically significant piece of property in the Keys, this bayside 63-acre nature preserve of tropical hardwoods and mangrove wetlands contains many exotic tree specimens, archaeological sites and a historic Bahamian conch-style house. Admission. ~ MM 50; 305-743-3900.

Crane Point Hammock is also home of the **Museum of Natural History of the Florida Keys**, which features a re-created coral reef, displays on pirate life and American Indian and shipwreck artifacts. Admission. ~ 5550 Overseas Highway; 305-743-9100.

Exhibits at the **Florida Keys Children's Museum**, also in Crane Point Hammock, include a tropical Caribbean lagoon, marine touch tank, hawk habitat, iguana exhibit, historic sailing vessel and an American Indian hut built with palm fronds. Ideal for the entire family. Admission. ~ Crane Point Hammock; 305-743-9100.

LODGING   If you like a resort where everything is at your fingertips, the 60-acre **Hawk's Cay Resort and Marina** will fulfill your dreams. Here you can sleep in a spacious room decorated in salmon and teal and furnished with wickerwork rattan, dine in several very fine restaurants, bask beside the pool or on a pleasant manmade beach, play tennis and golf, or make arrangements with the concierge for charter fishing, diving or just about anything the Keys have to offer. The entire huge property is elegant but casual. The rates include a big gourmet breakfast buffet. ~ MM 61, Duck Key; 305-743-7000, 800-432-2242. ULTRA-DELUXE.

HIDDEN ►   You can have a basic motel room or a fully equipped efficiency at the **Valhalla Beach Resort Motel** and feel as if you are on a private island with a quiet Atlantic inlet and waving palms. The dozen units are strictly basic, but the tiny beach, little boat docks and considerable distance from traffic make this a quiet and special place. ~ MM 56.5, Marathon; 305-289-0616. MODERATE.

At roadside, it looks like the front of an ordinary motel. But don't be fooled by the plain exterior. Follow the lane that leads to the bay, and you'll find yourself in a shady oasis. This is **Banana Bay Resort**, ten secluded acres that will make you totally forget the endless stream of cars buzzing by at the doorstep on Route 1. The 61 guest rooms are decorated in Caribbean plantation–style, and most have private verandas. The resort offers a spa, a large fresh-water pool with restaurant and lounge, tennis courts, boat and wa-tersport rentals and charters for fishing, sailing and diving. There's a poolside continental breakfast buffet. ~ MM 49.5, Vaca Key; 305-743-3500, 800-226-2621. DELUXE TO ULTRA-DELUXE.

Several motels and small hotels line the narrow but pretty Atlantic Beach at Key Colony Beach. The **Key Colony Beach Motel** offers small, carpeted, functional rooms, and you can dive into the large heated pool on those rare days when the ocean is too cold. ~ 441 East Ocean Drive; 305-289-0411. MODERATE.

The **Ocean Beach Club** is a three-story coral affair with cool blue decor that suits its oceanside setting. Besides the deluxe-priced rooms, there are ultra-deluxe-priced apartments with fully fur-nished kitchens, a small pool, a jacuzzi and lots of beach chairs for sunbathing on the rare (for the Keys) strip of sand. Guests can watch the waves or fish from the pier. ~ 351 East Ocean Drive; 305-289-0525, 800-321-7213, fax 305-289-9703. DELUXE TO ULTRA-DELUXE.

Sombrero Resort and Lighthouse Marina offers bright, com-fortable garden and waterfront suites that have kitchens or kitch-enettes. Everything about the place is appropriately light and airily tropical, from the sparkling pool to the breezy restaurant and cheerful lounge. There are tennis courts, a pro-shop, sauna and 54-slip marina. Children are encouraged, making it a good family lodging. ~ 19 Sombrero Boulevard, Marathon; 305-743-2250, 800-433-8660, fax 305-743-2998. DELUXE TO ULTRA-DELUXE.

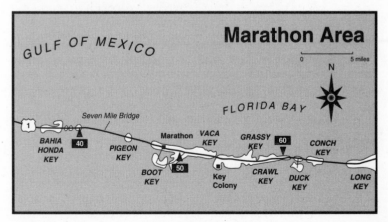

HIDDEN ▶   If you're looking for a bed and breakfast—and they are scarce in the Keys—try the **Hopp-Inn Guest House**, situated in an ocean-side home. There are four rooms for rent, each with private bath and entrance, air-conditioning, views of the ocean, good breezes and a full breakfast. Owners Joe and Joan Hopp also offer several apartments, without breakfasts but with full kitchens, at deluxe to ultra-deluxe rates. Papayas, bananas and figs grow right outside the door. Closed from May to October. ~ 500 Sombrero Beach Road, Marathon; 305-743-4118. MODERATE TO ULTRA-DELUXE

If you're in search of unique lodging, you might consider the double-decker houseboats at **Faro Blanco Marina Resort**. Securely moored, the boats are accessible from little private docks in a sheltered basin. These sedate blue-grey craft provide handsome quarters furnished formally enough for any ship's captain, and you can throw open the French doors to enjoy the comings and goings in the harbor. Cottages on the bay are also available. Guests have access to an Olympic-size swimming pool, four restaurants and two full-service marinas. Even more unusual are the two apartments in a four-story lighthouse dominating the marina. The interiors have a cozy, timeworn feel, with scads of old wood, creaking stairs and odd-shaped cubbyholes and cabinets. ~ 1996 Overseas Highway, Marathon; 305-743-9018, 800-759-3276, fax 305-743-2918. MODERATE TO ULTRA-DELUXE.

HIDDEN ▶   Reminiscent of old-time tourist cabins, **Conch Key Cottages** are located on their own tiny island accessible by a short causeway. This handful of rustic wooden cottages comes in a variety of sizes; some have screened porches and all are within easy access of a pleasant little beach. There's a swimming pool for all guests to use. Best of all, the cottages and apartments are away from busy Route 1. ~ Off Route 1 between MM 62 and 63; 305-289-1377, 800-330-1577, fax 305-743-8207. DELUXE TO ULTRA-DELUXE.

HIDDEN ▶   **Knights Key Inn** is a two-story unit of older vacation apartments, almost hidden alongside a neighboring campground, where you can dock your boat for free. If your efficiency is on the west side, you have a great view of the Seven Mile Bridge. Rooms are old-fashioned with a slightly nautical decor, and the whole place is submerged in lush tropical flora. There is a small picnic area with bougainvillea and palm trees; a few retirees stay here all winter. ~ MM 47, Marathon; 305-289-0289, 800-743-4786. MODERATE.

DINING   As its name suggests, this large nautical-themed restaurant is at the **Water's Edge**. It's on an inlet, rather than the open ocean, and overlooks an informal marina area. However, the setting is attractive, and the activity surrounding the boats moored just outside the windows is endlessly entertaining. The restaurant is actually part of

Hawk's Cay Resort, but is several blocks away—far enough to allow hotel guests to feel they've "gone out" to dinner. The American menu is varied and interesting, with an emphasis on fresh seafood. There's also a children's menu and an all-you-can-eat soup and salad bar. ~ MM 61, Duck Key; 305-743-7000. MODERATE TO DELUXE.

A teeny roadside stop with filmy jalousy windows and a handful of vinyl-topped tables, **Gallagher's** seems an unlikely candidate for gourmet food. But gourmet it is, from the filet mignon *au poivre* to the lobster chunks sautéed in escargot butter with garlic and shallots. For those who desire simpler dishes, there is broiled yellowtail and sometimes chicken and dumplings, and always a homebaked pie. Little extras like a relish tray and homemade rolls with honey only add to this unusual dining experience. Dinner hours are limited and reservations are recommended, so call ahead. Open Thursday through Monday. ~ MM 57.5, Marathon; 305-289-0454. MODERATE TO DELUXE.

> If you head toward the ocean at MM 47.5, you'll end up around the commercial fishing docks, where you can watch the comings and goings of shrimp boats and other crafts. ~ 11th Street.

Don Pedro demonstrates a creative use of a strip shopping center unit. Cuban cuisine is the feature of this sparkling blue-and-grey eatery located on an insignificant corner. All the entrées, such as *lechón asado* (roast pork), *churrasco* (Argentine steak), *boliche asado* (pot roast), and *picadillo* (a tasty hamburger dish), come with yellow rice, black beans, fried bananas and crispy Cuban bread. The very filling meals may be accompanied by steamy, thick Cuban coffee and topped off with a dessert of flan, a traditional baked custard. Closed Monday and Tuesday. ~ MM 53, Marathon; 305-743-5247. BUDGET TO MODERATE.

Brian's in Paradise has a menu with 12 large pages featuring humorous drawings of Keys wildlife and something to eat for everyone. The emphasis is on seafood, the most popular item being the "Marathon meal" that provides a good way to sample local favorites—conch chowder, conch fritters, fried shrimp and Key lime pie. Dinner selections include a spit-roasted chicken entrée appealingly named "Bird of Paradise." The wide variety of sandwiches are served all day. ~ MM 52, Marathon; 305-743-3183. BUDGET TO MODERATE.

The art deco menu plus the comical cartoons of fictional chefs beaming at you from the walls hint that **Chef's** is probably a fun place to eat. The small but well-balanced menu offers such items as rack of lamb, lobster sombrero and lobster sautéed with artichokes and mushrooms and served on pasta in a garlic and wine sauce. The fish du jour is prepared five different ways including blackened and baked with a pecan-butter topping. There is an open grill and a glassed-in dining area alongside the tennis courts. ~ Sombrero Resort, 19 Sombrero Boulevard, Marathon; 305-743-4108. MODERATE TO DELUXE.

You'd better like seafood if you stop at **The Cracked Conch**, which claims to have been "cracked up and conched out since 1979." Concessions are made for landlubbers, however, in the steak and chicken entrées. The main thing, of course, is the mollusk that comes out of the pretty pink shell—chowdered, frittered, cracked, burgered and sautéed. This is an unpretentious little place that is Keys to the core—that is, it sports a spacious bar and is not air-conditioned. But it's wide open to whatever breezes can be captured, and there's open-air seating out back under the branches of a great mahogany tree. ~ MM 49.5, Vaca Key; 305-743-2233. MODERATE TO DELUXE.

The lighthouse that distinguishes Faro Blanco Resort is authentic, and so is the fine dining at the resort's restaurant, **Kelsey's**. Along with creative treatments of local seafood, this sedately casual place prepares rack of lamb, roast Long Island duckling and grouper sautéed with mushrooms, roasted almonds and artichokes. The restaurant is lush with greenery, and its windows overlook the marina. Closed Monday during the summer. ~ MM 48.5, Marathon; 305-743-9018. MODERATE TO DELUXE.

HIDDEN ► If you wind down 15th Street past where you think it ends, you'll come to **Castaway**, a no-nonsense eatery on the working wharf where locals have been coming for several decades. There is a basic seafood menu with chicken and steak for the misguided, but the big come-on here is shrimp "steamed in beer—seconds on the house." They ply you with luscious hot buns dripping with honey even before you begin. There's a varied selection of wines. Dinner only. Closed Sunday and from September through mid-October. ~ Turn toward the ocean just below MM 48; 305-743-6247. MODERATE.

SHOPPING Don't miss **The Quay Shops**, a little cluster of weathered-grey boutiques that includes **Bayshore Clothing** for tropical fashions and **It's HIDDEN ► a Small World** (305-743-8430) for out-of-the-ordinary children's togs and toys. **Dangerous John Hubert's Hot Sauces and Cigars**, guaranteed to make smoke come out of your ears one way or another, is housed together with **Martha's Caribbean Cupboard** (305-743-9299), stocking mango marmalade and other delicacies, Key lime lotion, coffees and teas, and local pottery and carvings. **Marine Jewelry** (305-289-0628) offers gold and coral jewelry with nautical and sea-related themes (gold-capped shark teeth and gold Florida lobsters), while **Enchanted Elephant** (305-289-0646) has interesting eco-friendly gifts and an elephant "museum." ~ MM 54.

Being the largest populated area in the Middle Keys, Marathon has several shopping plazas and all the basic stores needed for daily living, as well as the usual souvenir dens. For originally designed, handpainted Florida Keys handbags and tropical clothes, stop at the **Brown Pelican Store**. ~ Kmart Shopping Plaza, MM 50; 305-743-3849.

If you are doing your own cooking, or you'd just like to peruse the catches-of-the-day, explore the collection of **seafood markets** along the wharves at the end of 11th or 15th Street. These are outlets for some of the area's serious commercial fishing. ~ On the oceanside near MM 48.

The **Water's Edge** overlooks the water beside the showy marina at Hawk's Cay. There's a casual mood and live music on weekends. ~ MM 61, Duck Key; 305-743-7000.

NIGHTLIFE

For dancing Thursday through Saturday nights try the **Hurricane Raw Bar**. There's usually a live band during the summer. ~ MM 49.5, 4650 Overseas Highway; 305-743-5755.

Happy hour offers live entertainment and hors d'oeuvres at **Royal Pelican**. ~ MM 54, at the Holiday Inn; 305-289-0222.

The Quay is so popular that it has clones in Key Largo and Key West. You can enjoy the sunsets, full seafood meals and tropical drinks at this wicker-furnished, brightly decorated Gulfside spot. ~ MM 54, Marathon; 305-289-1810.

Chef's Lounge, at the Sombrero Resort, is a tiki bar where your drink will be delivered to you poolside. ~ 19 Sombrero Boulevard, Marathon; 305-743-4108.

You can dance or play darts as local and imported bands play soft rock and other music every night at **Angler's Lounge** at Faro Blanco Resort. This second-story nightspot has windows all around and a wonderful view of the harbor and bay. ~ MM 48.5, Marathon; 305-743-9018.

Several arts organizations are active in the Marathon area, sponsoring or producing concerts and plays from time to time. For information on what may be going on during your stay, contact the **Marathon Community Theatre**. ~ 305-743-0994.

SOMBRERO BEACH PARK ⚓ This community park is mostly a generous windswept grassy area with a few palm trees and a long, narrow spit of sand along the ocean, offering one of the few public beaches around. Though not spectacular, it is a good place for some sun and relaxation and an ideal romping spot for children. Swimming is pleasant in usually clear, calm ocean water. There are picnic areas, restrooms and a playground. ~ The park is located on Sombrero Beach Road at MM 50 in Marathon.

PARKS

◀ *HIDDEN*

▼▼▼▼▼▼▼▼▼▼▼▼
Lower Keys Area

The Lower Keys, which begin at MM 40 just below the Seven Mile Bridge and extend to around MM 5, are *different*. They are different in geological makeup, in flora and fauna and even in ambience and pace from the rest of the Keys. Geologically, their fossil coral base is layered with a limestone that's called oolite (for its egg-shaped granules). Some of the islands of the Lower Keys are forested with sturdy pine trees, others with tall tropical hardwoods where orchids and bromeliads thrive. A number of endangered species, including the unique Key deer, struggle for survival on these low-lying islands.

Big Pine Key is the largest of the islands and second in area only to Key Largo in the entire Keys. Wildlife refuges and shopping centers share this island, the former protecting much of the unique plant and animal life, the latter offering necessary services for the people who choose to live in what seems a quieter, lonelier region than those on either side.

The Lower Keys boast the best beach south of the mainland and access to a fine protected section of coral reef offshore in the Atlantic. Though there are pockets of development, from collections of little frame houses to assorted elegant residences, frenetic modernization seems to have been held at bay. With some unassuming screened-in eateries, scattered modest lodgings and significant protected wild areas, this region offers more chances to experience the "old Keys" than any other.

SIGHTS

Perhaps the most impressive sight in the Lower Keys is its initial access, the magnificent **Seven Mile Bridge**, spanning the sea between Marathon and Sunshine Key. The bridge that carries the Overseas Highway today is the "new" bridge, built in 1982 to replace the terrifyingly narrow but equally impressive structure that parallels it on the Gulf side. The old bridge, referred to as "the longest fishing pier in the world," crosses **Pigeon Key**, which you can't reach but can view from your lofty height above the sea. Once a railroad camp for Henry Flagler's crew, Pigeon Key is an important historic site; efforts are underway to preserve its natural state and historic old conch-style houses.

Unlike the upper and middle Keys, most of the Lower Keys seem to lie at right angles to the highway. Their geology, and hence their vegetation and wildlife, differ in many respects from that of their neighbors to the northeast. **Bahia Honda Key**, for example, features some white sand beaches; many unusual species of plants and birds are found throughout the Lower Keys. ~ MM 37–38.

As you look across to the southern peninsula of Bahia Honda Key, you will see a magnificent section of the old **Flagler Bridge**, with the railroad trestle on one level and the automobile highway arching above it, a masterpiece of engineering for its day.

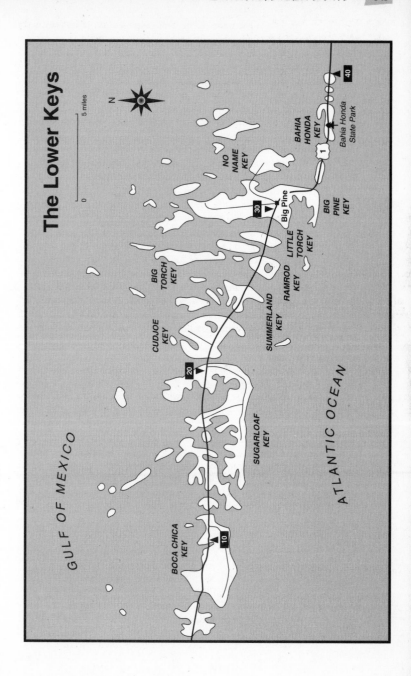

At MM 33 you arrive at **Big Pine Key**. Stop at the **Lower Keys Chamber of Commerce** for a lot of good information about this area. Big Pine Key is second only to Key Largo in size, but its character is quite different. Here there are blooming subdivisions, pine trees, good-sized shopping centers and freshwater sink holes formed in the oolic rock foundation of the island. The contest between development and the wild is apparent. ~ MM 31; 305-872-2411.

Living in uneasy relationship with the ever-growing population of Big Pine Key are the Key deer, a miniature subspecies of white-tailed deer that grow to be only about two feet in height. In the 1940s, the population almost disappeared, inspiring the establishment of the 7962-acre **National Key Deer Refuge**. Occasionally you can spot the world's tiniest deer in the wilderness areas of the refuge, especially in the early morning or late afternoon, but be warned that there are heavy fines for feeding or harming these endangered, fragile animals. ~ Headquarters at the Winn Dixie Shopping Center on Key Deer Boulevard; 305-872-2239.

Not far from the town of Big Pine lies a good-sized freshwater rock quarry pond called **Blue Hole**, the only one of its kind in the entire Keys. It is inhabited by several alligators, who often lie near the shore, as well as turtles and various wading birds and fish. ~ 2.25 miles north of Route 1 on Key Deer Boulevard. The nearby **Jack C. Watson Nature Trail** meanders through a typical Big Pine Key habitat of palms and slash pine and skirts a unique hardwood hammock.

HIDDEN ► Only reachable by boat, **Looe Key National Marine Sanctuary** is an exceedingly popular diving site. The spectacular coral formations of this five-square-mile area and the crystal-clear waters make it delightful even for novice snorkelers. Several wrecked ships also lie within the sanctuary, including the 1744 British frigate HMS *Looe*. ~ 6.7 nautical miles southeast of Big Pine Key; headquarters at 216 Ann Street, Key West; 305-292-0311. Please call the Chamber of Commerce for snorkeling and diving information.

HIDDEN ► Enjoy a sea kayaking adventure in the Great White Heron National Wildlife Refuge by calling **Reflection Nature Tours**. Their wildlife and educational trips give you a chance to see coral and

HEY, HEY, HEY

If you survey the sky on the Gulf side, you'll catch a glimpse of **Fat Albert** floating high above the water. A large, white, blimp-shaped radar balloon, he's diligently on the lookout for illegal drug traffickers and other inappropriate interlopers. To keep him from being *too* diligent, he is moored to a missile tracking station on Cudjoe Key.

sponges in the shallow water of the red mangroves. ~ One half mile north on Barry Avenue, Little Torch Key; 305-872-2896.

By now you have probably noticed that some of the telephone poles along the Overseas Highway seem to be topped with great untidy piles of sticks and twigs. These are **osprey nests**. If you look closely, you will occasionally see a bird with its young. Ospreys are regular residents of the Keys; some seem uninhibited by the cars and 18-wheelers that constantly whiz beneath them.

If you take a detour toward the Gulf on lower Sugarloaf Key, you'll get a glance at the **Perky Bat Tower**. This Dade County pine curiosity was built in 1929 as the brainchild of Richter C. Perky, who hoped to get the menacing mosquito population under control by importing a population of insect-devouring bats to take up residence in this louvered bat condo. Some say the bats never arrived, others claim that they came and, not satisfied with their carefully designed accommodations, took off for preferable climes. At any rate, the novel structure still stands and is on the National Register of Historic Places. ~ Off Route 1 at MM 17.

◀ HIDDEN

Heading toward Key West, you will see increasingly less development and more mangroves. Here and there you'll spot folks fishing off the old bridges. The densest residential area surrounds the Naval Air Base on Boca Chica Key. When you reach Stock Island, you have arrived in the suburbs of Key West.

LODGING

Generic motels and small resorts appear here and there in the Lower Keys; rates are often lower than in nearby Key West. If you look hard, you'll also discover that some of the very best lodgings in this area are the hidden ones.

There are three handsome duplex cabins on the Gulf side of **Bahia Honda State Park**. Though the cabins are not really hidden because you can see them from the highway, many visitors are unaware that the six grey frame units on stilts are available for rental. The fully equipped lodgings with spacious decks can accommodate up to six people. Make reservations by phone or in person, up to a year ahead. ~ MM 37; 305-872-2353. DELUXE.

If you'd like to rent a vacation home away from the highway, contact **Big Pine Vacation Rentals**. All the homes are on the waterfront, some with boat dockage and fishing. Three-night minimum stay required. ~ MM 29.5, Big Pine Key; 305-872-9863. DELUXE.

The motto of **Barnacle Bed and Breakfast**, "barefoot oceanfront living with panache," says it all. The owners built their elegant home in the shape of a six-pointed star, creating a collection of interestingly designed, distinctive rooms around a central atrium where gourmet breakfasts are served. Guests stay in either of two rooms with private baths in the main house or in one of the two efficiencies in a many-angled annex. ~ 1557 Long Beach Drive, one

◀ HIDDEN

and a half miles from MM 33; 305-872-3298, 800-465-9100, fax 305-872-3863; e-mail barnacle@iamerica.net. DELUXE.

HIDDEN ► **Deer Run Bed and Breakfast** offers three rooms with separate entrances and private baths in a very attractive Florida-style house with high ceilings, Bahama fans and good views of the ocean. A 52-foot veranda overlooks the sea and the natural grounds where Key deer roam. The owner has cleverly decorated the outdoor area with driftwood and other jetsam deposited by the Atlantic currents onto the beach. Guests enjoy an outdoor hot tub and full American breakfasts. Outdoor hammocks, chaise longues and a barbecue grill help you feel at home. Adults only. ~ Long Beach Drive, two miles from MM 33; 305-872-2015. MODERATE TO DELUXE.

If you'd like to stay near the area where the Key deer roam, contact **Canal Cottage**. This quaint, natural-wood stilt home is so far off the beaten path that you'll have to ask for directions when you call to reserve for a two-night minimum stay. Depend on Bahama fans and breezes to keep you cool in this casual tropical setting; everything is furnished, including breakfast food. Guests have access to a swim and tennis club. ~ Big Pine Key; 305-872-3881. DELUXE.

HIDDEN ► The windswept, old-time one- and two-bedroom cottages at the **Old Wooden Bridge Fishing Camp** are especially popular with anglers and divers who don't need a lot of amenities other than a comfortable, plain cabin, a full kitchen and access to the water. Rental boats are available, or you can stroll on over to the Bogie Channel Bridge for some great fishing. ~ Bunta Risa at Bogie Channel; take Wilder Road at MM 30 and follow signs to No Name Key; 305-872-2241. MODERATE.

HIDDEN ► "Tropical paradise" is a worn-out phrase, but it really fits **Little Palm Island**. This five-acre island of waving palms and green lawns features 14 luxurious two-suite villas, each one facing the water. You'll enjoy generous thatched-roof quarters with abundant windows, tropical decor, a private sundeck, meals in the excellent restaurant, boat transportation from Little Torch Key and enough quiet to calm the most jangled nerves. If you want to go fishing, touring nature preserves, diving or sightseeing, Little Palm will make the arrangements; but if you want to stay around, you can sail, windsurf, browse in the library and the gift shop, get a massage or just luxuriate on the island once enjoyed by Harry Truman and other notables. ~ Offshore at MM 28.5, Little Torch Key; 305-872-2524, 800-343-8567, fax 305-872-4843. ULTRA-DELUXE.

Sugar Loaf Lodge is one of the "full service" resorts with average but pleasant motel rooms and efficiencies, most of them facing the water. Full service here means not only a pool, restaurant and lounge, but a three-times-a-day dolphin show by long-time resident Sugar, a marina, mini-golf, tennis and fishing charters. It's also very convenient to Key West. ~ MM 17, Sugarloaf Key; 305-745-3211, 800-553-6097, fax 305-745-3389. DELUXE TO ULTRA-DELUXE.

The **Cedar Inn Restaurant and Lounge** is plain but a little less so than some of the other popular Lower Keys eateries. Fresh fish is served broiled, fried, stuffed or Florentine. They also have stuffed lobster in season, prime rib and a 'gator appetizer that most people try just so they can say they have. ~ MM 31; 305-872-4031. MODERATE TO DELUXE.

DINING

Open for breakfast, lunch and dinner, the **Dip 'N Deli** is a nice place whose name tells all. There are fresh salads, 22 kinds of sandwiches, soups and lots of ice cream treats, including old-fashioned sodas and milkshakes. Dinner features barbecue, chicken and steak entrées. There's also lots of local chatter going on here, as well as the refreshing break from the ever-present seafood. ~ MM 31; 305-872-3030. BUDGET TO MODERATE.

The most Jamaican things about **Montego Bay** are its name and a few spicy dishes that emulate that island's fiery "jerk" seasoning. This MoBay is two large, pleasant rooms, one of which is a lounge. Both are dark-walled with bamboo accents, and there is a small rock garden and fish pond beyond sliding glass doors off the dining room. The menu is mostly American in character, with fresh local seafood, hand-cut steaks, veal and pasta. Red Stripe beer does show up, however. ~ MM 30, Big Pine Key; 305-872-3009. MODERATE.

To get away from it all in style, plan to dine at the restaurant on **Little Palm Island**. You have to call ahead for a reservation; they will tell you when the boat will pick you up to take you to the lovely, luxurious island resort. If you're wise, you'll go in time to watch the sunset while sipping a cocktail beside the sandy beach or partaking of the fish of the day, pan-seared Gulf shrimp, breast of chicken or any of the other Continental entrées. ~ Offshore from Little Torch Key, MM 28.5; 305-872-2524. DELUXE TO ULTRA-DELUXE.

◄ HIDDEN

Montes Restaurant & Fish Market is a bare-bones place with plastic-covered round picnic tables and good old-fashioned fried seafood platters and baskets with french fries, cole slaw and sauce. Sit on the porch beside the canal and enjoy what you're supposed to eat in the Keys—conch chowder, conch salad, conch fritters, stone crabs and shrimp in beer. ~ MM 25, Summerland Key; 305-745-3731. MODERATE.

Mangrove Mama's is such a wildly decorated, side-of-the-road, banana tree–surrounded eating establishment that you probably wouldn't stop unless someone recommended it—and plenty of Lower Keys folks do just that, with great enthusiasm. The floor is concrete, tablecloths are minimal, the chairs don't match and resident cats look longingly at your dinners. But the menu, though brief and to the point, is somewhat fancier than you'd expect, with such treats as baked stuffed shrimp and chicken and scallop Caribbean, sautéed with bacon and served in a creamy dijon sauce. The Key lime pie is superb and the herb teas and homemade rolls are as pleasant a surprise as the handsome brick fireplace, used on very rare chilly nights. Mama's has live music on weekends. ~ MM 20; 305-745-3030. MODERATE TO DELUXE.

SHOPPING

For all the basic necessities, the main place for shopping in the Lower Keys is the **Big Pine Key Shopping Plaza**. ~ On Key Deer Boulevard just off Route 1 at MM 30.

At **Blue Moon Trader**, the New Age is alive and well. Standing high on stilts, the pretty pink "earth-friendly" building welcomes visitors with the sound of wind chimes and houses several levels of gifts and services for "conscious living"—jewelry, pottery, crystals and lots of other things. Bring your kids to play, receive a tarot card reading or get a massage for yourself. ~ MM 29.7, Big Pine Key; 305-872-8864.

Edie's Hallmark Shop is far more than its name implies. Here you'll find gifts, party goods and a book section with top-notch vacation reading, as well as a good supply of Florida and Keys books and guides. ~ Big Pine Key Shopping Plaza; 305-872-3933.

NIGHTLIFE

The **Cedar Inn Restaurant and Lounge** has live entertainment on weekend nights and occasional special events such as sock hops and the like. ~ MM 31; 305-872-4031.

HIDDEN ▶

For an evening with the locals, drop in at the **No Name Pub**, a funky, run-down eating and drinking establishment with a carved-up wooden bar, over 20 kinds of beer and a pool table. There's occasionally a pig roast and always the "best pizza in the known universe." This is a fun place that just about anybody can direct you to. ~ North Watson Boulevard, Big Pine Key; 305-872-9115.

Three nights a week there's live rock-and-roll performed by local bands at **Looe Key Reef Resort**. ~ MM 27.5, Ramrod Key; 305-872-2215.

Pirate's Lounge is a typical resort-motel nightspot. This one has weekend entertainment and dancing, and boasts oversized piña coladas and strawberry daiquiris. ~ Sugar Loaf Lodge, MM 17, Sugarloaf Key; 305-745-3211.

PARKS

BAHIA HONDA STATE PARK 🏊 🚤 ⛱ This southernmost state park offers what many consider the best swimming beaches in the Keys—wider and leading into deeper water than most. Remnants of the undeveloped Keys remain in this beautiful park— silver palms, satinwood, dwarf morning glories and a number of rare birds such as the roseate spoonbill and white-crowned pigeon. You may camp in the wide open spaces (best choice during mosquito season) in view of a handsome segment of Henry Flagler's original old bridge, or in the shady hardwood hammock at Sandspur Beach. Fishing is excellent, both in the bay and the ocean; guides are available during tarpon season. Swimming is also excellent, both in the Atlantic Ocean and Gulf of Mexico. Facilities include picnic areas, restrooms, vacation cabin rentals, a bathhouse, nature trail, concession stand, marina, snorkel shop and limited groceries. ~ Entrance on ocean side of Route 1 at MM 36.5; 305-872-2353.

▲ There are 80 tent sites (48 with water and electricity); $24 per night ($2 more for hookups).

▼▼▼▼▼▼▼▼▼ Key West

Though not quite in the tropics, Key West is to all appearances a tropical island. Lying low on a shimmering sea, it boasts backyards lush with hibiscus, oleanders, frangipani and kapok and mango trees. Its generous harbors are filled with hybrid fleets of battered fishing craft, glass-bottom boats and handsome yachts. Date and coconut palms rustle like dry paper in the usually gentle and dependable breezes that come in off the sea. Heat pervades, but even in midsummer it's seldom unbearable. Key West is a small town sort of place where narrow streets are lined with picket fences and lovely old frame houses. At the same time, it's a traveler's haven with classy hotels and happy hours. The cul-de-sac of the Overseas Highway, it's unlike any other city in the United States.

Numerous well-known artists and writers, most notably Ernest Hemingway and Tennessee Williams, have found Key West a place of inspiration. The town boasts several Pulitzer Prize winners among its residents. Loafers have discovered Key West to be a comfortable spot for idling away the hospitably temperate days. Gays and others with alternative lifestyles have found a tolerant atmosphere. Jazz performers, country-and-western singers and classical musicians have contributed to the sounds of the little city.

Each group has added color and contrast to the rich island tapestry. Today, Key West is a tourist town, one of the nation's chief travel destinations. Here most visitors have no trouble finding something to their liking. They can find tours, nightlife, souvenir shops, arts events, festivals and a nightly sunset celebration. Fishing, diving and boat trips to the Gulf Stream and tiny out-islands are added attractions.

SIGHTS

It's easy to get around Key West; the entire island is only about four miles long and two miles wide. Stop in at the **Key West Welcome Center** for a taste of the area. This is near MM 4, but from here on you can stop counting mile markers and return to familiar street numbers. ~ 3840 North Roosevelt Boulevard; 305-296-4444.

By following Route 1 you will arrive in **Old Town**, the historic and main tourist area of Key West, just about where North Roosevelt Boulevard becomes Truman Avenue. This is a helter-skelter sort of place, with grand old Victorian houses, inviting alleys, junky souvenir shops, rocking-and-rolling bars, classy hotels, intimate guest houses, crowded marinas, street hawkers and incredible sunsets all tossed together into a colorful, noisy, artsy collage.

Away from Old Town, the remainder of the island includes settled residential areas, predictable shopping and a number of interesting sights that should pull you away from the tourist trappings. Here you are likely to run into those descendants of old Key West and the lower Keys who proudly refer to themselves as "conchs." The original settlers were named after the giant shells that were so much a part of their sea-oriented lives.

Although Old Town is small enough for pleasant walking, and the whole island for biking, it helps to get oriented on one of several available tours. Besides, you'll pick up some very interesting history of this unique island city. The trackless **Conch Tour Train** has been orienting visitors for over 30 years with narrated 14-mile island tours, leaving at regular intervals daily. ~ Two depots, one near the Welcome Center at 3850 North Roosevelt Boulevard and one at 303 Front Street; 305-294-5161.

Old Town Trolley Tour meanders through the historic old streets and has the added advantage of unlimited drop-offs and pick-ups on your ticket, so when you see something of particular interest, you can stop and explore, then hop back on the next trolley that comes by. ~ Leaves every 30 minutes from the trolley barn at 1910 North Mallory Square, the Welcome Center and most major hotels; 305-296-6688.

HIDDEN ►   For a more indigenous excursion, join the **Key West Nature Bike Tour**. It is hosted by Lloyd Mager, an environmentalist who, during his 20 years in Key West, has never owned a car or a motorbike. The 90-minute ride meanders down hidden side streets, visits little-known oddities (including several local people) and explores the island's luxurious foliage. A passionate guide, Mager started his tours because he "couldn't stand that someone would leave here never smelling a gardenia or tasting a mango or feeling the thrill of Key West by bike." ~ 305-294-1882.

If you'd rather get oriented on your own, stop at the **Key West Chamber of Commerce** and pick up a *Pelican Path* walking guide or *Solares Hill Guide to Old Key West*. The latter, definitely the best local guide to Old Town, is named for the island's highest point, which rises a whole 16 feet above sea level. In the old days, the Solares guide was witty and weird, but along with some of Key

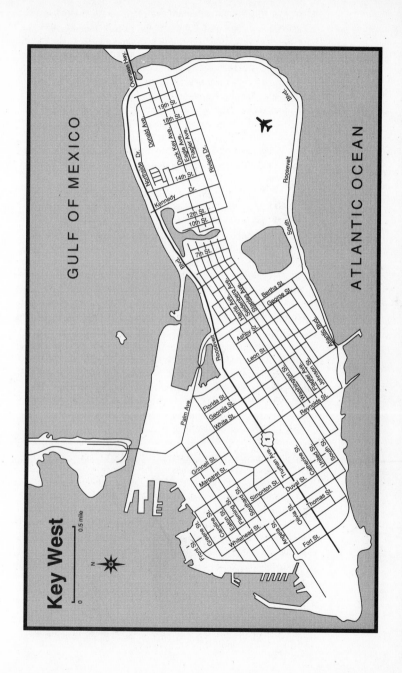

Key West

GULF OF MEXICO

ATLANTIC OCEAN

West, it has turned decidedly proper. Still, there are many historical and hidden gems and a few strange stops, including the old Busy Bee Bakery and a lane called Love and Grunt Bone Alley, where grits and grunts were once eaten. ~ 402 Wall Street; 305-294-2587.

The factory that was parent to the **Key West Cigar Factory** dates back to the mid-19th century. Though smaller than the original establishments, this shop is the place to watch cigars being hand-rolled the way they've always been. ~ 3 Pirates Alley at Front Street; 305-294-3470. Cigars are also rolled and sold at **Rodriguez Cigar Factory**. Closed Sunday. ~ 113 Kino Plaza; 305-296-0167.

The Richard Peacon House was built in the late 1800s by the owner of Key West's largest grocery store. It has distinctive octagon-shaped verandas and, some say, a ghost. ~ 712 Eaton Street.

History buffs will enjoy searching for the gun turret from the **Battleship USS Maine**. Not exactly hidden, but somewhat hard to find, this is a little monument to those who died in the tragic sinking that set off the Spanish-American War. ~ Near drop boxes at the Post Office, Front and Greene streets.

The impressive **Key West United Methodist Church** has two-foot-thick walls that were made from solid limestone quarried right beside the sanctuary. Built between 1877 and 1892, the handsome church has a native mahogany ceiling and a teakwood chancel. ~ Eaton Street at Simonton Street; 305-296-2392.

The most notable feature of Old Town is the architecture. Many of the beautiful old houses you see were built of wood by ships' carpenters in a blend of styles that came to be known as **conch-style houses**. Influenced by the varied backgrounds of their owners and the demands of the hurricane-prone climate, the result is an eclectic architectural heritage unique to this island city.

For an introductory sampling of these conch houses, start at the corner of Eaton and William streets, where two **Bahama Houses** stand side by side. These dwellings are the only ones known to have been shipped in their entirety to Key West from the Bahamas. Built in the mid-1800s by master shipbuilders, they feature unusual beaded siding, mahogany window sashes and broad verandas. ~ 730 Eaton Street and 408 William Street.

Next door, the **Samuel Filer House**, built around 1885, is a study in black and white contrasted with an etched cranberry glass transom and double-screen door. ~ 724 Eaton Street.

Only the front of the **Bartlum/Forgarty House** was floated over from the Bahamas on a schooner. The mid-19th-century dwelling is constructed with wooden pegs. ~ 718 Eaton Street.

No gimmicks, only immaculately preserved history awaits at the **Donkey Milk House**. The 1866 Classic Revival house is named for the donkey-drawn carts that once gathered in the courtyard to collect milk for their local deliveries. The home's original owner was Peter Williams, a U.S. marshal who saved his neighbor's house from Key West's devastating 1886 fire by dynamiting Eaton Street. In 1890, after his wife bore their second set of twins, he purchased another house, wheeled it across the island and attached it to the back of this one. Where the two houses meet, it's impossible to tell. There are, however, many gems here, including the 1890 Spanish tile floor and the black walnut staircase, the hand-decorated ceilings and the turn-of-the-century leather mirror and wooden thermometer in one of the bathrooms. The light fixtures—both gas and electric—tell the story of how modern conveniences came late to Key West. Admission. ~ 613 Eaton Street; 305-296-1866.

With delicate double balustrades, beveled glass and fan windows, ornate trim and 22 rooms, the Queen Anne–style **Curry Mansion** presents a three-story display of millionaire life at the turn of the century. Only the Bahama-style hinged shutters are common to other, less opulent homes of early Key West. The showcase house is open for tours daily, showing off the luxurious appointments and fine 19th-century furnishings. Admission. ~ 511 Caroline Street; 305-294-5349.

Although Key West's first lighthouse was built in 1825, a hurricane swept it away some 20 years later. A new structure was built inland in 1847 and guided ships through the water until 1969. Today, along with the adjacent lighthouse keeper's house, it contains the **Lighthouse Museum** operated by the Key West Art and Historical Society. For a panoramic view of this flat little island, climb the 88 steps to the top. See the huge Fresnel lens that cost $1 million back in the mid-19th century, vintage photographs and nautical charts, ship models and memorabilia from area lighthouses. Admission. ~ 938 Whitehead Street; 305-294-0012.

Though many famous authors have spent time in Key West, none has left as strong a mark as Ernest Hemingway. He and his wife Pauline bought a fine old coral-rock house in which they lived from 1931 until the end of their marriage in 1940. Today, the **Ernest Hemingway Home and Museum** is a tribute to "Papa's" life and work, for it was here that he created such masterpieces as *A Farewell to Arms* and *For Whom the Bell Tolls*. Tours are given daily, reflecting on Hemingway's works and his rigorous lifestyle. Through the marvelous house and luxuriant grounds roam sleek six-toed cats, said to be descendants of Hemingway's own; they lie irreverently on his works, snooze on his Spanish furniture and stalk the rooms that still reflect the writer's colorful personality. Admission. ~ 907 Whitehead Street; 305-294-1575.

The **Audubon House** is a fine sample of early Key West architecture; its restoration inspired a city-wide interest in preserving other historic structures. Furnished with fine antiques of the 18th and 19th centuries, the three-story frame house is held together entirely by wooden pegs and is an excellent example of the ship-builders' craft. It now serves as a museum housing an extensive collection of works by John James Audubon, the famous painter and naturalist. A lush one-acre tropical garden surrounds the house. Admission. ~ 205 Whitehead Street; 305-294-2116.

At the **Key West Municipal Aquarium** you can touch a starfish or watch a shark being fed. Opened in 1934, the aquarium was the first visitors' attraction built in the Keys. Today the exhibits include a turtle pool, shark tanks, live coral and many other samples of Atlantic and Gulf underwater life. The "Atlantic Shores" exhibit is a red mangrove ecosystem complete with wildlife. Guided tours and feedings take place four times a day. Admission. ~ 1 Whitehead Street; 305-296-2051.

If you've ever wondered how much a gold bar weighs or if rubies still sparkle after centuries on the bottom of the sea, visit **Mel Fisher Maritime Heritage Society Museum**. The place literally dazzles with gold chains, jewel-studded crosses and flagons, and great piles of gleaming coins—all treasures gathered by Fisher and his crew of divers from the sunken ships *Atocha* and *Margarita*. You really are allowed to lift the gold bar, though you can't take it with you. Admission. ~ 200 Greene Street; 305-294-2633.

Though nautical archaeologists may frown on treasure-seeking today, "wreckers" were once an important part of Keys society, varying from honest salvagers of broken, stranded ships to clever and unscrupulous opportunists. At **The Wrecker's Museum** you can learn about this unusual 19th-century profession while also admiring Key West's Oldest House. Built around 1829, this nine-room pine structure houses period antiques, as well as ship models and sea artifacts. Of particular interest is a built-to-scale mid-Victorian conch-style dollhouse complete with a miniature mural of early Key West in its dining room. Admission. ~ 322 Duval Street; 305-294-9502.

If, as many locals say, Key West is doomed to desecration by cheesy tourist shops, none could be a better example than the **Ripley's Believe It Or Not! Odditorium** settling into The Strand, the gloriously ornate 1930s movie house. It definitely is an odd place, with a pricey admission fee and 10,000 square feet of believable and unbelievable gimmicks. There's a "hurricane hallway" where you're nearly blown away and a "tropical rainforest" with drums, daggers and "authentic" shrunken heads. On the positive side, kids will love it. Admission. ~ 527 Duval Street; 305-293-9694.

Every visitor to Key West inevitably witnesses a sunset at **Mallory Square**, a Key West institution that will make you feel like you're part of a Mayan ritual. You'll find bagpipers, jugglers, fire-eaters and people who think it's fun to stand on one foot for half an hour. As the great moment nears, a cheer rises from the crowd, reaching fever pitch as the sun hits the horizon. ~ Northwest end of Duval Street.

The city of Key West grows many of its landscaping plants at the **Charles "Sonny" McCoy Indigenous Park**, a showplace for trees and plants native to the region. You may wander inside the gates of the park during the daytime and learn to recognize the lignum vitae, silver palm and a number of tropical trees found only in the Keys. There is a fish pond hidden away in the back. Closed weekends. ~ Atlantic Boulevard at White Street; 305-292-8157.

Also on the grounds is the **Wildlife Rescue of Florida Keys**, where injured birds are rehabilitated and then released back into the wild. From an observation platform that offers a view of the island's salt pond, you can see heron, ibis, gallinule and migratory birds that gather here. ~ McCoy Indigenous Park, White Street and Atlantic Boulevard; 305-294-1441.

The historic **West Martello Towers** are the enchanting home of Key West Garden Club's **Joe Allen Garden Center**. The remains of the once-upon-a-time fort, with its crumbling brick walls and arches and its massive banyan trees and old palms, create a pleasant, restful environment for permanent seed displays, numerous bromeliads and other tropical flora usually confined to green-

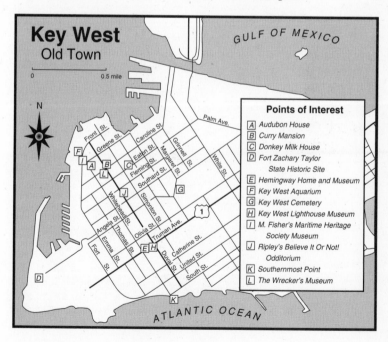

Key West
Old Town

GULF OF MEXICO

0 ____ 0.5 mile

N

Palm Ave.

Front St.
Greene St.
Caroline St.
Eaton St.
Fleming St.
Margaret St.
Grinnell St.
White St.
Southard St.
Whitehead St.
Simonton St.
Angela St.
Thomas St.
Olivia St.
Truman Ave.
Fort St.
Emma St.
Duval St.
Catherine St.
United St.
South St.

1

Points of Interest

- A Audubon House
- B Curry Mansion
- C Donkey Milk House
- D Fort Zachary Taylor State Historic Site
- E Hemingway Home and Museum
- F Key West Aquarium
- G Key West Cemetery
- H Key West Lighthouse Museum
- I M. Fisher's Maritime Heritage Society Museum
- J Ripley's Believe It Or Not! Odditorium
- K Southernmost Point
- L The Wrecker's Museum

ATLANTIC OCEAN

houses, and spectacular seasonal displays. Closed Monday and Tuesday. ~ Atlantic Boulevard and White Street; 305-294-3210.

"I Told You I Was Sick," reads the straightforward message immortalized on a gravestone in the **Key West Cemetery**. Due to the rocky geology of the island, many of the stone-encased caskets rest above ground, often carrying curious and, what seem now, humorous messages such as the one placed by a grieving widow: "At Least I Know Where He's Sleeping Tonight." History abounds in this enchanting and poignant spot, too, as in the special memorial to those who died at the sinking of the U.S. Battleship *Maine* in Havana harbor in 1898. You may stroll the cemetery until 6 p.m.; tours are given on Tuesday, Thursday and Sunday. ~ Angela and Margaret streets; 305-292-8177.

From the top of the citadel of the **East Martello Museum** you can get a magnificent view of the island and the Atlantic, just as the Union Army builders of this 1862 Civil War brick fortress planned. Today the historic structure houses 11 rooms and a large collection of Key West artifacts and serves as both a museum of Key West history and a gallery displaying the work of Keys artists. The fort's tower alone, with vaulted ceilings and spiral staircase, is worth a visit and, at the top, it affords you a view of the Gulf and the Atlantic. Admission. ~ 3501 South Roosevelt Boulevard; 305-296-3913.

Few developments have caused so much controversy on this tiny island as the **Truman Annex**. Owned for decades by the Navy, the quiet, shady 103-acre parcel was the last big piece of undeveloped land on Key West when it was auctioned in 1986 to a wealthy Sikh from Maine. Since then, expensive condominiums, a complex of Victorian-style houses, marinas and luxury hotels have been built. But the public is still welcome to tour the grounds and historic buildings, which include the surgeon's quarters, the old weather station and the marine hospital. ~ Main entrance at Thomas and Southard streets; 305-296-5601.

Today you can drive through the annex's wrought-iron gates, past the Bahama-style police with white pith helmets, and watch

RELIEF FOR REEFS

Before you visit the coral reef, stop by the **Reef Relief Environmental Center and Store**. The tiny place is packed with exhibits and information on the reef and how to protect it, as well as other fragile ecosystems such as mangrove forests and seagrass beds. It's run by the nonprofit Reef Relief, one of Florida's most powerful environmental organizations. ~ 201 William Street; 305-294-3100.

the new conch houses go up while the old ones tumble down. Here also is **Harry S Truman's Little White House**, built in 1890, where presidents Truman, Eisenhower and Kennedy vacationed. The handsome white clapboard building has two facades and spacious porches enclosed with wooden louvers. Admission. ~ 111 Front Street; 305-294-9911.

Recently rediscovered and unearthed from the sands, the **Fort Zachary Taylor State Historic Site** is a treasure trove of Civil War weaponry and memorabilia. The excavations of the 1845 fort have revealed beautiful mid-19th-century arched brickwork, parade grounds and the largest collection of Civil War cannons in the U.S. Admission. ~ Southwestern point of island, off Southard Street; 305-292-6713.

◄ HIDDEN

The Garden Club of Key West owns a small but nicely laid-out and well-marked **Botanical Garden** where you can get acquainted with many of the trees and other indigenous flora that grow in this distinctive region. There are two freshwater ponds, and if you look hard enough, you may catch sight of a rare butterfly. ~ College Road and Aguero Circle, Stock Island; 305-294-3168.

◄ HIDDEN

You won't find signs for **Nancy Forrester's Secret Garden**, a well-hidden spot of interest to environmentalists and plant fanciers. More than 25 years ago, Nancy began to create an informal rainforest for herself, and later opened it to the public. Narrow paths wind through the property, leading to small glades where benches and tables invite you to relax and enjoy the sounds of silence. Traipse down the lane that looks like a private drive beside a real estate company and you'll find the small white gate. You're welcome to bring your own lunch. Admission. ~ One Free School Lane, which leads off Simonton Street in the 500 block; 305-294-0015.

◄ HIDDEN

There are two choices for picture-window views of the coral reef in the Atlantic, as well as late afternoon sunset cruises. One is with the glass-bottom sightseeing boats **Fireball** and **Pride of Key West**. Admission. ~ World-Famous Glassbottom Boats, north end of Duval Street; 305-296-6293. The other is the glass-bottom boat of the **Coral Princess Fleet**, which makes snorkeling stops. Admission. ~ 700 Front Street; 305-296-3287.

As you might expect, in Key West you can find countless accommodations—from bare-basics motels to outrageously expensive resorts. Unfortunately, bare basics often carry a moderate price tag in Key West, now that the island is wildly popular year-round. Some of the best values can be found at the island's varied guesthouses, many with whimsical architecture splashed with tropical colors and surrounding exquisite little courtyards. A number of the guesthouses cater to gays only, so be sure to ask about the house

LODGING

policy. If you want help finding a place to stay, contact the **Key West Reservation Service**. ~ 628 Fleming Street; 305-296-7753, 800-327-4831, fax 305-296-6291.

Quietly dominating the edge of Old Town, the soft pink, metal-roofed **Hyatt Key West** is a maze of well-lit stairs and balconies from which you can observe Key West's famous sunsets without the folderol of Mallory Square. The cool pastel decor suits the location beside a small private beach and marina. A pool, jacuzzi, exercise room, fine restaurants and indoor/outdoor lounge make this one of the choicest lodgings—and one of the most convenient for Key West sightseeing. ~ 601 Front Street; 305-296-9900, 800-233-1234, fax 305-292-1038. ULTRA-DELUXE.

Pier House has long been one of Key West's most popular hotels. It sprawls along the Gulf with rambling tin-roofed villas and acres of docks. Here you get all the goodies of an elaborate resort—superb restaurants, lively nightspots, a therapeutic spa—with that classic laid-back Keys mood. A small beach is soft and picturesque, the swimming pool expansive, and the grounds jungly. Old Town shops and sights are a short stroll away. ~ 1 Duval Street; 305-296-4600, 800-327-8340, fax 305-296-7569. ULTRA-DELUXE.

The ultimate bed-and-breakfast (and dinner!) getaway is aboard the **Witt's End**, a 51-foot luxury sailing yacht manned by experienced sailors B.J. and Greg Witt, a husband-and-wife team. The ship has all the comforts of home and an accomplished chef to boot (featured in *Gourmet* magazine). Up to four people can book an overnight, weekend or longer stay that includes snorkeling. Reservations recommended. ~ Key West Bight Marina; 305-296-9916, fax 305-295-9232. ULTRA-DELUXE.

Don't let the "Holiday Inn" sign mislead you. **La Concha** is unlike any chain hostelry you've experienced. This is a downtown Key West landmark seven-story hotel with a wonderful old-fashioned feel. Holiday Inn was smart not to clone it but to keep its dark woodwork and marble floors and furnish it with appropriate 1920s wicker and wood and hazy old seaside pictures. Walking down the hall and into one of the rooms is like stepping into grandmother's attic trunk. The pool and sundeck, rooftop lounge, tiki bar, restaurants and sidewalk saloon, however, are appropriate toasts to modernity. ~ 430 Duval Street; 305-296-2991, 800-745-2191, fax 305-294-3283. DELUXE TO ULTRA-DELUXE.

The lushest place on the island is surely **The Gardens Hotel**. Now a small, luxurious European-style hotel, it was once the Peggy Mills Botanical Garden. The late Mills, known around town as Miss Peggy, searched the world for rare species, importing orchids from Hawaii and Japan, and palms and canopy trees from Latin America. She also brought in 87,000 bricks to create the footpaths that now curl through the garden. Five handsome buildings of crisp white, including Mill's original 1870s house, offer elegant rooms with French doors, wood floors, marble baths and porches. Continental breakfast can be taken in the glass sunroom or on the veranda. There's a pool and jacuzzi. ~ 526 Angela Street; 305-294-2661, 800-526-2664, fax 305-292-1007. ULTRA-DELUXE.

Built in 1890 and featuring a handsome metal-roofed turret on one corner, **The Artist House** is one of many conch houses turned hostelry. Guests may have one of six rooms with private bath, refrigerator and antique or period reproduction furnishings, including four-poster or genuine brass beds. A jacuzzi and sundeck are set among lush tropical plantings in the garden; breakfasts are continental. Rich period wallpapers and superb restoration make this an elegant lodging. ~ 534 Eaton Street; 305-296-3977, 800-593-7898, fax 305-296-3210. DELUXE TO ULTRA-DELUXE.

La Mer Hotel is one of many restored Victorian conch-style houses. This one has contemporary furnishings and definite flair, with many tropical plants, oceanview balconies and porches. Both a continental breakfast and high tea are served daily. ~ 506 South Street; 305-296-5611, 800-354-4455, fax 305-294-8272. ULTRA-DELUXE.

After a major renovation of this 1880s-era classic revival building, the **Marquesa Hotel** has landed securely on the National Register of Historic Places. Each of the 27 rooms is luxurious and formal, with antique appointments, pastel walls, gleaming white woodwork and distinctive fabrics. Every corner is a masterpiece of workmanship. The property includes an award-winning restaurant and two sparkling pools in a tropical garden. ~ 600 Fleming Street; 305-292-1919, 800-869-4631, fax 305-294-2121. ULTRA-DELUXE.

Newest of the island's lushly planted resorts, **Paradise Inn** is full of light and space—its winding footpaths, bubbling whirlpool and kidney of a pool open to sunshine. There is much floral exotica: pink tabebuias and night-blooming jasmine, purple-flowered sky vines trailing along gingerbread piazzas, and ylang-ylang trees whose heady blossoms smell like Chanel No. 5. Families like it here; the rooms are spacious suites or cottages with one or two bedrooms and baths of marble. There's plenty of on-site parking, too—a rare and welcome feature in Key West. ~ 819 Simonton Street; 305-293-8007, 800-888-9648, fax 305-293-0807. ULTRA-DELUXE.

Ethereal peach buildings trimmed in white gingerbread stand along a pretty beach at **The Reach**. This balmy address has lovely terraced suites with Mexican tile floors, Indian dhurrie rugs, ceiling fans, wet bars, commanding views of the ocean, a swimming pool, a health club and a palm courtyard. The tin-roofed dockhouse is a choice spot to loaf. ~ 1435 Simonton Street; 305-296-5000, 800-874-4118, fax 305-296-3008. ULTRA-DELUXE.

The **Curry Mansion Inn** provides 28 rooms with private baths. Most are in the beautiful backyard annex that surrounds the pretty deck and pool, eight are in the Victorian home across the street and four are in the fine old historic mansion itself. Furnishings are mostly fine wicker, and every bed is covered with a handmade quilt. Rooms in the annex are all pastel and white, creating a cool, fresh feel even on the hottest summer day. Rates include complimentary happy hour, a membership to a nearby beach club and a European breakfast with various freshly baked breads. Gay friendly. ~ 511 and 512 Caroline Street; 305-294-5349. ULTRA-DELUXE.

The Marriott Casa Marina was created as the final resort along Henry Flagler's railroad in 1921.

If you remember old-fashioned tourist courts, then you can indulge in a bit of nostalgia at **Key Lime Village**, a collection of 1920s and 1930s cottages surrounding an 1854 home. The accommodations are tiny but functional, including one studio, efficiency apartments and motel-type rooms with shared baths. Spanish lime, mango and ancient sapodilla trees abound. The peaceful surroundings include a swimming pool. ~ 727 Truman Avenue; 305-294-6222, 800-201-6222. MODERATE TO DELUXE.

HIDDEN ▶

A member of the international Youth Hostel Association, the **Key West Hostel** has dorm rooms for males, females and mixed couples in a quiet residential neighborhood. All ages are welcome, but nonmembers must have a valid picture. There are full kitchen facilities and lockers and bicycles to rent. ~ 718 South Street; 305-296-5719, 800-514-6783, fax 305-296-0672. BUDGET.

Even if you don't choose to stay at the **Marriott Casa Marina,** you should drop in and indulge in the Sunday brunch or at least explore the lobby of this 1921 historic landmark. This handsome Spanish-style hotel radiates historic elegance. The pine floors gleam like glass. The French doors leading to a spacious loggia and the restaurant's restored mahogany coffered ceiling pay tribute to Flagler's dreams for the Keys. A beachfront restaurant, two pools, lighted tennis courts, a water sports center and an airport shuttle add modern luxury. ~ 1500 Reynolds Street on the ocean; 305-296-3535, 800-626-0777, fax 305-296-4633. ULTRA-DELUXE.

Looking more like it should be in Disney World than Key West, the **Sheraton Suites** sports a cluster of faux Bahamas-style buildings coated in radiant peach and purple. In the lobby, teal benches and purple chairs look cartoonish; at the meandering pool, water cascades from fake boulders; and in the rooms, blue waves dance on the pastel bedside stands. All 180 rooms are 508-square-foot suites offering living rooms with sofa beds, wet bars with microwave ovens and refrigerators, louvered doors and two televisions. Many have jacuzzi tubs and some have balconies. The public beach is just across the street and there's a day-and-night shuttle to Duval

Street. ~ 2001 South Roosevelt Boulevard; 305-292-9800, 800-452-3224, fax 305-294-6009. ULTRA-DELUXE.

DINING

Marvelous Gulf views, candlelit tables and soothing piano music are reasons for reveling in the **Pier House Restaurant**, the only four-diamond restaurant in Key West. As an added treat, the cuisine is consistently outstanding, relying heavily on innovative treatments of local seafood, fruits and vegetables. Musts here are the conch bisque, conch eggroll with spicy island chili sauce and yellowtail with Key lime butter and papaya. A heady chocolate decadence dessert comes crowned with a fragrant red rosebud. ~ 1 Duval Street; 305-296-4600. DELUXE.

The sign above the **Crab Shack** promises "free crab tomorrow," but don't be discouraged if tomorrow never comes because the "one free refill" of spicy steamed shrimp is no hoax if you dine between 4 p.m. and 10 p.m. The crab selections are especially impressive for they include imports from Maryland and Alaska as well as the local side-crawlers. You can eat inside or out in dining areas that are rustic and functional. There's a good assortment of combination dinners that include both seafood and meat. ~ 908 Caroline Street; 305-294-9658. MODERATE.

Pepe's Café and Steakhouse is like a wonderful old boathouse, outfitted in battered wood walls, tiller-top tables and rumpled fishing snapshots. Opened in 1909 by a Cuban fisherman, it moved from prominent Duval Street to a lonesome byroad. All the better: except for locals, few know of the eatery's great burgers and gourmet coffees. There are also pork chops, steak, seafood and creamed chip beef on toast for breakfast. A vine-covered patio offers outdoor dining. ~ 806 Caroline Street; 305-294-7192. MODERATE.

◀ HIDDEN

Often when celebrities attach their name to a place it ensures mediocrity. Not so with **Kelly's Caribbean Bar, Grill & Brewery**, owned by actress Kelly McGillis and husband Fred Tillman. Their island fare is colorful, zesty and inventive, their home-brewed beer truly tasty, and their courtyard setting spacious and well-liked by locals. Some of our favorite dishes: jumbo coconut shrimp with a pineapple dipping sauce, whole yellowtail snapper with a tomato basil vinaigrette and Jamaican jerk chicken with tamarind sweet-and-sour sauce. ~ 301 Whitehead Street; 305-293-8484. MODERATE TO DELUXE.

If it weren't for the intoxicating aroma of garlic and olive oil and herb-spiked sauces, you might drive right by **Mangia Mangia**, hidden as it is in a quiet neighborhood. But find it you should, because the pasta is the freshest around. The rigatoni with jumbo shrimp is topped with a salad of radicchio, arugula and Belgian endive. The *bolito misto de mare* is a combination of seafood and *pappardello* pasta in a clam broth with white wine and herbs. It's

◀ HIDDEN

Text continued on page 366.

Fort Jefferson

Like a scattering of tiny emerald beads, a cluster of coral reel islands dot the Gulf of Mexico 68 miles west of Key West.
Ponce de León named them "Tortugas" for the turtles he found there, sailors called them "Dry" because they hold no fresh water. But the Dry Tortugas do hold a national monument centered around a magnificent 19th-century fort.

To see **Fort Jefferson** from the air, surrounded by azure sea, walled moat and white sand, is like conjuring up a fairy tale, enriched with popular legends of pirate treasure. Walking through the open sally port and arched hallways, one steps into a vast area whose silence is broken only by seagull cries and the calls of migratory birds.
~ For information, contact the Everglades National Park at 305-292-8798.

Fort Jefferson, from its perch on Garden Key, appears much as it did in its brief 19th-century heyday. German and Irish craftsmen, with the assistance of slaves, created the spectacular brick- and stonework from millions of bricks brought by sailing ships from Pensacola and Virginia, and granite and slate brought from New England. The eight-foot-thick walls stand 50 feet high and feature handsome arches and wide views of sea approaches. Fort Jefferson's half-mile hexagonal perimeter made it the largest link in the chain of coastal fortifications built from Maine to Texas in the first half of the 19th century. It encompasses almost all the land of its tiny key, creating the illusion that it floats on the glistening tropical sea.

Though at first glance the fort seems complete, it was never actually finished. Begun in 1846, work continued for 30 years, but Fort Jefferson's importance came to an end with the invention of the rifled cannon. When federal troops occupied the fort throughout the Civil War, they discovered its foundations were not built on solid coral reef as was originally thought, but on sand and coral boulders. The walls began to show cracks as foundations settled with the shifting of the sea floor.

Fort Jefferson's most inglorious claim to fame came in 1865. To this lonely and inescapable reef were sent the "Lincoln Conspirators," four men convicted of complicity in the assassination of President Abraham Lincoln. Most noted of these was Dr. Samuel Mudd, the physician who had innocently set the broken leg of John Wilkes Booth following the shooting of the president. Sentenced to life imprisonment at Fort Jefferson, Mudd was eventually pardoned following his gallant efforts at treating the almost 300 garrisoned men who were struck with yellow fever at the fort during the 1867 epidemic. Today visitors can explore Mudd's cell and envision the bleakness of his fate.

The Army formally abandoned Fort Jefferson in 1874, following more yellow fever and a serious hurricane; it never saw any military action. And many military men may have felt grateful, for duty at Fort Jefferson, where water was scarce, mosquitoes thick and hurricane winds ferocious, was not coveted. But fortunately for historians and travelers, President Franklin D. Roosevelt proclaimed Fort Jefferson a national monument in 1935, thus preserving its unique heritage and its spectacular architecture.

To visit Fort Jefferson, you can go by boat, or you can fly via chartered seaplane with **Seaplanes of Key West**. The plane trip rewards visitors with breathtaking views of the shallow waters, shipwrecks and coral reefs off the tip of the state. ~ 305-294-0709.

You can spread a picnic, pitch a tent in the shade of tropical trees or sunbathe on the tiny, pristine beach, but you must bring everything with you, for only restrooms are available on the island. An excellent self-guiding tour, introduced by an explanatory slide show, orients visitors to the wonderful wild fort that you may roam to your heart's content. Snorkelers need only wade out waist-deep from the little beach to behold the colorful array of marine creatures that dart among the patches of living coral in the crystal-clear Gulf water.

served on marble-topped tables inside or in a courtyard of many palm trees, with oil lamps flickering on your table. ~ 900 Southard Street; 305-294-2469. MODERATE.

Café des Artistes is so small and unspectacular on the outside, it's impossible to imagine that inside awaits the most elegant of spaces, with arches, crisp white linens and twinkling crystal lamps, offering rich, tropical cuisine of the most sensational order. From the roast half duckling with fresh raspberry sauce to the lobster tango mango (flambéed in cognac with saffron butter), every inspired dish tastes as luscious as it looks. ~ 1007 Simonton Street; 305-294-7100. ULTRA-DELUXE.

For such succulent Cuban dishes as black beans and yellow rice, sweet fried plantains, *picadillo* and those wonderful, famous sandwiches of thick slices of meat and cheese on crusty Cuban bread, run, don't walk, to **El Cocique**. Forget your diet; the theme here is pigs. Poster porkers line the walls, imparting such wisdom as, "a moment on the lips, forever on the hips" and "fat is beautiful." The food here should make you agree. ~ 3100 Flagler Avenue; 305-292-3700. BUDGET TO MODERATE.

HIDDEN ► **The Rusty Anchor** is run by a local family who have turned a one-time leaky-floored shrimpers' bar into a favored eating spot for locals from Key West and elsewhere. Charter boat captains send their customers here because, as one said, "It's just the best," a good example of the word-of-mouth publicity that keeps folks coming. The location is unlikely, proving that the reputation of good seafood, well-prepared conch fritters and, surprisingly, barbecued baby-back ribs, are all it takes to make an open-air eatery a success. ~ 5th Avenue off 5th Street across from the dog track, Stock Island; 305-294-5369. MODERATE.

SHOPPING Key West is the place to spend your money. The Old Town streets in the waterfront area are a mass of shops and boutiques offering everything from imported flamingos to artful fabrics. Visitors do most of their shopping in the dozens of glitzy and funky shops in Old Town; practical shopping is available in several centers in the newer areas.

HIDDEN ► **The Restaurant Store** is hidden down a sidestreet in a quiet part of Old Town and caters mostly to commercial kitchens. Home chefs, however, will go crazy over all the great gadgetry and great prices. ~ 313 Margaret Street; 305-294-7994.

Not quite all the sponge fishermen are gone from Key West, as explained on a continuous video at the **Sponge Market**. "Sponge King" C. B. McHugh demonstrates the harvesting and treating of sponges and tells their history on the film; the store has bins of these marvelous nonpolyfoam wonders and other gifts. ~ 1 Whitehead Street; 305-294-2555.

Because it's away from the bustling commercial area, you might miss **Whitehead Street Pottery**, located in what was once a Cuban grocery. Every piece here is one-of-a-kind, including many beautiful and durable copper-red and raku art pieces glazed with metallic oxides. ~ 1011 Whitehead Street; 305-294-5067.

◄ HIDDEN

Located in a historic old one-time waterfront grocery, the **Key West Art Center** is a cooperative for local artists. Works for sale include paintings and drawings of seascapes, sunsets and Key West street scenes, as well as sculpture and other art. ~ 301 Front Street; 305-294-1241.

Cavanagh's has a wide variety of rare and wondrous imported items for amazingly reasonable prices. This big store features furnishings and gifts from around the world, including Oaxacan pottery, Oriental accessories, Latin American treasures and African tribal artifacts. There is also a wide selection of women's clothing, but the main attractions here are the imports. ~ 520 Front Street; 305-296-3343.

Brightly colored silkscreened fabrics and designer clothing are for sale at **Key West Hand Print Fabric and Fashion**. ~ 201 Simonton Street; 305-294-9535.

If you don't plan to go deep-sea treasure hunting yourself, you can arrange to buy an authentic piece of booty at **Mel Fisher's Treasure Exhibit and Sales**. ~ 200 Greene Street; 305-296-9936.

For exotic kites, colorful nylon windsocks and just about any toy that flies, visit the **Key West Kite Company**, the first kite store in Florida. They also carry a wide variety of flags and banners. ~ 409 Greene Street; 305-296-2535.

Fast Buck Freddie's is a wonderful hodgepodge of a department store left over from the days before malls. Browse through racks of trendy tropical clothing, funny posters, fine candies, swimwear, home furnishings and gift items. ~ 500 Duval Street; 305-294-2007.

It's impossible to miss the **Environmental Circus**, parked as it is on the middle of Key West's main drag, sending billows of incense smoke into the street, beckoning with windows full of water pipes and counterculture patches. Inside this vintage establishment, one of Florida's biggest and oldest head shops, are postcards albums, and books on growing pot. ~ 518 Duval Street; 305-294-6055.

Haitian Art Co. imports metal and wood sculptures, carvings, papier-mâché and brilliantly colored paintings in handcrafted frames by Haitian artists. ~ 600 Frances Street; 305-296-8932.

Key West Island Books carries a large collection of natural history books, books about Key West and books by authors who have lived here. They have new, used and rare volumes, and have book signings and readings throughout the year. ~ 513 Fleming Street; 305-294-2904.

Lucky Street Gallery is a marvelous cache of paintings, glass-works, pottery, jewelry, metal sculptures and other zany pieces for the avant garde. ~ 1120 White Street; 305-294-3973.

HIDDEN ► Even for Key West, the **Lazy Way Shops** are strange. Tucked in-side a makeshift building is a helter-skelter maze of hammocks, crystals, wood pelicans and other tourist items, including "Conch Republic" silver coins. ~ In the alley just east of the intersection of Elizabeth and Greene streets; 305-294-3003.

NIGHTLIFE If you wondered where the nighttime action was as you traveled down the Keys, you'll discover it's almost all here in Key West. Entertainment begins long before sunset and goes on far into the early morning hours. A number of nightclubs seem to spill right out through their open windows and doors onto the street.

You should at least stick your head into **Sloppy Joe's** because it has hooked onto the Papa Hemingway legend in as many ways as it can. Papa and Sloppy Joe were drinking buddies, apparently, and it's said that some of the tales that showed up in literature were founded on stories they shared in the backroom here. Just follow your ears and you should find it most anytime of the day or night. There's live rock: softer music in the afternoon, rhythm-and-blues and a rockin' band until 4 a.m. ~ 201 Duval Street; 305-294-5717.

Capt. Tony's Saloon, "where everybody is a star," is said to be the location of the *real* Sloppy Joe's, and it just may be true. Anyway, the real star here is Cap'n Tony, a wiry white-haired cod-ger who has polished his role as local character until it shines. Rowdy and fun, with all sorts of live musicians from country to blues, it's a Key West institution. Come and see memorabilia of all the famous people who have had a drink here, or play pool. ~ 428 Greene Street; 305-294-1838.

On the sunset deck of second-story **Havana Docks Bar** you can get an eyeful of the Gulf and an earful of a calypso-soca band en-tertaining the crowd. Dancing and revelry goes on late into the night. ~ Pier House, 1 Duval Street; 305-294-9541.

The Top has the best view of any night spot in Key West, from the top of the 1925 La Concha hotel. Listen to relaxing music while you sip your drink and watch the sunset. ~ 430 Duval Street; 305-296-2991.

You'll find a bar, live rock-and-roll and, of course, plenty of Jimmy Buffet music at the **Margaritaville Café**, where Jimmy, no longer "wastin' away," makes occasional impromptu appearances. You can enjoy the music and the American-Caribbean food until closing time. ~ 500 Duval Street; 305-292-1435.

At the brick-floored bohemian grotto called **Baby's Place Coffee Bar**, you can indulge in such potent brews as Death by Chocolate, Hemingway's Hair of the Dog or Baby's Private Buzz, "the last legal high." ~ 1111 Duval Street; 305-292-3739.

Two Friends Patio Restaurant features live calypso, blues and Broadway tunes nightly in the winter season in its big, popular open-air lounge. The festivities sometimes spill out onto the street. There is a patio restaurant attached and a raw bar for late-night eating. ~ 512 Front Street; 305-296-9212.

There's often entertainment at the **Turtle Kraals Bar**, including live blues bands and turtle races. Once a turtle cannery, it's now an old-style Key West eating and drinking spot. You can see turtles and other sea creatures here while you relax and have a drink. ~ 2 Land's End Village, end of Margaret Street; 305-294-2640.

THEATER, OPERA, SYMPHONY AND DANCE   The arts are alive in Key West, too. A variety of popular and classical concerts, plays and dance programs are presented at the **Tennessee Williams Fine Arts Center**. ~ Florida Keys Community College, 5901 West Junior College Road; 305-296-1520.

The **Waterfront Playhouse** presents an assortment of plays, films, reviews and musical comedies throughout the winter and spring. ~ Mallory Square; 305-294-5015. The **Red Barn Theatre** is a resident company presenting several productions during the winter season. ~ 319 Duval Street; 305-296-9911.

BEACHES & PARKS

It's a surprise to many visitors that Key West has very few beaches, and those it does have are far from sensational. On the south side of the island, along the Atlantic Ocean, you can dip into the water or lie in the sun at one of several narrow public beaches that tend to get very crowded.

SMATHERS BEACH   This city-owned beach is where locals lie in the sun in the daytime and take walks at night. There's nice water for swimming but a rocky bottom. Facilities include restrooms, picnic areas, bathhouses, watersport rentals and concession stands. ~ Off South Roosevelt Boulevard west of the airport.

HIGGS BEACH   This beach area is popular with families, as swimming is possible and there are a number of recreational facilities nearby. Facilities include picnic areas, restrooms, a bathhouse, a playground, tennis courts, watersport rentals and concession stands. ~ Located along Atlantic Boulevard between White Street and Reynolds Road.

Key West Gay Scene

With so much to do concentrated on such an attractive little island, it's no surprise that Key West has become a popular destination. From its snorkeling trips and sunset cruises to its kitschy conch houses and trolley rides, Key West draws gay travelers from around the world. Even though it now appears that gay visitors are outnumbered by straights most times of the year, the gay community continues to have a strong presence in Key West. Gay visitors are welcomed everywhere and Key West's elected officials and business community continue to reach out to gay travelers. To see for yourself, check out Key West's excellent Web site at http://www.key-west.com/gaykw/, where you will not only find practical information, but a warm Key West welcome to greet you through the cold hardware of modern technology.

Speaking of warm, Key West's tropical maritime climate is the best year-round option among the gay resort towns. Its warm, sunny winters outshine Provincetown's unseasonably cold ones, and during the summer, when everyone in Palm Springs bakes in temperatures soaring above 100°, cool ocean breezes keep Key West's temperatures bearable. In fact, its average summer and winter temperatures generally vary only 10°; Key West has never recorded temperatures colder than 41° nor hotter than 97°.

The casual island atmosphere that prevails in Key West compels everyone who sets foot on its soil to let his or her hair down. Its gay guesthouses set the standard for elegance, amenities and decor, while most innkeepers provide the kind of personal service that is unmatched by any hotel staff. Whether you are sampling its many superb restaurants, browsing its shops or cruising its nightspots, you will find people in Key West extraordinarily sociable.

Although tourists visit all times of the year, two events boast an especially large attendance of lesbians and gays. In July, women take over the island for **WomenFest Key West**, a seven-day get-together of sun-filled days and party-hardy nights. This week is filled with theme parties, specially organized women-only tours and events, a film festival and sporting events—including a tennis tournament and even a wet T-shirt contest! ~ 210 Coppitt Road #106A, Key West; 305-296-4238, 800-374-2784, fax 305-296-4238.

The last week of October brings Key West's most popular event—**Fantasy Fest**. A Mardi Gras–style party that runs through Halloween, Fantasy Fest attracts all sorts of people in all types of costumes primed for a wild time. Just keep in mind that this small island can only hold a limited number of people, and during Fantasy Fest, it's advisable to make your reservations early if you hope to take part in the festivities.

The Key West Business Guild's **Key West Map and Directory** is filled with information and helpful touring suggestions. It's available at gay guesthouses or by contacting the guild, which is the island's gay business association. ~ 305-294-4603. The monthly publication, *Southern Exposure*, also offers information for gay travelers as well as timely listings of events and performances. But if you can't wait to find out the happenings in Key West before you arrive, tap into *Southern Exposure's* Web site, which is updated every month with the same timely details as the magazine. ~ 305-555-1212, http://www.kwest.com.

Gay visitors will find numerous guesthouses—many of which are exclusively for gay men and women. Several clothing-optional inns cater to young, single, party-minded males, while other, more intimate houses appeal to professional couples.

A 19th-century Victorian conch house, **Colours Key West** has 14-foot-high ceilings, hardwood floors and beautiful antiques. Bedrooms feature brass and wicker furniture, ceiling fans and, in some cases, balcony views of Old Town. A large clothing-optional pool is also popular at this 12-unit establishment favored by the gay crowd. ~ 410 Fleming Street; 305-294-6977, 800-934-5622, fax 305-534-0362. DELUXE TO ULTRA-DELUXE.

If you're looking for a relaxing house featuring a peaceful pool, jacuzzi and patio area, check into the **Curry House**. This 1890 Victorian home offers nine rooms, all furnished with antiques, and all with French doors that open onto a long veranda or a private deck. In the heart of Old Town, this three-story, white-and-green shuttered guesthouse is for males only. Rates include a full breakfast and poolside cocktails. ~ 806 Fleming Street; 305-294-6777, 800-633-7439, fax 305-294-5322. DELUXE TO ULTRA-DELUXE.

The Newton Street Station, now a guesthouse, was once home to the station master of the short-lived Florida East Coast Railway.

At the **Oasis** you'll find an early 1900s mansion, two restored conch houses and a young, swinging, all-male crowd. All 20 rooms are spacious and comfortable but nothing fancy, and there are two swimming pools, two hot tubs and a spacious nude sunbathing deck. ~ 823 Fleming Street; 305-296-2131, 800-362-7477. DELUXE TO ULTRA-DELUXE.

The elegant **Coral Tree Inn**, located across the street, has classical music piped through the lush, palmy grounds, while art deco sconces give off a special glow in the halls. The turn-of-the-century building has been painstakingly restored, and all 11 guest rooms are sumptuously furnished with gleaming pine and oak furniture and mauve and lavender prints. Rooms here are slightly more expensive than the Oasis. This inn is also exclusively for men. ~ 822 Fleming Street; 305-296-2131, 800-362-7477, fax 305-296-2131. ULTRA-DELUXE.

With its worn wood floors and ceilings and contemporary furnishings, **Alexander's** blends old with new and gives the feeling of a very comfortable home. In the jungly courtyard, flaming bougainvillea dangle above a cobalt blue pool, and 17 rooms and suites are spread among three houses. Each room is decorated individually, though particularly appealing are the second-floor treehouse rooms with their stained-glass windows and skylights. There's a primarily gay clientele, but straight visitors are welcome. ~ 1118 Fleming Street; 305-294-9919, 800-654-9919, fax 305-295-0357. DELUXE TO ULTRA-DELUXE.

Catering to gays and lesbians, the **Brass Key Guesthouse** is a beautiful two-story, plantation-style house surrounded by verandas and tropical gardens. A lovely pool and a spiral staircase leading up to the sundeck make this bed and breakfast particularly inviting. Sixteen rooms are furnished with English antiques, ceiling fans and all amenities. ~ 412 Frances Street; 305-296-4719, 800-932-9119, fax 305-296-1994. DELUXE TO ULTRA-DELUXE.

Newton Street Station, which bills itself as "a man's retreat in Key West," is an intimate, homey guesthouse exclusively for gay men, tucked away on a little-traveled street. The seven rooms are simply but comfortably furnished, and a complimentary bicycle is reserved for each guest. Although the building, is less interesting than some (gingerbread is notably lacking), the lush landscaping and clothing-optional pool offer an attractive setting for each morning's continental breakfast. ~ 1414 Newton Street; 305-294-4288, 800-248-2457, fax 305-292-5062. MODERATE TO DELUXE.

Open to women only, **Rainbow House** offers seven suites and nine rooms with private or shared kitchens. This Old Town inn serves an expanded continental breakfast poolside. Lush landscaping adds to the charm of the pavilion and veranda. Sitting areas are furnished with wicker and the tropical-style bedrooms feature print bedspreads. ~ 525 United Street; 305-292-1450, 800-749-6696. MODERATE TO DELUXE.

Big Ruby's Guesthouse is *Out & About's* favorite Key West guesthouse and received their palm rating in 1995. It's easy to see why. The 17 rooms, spread between three buildings, are tastefully decorated and have TVs, VCRs (with free movies), all-cotton bedding and extra-thick bath towels. The grounds are lushly landscaped and the pool is clothing-optional, open 24 hours and solar-heated in the winter. Every morning a substantial breakfast of eggs Benedict, breakfast burritos, french toast and the like is served poolside; the pool is also the place where guests gather in the evening for wine. Guests are mainly men, but women are always welcome. Proprietors George Chilson and Frank Rose will be happy to assist you in deciding on the island's various tours and activities. ~ 409 Appelrouth Lane; 305-296-2323, 800-477-7829, fax 305-296-0281. DELUXE TO ULTRA-DELUXE.

DINING   A dash of the Caribbean and a pinch of Italy, mixed well with a number of other worldly flavors, is brought to your table nightly at the **Palm Grill**. One of the five dining areas is sure to suit your dining aesthetic, be it a formal, casual or romantic affair. After wetting your palate at the 1878 mahogany bar, delight your gastronomic senses with the wahoo berber (wahoo coated in 17 different spices and then blackened), accompanied by a Moroccan sunflower salad. Or try the Cuban pork Wellington, enhanced with black bean pâté and served with fried plantains. There are also a number of tasty vegetarian items for the mixed clientele to choose from. Dinner only. Closed Monday and the month of September. ~ 1208 Simonton Street; 305-296-1744. ULTRA-DELUXE.

The owners of One Saloon bar can do no wrong with **La Trattoria Venezia**. Expect savory Italian fare dished out in a charming rustic setting decorated with statues and plants; its windows look out onto bustling Duval Street. Start with baked eggplant stuffed with ricotta and roasted red pepper. Then move on to the tortellini with cream sauce or crêpes filled with spinach, mushrooms and cheese. Also on the menu are veal, seafood, lamb and chicken dishes. Dinner only. ~ 524 Duval Street; 305-296-1075. MODERATE TO DELUXE.

For intimate, elegant dining New York style, saunter over to the **Square One**, which is popular with gays and straights alike. The atmosphere is enhanced by soft piano music and, if you're seated outside, the bubbling of the courtyard fountain. Try one of the different veal dishes, or perhaps the scallops, nestled on a bed of poached spinach. You'll also find steak, rack of lamb, duck and a variety of seafood prepared new American–style. Dinner only. ~ 1075 Duval Street; 305-296-4300. MODERATE TO ULTRA-DELUXE.

The chef at **La-Te-Da** will titillate your tastebuds with a "New World blend of Old World flavors." His preparations of local seafood are exquisite and his use of tropical fruits creative. Dine at the poolside or fountainside tables and try the shrimp with green apple curry with mango chutney or Florida lobster and shrimp served with a vodka sauce. There's also breakfast and lunch served daily. No dinner on Sunday. ~ 1125 Duval Street; 305-296-6706. MODERATE TO DELUXE.

SHOPPING

Key West offers a wide variety of shopping opportunities; you'll find many wonderful items tucked away in its boutiques and shops. As you would expect, all the stores in Key West welcome gay shoppers, but there are also establishments that cater specifically to the island's many gay visitors.

◄ *HIDDEN*

The best starting point for your shopping tour—and a recommended place to start any visit to Key West—is **Caroline St. Books**. Key West's alternative bookstore stocks mainly gay and lesbian literature but also offers well-kept selections of mainstream contemporary writings—especially that of Key residents. And if you can't wait to get home to begin your book, there's a friendly coffee bar where regulars meet to chat in this spot that has been a cigar factory, a ship's chandlery and a shrimpers' bar. ~ 800 Caroline Street; 294-3931.

Slip on a handful of handcrafted rainbow rings or other gay pride jewelry for sale at **Goldsmith Jewelers**. One of the first jewelers to market products for same-sex unions, you can have them custom-make commitment rings for you and your significant other. ~ 271 Front Street; 305-294-1243.

And if you *are* shopping for commitment rings, perhaps you're ready to take it a step further by visiting the **Chapel By the Sea of Key West, Inc.** This commitment and wedding service offers "stress-free" wedding packages for same-sex couples and is equipped to handle any—or all—details you can't attend to. Or, you might simply prefer to stop by and have them marry you right then and there in a lovely garden setting. It's advisable to call ahead first, though. ~ 201 Front Street; 305-292-5177, 800-603-2088.

Along with contemporary titles and works by local authors, **Blue Heron Books** carries an unbridled selection of gay and lesbian literature. They also have a wide array of cards and journals you can thumb through while your coffee cools off. 1014 Truman Avenue; 305-296-3508.

NIGHTLIFE   **One Saloon** is a popular gay dance bar that attracts the leather and denim crowd. Dance to disco in one of the three bars or watch live dancers perform. The saloon patio is also a popular retreat on balmy nights. ~ 524 Duval Street; 305-296-8118.

Formerly the Copa, **Epoch** is earning the crown as Key West's hottest danceclub—frequented by both gays and straights. The dancefloor, seemingly enclosed by rocky canyon walls, appears cavernous despite the number of bodies shimmying to the upbeat, high-speed dance music and breaking into a sweat under the state-of-the-art lighting. Take a breather upstairs in "celestial" surroundings and have the bartender mix you a drink before returning to the action downstairs. Wednesday, which is amateur drag night, is always a hit. Cover. ~ 623 Duval Street; 296-8522

The stage upstairs at the neighborhood **801 Bar**, where the entertainment ranges from live bands to comedy acts to drag shows, is guaranteed to keep you amused. If you prefer to create your own amusement, mosey on downstairs and hang out with the local crowd of gays and lesbians who frequent this place. There's also pool tables and pinball machines to keep you in shape. Cover occasionally. ~ 801 Duval Street; 305-294-4737.

On Sundays, gay happenings start before nighttime with Key West's famous afternoon tea dances. For years the most famous of all tea dances is **La-Te-Da**. Things heat up poolside with themed parties and disco music. For other entertainment at this laid-back and sophisticated spot, try the "Best in Drag" show six nights a week at the Treetop Bar. ~ 1125 Duval Street; 305-296-6706.

Near dusk, the party continues at the **Atlantic Shores Motel**, which has a bar and a clothing-optional pool side by side, and "Tea by the Sea" on the pier. ~ 510 South Street; 305-296-2491.

A neighborhood bar by day, **Numbers** transforms into a boisterous scene at night as male strippers take the stage. A mostly male clientele comprised of both locals and out-of-towners clamors in here in order to get the best view. ~ 1029 Truman Avenue; 305-296-0333.

HIGGS BEACH DOCK ⚓ Located along Key West's southern stretch of shoreline, Higg's Beach is popular with travelers for its fine beach and extensive park facilities (see the "Key West Beaches & Parks" section above). The dock, which juts out into the western end of the park, is active throughout the day with gay visitors enjoying the tropical atmosphere by swimming, sunbathing and socializing here. ~ Located at Atlantic Boulevard and Reynolds Road.

BEACHES & PARKS

▼▼▼▼▼▼▼▼▼▼▼▼
Outdoor Adventures

You can go sportfishing on a pricey, custom-designed charter or by joining one of the numerous party boats on a scheduled trip.

SPORT-FISHING

Tarpon, snook, redfish and trout are the four most popular fish that charter captains will help you locate in the western Everglades and Ten Thousand Islands region. Contact one of the following for a fishing trip: **Rod and Gun Club** will take you on a full- or half-day trip into the backcountry. ~ Everglades City, 941-695-2101. **Captain Dan** will guide up to four people in the shallow water of the outer islands. ~ Chokoloskee, 941-695-4573. About forty miles south of Naples, Captain Dave operates **Island Charters**, taking one or two people out after the elusive sheepshead and mangrove snapper. ~ Chokoloskee; 941-695-2286.

For charter fishing in the Upper Keys for such gamefish as amberjack, barracuda, bonefish, blackfin tuna and tarpon, contact Captain Jim of **Kersten Ann Charters**. ~ Miami Beach Marina, 1633 North Bayshore Drive, Miami, 305-358-4137. **Club Nautico** rents boats to Elliot's Key for dolphinfish and sailfish. ~ 300 Alton Road, Suite 104, Miami Beach; 305-673-2502.

Charters and guides for light tackle fishing in the creeks and deeper ocean waters out of Key Largo can be had from **Back Country Adventures**. Captain Harry Grigsby will take groups out after barracuda, grouper and porgy. ~ 59 North Blackwater Lane near MM 105, Key Largo; 305-451-1247. **The Sailor's Choice** is another good choice, among many, many other charter services. ~ MM 100 at the Holiday Inn; 305-451-1802.

In Islamorada, there are also dozens of sportfishing outfits to choose from, including **Gulf Lady**. ~ MM 79.8 at Bud N' Mary's Marina; 305-664-2626. **Holiday Isle Resorts & Marina** will make arrangements for both backcountry and offshore fishing trips and charters. ~ MM 84.5; 305-664-2321.

In Marathon, charter booking services are offered by **The World Class Angler** for flats, bridge or reef fishing. ~ 5050 Overseas Highway; 305-743-6139. **Marathon Lady Party Boats** offers day and night fishing trips. ~ MM 53 at Vaca Cut; 305-743-5580. For flats fishing, join Captain Barry Meyer on the **Magic**. He'll trailer his boat to meet you anywhere in the Keys for fly- or spincasting for tarpon or light-tackle bonefishing. ~ 305-743-3278.

In the Lower Keys, you can go tarpon fishing with **Outcast Charters**. ~ MM 27.5, Ramrod Key; 305-872-4680.Try **Fantasy Charters** for offshore and reef fishing. ~ MM 28, Big Pine Key; 305-872-3200. Try backcountry fishing with the **Outcast** at Sugarloaf Marina. ~ MM 17, Sugarloaf Key; 305-745-3135.

From Key West you can fish in the Atlantic or on the Tortuga Banks. Try **Yankee Fleet** for a two- or three-day trip on a headboat (complete with sleeping quarters, galley and onboard cook) November through April. ~ Oceanside Marina, Stock Island; 305-294-7009. **Sea Breeze Charters** is another choice. ~ 25 Arbutus Drive; 305-294-6027. There's also MV **Florida Fish Finders**. ~ 6810 Front Street, Stock Island; 305-296-0111.

DIVING

On any calm and beautiful day the sea to the east of Florida's Upper Keys is dotted with boats. They belong to the scuba divers and snorkelers who are captivated by the beauty of the continental United States' only living reef. Others search the remains of ships wrecked on that same lovely reef. Many communities in the Keys have dozens of scuba shops and dive centers designed to meet the needs of both novice snorkeler and sophisticated diver.

For scuba and snorkeling trips via glass-bottom boat to littletraveled, beautiful outer reefs and the patch reefs closer to shore, contact the **Biscayne National Underwater Park, Inc.** ~ Convoy Point, next door to the headquarters of the Biscayne National Park; 305-230-1100.

Route 1 in the Key Largo area seems like one continuous dive shop. To meet your diving needs, try **The Coral Reef Park Company, Inc.** ~ John Pennekamp Coral Reef State Park, MM 102.5; 305-451-1621. **American Diving Headquarters** is another choice. ~ MM 105.5; 305-451-0037. In Tavernier, try the **Florida Keys Dive Center**. ~ MM 90.5; 305-852-4599. Diving courses, gear and trips are available in Islamorada through **Lady Cyana Divers**. ~ MM 85.9; 305-664-8717. **Holiday Isle Resorts & Marina** has the same options. ~ MM 84; 305-664-2321. For trips, lessons and equipment in Marathon, contact **The Diving Site**. ~ MM 53.5; 305-289-1021. Or try **Fantasea Divers**. ~ 4650 Overseas Highway, Marathon; 305-743-5422. A full-service dive center in the Lower Keys is **Looe Key Reef Resort and Dive Center**. ~ MM 27.5, Ramrod Key; 305-872-2215. Another is **Cudjoe Gardens Marina and**

Dive Shop. ~ MM 21, Cudjoe Key; 305-745-2357. Or you can try **Inner Space Dive Shop.** ~ MM 29.5; 305-872-2319. From Key West, make arrangements with **Reef Raiders Dive Shop.** ~ 617 Front Street; 305-294-3635. Or call **Dive Key West Inc.** ~ 3128 North Roosevelt Boulevard; 305-296-3823.

SNUBA is the latest thing in underwater exploration. This is a shallow-dive system where the air supply (read tank) follows on the surface, allowing you to dive down to 25 feet. SNUBA Tours can arrange this and snorkeling and scuba trips; lessons are also available. ~ MM 97 at the Sheraton Key Largo; 305-451-6391.

Majestic Everglades Excursions offers a four-hour excursion on a small boat through the Ten Thousand Islands. ~ Everglades City; 813-695-2777.

BOATING

In Key Largo the best prices are at **John Pennekamp Coral Reef State Park Concession.** ~ MM 102.5; 305-451-1621. You can also rent boats at **Italian Fisherman Marina** ~ MM 104; 305-451-3726.

In Islamorada, try **Holiday Isle Resorts & Marina.** ~ MM 84; 305-664-2321. There's also **Robbie's Boat Rentals.** ~ MM 77.5; 305-664-9814. Or try **Bud N' Mary's Marina and Dive Center.** ~ MM 79.8; 305-664-2461. **Bayview Inn** rents powerboats and Sea Doos (waverunners). ~ MM 63, Conch Key; 305-289-1525.

Between Islamorada and Marathon, you can rent at **Pier 68 Boat Rentals.** ~ MM 68.2, Layton; 305-664-9393.

In Marathon you rent powerboats from **Fish 'n Fun Boat Rentals.** ~ MM 53.5; 305-743-2275. **Rick's Watercraft Rentals** is another option. ~ MM 49.5; 305-743-2450.

In the Lower Keys, you can rent boats at **Dolphin Marina.** ~ MM 28.5, Little Torch Key; 305-872-2685. Or try **Cudjoe Gardens Marina.** ~ MM 21; 305-745-2357. In Key West, contact **Key West Boat Rentals.** ~ 617 Front Street; 305-294-2628. **Club Nautico** also rents. ~ 717-C Eisenhower Drive; 305-294-2225.

✔ CHECK THESE OUT—UNIQUE OUTDOOR ADVENTURES

- Follow that old "when in Rome" advice—the Keys are *the* place to go sportfishing, but be careful you don't cross lines with one of your many fellow anglers! *page 375*
- Stare down an alligator, and perhaps an ibis, while hiking the Shark Valley Trail in Everglades National Park. *page 381*
- Search for sunken treasure or explore the continent's only living reef with a diving excursion in Biscayne National Park. *page 376*
- Kayak through a maze of mangrove-locked backwaters or out into the Great White Heron National Wildlife Refuge. *page 378*

**CANOEING
&
KAYAKING**

To explore the shoreline of Biscayne National Park by canoe, contact the **Biscayne National Underwater Park, Inc.** ~ Convoy Point, east of Homestead; 305-230-1100. For kayak and canoe rentals, outfitting and guided trips in the western Everglades, try **North American Canoe Tours**. ~ Ivey House Bed & Breakfast, 107 Camellia Street, Everglades City; 860-739-0791. You can canoe the streams and ponds of the southern Everglades through the **Flamingo Lodge Marina**. ~ Flamingo; 941-695-3101. **Coral Reef Park Company, Inc.** offers canoes for exploring the park. ~ MM 102.5, John Pennekamp Coral Reef State Park, Key Largo; 305-451-1621.

In Marathon, you can rent kayaks at **Ocean Paddler South**, which also has outlets in Summerland Key, Bahia Honda and Islamorada. ~ MM 48.5; 305-743-0131. In Big Pine Key, **Blue Water Tours** offers three-hour guided trips by sea kayak into a tranquil backwater mangrove habitat. ~ MM 11, Big Coppit Key, pickup point located at Circle K; 800-822-1386. In Big Pine Key, **Reflections Nature Tours** takes novice and experienced paddlers into the Great White Heron National Wildlife Refuge to see tropical wildlife in its native habitat. They also offer trips to Key Deer Refuge. ~ 305-872-2896.

Following are a number of popular canoe trails in Everglades National Park.

TAMIAMI TRAIL AREA **Wilderness Waterway** (99 miles) extends through a well-marked mangrove forest in the Ten Thousand Islands region of the national park. The entire trip can take from several days to a week. Backcountry permits are required, and arrangements must be made in advance for pickup and canoe transport.

MAIN VISITOR AREA All canoe trails are accessible from the main park road. Check with rangers before you set out, as varying water levels may close portions of some trails in dry seasons. The park provides maps and guides for canoe trails.

Nine Mile Pond Trail (5.2 miles) travels through a shallow sawgrass marsh and past islands of mangroves. It is the best summer trail in the park.

Noble Hammock Trail (2-mile loop) was once used by bootleggers, whose old "cutting" markers are still on the trees. This trail meanders across open country and small alligator ponds through buttonwood, red mangrove and sawgrass.

Hells Bay Trail (5.5 miles) travels through overgrown passageways of red mangrove and brackish water environments. A backcountry permit is recommended for this trip, even when not camping. There are campsites at the four- and eight-mile points.

West Lake Trail (8 miles) includes a long exposed crossing of the lake as well as a meandering trail through coastal lake country bordered by red and black mangrove and buttonwood trees and through the remains of a once-great living forest destroyed by hurricanes. Alligators and fish are numerous.

Cape Sable Trail (12 miles) begins north of the park road along the Buttonwood Canal and passes through dense mangrove/buttonwood regions into open flooded prairie where wading birds and ducks feed in winter. Several small lakes adjoin the trail; the last part skirts Florida Bay and is exposed, ending at the extensive beach at Cape Sable on the far southwestern tip of Florida's mainland.

Bear Lake Trail (5.5 miles) crosses shallow Mud Lake, which has a prairie, mangrove and buttonwood shoreline, making it good for birdwatching. The trip continues to Coot Bay through what may have once been a Calusa Indian canal and returns via the Buttonwood Canal.

Canoeing is also possible in **Florida Bay**, depending on wind and weather conditions. There is good birding in the shallows; during the dry months, the bay is the only realistic way to reach the beach at Cape Sable. But be sure to check with rangers on tides and weather conditions before setting out. It's a hefty jaunt to the beautiful but isolated sandy beach area, and sudden winds could make the return trip very difficult.

SAILING

In the Key Largo area you can rent sailboats from **Coral Reef Park Company, Inc.** ~ MM 102.5, John Pennekamp Coral Reef State Park; 305-451-1621. Sailing charters are available from **Witt's End Sailing Charters**. ~ MM 100, Key Largo; 305-451-3354. A similar but considerably shorter enviro-experience of about two hours' duration aboard either Zodiac inflatables or Hobie Cat sailboats is presented by **Caribbean Watersports**. ~ MM 97 at the Sheraton Key Largo; 305-852-4704.

In Islamorada, book sailing cruises through **Holiday Isle Resorts and Marina**. ~ MM 84; 305-664-2321.

Go sailing out of Marathon with ABC **Sailing Charters**. ~ Faro Blanco Marina Resort; 305-289-0373. Or sail aboard **Amantha**. ~ MM 48.3, Faro Blanco Marina Resort; 305-743-9020. Cruises for as many as six people on a 56-foot private yacht are available from **Latigo Charters**. Choose from a sunset dinner cruise, a bed-and-breakfast cruise and two types of wedding cruises. ~ 1021 11 Street, Marathon; 305-289-1066. **Hootmon Sailing Charters** is available for snorkeling trips and a sunset champagne cruise every evening. You can even take some learn-to-sail classes with licensed captains Ann and Dan Malone. ~ MM 49.5, at Banana Bay Resort, Marathon; 305-289-1433.

For catamaran cruises out of Key West, call **Sebago**. ~ 328 Simonton Street; 305-294-5687.

Enjoy an unforgettable five-hour, 45-mile tour aboard the *Emerald See*, **Strike Zone Charters**' 40-foot catamaran. Snorkel over the reef, visit the "back country" and relish a fish cookout on a private island. ~ MM 29.5, Big Pine Key; 305-872-9863, 800-654-9560.

You and five of your mates can spend several days aboard the 50-foot *Playmate*, enjoying day and night dives along the Florida Keys or the Dry Tortugas, snorkeling, fishing, birdwatching and the fine cuisine provided by **Sea-Clusive Charters**. One-day charters are also available. ~ Big Pine Key; 305-872-3940.

Keys visitors are increasingly interested in exploring the fragile ecosystems that surround the islands and Florida mainland. **Chic Charney Cruises** emphasizes sightings of birds and other wildlife, marine-science studies and photography from a comfortable, stable, shallow-draft boat. Mini and sunset cruises are available, but eco trips as long as five days are no problem. The captain and guide is Anne Baxter, a former Everglades National Park ranger. ~ MM 97; 305-852-4553.

WIND-SURFING

Windsurfers can find boards and lessons at **Caribbean Watersports**, which has two locations: MM 97, Key Largo, 305-852-4707; and the Cheeca Lodge Resort, MM 82, Islamorada, 305-664-4561. There's also **Coral Reef Park Company, Inc.** ~ MM 102.5, John Pennekamp Coral Reef State Park, Key Largo; 305-451-1621.

You can rent windsurfing equipment and Hobie Cats from several companies who set up shop at Key West's public beaches along South Roosevelt and Atlantic boulevards.

HOUSE-BOATING

One of the best ways to capture the essence of the Keys is to just laze away a few days aboard a slow-moving, pontoon houseboat. Just such a craft is available from **Coral Bay Houseboat Rentals**, which sleeps four comfortably (one state room). Available for three nights to a week. Thirty-day advance notice recommended. ~ MM 81.2, Islamorada; 305-664-3111, fax 305-664-4281. Another rental source is **Houseboat Vacations of the Florida Keys**. ~ MM 85.9, Islamorada; 305-664-4009.

To go houseboating in the southernmost Everglades and Florida Bay, contact **Flamingo Lodge**. ~ Flamingo; 941-695-3101.

GOLF

At Homestead, try the **Redland Golf & Country Club**. ~ 24451 Southwest Krome Avenue; 305-247-8503. At Key Colony Beach, near Marathon, the public may play at the nine-hole KCB. ~ MM 53.5; 305-289-1533. On Stock Island, **Key West Golf Club** has an 18-hole course with public tee-times. ~ 6450 College Road; 305-294-5232.

TENNIS

Many Keys resorts provide tennis for their guests. In Islamorada, the public is welcome to play at **The Net**. ~ MM 81; 305-664-4122.

The **Islamorada Tennis Club** is open to the public with both clay and hard courts and night lighting. ~ MM 76.8; 305-664-5340.

In Key West you can play for no charge at **Bayview Park**. ~ 1310 Truman Avenue; 305-294-1346. There are also public courts at **Higgs County Beach**. ~ Atlantic Boulevard between White Street and Reynolds Road.

Bikeways parallel Route 1 intermittently down through the Keys. **Bike Rentals** You can rent bikes at the **Equipment Locker Sport & Bicycle**. ~ MM 53, Marathon; 305-289-1670.

BIKING

Bicycling is a good way to explore Key West. Places to rent bikes include **The Bicycle Center**. ~ 523 Truman Avenue; 305-294-4556. **Adventure Scooter and Bicycle Rental** has three locations to rent from in Key West: Key Plaza, North Roosevelt Avenue, 305-293-9933; Hyatt parking lot at Simonton and Front streets, 305-293-9911; and Pier House, Duval Street, 305-293-0441.

Bicycles are for rent for exploring the **Shark Valley** day-use area of the Everglades National Park at **Shark Valley Tram Tours**. ~ Route 41, about 25 miles west of Florida's Turnpike; 305-221-8455.

Residential development and the lack of sandy beaches limit hiking possibilities in the Keys. There are some intriguing trails into the Everglades, however, suitable for both novice strollers and serious explorers. All distances for hiking trails are one way unless otherwise noted.

HIKING

EVERGLADES AREA Shark Valley Trail (7.5 miles) in Everglades National Park leads hikers and bicyclists across a sawgrass waterway where they are sure to see alligators and a wide assortment of birds such as snail kites, wood storks and ibis. They may also observe deer, turtles, snakes and otter. About half way is an observation tower that offers a good overview of the "river of grass." Because of a lack of shade and few facilities along this single-lane, paved walkway, only well-equipped, hardy hikers should attempt the entire 15-mile loop. Two short nature trails are located near the entrance to Shark Valley.

Florida National Scenic Trail (South Section) (33 miles) is a loop trail that begins at the Oasis Ranger Station on Route 41 west of Shark Valley. This wilderness trail, for experienced hikers only, plunges deep into the Big Cypress Swamp (the trail is usually under water from May to November), which is actually a vast region of sandy pine islands, mixed hardwood hammocks, wet and dry prairies and mysterious marshes. Stunted bald cypress stand amid the grasses; wildlife is abundant. Bring your own drinking water.

Longer trails allow hikers to explore the coastal prairie and delve deeper into the mysteries of the Everglades. As they are sometimes under water, be sure to check at the ranger station or visitors center before starting out. Between April and October most trails are impassable. These trails include the following:

Pinelands Trail (7 miles), beginning on the road to Long Pine Key, is a network of interconnecting trails running through an unusually diverse pineland forest. About 200 types of plants, including 30 found nowhere else on earth, grow here. Among the mammals you can spot along the trail are possums, white-tailed deer, raccoons and the seldom-seen, endangered Florida panther.

Snake Bight Trail (2 miles) commences about three miles northeast of Flamingo off the park road and heads due south to a boardwalk at Florida Bay. Two miles along, it is joined by **Rowdy Bend Trail** (2.6 miles). The two make a good loop hike through a variety of terrains and flora.

Old Ingram Highway Trail (11 miles) begins at the Royal Palm Visitors Center and follows an old road through hammocks, sawgrass prairie, and pine forest. This flat hike is ideal for birdwatching. Look for deer along the way.

Bear Lake Trail (1.6 miles) begins about three miles north of Flamingo's visitors center at the end of Bear Lake Road. This raised trail was made with fill dirt from the digging of the Homestead Canal and heads due west, skirting a canoe trail and the north shore of Bear Lake. Woodland birds are abundant here.

Christian Point Trail (1.8 miles), begins about one and a half miles northeast of Flamingo, travels across coastal prairie and winds through mangrove thickets to the shore of Florida Bay.

Coastal Prairie Trail (7.5 miles) follows an old road bed leading to Cape Sable. This trail can be quite demanding, depending on ground conditions, as it progresses through open salt marsh and tends to flood. The trail begins at Flamingo and ends at Clubhouse Beach on the edge of Florida Bay.

KEY LARGO AREA A hiking/biking path runs from Mile Marker 106 in upper Key Largo for about 20 miles. This is a walking route parallel to Route 1. It ties in with a short nature trail, passes the John Pennekamp Coral Reef State Park, follows an old road to a county park and leads to some historic sites.

BISCAYNE NATIONAL PARK Beginning at Elliott Key harbor in Biscayne National Park, the **East-West Trail** (.5 mile) is a self-guided nature trail that leads through a tropical hardwood hammock of rare vines, flowers and trees. If you're up for a longer hike, the **Spite Highway** (about 7 miles) runs the full length of the island.

▼▼▼▼▼▼▼▼▼▼▼
Transportation

CAR

From Miami, **Route 41**, the Tamiami Trail, heads due west through the middle of the Everglades, skirting the northern boundary of Everglades National Park. **Route 1** and the almost-parallel **Florida Turnpike** head toward Homestead and Florida City, where **Route 27** branches off into the heart of Everglades National Park. If you prefer the road less traveled, start from Naples and head east along Route 41. Route 1 and the slightly more northerly scenic **Card Sound Road** lead to Key Largo, where Route 1 becomes the **Overseas Highway**, continuing on through the Keys all the way to Key West.

Note: Mile markers, often called mile posts, can be seen each mile along Route 1 in the Keys. They appear on the right shoulder of the road as small green signs with white numbers, beginning with Mile Marker (MM) 126 just south of Florida City and ending at MM 0 in Key West. When asking for directions in the Keys, your answer will likely refer to a mile marker number. We use them throughout the Keys, except for Key West, where street addresses are used.

AIR

Many visitors to the Keys and Everglades choose to fly to Miami (see Chapter Two for more information). However, there are two small airports in the Keys located in Marathon and Key West. The **Marathon Airport** is serviced by Air Sunshine, Airways International, American Eagle and USAir Express. Carriers at **Key West International Airport** include American Eagle, Cape Air, Comair, Delta, Gulfstream International and USAir Express.

Servicing the Upper Keys, **The Airporter** provides regularly scheduled shuttle service from Miami International Airport to Key Largo, Homestead, Islamorada and other areas. ~ 305-247-8874, 800-830-3413. **Upper Keys Transportation, Inc.** provides limousine service to Miami International Airport 24 hours a day with personally scheduled reservations. ~ 305-852-9533, 800-749-5397.

Increasingly, travelers weary of the behemoths that large-city air terminals have become are looking for less stressful entry points into the 'glades. **Southwest Florida International Airport** in Ft. Myers, just 30 miles north of Naples, is served by most of the same domestic and international carriers as Miami International, including Air Canada, American Eagle, America TransAir, Canada 3000, Canadian Airlines, Cape Air, Carnival, Continental, Delta, LTU International, Midwest Express, Northwest/KLM, Spirit, TWA, United, USAir/British Airways and Valujet.

BUS

Greyhound Bus Lines (800-231-2222) services a few Keys and Everglades locations. They are in Homestead at 5 Northeast 3rd Road, 305-247-2040; in Key Largo at MM 102, 305-296-9072; in Big Pine Key at MM 27.5; and in Marathon at 12222 Overseas Highway, 305-296-9073.

CAR RENTALS

Avis Rent A Car (800-331-1212) is located at the Marathon Airport. **Value Rent A Car** (305-743-6100) at the Winn Dixie Shopping Center and **Enterprise Rent A Car** (305-289-7630) will arrange airport pickup. In Key Largo, call **Enterprise Rent A Car** (305-451-3998).

Rental agencies at the Key West airport include **Avis Rent A Car** (800-331-1212) and **Dollar Rent A Car** (800-800-4000). Pick up at the airport can be arranged through **Alamo Rent A Car** (800-327-9633), **Budget Rent A Car** (800-527-0700), **Enterprise Rent A Car** (800-325-8007) and **Hertz Rent A Car** (800-654-3131).

PUBLIC TRANSIT

In Key West, the **City of Key West Department of Transportation** operates buses that run the entire length and partial width of the island. The route does not currently include the airport. ~ 627 Palm Avenue; 305-292-8165.

TAXIS

Taxicabs that serve the Key West airport include **Friendly Cab** (305-292-0000), **Airport Taxi** (305-292-1111) and **Florida Keys Taxi** (305-296-7777). In Marathon, call **Action Express Taxi** (305-743-6800).

SEVEN

The West Coast

The West Coast is a Florida panther. Its beaches stretch tawny; its wilderness resists taming. And like the indigenous Florida cat, the Gulf Coast represents exotic intrigue and the continuing battle between the state's scenic wilds and civilization's growth gone wild.

American Indian tribes settled near Crystal River, on this coast's northern tip, as early as 200 B.C. Relics discovered there have been traced to Mayan civilizations. More recently, tribes such as the Timucuans and the Calusas made their living in Gulf Coast Florida, eating fish and oysters and creating tools and burial mounds out of seashells.

The first "sightseers"—Spanish explorers such as Hernando de Soto, Ponce de León and Panfilo de Narváez—visited the West Coast in the early 1500s, long before Jamestown was settled. They discovered warring American Indians, impenetrable swampland, vicious insects, and suffocating heat that quickly discouraged European settlement.

In the following centuries, Florida's Gulf Coast became home to some intriguing—albeit unsavory—European adventurers. Back in 1772, one explorer called the Charlotte Harbor coastline area below Tampa, "a haunt of the picaroons of all nations." Like the rest of West Coast shoreline, Charlotte Harbor's honeycombed maze of islands, keys, shoals, inlets, bayous and estuaries made the waters a sailor's nightmare. And a pirate's dream.

Gasparilla is the awe-inspiring name one hears most in these parts when talk turns to pirates. Serious historians refute his existence, while treasure hunters never give up the faith. Whether or not he ever lived, his legend matches the adventurous spirit of West Coast Florida. You will see his name everywhere today from Cedar Key to Naples—on street signs, hotel fronts, trails and on a Charlotte Harbor island that bears his moniker.

War was a great settler of Florida's rugged frontier. During the Seminole Wars of the 1800s, Tampa and Fort Myers were selected as U.S. Army outposts because of their strategic locations. Soldiers returning from western Florida after the Seminole and Civil wars talked about the area as a balmy paradise. Pioneers became more plentiful.

By the late 1800s, the area began attracting wealthy entrepreneurs. In Tampa, Henry Plant was to Florida's West Coast what railroad tycoon Henry Flagler was to the East. Both were men of insight and power who recognized Florida for its recreational, health and wealth potential. Noting the rich vacationers Flagler was enticing to the East Coast with his railroads and hotels, Plant figured he could do the same in the west. After all, the Gulf Coast was blessed with the same semitropical climate and flora. Plus it had something the Atlantic side never would: seaside sunsets.

When Plant brought his railroad to Tampa in 1884, only a handful of staunch settlers lived there. He built a causeway over the bay and deep water piers for a seaport. In 1891, he erected his fabulous Tampa Bay Hotel. The opulent Moorish palace served as a bastion for wealthy vacationers until the Spanish-American War, when Colonel Theodore Roosevelt brought his Rough Riders to train on the hotel grounds. The landmark hotel today houses University of Tampa offices and a historical museum.

At the turn of the century, Plant built another resort palace, the Belleview Hotel, in Clearwater. Down the coast, the Gasparilla Inn was established on Gasparilla Island to house the Vanderbilts, DuPonts and other wealthy northerners during their winter stays. Teddy Roosevelt, Shirley Temple, Charles Lindbergh and others came down to the once-forbidden islands of Charlotte Harbor to fish and relax.

Meanwhile, industry had come to Tampa in the form of phosphate shipping and cigar making. In 1886, Vincente Martínez Ybor moved his tobacco factories from Key West to Tampa. An influx of immigrant workers followed to settle in Ybor City, a section of Tampa that is today a center of Cuban culture.

At the same time Plant was building Tampa into a city, inventor Thomas Edison was putting the name Fort Myers up in lights. At his winter estate, he grew the bamboo and goldenrod needed for his experiments.

While Plant and Edison brought notice to Tampa and Fort Myers, another name stands out in Sarasota: John Ringling. The circus man bestowed a legacy of culture to the fledgling town south of Tampa. A devotee of Italian arts, Ringling designed his palatial Sarasota home, Ca'd'Zan, in imitation of the Doge's Palace in Venice. In 1927 he brought his Ringling Brothers and Barnum & Bailey Circus to the area for wintering, thereby stoking the city's economy. He built island causeways, hotels and an art museum, often using his circus elephants for construction.

In Naples, the 1920s brought an Ohio man named E. W. Crayton to develop this city that avid sportsmen had been keeping to themselves since 1887, when *Louisville Courier Journal* publisher Walter N. Haldeman discovered the area. On Marco Island, settler Bill Collier had turned his home into a fishing inn that in 1883 had advertised its rooms for "$1 a day. You furnish the meat." The '20s along Florida's West Coast not only roared, they boomed. By the next decade, tourism had developed into a bustling business that threatened to run amok, unchecked. Fortunately, the area's incredible natural endowment continued to bring lovers of the outdoors to the West Coast. Many of the islands, bays and villages were settled by vacationing fishermen, hunters and conservationists, who saw to it that wilderness areas were preserved.

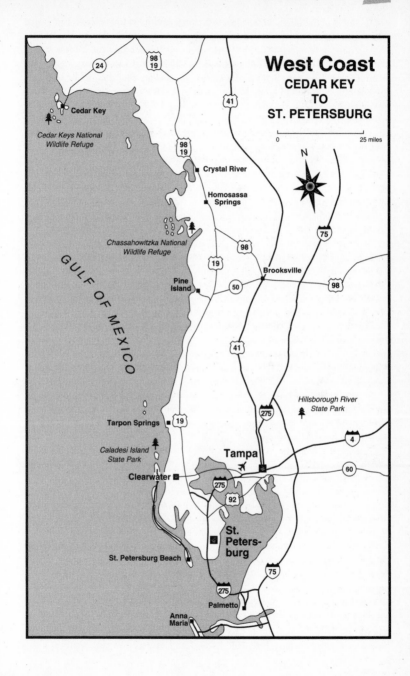

West Coast
CEDAR KEY
TO
ST. PETERSBURG

0   25 miles

N

GULF OF MEXICO

Cedar Key

Cedar Keys National
Wildlife Refuge

Chassahowitzka National
Wildlife Refuge

Crystal River

Homosassa
Springs

Pine
Island

Brooksville

Tarpon Springs

Caladesi Island
State Park

Clearwater

St. Petersburg Beach

Tampa

Hillsborough River
State Park

**St. Peters-
burg**

Palmetto

Anna
Maria

A couple of decades later, bulldozers began again to threaten the fabric of tamed and untamed life on Florida's West Coast. Glitz brought the demise of much old architecture; developers' insatiable greed threatened precious wildlife. But during the 1980s, Floridians developed a renewed sensibility about their past, which gave pause to the bulldozers. A style of architecture recalling Florida's belle epoch was revived. Known as Old Florida style, it features white clapboard, tin roofs and airy verandas.

Today, the visitor to Florida's West Coast finds a pleasing balance between the wild and the wilds. In big-city Tampa, skyscrapers seem to shoot up overnight. The town's pace is set by whizzing jai alai orbs, zooming corporate successes and neon nightlife. Yet wildlife can be found even in this soaring metropolis, on the Serengeti Plains of Busch Gardens/The Dark Continent, where thousands of exotic animals roam freely. The old ways are preserved in parks, the renovated downtown area and at shrimp docks.

Much like the state's East Coast, cities on the segment of shoreline below Tampa are beginning to melt together, leaving little rural area in between. Yet each community has its distinctions. Sarasota, the cultured pearl in this string of gems, has been drawing educated, upscale young people with its arts and cultural attractions. Bradenton, its sister city, maintains a homier ambience.

Down the coast, beaches remain to be discovered; Charlotte Harbor cities hide quietly behind great resort villages that are popping up. Islands where pirates and powerbrokers once fled still shelter adventurous refugees.

Fort Myers and its environs comprise one of the fastest growing areas in the United States, but the reins are held tightly to control development. Naples sits in sophistication on the verge of Florida wilds at their best—Everglades National Park. Olde Marco Inn still receives guests at Bill Collier's place. It even provides meat these days.

St. Petersburg, once the butt of retirement-home jokes, now projects a younger, livelier image. Directly north of that city, Pinellas County has become one of the coast's most popular playgrounds, owing to such features as a futuristic pier and its swinging, sun-soaked beaches.

Along the way up the coast from St. Pete, you can find pockets of cultural diversity. In Dunedin, the squeal of bagpipes reaffirm a Scottish flavor; in Tarpon Springs, where icons weep and divers pick sponges, all the world is Greek.

Nature thickens and the glitz thins out en route to Crystal River, where the endangered one-ton manatee symbolizes the endurance of things wild. Attractions in this part of the apart-from-things world give window to old Florida soul: crystal-clear springs, ancient American Indian relics and funky mermaid shows.

Cedar Key, once a thriving port and now an artists' community, has reverted back to a time that reality-escapees find refreshing. Up in these far reaches of the West Coast, palm trees are joined by pines and oaks, beaches turn marshy and life seems simpler.

The satisfaction of Cedar Key's rediscovered way of life represents a new awareness in Florida development. Residents no longer feel that this area exists merely as a playground. A new sense of place has emerged on the West Coast of Florida that lauds the merits of being relaxed and homey. And wild as a Florida panther.

To many, Tampa means Busch Gardens and Buccaneer football. But to those who take the time to explore, and to the increasing numbers who are making this West Coast hub home, Tampa is seen as a sophisticated network of growth stemming from carefully nurtured agricultural and fishing roots.

Tampa Area

DOWNTOWN In downtown Tampa, there beats the heart of a thriving city. Dazzling corporate towers now rub elbows with spruced-up historic buildings and re-created street markets. The result is sophistication with a homey feel.

SIGHTS

One of the biggest renovation projects undertaken was **Harbour Island**. Once weed-infested, today its cobblestone streets lead to a world-class hotel, luxury condominiums and the **Shops at Harbour Island**, an indoor fantasy mall. ~ 813-202-1830. The PeopleMover monorail carries passengers to and from the island and around the downtown area.

The neighborhood across the water from the island is also looking up. The **Franklin Street Mall** allows pedestrian outdoor shopping among restored boutiques that sit in marked contrast with Tampa's skyscraping and skyrocketing downtown commercial image. The **Tampa Theatre** resides in the same neighborhood. Built in 1926, it has been revived to the original glamour that once earned it a reputation as "The Pride of the South." ~ 711 North Franklin Street; 813-274-8981.

A block away, sitting humbly amid Tampa's modern highrises, is the historic **Sacred Heart Catholic Church**. Completed in 1905, its Romanesque architecture features a remarkable rose window in front. ~ 509 Florida Avenue; 813-229-1595.

Located at the Garrison Seaport Center is **The Florida Aquarium**, a 152,000-square-foot behemoth that encourages harmony between people and their natural environment. Boasting over one

---

✔ **CHECK THESE OUT—UNIQUE SIGHTS**

- At the **Mind's Eye Museum**, you can rev up your *om* at a free meditation class after a fiberoptic light show on reincarnation. *page 392*
- Juggle the many activities at **The John & Mable Ringling Museum of Art**, the estate of the famous circus man and Sarasota developer. *page 402*
- Bone up on science and history—and enjoy an impressive botanical display, too—when you visit the **Thomas A. Edison Winter Estate and Botanical Gardens**. *page 417*
- Feel surreal as you gaze at the impressive collection of Dali's paintings in St. Petersburg's **Salvador Dali Museum**. *page 430*

million gallons of water, the aquarium is home to 4300 plants and animals native to Florida, and showcases four of the Sunshine State's environments (wetlands, bays and beaches, coral reefs and offshore) by tracing the path of a drop of water from the ground in the northern part of the state to the open ocean of the keys. There are also a number of hands-on exhibits and a rather unusual exhibit demonstrating how an underwater piling for a bridge can become a whole ecosystem of its own. Admission. ~ 701 Channelside Drive; 813-273-4020.

"Hands-on" displays at the **Museum of Science and Industry** mean experiencing a hurricane and touching a shark's tooth. This—the largest science center in the southeast United States—is a facility that has fun with scientific phenomena. Admission. ~ 4801 East Fowler Avenue; 813-987-6300.

The permanent collection at the **Tampa Museum of Art** displays contemporary sculpture, paintings and photographs, as well as the largest collection of Greek and Roman antiquities in the Southeast. The facility hosts about ten special traveling exhibitions annually. Admission. ~ 600 North Ashley Drive; 813-223-8130.

The long-standing landmark and historical anchor of Tampa is marked by the silver Moorish minarets of the **Tampa Bay Hotel**, now the University of Tampa administrative offices. The **Henry B. Plant Museum** within the university collects memorabilia from the days when its ambitious namesake settled Tampa with visions of luxury hotels in the early 1890s. Some of the wicker and imported furnishings from the opulent hotel are displayed in the museum. Also recalled in the museum's memory banks are the days when Teddy Roosevelt headquartered his Rough Riders at the hotel, to train for the Spanish-American War. ~ 401 West Kennedy Boulevard; 813-254-1891.

Another pastime is watching the shrimp boats come in to unload their catches at the **shrimp docks**. If you don't catch any activity from the shrimpers, it's still a good place to watch waterfront activity and see gargantuan sea craft passing by. ~ 22nd Street Causeway.

For information on Tampa and its environs, stop in at the **Tampa/Hillsborough Convention and Visitors Association**. ~ 111 East Madison Street, Suite 1010; 813-223-1111. Another resource, also located in downtown Tampa, is the **Greater Tampa Chamber of Commerce**. ~ 801 East Kennedy Boulevard; 813-228-7777.

YBOR CITY AREA   Visitors to Ybor City, the well-known cigar-making center, can still see expert craftsmen roll cigars by hand and view factories as they operated in their heyday. Cobblestone streets, Spanish-tiled storefronts and wrought-iron detailing take you back to the days when Cuban, Jewish, German and Italian immigrants lived here.

The **Ybor City State Museum**, once a Cuban bread bakery, depicts the history of the area near Preservation Park, a turn-of-the-century street of cobblestone and wrought iron. Three buildings have been renovated to re-create typical cigar workers' homes. Closed Sunday and Monday. Admission. ~ 1818 East 9th Avenue; 813-247-6323. The **Ybor City Chamber of Commerce** is housed in one of these buildings. Stop here for a self-guided walking tour map of Ybor City. ~ 1800 East 9th Avenue; 813-248-3712.

At **Ybor Square**, arts-and-crafts, antique marts, specialty shops and a nostalgia market are located where cigars were once manufactured. ~ 8th Avenue and 13th Street; 813-247-4497. In the square at **Tampa Rico Cigars**, visitors can still watch a craftsman roll cigars by hand. ~ 813-248-0218.

While you're in the area, you might consider a sidetrip to the nearby **Bobby's Seminole Indian Village**, which contains a community of chickee (thatched-roof) structures and a museum demonstrating the way of life of these long-time Florida residents. Sensational alligator wrestling and snake shows can be arranged for groups of 30 or more. Admission. ~ 5221 North Orient Road; 813-620-3077.

BUSCH GARDENS AREA   Busch Gardens/The Dark Continent remains the number-one attraction in the metropolitan area, number

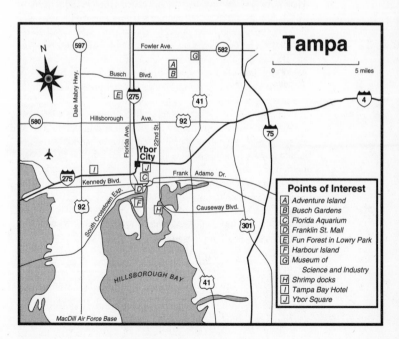

Tampa

0   5 miles

Points of Interest

A *Adventure Island*
B *Busch Gardens*
C *Florida Aquarium*
D *Franklin St. Mall*
E *Fun Forest in Lowry Park*
F *Harbour Island*
G *Museum of
       Science and Industry*
H *Shrimp docks*
I *Tampa Bay Hotel*
J *Ybor Square*

two in the state (after Disney World/EPCOT). The beer factory-cum-theme park takes visitors to 19th-century Africa via the 20th-century technology of a monorail system or skyride. The wilds are juxtaposed with the wild; jungle animals placidly roam the Serengeti Plains as thrill-seekers get dunked, spun and set on their heads by different amusement rides.

Tropical bird gardens, belly dancers, beer sampling and food and gift stands are all presented in exotic surroundings. Exhibits and rides carry African handles: the "Python" and "Scorpion" are torturous rollercoaster rides; an animal farm is found in Nairobi; visitors shoot the rapids on the Congo River; Stanleyville features a theater and log flume. Admission. ~ 3000 East Busch Boulevard; 813-987-5082.

Nearby **Adventure Island** is a 22-acre water theme park featuring an endless surf pool, water slides, inner-tubing chutes, beaches and picnic areas. The surf pool simulates the sea with manufactured churning. All is set in natural and manmade tropic surroundings. Admission. ~ 4545 Bougainvillea Avenue; 813-987-5660.

Down the road, the **Mind's Eye Museum** is operated by the Brahma Kamari's Raja Yoga Center. Colorful electronic video displays, fiberoptic light shows and recorded commentary illustrate metaphysical tenets such as karma, reincarnation and God. Other displays define the soul and the history of religion through high-tech media. This psychic museum is a Western-world prototype of facilities throughout India. You're welcome to attend free meditation classes. Closed Monday. ~ 2207 East Busch Boulevard; 813-935-0736.

At the Fun Forest Amusement Park in **Lowry Park**, storybook characters entertain the young and the young at heart. This attraction is set up as a city park, replete with bubbling fountains, shade trees and picnic areas. From there, childlike fancy takes over. Foot bridges look like rainbows and Ferris wheels spin. Safety Village is set up to look like a miniature town, complete with homes, a fire station and various shops. Here children learn the rules of the road in a universe their size. To top it off, there's even a zoo. Admission. ~ 7530 North Boulevard; 813-935-5503, 813-932-0245.

LODGING   Most of the accommodations in the city are chain hotels catering to the business traveler or overnight guest. Those looking for a fun-in-the-sun resort head across the bay to St. Petersburg and the necklace of islands that adorn it. If you plan on staying a while in the bay area, we recommend rooming there. For those seeking a few days of metropolitan stimulation and culture, we have found a few Tampa hotels that excel.

The **Radisson Bay Harbor Inn** offers private balconies in the 257 modern rooms overlooking the bay or the city. The lodgings come with a lot of extras: restaurant, lounge, tennis courts and pool. ~ 770 Courtney Campbell Causeway, Tampa; 813-281-8900, 800-282-0613, fax 813-281-0189. DELUXE.

On the outside, the **Double Guest Suites—Tampa Bay** looks like a Mayan temple dedicated to the god of bay waters. Inside the look is decidedly up-to-date, with subtle shades, dark woods and modern conveniences. All 203 units are suites. There are swimming and hot tub facilities, and parasail and waverunner rentals are available. ~ 3050 North Rocky Point Drive West, Tampa; 813-888-8800, 800-888-2223, fax 813-888-8743. ULTRA-DELUXE.

Holiday Inn Select Downtown—Ashley Plaza sits downtown on the riverfront near the Tampa Bay Performing Arts Center. Its 312 units include plushly carpeted rooms and suites decorated in modern mauves and teals. ~ 111 West Fortune Street, Tampa; 813-223-1351, 800-465-4329, fax 813-221-2000. DELUXE.

On Harbour Island in the downtown hub, the **Windham Harbour Island Hotel** spells luxury in the form of 300 posh rooms with bay vistas, along with sophisticated clubs and restaurants. Dark woods panel the lobby areas. ~ 725 South Harbour Island Boulevard, Tampa; 813-229-5000, 800-996-3426, fax 813-229-5322. ULTRA-DELUXE.

With its gleaming mirrored silhouette towering near the bay, the **Hyatt Regency** is easily Tampa's glitziest hotel. Formal and elegant, the lobby features a dramatic chandelier and a waterfall that cascades down two floors. The 517 guest rooms are cushy and oversized, adorned with designer pastel draperies and plush carpets. ~ 2 Tampa City Center, Tampa; 813-225-1234, 800-233-1234. ULTRA-DELUXE.

More homey and less glitzy is the family-operated **Tahitian Inn**, where you will find comfortable, clean rooms and a swimming pool. ~ 601 South Dale Mabry Highway, Tampa; 813-877-6721, 800-876-1397, fax 813-871-6218. MODERATE.

Howard Johnson Main Gate's theme comes from its proximity to Busch Gardens. The lobby fits in with its luxurious leather chairs and the bamboolike trim around the check-in area. The 99 rooms are decorated in jungle tones. There's also a pool, restaurant and lounge. ~ 4139 East Busch Boulevard, Tampa; 813-988-9191, 800-874-1768, fax 813-988-9195. MODERATE.

Tampa also offers many budget-priced chain establishments. **Days Inn Busch Gardens Hotel** features a pool and restaurant. ~ 2520 North 50th Street; 813-247-3300. **Red Roof Inn** offers a jacuzzi. ~ 2307 East Busch Boulevard; 813-932-0073.

DINING

Local seafood—pompano, grouper, shrimp and stone crab—makes a culinary splash at most Tampa restaurants, washed with the new wave of American cuisine. Standing at the crossroads of Cuban,

Spanish, Greek and Scottish subcultures, and influenced by its international port role, Tampa offers fare that tends to be Continental while maintaining the homespun flavor of its surrounding agricultural communities.

In the center of Tampa International Airport, **CK's** is a revolving rooftop restaurant overlooking the airport and the Tampa city skyline. The views are paralleled by the menu; the specialties include lobster in hollandaise sauce, swordfish steaks and tuna seared with black pepper sauce. Desserts are equally as imaginative, and the 5 to 6:30 p.m. early bird specials make this pricey place affordable for more moderate budgets. ~ 8th floor of TIA, Tampa; 813-879-5151. MODERATE TO DELUXE.

Crawdaddy's Restaurant & Lounge is a theme eating spot done in poor white trash chic. Outside, you feel you've stumbled into the backyard of a Carolina mountain man. A tin smokehouse, long johns on the clothesline and a junked truck, together with the broken-down shacks that house the facility, are some of the props. Inside, things are considerably more comfortable and pleasant. Parlor lamps, curtained booths and carved highback chairs are designed to look aged and to provide a unique eating experience with picture-window views of the bay. The menu concentrates on seafood, with steak, chicken and pasta for balance. ~ 2500 Rocky Point Road, Tampa; 813-281-0407. MODERATE TO DELUXE.

Saltwater aquariums, exotic music and a collection of articles that have washed ashore give **The Castaway** its South Seas ambience. However, the food is mainly steak and seafood with some pasta and chicken dishes. ~ 7720 Courtney Campbell Causeway, Tampa; 813-281-0770. MODERATE TO DELUXE.

Jasmine Thai's rendition of Thailand cuisine is dressed up with elegant touches. Offerings at this tiny restaurant include the "two-friend *panang*" (jumbo shrimp and chicken in *panang* curry sauce), salmon with chile sauce, garlic pork, Siam lobster and fancy duck. ~ 13248 North Dale Mabry Highway, Tampa; 813-968-1501. MODERATE.

Although you may feel a little spooked when you first enter **Bern's Steak House**, you have discovered Tampa's top shelf. The heavy, rococo decor gives Bern's a slightly somber feeling, but be assured, things don't get any fresher than Bern's homegrown herbs and vegetables. Only the steaks and wine are aged, the latter comprising the largest selection offered anywhere in the area. Desserts are enjoyed upstairs in glass booths equipped with televisions and radios for after-dinner relaxation. ~ 1208 South Howard Avenue, Tampa; 813-251-2421. MODERATE TO DELUXE.

Bella's Italian Café is a favorite of the artistic crowd. Paper tablecloths and a glassful of crayons decorate each table of this restaurant located in the historic Hyde Park section. The atmosphere is casual, the menu is Italian and the Bella! Bella! dessert is a triple-chocolate chocoholic's dream fix. Happy hours are animated. No lunch on weekends. ~ 1413 South Howard Avenue, Tampa; 813-254-3355. BUDGET TO MODERATE.

Despite its French name, **Mise En Place** serves American fare in this popular eatery across the street from the University of Tampa. Local ingredients combine with classics to offer entrées like roast duck with wild Jamaica strawberry sauce, Brazil nut–crusted rack of lamb and swordfish with melon and mint salsa. The menu changes daily. No lunch served on Saturday; no dinner on Monday. Closed Sunday. ~ 442 West Kennedy Boulevard, Tampa; 813-254-5373. MODERATE TO DELUXE.

One of the city's most visited delis is located in the heart of the downtown business district. Housed in a historic warehouse that once was the city's dock for loading foodstuffs, **The Loading Dock** offers the usual deli fare of sandwiches, soups and salads. Sandwiches are high and prices are good. ~ 100 Madison Street, Tampa; 813-223-6905. BUDGET.

Dishes at **Selena's** epitomize the Florida melting-pot effect. Creole and Italian influences are married together here to produce garlicked seafood with sides of sausage, red beans and rice. Furnishings are classic: refinished oak antiques and flowered wallcoverings. ~ 1623 Snow Avenue, Tampa; 813-251-2116. MODERATE.

Volvos, BMWs and other trendy cars regularly crowd the streets around **Jimmy Mac's**. Set in a 1920s brick house of creaky wood floors and fireplaces, the ever-popular meeting place feels like a cozy family room. Known for its dressed-up burgers, it also features fried grouper sandwiches, steaks and great dessert coffees. ~ 113 South Armenia Avenue, Tampa; 813-879-0591. BUDGET TO MODERATE.

◄ HIDDEN

Housed in a 70-year-old Spanish-style building, **Mojo** offers a melting pot of Cuban, Brazilian and South American influences in its menu. Enjoy citrus jicama-avocado salad, topped with Chilean salmon, with black-bean chorizo cakes. A fountained courtyard for outdoor dining is a plus. ~ 238 East Davis Boulevard, Davis Island, Tampa; 813-259-9949. MODERATE.

In the historic cigar factory district of Ybor City, restaurants principally feature Cuban food. The Cuban sandwich, Ybor City's gastronomic mainstay, creates a sense of friendly rivalry among restaurateurs, who all claim theirs is the best. Basically, this is little more than a sub sandwich. The difference is the Cuban bread, baked in yard-long loaves using a time-honored method that produces something totally unrelated to a sub bun. Other area specialties include Spanish soup, black beans and rice, paella, flan and Cuban coffee.

Ybor City's **Silver Ring Café** holds its reputation as maker of the best Cuban sandwich. These are produced in a showcase window for your entertainment. The decor of this long-established luncheonette is so old and out-of-date, it's "in." Seating is at a long formica counter, at tables or on stools facing little shelves along the wall. ~ 1831 East 7th Avenue, Ybor City; 813-248-2549. BUDGET.

The **Columbia Restaurant** is both landmark and restaurant extraordinaire. The block-long building demonstrates a Spanish influence in its ornate tiling, archways, balconies and grand chandeliers. Although the waiters wear dinner jackets and musicians serenade tableside, the Columbia is casual and reasonable. The menu features traditional and inventive Spanish dishes: paella, steak *salteado* and *boliche*, for example. ~ 2117 East 7th Avenue, Ybor City; 813-248-4961. MODERATE.

New Orleans ambience and food take diners on a cultural departure at **El Pasaje Café Creole**. Once a popular Spanish club, the restored building swings with jazzy background music, lively atmosphere, architectural drama and spicy Creole concoctions including blackened fish, crawfish, jambalaya and crab cakes. Live jazz Friday and Saturday. ~ 1330 9th Avenue, Ybor City; 813-247-6283. BUDGET TO MODERATE.

HIDDEN ► **Latam at the Centro** is our favorite find in the city because of its incredibly inexpensive châteaubriand. But if you desire elegant atmosphere with your fine food, you will be disappointed. The eatery is housed in an unassuming facility with naugahyde decor. It also serves Cuban specialties. Lunch is served weekdays; dinner is served Thursday through Saturday. ~ 1913 North Nebraska Avenue, Ybor City, 813-223-7338. BUDGET.

SHOPPING **Shops at Harbour Island** features exclusive shops and luxury boutiques in an indoor marketplace. That's why it is such a pleasant surprise to find a place like **Everything's $1.00** (813-223-6847), which sells items of use and of little use for a dollar, as promised. ~ 601 South Harbour Island Boulevard, Tampa.

Old Hyde Park Village features upscale shopping in a restored historic setting. ~ Located at West Swann and South Dakota avenues, Tampa; 813-251-3500. One of the many shops here that carry designer clothes is **Polo/Ralph Lauren**. ~ 701 Village Circle South; 813-254-7656.

Westshore Plaza is a popular Sun Coast shopping mall housing major area retailers plus an array of small boutiques and restaurants. ~ Westshore and Kennedy boulevards, Tampa; 813-286-0790.

The **Swiss Chalet Gift Shop** carries collectible figurines, T-shirts, citrus and other Floridiana. ~ 3601 East Busch Boulevard, Tampa; 813-985-3601.

Antique hunters can hit the jackpot at **El Prado Antique Center**. Close to 20 shops cluster within a three-block stretch, selling treasures such as Tiffany silver and 19th-century art. ~ MacDill and El Prado avenues, Tampa. **Village Antiques, Inc.** is one such antiquarian, specializing in Americana. ~ 4323 El Prado Boulevard, Tampa; 813-839-1761.

Contemporary fine glass and crystal can be found at **Smither's Gifts, Inc.** ~ 3225 South MacDill Avenue, Tampa; 813-831-1280.

In the market for a new kilt? **Dunedin Scottish Incorporated** carries a large stock of tartans, along with china and other Gaelic wares. ~ 5402 Airport Boulevard, Tampa; 813-885-5880.

The merchandise in Ybor City ranges from antique glassware to loaves of crusty Cuban bread. At **Ybor Square** an old cigar factory, a stemmery and a warehouse have been converted into a historic shopping mall. One shop here, **Tampa Rico** (813-248-0218), hand rolls and sells cigars. Another, **Chevere** (813-247-1339) is a cache of cool and colorful cotton dresses, flowing skirts and other women's clothing from Central and South America. The always-crowded **Red Horse** (813-248-8859) carries out-of-date newspapers and magazines as well as postcards from around the world. ~ 8th Avenue and 13th Street, Ybor City.

Buy your fresh Cuban bread at **La Segunda Central Bakery** in Ybor City. Around back, you can watch the bakers at their task. ~ 2512 15th Street, Ybor City; 813-248-1531.

J. J. Higgins offers an assortment of live entertainment nightly. Cover on weekends. ~ 10330 North Dale Mabry Highway, Tampa; 813-264-7811.

NIGHTLIFE

Country-and-western fans head 'em up for live music every Friday and Saturday at the **Dallas Bull**. Cover. ~ 8222 North Highway 301, Tampa; 813-985-6877.

The **Encore Bar** in the Ashley Plaza Hotel is the chic place to be seen after performances at the Tampa Bay Performing Arts Center. ~ 111 West Fortune Street, Tampa; 813-223-1351.

The Barn is a laid-back kind of place where the crowd wears blue jeans and the music wails softly in the background. The three pool tables beneath the soft glow of neon beer signs are almost always full. ~ 13815 Hillsborough Avenue, Tampa; 813-855-9818.

Blues, reggae, and progressive music are featured at **Skipper's Smokehouse**. Come for the Jimmy Buffett cover band on Tuesday or Grateful Dead Night on Thursday. Closed Monday. Cover. ~ 910 Skipper Road, Tampa; 813-971-0666.

◄ *HIDDEN*

442 is an upscale jazz/blues piano bar. A mixed crowd of mature sophisticates and young hipsters comes for the 1940s ambience. ~ 442 West Kennedy Boulevard, Tampa; 813-254-0442.

The Comedy Works manufactures mirth with top-name entertainers. ~ 3447 West Kennedy Boulevard, Tampa; 813-875-9129.

The **Tampa Bay Performing Arts Center** houses three theaters in a 290,000-square-foot facility. Everything from Broadway musicals to local concerts are hosted at this first-rate complex. ~ 1010 North MacInnes Place, Tampa; 813-229-7827.

One of the longer-standing clubs in town, **The Masquerade** is enduringly hip. A former theater, The Ritz tends to draw a young-ish crowd, with deejay-generated '80s, techno and house music. Cover. Adjacent to the main theater in a smaller room, **Apocalypse** is a get-down-and-dirty dance hall with a deejay who spins indus-trial tunes to an appreciative crowd body-jammed onto a modest-size dancefloor. Cover. ~ 1503 East 7th Avenue, Ybor City; 813-247-3319.

HIDDEN ▶   If you're looking for offbeat local color, visit **Showtown USA**, a carnival bar where you can mingle with circus stars and dance to live country and rock-and-roll music. ~ Route 41, Gibsonton; 813-677-5443.

GAY SCENE   Fridays, Sundays and Mondays are the busiest nights at **City Side**, a pleasant neighborhood bar with an outdoor patio to hang out in. Although it is primarily men who come here, women are always welcome. Have a drink and challenge your neighbor to a game of pinball, pool or darts. ~ 3810 Neptune Street, Tampa; 813-254-6466.

Tracks is a popular gay and lesbian bar with a clientele that is split almost 50/50. The dancefloor is surrounded by videos and smaller conversation areas are built in as well. Fridays are for women only. Cover after 10 p.m. and on weekends. ~ 1430 East 7th Avenue, Ybor City; 813-247-2711.

BEACHES & PARKS

HILLSBOROUGH RIVER STATE PARK 🧍 🚴 ⛵ 🛶 🛶 This spot includes 3000 forested acres and a suspension bridge that spans the placid river. Within Hillsborough River State Park sits Fort Foster, a reconstructed Seminole War fort garrisoned by sol-diers of the United States Second Artillery. Actually park service guides, they are dressed and equipped in exact replica outfits (weekends only). Fishing is good. Swimming is not safe in the river, but allowed in a pool. Facilities include nature trails, a bike trail, picnic areas, restrooms and canoe rentals; restaurants and groceries are nearby. ~ On Route 301, six miles southwest of Zephyrhills; 813-987-6771.

▲ There are 106 sites, 75 with hookups; $14 to $17 per night.

BEN T. DAVIS MUNICIPAL BEACH ⛵ 🛶 A stretch of sand lying along the Courtney Campbell Causeway, the nine-mile drive bridg-ing Tampa and Clearwater has pretty landscaping, and the sand is soft and white. This is the Tampa area's only saltwater beach, and the locals swarm here; the swimming is good as is fishing. True beach lovers go the distance to the other side of the Pinellas County peninsula across the causeway to the beaches of Holiday Isles.

Facilities include seasonal lifeguards, picnic areas and restrooms; restaurants are nearby, groceries a few miles away. ~ The park lies right on the Courtney Campbell Causeway's east end as it heads toward Rocky Point; 813-274-8615.

SIMMONS REGIONAL PARK ⚓ 🚴 🚤 🏊 ⛵ A popular   ◄ HIDDEN
birdwatching and canoe area on 450 acres of bayfront and channel land. Visitors find a good model of mangrove life and a bird sanctuary. The sand beach is not wide but very natural. The fine but ungroomed sands are favored by locals who prefer seclusion to aesthetics. It's a good place to swim and anglers fish in the saltwater for mangrove snapper and snook. There are picnic areas, a playground, restrooms and showers; restaurants and groceries are several miles away. ~ Located at 19th Avenue Northwest in Ruskin, off Route 41; 813-671-7655.

▲ There are 88 sites, 50 with hookups; $10 to $12 per night.

Home of America's most famous circus, Mediterranean-style villas and some of the best seafood on Florida's West Coast, the Bradenton–Sarasota area is also the place to find bald eagles and bobcats, as well as best beaches and remote islands. A variety of historic attractions may even tempt you away from the waterfront.

▼▼▼▼▼▼▼▼▼▼
Bradenton–
Sarasota Area

To find one such attraction, you must drive out of town and into   **SIGHTS**
antebellum Florida. The **Gamble Plantation**, plastered with a mixture of sand, oyster shells and fresh water, remains a relic of southern Florida's sugar plantations. A tour through the late 1840s home will give you a look at the life of a wealthy planter. Period antiques sit in their proper setting within the spacious, columned mansion. Also on the premises is a visitor center, complete with exhibits on the mansion's history. Closed Tuesday and Wednesday. Admission. ~ 3708 Patten Avenue, Ellenton; 941-723-4536.

Snooty, a West Indian manatee weighing in at 850 pounds, is one of the main attractions at the **South Florida Museum and Bishop Planetarium**. The complex includes artifacts of Florida history, science exhibits, a 16th-century Spanish chapel and a reproduction of Hernando de Soto's birthplace in Spain. Admission. ~ 201 10th Street West, Bradenton; 941-746-4131.

The **Manatee Chamber of Commerce** is ready to provide more information on the sights of the area. ~ 222 10th Street West, Bradenton; 941-748-3411.

Peppered along Sarasota's waterfront lie islands ranging from glitzy to laid-back. If you'd like to do an **island-hopping tour** of the Bradenton-Sarasota waterfront, follow Route 64 west from Bradenton through Palma Sola.

On your way to the islands, take a quiet sidetrip to **De Soto National Memorial**. You can drive to the point where the Manatee River meets the Gulf of Mexico, and where explorer de Soto purportedly met the New World. The view of old homes with landscaped spreads—not to mention the gumbo-limbo trees and cool Gulf breezes—is worth the drive. A visitor's center and interpretative trail tell the tale of the Europeans' arrival to this nation. In season, park rangers dress in period costume to greet visitors with demonstrations and talks. Admission. ~ 75th Street; 941-792-0458.

The first island you reach as you continue on Route 64 is **Anna Maria Island**. Anna Maria's personality is beach-oriented and youthful, and its twisty roads are dotted with beach shops and seafood restaurants.

South of Anna Maria lies **Longboat Key**, named for the long boat in which one of Hernando de Soto's scouts landed. The long island remains to this day a pleasant discovery. **Gulf of Mexico Drive** takes you on a tour of the island's exclusive shops and homes.

The next hop takes you onto **Lido Key**. To learn more about the sealife of Sarasota shores, visit **Mote Marine Aquarium** at the island's northern end. Here you can see sharks, lobsters, seahorses, barracuda and other species. Admission. ~ 1600 Ken Thompson Parkway, Lido Key; 941-388-2451.

Headed south on John Ringling Boulevard, you will reach **St. Armand Key**, a round little island synonymous with shopping. Circus man and Sarasota developer John Ringling once envisioned this area as a fantasy circle of fine shops, restaurants and Italian statuary, and so it has developed. On the other side of "The Circle" stretch fluffy white beaches.

If you continue on Ringling Boulevard, you will cross the Intracoastal Waterway onto Sarasota's mainland. Here in **Sarasota**, the wild has been tamed and dressed up in tails. Considered the cultural center of southwest Florida, the city and its surrounding islands and towns show a vast appreciation for the arts, a sensibility inherited from John Ringling.

Downtown Sarasota looks as if it has discovered Florida's fountain of youth. Clubs, pubs, restaurants, galleries and quirky boutiques have been popping up in old, restored buildings. In the heart of the city, one of Sarasota's oldest attractions blends a love of nature and aesthetics. **Marie Selby Botanical Gardens** spreads a banquet of exotic plant life that satisfies the most discriminating connoisseurs. The most brilliant display in the 15 gardens is the internationally acclaimed orchid center. Admission. ~ 811 South Palm Avenue, Sarasota; 941-366-5730.

To scout out all that Sarasota has to offer, check with the **Sarasota Convention & Visitor's Bureau**. ~ 655 North Tamiami Trail, Sarasota; 941-957-1877.

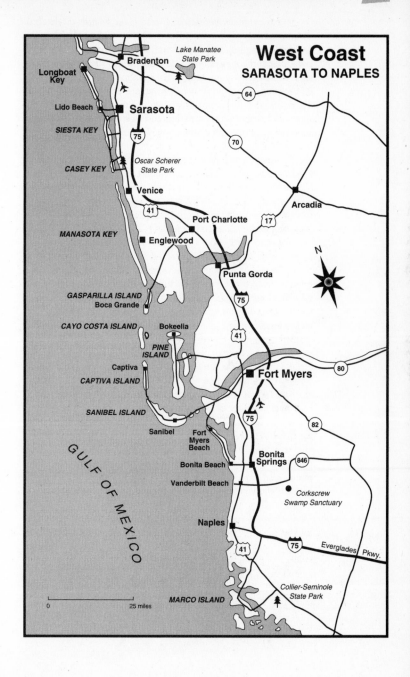

West Coast
SARASOTA TO NAPLES

Lake Manatee
State Park

Bradenton

Longboat
Key

Lido Beach

Sarasota

SIESTA KEY

Oscar Scherer
State Park

CASEY KEY

Venice

Arcadia

Port Charlotte

MANASOTA KEY

■ Englewood

Punta Gorda

GASPARILLA ISLAND
Boca Grande

CAYO COSTA ISLAND

Bokeelia

*PINE
ISLAND*

Captiva

CAPTIVA ISLAND

SANIBEL ISLAND

■ **Fort Myers**

Sanibel

Fort
Myers
Beach

Bonita Beach

Bonita
Springs

Vanderbilt Beach

*Corkscrew
Swamp Sanctuary*

Naples

Everglades Pkwy.

G U L F   O F   M E X I C O

0   25 miles

MARCO ISLAND

Collier-Seminole
State Park

Sarasota's greatest sightseeing attraction spreads bayfront at the northern end of town, on Route 41 near the airport. **The John & Mable Ringling Museum of Art** and its 66-acre entourage of sights and gardens pay homage to a man who shaped the city's cultural destiny. The museum focuses on Baroque, Ringling's favorite type of art, but includes other styles as well. Original Rubenses, Velasquez and El Grecos demonstrate the circus man's love of travel and fine art. Classic Greek and Roman statuary graces the courtyard gardens. Admission. ~ 5401 Bayshore Road, Sarasota; 941-355-5101.

The most impressive element on the Ringling grounds is **Ca'd'Zan**, Ringling's mansion, modeled after the Doge's Palace in Venice, with columned halls, ornately tiled towers and plazas, and awesome views from the living areas. Architectural elements and furnishings were shipped to the site from around the world. The 30-room mansion was completed in 1926 at a cost of $1.5 million.

Next door to the art museum sits **Asolo Theatre**, just as it once sat in a little town near Venice some centuries ago. When it came time to tear the building down, someone had the foresight to box up sections of the rococo-style, three-level theater. An antiquarian purchased the Asolo in its segmented fashion and later sold it to the Ringling Foundation, which had it shipped to Sarasota and pieced together.

After you leave the Ringling grounds, you might want to head south and hop over to **Siesta Key**, which can be reached by two bridges that cross the Intracoastal Waterway from Sarasota. **Ocean Boulevard** is where the action—and the beaches—are. Siesta's sands come from battered quartz rock, making them the whitest to be found and some of the most popular.

HIDDEN ► As you leave Sarasota, there is one more island to hop on. To get to **Casey Key**, you must turn off Route 41 at Blackburn Point, although there are no signs to point the way. This is no doubt intentional, as the population of this ribbon of sand smacks of old money that wants to escape crowds. When you get to the island, turn left and wind along the residential road with its mansions and

UNDER THE BIG TOP

A walk across the water-edged grounds at The John & Mable Ringling Museum of Art takes you to the **Circus Galleries**, a collection of displays and memorabilia that brings back the excitement and exotic feeling Ringling's shows once gave to the fledgling town of Sarasota. Displayed are ornate circus wagons, calliopes, costumes, photos, posters and exhibits featuring Tom Thumb, Emmett Kelly and other bygone circus celebrities.

landscaped yards. The road takes you to **Nokomis Beach** and then to the south end bridge back to the mainland.

The city of **Venice**, farther south, is known for its shark's teeth, and used to be known for its clown school. Named for Ringling's favorite city, the spot was once winter home to the circus.

As for shark's teeth, **Venice Beach** is the gathering place for serious and amateur collectors who comb the beaches and waters to find the specimens that wash up here in abundance.

In a terra-cotta-and-white-trimmed home on the river, **Five Oaks Inn's** four comfy rooms are rented out bed-and-breakfast style. You'll feel as if you've come to visit your grandmother, with the full breakfast service, high ceilings, wainscoted living room and quiet surroundings that await you. ~ 1102 Riverside Drive, Palmetto; phone/fax 941-723-1236. MODERATE TO DELUXE.

LODGING

◄ *HIDDEN*

Touches of charm add specialness to a motor inn called **Bradenton Inn**. The 200 rooms are done in shades of rose and blue and furnished with white-washed oak pieces. Suites with kitchenettes are also available. A keyhole-shaped swimming pool garnishes the grounds, and a complimentary continental breakfast is served daily. ~ 2303 1st Street, Bradenton; 941-747-6465. MODERATE TO DELUXE.

The most interesting accommodations in the immediate Bradenton vicinity lie offshore in Anna Maria Island's three communities of Anna Maria, Holmes Beach and Bradenton Beach, and on Longboat Key. At **Alamanda Villa**, personality is defined with a Mediterranean flavor and large, modern apartments with kitchenettes. The seven units look out on the beach and/or a wooden sunning deck. The hotel hides behind another building, so the rooms are not right on the main drag, though beach traffic can get pretty intense. ~ 102 39th Street, Holmes Beach; 941-778-4170. MODERATE.

Across the street from the Gulf of Mexico is the **Duncan House Bed & Breakfast**, a two-story Victorian home gussied up with gingerbread outside. Inside, four guest rooms with private baths are decorated with antiques and Victorian-era accessories. Efficient management and a top-of-the-line breakfast are included. Swimming pool on site. ~ 1703 Gulf Drive, Bradenton Beach; 941-778-6858, 941-778-3082. MODERATE TO DELUXE.

Surfside Econolodge offers miniature golf, a card room, a pool room, sunning deck with barbecue area, a swimming pool and 34 spacious guest rooms with its small beachfront. Fully equipped efficiencies make this place a popular spot for families. ~ 2502 Gulf Drive North, Bradenton Beach; 941-778-6671, 800-553-2666, fax 941-778-0360. DELUXE.

Sun 'n Sea Cottages look more like homes than cottages. Each of the 24 units (which are either one- or two-bedroom efficiencies) has its own neatly manicured yard, screened-in porch and carport. The beach area is small and seawalled to discourage erosion. ~ 4651 Gulf of Mexico Drive, Longboat Key; phone/fax 941-383-5588. DELUXE TO ULTRA-DELUXE.

The highly acclaimed **Colony Beach and Tennis Resort** caters to hedonistic fantasies. Townhouses and apartments (235 in all) are furnished with the most modern conveniences, including kitchenettes and marble bathrooms with whirlpool tubs. The grounds exude tropical lushness and recreational heaven with tennis, beach, fitness and swimming facilities. ~ 1620 Gulf of Mexico Drive, Longboat Key; 941-383-6464, 800-426-5669, fax 941-383-7549. ULTRA-DELUXE.

At the elegant **Radisson Lido Beach Resort** you can rent a room, efficiency or suite on the beach. The 116 units are decorated in subtle tones of green and sandy beige. The rooms' greatest features are their picture windows looking out on the beach. Extras include a lounge, coffee shop, pool and sundeck. ~ 700 Benjamin Franklin Drive, Lido Beach; 941-388-2161, 800-333-3333, fax 941-388-3175. DELUXE.

The gay- and lesbian-friendly **Normandy Inn** is a U-shaped, art deco–style motel in the heart of the city's theater district. A dozen rooms are fully carpeted and some units come with mirrored ceilings and spas. ~ 400 North Tamiami Trail, Sarasota; 941-366-8979, 800-282-8050. MODERATE TO DELUXE.

The **Crescent View Beach Club** has 26 one- and two-bedroom units with kitchens, balconies and living rooms on a quiet stretch of white sand beach. Decorated in Florida prints and rattan furniture, the hotel is clean, oriented for families and small groups. Facilities include a pool and a spa. ~ 6512 Midnight Pass Road, Siesta Key; 941-349-2000, 800-344-7171, fax 941-349-9748. ULTRA-DELUXE.

◆◆◆

✔ CHECK THESE OUT—UNIQUE LODGING

- *Budget:* Snag a room with a view of the water at the aptly named **Beach Front Motel**, a comfortable and convenient spot in Cedar Key. *page 445*
- *Moderate:* Lounge on your deck, enjoying the Mediterranean atmosphere of **Alamanda Villa** on Anna Maria Island. *page 403*
- *Moderate to deluxe:* Make music with the player piano and pump organ at **Bayboro House**, a bed and breakfast with private baths in one of St. Petersburg's oldest homes. *page 434*
- *Ultra-deluxe:* Escape to *Fantasy Island* when you stay at **Palm Island Resort**, a posh getaway on an island accessible only by boat. *page 412*

Budget: under $50 Moderate: $50–$90 Deluxe: $90–$130 Ultra-deluxe: over $130

A nice change of pace from the usual beachy accommodations on Siesta Key is a bed-and-breakfast inn called **Crescent House**. This historic home sits across the street from the beach. Its architecture and decor is 1920s Florida: a blend of Victorian and wicker with a cathedral ceiling and a fireplace in the lobby. The building houses four guest rooms (two with private baths) and a hot tub with a sundeck. Continental breakfast is served daily on lacy tablecloths. ~ 459 Beach Road, Siesta Key; 941-346-0857. MODERATE TO DELUXE.

Banyan House accommodates guests in a historic, residential setting. Nearby Sarasota's Mediterranean influence is evident in this neighborhood, with its red tile roofs and Spanish touches. Inside the home, the three efficiencies and five one-bedroom apartments draw on an Italian motif, with some modern touches added. Continental breakfast, pool and a hot tub bring this '20s structure into the present day. ~ 519 South Harbor Drive, Venice; 941-484-1385. DELUXE.

DINING

A legend in its time, the **Crab Trap** redefines native cuisine with a tendency toward the unusual: 'gator tail, octopus, shad roe, conch, Florida perch and, of course, crab. The surroundings are appropriately rugged and tropical. ~ U.S. 19, Palmetto; 941-722-6255. MODERATE.

◄ HIDDEN

Out-of-the-way but worth discovering, the **Sand Bar Restaurant** reigns as a local favorite. Casual dining on the deck beachside or in the picture-windowed dining room offers fresh fish, fried 'gator, Bali chicken, Cajun grouper, smoked salmon and caviar, soft shell crab and raspberry mousse cake. ~ 100 Spring Avenue, Anna Maria; 941-778-0444. MODERATE.

◄ HIDDEN

There's something fishy about the ambience and menu at **Moore's Stone Crab Restaurant**. Crab is the specialty, and Moore's freshness in that department cannot be beat, thanks to the owner's inventory of 3000 crab traps. Dine al fresco on the veranda or indoors with a water view. Florida lobster, scallops, clams, frog legs and shrimp keep the crab company on the menu. ~ 800 Broadway Street, Longboat Key; 941-383-1748. MODERATE.

Brick archways, wooden accents, wine racks and a long stretch of kudos decorate the walls at **Café L'Europe**. To complement the cozy dining room, Continental cuisine is served. Lunch offerings include German apple pancakes, veal piccata, Dover sole meunière and sautéed calf livers. Choose from European versions of beef, pasta, poultry, veal, lamb and seafood dishes for dinner. ~ 431 St. Armand's Circle, Lido Key; 941-388-4415. DELUXE TO ULTRA-DELUXE.

Sashimi, tempura, tofu, teriyaki, egg rolls and octopus can be enjoyed at the sushi bar, or from a floor or chair seat at **Kyoto Japanese Restaurant**. Small, as are most of the eateries downtown, this slip of Asian culture packs a lot of authentic Japanese experience into its narrow setup. No lunch on Saturday. Closed on Sunday. ~ 1519 Main Street, Sarasota; 941-955-7899. MODERATE TO DELUXE.

Ristorante Bellini is not just another Italian restaurant in a world of too many mediocre spaghetti houses. Some of the staff have a difficult time with the English language, which speaks well for its authenticity. Northern Italian cuisine is featured in a bright café atmosphere where unusual photographs and prints decorate the walls. The pasta, meat and seafood selections include gnocchi with gorgonzola sauce, *costoletta al ferri* (grilled veal) and snapper with wine and fresh tomatoes. Closed Sunday. ~ 1551 Main Street, Sarasota; 941-365-7380. MODERATE.

For an incomparably fine dining experience, try **Carmichael's**. A historic landmark, the building was the '20s-era home of a Sarasota newspaper publisher. Restored to a lovely freshness, the restaurant itself is a must-see. Pastel stained-glass windows, a tiled fireplace and antique furniture lend esoteric touches to the tiny dining rooms. The fare is also unique. In this totally tame environment, wild game is featured. Buffalo, wild duckling, ostrich, wild boar, king salmon, venison and other items appear on an ever-changing menu. Closed Sunday and Monday from July through October. ~ 1213 North Palm Avenue, Sarasota; 941-951-1771. DELUXE.

Sarasota comprises a large Amish population whose restaurants dot the city. Most are plain, cafeteria-style settings that serve the freshest of home-grown ingredients. One of the most popular is **Der Dutchman**. All of the lunch and dinner specialties—roasted chicken, liver and onions, desserts and bakery goods—are homemade, even the noodles. ~ 3713 Bahia Vista, Sarasota; 941-955-8007. BUDGET.

HIDDEN ► Good enough to make the top ten chart is the dizzying world of **Poki Joe's Café and Beer Emporium**. The founder-owner-cook, once a musician, has decorated his walls with old 78 discs and Christmas lights. Hits of the 1930s and 1940s provide some unique muzak. Stirfry chicken, vegetarian pasta, barbecue ribs, steak and fish are some of the specialties. Closed Monday. ~ 6614 Superior Avenue, Sarasota; 941-922-5915. MODERATE.

Old Florida meets new American at **Ophelia's On the Bay**. Cuisine is New American Continental. The menu provides eclectic temptations that range from classic Caesar salad to pompano in parchment. Patio seating is available overlooking the water. Dinner only. ~ 9105 Midnight Pass Road, Siesta Key; 941-349-2212. MODERATE TO DELUXE.

Fresh and natural describes the food at **The Wildflower**. The decor is just as healthy and bright looking. Have a breakfast of grilled tofu or a fresh fruit salad; a lunch of Mexican specialties or avocado Reuben; and a dinner of grouper, shrimp, sweet and sour tempeh, steamed vegetables or other healthful concoctions. Breakfast served on weekends only. ~ 5218 Ocean Boulevard, Siesta Key; 941-349-1758. BUDGET TO MODERATE.

While visiting Myakka State Park, you may want to make the short trip to an unusual backroads haunt known as **Snook Haven** Sitting right on the Myakka River, this local secret is known for its Sunday barbecue picnics and somewhat grisly legend of the Killer Turtles: local lore has it that a rare species of tree-climbing turtles inhabit nearby woods, and that they can fall on people—with fatal results. Regardless, exploring the grounds is as much a part of the experience here as earing the hearty food. Simple but tasty fare such as fish, burgers and chicken wings is available all week long. ~ 5000 East Venice Boulevard off River Road, Venice; 941-485-7221. BUDGET.

◀ HIDDEN

Pelican Alley serves unbelievably fresh seafood. The mood is comfortable and seaworthy. Locals and tourists alike head here for grouper, shrimp and novelty appetizers such as deep-fried artichoke hearts and pepperoncini. No lunch on Monday, Tuesday and Wednesday from June through November. ~ 1009 Albee Road West, Nokomis Beach; 941-485-1893. MODERATE.

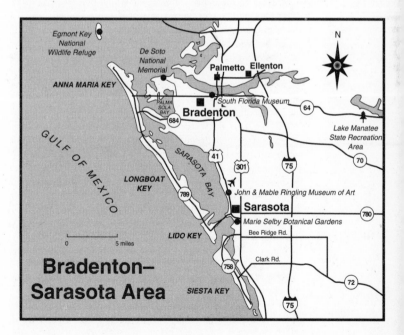

SHOPPING   **Ellenton Antiques & Gallery** sells historic furniture and other antiques and art in an old red-brick storefront, once the Ellenton State Bank. ~ 3711 Route 301 North, Ellenton; 941-729-1194.

Furry and dressed-up creatures reside at **Anything Goes**, a place for new and old-style collectibles priced from the moderate to thousand-dollar range. ~ 9801 Gulf Drive, Anna Maria Island; 941-778-4456.

Glassware, quilts, wicker, antique dolls and other collectibles await discovery at **Dotty's Depot**, where about two dozen dealers are gathered under one roof. ~ 1421 12th Avenue West, Bradenton; 941-749-1421.

When you say "shopping" in Sarasota, locals immediately free-associate **St. Armand's Circle Association**. It reigns with the great shopping meccas of the world: 5th Avenue, Rodeo Drive, Worth Avenue, etc. The 100-plus shops and dining rooms cover every conceivable need. Price tags in many of the stores make shopping on "The Circle" strictly a spectator sport for many. Designer labels abound. ~ 941-388-1554.

Authentic boomerangs and aboriginal earrings are the sort of oddities you'll find at **Binjara Traders, Ltd.** which also carries clothing, umbrellas and other things from all over the world. ~ 442 St. Armand's Circle, Sarasota; 941-388-3335.

Galleries are Sarasota's shopping long suit. One selling unusual art at the Circle is **The Tabby Cat**, which features calligraphy. ~ 9 Fillmore Drive, Sarasota; 941-388-3021.

Downtown Sarasota's restored storefronts have attracted the city's artists, who have opened many unusual boutiques and galleries in the area.

HIDDEN ▶   **Sarasota Emporium II** takes a trip back to the head shop days of the '60s. Rock-and-roll posters, tie-dyed T-shirts, jewelry, greeting cards and erotica are stocked. ~ 1448 Main Street, Sarasota; 941-957-1078.

Artwork with a New Mexico–American Indian flavor are sold at **Santa Fe Trails Gallery**, including carvings, pottery, silver jewelry and paintings. ~ 1429 Main Street, Sarasota; 941-954-1972.

In Venice, **Basketville** is a huge facility that sells every sort of straw item ever woven. It also features woodenware, silk flowers and other gifts. ~ 4011 South Tamiami Trail, Venice; 941-493-0007.

NIGHTLIFE   For entertainment local-style, stop in at **MarVista Backside Restaurant and Pub** to hoist a few with the fisherman crowd. ~ 760

HIDDEN ▶   Broadway, Longboat Key; 941-383-2391.

One of the most popular spots for nightlife in the Sarasota area is Siesta Key's **Beach Club**. This bar has a college tavern atmosphere but is favored by a mixed group. Live entertainment; reggae every Thursday. Cover. ~ 5151 Ocean Boulevard, Siesta Key; 941-349-6311.

THEATER, OPERA, SYMPHONY AND DANCE   The performing arts flourish in Sarasota's rich cultural medium. The largest and most impressive center of the arts in this area is the **Van Wezel Performing Arts Hall**. The purple seashell-shaped hall hosts touring theater, music and dance companies from the U.S. and abroad. ~ 777 North Tamiami Trail, Sarasota; 941-953-3366.

Asolo Center for the Performing Arts houses the professional troupe that once performed at the historic Asolo Theatre on Ringling Museum grounds. The facility is close by and is outfitted with two theaters plus film and television production studios. ~ 55 North Tamiami Trail, Sarasota; 941-351-9010.

Downtown's **Golden Apple Dinner Theatre** serves buffet dinner and theater in the musical/comedy vein. ~ 25 North Pineapple Avenue, Sarasota; 941-366-5454.

Sarasota Opera House hosts major musical artists from the U.S. and Europe. ~ 61 North Pineapple Avenue, Sarasota; 941-953-7030.

LAKE MANATEE STATE RECREATIONAL AREA 🏊 🚶 ⛺ 🚤 ⛵   An inland 556-acre park featuring natural vegetation and a manmade reservoir, this spot shelters the endangered gopher tortoise, indigo snake and other indigenous animal life. There's a beach area on the lake where there's a designated swimming area. Fishing is also allowed in the lake. Facilities include picnic areas, boat rentals and hiking trails. Day-use fee, $2. ~ Located on Route 64 east of Bradenton; 941-741-3028.

▲ There are 60 sites, all with RV hookups; $8.80 to $10.90 per night.

BEACHES & PARKS

EGMONT KEY NATIONAL WILDLIFE REFUGE 🚤 🎣 ⛵   A **◄ HIDDEN** remote island north of Anna Maria Island reachable only by boat. The threatened gopher tortoise abounds here, and the remains of a fort from the Spanish-American War, built in 1900, can be seen. The two-mile by half-a-mile island draws serious shellers and beachgoers devoted to seclusion. Fishing, shell-hunting, snorkeling and swimming are good here. There are no facilities.

The cheapest ride to the island, unless you have your own boat, is aboard the *Miss Cortez*, which operates every Tuesday, Wednesday and Thursday. ~ Cortez Road, Cortez; 941-794-1223.

The islands that front Bradenton and Sarasota show the Gulf a continuous run of sand. On these islands, all beach is public property. All accesses, however, are not. Each island has one or more marked public access points, often with parking facilities and other provisions. There are usually no perimeters to these beaches; they run into each other along the stretch of unbroken sand:

COQUINA BEACH 🚤 🎣   This is a long stretch of sand fringed in Australian pines at the south end of Anna Maria Island.

The beach runs up the face of the island, connecting with Anna Maria and Manatee beaches. Fishing is good off a dilapidated fishing pier on the Gulf side. Several fishing piers are located up the beach. Bradenton Beach City Pier at Cortez Road juts into the Intracoastal Waterway: sea trout, snapper and other local fish can be found here. Swimming is great on the Gulf side; avoid the bay side. You can also snorkel around the old pier, where the water is fairly clear and you'll see an array of sea life. Facilities include picnic areas, restrooms, showers and a lifeguard; restaurants and groceries are nearby in Bradenton Beach. ~ Located on Gulf Boulevard at the southern tip of Anna Maria Island; 941-951-5572.

NORTH LIDO BEACH 🏊 A natural, secluded area that invites birds and birdwatchers, this beachfront stretches a half mile. It's a great place to swim and fish. A nature trail is the only development; restaurants and groceries are nearby. ~ The park is located on Benjamin Franklin Drive at Lido Key's northern end; 941-951-5572.

LIDO BEACH 🏊 🐟 This is really a continuation of North Lido Beach, which stretches the entire length of the island's Gulf face, onto South Lido Beach, which wraps around to the Intracoastal Waterway. There are more public facilities available here in this central location, but the beach continues on in much the same sugar fineness and whiteness. It's a good place to swim and fishing is best at the southern end pass for sea trout, snook and snapper. Facilities include picnic areas, a playground, restrooms, showers, lifeguards, a 25-meter swimming pool, a snack bar and a volleyball court; restaurants and groceries are nearby. ~ On the 700 block of Benjamin Franklin Drive on Lido Key; 941-951-5572.

SIESTA KEY PUBLIC BEACH 🏊 🐟 🛶 An island-long stretch of beach. The quartz sand on Siesta Key was judged first place by a national beach expert who studied the whiteness and fineness of beaches around the world. The water is clear and intoxicating as vodka here. Fishing is good for local saltwater fish; there's great visibility for snorkeling, although not much to see (the best it gets is at Point of Rocks farther north on Crescent Beach); swimming is excellent. For the bad news, it's often crowded. Condos crowd at the edge of the beach no matter where you go. Facilities include picnic areas, restrooms, showers, a lifeguard, a snack bar, tennis and volleyball courts and a playground; restaurants and groceries are nearby in Siesta Village. ~ Located along Midnight Pass Road at Beach Road on Siesta Key; 941-951-5572.

OSCAR SCHERER STATE PARK 🚶 🚴 🏊 🎣 🛶 Home to some of Florida's endangered and threatened species, such as the bald eagle, bobcat and scrub jay, this 1384 acres of flatwoods is a naturalist's paradise. Fishermen enjoy this park for its versatility:

both freshwater and saltwater life dwell in the confines of lake, creek and salt marshes. Above the dam are freshwater fish such as bass and catfish; below the dam redfish and snapper are plentiful. Swimming is good in the small freshwater lake. There are nature trails, hiking and bike trails, trails for the disabled, picnic areas, restrooms, showers and canoe rentals; restaurants are a few miles away. ~ Located off Route 41 south of Sarasota; 941-483-5956.

▲ There are 104 sites, all with RV hookups; $12 to $16 per night.

CASPERSON BEACH This Venice Gulf–front beach boasts a lot of native vegetation. Seagrapes, sea oats and palmettos grow along this ribbon of beach with its greyish sand. Casperson Beach is known for its shark-teeth fossils and its proximity to one of the longest fishing piers on the West Coast of Florida— Venice Gulf Pier, measuring 750 feet. Fishing is popular from the pier; swimming is good; and snorkelers frenzy for fossilized shark's teeth. Facilities include a picnic area, restrooms, showers, restaurants and a snack bar on the pier; groceries are a few miles away. ~ Located at the southern end of Harbour Drive in Venice; 941-316-1172.

▼▼▼▼▼▼▼▼▼▼▼▼

Charlotte County

Just because you've never heard of Charlotte County doesn't mean you should pass it by. People who really know Florida adore this area's off-the-beaten-track locations like Gasparilla Island and Boca Grande Beach Park. Picturesque lighthouses, bird sanctuaries and fine art galleries reward travelers who take the time to explore this region. Laid back and low key, Charlotte County is nirvana for beachcombers.

SIGHTS

You can enter Charlotte County from the north in the Port Charlotte area on Route 41. One of two **Charlotte County Chamber of Commerce** offices is found here. ~ 2702 Tamiami Trail, Port Charlotte; 813-627-2222.

To escape the beaten path and discover the true rural and seaside beauty of the area, jump onto Route 776 south of Venice and wind down the island road through **Manasota Key** to Englewood Beach. You will enter Manasota at Manasota Beach, a popular coarse-sand beach to which the locals flock. The beach stretches the length of the island. At the other extreme lies **Englewood Beach**. In between, you'll experience a twisty ride among native vegetation hiding discreet private homes.

◄ HIDDEN

A truly hidden destination on this backroad tour is **Gasparilla Island**, reputed erstwhile headquarters of the West Coast's favorite pirate. Following Route 771, you will reach the toll bridge that takes you out to this island home of millionaires and tarpon enthusiasts. Past secluded mansions and private resorts, the road leads

◄ HIDDEN

to the village of Boca Grande. Drive down **Banyan Street** with its canopy of gnarled and shady namesake trees.

Boca Grande Lighthouse Park lies at the island's tip where the remnants of a thriving phosphorus shipping business can still be seen in railroad bridge ruins. The 1890-era lighthouse overlooks the Gulf and the deep waters of Boca Grande Pass, where thousands of vessels congregate in the summer for tarpon fishing.

Back on Route 41, take Marion Avenue out of Punta Gorda, on a quick sidetrip to **Ponce de León Park**. The park is a wildlife area and popular fishing spot, with picnic facilities and a bird sanctuary. A monument with a cross marks the spot where many believe Ponce de León was fatally wounded in a American Indian attack after trying to colonize the area in the early 1500s.

LODGING

HIDDEN ▶

Pelican Shore Cottages reflect the natural, quiet island life around them on Manasota Key. The thick cypress wood siding has a salt-worn appearance that makes the eight cottage units seem as if they belong just where they are, sitting on the soft white beach of Manasota Key, tucked away among palms and pines between Englewood and Blind Pass beaches. Inside, dark wood and braided rugs lend a comfortable, homey atmosphere. All of the fully equipped units contain two bedrooms. Only weekly and monthly rates are offered. ~ 4076 North Beach Road, Englewood; 941-474-2429. MODERATE.

Resort communities are the new wave in Florida vacationing. One such playground, **Palm Island Resort**, has settled its own, unbridged island. The experience starts on the mainland at Harbortown, where a swimming pool, marina and villas are situated. If this isn't far enough removed from civilization, a launch takes those with Gilligan fantasies out to Palm Island to abide in luxurious efficiencies. The rooms provide airy, beautiful living that recalls Old Florida. A tram shuttles guests about the beaches, shops, restaurant, bar, pools and spa facilities. This type of vacation does not come cheap, but if you are looking for the ultimate in getaways, you'll definitely find it in this 160-unit community. ~ 7092 Placida Road, Cape Haze; 941-697-4800, 800-824-5412. ULTRA-DELUXE.

If you go to **Gasparilla Inn** during the winter (social season for the wealthy), there's a good chance that you'll be turned away. If you're around during the off-season, do schedule at least a visit to this pale yellow palace that offers a yesteryear lifestyle. The rooms and cottages (140 units in all) remain as spartan as they were in the early 1900s. The civility of the era has been preserved at this unadvertised remnant of social graces situated near the beach. ~ 5th Street and Palm Avenue, Boca Grande; 941-964-2201. ULTRA-DELUXE.

Dine with a view at **Pepine's on the Water**. Neither well-advertised nor easy to find, this place is tucked behind a motel called Harbour Inn. The restaurant and lounge reflect a small town locale, in all its best connotations. But the menu is quite sophisticated: filet mignon, pepper steak, châteaubriand, lobster tail, rack of lamb, etc. Deck dining with a superb outlook on the Peace River is available. Dinner only. ~ 5114 Melbourne Avenue, Charlotte Harbor; 941-629-0007. MODERATE.

◄ HIDDEN

On Englewood Beach, **Barnacle Bill's** is famous for Dagwood-sized sandwiches that usually require a doggy bag. The ambience is picnic-table casual. Closed Sunday. ~ 1975 Beach Road, Englewood; 941-474-9703. BUDGET.

◄ HIDDEN

The aptly named **Temptation Restaurant** is an Old Florida–style place where white linen graces the tables and the murals depict the life of Boca Grande Island and its people. Specialties include red snapper baked in a herb sauce, crab au gratin and grilled pompano. ~ 350 Park Avenue, Boca Grande; 941-964-2610. MODERATE TO DELUXE.

Lighthouse Hole, on Millers Marina in Boca Grande, is a favorite with both the locals and the boating crowd. The sea-cooled porch overlooks the activities of the marina below. The menu features standard seafare, including all-you-can-eat shrimp night on Wednesday and an all-you-can-eat fishfry on Friday. ~ On Bayou Drive, Boca Grande; 941-964-0511, MODERATE TO DELUXE.

A well-known eatery at Fishermen's Village, **Smugglers** rises two stories, with dining upstairs and a raw bar downstairs. Fresh seafood, crab cakes, steak and chicken are offered along with great sunsets. ~ 1200 West Retta Esplanade, Punta Gorda; 941-637-1177. MODERATE TO DELUXE.

✔ **CHECK THESE OUT—UNIQUE DINING**

- *Budget:* Pull up to **The Loading Dock** in Tampa and load up on soups, sandwiches and other deli delights. *page 395*
- *Budget to moderate:* Boost your health at Siesta Key's **The Wildflower**—nosh on grilled tofu, fruit salad and sweet-and-sour tempeh. *page 406*
- *Moderate to deluxe:* Steal away to Punta Gorda and sneak into **Smugglers**, a popular seafood spot where you can munch on crab cakes and watch the sunset. *page 413*
- *Ultra-deluxe:* Relax in the rustic ambience of **Tierra** in Naples and enjoy skillet-roasted mussels, seafood risotto or a variety of Mediterranean-influenced entrées. *page 428*

Budget: under $8   Moderate: $8–$16   Deluxe: $16–$24   Ultra-deluxe: over $24

Salty's Harborside Restaurant at Burnt Store Marina features an elegantly nautical atmosphere. Seafood and landlubber specialties such as soft shell crab, oysters on the half-shell, swordfish, poached salmon, shrimp salad sandwiches, marinated duckling and lobster can be enjoyed with a dash of salt marinaside. ~ 3150 Matecumbe Key Road, Punta Gorda; 941-639-3650. MODERATE.

SHOPPING

All kinds of whimsical gifts, from pelican figurines to music boxes, are sold at **Silk 'N Sea**. ~ 3527-C Tamiami Trail, Port Charlotte; 941-625-5889.

Sea Grape Artists Gallery Co-op brokers the work of local artisans. ~ 117 West Marion Avenue, Punta Gorda; 941-575-1718.

Fishermen's Village is the place to shop in Charlotte County. The shops carry an array of clothing, gifts and Florida souvenirs. You will find gifts with a difference at **Caged Parrot** (941-637-8949). Unique wallhangings and other fine trinkets fill the shop. In the same mall, **The Scarlet Macaw** (813-639-8801) carries brand-name sportswear. ~ 1200 West Retta Esplanade, Punta Gorda.

NIGHTLIFE

Charlotte County is not known for its nightlife. Most entertainment is tailored to a senior crowd, except in the beach areas to which younger audiences gravitate. Cultural entertainment is just beginning to develop in this area.

In Boca Grande, **The Pink Elephant** is a restaurant first, but in the evenings folks cluster around the bar and tell fish stories. ~ On the bayou at Fifth Street; 941-964-0100.

The Temptation is a restaurant, small bar and package store mostly frequented by locals. ~ 350 Park Avenue, Boca Grande; 941-964-2327.

The **Charlotte County Memorial Auditorium** showcases international entertainers ranging from classic musicians and jazz bands to theater troupes. ~ 75 Taylor Street, Punta Gorda; 941-639-5833.

BEACHES & PARKS

Charlotte County itself is hidden. Many travelers tend to pass it by, finding little of interest on its highway face. But the adventuresome who veer off the main thoroughfare find that the county's best side lies seaside. Its many beaches and islands offer remote havens of unfettered nature.

HIDDEN ▶

MIDDLE BEACH ▲ ⌡ For those who can sacrifice convenience for seclusion, this long strip of beach fronting private homes is best mid-island at Blind Pass. The island, stretching between Venice and Englewood, is populated by private home owners but includes three public beaches. The one in the center is a largely neglected segment where the beach widens its shell-strewn sands. Pines and palms gather on the edges to separate it from the nearby road. Swimming is good here and you can fish for snook, tarpon and redfish. There are no facilities. ~ Enter at either the south (Venice) or north (Englewood) end on Route 776.

GASPARILLA ISLAND STATE PARK 🏊🎣 A white sandy beach ◄ *HIDDEN* with plenty of shade trees, this park lies at the southern tip of Gasparilla Island. Only the locals have discovered this patch of natural escapism. This island is famous for its tarpon fishing, especially in Boca Grande Pass at the southern end; there's also good local fishing from the North Pier and South Pier, both on Route 771. Swimming is also recommended here. Picnic areas, showers and restrooms are the only facilities; restaurants and groceries are several miles away. ~ Located off Route 771 at the south end of Gasparilla Island; 941-964-0375.

Island hopping provides one of the most enjoyable activities in this region. Within easy reach of Fort Myers are the resort islands of Estero, Sanibel and Captiva.

▼▼▼▼▼▼▼▼▼▼▼
Fort Myers Area

While the first contains the sun-soaked community of Fort Myers Beach, Sanibel and Captiva offer world-class shell gathering and luxurious barrier-island beaches.

The adventure begins at **Pine Island**, the northernmost of the **SIGHTS** bridged islands. It is often called the "forgotten" island because its lack of beaches has left it behind in the condo race. By car, you enter the island from Cape Coral at **Matlacha**, where waterside fish houses demonstrate the island's way of life as it has remained for centuries. Before the bridge, stop at the **Pine Island Chamber of Commerce**. ~ Pine Island Road; 941-283-0888.

To the north of Matlacha, **Bokeelia** lies on an isle of its own, ◄ *HIDDEN* cut off from the rest of Pine Island by a creek. There's not much to see in this quiet spot except a few modern condos trying to make

◆◆

FREEBIRDS

Visit **J. N. "Ding" Darling National Wildlife Refuge** for a look at uncaged bird life. This 5000-acre sanctuary is a nature-lover's mecca. You can drive, bicycle or canoe through the maze of estuarine wetlands to see roseate spoonbills, alligators, herons, armadillos, seagrape trees, gumbo-limbos and buttonwood. Trails off the main road take you to quiet brackish pools populated with alligators snapping at egrets. An observation tower provides an overview of this wild world. A visitor's center offers education on the area's flora and fauna, and on the life of Ding Darling, the Pulitzer Prize–winning cartoonist who took the area's waterfowl protection under his wing. Admission. ~ 1 Wildlife Drive, Sanibel; 941-472-1100.

it in a town that hasn't yet woken to the times. Bokeelia serves as the mainland lifeline for some of the unbridged islands nearby. Cayo Costa, Cabbage Key and Useppa Island visitors use Bokeelia marinas as departure points.

These intracoastal islands still retain independence from the mainland and make for secluded and time-frozen destinations. **Useppa** is a private island that is home to a luxury members-only club. Passing it on the way to Cabbage Key, you'll notice the restored 1920s style that remembers the days when Teddy Roosevelt, Hedy Lamarr and Shirley Temple signed the guest book at Useppa's Collier Inn.

HIDDEN ► **Cabbage Key** is a shred of island greenery dominated by a quaint inn and restaurant. A boater's pit stop, it offers nature and history lessons besides refreshments. Here, atop an ancient American Indian shell mound, author Mary Roberts Rinehart built a home that now serves as the simplistic **Cabbage Key Inn**. A short nature trail takes you on a tour of this sand spit, after which refreshment within walls papered in autographed currency is a must. ~ Cabbage Key; 941-283-2278.

HIDDEN ► **North Captiva** sits just north of Captiva, having been separated by a hurricane of yore. This island of mostly private residences, waterside restaurants and a lovely beach makes for a refreshing escape. The departure point to this island is Captiva. **Island Charters** provides boat transit to North Captiva, Useppa and Boca Grande from Pine Island. ~ 941-283-2008.

On the scenic causeway road to **Sanibel Island**, you'll spot the **Sanibel-Captiva Chamber of Commerce**. ~ 1159 Causeway Road; 941-472-1080.

HIDDEN ► A little known attraction on this island is hidden at the **Periwinkle Park**. The long-time owner here is an avid exotic bird breeder and maintains a couple of aviaries. One sits outdoors for public viewing and the lawns are populated with macaws, toucans, parrots and cockatiels. If you can persuade him, the breeder may show you his private rare collection. ~ 1119 Periwinkle Way, Sanibel; 941-472-1433.

Captiva Island lies at the northern end of Sanibel across the Blind Pass Bridge. Though little is offered in the way of attractions, the drive through tunnels of untamed vegetation warrants a visit. HIDDEN ► Take a meditational pause at the **Chapel-by-the-Sea**, a romantic spot many choose for weddings. ~ 11580 Chapin Lane, Captiva; 941-472-1646.

Away from the islands, the attractions take a historic bent in the "City of Palms," **Fort Myers**. In downtown Fort Myers is found the **Metropolitan Chamber of Commerce**. ~ 1365 Hendry Street; 941-334-1133. Nearby, housed in a former railroad depot, the **Fort Myers Historical Museum** starts history buffs down the road to old Fort Myers and back to its days as a Calusa Indian settlement and Seminole War fort. Admission. ~ 2300 Peck Street, Fort Myers; 941-332-5955.

The **Thomas A. Edison Winter Estate and Botanical Gardens** will not disappoint sightseers looking for a taste of history with their Florida sunshine. Located on a street flanked by the royal palms Edison planted to give the city its nickname, the Edison Estate spreads out along the Caloosahatchee River. The 1880-era house is actually two look-alike clapboard homes in which Edison and his wife lived and housed guests. More impressive is Edison's home-away-from-home laboratory, the museum of his inventions and the gardens he nurtured. In the museum, you'll see developmental stages of the phonograph, Edison's furniture creations and the Model T Henry Ford custom-made for the inventor. The exotic botanical gardens feature a giant banyan tree and specimens of goldenrod the inventor first planted for his experiments in discovering other methods of producing rubber. Admission. ~ 2350 McGregor Boulevard, Fort Myers; 941-334-3614, 941-334-7419.

LODGING

The elegant **Sheraton Harbor Place** overlooks the Fort Myers Yacht Basin near the downtown district. Done up in an impressive modern style, the 417 rooms offer plush comfort. The rates also get you an exercise room, three pools and whirlpool. ~ 2500 Edwards Drive, Fort Myers; 941-337-0300. DELUXE TO ULTRA-DELUXE.

One of the few nonchain facilities in town, **Fountain Motel** offers 18 reliably clean units, a swimming pool and its own brand of understated charm. Both overnight rooms and apartments are available. All are adequate in space and decorated in pastels with carpeting. ~ 14621 McGregor Boulevard, Fort Myers; 941-481-0429. MODERATE.

Close to Sanibel Island, the **Radisson Inn** offers accommodations with a south-of-the-border theme. Plush and pleasant, each of the 156 units come equipped with a refrigerator. Bar and grill, bike rentals, pool and whirlpool complete the services offered at this tidy property. ~ 20091 Summerlin Road, Fort Myers; 941-466-1200, 800-333-3333, fax 941-466-3797. ULTRA-DELUXE.

Sanibel's Song of the Sea captures the personal touches and ambience of a Mediterranean villa: pink stucco walls with red tile roofs and statued gardens on a beach with private access. Guest accommodations are decorated with country French furnishings, tile floors and ceiling fans. Kitchen facilities, pool and jacuzzi, use of the hotel's bicycles, barbecue area and continental breakfast are included. ~ 941 East Gulf Drive, Sanibel; 813-472-2220, 800-231-1045, fax 941-472-8569. ULTRA-DELUXE.

Kona Kai Motel, a 13-room facility offers Hawaiian garden ambience in a location central to island shops and restaurants.

Rooms or efficiencies are housed in Maui-inspired cottages with witch cap peaks. Rooms are moderate, efficiencies moderate to deluxe. ~ 1539 Periwinkle Way, Sanibel; 941-472-1001. MODERATE TO DELUXE.

South Seas Plantation is a 330-acre resort, extending over one-third of Captiva Island. This is one of those provide-everything places where even the rich and famous find solitude. Guest rooms come in every shape and size, and amenities include a full-service marina, an open-air trolley, golf, tennis, water sports and organized children's activities. South Seas earns its reputation through attention to detail and by projecting a *Fantasy Island* feeling to its guests. ~ Captiva; 941-472-5111. DELUXE TO ULTRA-DELUXE.

The town of Fort Myers Beach lies on Estero Island, where the hotels are as plentiful as sand. Most accommodations lie along the main drag, Estero Boulevard. At the northern end of Estero you will find a less-discovered section of "The Beach," as locals call it.

Occupying a good half block at the northern tip is the **Best Western Pink Shell Beach and Bay Resort**. Accommodation options include apartments, condominiums, motel rooms and cottages—208 units altogether. All are equipped with kitchen facilities. Facilities such as tennis and shuffleboard courts, pools on the beach, grass-roofed tiki huts, a fishing pier, game room and powdery beach are provided. Bike and boat rentals are also available. The rooms are adequate, but the focus here is on outdoor activity. ~ 275 Estero Boulevard, Fort Myers Beach; 941-463-6181. ULTRA-DELUXE.

In the thick of things on Estero Island, **Beacon Court Motel** is a small, family-type operation. Its 14 rooms are clean and comfortable. The one-level building is pretty in Gulf blue, and its wide balcony porch is generous, if not fancy or private. ~ 1240 Estero Boulevard, Fort Myers Beach; 941-463-5264, fax 941-463-5972. MODERATE.

Like a flower in a concrete jungle, **The Beach House** blossoms among huge condominiums. The 14-room complex looks just as its name suggests: a blue-grey sprawling home with white shutters and trim. A breezy walk-through area is paved with bricks and draws you to its sea-walled private beach area. The rooms are small, and the place has an informal, unassuming appeal that induces immediate relaxation. ~ 4960 Estero Boulevard, Fort Myers Beach; phone/fax 941-463-4004, 800-226-4005. MODERATE TO DELUXE.

DINING

Along Fort Myers and her islands, seafood is the favored fare, as well it should be. Since much of the area's transplanted population comes from the Midwest, meat and home cooking have found their place here as well. Continental and ethnic flavors also sweeten the melting pot.

The Veranda, in downtown Fort Myers, maintains a Southern regional style in a fine dining atmosphere. The restaurant is actually two antebellum homes connected by a courtyard garden. Entrées such as roast duckling and the Bourbon Street filet (beef with garlic, shallots, white wine, fresh mushrooms and a touch of sour whiskey) are served with fresh honey molasses bread and pepper jelly. No lunch on Saturday. Closed Sunday. ~ 2122 2nd Street, Fort Myers; 941-332-2065. DELUXE.

If you seek the freshest down-home meal for your money, try **Farmer's Market Restaurant**. The atmosphere is plain, but the food is like mom's—if mom cooks fried chicken livers, smoked ham hocks and sweet barbecued ribs. ~ 2736 Edison Avenue, Fort Myers; 941-334-1687. BUDGET.

◄ HIDDEN

Cape Coral—across the river from Fort Myers—boasts an Italian restaurant whose popularity brings knowing hordes despite a low profile. **Dario's Restaurant & Lounge** satisfies any Italian craving. The large menu does seafood, beef, poultry and pasta a dozen different ways each. An unpretentious shopping mall atmosphere. No lunch on the weekend. ~ Coral Point Shopping Center, 1805 Del Prado Boulevard, Cape Coral; 941-574-7798. MODERATE.

For barbecue at its roots level, go to **Hickory BBQ**. Beef and pork sandwiches or ribs are served with the best sauce ever concocted. They smoke their meat on the premises of this spartan facility. Closed Sunday. ~ 15400 McGregor Boulevard, South Fort Myers; 941-481-2626. BUDGET.

The names of Sanibel restaurants seem to change with the tides. One that has endured is **McT's Shrimphouse and Tavern**. Hidden from its busy surroundings by natural vegetation, the triple-peaked building looks like an Old Florida home. The dining room allows outside views through latticed plexiglass walls. Ceilings soar and floors look as though they'd leave splinters in bare feet. The menu swims with mermaids, and dishes overflow with jumbo shrimp: shrimp marinara, shrimp Oscar, stuffed shrimp and all-you-can-eat steamers. The menu also includes beef, chicken and fish dishes. ~ 1523 Periwinkle Way, Sanibel; 941-472-3161. MODERATE.

◄ HIDDEN

For relief from the tab-shock you experience at most Sanibel restaurants, check out **Island Pizza** for pizza, sandwiches, ribs and shrimp baskets, all served in a small but airy facility. ~ 1619 Periwinkle Way, Sanibel; 941-472-1581. BUDGET TO MODERATE.

French restaurants often bring to mind condescending waiters and stuffy surroundings. *Au contraire* at **Jean-Paul's French Corner**. In a tiny room reminiscent of provincial inns, great food comes from humble surroundings. The staff is refreshingly casual; the food is a pure gift to the tongue—fine dishes such as filet mignon *au poivre* and sole stuffed with salmon mousse. Closed on Sunday and in the summer. ~ 708 Tarpon Bay Road, Sanibel; 941-472-1493. DELUXE.

◄ HIDDEN

Text continued on page 422.

Collecting Seashells by the Seashore

It begins innocently with a thumbnail-sized scallop blushing in the morning sun. You bend over to pick it up, to hold it in your hand and consider what a nice souvenir it would make of your visit to Florida's West Coast. You slip it into your beach bag and continue strolling down the beach.

Suddenly you are more aware of what lies at your feet than of anything else in this seashore world of wonders. The rest of your walk— alas, the rest of your beaching days—is spent head down, eyeing cockles, conches, whelks and sand dollars. Your life has taken a new direction: you are shell-bent.

On **Sanibel Island**, the classic bent-from-the-waist shelling stance has been given a special name. Here in the Shelling Capital of the Western Hemisphere, the literally shell-bent are said to do the "Sanibel Stoop." The eastward hook on Sanibel's southern end allows it to snag shells the sea throws up from all directions. Its shelling fame has made it a prime destination for serious conchologists and amateurs for decades.

In early March, the island hosts an annual **Sanibel Shell Fair** that draws participants from around the world. Nearby, on the mainland, the **Fort Myers Festival of Shells** is celebrated every year. Along the West Coast, annual shell shows are also scheduled weekly during the last week of January through mid-March in St. Petersburg, Treasure Island, Sarasota, Naples and Marco Island.

The best place to find shells on Sanibel Island is **Bowman's Beach**. Because of Sanibel's worldwide shelling reputation, however, the competition is fierce. Serious collectors are out before dawn in miner's hats and mesh slippers, equipped with flashlights, collecting bags and shovels, hoping to find a prize junonia or lion's paw left by the ebbing tide. These are the only vacationers in the world who cheer for bad weather. They pray for storms to bring caches of live shells onto the beach for easy pickings. Because of the popularity of shelling on Sanibel, the city has passed a law that limits the taking of live shells to two per species.

Although Sanibel boasts shelling ascendancy, the entire Gulf Coast attracts collectors. **Captiva Beach** also provides good shelling. Here you will actually find shin-deep piles of washed-up shells—all you have to do is sit in one spot and sift through to find your treasures.

In fact, this beach inspired Anne Morrow Lindbergh, author and wife of the famed aviator Charles Lindbergh, to write *Gift from the Sea* back in 1955. This book of essays compares different types of seashells with stages in a woman's life. You will find this slim volume, as well as a myriad of how-to-shell guides, for sale in most book and gift shops on Sanibel and Captiva.

To escape the hordes of the shell-bent on Sanibel, try some of the outlying islands for less-populated collecting. Shelling charters leave daily from Sanibel and Captiva marinas and resorts. A locally famous shell writer, **Captain Mike Fuery**, works out of 'Tween Waters Marina on Captiva. ~ 941-472-1015. He takes his shellers to **Johnson Shoals** off the coast of Cayo Costa, where they can find up to 60 different kinds of shells.

Cayo Costa and **Upper Captiva** islands, because of their seclusion, are popular shelling spots. The same goes for **Egmont Key**, north of Sarasota, and the **Cedar Keys National Wildlife Refuge** at the West Coast's northern extreme. The abundance of shells often comes in direct proportion to the absence of bridges and crowds.

For the less ambitious shell appreciator, there are easier ways to find shells than rising at dawn and mucking around in tidal pools. Hunt instead at the numerous shell shops scattered along the West Coast. The largest and most famous is North Fort Myers' **Shell Factory**, which through the years has evolved from selling shells and coral to marketing jewelry, clothes, gourmet food and other gifts. ~ 2787 North Tamiami Trail; 941-995-2141.

On Sanibel, there are two shell shops owned and operated by knowledgeable conchologists who share advice about their gifts from the sea.

Neptune's Treasures is one. ~ 1101 Periwinkle Way; 941-472-3132. **Showcase Shells** is the other. ~ 1614 Periwinkle Way; 941-472-1971.

The 13-table **Sunshine Café** is good for take-out picnic food or sit-down dining inside or out. The menu includes pasta dishes, New Orleans–style sandwiches, a healthy wine list and a handful of desserts that change daily. Closed Monday and Tuesday during the summer. ~ Captiva Village Square, Captiva; 941-472-6200. MODERATE.

The idea behind **The Bubble Room** is that "you use your five senses," explains a manager, referring to the three levels of whirring, blinking antique toys and trains, Christmas decorations and strands of bubble lights. Waiters buzz around in Boy Scout–type uniforms, pushing the restaurant's superb prime rib. The "festive American" menu also features shrimp and chargrilled mahimahi in sherry butter. ~ 15001 Sanibel-Captiva Road, Captiva; 941-472-5558. DELUXE.

The place to settle a seafood hankering on Fort Myers Beach is indisputably **Snug Harbor Waterfront Restaurant and Café**. The experience begins with a stroll through brick-paved tropical gardens of hibiscus, screw pines and birds-of-paradise. Inside, the casual ambience is nautical in an uncontrived sense. The view out the window is of a shrimp boat rubbing gunwales with a luxury yacht. The seafood tastes as fresh as the flowers on the table look. ~ 645 San Carlos Boulevard, Fort Myers Beach; 941-463-4343. MODERATE TO DELUXE.

For authentic Greek food, try **Plaka Restaurant**. Served in the most casual of beachside atmospheres (the name means beach in Greek), this spot is a favorite. Gyro sandwiches, *moussaka*, spinach pie, baklava and all the Greek standards are offered. ~ 1001 Estero Boulevard, Fort Myers Beach; 941-463-4707. BUDGET.

HIDDEN ▶ For a delicious sense of discovery, find **Café du Monde**. The owners have transferred their Key West–style eatery into a Seattle cybercafé. Have a foamy cappuccino with a decadent slice of chocolate turtle cheesecake, a hefty poppyseed muffin or a flaky croissant. The atmosphere is as delicious as the food: inside, lots of bookshelves and polished wood give things a homey feel; outside, there's a bricked courtyard that hides from busy Estero Boulevard behind a low cement wall handpainted with roses. Umbrellas cover the tables surrounded by potted plants. ~ 1740 Estero Boulevard, Fort Myers Beach; 941-765-7188. BUDGET.

The Mucky Duck earned its reputation on nearby Captiva Island. This second in a series of British-inspired pubs continues its success at this historic beachfront location. Restored to a warm, country-style rendition of life in England, the menu blends Old World flavors with local specialties, offering fish 'n' chips, several preparations of shrimp and "whatever the fish." Dinner only. Closed Sunday during the summer; ~ 2500 Estero Boulevard, Fort Myers Beach; 941-463-5519. BUDGET TO MODERATE.

Royal Palm Square is one of two shopping centers in Fort Meyers **SHOPPING** offering specialty merchandise in tropically landscaped settings. While there, check out **The Wine Merchant** (941-939-0090), a purveyor of fine imported and domestic wines, cheeses, accessories and gift baskets. ~ 1400 Colonial Boulevard, Fort Myers.

Another open-air mall is **Bell Tower Shops**. **Anna's** (941-482-5600) carries a variety of exquisite Moroccan clothing and accessories for the exotic and adventurous. ~ 13499 Route 41 Southeast, Fort Myers.

Fort Myers' largest shopping center houses more than 150 merchants. **Edison Mall** hosts major retailers plus a multitude of specialty shops and food court eateries. ~ Route 41 and Colonial Boulevard, Fort Myers; 941-939-5464.

For discounted goods, shop at a local retail center, **Metro Mall**. ~ Metro Parkway and Colonial Boulevard, Fort Myers; 941-939-3132. Or, join bargain hunters flocking to **Fleamaster Fleamarkets**. ~ 4135 Dr. Martin Luther King, Jr. Boulevard, Fort Myers; 941-334-7001.

Touch of Sanibel Pottery sells fine clayware thrown and fired right on the premises. Their bright colors and intricate designs are inspired by the island's flora and fauna. ~ 1544 Periwinkle Way, Sanibel; 941-472-4330.

For T-shirts with a difference, swing by the **Tee Station**. You'll find unusual designs by local nature artists gracing quality resort wear, as well as more touristy items. ~ 1700 Periwinkle Way, Sanibel; 941-472-2251.

Schoolhouse Gallery stocks original paintings, sculpture and shelligrams. ~ 520 Tarpon Bay Road, Sanibel; 941-472-1193. **Matsumoto Gallery**, nearby, displays the work of island artists. ~ 751 Tarpon Bay Road, Sanibel; 941-472-6686.

At **Discovery Bay** you'll find a wide array of gifts including glassware, 14-karat jewelry and fashion jewelry. ~ 7205 Estero Boulevard, Fort Myers Beach; 941-463-4715.

For casual women's clothing, beachwear and accessories, try **Eastwind**. ~ 159 San Carlos Boulevard, Fort Myers Beach; 941-463-3232.

Touted as the world's largest shell shop, **The Shell Factory** is the only souvenir stop you'll ever need. Lamps, trays and jewelry are made of shells as is mostly everything else inside this cavernous place. Everything from kitsch to clothing is stocked. ~ 2787 North Tamiami Trail, North Fort Myers; 941-995-2141.

Rabid sports fans without portable TVs need not fear: there are 27 **NIGHTLIFE** televisions and two big screens at the **Courtside Sports Bar & Grill** in Sanibel Harbour Resort and Spa. ~ 17260 Harbour Pointe Drive, Fort Myers; 813-466-2138.

The Crow's Nest at 'Tween Waters Inn swings nightly with rhythm-and-blues, soft rock and funk. ~ Captiva Road, Captiva; 941-472-5161.

Fort Myers Beach is nightlife incarnate. Walk the beach or Estero Boulevard and stop in at the many clubs and bars for a people-packed and fun-filled evening out. One of the most notorious bars is **Top O' Mast Lounge**, where there's deejay music and dancing day and night. ~ 1028 Estero Boulevard, Fort Myers Beach; 941-463-9424.

The beachfront action at **Lani Kai Island Resort** draws crowds with rock-and-roll bands, Caribbean musicians and a piano bar. ~ 1400 Estero Boulevard, Fort Myers Beach; 941-463-3111.

THEATER, OPERA, SYMPHONY AND DANCE   As far as theater goes, the Fort Myers area has just begun to develop. **Barbara B. Mann Performing Arts Hall** hosts touring theater, music and dance troupes. ~ 8099 College Parkway, Fort Myers; 941-489-3033.

HIDDEN ►

The **Pirates Playhouse** presents intimate theater-in-the-round productions by professional and community companies. ~ 2200 Periwinkle Way, Sanibel; 941-472-0006.

BEACHES & PARKS

HIDDEN ►

CAYO COSTA STATE PARK 🏃 🚲 🏊 🛶 🚤 ⛵ This island of 640 acres can be reached only by boat. Because it is less populated than the lower islands, the shell pickings are great. Shell-studded white beaches run the length of the island on both the Gulf and bay side. All varieties of indigenous wildlife, including wild boars and bald eagles, thrive here. Fishing is very good at the northern end of the island where Boca Grande Pass separates the island from the famous tarpon mecca on Gasparilla Island. The pass that separates Upper Captiva from Captiva is named Redfish Pass for the fish found in abundance there. Facilities include nature trails, bike rentals, picnic areas, outdoor restrooms and cold-water showers. Day-use fee, $2. ~ Many tours and charters out of Sanibel, Captiva and Pine Island will take you there; 941-964-0375.

▲ Primitive camping is allowed; $13 per night. Twelve austere cabins are also available; $20 per night.

LIGHTHOUSE BEACH 🏊 ⛵ Wrapping around the southwestern end of Sanibel Island, this beach benefits from Gulf and bay frontage. The sand is cushiony and shell-littered. The historic Sanibel Lighthouse sits here in old Florida glory. This is the most popular beaching spot for newcomers because it is so easy to find. It's as good place to swim but waters tend to be murky in this part of the Gulf. Fishing is great at the pier on the bayside for snook, shark, sheepshead and red snapper. There are restrooms; restaurants and groceries are nearby. ~ Located on the southeastern end of Sanibel Island where Periwinkle Way deadends; 941-472-1080.

GULFSIDE PARK 🏊 ⛵ A secluded picnic area underneath ◀ *HIDDEN*
Australian pines, this spot attracts folks looking for alligators in
the canal that borders one side. The beach is narrow here but shell-
strewn and relatively unpopulated. A stand of sea oats separates
the beach from the picnic grounds. There's good ocean swimming.
The only facilities are picnic areas and restrooms; restaurants and
groceries a few miles away on Periwinkle Way. ~ Located on Sanibel Island, at the end of Algiers Lane, off Casa Ybel Road; 941-
472-1080.

BOWMAN'S BEACH 🏊 🐟 ⛵ A long, secluded stretch of sand,
probably Sanibel's finest. The shells are usually more plentiful on
this northern end of the island, and the people less so. The Sanibel
River cuts through, and two bridges cross its brackish waters. A
short hike will take you past a plethora of native jungle vegetation.
Bowman's Beach has wonderful swimming and snorkeling. There
are picnic areas, restrooms, showers and nature trails; restaurants
and groceries are a few miles away at Blind Pass. ~ The beach is
located on Bowman's Beach Road off Sanibel-Captiva Road; 941-
472-1080.

CARL E. JOHNSON PARK–LOVER'S KEY 🚶 🏊 ⛵ This park is actu- ◀ *HIDDEN*
ally a system of protected wetlands that covers three small islands—Lover's Key, Inner Key and Black Island. At Johnson Park,
a tram takes you across wooden bridges and down sandy paths to
view the area's unique mangrove ecosystem. The tram's ultimate
destination is the beach and its picnic ground facilities on Lover's
Key. It seems as though few have discovered this secluded beach
spot invitingly shaded with pines and landscaped in native shrubbery. Hikers will find it pleasant to hoof it to the beach here, or
they can turn north to Black Island. The swimming is good.
Facilities include picnic areas, restrooms and showers; restaurants
and groceries are several miles away in Fort Myers Beach or Bonita
Beach. ~ Located south of Fort Myers Beach on Estero Boulevard;
941-338-3300.

KORESHAN STATE HISTORIC SITE 🚣 🚤 ⛵ This place is
an interesting historic and recreational park built on a religious
theory. Founded by Cyrus Reed Teed, the Koreshan cult believed
the earth was hollow and that the sun revolved in its center while
life was contained around this nucleus. The Koreshans' legacy to
this state was the introduction of exotic plants that continue to
thrive here: avocados, mangos, royal palms and bromeliads. There
are canoe rentals, a nature trail, a picnic area and restrooms. ~ The
park entrance is located right off Route 41, south of Fort Myers;
941-992-0311.

▲ There are 60 sites, all with hookups; $10 to $16 per night.

▼▼▼▼▼▼▼▼▼▼▼▼
Naples Area

On the edge of the Everglades, the Naples area is one of the West Coast's more popular resort regions. Romantic beaches, grand cypress trees and wind-sculptured dunes are the region's calling card. Here you can choose between glamorous resorts and quiet inns. For a taste of contemporary Florida, check out the highrise world of Marco island.

SIGHTS

The fast-growing city of **Bonita Springs** sits south of Fort Myers along Route 41. Almost as old as Florida is the **Everglades Wonder Gardens**. This attraction offers a contained environment for viewing indigenous wetlands wildlife: the American eagle, toy deer, alligators, panthers and rattlesnakes. The nonlive exhibits show their age with tinges of yellowing and fading, but therein lies much of the charm of this vintage tourist attraction. Admission. ~ Old Route 41, Bonita Springs; 941-992-2591.

HIDDEN ►

Visit one of southwest Florida's finest wilderness refuges near Naples on Route 846 off Route 41. **Corkscrew Swamp Sanctuary** shelters breeding wood storks among its native plant and animal populations. Lakes of lettuce fern and 500-year-old cypress trees dripping with Spanish moss make you feel as though you have entered a different dimension of space and time. Admission. ~ Sanctuary Road; 941-657-3771.

The city of **Naples** sits prettily on a peninsula between the Gulf of Mexico and Naples Bay. Boutiques, fine restaurants and a perfect beach count as the city's greatest draws.

HIDDEN ►

Not far from the pier in old Naples, the **Palm Cottage** is one of the few remaining structures from the city's infancy days of the 1890s. It once served as winter home to *Louisville Courier Journal* editor Henry Watterson, and later as an annex to the town's first hotel. Today, the seashell mortar home serves as a museum and the home of the Collier County Historical Society. (Currently, Palm Cottage is undergoing restoration and is closed to the public, but architectural buffs will still enjoy passing by this graceful turn-of-the-century dwelling.) ~ 137 12th Avenue South, Naples; 941-261-8164.

The **Naples Chamber of Commerce and Visitors Center** has more information on area sights. ~ 895 Fifth Avenue South, Naples; 941-262-6141.

Marco Island counterpoints soaring condominium towers with bald eagle nests. You can examine this island group's past and present on a ride aboard the **Marco Island Trolley**, an excursion back to the years of the ancient Calusa Indians, whose shell mounds have survived the onslaught of bulldozers and concrete. You'll also see a sample of the estuarine life of the Everglades' Ten Thousand Islands, of which Marco is the northernmost. Admission. ~ 601 Elkcan Circle, Marco Island; 941-394-1600.

For more information on the island, visit the **Marco Island Area Chamber of Commerce**. ~ 1102 North Collier Boulevard, Marco Island; 941-394-7549.

In Naples proper, the hostelries reflect the town's upscale, sophisticated image. North of the city, beach hotels show more personality and less expense. A sweet little five-unit place called **Inn on the Bay Motel** sits on the water. The building looks like a seaside shanty of white clapboard and blue trim. The comfortable, homey rooms are within easy walking distance of the beach. ~ 4701 West Bonita Beach Road, Bonita Springs; 813-992-2655. MODERATE.

LODGING

◀ HIDDEN

Down the road at Vanderbilt Beach, the **Vanderbilt Inn on the Gulf** has a location that best suits beachgoers. Metropolites, however, don't have far to go to reach Naples shops and restaurants. The simple two-story structure offers some interior intrigue with a Florida-living motif in the rooms and a New Mexico-gone-tropic theme in the lobby. ~ 11000 Gulf Shore Drive North, Naples; 941-597-3151, 800-643-8654, fax 941-597-3099. ULTRA-DELUXE.

The Naples Pier, a landmark that predates the city itself, juts out from golden sands at a perfect angle from which to view a sunset.

When the occasion calls for first-class accommodations with impeccable service, elegant rooms and tea served in the afternoon, **The Ritz Carlton** is the right choice. Hospitality that combines Old World graciousness with ultramodern convenience makes a stay here top notch. Tennis courts, golf course, fitness center, three miles of private beach, six eateries and 463 rooms are offered at this majestic Mediterranean palazzo set amid unspoiled coastlands and back bays. ~ 280 Vanderbilt Beach Road, Naples; 941-598-3300, 800-241-3333, fax 941-598-6690. ULTRA-DELUXE.

Cove Inn Marina Resort rents 102 rooms with a lovely view of Naples Bay. The rooms huddle around a marina and boast some splashes of character, such as the cypress cross-section table in one of the efficiencies. Extras include a pool and chickee bar. ~ 900 Broad Avenue South, Naples; 941-262-7161, 800-255-4365, fax 941-261-6905. DELUXE TO ULTRA-DELUXE.

Fabulous blue vistas of sky and water and consistently fine seafood and steaks have continued to keep **McCully's Rooftop Restaurant** popular through the years. The mood is relaxed elegance. Closed Monday. ~ 25999 Hickory Boulevard, Bonita Beach; 941-992-0033. MODERATE TO DELUXE.

DINING

Riverwalk Fish & Ale House is found waterside in the Tin City shopping center. Casual, woody and open to the activity on the charter docks, the restaurant offers simply good seafood and a few chicken and steak entrées for dinner and sandwiches and salads for lunch. ~ 1200 5th Avenue South, Naples; 941-263-2734. MODERATE TO DELUXE.

The **Chart House** serves fine food in a casual dining room with a stunning view of Naples Bay. Dinners feature prime rib, steak and seafood. ~ 1193 9th Street South, Naples; 941-649-0033. DELUXE.

For northern Mediterranean cuisine in a comfortable rustic setting, try **Tierra**. You can choose from a light bar menu that includes skillet-roasted mussels, *focaccia* pizza and seafood risotto, or go for heartier dishes such as savory herb-encrusted tuna or mushroom lasagna. ~ 1300 3rd Street South, Naples; 941-262-5500. ULTRA-DELUXE.

For barbecue, try **Michelbob's**. Baby back ribs and barbecue chicken are favorites at this busy spot which offers bench seatings. Juicy New York steaks are another specialty. ~ 371 Airport Road, Naples; 941-643-2877. BUDGET.

The **Olde Marco Inn** serves history with its fine German and Continental fare: *jaeggerschnitzel*, sauerbräten with red cabbage and potatoes, beefsteak à la Meyer and, in keeping with its Florida setting, succulent seafood combinations, such as scallops, lobster, grouper and shrimp smothered in creamy sauces. The setting is a historical landmark where the island's founding father once lived. In a rambling home scenario, tables are set in six dining rooms, each with its own personality: from the casual and sun-touched veranda, to the formal dining room with its cranberry glass chandelier, to the Audubon room decorated with wildlife prints dating back to 1850. ~ 100 Palm Street, Marco Island; 941-394-3131. MODERATE TO DELUXE.

HIDDEN ►   **Stan's Idle Hour Seafood Restaurant** is a slice of old, real Florida in this rustic fishing village on the skirts of the Everglades. The menu is pure Everglades: frog legs, stone crab, fresh grouper made into sandwiches and fried oysters. (Be adventurous and try the buzzard wings.) The owner is a Hemingway look-alike. The patrons are heavy on the local color; many arrive by boat and sit outside on the patio and trade fish stories. ~ On the main street in Goodland; 941-394-3041. BUDGET TO MODERATE.

SHOPPING   **Old Marine Marketplace**, a waterfront relic also known as "Tin City," has become a rustic mall housing more than 30 high-class shops. For instance, **Things From the Sea** (941-261-3820) deals in quality nautical niceties. ~ 1200 5th Avenue South, Naples.

The shops of **5th Avenue South** are strictly upscale. **Gingerbread & Old Lace** has fine consignment items: art, antiques, and handmade pieces. ~ 995 5th Avenue South, Naples; 941-649-5755.

The Southwest American Indian art sold at **Four Winds Gallery** includes uniquely stylized and contemporary pottery, weavings as well as beautiful silver, gold and turquoise jewelry. ~ 340 13th Avenue South, Naples; 941-263-7555.

Located at the Registry Resort, **Club Zanzibar** is a popular weekend dancing spot with deejay music Tuesday, Wednesday, Thursday and Saturday. On Friday you can hear live blues and jazz. ~ 475 Seagate Drive, Naples; 941-597-3232.

The **Naples Playhouse** produces fine shows during its winter and summer seasons. ~ 399 Goodlette Road South; 941-263-7990.

BAREFOOT BEACH ACCESS   A shelly spread of sand with little vegetation. Although the nearby condominium congestion seems to be creeping ever nearer, the beach stays relatively unpopulated and has an unsophisticated air about it. The sands somehow seem homier than its neighboring beaches. Try fishing for snook and redfish. There are picnic tables; restrooms, restaurants and groceries are nearby. Parking fee, $3. ~ Off Bonita Beach Road on Lely Beach Boulevard; 941-353-0404.

DELNOR–WIGGINS PASS STATE RECREATION AREA   A natural mile-long beachfront park where the Cocohatchee River lets out into the ocean. The narrow peninsula protects native flora such as cactus, seagrapes, sabal palms, knickerbean and yucca. The lush white beach parallels low dunes and strands of sea oats. This area is protected to encourage turtle nesting. A trail at the southern end of the park leads to an observation tower. Swimming is good and fishing is rewarding at the north end along the pass for trout, snook and redfish; you can cast-net for mullet in the bay. Facilities include a picnic area, grills, restrooms, showers and lifeguards; restaurants and groceries are nearby. ~ At 11100 Gulf Shore Drive North in Naples; 941-597-6196.

LOWDERMILK PARK   A shady city park with over 1000 feet of fine sandy beach where volleyball is a popular activity. This beach teems with teens on weekends. During the week, you'll find a different crowd, but a crowd nonetheless. Despite its masses, it's a wonderful place to spend a party day on the beach. You can swim and fish (the best spot is at the pier, south of the park). You'll find picnic areas, two covered gazebos, restrooms, showers, dressing rooms and a snack bar; restaurants and groceries are nearby. ~ Gulfshore Boulevard North at Banyan Boulevard, Naples; 941-434-4687.

COLLIER-SEMINOLE STATE PARK   On the edge of the Everglades, this 6423-acre preserve offers a taste of the area's salt marsh and hardwood forest wildlife to a limited number of visitors each day. Exhibits throughout the park include a Bay City walking dredge. Facilities at this park include picnic areas, restrooms, a nature trail, canoe rentals and a snack bar. ~ The entrance is located east of Naples on Route 41; 941-394-3397.

▲ There are 130 sites, 80 with RV hookups, and a backpacker camp; $13 to 15 per night.

TIGERTAIL BEACH PARK 🦅 ⚓ 🏄 🏖 This 31-acre Gulf-front beach sits on Marco Island apart from the conglomeration of condos. A system of wooden ramps takes you over the sea-coated dunes to a marvelous beach. There are picnic areas, a playground, a snack bar, restrooms, showers and windsurfing and sailboat rentals; restaurants and groceries nearby. Parking fee, $3. ~ At the end of Hernando Drive on Marco Island; 941-394-2793.

▼▼▼▼▼▼▼▼▼▼▼▼▼
St. Petersburg–Clearwater Area

Bordered by Tampa Bay to the east and the Gulf of Mexico on the west, this popular peninsula offers a wealth of opportunity. What brings travelers here from all over Florida and the world is a dazzling thread of islands woven to the mainland by five bridges. This thread, often known as the Holiday Islands, has developed into highrise heaven thanks to its gorgeous beaches and lucid waters. Pleasure seekers of all ages are attracted to this paradise playground, where the most strenuous activity is building sandcastles.

SIGHTS

DOWNTOWN ST. PETERSBURG The city of St. Petersburg lies on a peninsula across the bay from Tampa. Its pitted bay face smiles with calm waters and sunshine. Activity downtown centers around **The Pier**, an inverted pyramid-shaped structure that houses shops, restaurants and an observation deck. The view from here overlooks the seaside city in all its splendor and is especially scenic at night. ~ 800 2nd Avenue Northeast; 813-821-6443.

One office of the **St. Petersburg Chamber of Commerce** is located in the lobby of The Pier. Another Chamber office is nearby. ~ 100 2nd Avenue North; 813-821-4069.

One of the most impressive downtown features is the **Salvador Dali Museum**, which boasts over 1000 prints and originals—including 94 oils—created by Spanish surrealist artist Salvador Dali. This collection of Dali's works, executed between 1914 and 1980, is contained within a spacious, modern garret. Admission. ~ 1000 3rd Street South; 813-823-3767.

Another downtown attraction, the **St. Petersburg Museum of History**, features a full-size replica of the world's first passenger airline. The Benoist airboat, a biplane that carried passengers over the bay, one at a time, was the first airline to offer scheduled flights. The museum also offers a variety of interactive exhibits on the history of the area from prehistoric times to the present. Admission. ~ 335 Second Avenue Northeast; 813-894-1052.

SOUTHERN PINELLAS COUNTY Around the city's peninsular Gulf front, a thread of islands, often known as the Holiday Isles, is woven to the mainland by five bridges.

To make the island tour, take Pinellas Bayway across the peninsula that comprises Pinellas County, to Fort de Soto Park. North

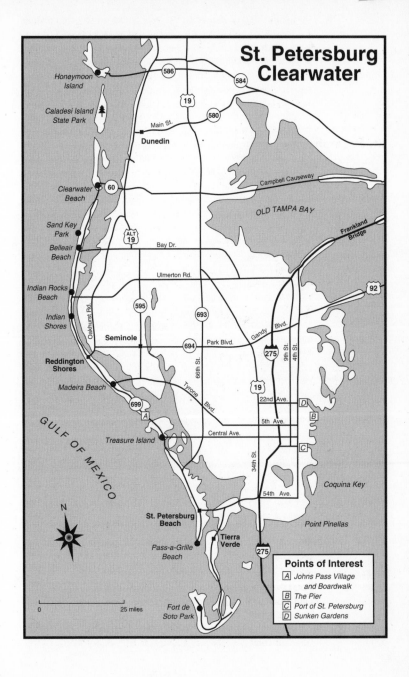

St. Petersburg Clearwater

Honeymoon Island

Caladesi Island State Park

Main St.

Dunedin

Campbell Causeway

OLD TAMPA BAY

Clearwater Beach

Frankland Bridge

Sand Key Park

Belleair Beach

Bay Dr.

Ulmerton Rd.

Indian Rocks Beach

Indian Shores

Oakhurst Rd.

Seminole

Park Blvd.

Gandy Blvd.

Reddington Shores

Madeira Beach

66th St.

Tyrone Blvd.

9th St.

4th St.

22nd Ave.

5th Ave.

Central Ave.

Treasure Island

34th St.

Coquina Key

54th Ave.

Point Pinellas

St. Petersburg Beach

Tierra Verde

Pass-a-Grille Beach

GULF OF MEXICO

N

0   25 miles

Fort de Soto Park

Points of Interest

A Johns Pass Village and Boardwalk
B The Pier
C Port of St. Petersburg
D Sunken Gardens

of the five islands that form the park, the town of Tierra Verde eases into the holiday carnival scene that its neighbor, **St. Petersburg Beach**, begins. Besides the wide beach and watersports action, other sights beckon the sightseer along this sandy rim.

From St. Petersburg Beach, the **island chain** along Gulf Boulevard includes Treasure Island, Madeira Beach, Indian Rocks Beach, Belleair Beach and Clearwater Beach. These Gulf-front islands are separated from the mainland by a narrow trickle of water that broadens at both ends.

Between Treasure Island and Madeira, a boardwalk with salty shops, restaurants and charter boats has cropped up at **Johns Pass Village and Boardwalk**. Patterned after a fishing community of yore, it pays tribute to the community's commercial fishing industry. ~ 12925 East Gulf Boulevard, Madeira Beach; 813-397-1571.

The **Suncoast Seabird Sanctuary** works to restore sky-dwellers. You'll find over 250 birds of many species here, among them the cormorant, white heron, brown pelican, sandhill crane and snowy egret. ~ 18328 Gulf Boulevard, Indian Shores; 813-391-6211.

NORTHERN PINELLAS COUNTY   To get back to the mainland segment of Pinellas County, cross into **Clearwater** at the nicely landscaped Courtney Campbell Causeway. The inland Route 19 takes you along small peninsula towns. In one of them, **Heritage Village** comprises a collection of historic structures that reflect the area's pioneer days. One building, the McMullen-Coachman loghouse, dates back to the 1850s and is the oldest building in the county. Others include a sugar mill, railroad depot, school and church. At the museum period craftsmen wear authentic costumes, and exhibits demonstrate such folk crafts as rug hooking and loom weaving. ~ 11909 125th Street North, Largo; 813-582-2123.

Nestled in the far reaches of Old Tampa Bay, **Philippe Park** commemorates the three groups that settled in this area: ancient American Indians, Spanish conquistadors and European settlers (who first introduced grapefruit to the New World at this spot). The large Timucuan Indian mound is listed in the National Register of Historic Places. ~ 2355 Bayshore Drive, Safety Harbor; 813-726-2700.

SUNKEN TREASURE

The **Sunken Gardens** is a pleasant surprise, with its jungle-like ambience. The grounds were created in a sinkhole from which the water was drained. The fertile pit was then landscaped with exotic plants and stocked with tropical birds. You'll see monkeys, crowned cranes, muntjac deer and hornbills wandering among bougainvillea and hibiscus. Admission. ~ 1825 4th Street North, St. Petersburg; 813-896-3186.

Dunedin is a Scottish-rooted city at the northern end of St. Petersburg's Pinellas County, where the peninsula attaches to mainland, reachable from Clearwater on Route 19A. Along the scenic bay drive, you'll begin to notice names like Aberdeen and Locklie on the street signs. The **Greater Dunedin Chamber of Commerce** hands out material on area attractions and accommodations. ~ 301 Main Street, Dunedin; 813-736-5066.

Tarpon Springs is Florida's Little Greece, an unexpected pocket of Aegean culture in a rural area of freshwater lakes and old southern neighborhoods. The community developed as a sponge divers' settlement in the 1890s. Along Dodecanese Boulevard one can still see the sponge docks, now used more by shrimpers than spongers. Shops and markets line the street, operated by Greek-American ladies and frequented by bearded sailors in Greek hats who converse in their ancestral tongue.

Spongearama, a museum that exhibits photos and memorabilia from the great sponging era, remembers the settlement days of Tarpon Springs. On display are animated scenes from the erstwhile world of sponge diving. The complex also features several shops and an operating sponge factory. Admission. ~ 510 Dodecanese Boulevard, Tarpon Springs; 813-943-9509.

St. Nicholas Greek Orthodox Cathedral is a relic of the Old World way of life. Its classic neo-Byzantine architecture features icon-studded walls, sculptured Grecian marble and a statue of the Blessed Mother that is said to weep. ~ 36 North Pinellas Avenue, Tarpon Springs; 813-937-3540.

In the **Unitarian Universalist Church**, the works of noted landscape artist George Inness, Jr., are collected. While living in Tarpon Springs, this early 20th-century artist executed many of his most renowned works, inspired by the beauty and spirituality of his natural surroundings. When a hurricane blew out the church's stained-glass windows in 1918, they were eventually replaced with murals that Inness painted. ~ 230 Grand Boulevard, Tarpon Springs; 813-937-4682.

If you seek the unusual in your sightseeing routines, consider **Noell's Ark Chimp Farm**. This home for retired zoo and circus primates features athletic apes and tame gorillas. You can't miss it: just watch for the big homemade sign that announces "Slow! Gorilla Ahead." Admission. ~ 4612 South Pinellas Avenue, Tarpon Springs; 813-937-8683.

The Tarpon Springs Chamber of Commerce distributes literature on things to see and do in the city. ~ 210 South Pinellas Avenue, Suite 120, Tarpon Springs; 813-937-6109.

DOWNTOWN ST. PETERSBURG   St. Petersburg's downtown accommodations combine a distinct historical flavor with born-again energy.

LODGING

Sitting with quiet majesty in an old residential downtown neighborhood, **The Heritage** wears its glamour like old money. The 71-room hotel was renovated in the 1980s to its '20s era birthright; rich mahogany bars and antique furnishings were liberated from years of paint. Subtle color tones in wallpaper, dhurrie rugs and polished oak floors lend a modern Florida look. Besides offering easy access to downtown attractions, The Heritage possesses in-house benefits such as a swimming pool and a restaurant. ~ 234 3rd Avenue North; 813-822-4814, 800-283-7827, fax 813-823-1644. MODERATE TO DELUXE.

One of St. Petersburg's earliest homes, the **Bayboro House** now stands as a bed and breakfast. The 19-room home, with its four guest rooms (all with private baths), was built by an early St. Petersburg settler in 1905. Its quirky old personality can be seen in its irregular architecture, asymmetrical windows and mixed bag of interior design styles. The front porch is white picketed, the steps edged in conch shells. A player piano, pump organ, marble tables and grandfather clocks furnish the inn. ~ 1719 Beach Drive Southeast; phone/fax 813-823-4955. MODERATE TO DELUXE.

SOUTHERN PINELLAS COUNTY Accommodations of both skyscraper and mom-and-pop nature have mushroomed along the coastline in southern Pinellas County, fronting St. Petersburg Beach and nearby beach communities.

A historic masterpiece in cotton-candy pink, the **Don CeSar Beach Resort** greets visitors to this beach town. It stands stately and fancifully to woo guests with complete resort services. Classic Florida resort style is embodied here. You'll find 275 rooms, plus restaurants, lounges, conference facilities and banquet halls, in prime condition. The Don's personality combines equal doses of Mediterranean, fairy castle and beach resort. ~ 3400 Gulf Boulevard, St. Petersburg Beach; 813-360-1881, 800-282-1116, fax 813-367-3609. ULTRA-DELUXE.

On Pass-a-Grille Beach, low-key motels and beach houses line one side of Gulf Way, dusty sand beach the other. One colorful lodging option is the **Sunset View Guest House**, where you can sleep with sea breezes wafting through jalousy windows. Refrigerators and microwaves come with each cozy room in this circa-1940 building that makes you feel right at home. Three-night minimum stay. ~ 1107 Gulf Way, St. Petersburg Beach; 813-360-1333. BUDGET.

HIDDEN ▶

Long Key Beach Resort provides some architectural interest with its 44 beachfront rooms, efficiencies and apartments. Peaked roofs, a wooden observation sundeck and a rounded bay window front upgrade the court hotel look. The rooms are pleasant, the efficiencies not without character. Two pools, a poolside lounge, a boat dock for guests and 180 feet of expansive beach comprise other amenities. ~ 3828 Gulf Boulevard, St. Petersburg Beach; 813-360-1748, fax 813-367-9026. DELUXE.

Guests can tour the grounds via gondolas at the exotic **Tradewinds Beach Resort**. Housing 577 rooms, Tradewinds takes complete care of guests with four pools, a sauna, a whirlpool, tennis and croquet courts, a fitness center, sailing equipment, four restaurants, a wide beach and children's activities. Each room includes a wet bar, refrigerator and exclusive furnishings. ~ 5500 Gulf Boulevard, St. Petersburg Beach; 813-367-6461. ULTRA-DELUXE.

A dramatic spiral staircase is the centerpiece of the elegant lobby at **Dolphin Beach Resort**. The 173 rooms are in a jagged lowrise building fronted by white beach and brightened by colorful sails and cabañas. The rooms are spacious and earth-toned with separate dressing areas. The on-site restaurant serves Continental and American cuisine. ~ 4900 Gulf Boulevard, St. Petersburg Beach; 813-360-7011, 800-237-8916, fax 813-267-5909. DELUXE.

The **Sandpiper Beach Resort** sits veiled from the main beach road by a wall of well-tended tropical shrubbery. This six-story complex boasts copious sports facilities: handball, squash and racquetball courts, an exercise room, shuffleboard courts, two swimming pools and a game room. Some units come equipped with kitchenettes. Piper's Patio offers poolside service for drinks and munchies. Rooms are decorated in Standard Florida Hotel—rattan, colorful prints and breezy colors. Child care service is also available. ~ 6000 Gulf Boulevard, St. Petersburg Beach; 800-237-0707, fax 813-562-1222. ULTRA-DELUXE.

A row motel called **Surfs Inn** shows a white face with a blue porte-cochère and colored shutters. The 27 rooms, efficiencies and suites in this mom-and-pop facility are compact and front the pool and beach. Blue awnings and table umbrellas in the sunning area perk up this pleasant little place. ~ 14010 Gulf Boulevard, Madeira Beach; 813-393-4609. MODERATE.

The eight, fresh little gingerbread cottages at **Villa St. Tropez Motel** The sit across the street from the beach and include full kitchen facilities and a pleasant grassy sunning area with shuffleboard courts. ~ 1713 North Gulf Boulevard, Indian Rocks Beach; 813-596-7133. BUDGET.   ◄ HIDDEN

The **Holiday House Motel Apartments** lie low along blindingly white sands. Typically beach oriented, the 27 apartments won't win awards for interior decoration but are clean and roomy and provide full kitchen facilities. You get a full apartment for what you would pay for a room at other hotels in the area. ~ 495 North Gulfview Boulevard, Clearwater Beach; 813-447-4533, fax 813-449-2083. MODERATE TO DELUXE.

Fine resort style at **Adam's Mark** is defined with accommodations and location that create a Caribbean atmosphere. The 213 modern rooms corner a wide stretch of beach and are custom designed with elegant tropical touches. ~ 430 South Gulfview Boulevard, Clearwater Beach; 813-443-5714, 800-444-2326, fax 813-442-8389. DELUXE TO ULTRA-DELUXE.

NORTHERN PINELLAS COUNTY The city of Clearwater owes its existence to the **Belleview Mido Hotel**, built here at the turn of the century. The rambling mansion displays its heritage with clapboard and dormers, capped with peaks as green as the property's golf course. Green is also used on the interior and in the 292 guest rooms. The voluminous lobby is a vision of beveled glass. Accents come in rich reds and mauves, with vintage touches such as Tiffany stained-glass ceiling panels and brass fixtures. Elegance settles in here without pretentiousness; the surroundings inspire complete comfort. ~ 25 Belleview Boulevard, Clearwater; 813-442-6171, 800-237-8947, fax 813-441-6171. ULTRA-DELUXE.

For very inexpensive accommodations a short walk from the beach, try the **Clearwater Beach International Hostel**. The hostel provides guests an outdoor pool, a fully equipped kitchen, a living room with a ping-pong table and games, and 40 to 50 beds in the dormitories. Bike rentals and free canoe usage are also available. ~ 606 Bay Esplanade Avenue, Clearwater; 813-443-1211, phone/fax 800-909-4776, ext. 16. BUDGET.

Built in the 1920s, when F. Scott and Zelda Fitzgerald supposedly visited, Don CeSar Beach Resort was converted into an army hospital during WWII.

A Swiss touch brushes the architecture of **Best Western—Yacht Harbor Inn**. The 55 rooms sport peaked ceilings, marina views and pastel color schemes. The lobby and restaurant have chalet nuances. ~ 150 Marina Plaza, Dunedin; 813-733-4121, 800-447-4728, fax 813-736-4365. MODERATE TO DELUXE.

Those looking for a place to play in the Tarpon Springs area should consider a vacation at **Innisbrook Hilton Resort**. Serious golfers, tennis and racquetball whackers, and lake beachers congregate at this 1000-room facility. Rooms range from spacious to more spacious. The best of the ambience awaits outdoors in the woodsy, landscaped, lake-graced grounds. ~ Route 19 North, Tarpon Springs; 813-942-2000, 800-456-2000, fax 813-942-5577. ULTRA-DELUXE.

The **Golfview Motel** is a 14-unit, clean mom-and-pop-type motel with flowered trellises adding a splash of tropical color to the well-kept grounds. ~ 1475 South Pinellas Avenue, Tarpon Springs; 813-937-7342. BUDGET.

Sunbay Motel is in a great location within walking distance of the sponge docks and the antique shops. It is located on Spring

Bayou. ~ 57 West Tarpon Avenue, Tarpon Springs; 813-934-1001.
BUDGET.

The Livery Stable is another bed and breakfast facility with ◄ HIDDEN
nine comfortable rooms and full breakfast. The white blockhouse
building sits in an old residential area of town. The guest quarters
are clean and comfortable. ~ At 100 North Ring Avenue, Tarpon
Springs; 813-938-5547. BUDGET.

DOWNTOWN ST. PETERSBURG   At the pier in downtown St. Pete, **DINING**
Alessi Café At the Pier impresses with blond woods, a brass espresso machine and a showcase of sinful pastries. The menu features
Italian specialties such as meat- and veggie-stuffed calzones and
gourmet pizzas, as well as hearty deli sandwiches and freshly baked
breads. ~ 800 2nd Avenue Northeast; 813-894-1133. MODERATE.

SOUTHERN PINELLAS COUNTY   Continental cuisine with a difference is served at **Good Times Continental Restaurant**. The Old
World influence takes a refreshing departure from France and Italy
to offer tastebud tantalization in the form of Hungarian chicken
paprikash, beef stroganoff, filet mignon topped with glazed
peaches and béarnaise, black forest cake and Czechoslovakian
beer. All is served in a plain-looking facility with vinyl chairs and
pool-hall paneling. Closed in August. ~ 1130 Pinellas Bayway,
Tierra Verde; 813-867-0774. MODERATE.

On Pass-a-Grille Beach, **Hurricane Seafood Restaurant** seats
you outdoors with a beach view, or inside its wood-accented, casual, dining room. Seafood comes in every form imaginable. The
grouper sandwich is a local favorite. ~ 809 Gulf Way, St. Petersburg Beach; 813-360-9558. MODERATE.

Pelican Diner serves homestyle meals in an authentic dining car
atmosphere—authentic meaning this is a survivor of a bygone era,
not a replica. Corroded chrome, vinyl counter stools and blue-and-
white tiled walls are the setting; pork chops, liver and corned beef
and cabbage are the fare. ~ 7501 Gulf Boulevard, St. Petersburg
Beach; 813-363-9873. BUDGET TO MODERATE.

Scandinavian specialties with names like *frikadeller* (meatballs),
medister polser (seasoned sausage) and *hakkobof med log og spei-
jlag* (beef topped with fried egg) taste as exotic as they sound at
Scandia. Other meat and seafood dishes with more common names
are also served in this Bavarian ski lodge setting. Closed Monday
and during the month of September. ~ 19829 Gulf Boulevard,
Indian Shores; 813-595-5525. MODERATE.

Crabby Bill's is your basic beach seafood eatery where the food
is terrific and the prices even better. The oyster stew is made to
order, and the catfish, shrimp, crab and fish have earned the place
a reputation that means long waits. ~ 401 Gulf Boulevard, Indian
Rocks Beach; 813-595-4825. BUDGET.

Rolls of paper toweling hang on coat hangers above the tables at **P. J.'s Oyster Bar**. In an ultracasual atmosphere, oysters, clams, crab and shrimp are served in their unadulterated state (raw and/or steamed, hold the sauce). The menu also includes fried, broiled, baked or steamed seafood, sandwiches, ribs, steak, chicken and blackened specialties. P.J. the parrot runs the show. ~ 500 1st Street North, Indian Rocks Beach; 813-596-5898. BUDGET TO MODERATE.

For more than a decade, folks across Tampa Bay have made faithful sojourns to the **Lobster Pot**, a place that can feed any lobster fetish. Danish, Maine, African and Florida lobsters, served unadorned or in creamy garlic or curry sauces, headline the menu. There are fish and prime steaks as well. Fresh flowers, candles and linens assure subtle formality amid fishing nets, mounted lobsters and other seaside decor. Dinner only. ~ 17814 Gulf Boulevard, Reddington Shores; 813-391-8592. DELUXE TO ULTRA-DELUXE.

A side dish of fun comes with your meal at **Seafood & Sunsets at Julie's**. As the name suggests, this casual eatery sits across from the public beach, which calls for dusk rituals every night with happy hour specials. The menu offers wonderful seafood items (such as barbecued shrimp, Bohemian conch or blackened 'gator bites) and sandwiches. You may want to order the Ron Petrini sandwich: one bottle of Budweiser with two slices of white toast. Sit outside under an umbrella, upstairs in the beach room, next to a showcase of crab claws, or in an intimate boothed corner. ~ 351 South Gulfview Boulevard, Clearwater Beach; 813-441-2548. BUDGET TO MODERATE.

Heilman's Beachcomber is known for its bargain southern-style dinners of fried chicken, gravy and mashed potatoes. Locals will tell you that this is the best place in the bay area to get good stone crab. The decor is simple, the menu diversified, the quality consistent. ~ 447 Mandalay Avenue, Clearwater Beach; 813-442-4144. MODERATE.

NORTHERN PINELLAS COUNTY **Bill Irle Restaurant** serves German fare with fresh vegetable and seafood twists. The house salad is blessed with sprigs of watercress and a tasty sweet-sour dressing. Sauerbraten and schnitzel share the menu with *coquilles* of seafood Newburg and sole amandine. Plastic placemats top linen tablecloths, demonstrating the restaurant's mix of casualness and elegance. ~ 1310 North Fort Harrison Street, Clearwater; 813-446-5683. BUDGET TO MODERATE.

Jesse's Seafood House is a class act near Honeymoon Island. Inside a grey clapboard-and-brick building the decor is very modern with pickled oak tables and rattan chairs set for marina views in one room, and a captain's stateroom motif in another. The menu gives you a choice of preparation for your salmon, mahimahi or grouper blackened, charbroiled, broiled, fried, island-style, stuffed and so on. Lunch served only on Sunday. ~ 345 Causeway Boulevard, Dunedin; 813-736-2611. BUDGET TO MODERATE.

A restaurant named **Molly Goodheads Raw Bar and Seafood** more or less invented the town of Ozona, between Dunedin and Tarpon Springs. The town's name gives you an idea of the whimsical nature of this two-floor one-time home. The bathtub full of beer and waitresses in T-shirts and shorts contribute to a casual, fun atmosphere. The menu offers seafood and burgers for lunch and dinner. ~ 400 Orange Avenue, Ozona; 813-786-6255. MODERATE.

> The southernmost islands of Pinellas County are the least populated.

In Tarpon Springs, where many of the local dishes may sound Greek to you, **Louis Pappas' Riverside Restaurant** is renowned for serving ethnic dishes inspired by the city's Greek population. From the outside, the restaurant looks like a bank. Inside, the decor positively spews Greek feeling with family portraits, statues of gods and sponge-diving memorabilia. Besides authentic *pastitsio*, moussaka, lamb kebabs and other traditional Greek fare, Pappas does local favorites such as frogs' legs and blackened grouper. A lounge with a tropical theme serving light Floridian fare will be added in late 1996. ~ 10 West Dodecanese Boulevard, Tarpon Springs; 813-937-5101. MODERATE TO DELUXE.

Less ostentatiously Greek than Louis Pappas', **Costa's Restaurant** homecooks dolmades and broiled octopus. The small café goes light on atmosphere, with vinyl chairs and formica tables. But chances are you'll find more Greek locals than vacationers eating here. ~ 521 Athens Street, Tarpon Springs; 813-938-6890. BUDGET TO MODERATE.

SHOPPING

The Pier, in downtown St. Petersburg, contains a variety of specialty shops that sell hats, curios and clothing, all in a high price range. ~ 800 2nd Avenue Northeast, St. Petersburg; 813-821-6164.

Glass Horizons is a good place to find artistic stained-glass creations. ~ 2225 Central Avenue, St. Petersburg; 813-823-8233.

Lovers of books will find it difficult to leave **Haslam's Book Store, Inc.**, Florida's largest bookseller. ~ 2025 Central Avenue, St. Petersburg; 813-822-8616.

Out at Madeira Beach, **John's Pass Village and Boardwalk** sets the mood of an old fishing village. Gift shops, resort wear outlets and numerous other stores congregate here. One shop, **The Bronze Lady, Inc.** (813-398-5994) is noteworthy for its clown motif. The shop's specialty is clown paintings rendered by Red Skelton and also carries clown statuettes and other novelty items. ~ 12th Avenue North and Gulf Boulevard, Madeira Beach.

The **Wagon Wheel Flea Market** overflows with goods at over 1000 booths on the weekend. ~ 7801 Park Boulevard North, Pinellas Park; 813-544-5319.

Near the St. Petersburg–Clearwater airport, **Boatyard Village** simulates nature's effect on seaside docks to create a trendy atmosphere for specialty shopping. Rusted tin, cracked windows and broken-down shacks house expensive boutiques. **Village Gem Shop** (813-539-6991) offers handmade jewelry crafted from rough and polished stones. ~ 16100 Fairchild Drive, Clearwater.

Dodecanese Boulevard is a Hellenic marketplace in the tradition of old Tarpon Springs. Here you'll find natural sponges, cotton and gauze fashions, olive oil, Greek olives and pastries with names like *kourambiethes*, *finikia* and *kataifi*. ~ Tarpon Springs.

Try **The Sponge Exchange**, a theme courtyard mall, for fine, pricey gifts and clothing. ~ Dodecanese Boulevard, Tarpon Springs.

NIGHTLIFE   At **Cha Cha Coconuts**, jazz, reggae, Top-40 and rhythm-and-blues bands jam outdoors overlooking the bay seven nights a week. ~ 800 2nd Avenue Northeast, St. Petersburg; 813-822-6655.

For that country twang in your evening, listen to the music over at **Carlis**. ~ 5641 49th Street North, St. Petersburg; 813-527-5214.

Deejays spinning Top-40, '70s hits and oldies are featured at the **Hurricane Seafood Restaurant** on Wednesday through Sunday nights. ~ 807 Gulf Way, Pass-a-Grille Beach; 813-360-9558.

There's live entertainment nightly, mostly Top-40 stuff, at **Cadillac Jack's**. ~ 145 107th Avenue, Treasure Island; 813-360-2099.

Another hopping nightspot is **The Beach Place**. Live entertainment on weekends, usually rock. ~ 2405 Gulf Boulevard, Indian Rocks Beach; 813-596-5633.

HIDDEN ►   Techno and a variety of high-energy dance music can be heard at the colorful **Penrod's Palace**. Cover. ~ 2675 Ulmerton Road, Clearwater; no phone.

Visiting performing artists are sponsored at **Ruth Eckerd Hall**, home to the Florida Orchestra and the Florida Opera. ~ 1111 McMullen-Booth Road, Clearwater; 813-791-7400.

In keeping with the Greek culture that is prominent in Tarpon Springs, **Zorba's Nightclub** is the local favorite for belly dancing performances toasted with ouzo. ~ 508 Athens Street West, Tarpon Springs; 813-934-8803.

HIDDEN ►   The **Frog Prince Puppetry Arts Center & Theatre** features animated puppet shows, workshops and exhibits. ~ The Arcade, 210 South Pinellas Avenue, Suite #158, Tarpon Springs; 813-784-6392.

GAY SCENE   A popular gay dance bar near St. Petersburg, **Fourteen Seventy West** is a high-tech, high-energy establishment. Stainless steel, purple neon and laser shows set the tone for this club where there's dancing to Top-40 music played by a deejay. Special events include Saturday night drag shows. ~ 325 Main Street, Dunedin; 813-736-5483.

If you're itchin' to kick up your heels, head over to the ever-popular **Sharp A's** on Thursday and Sunday, when they have country-and-western dance nights. Friday and Saturday are host to a number of live performances that keep the gay clientele entertained. If you've got two irreversible left feet, there's always the game room and a bunch of friendly folk to keep things lively. ~ 4918 Gulfport Boulevard, Gulfport; 813-327-4897.

Twenty-eight miles of sugar sand sweetens Pinellas County's Gulf front. Its public beaches spread wider than anywhere else along the coast.

BEACHES & PARKS

FORT DE SOTO PARK A precious natural respite from the beach crowds lies on five road-connected islands at the southern tip of Tierra Verde. Hiking trails take you to cannons marking an uncompleted Spanish-American War fort and around quiet paths shaded by Australian pines and live oaks dripping with Spanish moss. Secluded areas are available at both East Beach and North Beach. The sand is coarse, shelly and booby-trapped with sand spurs. The natural vegetation along the beaches grows low to the ground: cactus, seagrape shrubs and sea oats. You get a true deserted feeling with none of the development on the northern islands to clutter the view. Fishing is excellent from shore and the 1000-foot pier. A three-mile area of the seven-mile-long beach is approved for swimming. At the north end, currents are dangerous. Facilities include picnic areas, restrooms, showers and a snack bar; restaurants and groceries can be found a few miles away in Tierra Verde. ~ Off Pinellas Bayway, south of Tierra Verde; 813-866-2662.

◄ **HIDDEN**

▲ There are 233 sites, all with RV hookups; $17.75 per night. Reservations must be made at the camp office in person or at the St. Petersburg County Building, at 150 5th Street North, Room 63, St. Petersburg.

PASS-A-GRILLE BEACH A popular gathering place for young sunbathers, this strand of fluffy sand loops around the southern point of the island of St. Petersburg Beach. The long, wide beach is flanked by Gulf Way and its quaint homes and lowrises. It's a good place to swim. You'll find picnic areas, restrooms, showers, dressing rooms and a snack bar; restaurants and groceries are nearby. ~ Located on Gulf Way on southern St. Petersburg Beach; 813-367-2735.

SAND KEY PARK Like a majority of the parks in Pinellas County, this one is beautifully landscaped. The facility looks more like a resort than a city park, with lush greenery and beautiful sun-bleached blond sands. A rock barrier tumbles from the beach out into the Gulf at the southern end of the park. Swimming is good here and you can fish near the rocks and off the pier for snapper, pompano and snook. Facilities include picnic areas, cabana rentals, lifeguards, restrooms and showers; restaurants and groceries are a few miles away. ~ At the northern end of Belleair Beach on Gulf Boulevard; 813-464-3347.

HIDDEN ▶   **CALADESI ISLAND STATE PARK** The English translation of this island's name tells the story: beautiful bayou. The park, set adrift from the hectic pace of Holiday Isles, must be reached by boat. Spread across 1400 acres, this natural island environment is frequented by families as well as being home to birds like great blue herons, snowy egrets and double-crested cormorants. The three-mile beach is wide, natural and a good place to swim and fish for snapper, snook and trout. The picnic area is shaded by sabal palms. Other facilities include barbecue grills, a playground, restrooms, showers, nature trails, a lifeguard and a snack bar; restaurants and groceries are in Dunedin. Boaters can dock overnight at the island marina for $88. ~ Charters out of Dunedin or a ferry from Honeymoon Island (813-734-1501) take visitors to Caladesi; 813-469-5917.

HONEYMOON ISLAND A small island connected to northern Dunedin by a causeway, this beach is practically immune from modern life. It's used mostly by locals. The sand isn't as fine as that of its neighbors, and large rocks make barefooting uncomfortable. The park's boast is its virgin slash pine stands populated by the endangered osprey, a native fishing bird. You can swim here and fish in the surf and pass for snook, redfish, trout, whiting and tarpon. There are picnic areas, nature trails, restrooms, showers and concessions; you'll find restaurants and groceries nearby. ~ On Route 586, west of Route 19A; 813-469-5942.

HIDDEN ▶   **FRED HOWARD PARK AND BEACH** This unique and hidden recreational area lies in the Greek community of Tarpon Springs. The park incorporates mainland picnic grounds and a wildlife sanctuary with an offshore beach. The two areas are connected by a mile-long causeway crossing waters blue as a Greek god's eyes. The two parts of the park portray completely separate worlds. The mainland area is sheltered in lovely old live oaks and carpeted in thick grass. The island totally covered with sand and sits open to the elements, with only cabbage palms and seagrapes by way of vegetation. Swimming is great here and fishing is good off the causeway for trout, snapper and snook. Facilities include picnic areas, a playground, restrooms, showers and a lifeguard; restaurants and groceries are located a few miles away in Tarpon Springs. ~ Located on Howard Park Road near Tarpon Springs; 813-937-4938.

Up past Port Richey, tourism venues thin out and the slow pace along Route 19 offers travelers an opportunity to discover one of the nicest stretches of western coastline. It is also where wildlife and archaeological sites are the star attractions—with manatees the major draw come winter. Crystal River–Cedar Key is where Florida reverts to the personality of its youth, a kind of wild adolescence.

Crystal River– Cedar Key Area

SIGHTS

◀ HIDDEN

For a pleasant backroad sidetrip, take **Route 595** out of Hudson, north of Port Richey. This takes you through the town of **Aripeka**, where old, abandoned buildings sit by the side of the road.

En route to **Bayport**, you'll drive along rural roads through a canopy of trees. When you drive back to a crossroad at the Bayport Inn, swing up on Pine Island Drive to **Pine Island**, a remote and exclusive spit of sand with a small park at its western end.

You'll return to the main road at **Weeki Wachee**, a town whose main attraction and raison d'être (heaven help us) is an underwater mermaid theater. Here lovely, gold-clad young women perform complicated acrobatics in the crystalline waters of Weeki Wachee Springs. Admission. ~ Route 19, Weeki Wachee; 352-596-2062.

North of Weeki Wachee, at **Yulee Sugar Mill Ruins State Historic Site**, sits the remains of a sugar plantation in a tree-sheltered park. You can see the ruins of Florida's last standing sugar mill and its machinery. ~ Route 490, Homosassa; 352-795-3817.

The name "Cedar Key" refers to a scattering of about 100 wildlife refuge islands, of which Cedar Key is the largest and only inhabited one.

At **Homosassa Springs State Wildlife Park** you can enter an underwater fish bowl observatory and plunge over 30 feet deep in a natural spring to observe intermingling freshwater and saltwater life forms. Then a boat ride will take you through virgin Florida forest to see ospreys, turtles and other native Florida fauna. Admission. ~ Homosassa; 352-628-2311.

More manatees are found in abundance farther north. These "sea cows," mistaken for mermaids by early sailors, have become synonymous with **Crystal River**, whose warm springs attract them. The endangered sea mammals come to winter here, and to entertain divers in the one place where humans are allowed to interact with the 2000-pound gentle giants. The mammoth vegetarians are known to encourage petting by rolling over on their backs.

The **Crystal River Chamber of Commerce** distributes information on manatee preservation and area sights. ~ 28 Northwest Highway 19, Crystal River; 352-795-3149.

The **Crystal River State Archaeological Site** has been deemed an important ceremonial ground for ancient American Indian cultures. Excavators have opened over 400 graves to find valuable prehistoric relics, including a sophisticated astronomical calendar system. Visitors can climb to the highest temple mound, which overlooks the river. A small museum displays pottery, arrowheads and many other remnants of American Indian societies dating back to 500 B.C. Admission. ~ At 3400 North Museum Point, Crystal River; 352-795-3817.

HIDDEN ►   Up on **Cedar Key**, Florida time moves in reverse. Once a thriving fishing and commercial center, it now boasts seclusion from the state's quickening pulse. The drive to this fishing village island accounts for its unspoiled nature. Once north of Crystal River, you feel as though you are driving to the ends of the earth. Towns are tiny and signs warn of bear crossings. At Otter Creek, take Route 24 to reach Cedar Key.

The **Cedar Key State Museum** documents the days when trains operated on the island, before the hurricane of 1896 destroyed many of the cedar trees on which the local economy thrived. The museum also houses a special seashell collection. Closed Tuesday and Wednesday. Admission. ~ Museum Drive, Cedar Key; 352-543-5350.

For more information, visit the **Cedar Key Chamber of Commerce**. ~ In the Volunteer Fire Station, 2nd Street, Cedar Key; 352-543-5600.

LODGING   Near Homosassa Springs Nature World and the Yulee Sugar Mill, **Howard Johnson Riverside Inn Resort** offers character as well as a
HIDDEN ►   good location. The place is situated right on a river, from which it derives its personality. The marina atmosphere is complemented by an ambience best described as "old Florida elegance" in the 72 rooms. Golf courses, volleyball, tennis and shuffleboard courts, a swimming pool, restaurants and lounges come with this resort. ~ Homosassa Springs; 352-628-2474, 800-442-2040, fax 352-628-5808. MODERATE.

The antebellum South is re-created at **Plantation Inn & Golf Resort** and southern hospitality reigns throughout the 142-room property. Golf is the sporting focus, but fishing and canoeing keep this secluded spot activity-filled. Columned white buildings house rather generic rooms with plush carpeting. ~ West Fort Island Trail, Crystal River; 352-795-4211, 800-632-6662, fax 352-795-1368. DELUXE TO ULTRA-DELUXE.

Affordable accommodations are found at **Port Paradise Resort**. Catering to the scuba-diving trade that flocks to Crystal River, this resort offers comfortable rooms, all with efficiencies. The 100 rooms flank a marina where all the accoutrements for diving the springs are available. ~ 1610 Southeast Paradise Circle, in Crystal River; 352-795-3111. BUDGET TO MODERATE.

HIDDEN ►   The **Izaak Walton Lodge** began as a sportsman's lodge in 1924 and has been revived into a get-away-from-it-all bastion of hospitality. Dressed in a new tin roof and hunter green porch, the still-rustic facility sits on the river near a stretch of forested coastline. Variable rates are asked for the 12 units (the seven lodge rooms have shared baths). Two restaurants are located on the premises. A scenic boat tour, canoe packages and outfitting are available. ~ Riverside Drive at 63rd Street, Yankeetown; 352-447-2311, fax 352-447-3264. BUDGET TO DELUXE.

The Island Place testifies that Cedar Key has been discovered. Thirty luxury condo units decorated with designer touches simulate Old Florida with tin-roofed Victorian architecture. Prices for luxury are still lower here than in the rest of the Sunshine State. Within walking distance of downtown shops and eateries. ~ 1st Street, Cedar Key; 352-543-5307, 800-780-6522, fax 352-543-9141. MODERATE.

Beach Front Motel sits with unpretentious presence along a curve of rocky island shoreline. Its 23 rooms and efficiencies are comfortable and modern, most with waterfront views. ~ 1st and G streets, Cedar Key; 352-543-5113. BUDGET.

Island Hotel looks like an old frontier lodge, with its wooden two-story facade. Since this hotel is listed in the national register of historic places, the mosquito netting over the bed, sepia photos and antique furniture in the rooms fit perfectly. There is air-conditioning, but not a lot of other modern conveniences. Only six of the ten rooms have a private bath. A cedar-scented bar, gourmet seafood restaurant and lobby are outfitted with a potbelly stove, church pews and other frontier-era furniture. Rates include breakfast. ~ 2nd and B streets, Cedar Key; 352-543-5111. MODERATE.

DINING

K. C. Crump on the River resides in an 1870 home overlooking the Homosassa River. Meat and seafood lunches and dinners done in creamy, fruity sauces are served to diners at rattan tables with commanding views. No lunch on Thursday or Friday. Closed Monday through Wednesday. ~ 11210 West Halls Road, Homosassa Springs; 352-628-1500. MODERATE.

Except for locals, few attempt the lonely, sinuous nine-mile trek to **Peck's Old Port Cove**. There's not much here but crab traps and a little shack with a few rickety tables, along with the blue Gulf that falls off the horizon. Calvin Peck is famous for his fresh oysters, thick fried grouper and soft shell crab sandwiches. The crabs are grown out back in Peck's blue crab farm—one of the few in the country. As you might expect, no credit cards are accepted. ~ 139 North Ozello Trail off Route 19, Ozello; 352-795-2806. BUDGET TO MODERATE.

◄ HIDDEN

For unpretentious seafood enjoyment in Crystal River, visit **Oysters**. This restaurant is a favorite of the locals. From mullet to seafood pasta, fresh seafood is prepared reliably, if not exotically.

Closed Monday. ~ 606 Route 19 South, Crystal River; 352-795-2633. MODERATE.

At **The Compleat Angler**, don't be surprised to find a luxury yacht pulled up to the dock outside on the river. This country eatery has been discovered by jet setters in the know. In its restored fishing haven setting at Izaak Walton Lodge, the warm dining room features a rock fireplace and overlooks the Withlacoochee River. The menu features fine meats such as steak *au poivre* and châteaubriand, and fresh seafood: oysters, snapper topped with crab, scallions and mushrooms in a béarnaise sauce, and grouper with seasoned breadcrumbs pan-fried in peanut oil. ~ 1 63rd Street, Yankeetown; 352-447-2319. MODERATE TO ULTRA-DELUXE.

Cedar Key boasts a few food specialties of its own. Swamp cabbage (known in trendier terminology as hearts of palm) salads have always been associated with Cedar Key eateries. With its tenacity to fishing traditions, fresh seafood is the forte, especially crab, oysters, mullet and clams.

Sitting on the dock, **The Captain's Table** looks as though it's been around a while. The menu makes a slight concession to non-seafood lovers, but the specialty is definitely Cedar Key–style seafood: mullet, oysters, crab fingers, stone crab and a combination platter for two that will appease even the hardcore shellfish fancier. Closed from September to October. ~ Dock Street, Cedar Key; 352-543-5441. MODERATE TO DELUXE.

Seabreeze sits up on pilings over the water, surrounded by in floor-to-ceiling windows and spectacular views. The bill of fare is steak, chicken and seafood served every-which-way—including the traditional fried and broiled styles plus the fancier Florentine style. Laminated tables give this spot the requisite nautical appeal. Seabreeze is closed on Wednesday. ~ Dock Street, Cedar Key; 352-543-5738. MODERATE.

Natural gourmet food describes the fare at **Island Hotel**. In deference to the survival of the state tree, no palm salads are served here. What you can expect to find in this diamond-in-the-rough facility is baked garlic, phyllo Florentine—a flaky phyllo pastry stuffed with spinach, feta and almonds—and Cedar Key soft shell crabs. Breakfast and dinner are served. Closed Tuesday. ~ Main Street, Cedar Key; 352-543-5111. MODERATE TO DELUXE.

SHOPPING   For a cuddly souvenir of your Crystal River visit, try **The Manatee Toy Company**. ~ 31 Citrus Avenue, Crystal River; 352-795-6126.

Heritage Village houses seven shops with antiques, collectibles, quilts and artsy clothing. ~ North Citrus Avenue east of Route 19, Crystal River.

Cedar Key has become known for its artist residents. **Cedar Keyhole** carries works of local artists in the form of woodcarvings, pottery, folk art and macramé. ~ 2nd Street, Cedar Key; 352-543-5801. Fine arts and American crafts are featured at the **Suwannee Triangle Gallery.** ~ 5 Dock Street, Cedar Key; 352-543-5744.

Up in the rural northern coastal regions, nightlife is limited to local taverns. A good place for imbibing and mingling in Homosassa Springs is the **Ship's Lounge** at Riverside Inn resort on the Homosassa River. ~ 352-628-2474.

NIGHTLIFE

Live rock bands play on weekends at **L & M,** a laid-back local hangout. ~ 2nd Street, Cedar Key; 904-543-5827.

The coastline gets marshier north of Pinellas County. The good news is the parks are more secluded.

BEACHES & PARKS

FORT ISLAND BEACH You won't hear Crystal River locals talking about this out-of-the-way park, nor will you see signs advertising it. The beach is more natural than those developed farther south, but the sand is just as white and fine. Swimming is good in the roped-off area. Facilities include picnic areas, restrooms, outdoor showers, summer lifeguards and a boat ramp; restaurants and groceries are about ten miles away in Crystal River. ~ Located at the western end of Route 44; 352-795-2202.

◄ *HIDDEN*

CHASSAHOWITZKA NATIONAL WILDLIFE REFUGE A natural shelter for over 250 species of birds, as well as mink, otter, raccoon, bobcat, deer and alligator. Its 309,500 acres of estuarine habitat used to attract waterfowl by the thousands, but their numbers have steadily declined. Today the refuge serves as a crucial haven for West Indian manatees. Other natural landscape here includes brackish marshland, swamps, island hardwood forests and oyster bars. Fishing is excellent. There are no facilities here. ~ The fragile environment is accessible only by boat. Headquarters are located at 1502 Southeast Kings Bay Drive, Crystal River; 904-563-2088.

CEDAR KEYS NATIONAL WILDLIFE REFUGE This is a closely guarded area that places its importance as a wildlife sanctuary above its role as a human resource. The refuge incorporates several offshore islands ranging in area from 6 to 165 acres, five miles from the town of Cedar Key. Over 50,000 nesting birds colonize here annually, including ibis, egrets, Louisiana herons and great blue herons. Birdwatching enthusiasts will also find white pelicans, roseate spoonbills and bald eagles migrating through the refuge. Because of its importance to wildlife, public use is limited. Swimming is good off the beach at Seahorse Key. There are no facilities. (Seahorse Key is closed to the public from March through June.) You must take a boat to reach the refuge. Many charters leave daily from the dock at Cedar Key. ~ 352-493-0238.

◄ *HIDDEN*

▼▼▼▼▼▼▼▼▼▼▼▼▼▼

Outdoor Adventures

**SPORT-
FISHING**

Deep-sea fishing is one of western Florida's most popular sports. Private charters and excursion boats are practically as plentiful as the grouper, shark, triple tail and flounder they seek.

In the Sarasota area, contact **Flying Fish Fleet**. ~ Marina Jack Pier, Sarasota; 941-366-3373. For deep-sea fishing from a head boat, try **Getaway Marina**. ~ 18400 San Carlos Boulevard, Fort Myers Beach; 941-466-3600. Party boat offshore fishing trips can be booked at **Lady Brett and Double Sunshine Boat Charters** at Old Marine Market in Naples. ~ 1200 5th Avenue South, Naples; 941-263-4949. **Florida Deep Sea Fishing** offers offshore excursions. ~ 4737 Gulf Boulevard, St. Petersburg Beach; 813-360-2082. In the Crystal River area, contact **Robbie's Charters**. ~ 2060 South Melanie Drive, Homosassa; 352-628-3274.

DIVING

You'll find plenty of scuba shops up and down the West Coast, but most of them take their clients to the East Coast or the Florida Keys. Gulf of Mexico waters are mostly cloudy and/or devoid of reef life. Terrific freshwater diving, however, is available at Crystal River, where spring-fed waters populated with manatees draw divers in droves.

A full-service diving shop in Tampa is **Scuba Unlimited**. ~ 4119 Gunn Highway, Tampa; 813-960-7748. **Underwater Explorers Diving Center and School** is a qualified scuba instructor and dealer. ~ 12600 McGregor Boulevard, Fort Myers; 941-481-4733. In Crystal River, **Port Paradise** features a full-service dive shop. ~ 1610 Southeast Paradise Circle; 352-795-3111.

**SURFING
& WIND-
SURFING**

West Coast waters are generally too calm for anyone but the beginning surfer. Occasionally the waves on the beach that runs parallel with Captiva Road on Captiva Island will swell into good rides. For windsurfing enthusiasts, there's some good news; the entire coast makes for windsurfing fun, and many resorts rent equipment and offer lessons. Especially known for its fine winds and windsurfing competitions are the waters off the Sanibel Causeway on Sanibel Island. Many resorts in this area rent sailboard equipment and offer instruction. These services can also be found at surf shops up and down the coast.

Bradenton Beach Sailboat Rentals rents Hobies and G-Cats. ~ 1325 Gulf Drive North, Bradenton Beach; 813-778-4969. **Totally Active Sports** teaches windsurfing and rents equipment. ~ 7859 Blind Pass Road, St. Petersburg Beach; 813-367-7059.

BOATING

On Florida's West Coast, island hopping rates high on the activities list. Boating to unhitched islands for lunch is a favorite vacation activity. If you prefer to do your own navigating, boats can be rented at many resorts and marinas.

Try **O'Leary's Sarasota Sailing School** for instruction and charters. ~ 5 Bayfront Drive, Sarasota; 941-953-7505. **Don and Mike's Boat and Ski Rentals** rents jet skis, powerboats and pontoon boats. ~ 520 Blackburn Point Road, Osprey; 941-966-4000. On Sanibel, powerboats can be rented at **The Boat House.** ~ 634 North Yachtsman Drive, Sanibel Marina; 941-472-2531.

In Naples, **G. R. Boating** rents canoes, kayaks, powerboats and pontoons. ~ 4892 Bonita Beach Road, Bonita Springs; 941-947-4889. For powerboats in Naples, contact **Port-O-Call Marina.** ~ 505 Port-O-Call Way; 941-774-0479. In the St. Petersburg area, try **Jack's Boat Rental.** ~ 194 128th Avenue, Madeira Beach; 813-392-6912.

The area's state parks have excellent waters for paddling along in unhurried enjoyment of nature. Most parks rent canoes, including **Oscar Scherer State Park.** ~ Route 41 south of Sarasota; 941-483-5956. Another good bet is **Koreshan Historic Site.** ~ Route 41, Bonita Springs; 941-992-0311. Give **Collier-Seminole State Park** a call. ~ Route 41 east of Naples; 941-394-3397. **Tarpon Bay Marina** rents canoes for touring J. N. "Ding" Darling National Wildlife Preserve. ~ Tarpon Bay Road, Sanibel; 941-472-8900. **CANOEING**

For a bird's-eye view of Florida's West Coast, take the sunrise hot-air balloon tour offered by **Balloon Rides, Inc.** ~ North Port, Port Charlotte; 941-492-9792. **BALLOON RIDES**

Running along the multitude of beautiful beachscapes in western Florida makes exercise almost painless. In Tampa, joggers enjoy the bay and stately home view along **Bayshore Boulevard,** a six-and-a-half-mile-long sidewalk route. This is also where the **Gasparilla Classic** is run each February in conjunction with the city's annual pirate festival. **JOGGING**

Tampa has a few public courses. One is **Rocky Point Golf Course.** ~ 4151 Dana Shores Drive; 813-673-4316. Another is **Babe Zaharias Golf Course.** ~ 11412 Forest Hills Drive; 813-631-4374. **GOLF**

Sarasota is considered the birthplace of the American golf scene. Back in 1887, one of her first citizens, John Hamilton Gillespie, a Scotsman, cured his homesickness by building a two-hole link on what is now Main Street. Today, golf courses are uncountable here. Many are open to the public. Tee off at **Bobby Jones Golf Complex.** ~ 1000 Azinger Way, Sarasota; 941-955-8041. Or try **Sarasota Golf Club.** ~ 7280 North Leewynn Drive, Sarasota; 941-371-2431.

In Sanibel, **The Dunes Golf & Tennis Club** offers an 18-hole course with rentals and a pro shop. ~ 949 Sand Castle Road, Sanibel; 813-472-3355. **Golf Harbor Country Club** is a lovely fountained course. ~ 15000 McGregor Boulevard, Fort Myers; 813-433-4211.

Clearwater Golf Park is a public course in Pinellas County. ~ 1875 Airport Drive, Clearwater; 813-447-5272. **Tarpon Springs Golf Club** is another public course. ~ 1310 Pinellas Avenue South, Tarpon Springs; 813-937-6906.

TENNIS

Several public tennis courts are located along the West Coast. In Tampa, **Riverfront Park** is a public facility with courts for tennis, racquetball and handball. ~ 900 North Boulevard, Tampa; 813-254-4034. Tennis courts are also found at **City of Tampa Courts.** ~ 59 Columbia Drive, Tampa; 813-253-3782. In the Sarasota area, there are public courts at **Siesta Key Public Beach.** ~ Midnight Pass Road, Siesta Key. **Forest Lakes Tennis Club** has public courts as well. ~ 2401 Beneva Road, Sarasota; 941-922-0660. **Sanibel Elementary School** has four lighted courts. ~ 3840 Sanibel-Captiva Road, Captiva; 941-472-0345. **St. Petersburg Tennis Center** has 15 courts. ~ 650 18th Avenue South, St. Petersburg; 813-893-7301.

BIKING

A nature-view bike path runs through **Oscar Scherer State Recreation Area** south of Sarasota.

Twelve miles of bike path run the length of **Longboat Key** and onto **Lido Key. Boca Grande** on Gasparilla Island has a scenic bike path. **Sanibel Island**'s system of bike paths covers over 20 miles, providing access to all of the beaches, shops and restaurants. The path ends at the bridge to Captiva. You cannot ride over the causeway, however, so you must transport your vehicle.

You'll find paths in some areas of Fort Myers, notably on **Summerlin Road,** and in Naples as well, mostly around the beach areas.

Though established bike paths are not always provided in these areas, West Coast beach routes and city parks make for easy pedaling along flat terrain.

✔ CHECK THESE OUT—UNIQUE OUTDOOR ADVENTURES

- Tiptoe across suspension bridges into the forest primeval, and keep an eye out for alligators or turtles as you hike the trails in Hillsborough River State Park. *page 451*
- Glide past 'gators and maneuver through mangroves on a canoe jaunt in one of Florida's state parks. *page 449*
- Saunter out to Sanibel Island with a sailboard, and enjoy the steady winds and warm Gulf waters. *page 448*
- Try freshwater scuba diving in manatee-filled Crystal River, which lives up to its name in the clarity of its spring-fed waters. *page 448*

Bike Rentals   Many large resorts rent bikes to guests as well as to the public, in addition to the following:

In the Bradenton-Sarasota area bikes can be rented from **The Bicycle Center**. ~ 2610 Cortez Road, West Bradenton, 941-756-5480. You can also cruise by the **Backyard Bike Shop**. ~ 5610 Gulf of Mexico Drive, Longboat Key; 813-383-5184.

On Sanibel Island, try **Island Moped**. ~ 1470 Periwinkle Way; 941-472-5248. Another place for rental bikes is **Finnimore's Bike Shop**. ~ 2353 Periwinkle Way; 941-472-5577.

Trikes & Bikes in Fort Myers has bike rentals. ~ 3451 Fowler Street, Fort Meyers; 941-936-1851. In St. Petersburg Beach, you can rent bikes at **The Beach Cyclist Sports Center**. ~ 7517 Blind Pass Road, St. Petersburg Beach; 813-367-5001.

HIKING

Florida's West Coast offers the most scenic hiking along its hard-packed and often shell-strewn beaches. No established system of paths guides you along these sandy trails, fraught with wading birds, sand crabs and other beach life; most beaches are self-guiding. Off the beach, a few sanctuaries and state parks provide hiking opportunities that take you back to presettlement Florida. All distances for hiking trails are one way unless otherwise noted.

Hillsborough River State Park Trails (8 miles) skirt river rapids, cross suspension bridges and penetrate forests of hardwood, oak, magnolia and sabal palm. Several species of wading birds and waterfowl can be spotted along these gentle hikes, as well as alligators, turtles and other freshwater fauna.

A system of easy trails has been established at the **Sanibel-Captiva Conservation Center** (4 miles total) on Sanibel Island. This area is a favorite for bird lovers; other types of indigenous fauna and flora also can be enjoyed from the trail and from the observation tower along it.

Cayo Costa State Park stretches for ten miles, allowing unparalleled opportunity for uninterrupted exploration of Gulf sands and bay mangroves. A nature trail (3 miles) crosses the island, where pine forests and cactus sandlands, white pelicans and an occasional wild boar can be seen. The park is accessible only via the Tropics Star Ferry from Pine Island, or by private boat.

Koreshan State Historic Site Nature Trail (1 mile) loops along the Estero River and through tropical gardens planted by religious settlers at the turn of the century. Avocado, mango, royal palm and sapote trees now grow wild here.

Collier-Seminole Trail (6.5 miles) winds through saltwater and freshwater marshland and mangrove forests. Rare finds here include a stand of native royal palms and the Florida black bear. This is the starting point of over 800 miles of the Florida National Scenic Trail, which travels in starts and stops up to the northern Panhandle area of the state.

Boyd Hill Nature Trail features six trails that lead through 245 acres of various Florida ecosystems. ~ 1101 Country Club Way South, St. Petersburg; 813-893-7326.

▼▼▼▼▼▼▼▼▼▼▼

Transportation

CAR

The Tamiami Trail, **Route 41**, marks the original path between Miami and Tampa, thus its name. For getting to know the area, this southern-bound route allows the best insight into the cross-section it bisects. It crosses most of the cities from Tampa to Naples mentioned in this chapter. **Route 75**, from Georgia to Naples, is more often traveled by those looking at time schedules rather than regional personality. Tampa is connected to the Orlando–Disney World area via **Route 4. Route 19** stitches together the coastal cities from St. Petersburg north.

AIR

There are three major airports that service Florida's West Coast. Tampa is the coast's transportation hub; the Tampa International Airport is thereby the largest airport of the Gulf Coast. In Fort Myers, the Southwest Regional Airport receives both international and domestic flights. The Sarasota-Bradenton Airport is a somewhat smaller facility.

Tampa International Airport is serviced by a number of international carriers as well as domestic companies, including: Air Canada, American Airlines, British Airways, Carnival Airlines, Cayman Airways, Comair Inc., Continental Airlines, Delta Air Lines, Holland Airlines, Kiwi Airlines, Martinair, Midwest Express, Northwest Airlines, Trans World Airlines, United Airlines and USAir.

The major transportation company servicing the Tampa airport for Hillsborough County is **Central Florida Limousine**. ~ 813-396-3730. For Tampa airport service to and from Hillsborough, Sarasota and Pinellas counties, contact **The Limo**. ~ 813-572-1111.

Most of the major domestic carriers fly in and out of **Sarasota-Bradenton Airport**: American Eagle, Continental Airlines, Delta Air Lines, Northwest Airlines, TWA, United Airlines and USAir.

Ground transportation from Sarasota-Bradenton Airport is provided by **Diplomat Taxi** (941-355-5155) and **Westcoast Airport Limousine** (941-355-9645).

Southwest Regional Airport carriers include: American Airlines, Continental Airlines, Delta Airlines, Northwest Airlines, TWA, United Airlines and USAir.

BUS

Greyhound Bus Lines (800-231-2222) makes stops along the West Coast in Tampa at 610 Polk Street, 941-229-2112; in Sarasota at 575 North Washington Boulevard, 941-955-5735; in Fort Myers at 2275 Cleveland Avenue, 941-334-1011; in Naples at 2669 Davis Boulevard, 941-774-5660; and in St. Petersburg at 180 9th Street North, 813-822-1497.

Amtrak (800-872-7245) makes West Coast stops in Tampa at Nebraska Avenue and Twiggs Street; in Bradenton at the Manatee County Court House Bus Terminal, located on Manatee West at 12th Street West; in Sarasota at City Hall Bus Terminal, located on Lemon Avenue between 1st and 2nd streets; and in Pinellas Park (suburb of Clearwater) at 7200 Route 19 North.

TRAIN

Rental agencies located or with pick-ups at the Tampa airport include **Alamo Rent A Car** (800-327-9633), **Avis Rent A Car** (800-331-1212), **Budget Rent A Car** (800-527-0700), **Dollar Rent A Car** (800-800-4000), **Hertz Rent A Car** (800-654-3131) and **National Interrent** (800-227-7368).

CAR RENTALS

In the Sarasota-Bradenton area, the following agencies provide free pick-up from the airport: **A-Plus Car Rentals** (813-355-9621), **Alamo Rent A Car** (800-327-9633), **Budget Sears Rent A Car** (800-527-0700), **Dollar Rent A Car** (800-800-4000), **Hertz Rent A Car** (800-654-3131) and **National Interrent** (800-227-7368).

In Fort Myers, airport location and/or free pick-up service is provided by the following rental car agencies: **Alamo Rent A Car** (800-327-9633), **Avis Rent A Car** (800-331-1212), **Budget Rent A Car** (800-527-0700), **Dollar Rent A Car** (800-800-4000), **Value Rent A Car** (800-327-2501), **Hertz Rent A Car** (800-654-3131), **National Interrent** (800-227-7368) and **Sears Rent A Car** (941-768-2500).

For used rental vehicles, call **Rent A Wreck**. ~ 941-337-1633.

To get around Tampa, **HART** (Hillsborough Area Regional Transit) runs very dependably to most areas in the county. ~ 813-254-4278. The monorail **PeopleMover** provides state-of-the-art transportation in the downtown Tampa business district and to and from Harbour Island.

PUBLIC TRANSIT

In Sarasota, you will find comfort and reliability in **SCAT** (Sarasota County Area Transit) buses, which cover the in-town area and go to the beaches, Venice and Englewood. ~ 813-951-5851. **Lee-Tran** buses provide service to Fort Myers Beach, eastern and northern Fort Myers, Edison Mall, Lehigh Acres and Cape Coral. ~ 941-275-8726.

The **PSTA** (Pinellas Suncoast Transit Authority) operates buses with routes through downtown St. Petersburg and Clearwater. There is also service to other parts of the county. ~ 813-530-9911.

BATS (Bay Area Transit Service) city buses connect with PSTA routes to service St. Petersburg Beach. ~ 813-367-3086.

TAXIS   Several cab companies serve the Tampa airport, including **Yellow Cab** (941-253-0121) and **United Cab of Tampa** (941-253-2424). **Diplomat Taxi** (941-355-5155) is the designated airport cab service at Sarasota-Bradenton.

EIGHT

The Panhandle

It is curious that the section of Florida most accessible to the rest of the country should be its least known. "The Panhandle?" outsiders ask. "Is there really anything there?" Of course, there have long been visitors to Panhandle beaches, wise lovers of sand and sea who come in the summer months from Alabama, Georgia and Mississippi to work on their tans and romp in the crystal water or ride the occasionally challenging waves. They, and their ways of having vacation fun, explain why certain sections of the glistening shore have been dubbed the "Redneck Riviera."

Some retired folk have chosen to settle along this coast where the seasons change; many first fell in love with the place while stationed at Eglin Air Force Base (the nation's largest) or Pensacola's Naval Air Station. In recent years, Canadians have been heading this way in the winters, not minding the chilly sea breezes and thriving on the phenomenally low seasonal rates.

But the large majority of Florida's tourists skims across the Panhandle's eastern edge or zips through its inland middle on efficient allegro interstates, hastening to Daytona and Disney World and the pleasures of the tropics. In doing so, they miss one of the state's hidden treasures.

Over four centuries ago the Panhandle, already populated by American Indian tribes hunting its hills and harvesting its waters, attracted some of America's first European visitors. Spanish explorer Hernando de Soto set out in 1539 to conquer and to search for treasure. He and his band of soldiers, horses, livestock and followers slogged through the swamps and trails east of present-day Tallahassee and up into what would become Georgia. Tristan de Luna tried to set up a colony at Pensacola in 1559 but was forced to give up due to hurricane and hardship. Much of the region remained inhabited by American Indians, inspiring the Spanish to set up a chain of forts and missions from St. Augustine to Pensacola.

As later explorers made further attempts to tame the wild region, trades and treaties tossed the ownership of Florida back and forth between the hands of Spain, France and Great Britain for almost 200 years. When the British acquired the land in 1763, they divided it into two parts, East and West Florida, before returning it to Spanish hands twenty years later. The United States gained permanent ownership of the still-divided land with a final purchase from Spain in 1821.

Immediately, Andrew Jackson established a new territorial government, and the two Floridas merged. In 1824, Tallahassee was chosen as the new capital, not because of any intrinsic value but because it was about half way between Pensacola and St. Augustine, as confirmed by two delegates setting out toward each other from those cities. By 1840, steamboats were navigating the Apalachicola River and in 1845, Florida became a state. But the Civil War was still to come, and the Panhandle would feel its ravages for many years. Tallahassee escaped largely intact, however. Although federal troops occupied the city very briefly, this southern capital would remain the only one east of the Mississippi to avoid capture.

After the Civil War came reconstruction and its accompanying poverty. Though Tallahassee remained the capital and Panhandle ports flourished as the demand for wood and forest products grew, the state's real action lay to the south. As the East and West coasts of the peninsula boomed with development and tourism, the lands of the Panhandle came under the cultivation of sharecroppers and tenant farmers. The Panhandle story was more closely tied to the Deep South of Georgia and Alabama than to its own Florida family.

Today, much of the Panhandle still has a Deep South feel to it. Perhaps this is why tourists tend to pass it by for the distinctive glitter to the south. But though it still has remnants of plantations, small towns where natives speak in slow drawls and offer genteel hospitality, healthy pecan groves and more churches than you could ever count, the Panhandle has its own distinctions that make it truly Florida.

On the eastern boundary, the swift and clean Suwannee River flows through deep woods of pine and oak and cypress. Near the western edge, the Perdido and Blackwater rivers also run clean, dark-stained with tannin, dotted with tiny white sand beaches, meandering through rich forest lands. The broad Apalachicola River, once an important water highway, cuts the Panhandle nearly in two. These rivers and others, along with myriad creeks and streams, flow to the Gulf of Mexico, creating valuable estuaries and brackish marshes crucial to coastal wildlife.

Several vastly differing sections of coastline mark the Panhandle's expansive contact with the Gulf. From the Suwannee's mouth to St. Marks lies the "big bend," a great marshy shore with almost no beaches, dotted with old-fashioned fishing villages and containing vast regions devoted to wildlife management. Westward toward Apalachicola and beyond, the protected shores of the bays abound in rich estuarine life; the waters produce a bounty of seafood and oysters that are world-famous. Here one must travel to the barrier islands or peninsulas for beachcombing and swimming; those who do so are rewarded with miles of dunes, abundant wildlife and fine Gulf waters.

From touristy Panama City westward lies the pièce de résistance of the Panhandle: a hundred miles of quartz sand and turquoise water said to be the whitest and clearest in the country. Visitors may choose their ways to enjoy this region, from

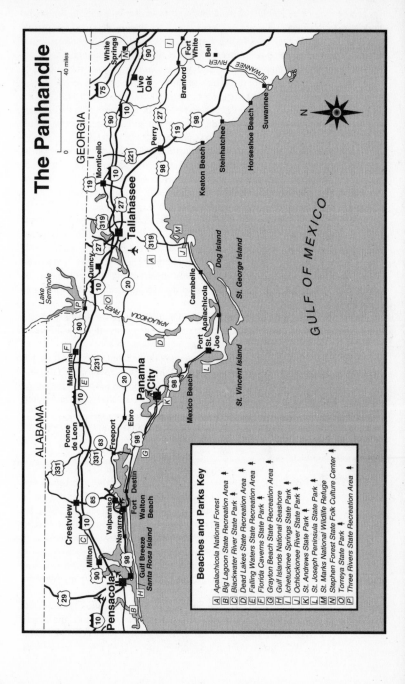

The Panhandle

0 ——— 40 miles

N

GEORGIA

ALABAMA

GULF OF MEXICO

SUWANNEE RIVER

APALACHICOLA RIVER

Lake Seminole

White Springs

Live Oak

Branford

Fort White

Bell

Suwannee

Horseshoe Beach

Steinhatchee

Keaton Beach

Perry

Monticello

Tallahassee

Quincy

Crestview

Milton

Pensacola

Valparaiso

Navarre

Gulf Breeze

Santa Rosa Island

Fort Walton Beach

Destin

Freeport

Ponce de Leon

Marianna

Ebro

Panama City

Mexico Beach

Port St. Joe

Apalachicola

Carrabelle

St. Vincent Island

St. George Island

Dog Island

Beaches and Parks Key

A Apalachicola National Forest
B Big Lagoon State Recreation Area
C Blackwater River State Park
D Dead Lakes State Recreation Area
E Falling Waters State Recreation Area
F Florida Caverns State Park
G Grayton Beach State Recreation Area
H Gulf Islands National Seashore
I Ichetucknee Springs State Park
J Ochlockonee River State Park
K St. Andrews State Park
L St. Joseph Peninsula State Park
M St. Marks National Wildlife Refuge
N Stephen Foster State Folk Culture Center
O Torreya State Park
P Three Rivers State Recreation Area

the honky-tonk of overbuilt Panama City Beach to modest little villages to the towering condos and classy resorts of Destin and Fort Walton Beach to the pristine dunes of the Gulf National Seashore at historic Pensacola. With only minimal searching, you can even discover miles of beach that remain almost deserted.

An even more hidden part of Florida, however, lies inland, from the Gulf all the way to the Georgia line. Here meandering country roads wander through miles of rural countryside, sometimes rolling, sometimes flat and sprawling. At its heart is Tallahassee, a suddenly sophisticated capital city with two large state universities, respectable hills, oak-canopied roads and a lot of southern charm. At its back door lies the vast Apalachicola National Forest. In the hinterlands to the east and west are small towns, some poor, some prosperous, many reached only by lonely roads that travel in and out of forested areas, through scrub land and clear-cut woods, alongside murky swamps or past fine horse farms, hunting plantations and productive dairies. Peanuts grow well in the Panhandle, along with cotton, Spanish moss and hogs. Land still sells, in some places, for affordable prices.

Within this inland terrain, scattered like jewels dropped into unexpected pockets, clear fresh springs bubble up across the Panhandle. Some, like Wakulla and Ichetucknee, have been made easily accessible; others still wait to be discovered by adventurous visitors to the sparsely populated counties in which they lie. In recent years, scuba divers and snorkelers have been attracted by the challenge of the springs' crystal-blue depths as well as their proximity to equally clear Gulf waters from Panama City westward.

Fishing has been a chief attraction of the Panhandle since the era of the Paleo-Indians; rivers, lakes, springs and marshes each offer up their unique prizes. Hunters thrive on the bounty of the deep forests and preserves.

So to those who ask, "Is there really anything in the Panhandle?" this chapter provides an answer. For the seeker of hidden destinations there is much. The greatest appeal of this land lies in the open spaces, the undeveloped fields and forests and beaches, the protected wetlands and unpolluted springs and rivers that can only be discovered by leaving the beaten path. In the Panhandle one can still walk in solitude, listen to mockingbirds and gulls instead of jam-boxes and, if one braves the backroads, drive for hours without seeing another car.

▼▼▼▼▼▼▼▼▼▼▼
Eastern Area

Most tourists zip through the Panhandle's eastern area on Route 10, or bypass it altogether as they head south. For the backroad-wanderer, however, hidden treasures of an undeveloped Florida wait to be discovered here. Just about any route you choose will take you through pine woods, past tree farms and pig farms, and along lonely roads whose miles seem to be inhabited by nothing but churches—some very old, others appearing to have been thrown up in haste overnight. Through it run rivers and streams—swift, dark, beautiful and remarkably unpolluted.

SIGHTS

Not to be missed, the **Stephen Foster State Folk Culture Center** celebrates the man who, though he never saw it, made the Suwannee River famous by setting it to music. "Old Folks at Home" ("Way down upon the Suwannee River . . ."), Florida's state song, and other familiar Foster melodies ring out from the park's carillon tower, entertaining the visitors who come to learn about the composer and area folklife through dioramas and exhibits. The riverside park is a beauty, full of trees and flowers and site of the remnants of a Victorian-style health resort where Teddy Roosevelt joined thousands of others to bathe in the smelly sulphur spring that flows into the Suwannee. Admission. ~ Route 41 and Route 136, White Springs; 904-397-2733.

In traversing the Panhandle interior, you have a choice of routes. If you take Route 90 westward, the countryside becomes more rolling as it follows the old **Hernando de Soto Trail**. Historical markers explain that the Spanish explorer, along with 600 soldiers and assorted livestock and servants, trekked along mosquito-infested American Indian paths here in 1539.

Today's travelers fare better, especially those who take the time to admire the Victorian and Greek revival houses in **Madison** and **Monticello**, where time seems to stand still. You can pick up a self-guided walking tour of Monticello at the **Chamber of Commerce**. Drive around the square and gaze at the Jeffersonian-classic 1909-era courthouse, a dramatic domed structure built for only $40,000. ~ 420 West Washington Street; 904-997-5552.

Routes heading south and southwest through this eastern area travel through vast areas of seeming nothingness—here tangled woods, there close regiments of planted pines, many clear-cut fields and acres of farmland. Much of the area is reserved for wildlife management. Along the eastern border flows the Suwannee River, its swift, clean water tannin-stained like tea and abundant in fish.

The greatest treasures are the springs, scattered like jewels tossed on a tattered quilt, occasional manifestations of the giant aquifer that lies beneath Florida. Some are unnamed, many unknown except to local folk. A few have been made easily accessible, incorporated into lovely parks such as **Ichetucknee Springs**

✔ CHECK THESE OUT—UNIQUE SIGHTS

- Visit the **Stephen Foster State Folk Culture Center** on the Suwannee River; a carillon plays tunes and folklife exhibits provide the visuals. *page 458*
- Drive the beautiful and mysterious **canopy roads** outside of Tallahassee, where Spanish moss dangles low from live oaks, tickling your windshield. *page 466*
- Admire the historic buildings and quaint old storefronts in Pensacola's **Palafox Historic Business District** and stop off at the nearby fish markets to pick up dinner. *page 493*
- Slip down into a sinkhole and see the state's only natural waterfall when you visit **Falling Waters State Recreation Area**. *page 500*

State Park and Hart Springs Park (see the "Beaches & Parks" section below). For information on how to reach Charles Spring, Little River Spring, Peacock Spring and other hidden beauties, you'll need a county map and advice, both of which are available at the Suwannee County Chamber of Commerce. ~ 601 East Howard Street, Live Oak; 904-362-3071.

The marshy land and river estuaries attract myriad species of birds. Enjoy the birds—and the stellar sunsets—from docks and porches in Suwannee, Horseshoe Beach, Steinhatchee and Keaton Beach.

Many roads lead to the coastal region known as Florida's "big bend." There are no great white sandy beaches here, which explains why much of the area is pristine and most of the little villages still keep to the business of fishing, maintaining a naturalness and a local charm.

From the coast, you can head back to the crossroads town of Perry. Here you can learn about Florida's remarkable lumber industry at the Forest Capital State Museum. There are dioramas showing how the cutting of giant cypress and pine was done in the old days and explanations of such futuristic wood products as rayon airplanes and cellulose clothing. Walk down a pine-needle path and enter the turn-of-the-century cracker homestead behind the museum. Washpots in the sand yard, grandma's mosquito netting, bare worn floors and a struggling garden carry you back to a time when life was simpler, and harder. Closed Tuesday and Wednesday. Admission. ~ 204 Forest Park Drive; 904-584-3227.

LODGING Numerous mom-and-pop enterprises provide lodging in the towns scattered throughout the eastern area. Many of them change hands often, and, like ladies in Southern novels, may appear elegant on the outside while crumbling within. However, plenty of them are just fine, and most offer great bargains; just look over the room before committing yourself. The usual chains reside along the interstate routes.

In Live Oak, the Econo Lodge is an exceptionally fine economy motel with pool, jacuzzi and remote-control TV. The cheery rooms and abundance of towels put some higher-priced lodgings to shame. ~ Route 10 and Route 129, Live Oak; 904-362-7459, 800-424-4777, fax 904-364-6598. BUDGET.

The Suwannee River Motel is a compact little outfit with 16 tiny, neat rooms for rates so low they seem from another era. When we were there, folks sat around chatting outside—about the friendliest little motel we've encountered. ~ Route 41, White Springs; 904-397-2822. BUDGET.

"No frills" are the operative words at Colonial House Inn, an interstate stopover with 28 nondescript but comfortable rooms. The design is typical motel, with one long stretch of single-floor rooms. Most importantly, there's no seasonal inflation of the rates. ~ Routes 75 and 136, White Springs; 904-963-2401. BUDGET.

For a roadside motel, consider the **Deerwood Inn**. The wallpaper may not suit your taste, but the carpeted rooms are fresh and clean. Enjoy the gameroom, miniature golf course, mallet pool and nature trail. There's even an RV park nearby, so you have access to laundry facilities and a nice pool under the pines. ~ Route 10 and State Road, exit 37, Madison; 904-973-2504. BUDGET.

You can get a good-sized, well-kept, carpeted room at the **Cadillac Motel**, convenient to the nearby spring and the Suwannee River. ~ Routes 19, 98 and 27, Fannings Springs; 352-463-2188, fax 352-463-2914. BUDGET.

The old-fashioned fishing villages along the "big bend" of the coastline provide a variety of modest accommodations, most with kitchens, for people who come to fish or seek the serenity of this nontouristy, nonswimming beach area. Most provide fishing-guide services and all offer peace and quiet.

Two miles from the Gulf, beside the Suwannee River, the **Suwannee Shores Motor Lodge** offers 27 pleasantly ordinary units, some with kitchens, only a stone's throw from a marina and access to fine saltwater and freshwater fishing. ~ End of Route 349, Suwannee; 352-542-7560. BUDGET.

◄ HIDDEN

Travis at **The Keaton Beach Marina** operates the only motel and marina in this tiny Gulfside town. In addition to boat docks, lifts, rentals and a convenience store geared toward fishers, the Marina has 13 rooms refurbished since Hurricane Andrew in '92 and three quiet two-bedroom cottages completely outfitted (except no telephones). ~ Highway 361 where it dead-ends into the Gulf of Mexico; 904-578-2897. BUDGET TO MODERATE.

Especially attractive is **Sexton's Riverside Motel**, a set of small stuccoed cinderblock efficiencies. You get two-room suites, a nice kitchen, a screened porch with a picnic table and a lovely view of the Steinhatchee River emptying into the Gulf. ~ 3rd Street West and 1st Avenue North, Steinhatchee; 352-498-5005. MODERATE.

◄ HIDDEN

"It's not Suwannee River country without catfish," proclaims the menu at the **Dixie Grill**, and this is the place to try it. No filets here, just lots of big, crunchy, bony pieces served with homemade hushpuppies. You can order other seafood and steaks and dine in the plain café area or the fancy carpeted section. Breakfast, lunch and dinner are cooked up daily. ~ 101 Dowling Avenue, Live Oak; 904-364-2810. BUDGET TO MODERATE.

DINING

The **Ship's Wheel Restaurant** is typical of many coastal restaurants that are worth the drive. The number of fishermen who eat here tells you something. Grouper, mullet and shrimp plates always come with hushpuppies, cole slaw and french fries, and there are chowders and oyster stew to fit the season. Also on the menu are filet mignon and steak. Open for breakfast, lunch and dinner. ~ End of Route 349, Suwannee; 352-542-2344. BUDGET.

◄ HIDDEN

Though the name may be misleading, **Keaton Beach Hot Dog Stand** serves full seafood dinners at a waterside location in the heart of tiny Keaton Beach. Operating out of a carnival trailer with a wooden pavilion, Martha and William Hargesheimer preside. The atmosphere is rustic and laid back, the crowd is predominantly locals and the menu centers around seafood caught in the Gulf. ~ 2139 Keaton Beach Drive, Keaton Beach; 904-578-2675. BUDGET.

HIDDEN ►

Roy's delights diners who partake of the remarkable seafood platters, which include shrimp, scallops, deviled crab, oysters and crab claws. The salad bar features unlimited feta cheese and other Greek treats; steaming grits come with dinner if you wish. The place appears unassuming, but tinted windows offer wonderful sunset-viewing and shorebird-watching. ~ Route 51, Steinhatchee; 352-498-5000. MODERATE.

SHOPPING

Most of the eastern area towns are far enough away from shopping malls to be able to maintain healthy downtowns with assorted clothing shops, drug stores, hardware and even old-fashioned dime stores. If you long for some down-home, old-timey small-town browsing, you can find it. You may even find some antique bargains by getting off the beaten path; little shops spring up on town squares and in homes.

Handwritten signs along the road announce "boiled peanuts," and, though an acquired taste, many folks get hooked on this north Florida delicacy. From the back of a truck or a tiny stand you can buy a steaming paper sack of these moist, soft-shelled, salty treats.

NIGHTLIFE

There are plenty of local drinking places along country roads and near little towns, but unless saloon-hopping is your style, you won't find much nightlife in this area.

One exception is **The Spirit of the Suwannee**, a huge park that puts on a variety of concerts and programs throughout the year. There are bluegrass festivals, storytelling events, square dancing and clogging, and other down-home entertainment. ~ Route 129 just south of Routes 75 and 10, Live Oak; 904-364-1683.

For local color, latch onto one of the church suppers, fish fries or political rallies advertised from time to time on signs along the road. Most of these are money-raising events, so guests are quite welcome.

BEACHES & PARKS

SUWANNEE RIVER STATE PARK 🧍 ⚓ 🚤 ⛵ 🎣 The Withlacoochee and Suwannee rivers meet in this quiet 1843-acre park, creating a rich variety of pine forest, hardwood hammock and sand hills. When the rivers are low, springs may be seen bubbling from their banks, crystal clear in the tannin-tinted waters. An old cemetery and Confederate earthworks recall the steamboat heyday when the area bustled. It's a good place to try for catfish, bass and panfish. Facilities include a picnic area, restrooms and nature trails. Day-use fee, $2. ~ Just off Route 90, 14 miles west of Live Oak; 904-362-2746.

▲ There are 31 sites, all with RV hookups, water and electricity; $10 to $12 per night.

HART SPRINGS PARK 🏊 🎣 ⛴ 🚣 🛥 ⛵ ⛵ This 275-acre county park is built around one of the many surprising springs that seem to appear from nowhere in this part of the country. A small footbridge crosses the crystal-clear run that flows to the Suwannee River, and cypress tress grow in the middle of the sand-bottomed swimming area. There are picnic areas, volleyball courts, restrooms and a concession stand. ~ Finding this park is tricky, so go with map in hand. From Live Oak, head south on Route 129 to Bell; go west on Route 341 and continue on 341 when it heads south. At C-344 head west and go about eight miles to the spring (at four miles, C-344 jogs right, then left); 352-463-3444.

◄ HIDDEN

▲ There are 50 sites, some with RV hookups, electricity and water; $11 per night.

ICHETUCKNEE SPRINGS STATE PARK 🏃 🚴 🏊 🎣 ⛴ ⛵ The heart of this lovely 2250-acre park is the crystal-clear, icy cold Ichetucknee River and the series of springs that rise from the Florida aquifer to feed it. Canoeing, tubing, snorkeling and swimming are so popular here that folks often wait in line for entrance on summer weekends. The river winds through hardwood hammock and jungle-like swampland; on quiet days folks floating on the river may spy otter, beaver, turtles or wading birds that make their homes here. Facilities include picnic areas, restrooms, dressing rooms, a nature trail and canoe and tube ramps. Day-use fee, $3.25. ~ The south entrance is off Route 27 between Branford and Fort White; the north entrance is off Route 238; 904-497-2511.

▲ Not allowed in the park but there are private campgrounds near each entrance and camping in **O'Leno State Park** (904-454-1853) near Lake City.

Tallahassee Area

Unlike most Florida cities, Tallahassee is hilly, green and abounding in trees. More Deep South than tropical, its sights include the trappings of a fascinating state capital, the campuses of two state universities, the vestiges of plantation days, a bit of prehistory and a neighboring wilderness that comes right up to the city limits.

SIGHTS

Because it's not on a major north–south route, Tallahassee isn't a tourist city. But despite its lack of tourist glitz, there's plenty to see and do here. Begin with a trip to the **Tallahassee Area Convention** and Visitors Bureau, where you can arm yourself with brochures, maps and a self-guided walking and driving tour. ~ 200 West College Avenue, Tallahassee; 904-413-9200.

Most of the downtown sights are within walking distance of The Columns. Even so, you might want to use the Old Town Trolley. Designed primarily for local commuters, this colorful diesel-powered conveyance circles the downtown area, operating only on weekdays.

Near the Chamber of Commerce you'll discover the First Presbyterian Church, a white-spired building that is Tallahassee's oldest house of worship. In 1838, the year it was built, townspeople sought refuge within its walls during Seminole Indian raids. Beautifully restored, even the galleries where slaves once sat still provide seating for worshippers. ~ 110 North Adams Street.

Continue along Park Avenue for a few blocks and admire a crop of fine antebellum homes that distinguish this lovely tree-lined promenade.

At the Adams Street Commons you'll find a serpentine, brick-paved block that has been redesigned and now features several fine hotels and restaurants, and some detailed landscaping. ~ 200 South Adams Street.

Straight ahead stand two startlingly contrasting structures. The modern, 22-story Florida Capitol was designed by Edward Durrell Stone. Tours of the new Capitol, including a scenic view from the top, are available daily. ~ Apalachee Parkway and South Monroe Street; 904-488-6167. The 1902 Old Capitol, with its handsome dome and red-striped awnings, has been restored. The Old Capitol is also open daily and houses exhibits of Florida political history. ~ 904-487-1902.

One block east of the Old Capitol is Florida's oldest surviving bank building, the Old Union Bank. Built around 1840, it has been restored and is open Tuesday through Sunday for tours. ~ Apalachee Parkway; 904-487-1902.

Two blocks west of the new Capitol, the Museum of Florida History reflects a new interest in preserving the diverse and colorful story of the state. Here you'll see the interior of a citrus packing house, climb aboard a river boat, marvel over Spanish treasure and examine American Indian relics. ~ 500 South Bronough Street; 904-488-1673.

Along nearby Martin Luther King Boulevard you can explore the Old City Cemetery, which has graves dating back to 1829, including those of pioneers and slaves and Confederate and Union soldiers. ~ Martin Luther King Boulevard and Park Avenue. Adjacent to it, the St. Johns Episcopal Cemetery contains the graves of Prince Achille Murat, son of the King of Naples and nephew of Napoleon Bonaparte, and his wife, Madame Catherine Murat, great-grandniece of George Washington. Several Florida governors are also buried here.

Within driving distance of downtown is **The Governor's Mansion**. Modeled after Andrew Jackson's Tennessee mansion, "The Hermitage," the mansion is open for tours three days a week during the legislative session (late February to early May) and a few weeks in December. ~ 700 North Adams Street; 904-488-4661.

Nearby is **The Grove**, built in 1825 by an aide to Jackson, and now the private residence of former Governor Leroy Collins. ~ North Adams Street and 1st Avenue.

The **Brokaw-McDougall House**, built in 1856, is a fine example of Italianate architecture, distinguished by pleasing proportions and spaciousness. Six Corinthian columns support a second-story porch overlooking grounds restored by landscapers to their 19th-century appearance. Closed weekends. ~ At 329 North Meridian Street; 904-488-3901.

The **LeMoyne Art Foundation** is located in a restored antebellum home and features permanent collections of pottery, paintings, sculpture and photography by area artists. Occasional traveling exhibits also grace the rooms of this handsome house. The backyard garden is tended as a sculpture and butterfly showplace. ~ 125 North Gadsden Street; 904-222-8800.

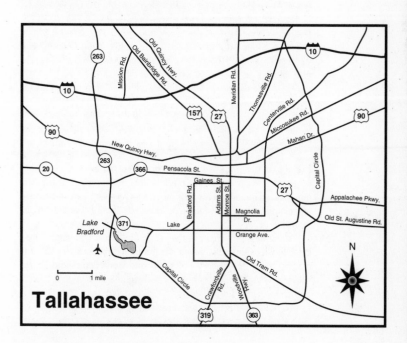

Tallahassee

Florida State University and Florida A&M University both offer some interesting sightseeing. Once an all-black school, **Florida A&M** houses its **Black Archives Research Center and Museum** in one of Tallahassee's oldest buildings. Here you are greeted by an impressive display of photos of African-Americans who have served in Congress; there is also a wide assortment of artifacts and exhibits on African-American culture and history. Closed weekends. ~ Carnegie Library; 904-599-3020. The **Foster Tanner Fine Arts Gallery**, also on the A&M campus, presents the works of many African-American artists. ~ 904-599-3161.

On the **Florida State University** campus, the **Museum of Fine Arts** features permanent collections of Japanese, Dutch and American paintings, pre-Columbian artifacts and traveling exhibits. ~ Fine Arts Building, Copeland and Call streets; 904-644-6836.

If you'd like to see a museum-in-the-making, visit the **San Luis Archaeological and Historic Site**. During the mid-17th century, an Apalachee Indian town and Spanish mission existed here. Excavations are conducted annually and the archaeology of the site is explained during guided tours. Some of the uncovered artifacts are on display at the visitors center. ~ 2020 West Mission Road; 904-487-3711.

Tallahassee's most enchanting feature is its collection of **canopy roads**, lovely country byways that begin within the city limits and go for miles beneath towering live oaks draped with Spanish moss. Distinctive road markers designate these protected highways, which include Old St. Augustine Road, Miccosukee Road (Route 146), Centerville Road (Route 151), Meridian Road (Route 155) and Old Bainbridge Road.

For a fine trip down one of these Old South lanes, head northeast on Centerville Road. After eight miles of gentle turns, you will come to the 1859 **Pisgah Church**, a grand old meetinghouse with hand-hewn pews and clerestory windows. Continue beneath the oaks for another seven miles, and you will reach the old metal-sided **Bradley's Country Store**, little changed since the 1920s. ~ Centerville Road, Moccasin Gap; 904-893-1647.

MOUNDS OF HISTORY

The **Lake Jackson Indian Mounds** look like a couple of ordinary hills in a park setting but are actually the remnants of an American Indian village. It's a nice place to contemplate history and have a picnic. A nature trail leads to the remains of an old grist mill and irrigation lake. ~ North of Route 10 off Crowder Road and Route 27; 904-562-0042.

Many other interesting destinations lie outside the Tallahassee city limits. Just north of Route 10, the **Maclay Gardens**, built as a private winter retreat, present an astounding array of azaleas, redbuds, camellias, magnolias, amaryllises and other native flora in the spring months. The grounds, where something is always blooming, are open year-round, the house from January through April. Admission. ~ 3540 Thomasville Road; 904-487-4115.

For a large variety of exhibits, visit the **Tallahassee Museum of History and Natural Science**. This wonderful combination zoo-park-farm-plantation primarily consists of outdoor exhibits and provides information and entertainment for folks of all ages. It's hard to believe that only 52 wooded acres could communicate so much about north Florida in such a captivating and authentic manner. See a late-19th-century schoolhouse, church and farm, and traverse the nature trail. Be sure to take your children here, and if you don't have children, go anyway. Admission. ~ 3945 Museum Drive; 904-575-8684.

Also located on the grounds of the museum is **Bellevue**, the former home of Catherine Dangerfield Willis, great-granddaughter of George Washington and widow of Achille Murat, Prince of Naples and nephew of Napoleon. The 1830-era home is a modest and excellent example of indigenous southern architecture.

The **San Marcos de Apalachee State Historic Site** is located at the confluence of the Wakulla and St. Marks rivers. A Spanish fort and mission stood here in the 17th century, and Confederate troops once occupied the area, too. You can see the old earthworks, pieces of walls and moats, and stroll a nature trail and boardwalk along the riverside. The visitors center displays artifacts from the fort's various eras. Closed Tuesday and Wednesday. Admission. ~ At the southern end of Route 363; 904-925-6216.

In 1829 the **St. Marks Lighthouse**, located in the **St. Marks National Wildlife Refuge**, was built with stones from the old fort at San Marcos de Apalachee. One of the oldest lighthouses in the Southeast, its remarkable pineapple-shaped lens has served to guide ships from Civil War times to the modern age. ~ County Road 59; 904-925-6121.

Ever since Tallahassee built its new state capitol building and spruced up its downtown, the ultimate place in elegant lodging has been **The Governors Inn**, an amazing reconstruction of an old downtown business place with high soaring ceilings and exposed heartpine trusses. Each of the 40 distinctive rooms is named for a Florida governor and furnished with appropriate antiques. Any head of state should be pleased to stay here, whether it be in a loft-bedroom overlooking a wood-burning fireplace or in a whirlpool bath–equipped suite. Government and business folk keep the

LODGING

inn booked during the legislature's session, but if you can book a reservation far enough in advance, this is the place to stay. Amenities include continental breakfasts and complimentary cocktails in the pine-paneled Florida room. ~ 209 South Adams Street, Tallahassee; 904-681-6855, fax 904-222-3105. ULTRA-DELUXE.

In the downtown area, the **Holiday Inn Capitol Plaza** contributes its stature to the city's ever-reaching skyline. Many of the 244 rooms and 12 suites offer good views of downtown Tallahassee, the university campuses and the lush green countryside. The hotel offers all you'd expect, from large rooms to an assortment of eating and watering places. Decor is up-to-date and spacious. ~ 101 South Adams Street, Tallahassee; 904-224-5000, 800-598-7777. DELUXE.

Just about all the usual chain motels, from economy to top-of-the-line, can be found north of the city near Route 10 exits. **Cabot Lodge** belongs to a small southern chain that offers more charm than most of its counterparts, and complimentary cocktails and a continental breakfast, too. The 160 rooms occupy an assortment of yellow buildings with wide porches and green-and-yellow trim. There's an Old South feeling about the place, even though the rooms are modern. ~ 2735 North Monroe Street, Tallahassee; 904-386-8880, 800-223-1964, fax 904-386-4254. MODERATE.

In the summer, you can save a lot of money by taking a room or suite at the privately owned dormitory, **Osceola Hall**. On the edge of the Florida State University campus, this comfortably functional dorm is made up of two-room/one-bath suites. A food service, fitness facilities and pool are available. ~ 500 Chapel Drive, Tallahassee; 904-222-5010. BUDGET.

Moorish architecture, handpainted Toltec and Aztec designs and Spanish tile set the **Wakulla Springs Lodge and Conference**

✔ CHECK THESE OUT—UNIQUE LODGING

- *Budget:* Stay at the friendly little **Suwannee River Motel**, where both the atmosphere and the prices will remind you of bygone days. *page 460*
- *Moderate:* Climb into your four-poster bed at **The Gibson Inn**, a restored turn-of-the-century Apalachicola hotel with period decor. *page 476*
- *Deluxe:* Sleep comfortably in a train station at the **Pensacola Grand Hotel**, where modern rooms are built onto a 1912 L&N depot. *page 494*
- *Ultra-deluxe:* Catch the end of a legislative session and, when the governors check out, you can check in to **The Governors Inn**, *the* place to stay in Tallahassee. *page 467*

Budget: under $50   Moderate: $50–$90   Deluxe: $90–$130   Ultra-deluxe: over $130

Center apart from anything else north Florida has to offer. Built in 1937, this fine old hostelry overlooks Florida's deepest spring. Rooms look much as they did in the 1930s, with marble floors, area rugs and functional furniture. But you reach them by climbing broad marble steps, and you sleep in another era, in the quiet of a wonderful park full of wildlife. ~ Route 61 and Route 267, Wakulla Springs; 904-224-5950, fax 904-561-7251. MODERATE.

About 35 miles from town, **George's Lighthouse Point Condominiums & Resort** has transformed itself from a run-of-the-mill motel into a riverside marina and lodge. Each condominium is individually decorated and fully furnished, and many of them overlook the broad river. Boating, swimming and tennis are available at the resort. Two-night minimum. ~ 11 Mashes Road, Panacea; 904-984-0171. MODERATE TO DELUXE.

DINING

Andrew's North offers elegant dining for every taste and pocketbook size. The ten-plus-page menu comprises salads, pasta, burgers, sandwiches and gourmet pizzas. Some entrées you'll find include oak-roasted salmon and Rio Grande pasta (grilled chicken, pecans, artichokes, prosciutto and much more over pasta). Dinner only. ~ 1700-3 Halstead Boulevard, Tallahassee; 904-894-0919. BUDGET TO DELUXE.

If the display of luscious pastries doesn't stimulate your appetite, the menu at **Chez Pierre** will. High-backed booths and flowered print tablecloths create a French café setting. You can enjoy chicken crêpes, onion soup, chicken breasts with mushrooms, and fish and scallops served in a lobster sauce. Closed Sunday. ~ 1215 Thomasville Road, Tallahassee; 904-222-0936. MODERATE TO DELUXE.

There are 120 items on the menu at **Bahn Thai**, all written in Thai and carefully explained in English. Despite its unassuming appearance and unlikely location among used car lots, diners come in to eat such traditional Asian fare as whole fish with hot sauce, sweet-and-sour shrimp and coconut milk soup. The menu also includes Chinese dishes. ~ 1319 South Monroe Street, Tallahassee; 904-224-4765. BUDGET.

The Spartan has been offering Greek food to Tallahasseans for years. Here you can choose *souvlaki* or spanakopita or try "Yorgo's Platter" for a wide sampling of Greek dishes. There is also non-Greek fare, such as beef Wellington and grilled chicken breast. Seafood platters are popular at this intimate eatery, and include Florida lobster in season. ~ 220 South Monroe Street, Tallahassee; 904-224-9711. MODERATE.

Anthony's offers traditional Italian dishes, as well as saltimbocca and fettuccine Eduardo (a shrimp and crab combination in cheese sauce served over pasta). The high-backed wicker chairs, booths and small tables make this an intimate place for romantic dining. Dinner only. ~ 1950-G Thomasville Road, Betton Place, Tallahassee; 904-224-1447. MODERATE.

Join the thousands of Tallahassee folk who have made a tradition of "fish dinners down at the bridge." "The bridge" is just below Panacea on the Ochlockonee Bay, and restaurants there are known for their excellent seafood. At **The Oaks Restaurant**, in spite of a seating capacity of over 200, you may still have to wait in line. This place serves up the usual platters with hushpuppies and grits; the shrimp boats, cold dinners and Florida lobster are added specialties. Breakfast, lunch and dinner are cooked up daily. ~ Route 98, south of Panacea; 904-984-5370. MODERATE.

Diners at **Angelo's** partake of sumptuous seafood "over the water," enjoying a spectacular view of the bay through huge windows or from the deck. The entrées include the usual seafood offerings, plus charbroiled seafood, creoles and stuffed fish. The grouper marguerite with a wine and cheese sauce reveals how this one-time fish camp has become sophisticated in recent years. Dinner only, brunch on Sunday. Closed Tuesday. ~ Route 98, south of Panacea; 904-984-5168. MODERATE TO DELUXE.

HIDDEN ▶ Not sophisticated but worth the search, the **Spring Creek Restaurant** concentrates on regional and seasonal "fruits of the sea" in a quiet setting under tall trees in the fishing village of Spring Creek. It's places like this that have finally put mullet on the list of respectable fish. Don't forget to BYOB. Dinner only, but there's brunch on the weekend. Closed Monday and Tuesday. ~ 25 miles south of Tallahassee at the end of Route 365 off Route 98; 904-926-3751. MODERATE.

Some 18 miles northwest of Tallahassee is a place so hidden you'll find maps on the menus and business cards. Stashed down a HIDDEN ▶ dirt lane on 30 forested acres, **Nicholson Farmhouse** abides in a trio of marvelous old buildings. A mule wagon ride starts the historical tour of the antique-filled farmhouse, built in 1828 by slave craftsmen and owned by the fourth generation of Nicholsons. There's also an antique and country store to browse through. Dine here or in the home's original rustic smokehouse and its adjacent 1890s frame home. The place specializes in steaks that are "wet aged" at 34° for 21 days. The process works: This is some of the choicest beef in Florida. ~ Route 12, 3.5 miles west of Havana; 904-539-5931. MODERATE TO DELUXE.

SHOPPING Because Tallahassee serves as the major shopping center for north central Florida, just about anything you might wish to buy is available in the town's malls and shops. The fastest-growing area for specialty shops lies along Thomasville Road, serving the prestigious suburb of Killearn.

Betton Place is the only shopping complex I've ever seen that made its home in a fine brick church building. The adaptation is clever and lovely, and the center features small specialty shops. ~ Bradford Road and Thomasville Highway.

Market Square also offers many specialty shops as well as an open-air market where local farmers bring their produce. Depending on the season, you may find anything from peaches to peanuts to fresh cane syrup. ~ Thomasville and Timberlane roads.

Across from Market Square is a medley of specialty stores and restaurants called **The Pavilions**. One eye-catcher, **Narcissus** (904-668-4807) proffers snazzy women's swimsuits and elegant lingerie. ~ 1410 Market Street.

For anyone planning to explore the wilds of north Florida, a trip to the **Outdoors Shop** is the place to begin. Not only do they have everything you'll need for hunting, backpacking, camping or fishing, they can tell you where to go and how to get there. They also carry a huge selection of outdoor and sporty clothing. ~ 2555 North Monroe Street; 904-386-4181.

If you're seeking souvenirs of substance, visit the gift shop at the **Museum of Florida History**. ~ 500 South Bronough Street; 904-488-1673. At the **Tallahassee Museum of History & Natural Science** you'll find items for children and adults ranging from T-shirts to history books to posters and calendars. ~ 3945 Museum Drive; 904-575-8684.

Antique shops abound in Tallahassee and in nearby Havana. The serious connoisseur and the casual hobbyist can spend days browsing in small shops in private homes.

A classy country store residing under ancient oak trees, **Bradley's Country Store** is probably the only place of its kind to be listed on the National Register of Historic Places. Selling homemade sausage since 1910, the Bradley family also has stone-ground meal and grits, mayhaw jelly and other seasonal delights. ~ Centerville Road, Moccasin Gap; 904-893-1647. ◄ HIDDEN

In the tiny town of Sopchoppy, artist **George Griffin's Pottery on Suncat Ridge** features original pieces by a master potter. Take time to enjoy the garden and resident animals. ~ Route 319, Sopchoppy; 904-962-9311. ◄ HIDDEN

NIGHTLIFE

Tallahassee nightlife is limited chiefly to quiet hotel and restaurant bars and noisy college gathering places. Check the Friday edition of the *Tallahassee Democrat's* "Limelight" section for complete listings of local nightspots and performances.

Big-name stars perform at the **Donald Tucker Civic Center**. ~ 505 West Pensacola Street, Tallahassee; 904-222-0400.

The Moon is a big dancehall with four bars and a lounge that features local acts and live music on some evenings and shows on others. Stars are booked on occasion. Cover. ~ 1105 Lafayette Street, Tallahassee; 904-222-6666.

Club Park Avenue features three bars, three dancefloors, a patio, video screens and deejay music. Raucous drag shows entertain the gay crowd Saturday and Sunday nights. Here you can move from one room to the other two in search of your favorite dance beat, or keep an eye out for drag queen appearances. A mixed crowd frequents this brick-walled, neon-lit club the rest of the week. No cover on Saturday. ~ 115 East Park Avenue, Tallahassee; 904-599-9143.

The **Riverfront/Rock Dock Saloon** is actually two bars in one with a dancefloor to kick up your heels on. The front portion is the Riverfront, which showcases country-and-western bands. Southern rock bands take the stage at the Rock Dock. The saloon stays open until 2 a.m., which is late by Tallahassee standards. ~ 9330 West Tennessee Street, Tallahassee; 904-575-1100.

For local yuks, duck into **Dooley's Downunder** in the Ramada Inn. Open only on Friday and Saturday nights for two shows each night, the small club features a double billing of local and regional comedians. Cover. ~ 2900 North Monroe Street, Tallahassee; 904-386-1027.

THEATER, OPERA, SYMPHONY AND DANCE   Tallahassee has a thriving arts scene. The **Tallahassee Symphony Orchestra** presents a full season of fine orchestral music. ~ 904-224-0461. The students and faculty of FSU perform in concerts by the **University Opera** and the **Florida State University Symphony Orchestra**. ~ 904-644-6500. In addition, the **Dance Repertory Theatre** at FSU gives annual shows. ~ 904-644-1023. Baroque concerts are presented by the very popular **Bach Parley, Inc.** ~ 904-385-3487. The **Tallahassee Little Theatre** has been entertaining the community with its performances for almost 50 years. ~ 904-224-8474. A variety of plays and concerts are presented regularly on the campus of **Florida A&M**. ~ 904-561-2871.

BEACHES & PARKS

APALACHICOLA NATIONAL FOREST The largest of the Sunshine State's three national forests, this 557,000-acre preserve contains pine and hardwood forests, swamps, four rivers and a multitude of streams, springs and sinkholes. The variety of natural phenomena is extraordinary, creating numerous recreational opportunities from wilderness canoeing to birdwatching to hunting and hiking. It's also an excellent place to fish and swimming is permitted in some recreation sites. Several developed recreation areas with picnic areas and restrooms lie within the national forest. In addition, there are some semideveloped wilderness areas with picnic areas, fire pits, water and pit toilets. Hiking trails run throughout the forest. ~ A number of main highways and secondary roads—including Routes 375 and 65—offer access to the forest, which is located southwest of Tallahassee; 904-926-3561.

▲ At **Silver Lake Recreation Area** there are 25 sites; $5 per night. Primitive camping is allowed throughout the forest; no fee.

LAKE TALQUIN STATE FOREST 🏃 🐎 🚣 🎣 ⛴ 🚤 🛶 This lovely, long lake, impounded in the gently rolling countryside, is most popular with local anglers for the fine bass and other freshwater catches. Picnics and nature walks among tall oaks and pines and breezes off the water make it a welcome getaway place. Other facilities include nature trails and restrooms. ~ Located ten miles west of Tallahassee off Route 20; 904-487-4250.

▲ Not permitted, but available in the county park on the north side of the lake (off Route 20, follow signs); information, 904-487-3070. There are also some privately owned campgrounds in the area that offer tent sites and RV hookups. These include Pat Thomas Park at Hopkins Landing (904-875-4544) with 30 sites, $5 to $10 per night; Ingram's Marina (904-627-2241) with 65 sites, $12 per night; and Gainey's Talquin Lodge (904-627-3822) with 60 sites, $15 per night.

EDWARD BALL WAKULLA SPRINGS STATE PARK 🏃 🚲 🚣 Spanish explorer Ponce de León is said to have wintered here, and one can easily see why he might choose this spot. The claim is that the beautiful spring is the world's deepest, and it was a favorite of swimmers and divers long before it became a state park. (It has some of the best spring swimming in the state.) Boat trips along the Wakulla River allow visitors to see an unusual array of bird species. The wild beauty of the place explains why Hollywood has filmed a number of movies here. Facilities include a picnic area, restrooms, a bathhouse, lifeguards in swim areas, a lodge, a restaurant, glass-bottom boat and jungle-river cruises and nature trails. Day-use fee, $3.25. ~ Off Route 61, 13 miles south of Tallahassee; 904-922-3632.

ST. MARKS NATIONAL WILDLIFE REFUGE 🏃 🚲 🐎 🎣 🚣 🚤 🛶 One of the nation's oldest wildlife refuges, St. Marks encompasses thousands of acres of land and a large portion of Apalachee Bay. Visitors come chiefly for the wildlife, such as black bear, otter, alligator, white-tailed deer and raccoons, and for the thousands of migratory and native birds. The southern bald eagle is protected here, as are many other species. The refuge is also popular with anglers who fish year-round in the bay, lakes and rivers. There are picnic areas, restrooms, hiking trails, canoe access, an observation tower and a visitors center. Day-use fee, $4. ~ Several routes enter the refuge; the main one is Lighthouse Road off Route 98, south of Tallahassee; 904-925-6121.

▲ If you are hiking the full length of the Florida National Scenic Trail through the refuge, you may camp (two weeks' notice is required; call 904-925-6121); otherwise camping is not permitted in the refuge, but available at Wakulla County's Newport Park (Route 98 and 59, east of Newport; 904-926-5769). There are 38 sites; $9 per night.

OCHLOCKONEE RIVER STATE PARK
This 392-acre park gives you a taste of the southern part of the Apalachicola forest without roughing it. The pine flatwoods are open here, providing good opportunities for spotting the endangered red-cockaded woodpecker and other birds. Deer, fox squirrel, bobcat and grey fox are attracted by the small grass ponds, bay heads and oak thickets; alligator warnings are posted. There are opportunities for both freshwater and saltwater fishing. There's a small protected swimming beach on the Dead River, which is quite lively as it empties into the Ochlockonee. You'll find picnic areas, restrooms, nature trails and a scenic drive. Day-use fee, $2. ~ Off Route 319, four miles south of Sopchoppy; 904-962-2771.

▲ There are 30 sites, all with RV hookups; $8 to $10 per night.

Apalachicola Area

A Florida coast without beaches? Improbable as it sounds, that's what awaits along Route 98 in the Panhandle's Apalachicola Bay region. Protected by a distant barrier reef, this pretty stretch shows you what the Sunshine State looked like before the arrival of the unofficial state bird, the construction crane. The lack of beaches means minimal development, beautiful bayous, marshes, islands and quiet fishing villages.

SIGHTS
The Gorrie Bridge (Route 98) leads into Apalachicola, a struggling but charming old fishing and riverboat town with a glorious past. At the **Apalachicola Chamber of Commerce** you can pick up a self-guided walking tour brochure. Little remains of the town's cotton business (which dates back to the 1820s) except for a few historical markers and a crumbling warehouse, but the grand homes built by men who made their fortunes from cotton, lumber and sponges still stand in various states of glory. ~ 84 Market Street; 904-653-9419.

You can tour **The Raney House**, a 1838 Greek revival mansion that reflects the prosperity of its original owner, an Apalachicola cotton commission merchant. Built in the temple-pediment style, the house has four tall columns across the front. The wide halls, now displaying antiques and museum pieces, once served as breezy rooms during hot summer days. Tours on Saturdays. ~ 128 Market Street.

Only two of Apalachicola's 43 original **cotton warehouses** remain. Compressed bales no longer stand in great piles, waiting for shipment around the world, but you can view the massive old buildings and imagine the dockside activity that followed a prosperous growing season. ~ Water Street and Avenue E. Next door stands the abandoned **sponge exchange**, a memorial to the days when the sponge trade at this port ranked third in the state.

Yellow fever was a serious problem during Apalachicola's early days. In an attempt to treat his patients by cooling them down, Dr. John Gorrie invented a machine for which all summer visitors to Florida must be grateful. At the **John Gorrie State Museum** you can see a replica of the first ice-making machine, the Gorrie invention that would one day lay the groundwork for modern air-conditioning. The small museum also features displays explaining the history and ecology of the bay. Closed Tuesday and Wednesday. Admission. ~ 46 6th Street in Gorrie Square; 904-653-9347.

For a meditative visit, stroll under the moss-draped oaks in Apalachicola's **Chestnut Street Cemetery**, where you can find markers dating from 1832. Confederate and Union soldiers are buried here, as are a number of the area's leading citizens. ~ Avenue E and 7th Street.

From the old waterfront area and **Battery Park**, you can watch the shrimp boats returning from a day's fishing, their nets spread out like dragonfly wings to dry. During oyster season the fishermen harvest the bay waters from their tiny boats, just as their fathers and grandfathers did before them, "tonging" with specially made long tongs for the shellfish that keep Apalachicola famous. ~ Bay Avenue and 6th Street.

A large portion of the rivers, bays, bayous, marshes and islands of this region are included in the **Apalachicola National Estuarine Research Reserve**. Though not really a traveler's destination, the headquarters will provide interested visitors with information on bird species, endangered animals, sea life and the importance of protecting the nation's ever-dwindling estuaries. Closed weekends. ~ Headquarters at 261 7th Street; 904-653-8063.

AMAZING GRACE

Trinity Episcopal Church was shipped in pieces from New York and assembled with wooden pegs in 1837 and 1838. The beautiful Greek revival building houses two historic organs, stained glass from several periods and a gallery designed for slaves who attended services here. Hand-stenciled designs grace the curved wooden ceiling. The church is on the National Register of Historic Places. ~ Avenue E and 6th Street.

Westward from Apalachicola, Route 98 travels inland, returning to the coast at **Port St. Joe**, home of a monstrous and smelly paper mill. The town is attractive, though, and a short detour will take you to the **Constitution Convention State Museum**. Here talking mannequins re-enact the finalizing of Florida's original constitution. Of interest, also, is a display of tools, china and personal items found at the site of short-lived Saint Joseph, an 1840-era boom town that was wiped out almost overnight by yellow fever and a hurricane. Closed Tuesday and Wednesday. Admission. ~ 200 Allen Memorial Way, Port St. Joe; 904-229-8029.

LODGING

The little coastal towns along Route 98 to the east of Apalachicola have a number of mom-and-pop motels that cater to folks who enjoy the peace and quiet and the fine saltwater and river fishing. One of the nicest is **Sportsman's Lodge**, a big, sprawling place whose spacious rooms include kitchenettes. At your doorstep is a large marina where you can charter a boat for bay or deep-sea fishing. ~ Route 98 and Magnolia Bluff, Eastpoint; 904-670-8423, fax 904-670-8316. BUDGET.

Coombs House Inn is a restored, three-story Victorian mansion with nine rooms, Oriental carpets, cypress and oak woodwork and a huge dining room where breakfast is served. Three suites include jacuzzi tubs. ~ Highway 98, Apalachicola; 904-653-9199, fax 904-653-2785. DELUXE.

The queen of Apalachicola's lodging is the product of a million-dollar, historically faithful restoration of a circa-1907 wooden hotel. **The Gibson Inn**, a handsome blue-and-white building, offers 31 rooms and suites, each individually decorated with period wallpaper, four-poster beds and antique armoires. The wraparound double galleries invite rocking and relaxation. The lounge features a great old wooden bar, and the restaurant completes the gentle sense of stepping back in time that the entire Gibson brings off so well. ~ 51 Market Street, Apalachicola; 904-653-2191. MODERATE.

You can dock your boat and clean your fish right at your door if you stay at the **Rainbow Inn and Marina**. The rooms are ordinary and only slightly musty, but the old waterfront location exudes a salt-air charm. ~ 123 Water Street, Apalachicola; 904-653-8139. BUDGET.

DINING

Florida's Panhandle coast is the place for seafood, and you won't find oysters better than those from the Apalachicola Bay. Most of the restaurants here serve everything the sea offers up; in fact, menus often seem cloned, featuring grouper, scallops, crab, mullet and whatever else is in season.

At **Julia Mae's Town Inn** you'll get a big helping of oysters and other seafood dishes, along with french fries, hushpuppies and cole slaw. You may even meet the venerable Julia Mae, whose scallop burgers, Florida lobster, seasonal fish platters, stews and creoles have kept this slightly rundown Carrabelle café overlooking the marsh hopping for many years. ~ Route 98, Carrabelle; 904-697-3791. MODERATE.

The Hut is one more popular seafood-and-steak place that attracts folks who love Apalachicola oysters. Both local folk and visitors wait in line for the sumptuous seafood, beer and cocktails. ~ Route 98, west of Apalachicola; 904-653-9410. MODERATE.

At **The Seafood Grill and Steakhouse** you'll find local folks having a down-home, Southern-cooked lunch or dinner. If you've forgotten what good hamburgers are like, you'll be pleased to find them here. ~ 100 Market Street, Apalachicola; 904-653-9510. MODERATE.

The restaurant at the restored **Gibson Inn** brings elegance to this modest fishing town, with crystal, white tablecloths, brass lamps and probably the only official chef in the area, resulting in gourmet treatments of seafood, such as oysters *duxell* with brandied butter sauce or charbroiled dolphin with an avocado salsa. Lots of fresh vegetables and a varied menu make this a nice change for anyone tired of local fare; the ambience is old-fashioned and relaxed, the prices surprisingly affordable. Breakfast, lunch and dinner are served. ~ 51 Market Street, Apalachicola; 904-653-2191. MODERATE TO DELUXE.

Three miles up the Apalachicola River from town, the **Breakaway** serves up wonderful local seafood and steaks to fishermen and riverboaters who do business at the marina next door, and to anyone else who has picked up rumors of this fish camp's dependable fare. Nothing fancy here, just a view of the river and plenty of hushpuppies. Closed Monday and Tuesday. ~ 200 Wadell Road; 904-653-9988. BUDGET TO MODERATE.

◄ HIDDEN

✔ CHECK THESE OUT—UNIQUE DINING

- *Budget:* Step back in time at Pensacola's **Hopkins House**, a restaurant where diners sit at one long table to enjoy the Southern food. *page 496*
- *Moderate:* Join the three-ring circus at **Harry T's Boathouse** in Destin, a wacky joint opened by an injured circus man that serves a wide selection of dishes on a waterfront patio. *page 489*
- *Moderate to deluxe:* Discover **Angelo's** in Tallahassee; dine on seafood and enjoy a spectacular view of its source—the sea. *page 470*
- *Deluxe to ultra-deluxe:* Call the tune at **Fiddler's Green**, one of the area's poshest restaurants, at Marriott's Bay Point Resort. *page 483*

Budget: under $8   Moderate: $8–$16   Deluxe: $16–$24   Ultra-deluxe: over $24

Text continued on page 480.

Apalachicola Area Barrier Islands

Look across the waters of St. George Sound and Apalachicola Bay and you will see a set of long islands hovering low on the brink of the horizon. Guarding some of the most productive fishing waters in the state and protecting the mainland from wind and storm, they provide nesting grounds for thousands of native and migratory birds. Their dunes and pinewoods harbor raccoons, ghost crabs, salt marsh snakes and diamondback terrapin. Their beaches glisten white and brilliant, attracting visitors in search of solitude and seashells.

Each of these barrier islands has a distinctive character. Easternmost **Dog Island** lies about three miles across the sound from Carrabelle, boasting some of the highest and most unspoiled dunes in the state. Only a handful of residents live here year-round; only 100 houses and cottages stand among the dunes. Today most of Dog Island is a wildlife preserve, protecting at least 30 species of endangered animals, plants and birds. In the higher regions you can walk among ancient sand pines, rosemary and reindeer moss. The lower ridges are rich in slash pine, live oak, dune goldenrod, morning-glory and sea lavender. Black mangrove and marsh grasses thrive in the rich bayside estuaries. Just be prepared: There are no public facilities.

Best of all, Dog Island provides lodging in its comfortable eight-unit **Pelican Inn**, one of Florida's most hidden hostelries. These are studios featuring decks, balconies and full kitchens. You must bring all your food by boat or charter ferry (which the inn will help you arrange), but the rewards are beachfront accommodations in fully equipped efficiency apartments with not even a streetlight to mar your enjoyment of the pristine environment. Daytrippers may come by their own boats or check dockside in Carrabelle for a varying schedule of ferry services provided by local skippers. ~ 904-653-8848, 800-451-5294. ULTRA-DELUXE.

More accessible and more populated is **St. George Island**, a 25-mile-long narrow strip of land, much of which is being rapidly developed. It is reached by the St. George Island Bridge and Causeway, off Route 98 at Eastpoint. Seven glorious miles of undeveloped beaches and dunes, pine and oak forests, bayshore and sandy coves and salt-marshes have been set aside in the beautiful 1883-acre **Dr. Julian G. Bruce St. George Island State Park**. A 2.5-mile hiking trail, beginning at the campground, leads through pine flatwoods and coastal scrub to Gap Point beside the rich bay waters. Amenities include observation decks, picnic areas and restrooms. Swimming off the glistening white beach is excellent. Surf and bay fishing can result in catches of redfish, ladyfish, Spanish mackerel, bluefish or pompano. Day-use fee, $3.25. Camping is allowed at 60 sites with RV hookups; $13 to $15 per night. ~ 904-927-2111.

St. George's most interesting lodging is the **St. George Inn**. All eight rooms on the second floor feature cannonball beds, as well as French doors leading onto the broad wraparound veranda. Antebellum in style and appearance, this inn has both restaurant and lounge. ~ Franklin Boulevard and Pine Street; 904-927-2903. MODERATE.

Little St. George, an appendage to the main island but now separated by a manmade channel, lies to the west. Site of a 78-foot historic lighthouse, Little St. George is now a state reserve and can only be reached by boat. ~ 904-653-8063.

Covering the entire 12,358 acres of a triangular-shaped island, **St. Vincent National Wildlife Refuge** is also accessible only by boat, for day use only. St. Vincent is unlike most barriers. Four miles wide at one point, it has 14 miles of beaches and 80 miles of crisscrossing sand roads and features several freshwater lakes and swamps. More than 200 species of birds have been spotted; loggerhead turtles lay eggs on the beaches; bald eagles nest in the pines; alligators bask in the sun. Sambur deer and feral hogs recall the times when the island was a private hunting estate. ~ 904-653-8808.

An outdoor kiosk at the end of Route 30-B provides information about St. Vincent Island. The refuge hosts an open house each October; otherwise you must get there on your own. If you do, your reward will be a rich experience of a varied natural Florida.

SHOPPING

The best shopping in the area is in Apalachicola, where local merchants still provide the personal attention so often missing in sprawling malls. Across from the Gibson Inn, the **Pied Piper Boutique** offers up-to-date women's styles. ~ 49 Market Street, Apalachicola; 904-653-8196.

Kristin Anderson sells her fine gold, silver and enamel "Kristinworks" jewelry at the **Long Dream Gallery**. The shop also features pottery, textiles, glass and wood items created by top-notch craftspeople. ~ 32 Avenue D, Apalachicola; 904-653-2249.

NIGHTLIFE

Except at occasional local lounges and roadside joints, nighttime is best for sleeping in this area. In Apalachicola local folks gather to drink at **The Hut** restaurant. ~ Route 98, west of town; 904-653-9410. Or for a quiet cocktail you can sit at the antique bar or out on the porch of the **Gibson Inn**. ~ 51 Market Street, Apalachicola; 904-653-2191.

BEACHES & PARKS

DEAD LAKES STATE RECREATION AREA The thousands of dead trees still standing in the lake (formed when levees on the Apalachicola River blocked the Chipola River) give this 83-acre park its name. Two ponds, lake access, marshes and an abundance of longleaf pines make this an interesting spot for campers, nature lovers and anglers (common catches are bass, bream, perch and catfish). Facilities here include picnic area, restrooms, showers and nature trails. Day-use fee, $2. ~ Located north of Wewahitchka along Route 71; 904-639-2702.

▲ There are 20 sites, ten with RV hookups, electricity and water; $8 to $10 per night.

ST. JOSEPH PENINSULA STATE PARK Strung out on a long, pencil-shaped peninsula, this 2516-acre park provides gifts of the sea and shore usually reserved for barrier islands. With the Gulf on one side and Saint Joseph Bay on the other, the seemingly endless stretches of white beach and high dunes and the rich waters attract over 200 species of migratory and nesting birds. Scallops, octopi, crabs and flounder reside in the bay, small mammals in the marshes and dense woods. A 1650-acre wilderness preserve enhances the natural attractions offered by this beautiful park. There are miles and miles of beach for swimming. You can also go crabbing, scalloping in the bay and fishing in the Gulf and the bay. You'll find picnic areas, restrooms, nature trails, a marina and a bathhouse here. Day-use fee, $3.25. ~ Located off Route C-30, west of Route 98 near Port St. Joe; 904-227-1327.

▲ There are 119 sites, all with hookups, water and some electricity; $15 to $18 per night. Also available are moderately priced cabins that can sleep up to seven people.

The white, sugary beaches, clear green, blue and ▼▼▼▼▼▼▼▼▼▼▼▼▼
turquoise Gulf water and the rather glitzy Coney **Panama City Area**
Island–style attractions seem to keep the crowds of
visitors to Panama City Beach occupied. However, there are a few
other things to see and do should it rain, or if you've had too much
sun. Stop in at the **Convention and Visitors Bureau** for suggestions.
~ 12015 Front Beach Road, Panama City Beach; 904-234-6575.

Visit the **Junior Museum of Bay County** and learn how Florida pio-   **SIGHTS**
neers lived and worked. Stroll the nature trail or explore the log
houses and the grist mill. A special room highlights hands-on activities relating to the current main exhibit. Closed Sunday. ~ 1731
Jenks Avenue, Panama City; 904-769-6128.

You'll have plenty to enjoy along Panama City Beach's Gulf-
front road, which leads past neon motels, towering condominiums,
beautiful beaches and a string of amusement park rides. Dragons
and monsters and rattling rollercoasters lure crowds to the **Miracle
Strip Amusement Park**. Admission. ~ 12000 Front Beach Road;
904-234-9873. Bumper boats, go-carts and video arcades draw
them to **Fun City**. ~ 13626 Front Beach Road; 904-234-5507.

You can observe dolphins, bait some crab traps and watch a
shrimp net being reeled in aboard the **Glass Bottom Boat**. The
company also offers shelling tours to prime spots on Shell Island.
~ 3605 Thomas Drive at the Treasure Island Marina, Panama City
Beach; 904-234-8944.

You can discover a lot about the creatures of the sea at **Gulf-
world** as you watch stingrays and performing dolphins. There are
also talking parrots, trained seals and a walk-through shark tank.
Admission. ~ 15412 Front Beach Road, Panama City Beach; 904-
234-5271.

Because the coast itself is the area's main attraction, treat yourself to an tour of **Shell Island**, a pristine state-owned island with   ◄ *HIDDEN*
seven miles of undeveloped beach and pine land. Sightseeing trips
from Panama City Beach are offered by **Lady Anderson Cruises**. ~
5550 North Lagoon Drive, Panama City Beach; 904-234-3435.

◆◆

UNDER-THE-SEA TREASURES

Stop by the **Museum of Man in the Sea**, a small but impressive undersea
museum. You'll see 19th-century underwater equipment and sea-lab
chambers used in modern oceanographic exploration, as well as
treasures from Spanish shipwrecks and an informative display on
underwater oil drilling. Admission. ~ 17314 Panama City Beach
Parkway, Panama City Beach; 904-235-4101.

For an entirely different outlook on the coast, **Coastal Helicopters** will take you up for a glorious view of the white beaches and islands. ~ 12204 Front Beach Road, Panama City Beach; 904-769-6117.

LODGING   With over 16,000 rooms to choose from in the Panama City area, from massive highrises to modest motels, decision-making can be a bit tough.

Some of the best lodging buys are found near downtown Panama City, seven or more miles from the beach. For example, at the **Best Western Bayside Inn** you'll find spacious rooms with blue-and-white appointments appropriate to the coast, some with efficiency kitchens and many with lovely views of the bay. ~ 711 West Beach Drive, Panama City; 904-763-4622, 800-528-1234, fax 904-747-9522. MODERATE.

Marriott's Bay Point Resort shows how $40 million can turn a country club into an exclusive resort. Most visitors stay in the luxurious 350-room pink hotel overlooking St. Andrew's Bay; there are also villas to rent. Everything you need is on the grounds, including numerous restaurants, lounges, shops, pools, tennis courts and two golf courses. The resort's own paddlewheeler will take you and your ice chest across St. Andrews Bay to pristine Shell Island for miles of white sand and crystal-clear water. ~ 4200 Marriott Drive, Panama City; 904-234-3307, 800-874-7105, fax 904-233-1308. ULTRA-DELUXE.

For those who prefer being in the big middle of the Panama City Beach hubbub, the **Bikini Beach Resort** offers bedrooms and suites, some with all-electric, fully equipped kitchens. The decor is ordinary-motel, but the Gulfside rooms have nice balconies overlooking a fabulous beach. ~ 11001 Front Beach Road, Panama City Beach; 904-234-3392, 800-451-5307, fax 904-233-2921. MODERATE TO DELUXE.

For a luxurious escape from the glitz, the **Edgewater Beach Resort** provides guests with all the beauties of Panama City Beach in a classy, protected environment. With property extending from shore to shore, there are both tower and midrise condominiums featuring individually decorated apartments overlooking the turquoise Gulf waters and wide white beach. Intimate golf villas sit closer to the beach. Everything, from the excellent restaurants to golf and tennis and swimming pools, is reserved for the guests. ~ 11212 Front Beach Road, Panama City Beach; 904-235-4044, 800-874-8686, fax 904-233-7577. DELUXE TO ULTRA-DELUXE.

If you like being where the action is, you'll appreciate the easy walk to shops, amusements, restaurants and fishing pier from the five-story **Osprey Motel**. Though this popular beach area can get pretty crowded, you can escape to your private balcony and a spacious room, tastefully decorated and featuring a fully equipped kitchen. The rates, as well as a pool and hot tub, make it attractive to families. ~ 15801 Front Beach Road, Panama City Beach; 904-234-0303, 800-338-2659, fax 904-234-0303 ext. 700. MODERATE.

Comfortably removed from Panama City Beach's main hullabaloo, the **Sugar Sands Resort** offers a variety of accommodations from single rooms to various-sized apartments. Best of all, the beautiful white beach is reasonably uncluttered, and the rates for modest well-kept rooms are modest. ~ 20723 Front Beach Road, Panama City Beach; 904-234-8802. MODERATE.

DINING

It's said that people drive a hundred miles to eat amid the lush flora of **The Greenhouse**, an intimate Continental café in downtown Panama City. If you try the Tuna Markel, charbroiled yellowfin tuna topped with orange pesto beurre blanc on a bed of angel hair pasta, you'll see why. Closed Sunday. ~ 450 Harrison Avenue, Panama City; 904-784-9880. MODERATE TO DELUXE.

The sign is fading but the aroma wafting out the door summons you through the leaded glass doors of **The Pasta Peddler**, an unadorned downtown café in Panama City right next to the Greenhouse and owned by the same people. In fact, the place smells so good that the lack of distinctive decor matters not. The homemade minestrone contains 15 vegetables; the broiled Italian sausage with green peppers and onions is a tasty addition to the selection of traditional seafood, veal and chicken dishes. Only dinner is served on Sunday. ~ 448 Harrison Avenue, Panama City; 904-763-0059. MODERATE.

The very popular **Harbour House** offers a pretty view of St. Andrews Bay, a few blocks from downtown Panama City. This family-style airy restaurant has a seafood and beef menu, but folks come from all around for the budget lunch buffet, which offers 40 or more of the restaurant's specialties. Friday and Saturday are host to a prime rib and seafood dinner buffet, and expect a breakfast buffet on Sunday. Breakfast is served as well. ~ 3001-A West 10th Street, Panama City; 904-785-9053. MODERATE.

Marriott's Bay Point Resort is home to several excellent restaurants. For a dining experience rare since the passing of Florida's grand old hotels, get dressed up, stroll through the posh main lobby and spend a couple of gourmet hours in the hushed elegance of **Fiddler's Green**, whose high windows overlook the grounds and lagoon. At the casual **Teddy Tucker's** you'll be served sandwiches, burgers and salad out on the dock. The moderately priced **Dockers** offers traditional but excellent seafood, pizza and pasta; you can watch the yachts slip in and out of the marina as you dine. ~ 4200 Marriott Drive, Panama City; 904-234-3307. MODERATE TO ULTRA-DELUXE.

As you would expect, seafood tops the list of restaurant offerings in Panama City Beach. **Captain Anderson's** serves it up by the ton (the restaurant seats 600) quite successfully. Greek salads and homemade breads and desserts set this popular place apart from many of the seafood-platter establishments; so do the varied grilled fish and steak entrées. Dinner only. Closed Sunday. ~ 5551 North Lagoon Drive, Panama City Beach; 904-234-2225. MODERATE TO ULTRA-DELUXE.

Despite the medieval armor and the noble prices, the **Boar's Head Restaurant** is a casual, rustic, big-barn of a place for a leisurely, luxurious meal. The house specialty is prime rib, but they also chargrill and blacken fish and do lots of interesting things with shrimp and lobster. There's also an impressive wine list. Dinner only. ~ 17290 Front Beach Road, Panama City Beach; 904-234-6628. MODERATE TO DELUXE.

SHOPPING   If teenagers can't find a seaside souvenir or a bathing suit in the Panama City area, they might as well give up. Dozens of stores that seem to be designed just for them are bulging with air-brushed T-shirts, sunglasses, crazy hats, beach toys and disappearing bikinis.

You'll find a variety of bargains from name-brand companies at the **Manufacturer's Outlet Center**, where over a dozen stores feature clothing, shoes and stylish accessories. ~ 105 West 23rd Street, Panama City.

Anglophiles can have a great time among the china, tinned biscuits, teas, jams and English toys at **British Quality Imports**. This wholesale outlet is open one day a week for retail shopping. ~ 304 Harrison Avenue, Panama City; 904-763-9781.

Essentially a store for teachers, **The Learning Shoppe** has a wonderful selection of educational toys and games for children of all ages. ~ 500 Harrison Avenue, Panama City; 904-769-8738.

The **Promenade Mall** is a festive specialty mall with pine siding and a red roof. ~ 8317 Front Beach Road, Panama City Beach.

NIGHTLIFE   Much of the area's nightlife rocks during the summer months and hibernates in the winter. But you can find some things to do year-round.

The Rader family's Nashville-imitation **Ocean Opry Theater** keeps drawing crowds to its big auditorium for country music and comedy. They sing, they dance, they make you part of the family, and audiences love it. Cover. ~ 8400 Front Beach Road, Panama City Beach; 904-234-5464.

Sunset cruises are a good way to spend a balmy evening in these parts. You can go on a dinner-and-dancing or gospel-music cruise with **Lady Anderson**. ~ 5550 North Lagoon Drive, Panama City Beach; 904-234-5940.

With decks over the beach and plenty of tropical drinks, **Pine-apple Willies** has a Caribbean feel. Look forward to reggae bands in the spring and jazz bands during the summer. Cover occasionally. ~ 9900 Beach Boulevard, Panama City Beach; 904-235-0928.

With 23 bars, six levels (three inside) and perpetual day-and-night crowds, **Spinnaker** is one hot sand spot. Regular live bands include national artists like Three Dog Night, Cheap Trick and The Byrds. Cover. ~ 8795 Thomas Drive, Panama City Beach; 904-234-7882.

ST. ANDREWS STATE PARK 🏃 ⛵ 🎣 🛶 🚣
Its proximity to Panama City and its beautiful 1063 acres of beaches, dunes, pine woods and marshes account for this being one of Florida's most popular recreation areas. It is bounded by the Gulf of Mexico, the Grand Lagoon and the ship channel so just about every water sport is available. The sand is like snow, the water clear as glass, the dunes rolling and covered with sea oats. A reconstructed cracker turpentine still can be found in the park. There is one fishing pier and a jetty that provide excellent year-round fishing for Spanish mackerel, redfish, flounder and more. Swimming is excellent in both the clear Gulf waters and the shallow pool behind the jetty. Other facilities include picnic areas, restrooms, bathhouses, snack and grocery concessions, nature trails and canoe rentals. Day-use fee, $4. ~ Take Route 392 (Thomas Drive) off Route 98, east of Panama City, to the park entrance; 904-233-5140

▲ There are 176 sites, all with RV hookups; $18 to $20 per night.

BEACHES & PARKS

SHELL ISLAND This "adjunct" to St. Andrews State Recreation Area can be reached only by boat. There are no facilities, but there are seven miles of beach and wilderness, a pristine oasis where Panama City's condo skyline is almost out of sight and certainly out of mind. A number of charter boats will ferry you over from the mainland for a fee, which is well worth it, especially if you take along a cooler and an umbrella and spend the day. ~ Information on shuttle boats available at St. Andrews State Park (904-233-5140) or local private boat tour companies.

◄ *HIDDEN*

▼▼▼▼▼▼▼▼▼▼▼▼▼▼▼▼
Fort Walton Beach Area

Looking for a spot where alligators roam and traffic isn't crowding you all day? Then you've come to the right place. The Fort Walton Beach area is graced by beautiful salt marshes and miles of rolling dunes not yet leveled by overdevelopment. Wide expanses of deep turquoise water and sugary sand invite serendipitous strolls.

You'll find the alligators in rivers and streams that empty into Choctawhatchee Bay. This rich jungle wilderness, shaded by majestic magnolia trees, also attracts birds and an abundance of other wildlife.

SIGHTS

Long ago, steamers plied the bay's beautiful waters, carrying the cypress, pine and oak exploited from inland forests. Once the site of a giant lumber company, **Eden State Gardens** still exhibits the remains of long ship-loading piers stretching into Choctawhatchee Bay. The main attraction, though, is a handsome two-story restored lumber baron's house, built in 1896 to look like an antebellum mansion and now filled with fine antiques. Broad landscaped lawns, shaded by moss-draped oaks, blaze with camellias and azaleas in the spring and winter. Closed Tuesday and Wednesday. Admission to the house. ~ North of Route 98 or Route 395, Point Washington; 904-231-4214.

HIDDEN ►

There is a small, homegrown **Heritage Museum** in the little town of Valparaiso, which has a number of artifacts and a reference library focusing on local and Florida history. You can learn how the Florida pioneers lived before the coming of the condos, and how the American Indians lived in this historically rich region centuries before the pioneers came. Closed Sunday and Monday. ~ 115 Westview Avenue, Valparaiso; 904-678-2615.

The chief attractions in Destin and Fort Walton Beach will always be the sand and the sea. For pointers on other sightseeing destinations, check with the **Destin Chamber of Commerce**. ~ 1021 Highway 98 East, 904-837-6241. You may also try the **Fort Walton Beach Chamber of Commerce**. ~ 34 Miracle Strip Parkway; 904-244-8191.

The Air Force Armament Museum presents seven decades of history in displays of aircraft, missiles and guns. ~ 100 Museum Drive, Eglin Air Force Base, Fort Walton Beach; 904-882-4062.

People who enjoy fishing the Gulf will like the interesting **Destin Fishing Museum** which presents video programs and includes game-fish mounts, antique fishing equipment and old photos of the area's important fishing industry. Closed Sunday. Admission. ~ 20009 Emerald Coast Parkway, Destin; 904-654-1011.

For dolphin and sea lion shows and an underwater zoo, you might consider the **Gulfarium**. The Living Sea exhibit features sharks, moray eels, sea turtles and other exotic creatures in natural habitats. There's also a penguin exhibit. Admission. ~ 1010 Miracle Strip Parkway Southeast, Fort Walton Beach; 904-244-5169.

The **Indian Temple Mound Museum** explains the story of the Fort Walton area from the days of prehistoric peoples. Artifacts of the southeastern American Indians and a series of exhibits appeal to all ages. The actual mound beside the small but excellent exhibit area is a National Historic Landmark. Closed Sunday. Admission. ~ 139 Miracle Strip Parkway, Fort Walton Beach; 904-243-6521.

Children and nostalgic adults will enjoy the restored one-room **Camp Walton School House Museum**, which recall the days of spelling primers and hickory sticks. A pine-needle path leads to a restored old post office, with letters and magazines still waiting to be picked up from rustic wooden mailboxes. The museum requires reservations for tours. Open Tuesday and Thursday in the summer. Admission. ~ 107 1st Street, Fort Walton Beach; 904-244-3433.

◀ *HIDDEN*

There is much to choose from in the way of lodging in the Fort Walton Beach area, from simple beach cottages to elegant resort townhouses and condominiums. For detailed information on lodging in the quiet beach communities that lie along Route 30-A from Inlet Beach to Dune Allen as well as the more developed beaches from Four Mile Village to Frangista Beach, write the **South Walton Tourist Development Council.** ~ P.O. Box 1248, Santa Rosa Beach, FL 32459; 800-822-6877.

LODGING

For a grand experience of nostalgia wrapped in newness, rent a pastel pretend-Victorian cottage at **Seaside**, a resort community built as an experiment in urban design and modeled on the old-fashioned East Coast resorts. You'll find it just west of Seagrove Beach. The frame houses are individually furnished and designed to a strict picket-fence-and-gingerbread code. Tennis courts, beach pavilions, pool, restaurants and shops are on-site. ~ Route 30-A, Seaside; 904-231-4224, 800-277-8696. ULTRA-DELUXE.

Destin claims to have more luxury condominiums than motel rooms, giving you plenty to choose from. Several large resorts offer golf, tennis and swimming pools as well as miles of beach, luxurious accommodations and the usual resort amenities. Chief among these is **Sandestin Beach Resort.** ~ 9300 Highway 98 West, ten miles east of Destin; 904-267-8000, 800-277-0800, fax 904-267-8222. A mile and a half farther west is **Seascape Resort.** ~ Highway 98 West; 904-837-9181, 800-874-9106, fax 904-837-4769. DELUXE TO ULTRA-DELUXE.

Four nine-hole golf courses, 21 tennis courts, two pools and a huge marina make **Bluewater Bay** the ideal resort for anyone who doesn't need the beach. Located across broad Choctawhatchee Bay from Destin, Bluewater offers beautifully appointed townhomes, suites, studios, hotel-style rooms and patio homes among the oak groves that set this place apart from so many sun-baked lodgings. A restaurant and shops are available on the property. ~ 1950 Bluewater Boulevard, Niceville; 904-897-3613, 800-874-2128, fax 904-897-2424. DELUXE TO ULTRA-DELUXE.

For lodgings right on the beach, try the 38-unit **Sea Oats Motel** The carpets in these plain rooms have a few stains but are very clean, and all front the beach. Kitchenettes and picnic tables make this a good place for families. ~ Scenic Route 98, Destin; 904-837-6655, 888-732-6287. DELUXE.

Fort Walton Beach offers a number of the usual motels, but there is luxury to be found here, too. **The Breakers of Fort Walton Beach** has luxurious, fully furnished beachfront condominiums. Along with a beautiful beach, the seven-story complex offers tennis courts, a grocery store and other amenities for convenience and contentment. ~ 381 Santa Rosa Boulevard; 904-244-9127, 800-395-4853, fax 904-244-4277. ULTRA-DELUXE.

Leeside Inn is across a busy highway from a nice beach park and next to a tiny piece of National Seashore land on the bay. The traffic is a drawback if you are trying to get to the beach, but you won't find a nicer room at this price, and the bayside rooms are amazingly quiet. Kitchenettes available. ~ 1350 Highway 98 East, Okaloosa Island, Fort Walton Beach; 904-243-7359, 800-824-2747. MODERATE.

DINING

Word has it that **Nick's** changes hands among family members every seven years, but the happy clientele of this rowdy and fun concrete block oyster house remains consistent. The drawing card is terrific fried, steamed and grilled seafood. Closed Monday. ~ Route 1, Basin Bayou, Freeport; 904-835-2222. MODERATE.

At the avant-garde community of Seaside, you can dine at nationally prominent **Bud & Alley's** on local seafood, pasta dishes, steaks and hearty soups. Their dinners include such tempting fare as sautéed shrimp with fresh rosemary, roasted garlic and tomatoes and wood-grilled beef stuffed with fried oysters and topped with béarnaise sauce. The setting is upscale and airy—very Seaside. Closed Tuesday. ~ Route 30-A, Seaside; 904-231-5900. DELUXE.

HIDDEN ▶

Unless you are staying in Grayton Beach, you might miss the **Grayton Corner Café**, a casual old beach house facing the dunes. A sign warns that if the surf is good the chef may close early; otherwise he'll serve you grilled marinated seafood, a great shrimp salad or the nightly seafood/duck/quail/beef special. Closed Monday. ~ Route 283 off Route 30-A, Grayton Beach; 904-231-1211. BUDGET TO MODERATE.

Bayou Bill's makes up for its nonbeach location by serving terrific seafood in a spirited nautical setting. Crowds wait cheerfully for the assortment of platters, blackened fish, steamed buckets and rib and steak entrées. Dinner only. ~ Route 98 East, Santa Rosa Beach; 904-267-3849. MODERATE.

For fine dining in Destin, try the **Flamingo Café**. The decor is very tropical, with teal, white and warm Caribbean colors. The menu features specially prepared seafood dishes such as roast garlic–rubbed Gulf snapper with sweet potato hay and cheese grits. Or try the angel hair pasta topped with lemon-seared jumbo shrimp or the oysters Bienville (with fresh bay shrimp). Dinner only. ~ 414 Route 98 East, Destin; 904-837-0961. DELUXE.

Enjoy the spectacular view of the Destin harbor and seafood prepared in a Continental manner with a touch of Louisiana, at the casually elegant **Marina Café**. The menu includes gourmet pizza, chicken, lamb and veal dishes along with local shellfish dishes. Dinner only. ~ 404 Route 98 West, Destin; 904-837-7960. DELUXE TO ULTRA-DELUXE.

Several decades ago, circus entertainer Harrison Thomas Babe took a bad fall during a show. He scooped up the insurance money, moved to Destin and opened **Harry T's Boathouse**. Harry Babe died in 1974, but this zany place is a testament to his crazy escapades. There's a stuffed giraffe's head dead center as you walk in, plus a great collection of circus memorabilia parked all over the walls. Tucked inside a yacht club, the popular eatery features a waterfront patio and 85 dishes, including chicken, fish, blackened steaks and pasta. ~ 320 Route 98 East, Destin; 904-654-4800. MODERATE.

The Backporch is so popular with travelers that it sells its own T-shirts. The small menu features broiled, baked, steamed, chargrilled and fried seafood served in baskets and a nice smoked yellowfin tuna dip. You can eat on butcher-block tables inside or at picnic tables on a deck right by the beach. ~ Route 98 East, Destin; 904-837-2022. MODERATE.

Scampi's is a three-ring-circus sort of place with a huge buffet, perfect for a family or a seafood-lover who can't make up his mind. The pretend pilings, nets and ropes may seem a bit hokey, but hungry diners flock to this big, noisy place. Dinner only. ~ Route 98 East, Destin; 904-837-7686. MODERATE.

SHOPPING

There are shopping malls and strip centers in Fort Walton and Destin, as well as souvenir and shell shops in the more populated beach areas.

The most colorful shopping experience awaits visitors to **The Market at Sandestin**, a very trendy festival mall with lots of neon and color and many upscale shops. It's hard to pass by **Classic Cargo** (904-837-8171) without stopping to gaze in the gleaming windows at the classic collections of crystal, silver and porcelain figures and gifts. ~ 9375 Route 98 West, Destin.

Modica Market is lined to its high ceilings with shelves of gourmet groceries, a deli and a produce stand. One of Seaside's hubs, the market also has a small eat-in deli for the sandwiches, salads and desserts the market sells. ~ Route 30-A, Seaside. ~ 904-231-1214.

Sundog Books offers a small selection of the requisite trashy beach reading, but its main stock consists of top-notch fiction and nonfiction and a good supply of wonderful children's books. ~ Route 30-A, Seaside; 904-231-5481.

Modeled on a Mediterranean open-air market, colorful **Per-spi-cas-ity** has a wonderful assortment of trendy casual clothes and gift and household items. Shop under canvas awnings to the accompaniment of classical music and sea breezes. ~ Route 30-A, Seaside; 904-231-5829.

A seafarer's delight, **Armchair Sailor** stocks books on shipwrecks and pirates, sailing instruction and naval history. Navigational charts and instruments as well as nature guides are also featured at this nautical gold mine. ~ 546 Route 98, Destin; 904-837-1577.

If beachwear and seaside souvenirs are something you can't resist, you'll love **Alvin's Island**. Air-brushed T-shirts, shells that never saw a Florida beach, postcards for your friends and enemies back home—they're all at Alvin's. ~ 1204 Route 98 West, Okaloosa Island, 904-244-3913; and 1073 Route 98 West, Destin, 904-837-5178.

NIGHTLIFE The area swings, rocks or snoozes at night, depending on the season and the crowd. Some of the most popular year-round nightlife goes on at restaurants. **Bud & Alley's** at Seaside features live jazz and blues bands on summer weekends. There are outdoor movies and a variety of other entertainment at Seaside, too. ~ Route 30-A; 904-231-5900.

At **Harry T's Boathouse**, overlooking the harbor, you can dance to a contemporary jazz-rock band on Wednesday, Friday and Saturday or stroll along the docks. Thursday is disco night. Lots of glass and many levels make this a delightful place. ~ Destin Yacht Club, Route 98 East, Destin; 904-654-4800.

Yesterday's Rock 'n' Roll Cafe has a big dancefloor and a 1957 T-bird and a 1955 Chevy out front to let you know that nostalgia is featured here. Come enjoy the occasional Elvis and Neil Diamond impersonations and a '50s- and '60s-era house band. ~ 1079 Route 98 East, Destin; 904-837-1954.

Nightown, bright with laser lights, rocks with a deejay and dancing. There's also a rock-and-roll bar to shoot pool in. For a respite from the frenetic pace, you can escape to Nightown's second bar for a New Orleans–style mood and quieter music. Cover. ~ Palmetto Street and Azalea Drive, Destin; 904-837-6448.

At **A. J.'s** you can kick back under a giant tiki hut overlooking the bay. With live reggae or Caribbean vibes as a backdrop, who could ask for more? ~ 116 Destin Highway East, Destin; 904-837-1913.

Timbers Nitespot is festooned with motion picture posters. Drop by early for a drink by candlelight, or late for dancing to live Top-40 and rock Wednesday through Saturday. Cover. ~ 1220 Siebert Street, Fort Walton Beach; 904-243-5400.

"Hog's breath is better than no breath at all" is the slogan of **Hog's Breath Saloon,** a wild and outrageously fun bar. Acoustic and rock bands play Tuesday through Saturday in this ramshackle building. ~ 1239 Siebert Street, Fort Walton Beach; 904-243-4646.

Mellow out at **Fudpuckers on the Island,** a casual restaurant/ bar with outdoor patios and live reggae, rock-and-roll or acoustic music. ~ 108 Santa Rosa Boulevard, Fort Walton Beach; 904-243-3833.

BEACHES & PARKS

Drive the coastal roads through south Walton County toward Destin and Fort Walton, and you'll discover many miles of almost pristine coastline. Only an occasional highrise mars the vista. If you peel off Route 98 wherever you can, you will come to little pull-off roads where local folks park for a day at the beach. From Inlet Beach to Dune Allen there are blufflike dunes overlooking the snow-white beaches and the turquoise Gulf.

GRAYTON BEACH STATE RECREATION AREA

A sensational broad white beach and high dunes give this 400-acre park the reputation of being one of the loveliest on the state's coast. Boardwalks carry visitors across the ever-changing dunes and among the vital sand-holding sea oats. Besides the perfect swimming beach and clear blue-green water, the park offers easy access to a brackish lake abundant in both freshwater and saltwater creatures, an extensive salt marsh, remnants of a pine forest and shady live-oak and palmetto hammocks. There's fishing in both the surf and the lake. Facilities include picnic areas, restrooms, nature trails and vending machines. Day-use fee, $3.25. ~ Just west of Seaside on Route 30-A; 904-231-4210.

▲ There are 37 sites, all with RV hookups; $14 to $16 per night.

HENDERSON BEACH STATE RECREATION AREA

Though there are no dunes here, this beautiful public beach has snow-white sand and crystal-clear water. The swimming is excellent and there's good surf fishing. The beach is close enough to populated areas and the busy highway to guarantee wall-to-wall sunbathers during the summer months. In addition to a boardwalk and picnic areas, there are restrooms and showers. Day-use fee, $2. ~ East of Destin on Route 98; 904-837-7550.

FRED GANNON ROCKY BAYOU STATE RECREATION AREA

This park reveals why not everyone in the Panhandle goes to the beach. Located on a gentle bayou off sprawling Choctawhatchee Bay, the restful park provides walks among the pines, oaks and magnolias, as well as access to excellent freshwater and saltwater fishing and crabbing. You can also swim here but it's not as great as the beaches across the bay. The beautiful picnic area affords fine views of the broad bay. Other facilities include restrooms and nature trails. Day-use fee, $2. ~ Located five miles east of Niceville on Highway 20 East; 904-833-9144.

▲ There are 42 sites, some with RV hookups; $8 to $10 per night.

▼▼▼▼▼▼▼▼▼▼
Pensacola Area Almost in Alabama, the Pensacola Area has just about everything you'd expect to find in Florida: alligators and historic districts, old lighthouses and Latino landmarks, memorable seafood restaurants and excellent fishing tackle shops. Come for the Dixieland scene and the Gulf islands. Stay to enjoy the Naval Aviation Museum and the national seashore. This area is one sleeper that will keep you wide awake.

SIGHTS The loveliest approach to the Pensacola area is via Route 399, along the sugar-white beaches of **Gulf Islands National Seashore** (see "Beaches & Parks" section below). There are many places to cross the dunes on boardwalks or paths to enjoy the pristine beach.

West of the community of Pensacola Beach, with its water slides and amusement parks, the National Seashore extends for ten more miles. At the western tip of the island stands **Fort Pickens**, a beautiful 19th-century fortification built by slaves and incorporating over 21 million bricks. Geronimo was held prisoner here in the 1880s. The fort's museum features nature exhibits on marine and terrestrial life. Admission. ~ Fort Pickens Road; 904-934-2621.

About ten miles east of Gulf Breeze on Route 98 lies **The Zoo**, the *only* accredited zoo in the Panhandle. You'll find over 500 animals, a petting zoo for children and a small botanical garden on the zoo's 20 acres. A train takes you through another 30 acres that are inhabited by free-roaming animals. Admission. ~ 5701 Gulf Breeze Parkway; 904-932-2229.

Two miles east of Gulf Breeze, stop at the **Naval Live Oaks Visitors Center** and stroll through a large stand of live-oak trees, the site where President John Quincy Adams inaugurated the first federal timber conservation program. There are exhibits on shipbuilding and information about the National Seashore. ~ 1801 Gulf Breeze Parkway; 904-934-2600.

Stop at the **Pensacola Area Convention & Visitors Center** for helpful brochures, including a self-guided tour of the historic area and downtown Pensacola. ~ 1401 East Gregory Street, Pensacola; 904-434-1234.

Nearby **Seville Historic District**, bounded by Bayfront Parkway, Tarragona, Romana and Cevallos streets, recalls the city's first century of European settlement. Within the district is the **Historic Pensacola Village**, an area brimming with charm, delightful architecture and mementos of days gone by. ~ Bounded by Alcaniz, Government, Jefferson and Zaragoza streets.

Stop first at the Tivoli House and sign up for the village tour led by costumed docents. Admission. ~ Zaragoza and Tarragona streets; 904-444-8905.

Along the way you'll spot such gems as a colonial well, a weavers' cottage, the French creole Barkley House, the Julee Cottage, a black history museum, the furnished Victorian Dorr House, the Colonial Archaeological Trail and the Museum of Industry and Commerce.

Also in the district is the **Pensacola Historical Museum**. The museum is filled with exhibits depicting the area's history from the days of the American Indians to the arrival of the first white settlers in the 1500s up through the Victorian era. Admission. ~ 904-433-1559.

St. Michael's Cemetery contains interesting graves dating from the early 19th century, including a replica of Napoleon's tomb. ~ Alcaniz and Garden streets.

Also here is the **T. T. Wentworth, Jr. Florida State Museum**, housed in the 1908 Pensacola City Hall. Inside these ruddy brick and clay walls are captivating exhibits—a funky Coca-Cola collection and over 100,000 of Wentworth's artifacts, including a bizarre petrified cat and a shrunken head. Kids will love the third-floor discovery room filled with replicas of buildings found in a modern city, including a school and radio and television stations. Open on Sunday in the summer. Admission. ~ 330 South Jefferson Street, Pensacola; 904-444-8586.

> If explorer Tristan de Luna's 1559 colony hadn't been battered by hurricane and hardship, Pensacola might have survived to beat out St. Augustine as the state's oldest permanent settlement.

To learn more about the area's history and culture, stop by the **Historic Resource Center**. It's a library and archive covering Pensacola and northwest Florida. ~ 117 East Government Street, Pensacola; 904-434-5455.

Up Palafox Street, beginning at Belmont Street and continuing for over a dozen blocks, lies the **North Hill Preservation District**, a residential area filled with elegant homes reflecting the lumbering industry's turn-of-the-century heyday. Though none of the homes is open for public tours, the handiwork of gifted artisans and the wealth of the lumber barons make this an interesting area for driving or walking.

Downtown Pensacola is worth a turn, too, if only to admire the lovely wrought-iron work and balconies on the old store fronts in the **Palafox Historic Business District** along Palafox Street. If you'd like to see the catch of the day, turn off Main Street on B and C streets to the **fish markets**. The variety of seafood can be quite amazing.

The folks at the **Wildlife Sanctuary** will introduce you to pelicans, alligators, raccoons, owls and other wildlife. Closed Sunday through Tuesday. ~ 105 North S Street, Pensacola; 904-433-9453.

In a building that once served as the old city jail, you can view one of the many changing exhibits at the **Pensacola Museum of Art**. Closed Monday. Admission. ~ 407 South Jefferson Street, Pensacola; 904-432-6247.

As you cross over the Pensacola Bay Bridge toward downtown Pensacola, you can admire the three-mile fishing bridge that runs alongside. It's said to be the world's longest fishing pier.

To the southwest of downtown lies the vast **Naval Air Station**, home of the famous flying Blue Angels and the wonderful **National Museum of Naval Aviation**. From the first flying boat to cross the Atlantic to the Skylab command module and the newest fighter jets, this grand indoor/outdoor museum has exhibits that appeal to all ages. ~ 1750 Radford Boulevard; 904-452-3604.

A small piece of the Gulf National Seashore resides in the middle of the station and includes 65 acres of forest and historic **Fort Barrancas**, across the bay from Fort Pickens. Drive past the **Old Pensacola Lighthouse**, which has been on duty since 1825, and Sherman Field, where the precision-flying Blue Angels take off. ~ On Radford Boulevard; 904-455-5167.

LODGING

If a condo is your preference, **Navarre Towers Condominium** has 47 nicely furnished two- and three-bedroom highrise units for rent overlooking the beach at Navarre. When you get tired of swimming in the Gulf, there's a pool and tennis courts. ~ 8271 Gulf Boulevard, Pensacola Beach; 904-939-2011, 800-628-2773, fax 904-939-3880. ULTRA-DELUXE.

The refreshing grey-and-beige decor of **The Dunes** make even the hottest days seem cool at this handsome highrise. Overlooking the white sand and turquoise water, this understated art deco hotel has a café and lounge, outdoor and indoor pools and penthouse suites. ~ 333 Fort Pickens Road, Pensacola Beach; 904-932-3536, 800-833-8637, fax 904-932-5361. DELUXE.

At the **Barbary Coast Motel** you can hear the surf from every room, all paneled in imitation weathered board. The 12 spacious units resemble cottages and include living rooms and full kitchens. ~ 24 Via de Luna, Pensacola Beach; 904-932-2233, fax 904-934-5364. ULTRA-DELUXE.

Located on the sound instead of the Gulf, the plain but pleasant **Gulf Aire Motel** is close enough to the beach to be just fine for bargain hunters. Half of the rooms have kitchens. ~ 21 Via de Luna, Pensacola Beach; 904-932-2319. MODERATE.

Except for the spacious modern rooms, the **Pensacola Grand Hotel**, incorporated into the 1912 L&N train depot, is a tribute to the past. Nostalgia reigns in the classic lobby, through the dining areas and into the ballrooms, where antiques and other period fixtures help to recall the early days of train travel. Views are grand from the higher story rooms above the old station. ~ 200 East

Gregory Street, Pensacola; 904-433-3336, 800-348-3336, fax 904-432-7572. DELUXE.

Built into a block of warehouses near Pensacola's historic waterfront district, the **New World Inn** features 14 rooms and one suite, all named for historic personages of local significance, such as Andrew Jackson and Geronimo. Little history lessons and appropriate decor and furnishings make the inn interesting—each room reflects the nationality of its hero. Intimate architecture provides a secluded and elegant oasis on the edge of a struggling downtown. ~ 600 South Palafox Street, Pensacola; 904-432-4111. MODERATE TO DELUXE.

Moderately priced rooms do exist downtown. The **Park View Inn** provides draperies and bedspreads. The nondescript five-story building counts among its amenities a swimming pool. There are great shops within walking distance. ~ 901 North Main Street, Pensacola; 904-355-3744. MODERATE.

Condos are going up on Perdido Key. For all the amenities from swimming pools to boat docks to tennis courts, try **Sea Spray**, which features two- and three-bedroom highrise and condominium apartments for family groups only. ~ 16287 Perdido Key Drive, Pensacola; 904-492-2200, 800-336-7263, fax 904-492-3225. DELUXE TO ULTRA-DELUXE.

"Eat, Drink & Flounder," advises the motto of Pensacola Beach's **Flounder's Chowder and Ale House**. The menu is full of other such flounder puns, along with a selection of ordinary fare and a wide variety of hickory-grilled seafood. Okay, the place is corny, but it's fun, and the menu, designed by "Fred Flounder, Founder," has been a hit with beach folks for years. ~ 800 Quietwater Beach Road, Pensacola Beach; 904-932-2003. MODERATE.

DINING

Because it prides itself on very fresh, in-season seafood, **Jubilee** changes its menu every week. But it always features interesting combination dishes such as filet of chicken sautéed with crayfish or beef filets with artichoke hearts and crabmeat. A glorious overhead window and a lighted stairway give this casual spot an air of elegance. Lunch is served at the beachside café and dinner is served nightly topside. ~ 400 Quietwater Beach Road, Pensacola Beach; 904-934-3108. MODERATE TO DELUXE.

An adjunct to a fish market in an area near downtown Pensacola known as "Seafood Village," **Patti's Seafood Deli** attracts local folks to its bare-bones store by offering seafood in terrific sandwiches known as "Po-Boys," as well as gumbos, creole and platters. You can find hamburgers and chicken here, along with fish right off the boats. You eat at spotless little tables and watch folks buying the latest catch to take home for dinner. Closed Monday. ~ 610 South C Street, Pensacola; 904-434-3193. BUDGET.

◄ HIDDEN

Restaurant reviewers and diners alike give **Jamie's** continuous raves for the classic French cuisine and the selection of over 100 wines. The setting, in a cream-and-apricot Victorian cottage, is as much a drawing card as the splendid food. No lunch on Monday. Closed Sunday. ~ 424 East Zaragoza Street, Pensacola; 904-434-2911. DELUXE.

Skopelos on the Bay has proven for over three decades that a restaurant doesn't have to be next to the water to serve some of the best seafood possible. They also offer lamb, veal and steak, and add Greek touches to many of their entrées. Lunch served only on Friday. Closed Sunday and Monday. ~ 670 Scenic Highway, Pensacola; 904-432-6565. MODERATE TO DELUXE.

A part of New World Landing, an elegantly adapted warehouse near downtown Pensacola, **New World Restaurant** has several handsome rooms that offer choices of decor. Whether you dine in the brick-walled Barcelona Room with its tall windows or in the Pensacola Room beneath a pressed-tin ceiling and mirrors, you can enjoy an array of Continental entrées like grouper Palafox (fillet of grouper topped with shrimp, crabmeat, mushrooms and artichokes) and New York steak with mushroom and wine sauce. Try the praline à la crème dessert. Closed Sunday and Monday. ~ 600 South Palafox Street, Pensacola; 904-434-7736. MODERATE.

You can eat aboard a non-ocean-going vessel at **The Yacht Restaurant**. At night there is a wide assortment of seafood, veal and chicken dishes and Cajun blackened entrées. ~ Harbour Village Marina at Pitt Slip, Bayfront Parkway, Pensacola; 904-432-3707. MODERATE.

Loosen your cuffs and practice your boardinghouse reach for a meal at the **Hopkins House**, in the North Hill Historic District. You'll share a big table with whoever happens to be there, passing around heaping platters of fried chicken, roast beef, black-eyed peas and other Southern dishes. This popular old house with a wide porch reminds you that family-style can be enjoyable. Breakfast and lunch are cooked up daily, but there's no dinner on the weekend. Closed Monday. ~ 900 North Spring Street, Pensacola; 904-438-3979. BUDGET.

McGuire's Irish Pub is plastered with dollar bills signed by all the people who have delighted in McGuire's steaks, seafood, ale and Irish music. It's hard to know whether the long lines are because of the food or the entertainment, but the atmosphere is exceedingly cheerful and the food excellent. ~ 600 East Gregory Street, Pensacola; 904-433-6789. MODERATE.

SHOPPING   A number of small shops reside in restored cottages and mansions in the **Seville Historic District**. ~ The neighborhood of Zaragoza and Adams streets, Pensacola.

For top-quality paintings, watercolors, pottery and jewelry by local artists, go to the **Quayside Art Gallery**. ~ 15-17 East Zaragoza Street, Pensacola; 904-438-2363.

Handicrafts, antiques, collectibles, fancy coffees and imports are only a sampling of what you'll find Wednesday through Sunday at the **Quayside Thieves Market** in a restored waterfront warehouse. ~ 712 South Palafox Street, Pensacola; 904-433-9930.

As you might expect in a historic city like Pensacola, there is an abundance of antique shops, over 30 at last count. The Visitors Bureau will provide you with an up-to-date list. One all-day prospect, the **9th Avenue Antique Mall** houses 30 shops under one roof. ~ 380 North 9th Avenue, Pensacola; 904-438-3961.

Though Panhandle pecans drop from the trees only in the fall, you can buy them year-round in Pensacola at **J. W. Renfroe Pecan Company**. ~ 2400 West Fairfield Drive, Pensacola; 904-432-2083.

If browsing through dusty old volumes is your meat, go to **Farley's Old & Rare Books, Inc.** ~ 5855 Tippin Avenue, Pensacola; 904-477-8282. For bestsellers as well as neat gifts and T-shirts, try **Hurricane Books**. ~ 366 Gulf Breeze Parkway, Gulf Breeze; 904-932-6254.

The **Harbourtown Shopping Village** is one of those designer-type shopping malls where it's as much fun to window shop as it is to spend money. You stroll indoors in a village-like atmosphere past shops featuring clothing, gifts, jewelry and an assortment of other items. ~ 913 Gulf Breeze Parkway, Gulf Breeze.

For quality souvenirs, books and materials on the history and ecology of the area, try the book and gift shop at the **Fort Pickens Museum**. ~ Fort Pickens Road, Pensacola Beach; 904-934-2621. The **National Museum of Naval Aviation** is another good choice. ~ Naval Air Station, Pensacola; 904-452-3604.

There *are* things to do at night in Pensacola, although the place is considered pretty quiet and sedate, especially for a Navy town. To see what's going on while you are in town, check the "Weekender" section of the Friday *Pensacola News Journal*.

NIGHTLIFE

Flounder's Chowder and Ale House, where you can "eat, drink and flounder" overlooking the sound, has live reggae Thursday through Sunday. ~ 800 Quietwater Beach Road, Pensacola Beach; 904-932-2003.

Jubilee features a band six nights a week in the summer. You can enjoy the relaxing sounds inside or outside on the deck overlooking the water. ~ 400 Quietwater Beach Road, Pensacola Beach; 904-934-3108.

Since the late '60s, **Seville Quarter** has been one of Pensacola's most happening nighttime addresses. Located in the historic district, it boasts seven clubs with a wide variety of live tunes, from

Dixieland jazz and county-western twang to high-pep disco. Thursday through Saturday is when all the clubs are open. One price gets you into all the clubs. ~ 130 East Government Street, Pensacola; 904-434-6211.

Big name stars, circuses and concerts appear occasionally at the **Pensacola Civic Center**. ~ 201 East Gregory Street, Pensacola; 904-433-6311.

For all-round fun, locals and visitors head for **McGuire's Irish Pub and Brewery**. Perhaps it's the crowd, perhaps the live Irish entertainment, perhaps the house-brewed ale, perhaps the old-timey dark booths and the promise of "feasting, imbibery and debauchery" that make this pub popular. Sure'n it's grand, and that's no blarney. ~ 600 East Gregory Street, Pensacola; 904-433-6789.

THEATER, OPERA, SYMPHONY AND DANCE You can also find classical entertainment in Pensacola. The **Pensacola Symphony Orchestra** offers concerts. ~ 904-435-2533. For information on the various community groups that present jazz, chamber music, ballet and opera throughout the year, contact the **Arts Council of Northwest Florida**. ~ P.O. Box 731, Pensacola, FL 32594; 904-432-9906.

Theatrical performances are presented by the **Pensacola Little Theatre**. ~ 400 South Jefferson Street, Pensacola; 904-432-2042. The **University of West Florida Repertory Theatre** puts on great shows. ~ 11000 University Parkway, Pensacola; 904-474-2405. The handsomely restored **Saenger Theatre** hosts a number of dance, music and literary events, some big-name. ~ 118 South Palafox Place, Pensacola; 904-444-7686.

BEACHES & PARKS

GULF ISLANDS NATIONAL SEASHORE 🏃 🚲 ⛵ 🎣 🏖 🛶 Fortunately for us and for posterity, Congress has set aside 150 miles of coastal land, including several barrier islands, from Santa Rosa Island to West Ship Island, Mississippi. In the Panhandle this includes six distinct areas—Perdido Key; the vast western Fort Pickens section of Santa Rosa Island; the Historic Forts section on the Pensacola Naval Air Station; the Santa Rosa day-use area near Navarre Beach; the small Okaloosa area east of Fort Walton Beach; and the Naval Live Oaks area, site of the park headquarters, east of Gulf Breeze. Throughout the national seashore there is good surf and bay fishing and crabbing. Swimming is good at Perdido Key, Fort Pickens area and Santa Rosa, but watch out for undercurrents. Lifeguards are only on duty in certain sections during the summer. Nature trails are found at Perdido Key, Fort Pickens and Naval Live Oaks. There are picnic areas, restrooms and self-guiding trails; bathhouses and outdoor showers are in the beach sections. Day-use fee, $4. ~ Located south of Pensacola; vast stretches of the park are accessible from Route 399; 904-934-2621.

▲ There are 200 sites in Fort Pickens, most with RV hookups and electricity; $12 to $14 per night.

BIG LAGOON STATE RECREATION AREA 🏊 ⛵ 🚣 🚤 🛥 🎣
Because this 678-acre park contains beaches, salt marshes, dunes and pine woods, it is a good place to observe bird, animal and plant life. It's also an excellent place for fishing; bluefish, flounder and sea trout are caught in season. People also go crabbing and netting for mullet. There are several nice beaches on the lagoon for swimming, but proximity to the Intracoastal Waterway is a drawback. Boardwalks make many areas accessible; other spots convey a feeling of remoteness. Facilities include picnic areas, restrooms, bathhouses, nature trails and an observation tower. Day-use fee, $3.25. ~ Take Route 292-A southwest from Pensacola for about ten miles; 904-492-1595.

▲ There are 49 sites with electricity and water, 26 sites with water only; $11 per night.

▼▼▼▼▼▼▼▼▼▼

Inland Area

Florida's canoe capital, this tranquil area is the place to go to enjoy waterfalls, beautiful caverns, pine swamps and swinging bridges. The lack of bright city lights means you'll be able to see a lot more stars at night. A showcase for the state's past, you can explore the Panhandle's inland regions along major highways or country roads. Be prepared to make some detours to capitalize on what this area has to offer.

SIGHTS

Along Route 90, **Quincy** is a pretty town whose shady streets and historic homes give the place a gracious antebellum charm. The downtown district has been revitalized and many of the old brick buildings sport fresh paint and clean awnings. This is a good place for antique-browsing. The **Quincy Chamber of Commerce** can help you enjoy the town. ~ 221 North Madison Street, Quincy; 904-627-9231.

You can pick up a "Historic Sidewalk Tour" of **Marianna** from the **Chamber of Commerce**. This is another Old South town with restored buildings and elegant historic homes. ~ 2928 Jefferson Street, Marianna; 904-482-8061.

Most visitors to Marianna come to see **Florida Caverns State Park** (see the "Parks" section below), where you can explore live limestone caves or do some adventurous spelunking. Admission. ~ Route 166, three miles north of town; 904-482-9598.

If you drive on up to admire the Victorian houses in **Greenwood**, you can rummage in the old cooler for a soda at **Pender's Store**. Local farmers have been buying feed and seed, work boots, dry goods and groceries from the Pender family since the 1800s. The heartpine floors and sturdy shelves date to 1869, when the place was built. ~ 4208 Bryan Street, Greenwood; 904-594-3304.

◄ *HIDDEN*

A number of springs bubble up in surprising places in the central inland region. An easy one to enjoy is at **Ponce de León Springs State Recreation Area** (see the "Parks" section below). Two main boils below the concrete-walled pool produce 14 million gallons of crystal-clear water each day. Though the spring has never been proven to be a fountain of youth, the refreshing swimming and the tall cypress trees impart a sense of tranquility and well-being. Admission. ~ Route 181-A in Ponce de León; 904-836-4281.

Milton is called the "canoe capital of Florida" because of its easy access to the rivers and creeks in the Blackwater Forest.

Sinkholes, or sinks, are also quite common in Florida. Their evolution begins when the weak acids in rainwater seep through cracks in limestone beneath the ground, forming a cavern. If the surface collapses, the cavern, filled with water, is revealed and the result is a sink. The one at **Falling Waters State Recreation Area** (see the "Parks" section below) is unique, for its deep underground cavern is also fed by stream waters falling down a 100-foot smooth-walled chimney resulting in the state's only natural waterfall. Admission. ~ Route 77-A, three miles south of Chipley; 904-638-6130.

HIDDEN ►

By leaving Route 10 at Greensboro and winding down Route 12, you can visit **Torreya State Park** (see the "Parks" section below) and stroll the pretty walkway to the 1849-era **Gregory House**. Admission. This remnant of Florida's steamboat days was transported across the Apalachicola River from its original plantation setting. The classic Greek revival house is filled with 19th-century antiques, including a bedroom suite belonging to the original owner's daughter. Be sure to explore some of the park as well. The rare torreya tree is making a comeback here, and the high bluffs offer fine views of the river. ~ Route 271; 904-643-2674.

In the late 19th century, Chautauqua religious leaders selected **DeFuniak Springs** as their winter headquarters. A portion of the **Chautauqua Auditorium** with its handsome colonnaded dome is still in use. Stop in here for information on the town and the current Chautauqua renaissance. The auditorium houses the **Walton County Chamber of Commerce** (904-892-3191). As you round the lake on Circle Drive, you will see a number of turn-of-the-century homes and other elegant reminders of Florida Chautauqua's 40-year heyday, among them the 1896-era **St. Agatha's Episcopal Church** and the tiny **Walton-DeFuniak Library** (904-892-3624). ~ Circle Drive.

The **Bob Sikes Library**, a handsome brick building with curving staircase and marble floors, houses local American Indian artifacts as well as tributes to the former Congressman, who sponsored the Gulf Islands National Seashore. Closed Sunday. ~ Route 90, east of Crestview; 904-682-4432.

West of Crestview, Route 4 leads into the **Blackwater River State Forest,** so named for the beautiful tannin-stained river that meanders through dense woods. A number of sideroads make for varied exploration of this wild natural region.

Milton is a restored turn-of-the-century town with an interesting history rooted in lumber and shipping. Pick up information at the **Santa Rosa County Chamber of Commerce** and stroll along the Blackwater River. ~ 5247 Stewart Street, Milton; 904-623-2339.

Generic motels in budget and moderate price ranges can be found wherever Route 10 is crossed by a major highway. Many of the inland towns also have a variety of mom-and-pop lodgings, and most of them are budget. If you want luxury, you'll have to stay in Tallahassee or head for the coast.

LODGING

Seminole Lodge is more like a motel than its name suggests, but its location on the shore of Lake Seminole makes its ten rooms popular with fishermen and anyone who enjoys wonderful views of the water. The rooms are old-timey, spacious and well-kept, and some have kitchenettes. There's a tackle shop, a picnic area and a big park nearby. ~ Legion Road, two and a half miles north of Sneads; 904-593-6886. BUDGET.

Although **Tomahawk Landing** is primarily a camping spot for canoeists, the wide variety of cabin accommodations makes this a delightful place to stay and experience the Blackwater Forest area. You can put your whole family in a rustic cabin or escape to the lantern-lit honeymoon cabin on the banks of the Coldwater River; or live it up in one of the air-conditioned deluxe cabins in the pine woods, with a fully equipped kitchen and a fireplace to keep things cozy in the winter. ~ Off Route 87, 12 miles north of Milton; 904-623-6197. BUDGET TO MODERATE.

◄ *HIDDEN*

On the banks of the Apalachicola River, the **Morgan Motel** is an unpretentious establishment with clean, carpeted rooms. About 15 miles from the Three Rivers Recreation Area, this motel is popular with the angling crowd. ~ 116 Route 90, Chatahoochee; 904-663-4336. BUDGET.

During the day you know that the cars and pick-ups parked at Parramore Landing belong to folks out fishing. In the late afternoon you can join the ones who come ashore for fried catfish, shrimp or scallops at **Parramore Restaurant.** Even landlubbers eat at this rundown but popular fishcamp café restaurant. If you've never had cheese grits, try them here. Lunch served only on weekends. Closed Monday. ~ Off Route 271, 12 miles north of Sneads; 904-592-2091. BUDGET TO MODERATE.

DINING

Tony's Restaurant is one of those hometown eateries where gossip gets traded and plates get piled with fixin's such as ham steak and crisp-fried catfish with hushpuppies. Roomy booths and checkered tabletops provide a sunny ambience, and fresh-cooked field peas, string beans, candied yams and buttered carrots ensure a wonderful aroma. Closed Sunday. ~ 4133 Lafayette Street, Marianna; 904-482-2232. BUDGET.

It's said that lots of politicking goes on at **McLain's Family Restaurant,** which means that local folks like this high-ceilinged roadside stopping place. Specials of fried chicken and broiled seafood make this a nice alternative to the neighboring franchises along the interstate route. Breakfast, lunch and dinner are served daily. ~ Routes 10 and 85, Crestview; 904-682-5286. BUDGET TO MODERATE.

Looking for Cajun food like jambalaya or gumbo? Craving fried catfish, broiled halibut or grouper? Or perhaps you'd just like to try a country buffet featuring fried chicken and a dozen salads, side dishes and desserts. If so, why not stop in at **Grandma's Restaurant,** a paneled, antique-furnished dining room set in a wood building. ~ 5887 Route 90, Milton; 904-626-8788. BUDGET.

SHOPPING   Graceville is synonymous with shopping. Bargain hunters come from all points in search of good deals on name brands at the VF **Factory Outlet,** 904-263-3207. You can spend a day hunting for shoes, toys, jewelry, clothing, leather goods, cosmetics and more. ~ Route 77 South and West Prim Avenue; Graceville.

With 11,000 square feet of antiques and collectibles, **Blackwater River Antique Mall** is a great place to explore Florida's past. With more than 25 dealers, you'll find quite a collection of coins, clothing, furniture, jewelry and crystal. ~ 7080 Route 90 East, Milton; 904-626-4492.

Stop by **Etc.** for women's suits, dresses, separates, belts and jewelry. ~ 17 North Madison Street, Quincy; 904-875-1864.

HIDDEN ▶   In the late fall you may see signs for pecans. If you miss them, you can get plenty, shelled or unshelled, from **Lundy's Pecans** in November and December. Lundy's also has blueberries in July. ~ Route 89 north of Milton; 904-623-0652. And don't forget to try the boiled peanuts sold along the road. After the first shock of biting down on one of these soft, warm, chewy legumes, you may become a believer. We did.

NIGHTLIFE   Inland towns roll up their sidewalks early, so folks in search of serious nightlife either make do with local bars and pool tables or head for the coastal cities. The best entertainment probably happens in the forests and preserves, where no lights interfere with stargazing and campers can listen to the rustling of nighttime critters hunting for their dinners. Mockingbirds sometimes sing all night long.

To travelers who hug the coastline or zip through the Panhandle on Route 10, inland area parks will remain hidden. These parks are worth the short detours, however, as they offer a variety of natural phenomena found nowhere else in the state.

THREE RIVERS STATE RECREATION AREA

The three rivers are the Chattahoochee and Flint, which merge above Lake Seminole, and the Apalachicola, which flows out of it. The lake is the result of the flooding of a river swamp; many dead trees lie below the water, guaranteeing fine fishing (bass, catfish, bluegill, perch and bream are common catches). The park is somewhat hilly, with grassy shoreline-slopes in some areas, and deep and diverse woods abundant in deer, grey fox and raccoons elsewhere. Facilities include picnic areas, restrooms, a fishing dock, canoe rentals and nature trails. Day-use fee, $2. ~ Take Route 271 north off Route 90, west of Sneads or exit 23 off Route 10; 904-482-9006.

▲ There are 65 sites, many with RV hookups, electricity and water; $8 to $10 per night.

FLORIDA CAVERNS STATE PARK

This park is beautiful both above and below ground with its disappearing river, magnolia forest and dry cavern. Tours among the spectacular cavern's stalactites and stalagmites are available daily. There's refreshing spring swimming in Blue Hole and good fishing in the Chipola River. Facilities include a picnic area, stables, restrooms, nature trails and a visitors center. Day-use fee, $3.25. ~ Off Route 166, three miles north of Marianna; 904-482-1228.

▲ There are 32 sites with RV hookups and three primitive sites; $12 per night.

PONCE DE LEÓN SPRINGS STATE RECREATION AREA

This 443-acre park reveals one of the small, pretty Florida springs that has been developed for swimming. Like so many of these jewels, the spring creates an oasis in the dry, sandy inland region. Several trails lead you through surrounding pine woods. Other facilities are picnic areas and restrooms. Day-use fee, $2. ~ On Route 181-A, one mile off Route 90, in Ponce de León; 904-836-4281.

FALLING WATERS STATE RECREATION AREA

◄ *HIDDEN*

This small 155-acre park boasts the state's only natural waterfall, which actually starts at ground level and falls 100 feet into a mossy sinkhole to disappear into the ground. The tiny, lush region around this curiosity and the other ordinary sinks in the park provide a pleasant respite from the surrounding dry and sandy terrain. There's swimming in a small manmade lake. Facilities include a picnic area, restrooms and a nature trail. Day-use fee, $3.25. ~ Three miles south of Chipley off Route 77; 904-638-6130.

▲ There are 24 sites, all with RV hookups; $8 to $10 per night.

HIDDEN ► **TORREYA STATE PARK** 🚶🚴 This unusual park is named for the rare torreya tree that has made a comeback after near-extinction. In an almost magical setting, a trail winds up and down ravines and forested bluffs, rising as much as 150 feet, shaped by the Apalachicola River winding along the northwestern boundary. Because of the rapidly changing elevations, a wide variety of distinctive plant communities resides here. Many trees and plants commonly found in the Appalachian regions of north Georgia thrive, along with the rare Florida yew and the National Champion winged elm. A restored antebellum plantation house recalls the days when the river was an important waterway for steamers. Picnic areas and restrooms are the only facilities. Day-use fee, $2. ~ Off Route 10 between Quincy and Marianna. Take the Greensboro exit (Route 12) off Route 10 and head southwest to County Road 1641; go north to the entrance; 904-643-2674.

▲ There are 30 sites, many with RV hookups and electricity; $8 to $10 per night. Primitive camp sites are available; $3 per night.

BLACKWATER RIVER STATE PARK 🏊 🚶 🚣 This 590-acre, heavily wooded park on the southwestern corner of the 183,155-acre **Blackwater River State Forest** stands as a sort of mystical microcosm of its larger neighbor, with deep, dark areas of pine swamp hardwoods, white cedar and a wide variety of other flora. While the river is not really black, it is as dark as strong tea, stained by the tannin from cypress trees and decaying leaves. The water, however, is unpolluted and clear, dotted with broad white sandbars. Oxbow lakes, swamps, dry hills, ponds and swamps attract abundant wildlife to the park; wildflowers and birds lure naturelovers year-round. You can fish for catfish, bream and other freshwater fish. There's excellent swimming off a sandbar beach. Facilities include picnic areas, restrooms and nature trails. Day-use fee, $2. ~ Located off Route 90, 15 miles northeast of Milton, west of Floridale; 904-983-5363.

▲ There are 30 sites, all with RV hookups; $8 to $10 per night.

▼▼▼▼▼▼▼▼▼▼▼▼▼▼
Outdoor Adventures

SPORT-FISHING

Both freshwater and saltwater fishing opportunities are abundant in the Panhandle. Charters, boat rentals and guide services can be found just about anywhere water runs deep enough for a skiff. Fleets of fancy deep-sea craft carry parties out into Gulf waters for marlin, sailfish, black-fin tuna, barracuda, king mackerel, shark and dolphin (the fish, not Flipper, the mammal!). Inland lakes and rivers teem with largemouth bass, bream, panfish and catfish, while coastal areas produce speckled trout, redfish, Spanish mackerel and more.

Apalachicola Adventures offers deep-sea fishing charters. ~ 87 5th Street, Apalachicola; 904-653-9081. The people at **Sportsman Lodge** will make sure you get a heck of a deep-sea or bay charter guide. ~ 99 North Bayshore Drive, Eastpoint; 904-670-8423.

On Panama City Beach, try **Captain Bob Zales' Zodiac Charter Fleet** for deep-sea fishing. ~ 3605 Thomas Drive, 904-235-2628. **Davy Jones Charters** offers more of the same. ~ Anderson-Davis Pier; 904-234-5979. In Destin, board the party boat **Emmanuel**. ~ Highway 98; 904-837-6313. In Pensacola Beach, you can charter the **Moorings**. ~ 655 Pensacola Beach Boulevard; 904-932-0305.

If you want a licensed guide to introduce you to some areas unknown to most tourists, try **Pace's Cottages**. ~ 321 Riverside Drive, Steinhatchee; 352-498-0061. **Shell Island Fish Camp** is another good bet. ~ Shell Island Road, St. Marks; 904-925-6226.

Freshwater boat rentals and/or guide service can be found in any inland town within casting distance of a river or a stream. You'll see their signs along the road. Availability depends on the season and the guides are often natives who have been fishing their favorite spots all their lives. On the Steinhatchee River, **Ideal Fish Camp** rents open fishing craft. ~ Route 51, Steinhatchee; 352-498-3877. **Westwind Fish Camp** has flat-bottom boats. ~ Route 51, Steinhatchee; 352-498-5254.

In Destin, contact **Adventure Pontoon Rentals**. ~ 603 2nd Street, Destin; 904-837-3041. **Key Sailing** in Pensacola Beach offers parasailing and pontoon rentals. ~ 500 Quietwater Beach Boulevard, Pensacola Beach; 904-932-5520.

SAILING

Sailboarding is hotly pursued along Florida's northern Gulf beaches. For rentals, check with **Rogue Wave Windsurfing**. ~ 171 Brooks Street Southeast, Fort Walton Beach; 904-243-1962.

WIND-SURFING

The choice of experiences for divers in the Panhandle is broad indeed, from exploring wrecked ships in the Gulf to cave-diving in deep hidden springs. The less daring can rent snorkeling equipment and lazily watch fish in a blue spring. Many outfitters provide equipment and exploration trips in salt and freshwater, as well as scalloping, shelling, spear fishing and/or instruction.

DIVING

To explore more than two dozen hidden springs in the eastern area, contact **Branford Dive Center**. ~ Route 27 and the Suwannee River, Branford; 904-935-1141. In Tallahassee, organized dive trips can be arranged at either of the two **Coral Reef Scuba** locations. ~ 1362 Lake Bradford Road, 904-576-6268; 2783 Capitol City Northeast, Unit B, 904-385-1323.

For Gulf and bay exploration, as well as some spring diving, try **Apalachicola Divers Supply**. ~ 119 Water Street, Apalachicola; 904-653-9521. Or you can call **Captain Black's Marine**. ~ 301 Monument Avenue, Port St. Joe; 904-229-6330. **Hydrospace Dive Shop** is another good bet. ~ 3605 Thomas Drive, Panama City; 904-234-9463. **Panama City Dive Center** can show you a good time. ~ 4823 Thomas Drive, Panama City Beach; 904-235-3390. In the Fort Walton area, try **Aquanaut Scuba Center**. ~ 24 Highway 98, Destin; 904-837-0359. Explore with **Fantasea Scuba**. ~ 1 Route 98, Destin; 904-837-6943. Give the **Scuba Shop** a call. ~ 348 Miracle Strip Parkway, Fort Walton Beach; 904-243-1600. Or try **Captain J. Dive Shop**. ~ 301 Highway 98, Destin; 904-654-5300.

To explore Florida's westernmost waters, seek **Dive Mart**. ~ 5501 Duval Street, Pensacola; 904-494-9800. Or try **Scuba Shack**. ~ 719 Palafox Street, Pensacola; 904-433-4319.

Spring exploration in the central area is offered by **Cypress Springs**. ~ Cypress Springs Road, Vernon; 904-535-2960. Or learn with **Morrison Springs Diving Facility**. ~ On Morrison Springs Road off Highway 181-C, Ponce de León; 904-836-4223. **Vortex Spring Inc.** can show you a thing or two. ~ Route 81 north of Ponce de León; 904-836-4979.

CANOEING & TUBING

Milton calls itself the canoe capital of Florida, and you'll know why when you see hundreds of canoes on the Blackwater River or Coldwater Creek on a holiday weekend. There's canoeing on other Panhandle rivers and spring runs, too, from the Suwannee to the Perdido, and much of it can be handled by novices. There's no better way to explore the waters of hidden Florida.

Rental companies usually provide shuttle services and often rent tubes and rafts. To canoe the Suwannee River and the eastern area runs, try the **Suwannee Canoe Outpost**. ~ Off Route 129 north of Live Oak; 800-428-4147. Another choice is **River Run Campground**. ~ Route 27 east of Branford; 904-935-1086.

In the Tallahassee area, try **The Canoe Shop**. ~ 1115-B Orange Avenue, Tallahassee; 904-576-5335. Or call **TNT Hideaway Inc.** ~ Route 98 at the Wakulla River, St. Marks; 904-925-6412.

To explore the western Panhandle rivers, try **Andrew Jackson Canoe Trails**. ~ P.O. Box 666, Baghdad; 904-623-4884. **Adventures Unlimited** is a good choice. ~ 12 miles north of Milton on Route 87 North; 904-623-6197. Another bet is **Blackwater River Canoe Rental**. ~ Route 90 east of Milton; 904-623-0235. **Bob's Canoes** awaits your call. ~ Route 191 northwest of Milton; 904-623-5457. **Adventures Unlimited, Perdido** offers canoeing on Florida's western boundary. ~ 160 River Annex Road, Muskogee; 904-968-5529.

In the central inland area, try **Chipola River Canoe Trail**. ~ Route 280, Marianna; 904-482-4948. Or try **Cypress Springs**

Canoe Trails, Inc. ~ Cypress Springs Road, Vernon; 904-535-2960.
Sasquatch Canoe Rentals is another place to call. ~ Route 90 east
of Crestview; 904-682-3949.

To explore the Suwannee River, begin at its mouth on one of
Miller's Suwannee Houseboats for one-day to one-week trips. ~
Off Route 349, Suwannee; 352-542-7349.

**HOUSE-
BOATING**

The Panhandle's favorable climate and a wide variety of courses attract golf enthusiasts year-round. In Tallahassee, the public can
play at the **Hilaman Park Municipal Golf Course**. ~ 2737 Blair
Stone Road, Tallahassee; 904-891-3935. The **Seminole Golf Course**
is another course to try. ~ 2550 Pottsdamer Road, Tallahassee;
904-644-2582. There is a public course at **St. Joseph's Bay Country
Club**. ~ On C-30 off Route 98, Port St. Joe; 904-227-1751. In the
Panama City area, try **Signal Hill Golf Course**. ~ 9615 Thomas
Drive, Panama City Beach; 904-234-5051. Or test out **Holiday
Golf Club**. ~ 100 Fairway Boulevard, Panama City Beach; 904-
234-1800.

GOLF

The elegant resort **Seascape**, in the Fort Walton area, opens its
championship course to the public. ~ 100 Seascape Drive, Destin;
904-837-9181. You can also play at **Bluewater Bay**. ~ Off Highway 20, Niceville; 904-897-3241.

In the Pensacola area you can tee off at **Green Meadow Par 3**.
~ 2500 West Michigan Avenue, Pensacola; 904-944-5483. Or you
could try **Tiger Point Golf & Country Club**. ~ 1255 Country Club
Road, Gulf Breeze; 904-932-1333. Golfers traveling the inland
areas may play at **Florida Caverns Golf Course**. ~ 3309 Caverns
Road, Marianna; 904-482-4257. The **Bonifay Country Club** is
also in the inland area. ~ Route 177-A Northwest, Bonifay; 904-
547-9381. Or you might want to tee off at **Tanglewood Golf &
Country Club**. ~ Tanglewood Drive, Milton; 904-623-6176.

✔ **CHECK THESE OUT—UNIQUE OUTDOOR ADVENTURES**

- Spelunk and dive at the same time when you try cave-diving into the inland area's deep underground springs. *page 505*
  - Hop into a tube or canoe and float the Blackwater River, where tannin
    from the cypress tress have stained the water a deep golden brown.
    page 506
    - Bike along the Michael J. Kennan Memorial Bike Path at Pensacola
      Beach—a dip in the water provides respite from the heat. *page 508*
      - Trek along the 22-mile Florida National Scenic Trail—it crosses
        four rivers and explores the Panhandle's wild terrain. *page 509*

TENNIS

Some of the resorts and local country clubs provide courts for their guests and allow the public to play for a fee. **Sandestin** is one such place. ~ Emerald Coast Parkway, ten miles east of Destin; 904-267-8000. **Seascape** is another. ~ 100 Seascape Drive, Destin; 904-837-9181. Brush up on your serve at **Shalimar Pointe Tennis Club**. ~ 2 Country Club Road, Shalimar; 904-651-8872.

BIKING

Narrow roads and hot weather discourage many folks from biking in the Panhandle. On Pensacola Beach, the **Michael J. Kennan Memorial Bike Path** provides seven miles of safe and scenic biking that will eventually be linked to a path traversing the Gulf Islands National Seashore.

Three guides to biking in the Panhandle have been designed by the **Florida Department of Transportation** and may be obtained from the department at 605 Suwannee Street, M.S. 17, Tallahassee, 32399-0450; 904-487-1200. These include suggested routes from downtown Pensacola to the Gulf Islands National Seashore, a loop tour from Tallahassee to Monticello and back, and a tour from Tallahassee to St. Marks.

Bike Rentals Rent your bicycles from **About Bikes**. ~ 4780 Woodville Highway, Tallahassee; 904-656-0001. **Bob's Schwinn** will give you something to ride around on. ~ 415-G Mary Esther Boulevard, Fort Walton Beach; 904-243-5856. **Paradise Bicycle Rental** is another place to try. ~ 715 Pensacola Beach Boulevard, Pensacola Beach; 904-934-0014.

HIKING

Though most visitors to the Panhandle do their primary walking on the beaches, there are other hiking opportunities available. Almost every state park and recreation area contains at least one nature trail. The Florida Trail Association is in the process of creating unbroken hiking trails from Pensacola to Lake Okeechobee; several existing Panhandle trails are already part of the system. Because altitudes seldom go above 300 feet, most hiking is easy, especially in seasons when temperatures cool down and the mosquitoes disappear. All distances for hiking trails are one way unless otherwise noted.

TALLAHASSEE AREA **Stoney Bayou Trail** (6 miles) and **Deep Creek Trail** (13 miles) allow exploration of the vast St. Marks National Wildlife Refuge. These loop trails begin near the visitor's center off Route 59 south of Newport. Deep Creek Trail leads deep into coast swampland where you are likely to encounter wide varieties of birds and wildlife.

Ridge Trail (3 miles) and **Otter Lake Loop** (9 miles) lie in a secluded western portion of the St. Marks National Wildlife Refuge where ospreys nest. Both these loop trails begin and end at the Otter Lake Recreation area east of Panacea off Route 98.

St. Marks Trail (16 miles) begins off Route 98, and travels through beautiful and remote areas of the St. Marks National Wildlife Refuge to Route 319, five miles east of Sopchoppy.

Florida National Scenic Trail (22 miles) begins where the St. Marks Trail ends, near Sopchoppy. It crosses four rivers and explores both wilderness and scenic areas that display much of north Florida's natural phenomena.

The **Trail of the Lakes** (9 miles) is a loop trail which links up with the Florida National Scenic Trail in the western part of the Apalachicola National Forest. It begins at the Camel Lake Recreation Area 15 miles south of Bristol.

> Get a sampling of the forest's flora and fauna on the Trail of the Lakes, an excellent place for a family hike.

APALACHICOLA AREA St. Joseph Peninsula Trail (18-mile loop) begins at the ranger station in the state park of the same name and travels through the St. Joseph Peninsula Wilderness Preserve. You can make an interesting loop by going one way along the beach and returning through the interior. This will provide opportunities for shelling as well as observing marsh and piney woods wildlife. It's a long walk, but not difficult.

PANAMA CITY AREA Pine Log Trail (3 miles) is an easy loop trail popular with birdwatchers. It begins at the Pine Log State Forest Headquarters, off Route 79, south of Ebro.

INLAND AREA Torreya State Park Hiking Trail (7 miles) is a loop trail that traverses ravines, bluffs and streams and goes through hardwood forests unique to Florida. The short **Apalachicola River Bluffs Trail**, incorporated into this loop trail, passes Confederate gun pits and offers good views of the river.

Jackson Red Ground Hiking Trail (21 miles) runs through the center of Blackwater River State Forest. The trail traverses forest and swamp and crosses the Blackwater River.

Sweetwater Hiking Trail (4.5 miles) begins at the Krul Recreation Area near the intersection of Routes 191 and 4 and crosses Sweetwater Creek on a swinging bridge.

Transportation

CAR

Traveling with dispatch across the Panhandle is accomplished by driving the interstate highway **Route 10**, which is intersected by north–south **Routes 75** and **19** and many roads winding down from Georgia and Alabama and up from the coastal cities and towns. The slower but more scenic **Route 98** follows the curves of the coastline, while old **Route 90** parallels Route 10 through the inland towns.

AIR

You can fly into airports at Tallahassee, Panama City, Fort Walton or Pensacola. Airlines serving the **Tallahassee Regional Airport** include Delta Airlines and USAir.

Panama City-Bay County International Airport is served by Atlantic Southeast, Northwest Airlink and USAir Express. **Deluxe Coach Service** provides ground transportation. ~ 904-763-0211.

Okaloosa County Airport is served by Atlantic Southeast/Delta, Northwest Airlines and USAir Express.

Airlines serving the **Pensacola Regional Airport** include Continental Airlines, Delta Airlines, Northwest Airlink and USAir. There is no shuttle transportation service from Pensacola Airport into town.

For a wider choice of schedules, you might consider flying into Jacksonville (see Chapter Four) and driving west.

BUS

Greyhound Bus Lines (800-231-2222) serve the major cities and many of the small towns across the Panhandle. Stations are located in Tallahassee at 112 West Tennessee Street, 904-222-6614; in Panama City at 917 Harrison Avenue, 904-785-7861; in Fort Walton Beach at 101 Perry Avenue, 904-243-1940; and in Pensacola at 505 West Burgess Road, 904-476-4800.

CAR RENTALS

You'll find car rentals at each of the Panhandle airports. In Tallahassee, try **Alamo Rent a Car** (800-327-9633), **Avis Rent A Car** (800-331-1212), **Budget Rent A Car** (800-527-0700), **Hertz Rent A Car** (800-654-3131) or **National Interrent** (800-227-7368).

Rentals are available at the Panama City Airport from **Avis Rent A Car** (800-331-1212), **Budget Rent A Car** (800-527-0700), **Hertz Rent A Car** (800-654-3131), **National Interrent** (800-227-7368) and **Snappy Car Rental** (800-677-7627).

At Okaloosa County Airport you can pick up a car from **Budget Rent A Car** (800-527-0700), **Hertz Rent A Car** (800-654-3131) or from **National Interrent** (800-227-7368).

Franchises at the Pensacola Airport include **Avis Rent A Car** (800-331-1212), **Budget Rent A Car** (800-527-0700), **Hertz Rent A Car** (800-654-3131) and **National Interrent** (800-227-7368).

PUBLIC TRANSIT

Public transportation is limited in the Panhandle and is used mostly by folks going to and from work. In Tallahassee, contact **Taltran** for bus schedules. ~ 904-891-5200. The **Escambia County Area Transit System** provides local bus service in the Pensacola area. ~ 904-436-9383.

TAXIS

Several cab companies serve the Tallahassee airport, including **Yellow Cab** (904-222-3070). At the Panama City airport, you can also call **Yellow Cab** (904-763-4691). The airport in Fort Walton Beach is served by **A-1 Taxi** (904-678-2424) and **Checker Cab** (904-244-4491). At the Pensacola airport, contact **Express Lightning** (904-449-3018) and **Yellow Cab** (904-433-3333).

Index

Lodging Index

Dining Index

HIDDEN GUIDES

Adventure travel or a relaxing vacation?—"Hidden" guidebooks are the only travel books in the business to provide detailed information on both. Aimed at environmentally aware travelers, our motto is "Adventure Travel Plus." These books combine details on unique hotels, restaurants and sightseeing with information on camping, sports and hiking for the outdoor enthusiast.

THE NEW KEY GUIDES

Based on the concept of ecotourism, The New Key Guides are dedicated to the preservation of Central America's rare and endangered species, architecture and archaeology. Filled with helpful tips, they give travelers everything they need to know about these exotic destinations.

ULTIMATE FAMILY GUIDES

These innovative guides present the best and most unique features of a family destination. Quality is the keynote. In addition to thoroughly covering each destination, they feature short articles and one-line "teasers" that are both fun and informative.